Lecture Notes in Artificial Intelligence 1421

Subseries of Lecture Notes in Computer Science
Edited by J. G. Carbonell and J. Siekmann

Lecture Notes in Computer Science

Edited by G. Goos, J. Hartmanis and J. van Leeuwen

Springer
Berlin
Heidelberg
New York
Barcelona
Budapest
Hong Kong
London
Milan
Paris
Singapore
Tokyo

Claude Kirchner   Hélène Kirchner (Eds.)

Automated Deduction – CADE-15

15th International Conference
on Automated Deduction
Lindau, Germany, July 5-10, 1998
Proceedings

 Springer

Series Editors

Jaime G. Carbonell, Carnegie Mellon University, Pittsburgh, PA, USA
Jörg Siekmann, University of Saarland, Saarbrücken, Germany

Volume Editors

Claude Kirchner
LORIA-INRIA
Hélène Kirchner
LORIA-CNRS
615, rue du Jardin Botanique
F-54602 Villers-les-Nancy Cedex, France
E-mail: {Claude.Kirchner, Helene.Kirchner}@loria.fr

Cataloging-in-Publication Data applied for

Die Deutsche Bibliothek - CIP-Einheitsaufnahme

Automated deduction : proceedings / CADE-15, 15th International
Conference on Automated Deduction, Lindau, Germany, July 5 - 10,
1998. Claude Kirchner ; Hélène Kirchner (ed.). - Berlin ; Heidelberg ;
New York ; Barcelona ; Budapest ; Hong Kong ; London ; Milan ;
Paris ; Santa Clara ; Singapore ; Tokyo : Springer, 1998
  (Lecture notes in computer science ; Vol. 1421 : Lecture notes in
  artificial intelligence)
  ISBN 3-540-64675-2

CR Subject Classification (1991): I.2.3, F.4.1, F.3.1

ISBN 3-540-64675-2 Springer-Verlag Berlin Heidelberg New York

© Springer-Verlag Berlin Heidelberg 1998
Printed in Germany

Typesetting: Camera ready by author
SPIN 10637443   06/3142 – 5 4 3 2 1 0   Printed on acid-free paper

Preface

The CADE conferences are the major forum for the presentation of new research in all aspects of automated deduction. This volume contains the papers and system descriptions selected for presentation at the 15th International Conference on Automated Deduction CADE-15, held July 5-10, 1998, in Lindau (Germany).

Eighty-five research papers and twenty-five system descriptions were submitted by researchers from eighteen countries. Each submission was reviewed by at least three program committee members with the help of 129 subreferees. An electronic discussion through the World Wide Web allowed us to prepare the Program Committee meeting, which took place in Nancy (France) on March 14. We accepted twenty-four research papers and ten system descriptions for presentation at the conference.

The papers cover a wide range of topics on theorem proving based on resolution, superposition, model generation and elimination, or connection tableau calculus, in first-order, higher-order, intuitionistic, or modal logics, and describe applications to geometry theorem proving, computer algebra, or reactive systems. System descriptions address the implementation of various techniques such as constraint solving, decision procedures, proof planning, induction, model checking, and cooperation.

The program also included three invited lectures: "Reasoning About Deductions in Linear Logic" by Frank Pfenning, "ACL2 Support for Verification Projects" by Matt Kaufmann, and "Deductive vs. Model-Theoretic Approaches to Formal Verification" by Amir Pnueli. Abstracts or full papers of these lectures are also included in this volume.

Not covered in these proceedings are several other CADE-15 events. Four tutorials and nine workshops were offered to participants prior to the conference. The third automated theorem-proving system competition CASC-15 was organized by Christian Suttner and Geoff Sutcliffe. Immediately following the conference, the final meeting of the National Schwerpunkt Deduktion project, organized by Wolfgang Bibel, was open to all participants.

We would like to express our gratitude to Wolfgang Bibel and his Organizing Committee at Darmstadt University for their great organization of this fifteenth CADE, taking care of many different tasks including publicity for the Conference, raising outside funding, and local arrangements.

We would like also to thank the members of the Program Committee and all the referees for their care and time in reviewing and selecting the submitted papers. Finally, special thanks go to Horatiu Cirstea for his continuous help in maintaining the Web server of the program committee and facilitating our task in preparing the conference.

Nancy, April 1998   Claude and Hélène Kirchner

Conference Organization

Program Chairs

Claude and Hélène Kirchner (Nancy)

Conference Chair

Wolfgang Bibel (Darmstadt)

Program Committee

F. Baader (Aachen)
D. Basin (Freiburg)
W. Bibel (Darmstadt)
H. Comon (Cachan)
G. Dowek (Rocquencourt)
H. Ganzinger (Saarbrücken)
F. Giunchiglia (Trento)
S. Grumbach (Rocquencourt)
J. Hsiang (Taipei)
D. Kapur (Albany)
C. Kirchner (Nancy)
H. Kirchner (Nancy)

C. Kreitz (Ithaca)
C. Lynch (Clarkson)
D. McAllester (Florham Park)
M. Okada (Tokyo)
L. Paulson (Cambridge)
N. Shankar (Menlo Park)
A.P. Sistla (Chicago)
J. Slaney (Canberra)
M. Wallace (London, UK)
D. Wang (Grenoble)
S. Watt (London, Canada)

Organizing Committee

Holger Hoos (Darmstadt)
Hesham Khalil (Darmstadt)
Stephanos Padelis (Darmstadt)

Ulrich Scholz (Darmstadt)
Maria Tiedemann (Darmstadt)

CADE-15 Sponsors

Deutsche Forschungsgemeinschaft, Bonn
Bayerisches Staatsministerium für Unterricht, Kultus, Wissenschaft und Kunst, München
Daimler-Benz AG, Stuttgart
Siemens AG, München
SUN Microsystems GmbH, München
LORIA, INRIA & CNRS
Darmstadt University of Technology

List of Referees

I. Alouini	N. Hermann	M. Reynolds
J. Andrews	J. Hickey	J. Richts
A. Armando	H. H. Hoos	C. Ringeissen
L. Bachmair	D. Howe	R. Rioboo
R. Backofen	G. S. Huang	R. Rodosek
C. Ballarin	D. Hutter	M. Roveri
H. Barendregt	H. Khalil	A. Rubio
B. Barras	D. Korn	J. Rushby
P. Baumgartner	W. Küchlin	M. Rusinowitch
M. Beeson	G. Lakemeyer	C. Scharff
M. Benerecetti	A. Leitsch	T. Schaub
P. Bertoli	R. Letz	J. Schimpf
M. P. Bonacina	J. Levy	S. Schmitt
M. Bormann	J. Lobo	U. Scholz
A. Bouhoula	P. Loiseleur	R. Sebastiani
T. Boy de la Tour	J. J. Lu	D. Seipel
G. Brewka	D. Lugiez	L. Serafini
F. Bry	L. M Pereira	S. Soliman
R. Caferra	H. Mantel	L. Spalazzi
O. Caprotti	C. Marché	B. Spencer
A.-C. Caron	F. Massacci	J. Steinbach
C. Castro	A. Massarotto	G. Struth
J. Crow	S. Matthews	J. Stuber
M. Daniele	W. McCune	T. Stuetzle
G. Defourneaux	C. Munoz	A. Tacchella
J. Denzinger	G. Nadathur	T. Tammet
P. M. Dung	M. Nagayama	K. Terui
K. Eastaughffe	D. Nardi	V. Thomas
F. Fages	P. Narendran	S. Thompson
S. Fevre	R. Nieuwenhuis	C. Tinelli
B. Fronhöfer	T. Nipkow	C. Tollu
D. Galmiche	H. de Nivelle	L. Viganò
T. Genet	A. Nonnengart	L. Vigneron
C. Ghidini	J. Otten	A. Villafiorita
A. Gordon	S. Owre	U. Waldmann
R. Goré	S. Padelis	C. Walther
B. Gramlich	B. Pagano	C. Weidenbach
P. de Groote	N. Peltier	B. Werner
M. Hamano	F. Pfenning	B. Wolff
M. Hanus	F. Pirri	R. Yuge
J. Harrison	J. Pitt	H. Zantema
F. Henglein	S. Ranise	H. Zhang
H. Herbelin	T. Rath	

Previous CADEs

CADE-1, Argonne National Laboratory, USA, 1974
(IEEE Trans. on Computers C-25(8))
CADE-2, Oberwolfach, Germany, 1976
CADE-3, Massachusetts Institute of Technology, USA, 1977
CADE-4, University of Texas at Austin, USA, 1979
CADE-5, Les Arcs, France, 1980 (Springer-Verlag LNCS 87)
CADE-6, Courant Institute, USA, 1982 (Springer-Verlag LNCS 138)
CADE-7, Napa, California, USA, 1984 (Springer-Verlag LNCS 170)
CADE-8, University of Oxford, UK, 1986 (Springer-Verlag LNCS 230)
CADE-9, Argonne National Laboratory, USA, 1988 (Springer-Verlag LNCS 310)
CADE-10, Kaiserslautern, Germany, 1990 (Springer-Verlag LNAI 449)
CADE-11, Saratoga Springs, New York, USA, 1992 (Springer-Verlag LNAI 607)
CADE-12, Nancy, France, 1994 (Springer-Verlag LNAI 814)
CADE-13, Rutgers University, USA, 1996 (Springer-Verlag LNAI 1104)
CADE-14, Townsville, North Queensland, Australia, 1997 (Springer-Verlag LNAI 1249)

CADE Inc. Trustees

Table of Contents

Session 8:

Session 9:

Session 10:

Session 11:

Session 12:

— Invited Talk —
Reasoning About Deductions in Linear Logic

Frank Pfenning

Carnegie Mellon University
School of Computer Science
fp@cs.cmu.edu

Linear logic has been described as a logic of state. Many complex systems involving state transitions, such as imperative programming languages, concurrent systems, protocols, planning problems, games, or abstract machines, can be specified in linear logic at a very high level of abstraction. Generally, these encodings represent legal sequences of transitions as deductions in linear logic.

Proof search in linear logic then allows us to establish the existence of transition sequences, thereby, for example, solving a planning problem or modelling the execution of a protocol. But we often need to consider all possible computations, for example, to establish that an imperative programming language is type-safe or that a protocol is secure. This then requires reasoning about deductions in linear logic.

We describe our approach to proving properties of deductions in linear logic which is based on the linear logical framework LLF [CP96] and an explicit meta-logic with universal and existential quantifiers ranging over proof objects. Due to the immediacy of the encodings, the expressive power of the linear logical framework, and the design of the meta-logic this architecture offers excellent opportunities for automation, combining techniques from type theory, constraint logic programming, and inductive theorem proving. In the interactive setting, a related architecture has been proposed by McDowell [McD97] and applied to a less expressive linear framework.

Preliminary results with a non-linear prototype [SP98] have been very encouraging and include, for example, automatic proofs of Hilbert's deduction theorem, type preservation for mini-ML, and soundness and completeness of logic programming search.

References

[CP96]   Iliano Cervesato and Frank Pfenning. A linear logical framework. In E. Clarke, editor, *Proceedings of the Eleventh Annual Symposium on Logic in Computer Science*, pages 264–275, New Brunswick, New Jersey, July 1996. IEEE Computer Society Press.

C. Kirchner and H. Kirchner (Eds.): Automated Deduction, CADE-15
LNAI 1421, pp. 1–2, 1998. © Springer–Verlag Berlin Heidelberg 1998

[McD97] Raymond McDowell. *Reasoning in a logic with definitions and induction.* PhD thesis, University of Pennsylvania, 1997.

[SP98]   Carsten Schürmann and Frank Pfenning. Automated theorem proving in a simple meta-logic for LF, 1998. This volume. An extended version is available as Technical Report CMU-CS-98-123, Carnegie Mellon University.

A Combination of Nonstandard Analysis and Geometry Theorem Proving, with Application to Newton's Principia

Jacques D. Fleuriot and Lawrence C. Paulson

Computer Laboratory – University of Cambridge
New Museums Site, Pembroke Street
Cambridge CB2 3QG
{jdf21,lcp}@cl.cam.ac.uk

Abstract. The theorem prover Isabelle is used to formalise and reproduce some of the styles of reasoning used by Newton in his **Principia**.
The Principia's reasoning is resolutely geometric in nature but contains
"infinitesimal" elements and the presence of motion that take it beyond
the traditional boundaries of Euclidean Geometry. These present difficulties that prevent Newton's proofs from being mechanised using only
the existing geometry theorem proving (GTP) techniques.
Using concepts from Robinson's Nonstandard Analysis (NSA) and a powerful geometric theory, we introduce the concept of an *infinitesimal geometry* in which quantities can be infinitely small or infinitesimal. We
reveal and prove new properties of this geometry that only hold because
infinitesimal elements are allowed and use them to prove lemmas and
theorems from the Principia.

1 Introduction

Isaac Newton's *Philosophiæ Naturalis Principia Mathematica* (Mathematical
Principles of Natural Philosophy [9]), or *Principia* as it is usually called, was
first published in 1687 and set much of the foundations of modern science. We
now know that Newton's view of the world was only approximate but the laws
and proofs he developed are still relevant and used in our everyday world. The
elegance of the geometrical techniques used by Newton in the *Principia* is little
known since demonstrations of most of the propositions set out in it are usually
done using calculus.

In Newton's time, however, geometrical proofs were very much the norm.
It follows that some of the lemmas of the *Principia* can be proved using just
Euclidean geometry and we do so using our formalisation in Isabelle [11] of GTP
rules proposed by Chou, Gao, and Zhang [4,5]. According to De Gandt [6] many
of Newton's propositions and lemmas, however, do go beyond the boundaries
of traditional Euclidean geometry in important respects such as the presence of

C. Kirchner and H. Kirchner (Eds.): Automated Deduction, CADE-15
LNAI 1421, pp. 3–16, 1998. © Springer–Verlag Berlin Heidelberg 1998

motion and the admission of the infinitely small. Below we shall describe how we used the concept of the infinitesimal from Nonstandard Analysis (NSA) [12] to help formalise the notion of infinitely small geometric quantities.

Our initial aim is to study the geometric proofs of the *Principia* and investigate ways of mechanising them. We want to use some of the methods already developed for GTP in our own proofs. Moreover, we hope that some of Newton's reasoning procedures can be adapted to produce new methods in mechanised proofs of geometry theorems and in problem solving for classical mechanics. This work also hopes to expose some of the remarkable insights that Newton had in his use of geometry to prove propositions and solve problems.

In section 2 we briefly review the exposition of the *Principia* and the specific nature of its geometry. Section 3 gives an overview of the theory of infinitesimals from NSA that we formalised in Isabelle. Section 4 introduces our axiomatisation and use of parts of the area and full-angles methods first introduced by Chou et al. for automated GTP. We also have additional notions such as similar triangles and definitions of geometric elements such as ellipses and tangents. These are essential to our formalisation of Newton's work. In section 5 we describe some of the main results proved so far. Section 6 offers our comments on related work, conclusions and possible future work.

2   The Principia and Its Mathematical Methods

The *Principia* is considered to be one of the greatest intellectual achievements in the history of exact science. It has, however, been influential for over three centuries rarely in the geometrical terms in which it was originally written but mostly in the analytico-algebraic form that was used very early to reproduce the work. Below we examine some of the original methods used in the *Principia*.

2.1   The Style and Reasoning of the Principia

Newton's reasoning rests on both his own methods and on geometric facts that though well known for his time (for example, propositions of Apollonius of Perga and of Archimedes) might not be easily accessible to modern readers. Moreover, the style of his proofs is notoriously convoluted due to the use of a repetitive, connected prose. Whiteside [15] notes the following:

> I do not deny that this hallowed ikon of scientific history is far from easy to read... we must suffer the crudities of the text as Newton resigned it to us when we seek to master the *Principia's* complex mathematical content.

It is therefore one of our aims to show that we can use Isabelle to master some of the "complex mathematical content" of the work and give formal proofs of lemmas and propositions of Newton.

In the various figures used by Newton, some elements must be considered as "very small": for example, we encounter lines that are infinitely or indefinitely small or arcs that may be nascent or evanescent. De Gandt argues that there is a temporal infinitesimal that acts as the independent variable in terms of which other magnitudes are expressed. However, since time itself is often represented geometrically using certain procedures, the infinitesimal time or "particle of time" in Newton's own expression appears as distance or area[1].

2.2   The Infinitesimal Geometry of the Principia

On reading the enunciations of many of the lemmas of the *Principia* one often comes across what Newton calls **ultimate** quantities or properties— for example, ultimate ratio (lemma 2,3,4 . . .), ultimately vanishing angle (lemma 6), and ultimately similar triangles (lemma 8). Whenever Newton uses the term, he is referring to some "extreme" situation where, for example, one point might be about to coincide with another one thereby making the length of the line or arc between them vanishing, that is, infinitesimal.

Furthermore, as points move along arcs or curves, deformations of the diagrams usually take place; other geometric quantities that, at first sight, might not appear directly involved can start changing and, as we reach the extreme situation, new ultimate geometric properties usually emerge. We need to be able to capture these properties and reason about them. The use of infinitesimals allows us to "freeze" the diagram when such extreme conditions are reached: we introduce, for example, the notion of the distance between two points being infinitesimal, that is, infinitely close to zero and yet not zero when they are about to coincide. With this done, we can then deduce new or ultimate properties about angles between lines, areas of triangles, similarity of triangles and so on. This is what distinguishes our geometry from ordinary Euclidean geometry.

The infinitesimal aspects of the geometry give it an intuitive nature that seems to agree with the notions of infinitesimals from Nonstardard Analysis (NSA). Unlike Newton's reasoning, for which there are no formal rules of writing and manipulation, the intuitive infinitesimals have a formal basis in Robinson's NSA. This enables us to master motion, which is part of Newton's geometry, and consider the relations between geometric quantities when it really matters, that is, at the point when the relations are ultimate.

3   Introducing the Infinitesimal

For a long time, the mathematical community has had a strong aversion to the notion of an infinitesimal (Bishop Berkeley [3] wrote a famous and vitriolic attack). This was historically due to the incorrect and informal use of infinitesimals in the development of the calculus. We are used to the powerful intuitions that infinitesimals can provide in constructing proofs of theorems but we are not allowed to use them in the proofs themselves (though physicists might disagree) without formal justification.

---

[1] See our exposition below of Proposition 1. Theorem 1 (Kepler's law of Equal Areas) for an example.

3.1   The Nonstandard Universe $\mathbb{R}^*$

NSA introduces the nonstandard real field $\mathbb{R}^*$, which is a proper extension of the complete ordered field of the reals $\mathbb{R}$. We give here the algebraic facts about infinitesimals, proved in Isabelle, that follow from the properties above and that we have used in our geometric proofs. Notions of finite and infinite numbers are also defined and we have proved many algebraic properties about them as well. We follow the definitions and mechanically-proved the theorems given in section 1A of Keisler [8].

Definition 1. *In an ordered field extension* $\mathbb{R}^* \supseteq \mathbb{R}$, *an element* $x \in \mathbb{R}^*$ *is said to be an* **infinitesimal** *if* $|x| < r$ *for all positive* $r \in \mathbb{R}$; **finite** *if* $|x| < r$ *for some* $r \in \mathbb{R}$; **infinite** *if* $|x| > r$ *for all* $r \in \mathbb{R}$.

For an infinitesimal x, it is clear that $x \in \mathbb{R}^* \backslash \mathbb{R}$ or $x = 0$. This means that 0 is the only real infinitesimal and that other infinitesimals cannot be identified with any existing real numbers. We prove, in Isabelle, that the set Infinitesimal of infinitesimals and the set Finite of finite numbers are *subrings* of $\mathbb{R}^*$. Also, Infinitesimal is an *ideal* in Finite, that is the product of an infinitesimal element and a finite element is an infinitesimal.

Definition 2. $x, y \in \mathbb{R}^*$ *are said to be* **infinitely close**, $x \approx y$ *if* $|x - y|$ *is infinitesimal.*

It is easily proved that x is an infinitesimal if and only if $x \approx 0$ and that we have defined an equivalence relation above. Ballantyne and Bledsoe [1] observe:

> The relation $\approx$ now solves the problem Leibnitz encountered in that he was forced to make his infinitesimals simultaneously equal and different from zero. If one replaces the identity relation with the $\approx$ relation then all is well.

We can now formalise, for example, the idea of a point B about to meet another point A by saying that the distance between them, whether linear or curvilinear, is infinitesimal. We illustrate what we mean in the case of B moving along a circular arc of finite radius of curvature and about to meet A:

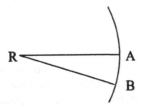

The length of the circular arc AB is infinitesimal and given that $\text{len}(R - A) \in$ Finite, we can deduce $\langle A - R, R - B \rangle \in$ Infinitesimal since $\text{arc\_len}\,R\,A\,B = (|\text{len}(R-A)| \cdot \langle A - R, R - B \rangle) \in$ Infinitesimal and Infinitesimal is an ideal in Finite.

The same reasoning can be applied if point B is moving away from A, that is to the start of motion. Thus, we can deduce how various geometric quantities behave when we reach conditions that existing GTP techniques would consider degenerate since they are infinitesimal. Furthermore, as mentioned previously, geometric theorems and lemmas that hold at the infinitesimal level do not necessarily hold in general and we now have tools to prove them.

4 A Formalisation of Geometry in Isabelle

There exist efficient techniques for GTP— many of which, though extremely powerful, are highly algebraic [16]. These have been developed mostly for automated proofs, which are usually long and extremely difficult to understand. They consist mostly of a series of algebraic manipulations of polynomials that could not be farther from the style of reasoning employed by Newton. Fortunately, there has been recent work in automated GTP by Chou et al. [4,5] that aim to produce short, human-readable proofs in geometry using more traditional properties. We introduce a geometry theory in Isabelle based on some of the rules used in the algorithms for these new approaches.

4.1 The Geometric Methods

In these methods there are basic lemmas about geometric properties called signed areas and full-angles. Other rules are obtained by combining several of the basic ones to cover frequently-used cases and simplify the search process. We have assumed the basic rules as axioms and formally proved that the combined rules also hold.

We represent the line from point A to point B by $A-B$, its length by $\text{len}(A-B)$, and the *signed* area $\text{S}_{\text{delta}}ABC$ of a triangle is the usual notion of area with its sign depending on how the vertices are ordered. We follow the usual approach of having $\text{S}_{\text{delta}}ABC$ as positive if $A-B-C$ is in anti-clockwise direction and negative otherwise. Familiar geometric properties such as collinearity, coll, and parallelism, $\parallel$, can be thus

$$\text{coll}\,abc \equiv (\text{S}_{\text{delta}}\,abc = 0)$$
$$a-b \parallel c-d \equiv (\text{S}_{\text{delta}}\,abc = \text{S}_{\text{delta}}\,abd)$$
$$\text{coll}\,abc \implies \text{len}(a-b) \times \text{S}_{\text{delta}}\,pbc = \text{len}(b-c) \times \text{S}_{\text{delta}}\,pab$$

A full angle $\langle u,v \rangle$ is the angle from line u to line v. We note that u and v are lines rather than rays and define the relation of *angular* equality as follows:

$$x =_a y \equiv \exists n \in \text{Integer}.\ |x - y| = n\pi$$

The relation $=_a$ is an equivalence relation that is also used to express the properties that we might want. For example the idea of two lines being perpendicular becomes

$$a-b \perp c-d \equiv \langle a-b, c-d \rangle =_a \frac{\pi}{2}$$

Our aim is not to improve approaches to GTP given by Chou et al. since they are essentially algorithmic and designed to perform automatic proofs. We have, however, provided a definition for the equality between full-angles. We can then easily prove that $\pi =_a 0$ and $\frac{3\pi}{2} =_a \frac{\pi}{2}$. Moreover, this enables us to combine the area and full-angles methods when carrying out our proofs and deduce, for example, $\langle a - b, b - c \rangle =_a 0 \iff S_{\mathtt{delta}}\, a\, b\, c = 0$. We avoid the problems, such as $\pi = 0$, that would arise if we had used the ordinary equality for angles.

The attractive features of these approaches, as far as we are concerned, are the short, clear and diagram-independent nature of the proofs they produce and that they deal easily and elegantly with ratios of segments, ratios of areas and angles and so on. These are the properties used in the geometry of the *Principia*.

4.2   Infinitesimal Geometric Relations

Having introduced the basic geometric methods, we can now provide geometric definitions that make use of infinitesimals. Since we have explicitly defined the notion of equality between angles, we also need to define the idea of two angles being infinitely close to one another. We use the infinitely close relation to do so:

$$a_1 \approx_a a_2 \equiv \exists n \in \mathbf{Integer}.\ |a_1 - a_2| \approx n\pi$$

This is an equivalence relation. We prove in Isabelle the following property, which could provide an alternative definition for $\approx_a$:

$$a_1 \approx_a a_2 \iff \exists \epsilon \in \mathbf{Infinitesimal}.\ a_1 =_a a_2 + \epsilon$$

Of course, we also have the theorem $a_1 \approx a_2 \implies a_1 \approx_a a_2$. We now introduce a property that can be expressed using the concepts that we have developed so far in our theory — that of two triangles being *ultimately similar*. Recall that two triangles $\triangle abc$ and $\triangle a'b'c'$ are similar ($\mathtt{SIM}\, a\, b\, c\, a'\, b'\, c'$) if they have equal angles at a and a', at b and b', and at c and c'. The definition of ultimately similar triangles follows:

$$
\begin{aligned}
\mathtt{USIM}\, a\, b\, c\, a'\, b'\, c' \equiv\ & \langle b - a, a - c \rangle \approx_a \langle b' - a', a' - c' \rangle\ \wedge \\
& \langle a - c, c - b \rangle \approx_a \langle a' - c', c' - b' \rangle\ \wedge \\
& \langle c - b, b - a \rangle \approx_a \langle c' - b', b' - a' \rangle
\end{aligned}
$$

This property allows of treatment of triangles that are being deformed and tending towards similarity as points move in Newton's dynamic geometry. Elimination and introduction rules are developed to deal with the USIM property. It follows also, trivially, that $\mathtt{SIM}\, a\, b\, c\, a'\, b'\, c' \implies \mathtt{USIM}\, a\, b\, c\, a'\, b'\, c'$. We also define the geometric relation of *ultimate congruence* UCONG and areas, angles and lengths can be made infinitesimal as needed when carrying out the proofs.

4.3   Other Geometric Definitions

The geometry theory contains other definitions and rules that are required for the proofs. These include length of arcs, length of chords and area of sectors.

Since Newton deals with circular motion, and the paths of planets around the sun are elliptical, definitions for the circle, the ellipse and tangents to these figures are also provided. A few of these are given below.

$$\texttt{circle}\, x\, r \equiv \{p. \, |\texttt{len}(x - p)| = r\}$$
$$\texttt{ellipse}\, f_1\, f_2\, r \equiv \{p. \, |\texttt{len}(f_1 - p)| + |\texttt{len}(f_2 - p)| = r\}$$
$$\texttt{e\_tangent}\, (a - b)\, f_1\, f_2\, E \equiv (\texttt{is\_ellipse}\, f_1\, f_2\, E \, \wedge \, a \in E \, \wedge$$
$$\langle f_1 - a, a - b \rangle =_a \langle b - a, a - f_2 \rangle))$$

The definition of the tangent to an ellipse relies on a nice property of the curve (which also provides an alternative definition): light emitted from one focus, say f_1 will reflect at some point p on the ellipse to the other focus f_2. Thus, light reflects from the curve in exactly the same way as it would from the tangent line at p. Since the law of reflection means that the angle of incidence is the same as the angle of reflection, the definition above follows. The tangent line is important as it shows in the case where the ellipse is the path of an orbiting object, like a planet, the direction of motion of the object at that point.

5   Mechanised Propositions and Lemmas

Some of the results obtained through the mechanisation of the ideas discussed above can now be presented. The methods have been used to investigate the nature of the infinitesimal geometry and formally prove many geometry theorems. Some of these results confirm what one intuitively might expect to hold when elements are allowed to be infinitesimal.

5.1   Motion Along an Arc of Finite Curvature

Consider Fig. 1 based on diagrams Newton constructed for proofs of his lemmas; let $A - D''$ denote the tangent to the arc ACB and $A - R$ the normal to the tangent, both at A. Let R be the centre of curvature, r be the antipodal of the circle of contact at A, the points D, D' and D'' be collinear and $B - D \perp A - D''$. With the point B moving towards A along the arc, we can prove several properties about this diagram, including some which become possible because we have infinitesimals:

- $\triangle BDA$ and $\triangle ABr$ are **similar** and hence $\texttt{len}(A - B)^2 = \texttt{len}(A - r) \times \texttt{len}(D - B)$. The latter result is stated and used but not proved by Newton in Lemma 11.
- $\triangle ABD'$ and $\triangle rAD'$ are similar and hence $\texttt{len}(D' - A)^2 = \texttt{len}(D' - B) \times \texttt{len}(D' - r)$.
- $\langle B - A, A - D'' \rangle =_a \langle B - R, R - A \rangle / 2$
- $\triangle ABR$ and $\triangle AD''R$ are **ultimately similar** since the angle $\langle B - A, A - D'' \rangle$ is infinitesimal when point B is about to coincide with point A. This proves part of Lemma 8.

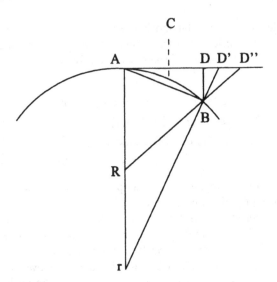

Fig. 1. Point B moving along an arc towards A

- the **ultimate ratio** of len($A - B$), arc_len RAB, and len($A - D''$) is infinitely close to 1. This is Lemma 7.

It is clear from the diagram above that $\triangle ABR$ and $\triangle AD''R$ are not similar in ordinary Euclidean Geometry. Infinitesimal notions reveal that we are tending towards similarity of these triangles when the point B is about to meet point A. This property cannot be deduced from just the static diagram above. The dynamics of Newton's geometry involves the reader using his or her imagination to incorporate motion and see what is happening to the relations between various parts of the diagram as points are moving. This task is not always trivial. The relation USIMABRAD''R can be illustrated by considering the relation between the parts of the diagram as point B moves towards point A (Fig. 2).

We can see as B moves towards A that $\langle B - A, A - D'' \rangle$ is decreasing, as one might intuitively expect, and when ultimately the distance between B and A is infinitely close to zero, then we have that $\langle R - A, A - B \rangle \approx_a \langle R - A, A - D'' \rangle$. From this we can deduce the ultimate similarity of the triangles as required.

We give below a detailed overview of our reasoning and theorems proved to show the ultimate similarity of these two triangles. We show that the angle subtended by the arc becomes infinitesimal as B approaches A and that the angle between the chord and the tangent is always half that angle:

```
[| arc_len R A B ≈ 0; len (A--R) ∈ Finite - Infinitesimal |]
 ⟹ <B--R,R--A> ≈ 0

[| c_tangent A D'' R Circle; B ∈ Circle |]
 ⟹ <B--A,A--D''> =ₐ <B--R,R--A>/2
```

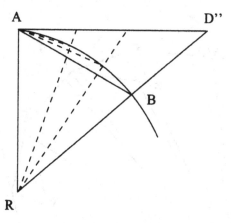

Fig. 2. Ultimately similar triangles

We use the theorem from NSA that Infinitesimal form an ideal in Finite and the results above to prove that the angle between the chord and the tangent becomes infinitely close to zero and that $\langle R - A, A - D \rangle$ and $\langle R - A, A - B \rangle$ are infinitely close:

```
[| <B--R,R--A>∈ Infinitesimal; 1/2∈ Finite |]
⟹<B--R,R--A>*1/2 ∈ Infinitesimal

[| c_tangent A D'' R Circle; B ∈ Circle; arc_len R A B ≈ 0;
   len (A--R) ∈ Finite - Infinitesimal |]
⟹ <B--A,A--D''> ≈ₐ 0";

<?--A,A--D''> ≈ₐ 0 ⟹ <R--A,A--D''> ≈ₐ <R--A,A--B>
```

Finally, since $\triangle ABR$ and $\triangle AD''R$ have two corresponding angles that are infinitely close (they have one common angle in fact), we can show that they are ultimately similar:

```
<B--R,R--A> =ₐ <B--R,R--A> ⟹ <B--R,R--A> ≈ₐ <B--R,R--A>

[|<B--R,R--A> ≈ₐ <B--R,R--A>; <R--A,A--D''> ≈ₐ <R--A,A--B> |]
⟹ USIM A B R A D'' R
```

5.2 Kepler's Law of Equal Areas

Kepler's equal area law was published in 1609 and was often regarded until Newton's *Principia* as one of the least important of Kepler's Laws. This law is established by Newton as the first mathematical Proposition of the *Principia*.

In Newton's diagram (Fig. 3), the polygons $ABCDEF$ are used to approximate the continuous motion of a planet in its orbit. The motion between any two points such as A and B of the path is not influenced by any force, though

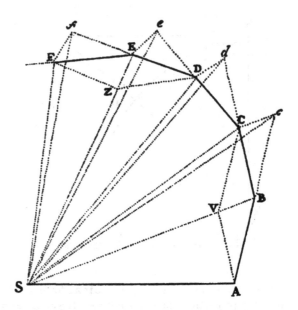

Fig. 3. Original diagram from the *Principia* showing a body moving under the influence of a series of impulsive centripetal forces

there are impulsive forces, all directed towards the fixed centre S, that act at $A, B, C, \ldots$. Newton proved that if the time interval between successive impulses is fixed then all the triangular areas $SAB, SBC, \ldots$, are equal, that is equal areas are described in equal times. The demonstration of this law makes no assumption about how this force varies with distance from the centre of force S; its only restriction is that it be directed toward S. Newton reduces the discontinuous motion along the straight edges $AB, BC, \ldots$, to continuous motion along a smooth orbital path by using an infinitesimal process that lets the size of the triangles become infinitely small.

We follow Newton's argument and prove that the area of SAB is equal to that of SBC using our geometric tools. We quote from the exposition of Proposition 1 in the *Principia*:

> Let time be divided into equal parts, and in the first part of the time let the body, by its inherent force, describe the straight line AB. In the second part of the time, the same body, if nothing were to impede it, would pass on by means of a straight line to c (by Law 1), describing the line Bc equal to AB, with the result that, radii AS, BS, cS being drawn to the centre, the areas ASB, BSc would come out equal.

We first observe that the area of SAB equals that of SBc because the triangles have equal bases (since the times are equal and no force has acted to change the velocity) and the same height:

```
[| coll A B C; len(A--B) = len(B--c)|]
 ⟹ S_delta S A B = S_delta S B c
```

The impulsive centripetal force at B makes the body depart from motion in a straight line and Newton makes the following construction (using the Parallelogram Law of Forces):

> Let cC be drawn parallel to BS, meeting BC at C; and, the second part of the time being completed, the body (by Corollary I of the laws) will be located at C, in the same plane as the triangle ASB ... Connect SC, and because of the parallels SB,Cc, triangle SBC will be equal to triangle SBc, and therefore to triangle SAB.

This leads to the following lemma, which is also easily proved in Isabelle since it follows from the definition of parallel lines:

```
[| S--B || c--C |] ⟹ S_delta S B c = S_delta S B C
```

The proof that the areas are equal follows. In fact, this first part of the proof of Kepler's Law of Equal Areas is proved automatically in one step by Isabelle thanks to the presence of powerful proof tactics.

The next step is to decrease the breadth of the triangles to be infinitesimally small and by Lemma 3 and its corollaries we can substitute the straight edge by a curved line:

```
<A--S,S--B> ≈ 0 ⟹ len(A--B) ≈ arc_len S A B
```

And furthermore using the same lemma, the area of the infinitesimal triangle SAB is infinitely close to the area of the arc and can be substituted:

```
<A--S,S--B> ≈ 0 ⟹ S_delta S A B ≈ arc_area S A B
```

As the triangles become infinitesimal, the perimeter of the path becomes infinitely close to a curvilinear one and the force can be viewed as acting continuously since the times between the impulses are infinitesimal. We can note here the geometrical representation of time since making the triangles infinitesimal effectively makes the time intervals also infinitely close to zero. The result that the area described is proportional to the time still holds for the evanescent triangles and hence also holds for the infinitely close curvilinear areas.

6   Related Work and Final Comments

The combination of concepts used in this approach relates it to work that has already been done in the field of NSA and GTP.

6.1 Nonstandard Analysis Theorem Proving

The theorem proving community does not seem to have shown much interest in NSA even though its importance has grown in many fields such as physics, analysis and economics, where it has successfully been applied. Ballantyne and Bledsoe [1] implemented a prover using nonstandard techniques in the late seventies. Their work basically involved substituting any theorem in the reals $\mathbb{R}$ by its analogous in the extended reals $\mathbb{R}^*$ and proving it in this new setting. Even though the prover had many limitations and the work was just a preliminary investigation, the authors argued that through the use of nonstandard analysis they had brought some new and powerful mathematical techniques to bear on the problem.

Despite this rather promising work, there does not seem to have been much done over the last two decades. Suppes and Chuaqui [13] have proposed a framework for doing proofs in NSA and Bedrax has implemented a prototype for a simplified version of Suppes-Chuaqui system called Infmal [2]. Infmal is implemented in Common Lisp and contains the various axioms (logical, algebraic and infinitesimal) required by the deduction system and extensions to the usual arithmetic operations. Unfortunately, Infmal is a simple experiment and though interactive is rather limited in the proofs it can carry out.

The parts of this work relating to NSA have used the definitions provided in Sect. 3.1 and have proved most of the facts about NSA built in Ballantyne and Bledsoe's prover. There are proofs involving *standard parts* and infinite numbers, for example, that have not been described in this paper.

6.2 Automated Geometry Theorem Proving

As mentioned already, the geometric methods based on signed areas and full-angles have been useful to the development of the geometry theory in Isabelle. The work of Chou et al. is intended to produce short and readable proofs of difficult geometry theorems. This represents a return to the original and more traditional ways of geometry theorem proving that had been superseded by the more powerful *algebraic* methods based mainly on Wu's characteristic set method [16] and the Gröbner basis method [7]. Unfortunately there are several drawbacks associated with the use of these algebraic techniques: they are computationally intensive and produce long proofs that do not have clear geometric meaning since they are manipulations of polynomials obtained by coordinatisation of points in the diagrams.

The recent work improves on various previous attempts to use geometrically meaningful properties for theorem proving through the use of geometric invariants, that is, areas, full-angles etc. In our work, techniques such as those of similar and congruent triangles that are needed for the proofs are also added as traditionally these have also been used in proofs of geometry. Though Chou et al. [4] note that they have limitations, our proofs are not affected since we are not concerned with completely automatic proofs. The resulting geometry theory of Isabelle is powerful and able to prove most of the results that the signed area and full-angles methods can tackle. Moreover, many of the lemmas from Chou et al. [4,5] obtained through the combination of various rules and used to help the automatic search have been verified in Isabelle.

Other methods that provide short and readable proofs, without introducing coordinates, include bracket and Clifford algebras. These two algebraic techniques, however, seem less relevant to the present work since they do not match closely the geometric concepts and infinitesimal nature of Newton's proofs. Excellent overviews of the bracket and Clifford algebras, of the methods used in this work, and of several other approaches to GTP can be obtained from the survey paper by Wang [14].

6.3   Problem Solving in Mechanics

There has been some interest in the past in problem solving in mechanics in the GTP community where, interestingly, Wu [17] algebraically proved Newton's Laws of Gravitation and even, with somewhat more difficulty, automatically derived them from Kepler's Laws (which Newton actually proved in the *Principia*).

There is also Novak, who implemented several systems to do problem solving in classical physics with the help of diagrams [10]. Though his work falls into the field of diagrammatic reasoning rather that GTP it does require the implicit applications of geometry theorems to derive relations between various physical quantities represented geometrically in the diagrams. This work also shows that it is possible to closely relate physical and geometric principles through diagrams.

6.4   Conclusions and Future Work

Reading the *Principia* and making sense of the reasoning of Newton is a difficult but rewarding task. As is common with proofs using geometric tools, once the hard task of constructing the diagram and proof is done, the result that follows usually looks simple and intuitive. We have shown that, though Newton does not provide a set of rules for carrying out his proofs, the reasoning is formal and can be mechanised. We can effectively give formal definitions and proofs of some of the ultimate properties Newton is trying to prove. We have tried to bridge the gap between intuition and formality.

Furthermore, the introduction of infinitesimal elements in the geometry is an exciting aspect that can lead to the discovery of interesting properties that cannot be seen ordinarily. We have scope for more work in the field of NSA, whose foundations in Isabelle we plan to investigate in more depth in the near future. Infinitesimals are always tricky and can lead to paradoxes if not used carefully.

We plan to mechanise other interesting propositions from the *Principia* and, since these are actually proofs in classical mechanics, it would be interesting to see how these techniques can be applied to problem solving in the field. Physics textbooks commonly use infinitesimals in informal reasoning, because it is intuitive. This material could also be mechanised.

Acknowledgements

We thank Clemens Ballarin and the anonymous referees for their comments on the work and for providing us with further pointers to the literature. Support from the ORS and Cambridge Commonwealth Trusts is gratefully acknowledged.

References

1. A. M. Ballantyne and W. W. Bledsoe. Automatic Proofs of Theorems in Analysis Using Nonstandard Analysis. *J. of the Association of Computing Machinery*, Vol. 24, No. 3, July 1977, 353–374.
2. T. Bedrax. Infmal: Prototype of an Interactive Theorem Prover based on Infinitesimal Analysis. Liciendo en Mathematica con Mencion en Computation Thesis. Pontifica Universidad Catolica de Chile, Santiago, Chile, 1993.
3. G. Berkeley. The Analyst: A Discourse Addressed to an Infidel Mathematician. *The World of Mathematics*, Vol. 1, London. Allen and Unwin, 1956, 288–293.
4. S. C. Chou, X. S. Gao, and J. Z. Zhang. Automated Generation of Readable Proofs with Geometric Invariants, I. Multiple and Shortest Proof Generation. *J. Automated Reasoning* **17** (1996), 325–347.
5. S. C. Chou, X. S. Gao, and J. Z. Zhang. Automated Generation of Readable Proofs with Geometric Invariants, II. Theorem Proving with Full-angles. *J. Automated Reasoning* **17** (1996), 349–370.
6. F. De Gandt. *Force and Geometry in Newton's Principia*. Princeton University Press, Princeton, New Jersey, 1995.
7. D. Kapur. Geometry Theorem Proving using Hilbert's Nullstellensatz. Proceedings of SYMSAC'86, Waterloo, 1986, 202–208.
8. H. J. Keisler. *Foundations of Infinitesimal Calculus*. Prindle, Weber & Schmidt, 20 Newbury Street, Boston, Massachusetts, 1976.
9. I. Newton. *The Mathematical Principles of Natural Philosophy*. Third edition, 1726. Translation by A. Motte (1729). Revised by F. Cajory 1934. University of California Press.
10. S Novak Jr. Diagrams for Solving Physical Problems. *Diagrammatic Reasoning: Cognitive and Computational Perspectives*, AAAI Press/MIT Press, 753–774, 1995. (Eds. Janice Glasgow, N. Hari Narayana, and B. Chandrasekaram).
11. L. C. Paulson. *Isabelle: A Generic Theorem Prover*. Springer, 1994. LNCS 828.
12. A. Robinson. *Non-Standard Analysis*. North-Holland Publishing Company, 1980. 1966, first edition.
13. R. Chuaqui and P. Suppes. Free-Variable Axiomatic Foundations of Infinitesimal Analysis: A Fragment with Finitary Consistency Proof. *J. Symbolic Logic*, Vol. 60, No. 1, March 1995.
14. D. Wang. Geometry Machines: From AI to SMC. 3rd Internationa Conference on Artificial Intelligence and Symbolic Mathematical Computation. (Stey, Austria, September 1996), LNCS 1138, 213–239.
15. D. T. Whiteside. The Mathematical Principles Underlying Newton's Principia Mathematica. Glasgow University Publication 138, 1970.
16. W.-t. Wu. On the Decision Problem and the Mechanization of Theorem in Elementary Geometry. *Automated Theorem Proving: After 25 years*. A.M.S., Contemporary Mathematics, **29** (1984), 213–234.
17. W.-t. Wu. Mechanical Theorem Proving of Differential Geometries and Some of its Applications in Mechanics. *J. Automated Reasoning* **7** (1991), 171–191.

Proving Geometric Theorems Using Clifford Algebra and Rewrite Rules*

Stéphane Fèvre and Dongming Wang

LEIBNIZ–IMAG, 46, avenue Félix Viallet, 38031 Grenoble Cedex, France

Abstract. We consider geometric theorems that can be stated constructively by introducing points, while each newly introduced point may be represented in terms of the previously constructed points using Clifford algebraic operators. To prove a concrete theorem, one first substitutes the expressions of the dependent points into the conclusion Clifford polynomial to obtain an expression that involves only the free points and parameters. A term-rewriting system is developed that can simplify such an expression to 0, and thus prove the theorem. A large class of theorems can be proved effectively in this coordinate-free manner. This paper describes the method in detail and reports on our preliminary experiments.

1 Introduction

It has been widely known that algebraic methods such as Wu's [21,22,3] and those based on Gröbner bases [11,13] and other variable elimination techniques [12,19] are very efficient for automatically proving theorems in geometry. In these methods, coordinates are introduced to formulate the geometric theorems in question. Several powerful coordinate-free techniques have also been proposed and developed recently for producing short and readable proofs [5,6,9,14,15,17,18,20], which represents further progress and success of research on this active subject. After many non-trivial geometric theorems have been proved using specialized techniques, researchers also turn to investigating how general deduction mechanisms can be adapted for geometry [2,6], the relationship between general and special-purpose systems and how they can be integrated [8]. One objective of this paper is to demonstrate how general term-rewriting techniques may be applied effectively to proving geometric theorems when they are formulated using Clifford algebra.

As in [20], we propose to start with geometric theorems that can be stated constructively by introducing new points step by step. Let each newly introduced point be represented in terms of the previously constructed points using Clifford algebraic operators (or *Clifford operators* for short). To prove a concrete theorem, one first substitutes the expressions of the dependent points into the

---

* Supported by CEC under Reactive LTR Project 21914 (CUMULI) and a project of LIAMA.

C. Kirchner and H. Kirchner (Eds.): Automated Deduction, CADE-15
LNAI 1421, pp. 17–32, 1998. © Springer-Verlag Berlin Heidelberg 1998

conclusion Clifford polynomial to obtain an expression that involves only the free points and parameters. Proving the theorem is then reduced to simplifying such ·ι expression to 0; the latter can be done by using term-rewriting techniques. In [20] we have shown that some difficult theorems may be proved in this way. However, the term-rewriting system could not address as many problems as the one presented in this paper. For instance, the previous version requires coordinates for proving Simson's theorem. Termination of the current method has also been proved.

Our preliminary experiments show that a large number of theorems can be proved by using Clifford algebra and the proposed term-rewriting system. The following example is used to explain the structure of the paper.

Example 1 (Desargues theorem – parallel version). Let ABC and $A'B'C'$ be two triangles such that the lines AA', BB', CC' are concurrent, $A'B' \parallel AB$ and $A'C' \parallel AC$. Then $B'C' \parallel BC$.

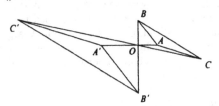

Let the common point of intersection of AA', BB', CC' be located at the origin O. Take A, B, C as free points and introduce a parameter u. Then the dependent points A', B', C' may be constructed step by step and represented as follows

$$A' = uA, \quad B' = \frac{A \cdot AB^\sim - A \cdot BA^\sim}{A \cdot B^\sim}, \quad C' = \frac{A \cdot AC^\sim - A \cdot CA^\sim}{A \cdot C^\sim},$$

where "." and "~" are operators in Clifford algebra. We s'·ll explain these operators and how Clifford (algebraic) expressions of this kind may be obtained in Sect. 2.

The conclusion of the theorem to be proved is

$$g = (B - C) \wedge (B' - C') = 0, \quad \% \ B'C' \parallel BC$$

where "$\wedge$" is another Clifford operator. Substituting the expressions of A', B', C' into g, one obtains the following

$$\begin{aligned}
g^* = (&A \cdot C^\sim A \cdot AB \wedge B^\sim - A \cdot C^\sim A \cdot BA \wedge B^\sim - A \cdot B^\sim A \cdot AB \wedge C^\sim \\
&+ A \cdot B^\sim A \cdot CA \wedge B^\sim - A \cdot C^\sim A \cdot AB \wedge C^\sim + A \cdot C^\sim A \cdot BA \wedge C^\sim \\
&+ A \cdot B^\sim A \cdot AC \wedge C^\sim - A \cdot B^\sim A \cdot CA \wedge C^\sim)/(A \cdot B^\sim A \cdot C^\sim),
\end{aligned}$$

which only involves the free points A, B, C. By using the term-rewriting system described in Sect. 3, g^* may be proved to be identically equal to 0. Hence, the theorem is true under the conditions $A \cdot B^\sim \neq 0$ and $A \cdot C^\sim \neq 0$, i.e., points B and C do not lie on line OA.

The overall proof method will be presented in Sect. 4, where some implementation issues and initial experiments are also discussed. The paper concludes with a few remarks and pointers to related work.

2   Clifford Algebra and Geometric Constructions

2.1   Clifford Algebraic Operators

Let $\mathbb{K}$ be a field of characteristic $\neq 2$, $\mathcal{V}$ an n-dimensional vector space, and Q a quadratic form on $\mathcal{V}$. Denote the tensor algebra over $\mathcal{V}$ by $\mathfrak{T}(\mathcal{V})$ and the tensor multiplication by $\otimes$. Let $\mathfrak{I}(Q)$ be the two-sided ideal of $\mathfrak{T}(\mathcal{V})$ generated by the elements $\mathbf{v} \otimes \mathbf{v} - Q(\mathbf{v})$, $\mathbf{v} \in \mathcal{V}$. The resulting associative quotient algebra $\mathcal{C} = \mathfrak{T}(\mathcal{V})/\mathfrak{I}(Q)$ is called the *Clifford algebra* associated to the quadratic form Q. Elements of $\mathcal{C}$ are also called *Clifford numbers*. The product of any two Clifford numbers $\mathbf{A}$ and $\mathbf{B}$ — called the *geometric product* of $\mathbf{A}, \mathbf{B}$ — is written as $\mathbf{AB}$.

Clifford algebra provides a powerful language for geometric calculus with diverse applications, see [1,10] for example. A short accessible introduction to Clifford algebra is given in [20]. In what follows, we recall a few Clifford operators that are used in this paper.

Any vector of $\mathcal{V}$ may be represented as a directed line segment in an n-dimensional space. For any two vectors $\mathbf{a}, \mathbf{b} \in \mathcal{V}$ the *geometric sum* of $\mathbf{a}$ and $\mathbf{b}$ is also a vector of $\mathcal{V}$, i.e., $\mathbf{a} + \mathbf{b} \in \mathcal{V}$. It has the familiar geometric meaning. The *inner product* $\mathbf{a} \cdot \mathbf{b}$ of $\mathbf{a}$ and $\mathbf{b}$ is defined by

$$\mathbf{a} \cdot \mathbf{b} = \frac{1}{2}(\mathbf{ab} + \mathbf{ba}) \in \mathbb{K}.$$

In the following sections, we shall fix an orthonormal base for $\mathcal{V}$ without further indication. In this case, the above definition leads to the familiar inner product of two vectors in Euclidean space.

The anticommutative *outer product* $\mathbf{a} \wedge \mathbf{b}$ of two vectors $\mathbf{a}, \mathbf{b}$ is defined as

$$\mathbf{a} \wedge \mathbf{b} = \mathbf{ab} - \mathbf{a} \cdot \mathbf{b}.$$

It is a bivector corresponding to the parallelogram obtained by sweeping the vector $\mathbf{a}$ along the vector $\mathbf{b}$.

The above definitions may be naturally extended to arbitrary multivectors, i.e., elements of the Clifford algebra $\mathcal{C}$. Starting from geometric sum, inner and outer products, one can define various other operators like the *cross product* $\times$, the *meet* $\vee$ and the *dual operator* $\sim$ for multivectors. The reader is referred to [10] for more details about these operators and their geometric interpretations.

The dual operator for $n = 2$ will be used in later sections; we explain it as follows. Let $n = 2$; $\mathbf{e}_1, \mathbf{e}_2$ be an orthonormal base of the vector space $\mathcal{V}$ and

$$I = \mathbf{e}_1 \wedge \mathbf{e}_2.$$

The *dual* $\mathbf{C}^\sim$ of any multivector $\mathbf{C} \in \mathcal{C}$ with respect to I is defined to be $\mathbf{C}I$, the geometric product of $\mathbf{C}$ and I. Geometrically, let $\mathbf{e}_1$ and $\mathbf{e}_2$ form an orthonormal frame of the Euclidean plane. If $\mathbf{v}$ is a vector, then $\mathbf{v}^{\sim}$ is the vector obtained by rotating $\mathbf{v}$ 90° anticlockwise in the plane. The duality considered in this paper is always for $n = 2$ and with respect to the fixed I.

We shall refer to such operators as the geometric sum and product, inner and outer products, dual operator, cross product and meet as *Clifford operators*. They obey some basic calculational laws and relate to each other; some of the laws and relations will be given as rewrite rules in Sect. 3.

2.2   Geometric Construction and Representation

Let a point P be regarded also as the vector from the origin O to P, $Q - P$ as the vector from P to Q, and $P + Q$ as the vector from O to the opposite vertex of the parallelogram formed by OP and OQ. We take points as the most fundamental geometric objects and represent other geometric objects by means of points: for instance, a line by two distinct points on the line, and a circle by three non-collinear points on the circle. The vector $Q - P$ also represents the line PQ which passes through P and Q.

We consider the following three kinds of constructions.

C1. Construct arbitrary points, lines, planes, circles, etc. In this simple case, take a finite number of free points. There is no constraint among these points.

C2. From already constructed points $P_1, \ldots, P_s$, construct a new *dependent* point X that is neither arbitrary nor completely determined by $P_1, \ldots, P_s$. In this case, determine the *degree* d of freedom of X, introduce d scalar parameters or free points $\mu_1, \ldots, \mu_d$, and represent X in terms of $P_1, \ldots, P_s$ and $\mu_1, \ldots, \mu_d$ using Clifford operators:

$$X = f(P_1, \ldots, P_s; \mu_1, \ldots, \mu_d).$$

C3. From already constructed points $P_1, \ldots, P_s$, construct a new *dependent* point X that is completely determined by $P_1, \ldots, P_s$. In this case, X may be represented in terms of $P_1, \ldots, P_s$ using Clifford operators:

$$X = f(P_1, \ldots, P_s).$$

The following is a list of example constructions for plane Euclidean geometry, in which the points P_i have already been constructed. The list contains some of the constructions given in [20], which are reproduced to help understand the examples.

– Construct a point X such that $XP_3 \parallel P_1P_2$:

$$X = \mathsf{par}(P_1, P_2, P_3) = P_3 + u(P_2 - P_1),$$

where u is a scalar parameter newly introduced.
Special case. Take a point X on the line P_1P_2:

$$X = \mathsf{on\_line}(P_1, P_2) = \mathsf{par}(P_2, P_1, P_2) = uP_1 + (1 - u)P_2.$$

- Take a point X on the circumcircle of $\triangle P_1 P_2 P_3$:

$$X = \mathsf{on\_cir}(P_1, P_2, P_3) = 2\,\mathsf{per\_ft}(U, \mathsf{cir\_ctr}(P_1, P_2, P_3), P_1) - P_1,$$

where $\mathsf{cir\_ctr}$ and $\mathsf{per\_ft}$ are defined below and U is a free point introduced.
- Construct the midpoint X of two points P_1 and P_2:

$$X = \mathsf{midp}(P_1, P_2) = (P_1 + P_2)/2.$$

- Construct the point X such that $XP_5 \parallel P_1 P_2$ and $XP_6 \parallel P_3 P_4$:

$$X = \mathsf{par\_par\_int}(P_1, P_2, P_3, P_4, P_5, P_6)$$
$$= \frac{\{(P_2 - P_1) \cdot [P_6 \wedge (P_4 - P_3)]\}^{\sim} - \{(P_4 - P_3) \cdot [P_5 \wedge (P_2 - P_1)]\}^{\sim}}{[(P_2 - P_1) \wedge (P_4 - P_3)]^{\sim}}.$$

The non-degeneracy condition is

$$(P_2 - P_1) \wedge (P_4 - P_3) \neq 0. \qquad \text{%} \ \ P_1 P_2 \nparallel P_3 P_4$$

- Construct the point X such that $XP_5 \parallel P_1 P_2$ and $XP_6 \perp P_3 P_4$:

$$X = \mathsf{par\_per\_int}(P_1, P_2, P_3, P_4, P_5, P_6)$$
$$= \frac{P_6 \cdot (P_4 - P_3)(P_2 - P_1) - (P_4 - P_3) \cdot [P_5 \wedge (P_2 - P_1)]}{(P_2 - P_1) \cdot (P_4 - P_3)}.$$

The non-degeneracy condition is

$$(P_2 - P_1) \cdot (P_4 - P_3) \neq 0. \qquad \text{%} \ \ P_1 P_2 \not\perp P_3 P_4$$

Special cases.
- Construct the foot X of the perpendicular drawn from P_3 to $P_1 P_2$:

$$X = \mathsf{per\_ft}(P_1, P_2, P_3) = \mathsf{par\_per\_int}(P_1, P_2, P_1, P_2, P_1, P_3).$$

- Construct the reflection point X of P_3 with respect to $P_1 P_2$:

$$X = \mathsf{ref}(P_1, P_2, P_3) = \mathsf{par\_per\_int}(P_1, P_2, P_1, P_2, 2P_1 - P_3, P_3).$$

In these two cases, the non-degeneracy condition is: the line $P_1 P_2$ is non-isotropic (or $P_1 \neq P_2$ over the reals).
- Construct the point X such that $XP_5 \perp P_1 P_2$ and $XP_6 \perp P_3 P_4$:

$$X = \mathsf{per\_per\_int}(P_1, P_2, P_3, P_4, P_5, P_6)$$
$$= \frac{P_5 \cdot (P_2 - P_1)(P_4 - P_3)^{\sim} - P_6 \cdot (P_4 - P_3)(P_2 - P_1)^{\sim}}{(P_2 - P_1) \cdot (P_4 - P_3)^{\sim}}.$$

The non-degeneracy condition is

$$(P_2 - P_1) \cdot (P_4 - P_3)^{\sim} \neq 0. \qquad \text{%} \ \ P_1 P_2 \nparallel P_3 P_4$$

– Construct the circumcenter X of $\triangle P_1 P_2 P_3$:

$$X = \mathsf{cir\_ctr}(P_1, P_2, P_3)$$
$$= \frac{(P_2 \cdot P_2 - P_1 \cdot P_1)(P_3 - P_1)^\sim - (P_3 \cdot P_3 - P_1 \cdot P_1)(P_2 - P_1)^\sim}{2\,[(P_2 - P_1) \wedge (P_3 - P_1)]^\sim}.$$

The non-degeneracy condition: P_1, P_2, P_3 are non-collinear.

– Construct a point X such that $XP_3 \perp P_1P_2$ and the perpendicular distance from X to P_1P_2 is equal to a given non-negative scalar d:

$$X = \mathsf{per\_dis}(P_1, P_2, P_3, d) = \mathsf{per\_ft}(P_1, P_2, P_3) \pm d\frac{(P_2 - P_1)^\sim}{\sqrt{(P_2 - P_1) \cdot (P_2 - P_1)}}.$$

The non-degeneracy condition: P_1P_2 is non-isotropic.

Using the above constructions and those in [20], one can express a big class of geometric theorems involving points, lines, circles and their relations such as collinearity, parallelism, perpendicularity and equi-distance. Some of the expressions for X above are derived from the solutions of vector equations given in [14]. Their correctness can be easily verified by taking coordinates for the involved points (see the δ-rules in [20]).

3   A Rewrite System for Clifford Algebraic Expressions

It will be shown in Sect. 4.1 how to prove geometric theorems using essentially substitutions of dependent points introduced by the hypotheses and simplifications of the resulting conclusion expressions to 0. As a lot of geometric relations may be expressed by linear constructions in Clifford algebra, this makes possible to use algebraic computing and term-rewriting techniques for proving many nontrivial theorems. This section describes the representation of Clifford numbers and the main rules for simplifying Clifford expressions.

3.1   Computation Rules

Consider expressions composed by means of the operators $\wedge$, $\cdot$ and $\sim$ as well as the usual sum and product among scalars and between scalars and multivectors. We describe a term-rewriting system that can effectively simplify such expressions.

The *grade* of any element of $\mathbb{K}$ is defined to be 0. The *grade* $\mathsf{gr}(\mathbf{C})$ of any $\mathbf{C} \in \mathcal{C} \setminus \mathbb{K}$ is defined to be k if there exist $\mathbf{v}_1, \ldots, \mathbf{v}_k \in \mathcal{V}$ such that $\mathbf{C} = \mathbf{v}_1 \wedge \cdots \wedge \mathbf{v}_k$, and -1 otherwise. Computationally, we have

$$\mathrm{gr}(\mathbf{C}) = \begin{cases} 0 & \text{if } \mathbf{C} \in \mathbb{K}, \\ 1 & \text{if } \mathbf{C} \in \mathcal{V}, \\ |k_1 - k_2| & \text{if } \mathbf{C} = \mathbf{C}_1 \cdot \mathbf{C}_2 \text{ and } k_i = \mathrm{gr}(\mathbf{C}_i) \geq 1 \text{ for } i = 1, 2, \\ k_1 + k_2 & \text{if } \mathbf{C} = \mathbf{C}_1 \wedge \mathbf{C}_2, k_i = \mathrm{gr}(\mathbf{C}_i) \geq 0 \text{ and } k_1 + k_2 \leq n, \\ 0 & \text{if } \mathbf{C} = \mathbf{C}_1 \cdot \mathbf{C}_2 \text{ and } \mathrm{gr}(\mathbf{C}_1) = 0 \text{ or } \mathrm{gr}(\mathbf{C}_2) = 0; \\ & \text{or } \mathbf{C} = \mathbf{C}_1 \wedge \mathbf{C}_2, k_i = \mathrm{gr}(\mathbf{C}_i) \geq 0 \text{ and } k_1 + k_2 > n, \\ -1 & \text{if } \not\exists \mathbf{v}_1, \dots, \mathbf{v}_k \in \mathcal{V} \text{ such that } \mathbf{C} = \mathbf{v}_1 \wedge \cdots \wedge \mathbf{v}_k \\ & \text{for any } k \geq 1. \end{cases}$$

$\mathbf{C}$ is called a k-vector or a *multivector* of grade k if $\mathrm{gr}(\mathbf{C}) = k \geq 0$.

It has been proposed in [20] to use four groups of selected computation rules to simplify Clifford expressions:

α.1–4. Trivial rules; $\qquad\qquad$ β.1–5. Elementary rules;
γ.1–5. Advanced rules; $\qquad\qquad$ δ.1–3. Coordinate rules.

Here our term-rewriting system is developed on the basis of these rules with one modification for γ.1. For any $\mathbf{a}, \mathbf{b} \in \mathcal{V}$ and $\mathbf{C}, \mathbf{D} \in \mathcal{C}$ with $\mathrm{gr}(\mathbf{C}) \geq 0$:

$$(\mathbf{C} \wedge \mathbf{a}) \cdot \mathbf{D} \rightarrow \mathbf{C} \cdot (\mathbf{a} \cdot \mathbf{D}); \quad \mathbf{a} \cdot (\mathbf{b} \wedge \mathbf{C}) \rightarrow \mathbf{a} \cdot \mathbf{b}\,\mathbf{C} - \mathbf{b} \wedge (\mathbf{a} \cdot \mathbf{C}).$$

The correctness of this and other rewrite rules follows from the known properties and relations among Clifford operators (see [10]). It can also be verified partially by using the coordinate rules. Some rules should only be applied according to the grade of some subterms; in this case the conditions are specified.

The δ rules are used only in case one fails to prove a theorem using other rules. The exact process is presented in the following subsections. Some rules are constrained by order conditions, others by grades; every condition may be easily computed as we only intend to apply them to *ground terms*. For the same reason, distributivity, associativity and commutativity may be used without termination problems under a suitable ordering.

3.2 Grading

Among the several problems that we address is the treatment of scalars. Scalars are expressions having a null grade and generally represented by a composition of constant symbols denoting elements of $\mathbb{K}$ and vectors or other Clifford numbers of higher grade.

There are two ways for coping with this problem. The first approach consists in using a rewrite system for computing rational numbers [7] and could be used to make our system entirely based on symbolic treatments. However we prefer to use a second approach, based on a specific representation of multivectors, for the purpose of efficiency.

In this representation, the key concept is the multivector. A new ternary symbol v is introduced, with the following semantics: $v(g, f, e)$ is the multivector

e of grade g multiplied by the scalar factor $f \in \mathbb{K}$ and three sorts are used, for grades, scalars and other Clifford numbers. Note that 0 may be represented by any of the $v(0,0,e)$ terms. Moreover, in the rule

$$v(g_1, f_1, x_1) \wedge v(g_2, f_2, x_2) \rightarrow v(g_1 + g_2, f_1 f_2, v(g_1, f_1, x_1) \wedge v(g_2, f_2, x_2)),$$

$g_1 + g_2$ denotes a natural or -1, and $f_1 f_2$ denotes a scalar. Using this rule, $v(1, 2, A) \wedge v(1, -3, B)$ is reduced to $v(2, -6, v(1, 1, A) \wedge v(1, 1, B))$. By successive applications of these rules to a term whose leaves have the form $v(.,.,.)$ using an innermost reduction strategy, it is clear that the grade of any term and its subterms are computed. But before applying these rules for computing grades, the following transformation is performed first.

A Clifford expression is said to be expanded iff every leaf has the form $v(g, f, x)$, where g denotes an integer positive or equal to -1, f a scalar, and x a Clifford number such that if g's interpretation is a positive integer k then x is interpreted as a k-vector and the term is in normal form modulo the following:

$$(x_1 + x_2)^\sim \rightarrow x_1^\sim + x_2^\sim; \quad x_1 \wedge (x_2 + x_3) \rightarrow (x_1 \wedge x_2) + (x_1 \wedge x_3);$$

$$(x_1 + x_2) \wedge x_3 \rightarrow (x_1 \wedge x_3) + (x_2 \wedge x_3); \quad x_1 \cdot (x_2 + x_3) \rightarrow (x_1 \cdot x_2) + (x_1 \cdot x_3);$$

$$(x_1 + x_2) \cdot x_3 \rightarrow (x_1 \cdot x_3) + (x_2 \cdot x_3).$$

A Clifford expression is graded iff it cannot be reduced by an application of any rule of the following system:

$$v(g_1, 0, x_1) \rightarrow v(0, 0, 1) \text{ if } g_1 \neq 0; \quad v(g_1, 0, x_1)^\sim \rightarrow v(0, 0, 1);$$

$$v(g_1, f_1, v(g_2, f_2, x_1)) \rightarrow v(g_2, f_1 f_2, x_1);$$

$$v(g_1, 0, x_1) + x_2 \rightarrow x_2; \quad x_1 + v(g_1, 0, x_2) \rightarrow x_1;$$

$$v(g_1, f_1, x_1) + v(g_1, f_2, x_1) \rightarrow v(g_1, f_1 + f_2, x_1);$$

$$v(g_1, 0, x_1) \cdot x_2 \rightarrow v(0, 0, 1); \quad x_1 \cdot v(g_1, 0, x_2) \rightarrow v(0, 0, 1);$$

$$v(0, f_1, x_1) \cdot x_2 \rightarrow v(0, 0, 1); \quad x_1 \cdot v(0, f_2, x_2) \rightarrow v(0, 0, 1);$$

$$v(0, f_1, 1) \wedge v(g_1, f_2, x_1) \rightarrow v(g_1, f_1 f_2, x_1);$$

$$v(g_1, f_1, x_1) \wedge v(0, f_1, 1) \rightarrow v(g_1, f_1 f_2, x_1);$$

$$v(g_1, f_1, x_1) \wedge v(g_2, f_2, x_2) \rightarrow v(g_1 + g_2, f_1 f_2, v(g_1, 1, x_1) \wedge v(g_2, 1, x_2));$$

$$v(g_1, f_1, x_1) \cdot v(g_2, f_2, x_2) \rightarrow v(|g_1 - g_2|, f_1 f_2, v(g_1, f_1, x_1) \cdot v(g_2, f_2, x_2)).$$

The above rules are applied using for priority their rank in the system. The normalization is performed on subterms first. The symbol 1 is interpreted as a multivector of grade 0. Thus, as we have already mentioned, the ring product in $\mathbb{K}$ may be replaced by the outer product, and the null element of $\mathbb{K}$ is represented by the term $v(0, 0, 1)$.

3.3   Flattening

After being expanded and graded, a Clifford expression becomes a sum of products and duals. When a dual is applied to a product it cannot be further reduced without knowing the dimension of the space. That is why we can consider that equal duals are replaced by identical symbols denoting a multivector. Thus we restrict ourselves to the case where no dual symbol appears in a product.

A flat form may be considered as a multiset of multivectors and the following order may be used to sort them. As before let $\mathrm{gr}(.)$ be the grade of a term; $\mathrm{gr}(v(g,.,.))$ is the integer represented by g. By convention, "$\sim$" $<$ "$\wedge$" $<$ ".", and if $\mathbf{V}$ is a constant symbol denoting a k-vector ($k > 0$) then $1 < \mathbf{V} <$ "$\sim$". Denote by $<_{\mathrm{lex}}$ the lexical order, induced by "$<$", which does not take into account the first two arguments of v. Let t_1 and t_2 be two ground terms in expanded form representing multivectors. We order $t_1 < t_2$ iff one of the following cases holds:

1. $\mathrm{gr}(t_1) < \mathrm{gr}(t_2)$;
2. $\mathrm{gr}(t_1) = \mathrm{gr}(t_2)$ and $t_1 <_{\mathrm{lex}} t_2$.

This defines an order over classes of ground terms interpreted by equal Clifford numbers up to a factor in $\mathbb{K}$. The following commutation and transposition rules are used to simulate a kind of sort:

$$v(g_1, f_1, x_1) \cdot v(g_2, f_2, x_2) \rightarrow v(g_2, f_3, x_2) \cdot v(g_1, 1, x_1) \text{ if } x_1 > x_2,$$
$$\text{where } f_3 = (-1)^{g_1 g_2 - \min(g_1, g_2)} f_1 f_2;$$

$$v(g_1, f_1, x_1) \wedge v(g_2, f_2, x_2) \rightarrow v(g_2, f_3, x_2) \wedge v(g_1, 1, x_1) \text{ if } x_1 > x_2,$$
$$\text{where } f_3 = (-1)^{g_1 g_2} f_1 f_2;$$

$$v(g_1, f_1, x_1 \cdot x_2) \cdot x_3 \rightarrow v(g_1, f_1, x_1 \cdot (x_2 \cdot x_3));$$
$$x_1 \cdot v(g_1, f_1, x_2 \cdot x_3) \rightarrow v(g_1, f_1, x_2 \cdot (x_1 \cdot x_3)) \text{ if } x_2 < x_1;$$
$$v(g_1, f_1, x_1 \wedge x_2) \wedge x_3 \rightarrow v(g_1, f_1, x_1 \wedge (x_2 \wedge x_3));$$
$$x_1 \wedge v(g_1, f_1, x_2 \wedge x_3) \rightarrow v(g_1, f_1, x_2 \wedge (x_1 \wedge x_3)) \text{ if } x_2 < x_1;$$
$$v(g_1, f_1, x_1) \cdot v(g_4, f_2, v(g_2, 1, x_2) \cdot v(g_3, 1, x_3)) \rightarrow v(g_1, f_3, x_1) \cdot [v(g_2, 1, x_2)$$
$$\cdot v(g_3, 1, x_3)] \text{ if } x_1 < x_2, \text{ where } f_3 = (-1)^{g_1 g_2 - \min(g_1, g_2)} f_1 f_2;$$

$$v(g_1, f_1, x_1) \wedge v(g_4, f_2, v(g_2, 1, x_2) \wedge v(g_3, 1, x_3)) \rightarrow$$
$$v(g_2, f_3, x_1) \wedge [v(g_1, 1, x_2) \wedge v(g_3, 1, x_3)] \text{ if } x_2 < x_1, \text{ where } f_3 = (-1)^{g_1 g_2} f_1 f_2;$$
$$(x_1 + x_2) + x_3 \rightarrow x_1 + (x_2 + x_3);$$
$$v(g_1, f_1, x_1) + v(g_2, f_2, x_2) \rightarrow v(g_2, f_2, x_2) + v(g_1, f_1, x_1) \text{ if } x_2 < x_1;$$
$$v(g_1, f_1, x_1) + [v(g_2, f_2, x_2) + v(g_3, f_3, x_3)] \rightarrow$$
$$v(g_2, f_2, x_2) + [v(g_1, f_1, x_1) + v(g_3, f_3, x_3)] \text{ if } x_2 < x_1.$$

3.4 Space-Dependent and Advanced Rules

Two general rules involve the dimension. The first one is related to the computation of the grade of a dual of a multivector; the second is related to the upper dimension axiom. Let n be the dimension of the vector space $\mathcal{V}$; then

$$v(g_1, f_1, x_1)^{\sim} \rightarrow v(n - g_1, f_1, x_1^{\sim}); \quad v(g_1, f_1, x_1) \rightarrow v(0, 0, 1) \text{ if } g_1 > n.$$

The following rules are essential in practice for proving most theorems:

$$v(g_1, f_1, x_1 \wedge v(1, f_2, x_2)) \cdot x_3 \rightarrow x_1 \cdot [v(1, f_1 f_2, x_2) \cdot x_3];$$
$$v(1, f_1, x_1) \cdot v(g_1, f_2, v(1, 1, x_2) \wedge x_3) \rightarrow$$
$$[v(1, f_1, x_1) \cdot v(1, f_2, x_2)] \wedge x_3 - v(1, f_2, x_2) \wedge [v(1, 1, x_1) \cdot x_3].$$

It is possible to append other axioms for specific dimensions. They correspond to the $\beta.4$ and γ groups. For instance, in two-dimensional space, the following rules are added:

$$v(1, f_1, x_1) \wedge v(1, f_2, x_1) \rightarrow v(0, 0, 1); \quad v(1, f_1, x_1) \cdot v(1, f_2, x_1^{\sim}) \rightarrow v(0, 0, 1);$$
$$v(1, f_1, x_1^{\sim\sim}) \rightarrow v(1, -f_1, x_1);$$
$$[v(2, f_1, v(1, 1, x_1) \wedge v(1, 1, x_2))]^{\sim} \rightarrow v(1, f_1, x_1) \cdot v(1, f_2, x_2)^{\sim};$$
$$v(1, f_1, x_1) \wedge v(1, f_2, x_2^{\sim}) \rightarrow v(1, f_2, x_2) \wedge v(1, f_1, x_1^{\sim}) \text{ if } x_1 > x_2.$$

It is useful to introduce the multivector I of grade 2 (see Sect. 2.1). The following rules are used to simplify expressions involving I and eliminate the outer product:

$$v(0, f_1, I^{\sim}) \rightarrow v(0, -f_1, 1);$$
$$v(1, f_1, x_1) \wedge v(1, f_2, x_2) \rightarrow [v(0, -f_1 f_2, v(1, 1, x_1) \cdot v(1, 1, x_2^{\sim}))] \wedge v(2, 1, I);$$

$$v(0, f_1, x_1^{\sim}) \rightarrow v(0, f_1, x_1) \cdot v(2, 1, I); \quad v(1, f_1, x_1) \cdot v(2, f_2, I) \rightarrow v(1, f_1 f_2, x_1^{\sim});$$
$$v(2, f_1, x_1 \wedge v(2, f_2, I)) \cdot v(2, f_3, x_2 \wedge v(2, 1, I)) \rightarrow v(0, -f_1 f_2 f_3, x_1 \wedge x_2);$$
$$v(2, f_1, I) \cdot v(2, f_2, x_2 \wedge v(2, 1, I)) \rightarrow v(0, -f_1 f_2, x_2);$$
$$v(2, f_1, x_1 \wedge v(2, 1, I)) \cdot v(2, f_2, I) \rightarrow v(0, -f_1 f_2, x_1);$$
$$v(2, f_1, I) \cdot v(2, f_2, I) \rightarrow v(0, -f_1 f_2, 1).$$

3.5 Normalization

For proving that a Clifford expression g is null, it is first graded and flattened. The grading process realizes most of the simplifications. Before every application of an advanced rule, the term is graded and flattened, following the idea of normalized rewriting [16].

If g with flat subterms is not equal to 0, then the space-dependent rules are applied using an innermost strategy. If it is not reduced to 0, the whole process restarts. If no further reduction can be made in the process then the coordinate rules δ are applied finally to transform the expression into a polynomial or a multivector with polynomial entries whose variables are coordinates. In this case, the expression is identically 0 iff the polynomial (entries) are all 0.

4 Method, Examples, and Experiments

4.1 Description of the Method

Let us be restricted to theorems in plane Euclidean geometry, each of which may be formulated constructively as follows.

Starting with a finite number of given scalar parameters $u_1, \ldots, u_e$ and free points $U_1, \ldots, U_h$, construct finitely many new points step by step using the three kinds of constructions listed in Sect. 2.2 and [20]. During the construction, some other scalar parameters $u_{e+1}, \ldots, u_d$ $(d \geq e)$ and free points $U_{h+1}, \ldots, U_m$ $(m \geq h)$ may be introduced so that the remaining points $X_1, \ldots, X_r$ are dependent and each X_i can be represented in terms of the scalar parameters $u_1, \ldots, u_d$, free points $U_1, \ldots, U_m$, and the previously constructed dependent points $X_1, \ldots, X_{i-1}$:

$$X_i = f_i(u_1, \ldots, u_d; U_1, \ldots, U_m; X_1, \ldots, X_{i-1}), \quad 1 \leq i \leq r, \tag{H}$$

using Clifford operators. Then the set of equational expressions

$$X_1 - f_1 = 0, \ldots, X_r - f_r = 0$$

constitutes the hypothesis of the theorem in question. In the above representation of X_i, the denominator d_i of each f_i is assumed to be non-zero, taking as a non-degeneracy condition. The conclusion of the theorem to be proved may be given as another Clifford expression

$$g = g(u_1, \ldots, u_d; U_1, \ldots, U_m; X_1, \ldots, X_r) = 0. \tag{C}$$

The problem of proving the theorem is reduced to verifying whether g is identically equal to 0 when the X_i are substituted by the corresponding expressions f_i. We refer to the class of theorems which can be stated in the above manner as class $\mathbb{C}$.

Method (for proving any geometric theorem in $\mathbb{C}$).

Step 1. Formulate the theorem in $\mathbb{C}$ using the constructions given in Sect. 2.2 and [20] so that d scalar parameters u_j, m free points U_k and r dependent points X_i are introduced, the Clifford expressions (H) constitute the hypothesis and (C) gives the conclusion of the theorem. Let d_i be the denominator of f_i in (H) for $1 \leq i \leq r$.

Step 2. Let $f_1^* = f_1$. Do the following substitution for $i = 2, \ldots, r$:

Compute $f_i^* = f_i^*(u_1, \ldots, u_d; U_1, \ldots, U_m) = f_i|_{X_1 = f_1^*, \ldots, X_{i-1} = f_{i-1}^*}$

$$= f_i(u_1, \ldots, u_d; U_1, \ldots, U_m; f_1^*, \ldots, f_{i-1}^*).$$

[Clearly, the obtained f_i^* involve only the parameters u_j and free points U_k.]

Step 3. Substitute all $X_i = f_i^*$ into g:

$$g^* = g^*(u_1, \ldots, u_d; U_1, \ldots, U_m) = g|_{X_1 = f_1^*, \ldots, X_r = f_r^*}$$
$$= g(u_1, \ldots, u_d; U_1, \ldots, U_m; f_1^*, \ldots, f_r^*).$$

Let h be the numerator of g^*.

Step 4. Apply the rewrite system presented in Sect. 3 to h. If h is simplified to 0, then the theorem is true under the non-degeneracy conditions $d_i \neq 0$ for $1 \leq i \leq r$. If h does not evaluate to 0 when the coordinate rules δ are applied, then the theorem is false under the conditions $d_i \neq 0$.

An alternative for steps 2 and 3 is to use a reversed substitution that reduces the conclusion expression g to 0 by $X_i = f_i$ for $i = r, \ldots, 1$; see [20] for details. The efficiency of the method may be seen partially from the following examples.

4.2   Two Examples

Example 2 (Pivot). Take three points P, Q, R on the three sides of an arbitrary triangle ABC. Let the circumcircles of $\triangle APR$ and $\triangle BQP$ meet at another point M. Then the four points C, R, M, Q are cocyclic.

Let the circumcenters of $\triangle APR, \triangle BQP$ and $\triangle CRQ$ be O_A, O_B and O_C respectively. Now A, B, C are free points. The constructions may be as follows

$P = \mathsf{on\_line}(A, B),$

$Q = \mathsf{on\_line}(B, C),$

$R = \mathsf{on\_line}(A, C),$

$O_A = \mathsf{cir\_ctr}(A, P, R),$

$O_B = \mathsf{cir\_ctr}(B, Q, P),$

$O_C = \mathsf{cir\_ctr}(C, R, Q),$

$M = \mathsf{ref}(O_A, O_B, P).$

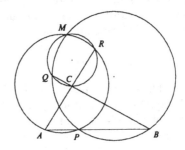

During the construction, three parameters are introduced. The algebraic expressions for the dependent points may be obtained easily from those given in Sect. 2.2. The conclusion of the theorem is

$$g = [\mathsf{midp}(M, R) - O_A] \wedge (O_C - O_A) = 0. \quad \text{\% } \mathsf{col}(O_A, \mathsf{midp}(M, R), O_C)$$

Note that $\mathsf{col}(A, B, C, \ldots)$ stands for "the points $A, B, C, \ldots$ are collinear." To simplify calculation, take A as the origin, i.e., $A = 0$. The theorem is then proved by substituting the expressions of P, Q, R, etc. into g and simplifying the result to 0 with application of the rules α–γ.

The following is another example that provides easy proofs of difficult theorems without using the coordinate rules. For any three points A, B, C, let $|AB|$ denote the distance between A and B, and $|C(AB)|$ the (perpendicular) distance from C to the line AB.

Example 3. Take three points C_1, A_1 and B_1 respectively on the three perpendicular bisectors of AB, BC and CA of any $\triangle ABC$ such that

$$|C_1(AB)| = t|AB|, \quad |A_1(BC)| = t|BC|, \quad |B_1(CA)| = t|CA|,$$

where t is an arbitrary non-negative number. Then:

(a) (Generalized Steiner theorem). The lines AA_1, BB_1, CC_1 are concurrent;

(b). If $t = \sqrt{3}/2$, the circumcircles of $\triangle ABC_1, \triangle BCA_1, \triangle CAB_1$ are concurrent;

(c) (Napoleon theorem). If $t = \sqrt{3}/6$, then $\triangle A_1 B_1 C_1$ is equilateral;

(d). If $t = 1/2$, then $CC_1 \perp A_1 B_1$ and $|CC_1| = |A_1 B_1|$.

Let the vertex C of the triangle be located at the origin, i.e., $C = 0$. The points A_1, B_1, C_1 may be constructed as follows

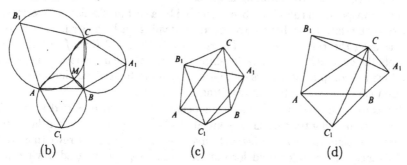

(b)   (c)   (d)

$$A_1 = \mathsf{per\_dis}(C, B, \mathsf{midp}(C, B), t|CB|) = B/2 + tB^\sim,$$

$$B_1 = \mathsf{per\_dis}(A, C, \mathsf{midp}(A, C), t|AC|) = A/2 - tA^\sim,$$

$$C_1 = \mathsf{per\_dis}(B, A, \mathsf{midp}(B, A), t|BA|) = (A + B)/2 + t(A^\sim - B^\sim).$$

(a). A proof of the generalized Steiner theorem using Clifford algebra has been given in [20]. Special cases of this theorem include the centroid theorem ($t = 0$), Steiner theorem ($t = \sqrt{3}/2$) and orthocenter theorem ($t = \infty$).

(b). As in the preceding example, let

$$O_A = \mathsf{cir\_ctr}(B, C, A_1), \quad O_B = \mathsf{cir\_ctr}(C, A, B_1), \quad O_C = \mathsf{cir\_ctr}(A, B, C_1),$$
$$M = \mathsf{ref}(O_A, O_B, C).$$

The theorem may be proved by substituting $t = \sqrt{3}/2$ and the expressions of the dependent points into the conclusion expression

$$[\mathsf{midp}(M, B) - O_A] \wedge (O_C - O_A)$$

and simplifying the result to 0 with application of the rules α–γ.

(c) and (d). The conclusion expressions

$$(B_1 - A_1) \cdot (B_1 - A_1) - (C_1 - A_1) \cdot (C_1 - A_1),$$
$$(B_1 - A_1) \cdot (B_1 - A_1) - (C_1 - B_1) \cdot (C_1 - B_1);$$
$$(B_1 - A_1) \cdot (C_1 - C), \quad (B_1 - A_1) \cdot (B_1 - A_1) - (C_1 - C) \cdot (C_1 - C)$$

may be easily simplified to 0 by substitution of $t = \sqrt{3}/6$ and $t = 1/2$, respectively, and the expressions of A_1, B_1, C_1 with application of the rules α–γ.

4.3   Implementation and Experiments

The method described in Sect. 4.1 has been implemented first in *Maple V* for our preliminary experiments and has proved a number of interesting geometric theorems. In order to achieve better performance and to explore the full power of rewriting techniques, we have started implementing another theorem prover using the rewrite rules on top of a sample rewriting package EZTerm written in the *Objective Caml* programming language.

The transposition rules have been replaced by a sort on the list of k-vectors. A new rewrite relation has been introduced for dealing with the scalar operations: $u \to v$ using the rule $l \to_f r$ iff $\sigma l = u$ and $v = f(\sigma, r)$. When $f : (\sigma, t) \to \sigma t$, one gets the classical rewrite relationship. This makes the incorporation of scalar functions for computing factors quite easy. It should be noticed that every such function could be simulated by rewriting.

It has been observed that the space-dependent rules may help to dramatically decrease the proving time when they are applied to the term just after flattening. We are investigating new strategies to avoid some unnecessary rewriting steps. For instance, actual rules used for our experiments preserve grades while it is possible, and grading is required only after an application of a simplification rule involving the null term. They are not listed here for the sake of clarity.

In EZTerm, we have a draft version ready for the last simplification step of the method; the implementation for the other steps is in progress. For the current experiments, the expression h in step 3 is obtained by using the Maple V implementation. It is reduced to 0 as in step 4 using our simplifier in EZTerm.

The following table shows the reduction of h to 0 for 12 typical theorems on a PC Pentium 90 with 24 Mb of RAM. The times T are given in seconds. The number n of parameters and free points and the size l (measured by the Maple function length) of h are also provided.

Theorem	n	l	T	Theorem	n	l	T
Orthocenter	2	93	0.4	Example 3 (d)	3	112	0.6
Example 3 (c)	3	154	0.8	Centroid	3	157	2.0
Pivot	5	274	81.2	Example 3 (a)	3	352	7.4
Desargues	3	457	2.2	Gauss line	4	489	6.1
Example 3 (b)	3	1741	36.9	Pappus	6	1919	8.6
Simson	4	3591	14.7	Butterfly	4	36828	28.0

We have no intention to compare our approach with others such as those based on characteristic sets and Gröbner bases in terms of computing time because the proofs produced by the two types of methods differ by their nature: the latter use coordinates and reduce geometric statements to polynomial relations; on the contrary Clifford algebra emphasizes the geometric aspect of a proof, in which every Clifford expression can be interpreted geometrically. However our experiments show that the method presented in this paper may compete with long-time studied coordinate-based proof methods.

5 Conclusion Remarks

This paper underlines the role of a term-rewrite system for geometric theorem proving, where the use of Clifford algebra is essential. The effectiveness of our coordinate-free approach has been demonstrated by some preliminary experiments with non-trivial examples. As a matter of fact, the rewrite system developed by us is geometry-independent and thus can be used for automated theorem proving in Clifford algebra in general. Investigations along this line with application to other areas beyond geometry remain for our future research.

Vector and Clifford algebra representations have been used for geometric theorem proving previously in [5,14,15,18,20]. Compared with [20], in which rewrite rules are given as a set of mathematical equations allowing to transform Clifford expressions, this paper presents rewriting in Clifford algebra from an operational point of view: it gives a slightly different system (notably with the addition of an important rule to $\gamma.1$, see Sect. 3.1), sketches the strategy used to reduce Clifford expressions and reports experimental results. From the presentation of the previous sections, one may observe the significance of simplifying Clifford expressions in the context of theorem proving. We have not been aware of any other work for such automated simplification in the literature.

The application of rewrite rules for proving geometric theorems has also been explored early in [4], where polynomial computations are performed by using specialized procedures; this is not the case in our implementation. In comparison with [2], our work illustrates the power and capability of general rewriting techniques for solving difficult problems.

References

1. Ablamowicz, R., Lounesto, P., Parra J. M.: Clifford algebras with numeric and symbolic computations. Birkhäuser, Boston (1996).
2. Balbiani, P., Fariñas del Cerro, L.: Affine geometry of collinearity and conditional term rewriting. In: Proc. French Spring School Theor. Comput. Sci. (Font-romeu, May 17–21, 1993), LNCS **909**, pp. 196–213 (1995).
3. Chou, S.-C.: Mechanical geometry theorem proving. Reidel, Dordrecht (1988).
4. Chou, S.-C., Schelter, W. F.: Proving geometry theorems with rewrite rules. J. Automat. Reason. **2**: 253–273 (1986).
5. Chou, S.-C., Gao, X.-S., Zhang, J.-Z.: Automated geometry theorem proving by vector calculation. In: Proc. ISSAC '93 (Kiev, July 6–8, 1993), pp. 284–291.
6. Chou, S.-C., Gao, X.-S., Zhang, J.-Z.: Machine proofs in geometry. World Scientific, Singapore (1994).
7. Contejean, E., Marché, C., Rabehasaina, L.: Rewrite systems for natural, integral and rational arithmetic. Technical report, L.R.I., Université de Paris-Sud, France (1997).
8. Fèvre, S.: Integration of reasoning and algebraic calculus in geometry. In: Automated deduction in geometry (D. Wang et al., eds.), LNAI **1360**, pp. 218–234 (1998).
9. Havel, T. F.: Some examples of the use of distances as coordinates for Euclidean geometry. J. Symb. Comput. **11**: 579–593 (1991).

10. Hestenes, D., Sobczyk, G.: Clifford algebra to geometric calculus. Reidel, Dordrecht (1984).
11. Kapur, D.: Using Gröbner bases to reason about geometry problems. J. Symb. Comput. **2**: 399–408 (1986).
12. Kapur, D., Saxena, T., Yang, L.: Algebraic and geometric reasoning using Dixon resultants. In: Proc. ISSAC '94 (Oxford, July 20–22, 1994), pp. 99–107.
13. Kutzler, B., Stifter, S.: On the application of Buchberger's algorithm to automated geometry theorem proving. J. Symb. Comput. **2**: 389–397 (1986).
14. Li, H.: New explorations on mechanical theorem proving of geometries. Ph.D thesis, Beijing University, China (1994).
15. Li, H., Cheng, M.-t.: Proving theorems in elementary geometry with Clifford algebraic method. Chinese Math. Progress **26**: 357–371 (1997).
16. Marché, C.: Normalized rewriting: An alternative to rewriting modulo a set of equations. J. Symb. Comput. **3**: 253–288 (1996).
17. Richter-Gebert, J.: Mechanical theorem proving in projective geometry. Ann. Math. Artif. Intell. **13**: 139–172 (1995).
18. Stifter, S.: Geometry theorem proving in vector spaces by means of Gröbner bases. In: Proc. ISSAC '93 (Kiev, July 6–8, 1993), pp. 301–310.
19. Wang, D.: Elimination procedures for mechanical theorem proving in geometry. Ann. Math. Artif. Intell. **13**: 1–24 (1995).
20. Wang, D.: Clifford algebraic calculus for geometric reasoning with application to computer vision. In: Automated deduction in geometry (D. Wang et al., eds.), LNAI **1360**, pp. 115–140 (1998).
21. Wu, W.-t.: Basic principles of mechanical theorem proving in elementary geometries. J. Syst. Sci. Math. Sci. **4**: 207–235 (1984).
22. Wu, W.-t.: Mechanical theorem proving in geometries: Basic principles. Springer, Wien (1994).

System Description: Similarity-Based Lemma Generation for Model Elimination

Marc Fuchs

Technische Universität München, Institut für Informatik, D-80290 München
fuchsm@informatik.tu-muenchen.de

ATP systems based on model elimination (ME) [5] or the connection tableau calculus [4] have become more and more successful. But a problem regarding the use of ME is the fact that ME proof procedures are among the weakest procedures when the length of existing proofs is considered. The use of lemmas offers a solution to this problem. Successful sub-deductions are stored in form of lemmas and the input clauses are augmented with these formulas. But although lemmas can help to decrease the proof length they also increase the branching rate of the search space. An unbounded generation of lemmas without filtering *relevant* lemmas is not sensible. Actually, filter mechanisms are in use that ignore the proof task at hand (cp. [1,8]). It may be more appropriate to use *similarity criteria* between the proof goal and a possible lemma (*lemma candidate*) in order to filter lemmas. Thus, we will present a model for similarity-based lemma use.

Connection Tableau Calculus. The connection tableau calculus (CTC) works on clausal tableaux and consists of three inference rules. Let $\mathcal{C}$ be a given set of clauses to be refuted. The *start* rule allows for a conventional tableau expansion applied to the trivial tableau which consists of only one unlabeled node. Tableau expansion attaches a clause from $\mathcal{C}$ at the leaf node of a tableau. *Reduction* allows for closing an open branch by unifying the literal at the leaf with the complement of another literal on the same branch. *Extension* is a combination of tableau expansion and immediately performing reduction.

In order to refute a clause set with CTC a closed tableau has to be enumerated starting with the trivial tableau. Normally implicit enumeration procedures are employed performing iterative deepening search with backtracking (cp. [9]). Iteratively, larger finite segments of the search tree $\mathcal{T}$ which is the tree of all possible derivations of tableaux are explored. The segments are defined by so-called *completeness bounds* which pose structural restrictions on the tableaux which are allowed in the current segment. Prominent examples for such bounds are the *depth* and *inference* bound (see [6]). The depth bound limits the maximal depth of nodes (the root node has depth 0) in a tableau (ignoring leaf nodes) according to a fixed *resource* $n \in \mathbb{N}$, i.e. only tableau with depth smaller or equal to n are allowed. The inference bound limits the number of inferences allowed for

C. Kirchner and H. Kirchner (Eds.): Automated Deduction, CADE-15
LNAI 1421, pp. 33–37, 1998. © Springer–Verlag Berlin Heidelberg 1998

the derivation of a tableau. Iterative deepening, using a bound $\mathcal{B}$, is performed by starting with a basic resource n and iteratively increasing n until a proof is found within the finite initial segment of T defined by $\mathcal{B}$ and n.

Bottom-Up Lemma Generation. We employ a *static* lemma generation technique as introduced in [8]. *Unit lemmas* are generated in a preprocessing phase and added to the clause set $\mathcal{C}$ to be refuted. In the preprocessing queries $\neg p(X_1, \ldots, X_n)$ (and $p(X_1, \ldots, X_n)$ in the case of non-horn clauses) are added to $\mathcal{C}$ and all solution substitutions $\sigma_1, \ldots, \sigma_k$ which can be obtained in the segment of the search tree defined by the depth bound and a fixed (small) resource n_D are enumerated. Subsumed facts from $\{\sigma_i(p(X_1, \ldots, X_n)) : 1 \leq i \leq k\}$ are deleted which results in a set $\mathcal{L}_0$. Then a top-down proof run takes place using $\mathcal{C} \cup \mathcal{L}_0$ and a fixed bound. With this method always a reduction of the proof length is obtained using horn clauses (see [2]). More interesting is whether the process of *finding* a proof profits from using lemmas ("macro operators").

Let us first consider the case that the *depth bound* $\mathcal{B}_D$ is used for the top-down proof run. Let n be the resource which is at least needed to obtain a proof when using no lemmas. We assume that the resource which is at least needed when using lemmas from $\mathcal{L}_0$ can be reduced from n to $n - n_D + 1$. This is guaranteed for horn clauses. Let T_1 or T_2 be the smallest segments (w.r.t. $\mathcal{B}_D$) of the search trees which are defined by $\mathcal{C} \cup \mathcal{L}_0$ or $\mathcal{C}$, respectively, that include a proof. In T_1 there are *no new solutions* of subgoals compared with T_2 (cp. [2]). If local failure caching (cp. [4]) is employed also no duplication of segments of the search space is incorporated into T_1 which is in opposite to classical macro operator learning (cp. [7, 2]). Instead, inferences possible in T_2 are *spared*, e.g. because of the subsumption test when generating lemmas (see [2]). The number of inferences saved is normally much larger than the number of inferences performed in the preprocessing phase. When using the *inference bound* similar effects occur. But new solution substitutions may be introduced to T_1 that are not possible in T_2. We have a more uncontrolled behavior in comparison to the depth bound (cp. [2]). A dramatic improvement for the search can be obtained by using only some few *relevant* lemmas which lead to resource reductions.

Principles of a Similarity-Based Lemma Selection. We introduce a notion of relevancy of a lemma set for a proof goal (*a posteriori similarity*). Let $\mathcal{C}$ be a set of clauses, $S \in \mathcal{C}$ a start clause for refuting $\mathcal{C}$, and $\mathcal{L}_0$ a set of lemma candidates. $\mathcal{L} \subseteq \mathcal{L}_0$ is *most similar* to S w.r.t. a completeness bound $\mathcal{B}$ if instances of all clauses from $\mathcal{L}$ appear in a closed tableau which can be found with start clause S, bound $\mathcal{B}$, and a minimal resource (no proof for $\mathcal{C} \cup \mathcal{L}_0$ can be found with a smaller resource). A selection of a most similar lemma set necessitates the consideration of all subsets of $\mathcal{L}_0$. Thus, we employ a *local notion* of relevancy. A lemma is *most weakly similar* to S if there is a lemma set that contains l and which is most similar to S. The lemmas most weakly similar to S form a set $\mathcal{L}_{loc}$ which can help to refute $\mathcal{C}$ (using start clause S) with a minimal resource. Since $\mathcal{L}_{loc}$ is normally much smaller than $\mathcal{L}_0$ it is a well-suited lemma set.

The following method (*lemma delaying* tableaux enumeration) allows for computing the set $\mathcal{L}_{loc}$. It provides a sound and complete test whether $l \in \mathcal{L}_0$ can be used to refute S in $\mathcal{T}^{C \cup \mathcal{L}_0, S, \mathcal{B}, m}$. ($\mathcal{T}^{C \cup \mathcal{L}_0, S, \mathcal{B}, m}$ is the finite search tree defined by $C \cup \mathcal{L}_0$, start clause S, a completeness bound $\mathcal{B}$, and the resource m which is at least needed to refute $C \cup \mathcal{L}_0$.) We enumerate the set $\mathcal{O}$ of all tableaux in $\mathcal{T}^{C \cup \mathcal{L}_0, S, \mathcal{B}, m}$. Then, we have to check whether a tableau $T \in \mathcal{O}$ exists which has only one subgoal (*front literal*) and whether the front literal can be solved by extension with l such that the resulting tableau is in $\mathcal{T}^{C \cup \mathcal{L}_0, S, \mathcal{B}, m}$. With the help of *similarity measures* we come to estimations for the maximal weak similarity. We compute such measures by *simulating* the complete test. We enumerate only a subset of the set of front literals occurring in $\mathcal{T}^{C \cup \mathcal{L}_0, S, \mathcal{B}, m}$ and compute some *unification distances* between the generated front literals and the facts from $\mathcal{L}_0$. Based on these distances the usefulness of a fact can be estimated.

Similarity Measures. At first we want to clarify how to generate front literals. We want to generate for each useful lemma a structural similar front literal. Since a priori not even the value m is given and thus the form of $\mathcal{T}^{C \cup \mathcal{L}_0, S, \mathcal{B}, m}$ is unknown we employ breadth-first search in the search tree defined by $C \cup \mathcal{L}_0$, S, and $\mathcal{B}$. We enumerate all front literals occurring in tableaux which can be reached with at most k ($\in \mathbb{N}$) inference steps. Thus, we can follow each inference chain needed to obtain a front literal f^l (in $\mathcal{T}^{C \cup \mathcal{L}_0, S, \mathcal{B}, m}$) that is unifiable with the complement of a lemma l until a certain depth. If we are able to generate a front literal f where inferences are performed similar to those needed to find f^l then it is quite probable that f and l are structurally similar (as described shortly). We used an inference value k which defines a compromise between computation effort and precision of the simulation and produced up to 500 front literals.

Normally the front literal f^l which can be closed with l cannot be generated with k inferences. Now, either it is possible that all inferences that have to be performed to literals on the path from S to f^l of the tableau T_{f^l} (whose front literal is f^l) can also be performed when generating a front literal f (with tableau T_f). Thus, some of the subgoals which occur when enumerating T_{f^l} and T_f have been solved, when generating f, by a sub-proof different to the sub-proof in T_{f^l}. Since the subgoals are variable-connected "unification failures" arise in f that prevent $\sim f$ and l from being unifiable. Or, inferences which have to be performed to literals on the path from S to f^l may not be performed when producing a front literal f. Then, f and l may even differ at the top-level position.

If no instantiations of f^l and l are needed a complete similarity test consists of a test of *structural equality* between the front literals (in $\mathcal{T}^{C \cup \mathcal{L}_0, S, \mathcal{B}, m}$) and l. This has to be weakened to a *structural similarity* test between the enumerated front literals and l. A common method in order to allow for such a similarity test of structures is to employ *features*. A feature is a function φ which maps a literal to $\mathbb{N}$. Normally, a set of features $\varphi_1, \ldots, \varphi_n$ is used and a literal u is represented by its *feature value vector* $(\varphi_1(u), \ldots, \varphi_n(u))$. Our features concentrate on simple syntactical properties (cp. [2, 3]). We define a distance $d_F(u, v)$ of two literals as the Euclidean distance of the feature value vectors of $\sim u$ and v.

If instantiations are needed in order to use lemmas normally the previous method will not allow for good estimations. Therefore, in [2] an instantiating method based on an inference system for unification has been developed. An instantiation (substitution) is computed by *pseudo-unifying* two literals (terms) based on an inference system $\mathcal{UD}$ which ignores certain unification failures during the unification process. A definition of $\mathcal{UD}$ and remarks for controlling $\mathcal{UD}$ can be found in [2]. After instantiating two terms d_F can be employed. In summary, we obtain the measure d_S by $d_S(u,v) = d_F(\sigma_u^v(u), \sigma_u^v(v))\}$ where σ_u^v is the substitution obtained with $\mathcal{UD}$ for $\sim u$ and v.

In order to *select* lemmas we generate for each clause which should serve as start clause front literals and choose for each front literal the lemma most similar to the literal w.r.t. a given distance measure (d_F or d_S).

Experiments. We have performed experiments with the CTC based prover SETHEO [6] and the lemma generator DELTA [8]. We experimented in four domains of the TPTP library, namely in the BOO, COL, and GRP domain. We employed SETHEO, an unfiltered combination of SETHEO and DELTA (SETHEO/U), a version where conventional filter criteria (cp. [8]) are used (SETHEO/C), and our similarity-based version SETHEO/S. In the BOO and GRP domain d_F, and in the COL domain the measure d_S was used. We employed the depth bound for the proof run with lemmas. Lemmas were generated with resource $n_D = 2$.

Problem	Setheo	Setheo/U	Setheo/C	Setheo/S	Problem	Setheo	Setheo/U	Setheo/C	Setheo/S
BOO003-1	35	19	1	3	COL003-2	—	481	238	705
BOO003-2	344	—	377	2	COL042-2	—	983	—	58
BOO004-2	497	—	628	2	COL042-3	—	—	—	907
BOO005-2	629	—	110	21	COL042-4	—	—	—	520
BOO006-2	387	—	42	25	COL060-2	532	264	—	11
BOO006-4	141	503	5	8	COL060-3	509	252	—	8
BOO012-2	—	—	—	131	COL063-5	541	267	—	37
BOO012-4	—	—	—	408	COL063-6	539	262	—	15
BOO013-3	485	44	—	2	COL064-3	566	275	—	23

In the table we show for some problems from the BOO and COL domain the run times in seconds on a Sun Ultra 2. The entry '—' denotes that no proof could be found within 1000 seconds. The run times include the time for lemma generation and selection. SETHEO/S significantly improves on the other versions. Similar results could be obtained *all over* the domains in a stable way (see [2]).

Conclusions and Future Work. Lemma use offers the potential to improve the performance of an automated theorem proving system. We discussed static lemma generation and investigated the potential of lemma use for proof length and resource reduction. In order to filter relevant lemmas, we developed efficient techniques based on similarity criteria between a proof goal and a set of lemma candidates. The future work will deal with the improvement of our similarity measures. It remains to be investigated whether a more intelligent generation of front clauses improves the reliability of our similarity test. Furthermore, machine learning techniques may allow for an improvement of our distance measures.

References

1. O.L. Astrachan and D.W. Loveland. The Use of Lemmas in the Model Elimination Procedure. *Journal of Automated Reasoning*, 19(1):117–141, 1997.
2. M. Fuchs. Controlled Use of Clausal Lemmas in Connection Tableau Calculi. AR-Report, AR-98-02, TU München.
3. M. Fuchs. Flexible proof replay with heuristics. In *Proc. EPIA-97*, LNAI 1323, pages 1–12. Springer, 1997.
4. R. Letz, K. Mayr, and C. Goller. Controlled Integration of the Cut Rule into Connection Tableau Calculi. *Journal of Automated Reasoning*, (13):297–337, 1994.
5. D.W. Loveland. *Automated Theorem Proving: a Logical Basis*. North-Holland, 1978.
6. R. Letz, J. Schumann, S. Bayerl, and W. Bibel. SETHEO: A High-Performance Theorem Prover. *Journal of Automated Reasoning*, 8(2):183–212, 1992.
7. S. Minton. Quantitative Results Concerning the Utility of Explanation-Based Learning. *Artificial Intelligence*, (42):363–391, 1990. Elsevier Science Publishers.
8. J. Schumann. Delta - a bottom-up preprocessor for top-down theorem provers. In *Proc. CADE-12*. Springer, 1994.
9. M.E. Stickel. A prolog technology theorem prover: Implementation by an extended prolog compiler. *Journal of Automated Reasoning*, 4:353–380, 1988.

System Description: Verification of Distributed Erlang Programs

Thomas Arts[1], Mads Dam, Lars-åke Fredlund, and Dilian Gurov[2]

[1] Computer Science Laboratory, Ericsson Telecom AB, 126 25 Stockholm, Sweden,
thomas@cslab.ericsson.se
[2] Swedish Institute of Computer Science, Box 1263, S-164 28 Kista, Sweden,
{mfd,fred,dilian}@sics.se

1 Introduction

Software written for telecommunication applications has to meet high quality demands. *Correctness* is one major concern; the activity of proving formally that a system is correct is called *verification*. Telecommunications software is highly concurrent, and *testing* is often not capable of guaranteeing correctness to a satisfactory degree. The software we are faced with consists of many, relatively small modules, written in the functional language Erlang [AVWW96]. These modules define the behaviour of a number of processes operating in parallel and communicating through asynchronous message-passing. New processes can be generated during execution. Because of the complexity of such software, our approach to verification is to prove that the software satisfies a set of properties formally specified in a suitable logic language. The specification language we use is based on Park's μ-calculus [Par76,Koz83], extended with Erlang-specific features. This is a very powerful logic, due to the presence of least and greatest fixed point recursion, allowing the formalization of a wide range of behavioural properties.

To facilitate verification of Erlang programs of realistic size we are developing a verification tool implementing a tableau-based proof system described in [DFG98]. Our main objectives are to achieve a satisfactory degree of automation, proof reuse, easy navigation through proof tableaux, and meaningful feedback about the current proof state, so as to require user intervention only when this is really necessary, and to assist in taking informed proof decisions.

2 The Erlang Programming Language

We consider a core fragment of the Erlang programming language with dynamic networks of processes operating on data types such as numbers, lists, tuples, or process identifiers (pid's), using asynchronous, first-order call-by-value communication via unbounded ordered message queues called mailboxes. Real Erlang

C. Kirchner and H. Kirchner (Eds.): Automated Deduction, CADE-15
LNAI 1421, pp. 38–41, 1998. © Springer–Verlag Berlin Heidelberg 1998

has several additional features such as communication guards, exception handling, modules, and a host of built-in functions. The abstract syntax of Core Erlang expressions is summarised as follows:

$$
\begin{array}{ll}
\text{Var} & := \text{X} \mid \text{Y} \mid \text{Z} \mid \ldots \\
\text{Atom} & := \text{a} \mid \text{b} \mid \text{c} \mid \ldots \\
\text{Pid} & := <1> \mid <2> \mid <3> \mid \ldots \\
\text{Pattern} & := \text{Var} \mid \text{Atom} \mid \text{Pid} \mid \{\text{Pattern, Pattern}\} \\
\text{Match} & := \text{Pattern} \rightarrow \text{Expr} \mid \text{Match; Pattern} \rightarrow \text{Expr} \\
\text{Expr} & := \text{Var} \mid \text{Atom} \mid \text{Pid} \mid \{\text{Expr, Expr}\} \mid [] \mid [\text{Expr}|\text{Expr}] \mid \\
& \quad \text{case Expr of Match end} \mid \text{Expr, Expr} \mid \\
& \quad \text{Atom(Expr)} \mid \text{spawn(Atom, Expr)} \mid \\
& \quad \text{self} \mid \text{Expr!Expr} \mid \text{receive Match end}
\end{array}
$$

Core Erlang expressions are built from variables, atoms (like integers and operations on integers), process identifiers (pid's), and patterns by forming tuples (pairs), lists, case expressions, sequential composition, function application, generating new processes (spawn), obtaining the identity of the current process (self), as well as constructs for input and output to a specified recipient.

3 The Specification Language

The property specification logic we use can be summarised as a first-order predicate logic, extended with labelled "box" and "diamond" modalities, least and greatest fixed point recursion, and some Erlang-specific atomic predicates. This is a powerful logic capable of expressing a wide range of important system properties, ranging from type-like assertions to complex reactivity properties of the interaction behaviour of a telecommunication system. For example, the formula $\mu X.(n = 0 \vee \exists n'.(X(n') \wedge n = n'+1))$ defines the type of natural numbers, i.e. the least predicate which is true at zero and is closed under successor. As another example, $\nu X.(\forall x.[p?x] (\exists y. <q!y> X))$ expresses the capability of a system to react to messages received by process p by sending replies to process q. Far more complicated properties, such as fairness and responsiveness properties, can be expressed by alternating least and greatest fixed points.

4 The Proof System

A large number of algorithms, tableau systems and proof systems for verifying processes against modal μ-calculus specifications can be found in literature, e.g. [EL86,SW91,Gur98] to cite but a few. However, most of these approaches are only applicable for finite-state processes, or at least processes where properties depend only on a finite portion of a potentially infinite-state process. The complexity of the software we consider and the properties we want to verify demand a new approach.

We build upon work begun by Dam in [Dam95], where instead of closed correctness assertions of the shape $S : \phi$ (where S is a system and ϕ a specification), *open correctness assertions* of the shape $\Gamma \vdash S : \phi$, where Γ expresses a set of assumptions $s : \psi$ on components s of S, are considered. Thus, the behaviour of S is specified parametrically upon the behaviour of its components.

This idea of open correctness assertions gave rise to the development of a Gentzen-style proof system [DFG98] that serves as the basis for the implementation of the verification tool. On top of a fairly standard proof system we added two rules: a "cut" rule for decomposing proofs of a system with multiple processes to proofs about the components, and a discharge rule based on detecting loops in the proof. Roughly, the goal is to identify situations where a latter proof node is an instance of an earlier one on the same proof branch, and where appropriate fixed points have been safely unfolded. The discharge rule thus takes into account the history of assertions in the proof tree. In terms of the implementation this requires the preservation of the proof tree during proof construction. Combined, the cut rule and the discharge rule allow general and powerful induction and co-induction principles to be applied. Examples include induction on the dynamically evolving architecture of a system, induction on datatypes, and co-induction on possibly infinite computation sequences.

5   The Erlang Verification Tool

From a user's point of view, proving a property of an Erlang program using the verification tool involves "backward" (i.e., goal-directed) construction of a proof tree (tableau). The user is provided with commands for defining the initial node of the proof tree, for expanding a proof tree node ('the current proof node can be considered proved if the following nodes are proved instead'), for navigating through the proof tree, for checking whether the discharge rule is applicable, and for visualizing the current state of the proof tree using the daVinci graph manipulation tool [FW94]. Since the whole proof tree is maintained, proof reuse and sharing is greatly facilitated. The verification tool provides also a scripting language which can be used for automating several proof tasks, such as model-checking of simple formulas.

As an example, consider a resource managing process rm, which accepts requests *req* from users u for using resources. The resource manager reacts to each such request by generating a new resource handling process rh, with the only task to serve this special request by sending a reply *rep* to the corresponding user. Naturally, such a system should not send spontaneous replies without having received initiating requests. To keep the example simple, we shall formalise an approximation of this property, namely that the system can never engage in an infinite sequence of output actions. This property (let us denote it with ϕ) can be expressed as $\nu X.\mu Y.(\forall u.\forall req.[u?req]X \wedge \forall u.\forall rep.[u!rep]Y)$. Our initial proof obligation is "$\vdash rm : \phi$". By applying a command which attempts to model-check process rm until some new process is generated, we automatically obtain a new proof obligation of the shape "$\vdash rm \parallel rh : \phi$", namely that the system after generating one request handler also has the same property. So, some form of induction on the global process structure is necessary here. This is easily achieved by applying (manually) the cut rule, reducing the previous obligation to "$s : \phi \vdash s \parallel rh : \phi$" (denote this proof obligation by ($*$)), namely to proving that *any* process s satisfying ϕ, when put in parallel with process rh, also satisfies ϕ. In fact, this is the only point at which human intervention is required. By invoking the same command, the tool explores the possible actions of s and rh, and ultimately completes the proof. If $s \parallel rh$ performs an input action, this can only be because of s, and if s evolves thereby to s', then the resulting proof obligation becomes "$s' : \phi \vdash s' \parallel rh : \phi$" which is automatically discharged against ($*$). Similarly, if $s \parallel rh$ performs an output action, this can only be because of rh, and since after this action rh ceases to exist, the resulting proof obligation becomes "$s : \phi \vdash s : \phi$" which is an instance of the usual identity axiom of Gentzen-style proof systems.

At the present point in time a first prototype tool has been completed with the functionality described above. A number of small examples have been completed, including, as the largest, a correctness proof concerning trust of a mobile billing agent reported in [DFG98]. Further information on the project and the prototype implementation can be found at http://www.sics.se/fdt/erlang/. We expect to announce a public release of the system by the end of 1998. Future work includes bigger case studies, increased support for proof automation, and better handling of fairness.

References

[AVWW96] J. Armstrong, R. Verding, C. Wikström and M. Wiliams, *Concurrent Programming in Erlang*. 2:nd edition, Pretence Hall, 1996.

[Dam95] M. Dam, Compositional proof systems for model checking infinite state processes. In *Proceedings CONCUR'95*, LNCS 962, p. 12–26, 1995.

[DFG98] M. Dam, L.-å. Fredlund and D. Gurov, Toward Parametric Verification of Open Distributed Systems. To appear in: H. Langmaack, A. Pnueli, W.-P. De Roever (eds.), *Compositionality: The Significant Difference*, Springer Verlag, 1998.

[EL86] E.A. Emerson and C. Lei, Efficient model checking in fragments of the propositional mu-calculus. In *Proceedings LICS'86*, p. 267–278, 1986.

[Gur98] D. Gurov, Specification and Verification of Communicating Systems with Value Passing. Ph.D. Thesis, Department of Computer Science, University of Victoria, March 1998.

[FW94] M. Fröhlich and M. Werner. The graph visualization system daVinci – a user interface for applications. Technical Report 5/94, Department of Computer Science, Bremen University, 1994.

[Koz83] D. Kozen, Results on the propositional μ-calculus. *Theoretical Computer Science*, 27:333–354, 1983.

[Par76] D. Park, Finiteness is mu-ineffable. *Theoretical Computer Science*, 3:173–181, 1976.

[SW91] C. Stirling and D. Walker, Local model checking in the modal mu-calculus. *Theoretical Computer Science*, 89(1):161–177, 1991.

System Description: Cooperation in Model Elimination: CPTHEO*

Marc Fuchs and Andreas Wolf

Technische Universität München, Institut für Informatik, D-80290 München
fuchsm,wolfa@informatik.tu-muenchen.de

Automated theorem proving can be interpreted as the solution of search problems which comprise huge search spaces. Parallelization of the proof task as well as cooperation between the involved provers offer the possibility to develop more efficient search procedures. In this description we present a concept for a cooperative parallel theorem prover which combines goal oriented search with a saturating approach. This concept has been realized within a prototype of the automated theorem prover CPTHEO which is based on the Model Elimination (ME) prover SETHEO [5]. Moreover, we give a short assessment of the results of first experiments with CPTHEO, followed by a listing of topics planned for the future improvement of the prover.

Cooperation. Cooperative parallel theorem proving aims to achieve synergetic effects between several prover instances by exchanging information on the search conducted so far. Basically, when dealing with cooperation among provers one has to deal with the following two aspects (see also [9]). Firstly, one has to deal with the system behavior in order to achieve cooperation, i.e., the exchange of some "interesting" data has to be controlled. Information to be exchanged between different ME provers may be symbolic information on proved subgoals in form of lemmas or on failed subgoals. Furthermore, information regarding the search control, e.g., in form of parameter settings or inference rates may be exchanged. In general the information may be exchanged on a *request* base (a prover asks for information) or on an *offer* base (a prover offers its results). Secondly, besides the behavioral aspects, the architecture of a cooperative prover is important, e.g., the hierarchical structure of the involved sub-provers, or the synchronous/asynchronous communication model.

Related Work. In the past there have been several approaches for cooperation among *bottom-up* theorem provers (e.g., based on superposition, unfailing completion, and resolution). Methods which partition the clauses among several sub-provers are used in [1]. Cooperation is needed there in order to preserve completeness. The methods introduced in [2,3] provide cooperation among

---

* This work is supported by the Deutsche Forschungsgemeinschaft.

C. Kirchner and H. Kirchner (Eds.): Automated Deduction, CADE-15
LNAI 1421, pp. 42–46, 1998. © Springer–Verlag Berlin Heidelberg 1998

(complete) competitive provers by periodically exchanging selected results. An approach to achieve sequential cooperation among a saturating component and a top-down prover has been developed in [6].

Computation Model. The prover CPTHEO is based on the cooperation among pairs (TD_i, BU_i), $1 \leq i \leq n$, of *top-down components* and *bottom-up components*. We employ as top-down components ME provers which are complete for first-order logic. As bottom-up components we use ME based unit-lemma generators similar to [6]. Note that the bottom-up components are complete provers for horn logic whereas they are incomplete for non-horn logic.

In order to prove a given set of input clauses, each component TD_i tries to enumerate a closed tableau, each bottom-up component generates unit lemmas. Furthermore, in order to achieve cooperation between TD_i and BU_i we repeatedly choose during the proof search a subset of the lemmas generated by BU_i with a *lemma selection component* LS_i. This selection is supported by information collected during the search conducted by TD_i. Then, a new *dependent sub-prover* (a ME prover) can be started which tries to refute the input clauses augmented by the selected lemmas. Thus, the whole system consists of *basic units* (TD_i, BU_i, LS_i) which work as competitive proof systems. Furthermore, the cooperation among TD_i and BU_i enables the use of a basic unit as an intelligent lemma generator which assists new dependent sub-provers in order to solve the given proof task. Different basic units employ different bottom-up, top-down components, and different lemma selection strategies in order to force the generation of different lemma sets. Thus, we employ some kind of strategy parallelism (see [10]). The whole system stops after a time-out is exceeded or one of the involved provers is able to refute the given input clauses.

In detail, in the actual version of CPTHEO we proceed as follows. We use two basic units (TD_i, BU_i, LS_i), $i = 1, 2$, where $BU_1 = BU_2$. Each component BU_i sends a data stream (generated lemmas) to LS_i. In order to reduce the amount of data some filter methods are used which discard some lemmas before sending them. Filter criteria are the complexity of a lemma w.r.t. the proof goal (too large lemmas are discarded).

In order to support the lemma selection each TD_i sends some information to LS_i. Our first method (realized in TD_1) sends information on subgoals which fail because of the lack of resources during the proof attempt. If a lemma is unifiable with such a failed subgoal it may be useful since the search for the proof, when additionally using the lemma, would succeed at this position and may lead to a proof. Our second method (realized in TD_2) sends information on all literals which are the only open subgoal (*front literal*) of an enumerated tableau to LS_2. As described in [4] in more detail these literals can give hints on the usefulness of a lemma in order to close an open tableau. By measuring a unification distance (as defined in [4]) between the front literal and a lemma the usefulness of a lemma can be estimated. Analogously to the bottom-up components filter criteria reduce the amount of data to be sent.

In each selection component the filtered data is refereed and ranked (after employing forward subsumption tests). Literals from TD_i representing more detailed proof attempts (more inferences are needed to infer them) are favored. The data from the bottom-up components are refereed regarding both general experiences and information transmitted from TD_i. General experiences lead to a preference of lemmas with large proofs and small term complexity. The idea is to use lemmas which can provide a rather large proof length reduction and may often be applicable in order to close open subgoals. Furthermore, in LS_1 the information is used whether a lemma is unifiable with a failed subgoal provided by TD_1 and thus applicable in order to avoid this fail (see above). In LS_2 we use similarity measures between the front literals and a lemma (see [4]).

In summation, in each component LS_i two dynamically refereed and ranked data bases of limited size are administered. The best k lemmas of the lemma pool in a lemma selection component represent possibly well-suited lemmas and form a lemma set $\mathcal{L}$. Everytime $\mathcal{L}$ has "significantly" changed, a new dependent sub-prover is started which tries to refute the original input clauses after augmentation with $\mathcal{L}$.

The table summarizes the cooperation model according to the classification scheme as introduced in [9].

system architecture	homogeneous system
communication model	asynchronous exchange of information
hierarchical structure	basic units on the same level, dependent sub-provers
goal-orientation/saturation	combination
cooperation/competition	cooperating components in the basic units, competition between dependent sub-provers and basic units
exchange of control info	no
exchange of lemmas	from the bottom-up components
exchange of failure info	from the top-down components

Implementation. CPTHEO uses the SETHEO [5] abstract machine. It is implemented in C, Prolog, and Perl. In the current implementation, within the basic units communication is achieved via named pipes. This restricts the parallelization possibilities of one basic unit to multiprocessor machines. Nevertheless, the sub-provers which process the proof tasks (input clauses) enriched with lemmas can be distributed within the local workstation cluster.

task	added lemmas	CPTHEO inferences	SETHEO inferences	speed-up	task	added lemmas	CPTHEO inferences	SETHEO inferences	speed-up
BOO003-1	3	640	13489	21.1	CAT004-4	5	4069	73231	18.0
COL061-1	3	611	*23221	>38.0	COL066-2	3	177	2453	13.9
FLD010-1	3	215	*39908	>185.6	FLD031-5	3	133	2377	17.9
GEO017-2	5	384	6554	17.1	GEO026-2	3	259	*121505	>469.1
HEN003-5	5	418	7341	17.6	LCL080-1	10	660	*13862	>21.0
LCL108-1	5	40	549	13.7	NUM180-1	5	836	*342886	>410.2
PUZ001-2	3	1452	14408	9.9	RNG004-3	5	1764	*241877	>137.1
ROB002-1	3	213	1408	6.6	SYN310-1	3	247	56953	230.6

Experiments. To determine the influence of the cooperation on the proof process, we compare the results of CPTHEO with those reached by SETHEO. We employ a version of SETHEO which uses the same search strategy as the subprovers of our cooperative prover. Since some parts of CPTHEO are still implemented in Prolog and thus rather inefficiently, we selected inferences as cost measure instead of the run time. We show the results of some problems from the TPTP [7]. In the table above we depict for each problem the number of lemmas added to the original proof task (each of the problems could be solved with the first lemma set selected from one of the LS_i's) and the number of inferences until the goal is proved or the time limit of 1000s is reached (for CPTHEO the inferences performed by the bottom-up and top-down components are included). A $\star$ denotes that a proof could not be found within 1000s. Furthermore, we depict the speed-up rate obtained when comparing CPTHEO with SETHEO.

Assessment. As the experimental results reveal cooperation among provers can achieve very high speed-ups. The main problem for cooperative theorem provers is the intelligent selection of data relevant for the proof from an ever growing amount of information. If this selection is not performed appropriately no improvement is reached and cooperation offers no gain. Our selection techniques were sufficient in order to solve problems which are unreachable with conventional search methods. Nevertheless, the methods and techniques for information assessment and selection still need further research. Of course lemma selection also imports additional costs to the proof procedure. Parallelization of LS_i's and limitation of the size of the stored formula sets (as realized in CPTHEO), however, allow for a lemma selection within an acceptable amount of time. Note that our cooperation approach can be combined with other parallelization paradigms like search space partitioning (see e.g. [8]). Thus, the good scalability of these models can easily be incorporated into our prover.

In future a more efficient implementation is needed. Specifically, we are interested in further parallelizing the basic units, e.g. by employing PVM. Further, no real tuning of the internal parameters of CPTHEO has been performed. If appropriate values are found, e.g. for the number of lemmas to be used in a proof run or the size of the internal data bases, a further gain of efficiency can be expected.

References

1. S. E. Conry et al., DARES: A Distributed Automated Reasoning System. Proc. AAAI-90, pp. 78–85, 1990.
2. J. Denzinger. Knowledge-based distributed search using teamwork. ICMAS-95, AAAI-Press, pp. 81–88, 1995.
3. D. Fuchs. Coupling Saturation-Based Provers by Exchanging Positive/Negative Information. Proc. RTA-98, LNCS 1379, Springer, pp. 317–331, 1998.
4. M. Fuchs. Similarity-Based Lemma Generation for Model Elimination. Proc. FTP-97 Workshop, RISC-Linz Report Series No. 97-50, pp. 63-67, 1997.

System Description: cardT^4P: The First Theorem Prover on a Smart Card

Rajeev Goré[1], Joachim Posegga[2], Andrew Slater[1], and Harald Vogt[2]

[1] Automated Reasoning Project, Australian National University, 0200, Canberra
[2] Deutsche Telekom AG, Technologiezentrum, IT Security, D-64276 Darmstadt

Abstract. We present the first implementation of a theorem prover running on a smart card. The prover is written in Java and implements a dual tableau calculus. Due to the limited resources available on current smart cards, the prover is restricted to propositional classical logic. It can be easily extended to full first-order logic.

The potential applications for our prover lie within the context of security related functions based on trusted devices such as smart cards.

1 Smart Cards: The Secure PC of Tomorrow

Smart cards are currently evolving into one of the most exciting and most significant technologies of the information society. Current smart cards on the market are in fact small computers consisting of a processor, ROM and RAM, an operating system, a file system, etc. Although their resources are still quite restricted, continuous advances in chip manufacturing will soon enable to market smart cards with 32 bit processors and up to 128 KByte of memory. Manufacturers are also thinking about integrating small keyboards and LCD displays on these plastic cards. Thus, the next generation of smart cards will be as powerful as PCs were a few years ago.

The evolution of smart card technology resembles the development of computer technology over the last 20 years: the separation of "physics" and "logic". While early computers had to be programmed in machine language because each bit of memory and each instruction cycle was valuable, the increase of resources and processing power made it affordable to trade resources for higher level programming concepts and languages. This separation of software and hardware was the basis for the spread of computers into everyday life during this decade.

The same phenomenon is about to take place in smart card technology: as resources and processing power increase, it will become affordable to neglect the optimal use of the card processor and memory. The most promising move in this direction are Java smart cards, where a Java virtual machine is implemented inside the card. The software determining the function of the card is no longer tied to the particular card, but multiple applications can be loaded onto, and removed from, the card as desired.

C. Kirchner and H. Kirchner (Eds.): Automated Deduction, CADE-15
LNAI 1421, pp. 47–50, 1998. © Springer–Verlag Berlin Heidelberg 1998

The primary purpose of smart cards will continue to be security-related applications since they will serve as a trusted device for their owner. The most important applications to date are of a cryptographic nature like authentication and encryption, eg for electronic cash. Today's smart cards are used essentially as simple authentication devices in these contexts. Future smart cards applications, however, will take advantage of the fact that more complex cards will be able to carry out more complex operations; so that the smart card of the future will be a secure, personal computer.

Current smart cards have security-related applications hard-wired onto them. Future smart cards will serve multiple purposes and will be adaptable by downloading one or more applications. Interactions between such applications, and between the card and the outside world therefore become non-trivial. Formal logic is not only well-suited for modelling such complex interactions but is also ideal for describing a given security model. Consequently, a trusted, secure, personal device should be able to perform logical reasoning to ensure that the card complies to its owner's security model. A concrete example is the use of formal logic in the context of proof-carrying code [1].

Here we outline the first successful implementation of a theorem prover on a Java smart card.

2   Implementation Details

card$T^A P$ is a theorem prover for propositional logic that uses a dual tableaux method based on lean$T^A P$ [2]. card$T^A P$ was specifically designed to reside on a smart card; the program executable size is less that 2 KByte, and the stack usage, heap space and allocated memory is minimal. To achieve this, card$T^A P$ naively simulates Prolog's run time stack and backtracking environment using recomputation. The trade off is efficiency: some work must be repeated since we cannot save all of the prover's previous states.[1] The theorem prover resides on the smart card as a Java applet which can down-load a formula from a card reader and determine its theoremhood.

Due to space constraints we only allow formulæ in Negated Normal Form using Reverse Polish Notation. The current prover is limited by statically defined restrictions on the length and complexity of the formula determined by the limited memory resources of the smart card [3]. Specifically, a formula can contain up to 26 distinct propositional variables, at most 20 disjunctions, and at most 20 nested conjunctions, with a total length of 126 symbols. Future cards with greater resources will be less restrictive.

Formulæ are written to an EEPROM file; excess EEPROM space is used as virtual memory. The efficiency of accessing the formula is somewhat enhanced by using a smaller buffer in local memory as a small "window" into the formula.

---

[1] Although backtracking is not necessary for propositional classical logic, card$T^A P$ has been implemented for extensions to other logics.

The prover traverses each path from the root of the proof tree to some leaf. If every leaf is closed then the formula is unsatisfiable. Typically a dual tableaux theorem prover is capable of remembering or copying information about some point in the proof tree before it takes a branch at some conjunction. By doing so it can efficiently return to that branching point and traverse the alternate path. cardT^4P does not have enough memory space to arbitrarily store a "state" for some branch. As an alternative, cardT^4P stores a simple binary map of the paths taken to implement a depth first traversal of the proof tree, but is thus required to return to the root to traverse its next path. In doing so it reaccumulates the state information it had previously acquired at the last branching point in the proof tree. Disjunctions are also mapped so that if the prover reaches a leaf node leading from some conjunction, it may look in the disjunction map to determine whether there is a disjunct to process that may result in the current path closing. If a disjunct is available then that subformula may be immediately processed as if it were attached to the open node. Each path, from root to leaf, generates its own disjunction map as the path is traversed. Each path also generates state information regarding the variables in the formula as they are identified.

3   Experimental Results

We successfully ran cardT^4P on a smart card provided by Schlumberger [3] implementing JavaCard API V1.0 [4]. This card handles applications of up to 2.8K and offers approximately 200 bytes of main memory during run time. Our test formulæ consisted of 17 theorems of propositional logic [5] converted into negated normal form and into reverse polish notation. We also tested some non-theorems, obtained by mutating some of these 17 theorems.

Each formula was loaded onto the card individually and tested using the proof procedure described above. The interaction was performed through *LoadSolo*, a simple tool for communicating with the card, which came with the Cyberflex Development Kit [3]. cardT^4P returned an answer code indicating whether or not the formula was a theorem. All measurements were made by hand: each theorem was proved 3 times, the fastest and the slowest times were discarded. The following run-times include communication overhead:

Pelletier's 17 theorems:			Non-theorems:		
P1 21.9 s	P2 6.9 s	P3 2.0 s	N1	&-pp	2.0 s
P4 22.1 s	P5 8.7 s	P6 1.7 s	N2	+pp	2.4 s
P7 1.7 s	P8 3.2 s	P9 27.6 s	N3	p	1.8 s
P10 1:33 min	P11 7.0 s	P12 -	N4	-p	1.8 s
P13 1:50 min	P14 2:40 min	P15 22.1 s	N5	+&&p-q&-qp&+-pq+qp	7.2 s
P16 2.0 s	P17 -		N6	+&+p-q&-qp&+-pq+qp	25.3 s
			N7	+&pp&p-p	2.7 s
			N8	++-pq+q-p	5.0 s
			N9	+p&+-pqp	6.7 s
			N10	+&pq+&-p-q+&-p-q&p-q	7.3 s

Timing constraints enforced by the card due to the corresponding ISO-Standards either raised an exception or garbled communication during some of the longer computations.[2] These problems could be partially solved by interspersing commands which send data from the card to the reader. These modifications are sufficient for proving the shorter theorems, theorems P10 and P13, but for the larger ones, like theorem P14, additional modifications had to be made. All modifications concern only additional commands for communication. Theorems P12 and P17 could not be proved with any version of cardT^AP.

3.1 Conclusion and Outlook

The current version of cardT^AP is a propositional logic theorem prover written in Java. The methodology is essentially the same as that of the Prolog first order logic theorem prover leanT^AP. With greater available resources on smart cards, an extension of cardT^AP to first-order logic is straightforward. The simplicity of the Java code is a direct result of the tableau methodology which nicely partitions the problem into multiple branches, each of which can be explored using the limited resources individually. In contrast, "global" procedures such as resolution would not have been as well suited since they accumulate information rather than partitioning it.

We are currently experimenting with prototypes of new smart cards, implementing Java Card V2.0. These cards offer a 32-Bit RISC processor and up to 16K space in the EEPROM. First tests indicate that our prover runs about one order of magnitude faster in these cards, and it might in fact be realistic to extend the prover to first order logic.

References

1. G Necula and P Lee. Proof carrying code. Technical Report CMU-CS-96-165, Carnegie Mellon University, School of Computer Science, Pittsburgh, PA, September 1996.
2. Bernhard Beckert and Joachim Posegga. leanT^AP: Lean tableau-based deduction. *Journal of Automated Reasoning*, 15(3):339–358, 1995.
3. Schlumberger Inc. Cyberflex. http://www.cyberflex.austin.et.slb.com, 1997.
4. JavaSoft Inc. Javacard API. http://www.javasoft.com/products/javacard/, 1997.
5. Francis J. Pelletier. Seventy-five problems for testing automatic theorem provers. *Journal of Automated Reasoning*, 2:191–216, 1986.

---

[2] The cardT^AP program itself has been independently run in a simulation environment where these problems did not surface.

System Description: leanK 2.0

Bernhard Beckert[1] and Rajeev Goré[2],[*]

[1] University of Karlsruhe, Institute for Logic, Complexity and Deduction Systems,
D-76128 Karlsruhe, Germany.
beckert@ira.uka.de

[2] Automated Reasoning Project and Department of Computer Science,
Australian National University,
Canberra, ACT, 0200, Australia.
rpg@arp.anu.edu.au

Abstract. leanK is a "lean", i.e., extremely compact, Prolog implementation of a free variable tableau calculus for propositional modal logics. leanK 2.0 includes additional search space restrictions and fairness strategies, giving a decision procedure for the logics **K**, **KT**, and **S4**.

Overview. leanK is a "lean" Prolog implementation of the free variable tableau calculus for propositional modal logics reported in [1]. It performs depth first search and is based upon leanT^4P [2]. Formulae are annotated with labels containing variables, which capture the universal and existential nature of the box and diamond modalities, respectively. leanK 2.0 includes additional search space restrictions and fairness strategies, giving a decision procedure for the logics **K**, **KT**, and **S4**. It has 87, 51, and 132 lines of code for **K**, **KD**, and **S4**, respectively.

The main advantages of leanK are its modularity and its versatility. Due to its small size, leanK is easier to understand than a complex prover, and hence easier to adapt to special needs. Minimal changes in the rules give provers for all the 15 basic normal modal logics. By sacrificing modularity we can obtain specialised (faster) provers for particular logics like **K45D**, **G** and **Grz**. It is easy to obtain an explicit counter-example from a failed proof attempt. The leanK (2.0) SICStus Prolog 3 code is at: http://i12www.ira.uka.de/modlean.

The Calculus. We describe leanK (2.0) in some detail since [1] does not contain the new search space restrictions and fairness strategies.

To reduce the number of tableau rules, we assume all formulae are in negation normal form (NNF). An NNF transformation comes with the leanK source code.

To test a formula A for theoremhood in logic **L**, leanK tests whether the formula $B = \mathrm{NNF}(\neg A)$ is **L**-unsatisfiable. The initial (single node) tableau contains the labelled formula $1 : B$. leanK repeatedly applies the tableau expansion and closure rules until (a) a closed tableau is constructed (whence B is unsatisfiable

---

[*] Supported by the Australian Research Council via a Queen Elizabeth II Fellowship.

C. Kirchner and H. Kirchner (Eds.): Automated Deduction, CADE-15
LNAI 1421, pp. 51–55, 1998. © Springer–Verlag Berlin Heidelberg 1998

and A is a theorem) or (b) no further rule applications are possible (whence B is
L-satisfiable and A is not a theorem). The following features distinguish leanK's
calculus from other labelled modal tableau calculi (see [4] for an overview):

Free variables in labels: Applying the traditional box-rule requires guessing the
correct eigenvariables. Using (free) variables in labels as "wildcards" that
get instantiated "on demand" during branch closure allows more intelligent
choices of these eigenvariables. To preserve soundness for worlds with no
successors, variable positions in labels can be "conditional" (i.e., a formula
labelled with a conditional label σ has only to be satisfied by a model if
the world corresponding to σ exists in that model). Similar ideas have been
explored in [6] and [5] using unification of labels, rather than just matching
(as in our calculus), and also using an analytic cut rule.

Universal variables: Under certain conditions, a variable x in a label is "universal" in that an instantiation of x on one branch need not affect the value of x
on other branches, thereby localising the effects of a variable instantiation to
one branch. The technique entails creating and instantiating local duplicates
of labelled formulae instead of the originals.

Finite diamond-rule: Applying the diamond-rule to $\Diamond A$ usually creates a *new*
label. By using instead (a Gödelisation of) the formula A itself as the label, we guarantee that only a finite number of different labels (of a certain
length) are used in the proof. In particular, different (identically labelled)
occurrences of $\Diamond A$ generate the same unique label.

The intuitive reading of a labelled tableau formula $\sigma : A$ (where σ is a label
and A is a modal formula in NNF) is "the possible world σ satisfies the formula A". Thus, $1 : \Box p$ says that the possible world 1 satisfies the formula $\Box p$.
Our box-rule then reduces the formula $1 : \Box p$ to the labelled formula $1.(x) : p$,
which contains the *universal* variable x in its label and has an intuitive reading
"the possible world $1.(x)$ satisfies the formula p". Since different instantiations
of x give different labels, the labelled formula $1.(x) : p$ effectively says that "all
successors of the possible world 1 satisfy p", thereby capturing the usual Kripke
semantics for $\Box p$ (almost) exactly. But, in a non-serial logic, the possible world 1
may have no successor worlds; so, in such logics, we read $\sigma : A$ as "for all instantiations of the variables in σ, if the world corresponding to that instantiation
of σ exists then the world satisfies the formula A". Our rule for disjunctions
retains free variables in the labels of the two disjuncts, but because $\Box$ does not
distribute over $\vee$, such variables then lose their "universal" force. These "rigid"
variables can be instantiated only *once* in a tableau proof. When the disjunctive
rule makes universal variables rigid, additional copies of the box-formula that
generated the original variables are needed. However, these additional copies are
not generated by the box-rule, but by the disjunctive rule itself. In the formulae
resulting from expansion rule applications, universal variables are renamed so
each universal variable occurs in only one formula in a tableau.

All of leanK's tableau expansion rules are *invertible*: some denominator (conclusion) of each rule is satisfiable *iff* the numerator (the premiss) is satisfiable.

Thus, unlike traditional modal tableau methods [3,4], the order of rule application is *immaterial*. The rules for expanding a branch can be found in [1].

The calculi for different logics differ mainly in the box-rule, with different denominators for different logics (see [1]). In addition, a simpler version of the closure rule can be used if the logic is serial. Since each rule corresponds to a separate Prolog clause, replacing one clause with another implements a different logic. The clauses for some logics require additional arguments so minor editing is also required to ensure all clauses contain the same number of arguments. If labels contain free variables, detecting closure in non-serial logics is non-trivial because the labels of apparently complementary literals may be conditional. The (apparently contradictory) pair $1.(1) : p$ and $1.(1) : \neg p$ is not necessarily inconsistent since the world represented by $1.(1)$ may not exist in the chosen model. We therefore have to ensure that this world exists in all interpretations satisfying the tableau branch $\mathcal{B}$, before closing $\mathcal{B}$. This knowledge can be deduced from other formulae on $\mathcal{B}$. Thus in our example, a formula like $1.1 : A$ on $\mathcal{B}$ would "justify" the use of the literal pair $1.(1) : p$ and $1.(1) : \neg p$ for closing the branch $\mathcal{B}$. The crucial point is that the label 1.1 is *unconditional* exactly in the *conditional* position of $1.(1)$. In that case, we say that the label $1.(1)$ is *justified* on the branch $\mathcal{B}$ (for a formal definition see [1]).

The Fair Proof Procedure. The calculus described above is sound. Using a fair proof search procedure it is also complete. leanK uses a fairness strategy for closing branches so backtracking over different choices of complementary literals on a tableau branch and the closing substitutions associated with them is unnecessary. For that purpose, each tableau formula ϕ has an attached list of all instantiations of the rigid variables in ϕ that have previously been applied to copies of ϕ occurring on the same branch. Closure on a pair of complementary literals on a branch is forbidden if the associated closing substitution would lead to a previous instantiation of the free variables. Furthermore, to avoid generating useless renamings of disjunctive formulae, leanK uses the following restriction: when the disjunctive rule is applied to a formula $\phi = \sigma : A \vee B$, the renamings of ϕ that are added to the new sub-branches are "put asleep". The disjunctive rule is not applied to these renamings until they are woken up, which is only allowed if at least one of the free variables in σ has been instantiated using (a descendant of) $\sigma : A$ (resp. $\sigma : B$) for closure.

The next branch for expansion and the next formula to which a tableau rule is applied are chosen using the following fair procedure: always choose the left-most open branch, and view the formulae on any particular branch as a queue. The first formula in the branch/queue is removed and is used as the numerator to update the tableau as follows (a disjunctive rule is only used if it is not asleep): If the chosen formula is not a literal then some (one) rule is applicable to it, and the formulae created by that rule application are added to the queue. To preserve fairness, if (the traditional part of) the created formula is more complex than the numerator, this new formula is added to the end of the queue, otherwise it is added to the front of the queue. In particular, renamings of disjunctive formulae added by the disjunctive rule, and the transitive part of the denominator of the box-rule are added to the end. If the queue is empty, the first sleeping disjunctive formula that can be woken up is used; if there are none, the proof search terminates.

This procedure is a semi-decision procedure for all basic modal logics and, due to the finite diamond-rule, a decision procedure for the non-transitive logics.

To ensure that proof search terminates in case the logic is transitive, leanK 2.0 employs additional search space restrictions to avoid loops: (1) A box-formula may only be used to expand a branch B if its label is justified on B. (2) A diamond-formula $\sigma : \Diamond A$ may only be used to expand a branch B if it is *not* "blocked" by a formula $\sigma' : \Diamond A$ that already has been used to expand B where $\sigma' \leq \sigma$ (i.e., σ' is an initial prefix of σ) up to instantiation of universal variables— except if $\sigma : \Diamond A$ is unblocked "behind" σ' by a *new* box-formula $\tau : \Box B$ ($\sigma' \leq \tau$ and $\tau \leq \sigma$). A formula $\tau : \Box B$ is *new* if, at the time it is used to expand the branch, there is no formula $\tau' : \Box B$ that already has been used to expand B (where $\tau' \leq \tau$). Intuitively, a diamond-formula $\Diamond A$ may not be used for expansion in a world w if we have already seen it in a world w' that is a predecessor of w, except if we have seen a new box formula in a world w'' that is on the path from w' to w. Now, if the logic is transitive, the next formula to which a tableau rule is applied is chosen from the branch/queue in the following order: (1) the first formula that is a literal, a conjunctive formula, or a disjunctive formula that is not asleep, (2) the first diamond-formula that is not blocked, (3) the first disjunctive formula that can be woken up, (4) the first box-formula whose label is justified; if none of these choices is possible, the proof search terminates.

Performance. The strength of leanK (2.0) clearly is its small size and adaptability and not its performance. The following table shows statistics for a set of 72 K-theorems kindly provided by A. Heuerding. These formulae are non-trivial; No. 55, has about 90 logical operators. leanK 2.0 could prove 58 of these theorems. The program was terminated if no proof had been found after 15sec. The table shows the number of branches that were closed, and the proof time (running under SICStus Prolog 3 on a SUN Ultra 1 workstation).

	No.	24	44	46	50	52	55	56	67	72
Vers.	Branches	22251	90	137	43	56	1011	68	26565	154
1.0	Time [msec]	4400	50	80	20	30	1000	30	9520	90
Vers.	Branches	–	6	46	27	15	5	42	–	–
2.0	Time [msec]	–	20	20	20	10	0	20	–	–

References

1. B. Beckert and R. Goré. Free variable tableaux for propositional modal logics. In *Proceedings, TABLEAUX-97*, LNCS 1227, pages 91–106. Springer, 1997.
2. B. Beckert and J. Posegga. leanT^AP: Lean tableau-based deduction. *Journal of Automated Reasoning*, 15(3):339–358, 1995.
3. M. Fitting. *Proof Methods for Modal and Intuitionistic Logics*, volume 169 of *Synthese Library*. D. Reidel, Dordrecht, Holland, 1983.
4. R. Goré. Tableau methods for modal and temporal logics. In *Handbook of Tableau Methods*, Kluwer, Dordrecht, 1998. To appear.

5. G. Governatori. Labelled tableaux for multi-modal logics. In *Proceedings, TABLEAUX-95*, LNCS 918, pages 79–94. Springer, 1995.
6. J. Pitt and J. Cunningham. Distributed modal theorem proving with KE. In *Proceedings, TABLEAUX-96*, LNAI 1071, pages 160–176. Springer, 1996.

Extensional Higher-Order Resolution

Christoph Benzmüller and Michael Kohlhase

Fachbereich Informatik, Universität des Saarlandes, Germany
chris|kohlhase@cs.uni-sb.de

Abstract. In this paper we present an extensional higher-order resolution calculus that is complete relative to Henkin model semantics. The treatment of the extensionality principles – necessary for the completeness result – by specialized (goal-directed) inference rules is of practical applicability, as an implentation of the calculus in the LEO-System shows. Furthermore, we prove the long-standing conjecture, that it is sufficient to restrict the order of primitive substitutions to the order of input formulae.

1 Introduction

The history of building automated theorem provers for higher-order logic is almost as old as the field of deduction systems itself. The first successful attempts to mechanize and implement higher-order logic were those of Huet [Hue73] and Jensen and Pietrzykowski [JP76]. They combine the resolution principle for higher-order logic (first studied in [And71]) with higher-order unification. The unification problem in typed λ-calculi is much more complex than that for first-order terms, since it has to take the theory of $\alpha\beta\eta$-equality into account. In particular the higher-order unification problem is undecidable and sets of solutions need not to have most general elements that represent them. Thus the calculi for higher-order logic have to take special measures to circumvent the problems posed by the theoretical complexity of higher-order unification.

Experiments like the TPS system [And89,ABI+96] (which uses a higher-order matings calculus) or our own LEO system [BK98,Ben97] (which uses a variant of Huet's resolution calculus [Hue73]) have shown the practical feasibility of higher-order automated theorem proving based on these ideas. Establishing completeness for higher-order calculi is more problematic than in first-order logic. The intuitive set-theoretic *standard semantics* cannot give a sensible notion of completeness, since it does not admit complete calculi [Göd31]. But there is a more general notion of semantics due to Henkin [Hen50] that allows complete calculi and therefore sets the standard for the deductive power of calculi.

The core of higher-order resolution ($\mathcal{HORES}$, see [Hue73,Koh94] for details) is a simple extension of the first-order resolution method to the higher-order language: the only significant difference is that $\beta\eta$-equality has to be build in by keeping formulae in normal form and that first-order unification has to be replaced by higher-order unification (i.e. unification with respect to the theory

C. Kirchner and H. Kirchner (Eds.): Automated Deduction, CADE-15
LNAI 1421, pp. 56–71, 1998. © Springer–Verlag Berlin Heidelberg 1998

of $\beta\eta$-equality). Since this is a semi-decidable search process itself, it cannot simply be used as a sub-procedure that is invoked during the application of the resolution or factoring rules. Rather resolution and factorization rules are modified, so that they record the induced unification problem in a unification constraint instead of trying to compute a complete set of unifiers. Furthermore, the calculus is augmented with the inference rules of higher-order unification that are lifted to act on the unification constraints of clauses. With this trick the search for empty clauses and that for higher-order unifiers are interleaved, which alleviates the undecidability problem.

Unfortunately, neither $\mathcal{HORES}$ nor the TPS procedure are complete with respect to Henkin semantics, since they fail to capture substitutivity of equivalence. In [Koh95], the first author has presented a higher-order tableau calculus that addresses the problem with a new inference rule that uses substitutivity of equivalence in a goal-oriented way, but still fails to capture functional extensionality of Leibniz equality.

For our extensional higher-order resolution calculus $\mathcal{ER}$ we extend higher-order resolution by ideas from [Koh95] and a suitable treatment of Leibniz equality and prove the resulting calculus sound and complete with respect to Henkin's general model semantics [Hen50]. Furthermore, we show that we can restrict the set of primitive substitutions that are necessary for flexible literals to a finite set.

Before we begin with the exposition, let us specify what we mean by "higher-order logic": any simply typed logical system that allows quantification over function variables. In this paper, we will employ a system $\mathcal{HOL}$, which is based on the simply typed λ-calculus; for an introduction see for instance [And86,Bar84].

2   Higher-Order Logic ($\mathcal{HOL}$)

The set $\mathit{wff}_\alpha(\Sigma)$ of well-formed formulae of type α is build up from the set $\mathcal{V}$ of variables, and the signature Σ (a set of typed constants) as applications and λ-abstractions. We will denote variables with upper-case letters ($X_\alpha, Y, Z, X_\beta^1, X_\gamma^2 \ldots$), constants with lower-case letters ($c_\alpha, f_{\alpha\to\beta}, \ldots$), and well-formed formulae with upper-case bold letters ($\mathbf{A}_\alpha, \mathbf{B}, \mathbf{C}^i, \ldots$)[1]. Furthermore, we abbreviate multiple applications and abstractions in a kind of vector notation, so that $\mathbf{A}\overline{\mathbf{U}^k}$ denotes k-fold application (associating to the left) and $\lambda\overline{X^k}.\mathbf{A}$ denotes k-fold λ-abstraction (associating to the right) and use the square dot . as an abbreviation for a pair of brackets, where . stands for the left one with its partner as far to the right as is consistent with the bracketing already present in the formula.

We will use the terms like free and bound variables in their standard meaning and we use $\mathbf{Free}(\mathbf{A})$ for the set of free variables of a formula $\mathbf{A}$. In particular alphabetic change of names of bound variables is build into our $\mathcal{HOL}$: we consider alphabetic variants to be identical (viewing the actual representation as a representative of an alphabetic equivalence class) and use a notion of substitution that avoids variable capture, systematically renaming bound variables. We

---

[1] We will denote the types of formulae as indices, if it is not clear from the context.

could also have used de Bruijn's indices [dB72] as a concrete implementation of this approach at the syntax level.

By $\mathit{wff}_\alpha^{cl}(\Sigma) \subseteq \mathit{wff}_\alpha(\Sigma)$ we denote the set of all closed well-formed formulae, i.e. which contain no free variables and we call the members of $\mathit{wff}_o(\Sigma)$ sentences.

We denote a substitution that instantiates a variable X with a formula $\mathbf{A}$ with $[\mathbf{A}/X]$ and write $\sigma, [\mathbf{A}/X]$ for the substitution that is identical with σ but instantiates X with $\mathbf{A}$.

The structural equality relation of $\mathcal{HOL}$ is induced by $\beta\eta$-reduction

$$(\lambda X.\mathbf{A})\mathbf{B} \longrightarrow_\beta [\mathbf{B}/X]\mathbf{A} \qquad\qquad (\lambda X.\mathbf{C}X) \longrightarrow_\eta \mathbf{C}$$

where X is not free in $\mathbf{C}$. It is well-known, that the reduction relations β, η, and $\beta\eta$ are terminating and confluent, so that there are unique normal forms.

In $\mathcal{HOL}$, the set of base types is $\{o, \iota\}$ for truth values and individuals, and the signature Σ contains logical constants for negation $\neg_{o\to o}$, conjunction $\wedge_{o\to o\to o}$, and quantification[2] $\Pi^\alpha_{(\alpha\to o)\to o}$. All other constants are called parameters, since the argumentation in this paper is parametric in their choice[3].

It is matter of folklore that equality can directly be expressed in $\mathcal{HOL}$ e.g. by the *Leibniz definition*, so that a primitive notion of equality (expressed by a primitive constant $=$ in Σ) is not strictly needed; we will use this observation in this paper to treat equality as a defined notion. Leibniz equality defines two terms to be equal, iff they have the same properties. Hence equality can be defined as

$$\doteq^\alpha := \lambda X_\alpha.\lambda Y_\alpha.\forall P_{\alpha\to o}.PX \Rightarrow PY$$

A **standard model** for $\mathcal{HOL}$ provides a fixed set $\mathcal{D}_\iota$ of individuals, and a set $\mathcal{D}_o := \{\mathrm{T}, \mathrm{F}\}$ of truth values. All the domains for the complex types are defined inductively: $\mathcal{D}_{\alpha\to\beta}$ is the set of functions $f: \mathcal{D}_\alpha \to \mathcal{D}_\beta$. The evaluation $\mathcal{I}_\varphi$ with respect to an interpretation $\mathcal{I}: \Sigma \to \mathcal{D}$ of constants and an assignment φ of variables is obtained by the standard homomorphic construction that evaluates a λ-abstraction with a function, whose operational semantics is specified by β-reduction.

Henkin models only require that $\mathcal{D}_{\alpha\to\beta}$ has enough members that any well-formed formula can be evaluated[4]. Note that with this generalized notion of a model, there are less formulae that are valid in all models (intuitively, for any given formulae there are more possibilities for counter-models). Thus the generalization to Henkin models restricts the set of valid formulae sufficiently, so that all of them can be proven by the resolution calculus presented in this paper. For our completeness proofs, we will use the abstract consistency method first introduced by Raymond Smullyan in [Smu63] for first-order logic and later

---

[2] With this quantification constant, standard quantification of the form $\forall X_\alpha.\mathbf{A}$ can be regained as an abbreviation for $\Pi^\alpha(\lambda X_\alpha.\mathbf{A})$.

[3] In particular, we do not assume the existence of description or choice operators. For a detailed discussion of the semantic issues raised by the presence of these logical constants see [And72].

[4] In other words: the functional universes are rich enough to satisfy the comprehension axioms.

extended to higher-order logic by Peter Andrews [And71]. The model existence theorem below is a variant of the latter for Henkin models. For the proof we .refer to [BK97].

Theorem 1 (Henkin Model Existence). *Let Γ_Σ be a saturated abstract consistency class for Henkin models (see the definition below), and $\Phi \in \Gamma_\Sigma$, then there is a Henkin model $\mathcal{M}$ such that $\mathcal{M} \models \Phi$.*

Definition 1 (Abstract Consistency Class for Henkin Models). *We call a class Γ_Σ of sets of sentences an **abstract consistency class for Henkin Models**, iff Γ_Σ is closed under subsets and such that for all sets $\Phi \in \Gamma_\Sigma$ (we use $\Phi * A$ as an appreviation for $\Phi \cup \{A\}$):*

∇_c *If A is atomic, then $A \notin \Phi$ or $\neg A \notin \Phi$.*

$\nabla_\neg$ *If $\neg\neg A \in \Phi$, then $\Phi * A \in \Gamma_\Sigma$.*

$\nabla_{\beta\eta}$ *If $A \in \Phi$ and B is the $\beta\eta$-normal form of A, then $B * \Phi \in \Gamma_\Sigma$.*

$\nabla_\vee$ *If $A \vee B \in \Phi$, then $\Phi * A \in \Gamma_\Sigma$ or $\Phi * B \in \Gamma_\Sigma$.*

$\nabla_\wedge$ *If $\neg(A \vee B) \in \Phi$, then $\Phi * \neg A * \neg B \in \Gamma_\Sigma$.*

$\nabla_\forall$ *If $\Pi^\alpha F \in \Phi$, then $\Phi * FG \in \Gamma_\Sigma$ for each $G \in wf\!f_\alpha^{cl}(\Sigma)$.*

$\nabla_\exists$ *If $\neg\Pi^\alpha F \in \Phi$, then $\Phi * \neg(Fw) \in \Gamma_\Sigma$ for a fresh parameter $w_\alpha \in \Omega_\alpha$.*

∇_b *If $\neg(A \doteq^o B) \in \Phi$, then $\Phi \cup \{A, \neg B\} \in \Gamma_\Sigma$ or $\Phi \cup \{\neg A, B\} \in \Gamma_\Sigma$.*

∇_q *If $\neg(F \doteq^{\alpha\to\beta} G) \in \Phi$, then $\Phi * \neg(Fw \doteq^\beta Gw) \in \Gamma_\Sigma$ for a fresh parameter $w_\alpha \in \Omega_\alpha$.*

*We will call Γ_Σ **saturated**, iff for all sentences $A \in wf\!f_o(\Sigma)$ we have $\Phi * A \in \Gamma_\Sigma$ or $\Phi * \neg A \in \Gamma_\Sigma$.*

Remark 1 (Counterparts for ∇_b, ∇_q). In Definition 1 positive counterparts for the two conditions ∇_b, ∇_q are not needed, since these conditions are automatically met (note that $\doteq$ is a defined construct). For details see [BK97].

In this paper the *extensionality principles* will play a major role. These formalize fundamental mathematical intuitions about functions and truth values. The **functional extensionality principle** says, that two functions are equal, iff they are equal on all arguments. This principle can be formulated by the following schematic λ-term:

$$\forall M_{\alpha\to\beta}.\forall N_{\alpha\to\beta}.(\forall X.(MX) \doteq (NX)) \equiv (M \doteq N)$$

The **extensionality principle for truth values** states that on the set of truth values equality and equivalence relation coincide: $\forall P_o.\forall Q_o.(P \doteq Q) \equiv (P \equiv Q)$. Note that in Henkin models both extensionality principles are valid and that Leibniz equality indeed denotes equality relation (see [BK97] for details).

3   The Calculus $\mathcal{ER}$

Now we introduce the higher-order resolution calculus $\mathcal{ER}$. Therefore we will review standard higher-order resolution $\mathcal{HORES}$ and use the extensionality principles to discuss why it is not complete. From the deficiencies we will develop the necessary extensions and give an intuition by exhibiting refutations that become possible.

$\mathcal{HORES}$ is a refutation calculus that manipulates sets of *clauses*, i.e. sets (which we will represent as disjunctions) of literals (e.g. $C := [q_{\alpha \to o} X_\alpha]^T \vee [p_{\alpha \to o} X_\alpha]^F \vee [c_\alpha = X_\alpha]^F$).

Definition 2 (Literal). *Literals are atomic propositions labeled with an intended truth value. We call a literal a* unification constraint, *iff it is negative (i.e. annotated by the truth value F) and the head is* =, *all the others we call* **proper literals**. *Clauses existing entirely of unification constraints are called* **almost empty**. *Since instantiation of a head variable will convert a literal into a general labeled propositions, we will sometimes call these* **pre-literals**.

Clause normalization is very similar to the first-order case, except for the treatment of existential quantification. Therefore, we will not present the transformation rules here, but simply discuss the differences and assume that each given higher-order proof problem $\mathcal{P}$ can be transformed into a set of clauses CNF($\mathcal{P}$). A naive treatment with Skolemization results in a calculus that is not sound with respect to Henkin models, since Skolem functions are special choice functions[5], which are not guaranteed to exist in Henkin models. A solution due to [Mil83] is to associate with each Skolem constant the minimum number of arguments the constant has to be applied to. Skolemization becomes sound, if any Skolem function f^n only occurs in a *Skolem term*, i.e. a formula $\mathbf{S} = f^n \overline{\mathbf{A}^n}$, where none of the $\mathbf{A}^i$ contains a bound variable. Thus the Skolem terms only serve as descriptions of the existential witnesses and never appear as functions proper. When we speak of a **Skolem term** $\mathbf{S}_\alpha$ for a clause C, where $\{X^1_{\alpha^1} \cdots X^n_{\alpha^n}\}$ is the set of free variables occurring in C, then $\mathbf{S}_\alpha$ is an abbreviation for the term $(f^n_{\alpha^1 \to \cdots \to \alpha^n \to \alpha} X^1 \cdots X^n)$, where f is a new constant from $C_{\alpha^1 \to \cdots \to \alpha^n \to \alpha}$ and n specifies the number of necessary arguments for f.

Remark 2 (Leibniz Equality). We assume that before applying clause normalization each primitive equality symbol is replaced by its corresponding Leibniz definition. Hence after normalizing a given input problem, the resulting clause set does not contain any equality symbol. However, during the refutation process, equality symbols may be introduced again as we code unification constraints by negated equation literals.

3.1 Higher-Order Unification in $\mathcal{ER}$

Higher-order unification is a process of recursive deterministic simplification (rules α, η, *Dec*, *Triv*, and *Subst* in figure 1) and non-deterministic variable binding (rule *Flex/Rigid*). The rules α and η are licensed by the functional extensionality principle and eliminate the top λ-binder in unification constraints of functional type. The Skolem term s_α is an existential witness for the fact that the functions are different. Since clauses are implicitly universally quantified, this witness may depend on the values of all free variables occurring in the

---

[5] They choose an existential witness from the set of possible witnesses for an existential formula.

$$\frac{C \vee [(\lambda X_\alpha.\mathbf{A}) = (\lambda Y_\alpha.\mathbf{B})]^F \quad s_\alpha \text{ Skolem term for this clause}}{C \vee [[s/X]\mathbf{A} = [s/Y]\mathbf{B}]^F} \; \alpha$$

$$\frac{C \vee [(\lambda X_\alpha.\mathbf{A}) = \mathbf{B}]^F \quad s_\alpha \text{ Skolem term for this clause}}{C \vee [[s/X]\mathbf{A} = (\mathbf{B}s)]^F} \; \eta$$

$$\frac{C \vee [h\overline{\mathbf{U}^n} = h\overline{\mathbf{V}^n}]^F}{C \vee [\mathbf{U}^1 = \mathbf{V}^1]^F \vee \dots \vee [\mathbf{U}^n = \mathbf{V}^n]^F} \; Dec \qquad \frac{C \vee [\mathbf{A} = \mathbf{A}]^F}{C} \; Triv$$

$$\frac{C \vee E \quad E \text{ solved for } C}{\mathrm{CNF}(\mathrm{subst}_E(C))} \; Subst$$

$$\frac{C \vee [F_\gamma \overline{\mathbf{U}^n} = h\overline{\mathbf{V}}]^F \quad \mathbf{G} \in \mathcal{GB}^h_\gamma}{C \vee [F = \mathbf{G}]^F \vee [F\overline{\mathbf{U}} = h\overline{\mathbf{V}}]^F} \; Flex/Rigid$$

Fig. 1. Lifted Higher-Order (pre-)unification rules

clauses, so it must be a Skolem term for this clause. Decomposition (rule Dec) is analogous to the first-order case and the rule $Triv$ allows to remove reflexivity pairs. Rule Dec will be discussed again in connection with the extensionality rules in section 3.3.

The rule $Subst$ eliminates variables that are solved in a clause: we call a unification constraint $U := [X_\alpha = \mathbf{N}_\alpha]^F$ or $U := [\mathbf{N}_\alpha = X_\alpha]^F$ **solved** iff X_α is not free in $\mathbf{N}_\alpha$. In this case X is called the **solved variable** of U. Let $C := L^1 \vee \dots \vee L^n \vee U^1 \vee \dots \vee U^m$ be a clause with unification constraints $U^1 \vee \dots \vee U^m$ $(1 \leq m)$. Then a disjunction $U^{i_1} \vee \dots \vee U^{i_k}$ $(i_j \in \{1, \dots, m\}; 1 \leq j \leq k)$ of solved unification constraints occurring in C is called **solved for** C iff for every $U^{i_j}(1 \leq j \leq k)$ holds: the solved variable of U^{i_j} does not occur free in any of the U^{i_l} for $l \neq j; 1 \leq l \leq k$. Note that each solved set of unification constraints E for a clause C can be associated with a substitution subst_E which is the most general unifier of E. Thus the rule $Subst$ essentially propagates the information from the unification constraints to the proper clause parts. Since the instantiation of flexible literals (i.e. literals, where the head is a free variable) may result in pre-literals, the result of this propagation may cease to be a clause, therefore it needs to be reduced to clause normal form.

Remark 3 (Eager Unification). The set of rules described up to now is terminating and confluent, so that higher-order unification applies it eagerly to filter out all clauses with an unsolvable unification constraint[6]. It leads to unification

---

[6] As we will see later this solution is too strong if we want to be complete in Henkin models since an unsolvable unification constraint might be solvable by using the extensionality rules.

constraints, where both sides are applications and where at least one side is flexible, i.e. where the head is a variable. In this case, the higher-order unification problem can be reduced to the problem of finding most general formulae of a given type and a given head symbol.

Definition 3 (General Binding). *Let* $\alpha = (\overline{\beta^l} \to \gamma)$, *and* h *be a constant or variable of type* $(\overline{\delta_m} \to \gamma)$ *in* Γ, *then* $\mathbf{G} := \lambda \overline{X^l_{\beta_l}}.h\overline{\mathbf{V}^m}$ *is called a* **general binding of type** α **and head** h, *if* $\mathbf{V}^i = H^i \overline{X^l_{\beta_l}}$. *The* H^i *are new variables of types* $\overline{\beta^l} \to \delta^i]$. *It is easy to show that general bindings indeed have the type and head claimed in the name and are most general in the class of all such terms.*

General bindings, where the head is a bound variable $X^j_{\beta_j}$ *are called* **projection bindings** *(we write them as* $\mathcal{G}^j_\alpha$*) and* **imitation bindings** *(written* $\mathcal{G}^h_\alpha$*) else. Since we need both imitation and projection bindings for higher-order unification, we collect them in the set of* **approximating bindings for** h **and** α $(\mathcal{GB}^h_\alpha := \{\mathcal{G}^h_\alpha\} \cup \{\mathcal{G}^j_\alpha \mid j \leq l\})$.

Since there are only finitely many general bindings (one imitation binding and at most l projection bindings) the *Flex/Rigid* rule is finitely branching. We never have to consider the so-called *Flex/Flex* literals[7], since *Flex/Flex* equations can always be solved by instantiating the head variables with suitable constant functions that absorb their arguments. This observation is due to Gérard Huet [Hue73] and defines higher-order pre-unification, a computationally more feasible (but still undecidable) variant of higher-order unification. However, even if *Flex/Flex* pairs are solvable, we cannot simply delete them like trivial pairs, since one or both of the heads may be instantiated making the term rigid, so that the pair has to be subject to pre-unification again.

3.2   Higher-Order Resolution

Definition 4 (Higher-Order Resolution). *The* **higher-order resolution calculus** $\mathcal{HORES}$ *consists of the inference rules in figure 2 together with the unification rules in figure 1. We call a clause* **empty**, *iff it consists entirely of Flex/Flex unification constraints and say hat a* $\mathcal{HORES}$*-derivation of an empty clause from a set* Φ *of clauses is a* **refutation of** Φ. *For a sentence* $\mathbf{A}_o$ *we call a refutation of* $CNF(\neg\mathbf{A})$ *a* **refutation for** $\mathbf{A}$.

As in first-order we have resolution and factorization rules *Res* and *Fac*. But instead of solving the unification problems immediately within a rule application we delay their solution and incorporate them explicitly as unification constraints in the resulting clauses. Note that the resolution rule as well as the factorization rule are allowed to operate on unification constraints.

To find a refutation for a given problem we may have to instantiate the head variables of flexible literals by material that contains logical constants. Unfortunately these instantiations cannot be generated by the unification rules, since

---

[7] For a refutation, we do not need to enumerate all unifiers for a given unification problem but to seek for one possible instantiation of a given problem which leads to the contradiction.

$$\frac{[\mathbf{N}]^\alpha \vee C \quad [\mathbf{M}]^\beta \vee D \quad \alpha \neq \beta}{C \vee D \vee [\mathbf{N} = \mathbf{M}]^F} \; Res \qquad \frac{[\mathbf{N}]^\alpha \vee [\mathbf{M}]^\alpha \vee C \quad \alpha \in \{T, F\}}{[\mathbf{N}]^\alpha \vee C \vee [\mathbf{N} = \mathbf{M}]^F} \; Fac$$

$$\frac{[Q_\gamma \overline{\mathbf{U}^k}]^\alpha \vee C \quad \mathbf{P} \in \mathcal{GB}_\gamma^{\{\neg, \vee\} \cup \{\Pi^\beta | \beta \in T^k\}}}{[Q_\gamma \overline{\mathbf{U}^k}]^\alpha \vee C \vee [Q = \mathbf{P}]^F} \; Prim^k$$

Fig. 2. Higher-order resolution rules

all logical constants have been eliminated from the clause set by normalization, thus they enter the refutation by unification. Therefore the rule *Prim* allows to instantiate head variables Q_γ by general bindings $\mathbf{P}$ of type γ and head in $\{\neg, \vee\} \cup \{\Pi^\beta | \beta \in T\}$. Thus the necessary logical constants are introduced into the refutation one by one, hence the name *primitive substitutions*.

For instance the sentence $\mathbf{A} := \exists X_o . X$ is valid in all Henkin models, but $\mathrm{CNF}(\neg \mathbf{A}) = \{[X]^F\}$ cannot be refuted without some kind of a primitive substitution rule, since none of the other rules apply. With *Prim*, we can deduce $[X]^F \vee [X = \neg H]^F$ and then $[Y]^T$ by *Subst*. These two unit literals can be resolved to $[X = Y]^F$, which is an empty clauses, since $[X = Y]^F$ is a *Flex/Flex* unification constraint.

The primitive substitution rules have originally been introduced by Peter Andrews in [And89] (Gérard Huet uses a set of so-called "splitting rules" for the same purpose in [Hue73]). Note that the set of general bindings is infinite, since we need one for every quantifier Π^α and the set of types is infinite. Thus in contrast to the goal-directed search for instantiations in unification, the rule *Prim* performs blind search and even worse, is infinitely branching. Therefore, the problem of finding instantiations for predicate variables is conceived as the limiting factor to higher-order automated theorem proving.

It has been a long-standing conjecture that in machine-oriented calculi it is sufficient to restrict the order of primitive quantifier substitutions to the order of the input formulae. In [BK97], we have established a finer-grained variant of theorem 1 that we can use as a basis to prove this conjecture. Let us now introduce the necessary definitions.

Definition 5 (Order). *For a type $\alpha \in T$, we define the **order** $\mathbf{ord}(\alpha)$ of α as* $\mathbf{ord}(\iota) = \mathbf{ord}(o) = 0$, *and* $\mathbf{ord}(\alpha \to \beta) = \max\{\mathbf{ord}(\alpha), \mathbf{ord}(\beta)\} + 1$. *Note that the set $T^k = \{\alpha \in T \mid \mathbf{ord}(\alpha) \leq k\}$ is finite for any order k. We will take the order of a formula to be the highest order of any type of any of its subterms, and the order of a set of formulae to be the maximum of the orders of its members.*

Theorem 2 (Model Existence with Order). *The model existence theorem holds even if we weaken the condition ∇_f of an abstract consistency class to*

$$\nabla_f^k \qquad \text{If } \Pi^\alpha \mathbf{F} \in \Phi, \text{ then } \Phi * \mathbf{FG} \in \Gamma_\Sigma \text{ for each } \mathbf{G} \in \textit{wff}_\alpha^{cl}(\Sigma) \text{ with } \mathbf{ord}(\mathbf{G}) \leq \mathbf{ord}(\Phi).$$

In [BK97] we establish this theorem for arbitrary well-founded orderings on types such that $\text{ord}(\alpha), \text{ord}(\beta) \leq \text{ord}(\alpha \to \beta)$. This allows us to restrict instantiation in $\mathcal{ER}$ to formulae of the order of the input formulae. Note that this only effects the primitive substitution rule, since all other instantiations are performed by unification, which is order-restricted by construction. In particular, the non-standard definition of order above ensures finite branching of the primitive substitution rule. This ordering, that takes the lengths of argument lists into account leads to an increased order of the input set compared to the standard definition of order $(\text{ord}(\overline{\alpha_n} \to \beta) = \max_n\{\alpha_i\} + 1)$ and effectively restricts the number of necessary instantiations.

Our result justifies the practice of higher-order theorem provers to restrict the search for primitive substitutions and gives a road-map towards complete procedures. Of course there is still a lot of room for experimentation with the respective orderings.

3.3   Extensionality

The higher-order resolution calculus $\mathcal{HORES}$ defined above is not complete with respect to Henkin models, as the following example will show.

Example 1. The following formulae E1-E5[8] are not provable in $\mathcal{HORES}$ without using additional axioms for functional extensionality and/or extensionality on truth values.

E1 $a_o \equiv b_o \Rightarrow (\forall P_{o \to o}.Pa \Rightarrow Pb)$
   This is the non-trivial direction of the extensionality property for truth values: if a_o is equivalent to b_o then a_o is equal to b_o $(a_o \equiv b_o \Rightarrow a = b)$.
E2 $\forall P_{o \to o}.P(a_o \wedge b_o) \Rightarrow P(b \wedge a)$.
   Any property which holds for $a \wedge b$ also holds for $b \wedge a$ (or simply that $a \wedge b = b \wedge a$).
E3 $(p_{o \to o}a_o \wedge pb_o) \Rightarrow p(b \wedge a)$
   In other words, an arbitrary property $p_{o \to o}$ which coincidently holds for a_o and b_o also holds for their conjunction.
E4 $(\forall X_\iota.\forall P_{\iota \to o}.(P(m_{\iota \to \iota}X) \Rightarrow P(n_{\iota \to \iota}X))) \Rightarrow (\forall Q_{(\iota \to \iota) \to o}.Q(\lambda X_\iota.mX) \Rightarrow Q(\lambda X_\iota.nX))$
   This formula can be interpreted as an instance of the ξ-rule $(\forall X_\iota.m_{\iota \to \iota}X = n_{\iota \to \iota}X) \Rightarrow (\lambda X_\iota.mX) = (\lambda X_\iota.nX)$ (See for instance [Bar84]).
E5 $(\forall X_\iota.\forall P_{\iota \to o}.P(m_{\iota \to \iota}X) \Rightarrow P(n_{\iota \to \iota}X)) \Rightarrow (\forall Q_{(\iota \to \iota) \to o}.Qm \Rightarrow Qn)$
   This is an instance of the non-trivial direction of the functional extensionality axiom for type $\iota \to \iota$: $(\forall X_\iota.(m_{\iota \to \iota}X) = (n_{\iota \to \iota}X) \Rightarrow m = n)$.

For a proof of **E1** note that the clause normal form of the succedent consists of the two unit clauses $[p^0a]^F$ and $[p^0b]^T$, where p^0 is the Skolem constant for the variable P. These can be resolved upon to obtain the clause $[p^0a = p^0b]^F$, which can be decomposed to $[a_o = b_o]^F$. Obviously, this unification constraint cannot be solved by higher-order unification, and hence the refutation fails. In

---

[8] In Problems **E1**, **E2**, **E4**, and **E5** we have used Leibniz definition of equality to remove the intuitive equality symbols.

$$\frac{C \vee [\mathbf{M}_o = \mathbf{N}_o]^F}{\mathrm{CNF}(C \vee [\mathbf{M}_o \equiv \mathbf{N}_o]^F)} \; Equiv \qquad \frac{C \vee [\mathbf{M}_\alpha = \mathbf{N}_\alpha]^F \quad \alpha \in \{o, \iota\}}{\mathrm{CNF}(C \vee [\forall P_{\alpha \to o}.PM \Rightarrow PN]^F)} \; Leib$$

$$\frac{C \vee [\mathbf{M}_{\alpha \to \beta} = \mathbf{N}_{\alpha \to \beta}]^F \quad s_\alpha \text{ Skolem term for this clause}}{C \vee [\mathbf{M}s = \mathbf{N}s]^F} \; Func$$

Fig. 3. Extensionality rules

this situation, we need the principle of extensionality on truth values, which allows to replace each negated equality on type o by an equivalence. This leads to the clause normal form of $[a_o \equiv b_o]^F$, which contradicts the antecedent of **E1** and finally gives us the refutation.

Similar investigations show that the other examples cannot be proven by $\mathcal{HORES}$ too.

Our aim is to find an extension of $\mathcal{HORES}$, which is both Henkin-complete and adequate for an implementation. Surely, the introduction of axioms for the extensionality principles can solve the completeness problem in theory, but this will lead to an explosion of the search space which has to be avoided in practice. In particular, we do not change the purely negative spirit of the resolution calculus by introducing axioms but introduce special inference rules.

Definition 6 (Extensional Higher-Order Resolution). *The* **extensional higher-order resolution** *calculus $\mathcal{ER}$ is $\mathcal{HORES}$ extended with the inference rules in figure 3.*

The Rule *Leib* instantiates the equality symbol by its Leibniz definition and applies clause normalization. Rule *Equiv* is directly motivated by the proof attempt of **E1** discussed in example 1. Thus rule *Equiv* reflects the extensionality property for truth values but in a negative way: if two formulas are not equal then they are also not equivalent. Rule *Func* does the same for functional extensionality: if two functions are not equal then there exists an argument s_α on which these functions differ. To ensure soundness s_α has to be a new Skolem term which contains all the free variables occurring in the given clause.

The new rules strongly connect the unification part of our calculus with the resolution part. In some sense, they make the unification part extensional, since they allow to modify unification problems, which are not solvable by preunification alone in an extensional appropriate way and to translate them back into usual literals, such that we can try to find the right argumentation for the solvability of the unification constraints in the general refutation process by possibly respecting the additionally given clauses in the search space.

Remark 4 (Rule Func). Note that we have already introduced two rules – α and η in unification (see figure 1) – which are very similar to this one. In fact we can restrict rule *Func* to the case were $\mathbf{N}$ and $\mathbf{M}$ are non-abstractions or vice-versa, we can remove the α and η rules from simplification as they are subsumed by the rule *Func* as purely type-based and apply β-reduction to both sides of the modified unification constraint.

Remark 5 (Unification Constraints). We have lifted the unification constraints to clause level by coding them into negated equation literals. Hence the question arises whether or not resolution and factorization rules are allowed to be applied on these unification constraints. In order to obtain a Henkin complete calculus this is not necessary – as our completeness proof shows – if we add the three extensionality rules discussed in the next subsection. Consequently the unification constraints do not necessarily have to be coded as negative equation literals, any other form will work as well.

The coding of unification constraints as negated equation literals becomes important if one considers an alternative version of extensional higher order resolution – which we will also motivate below –, where the rule *Leib* is avoided.

Note that none of the three new extensionality rules introduces any flexible literal and even better, they introduce no new free variable at all; even if they heavily increase the search space for refutations, they behave much better – as experiments show with the LEO theorem prover [BK98,Ben97] – than the extensionality axioms, which introduce lots of flexible literals in the refutation process.

3.4   Examples

We now demonstrate the idea of the extensional resolution calculus on examples **E3** and **E5**:

E3 $\forall P_{o \to o'}(Pa_o \wedge Pb_o) \Rightarrow P(a \wedge b)$

CNF($\neg$**E3**) ($p_{o \to o}$ is a new Skolem constant):

	$c1:\ [pa]^T$	$c2:\ [pb]^F$	$c3:\ [p(a \wedge b)]^F$
$Res(c3,c1):$	$c4:\ [p(a \wedge b) = pa]^F$		
$Res(c3,c2):$	$c5:\ [p(a \wedge b) = pb]^F$		
$Dec(c4):$	$c6:\ [(a \wedge b) = a]^F$		
$Dec(c5):$	$c7:\ [(a \wedge b) = b]^F$		
$Equiv(c6):$	$c8:\ [a]^F \vee [b]^F$	$c9:\ [a]^T \vee [b]^T$	$c10:\ [a]^T$
$Equiv(c7):$	$c11:\ [a]^F \vee [b]^F$	$c12:\ [a]^T \vee [b]^T$	$c13:\ [b]^T$

The rest is obvious: Resolve $c10$ and $c13$ against $c8$ (or $c11$). $\square$

E5 $(\forall X_\iota.\forall P_{\iota \to o}.P(m_{\iota \to \iota}X) \Rightarrow P(n_{\iota \to \iota}X)) \Rightarrow (\forall Q_{(\iota \to \iota) \to o}.Qm \Rightarrow Qn)$

CNF($\neg$**E5**) (q is a new Skolem constant):

$$c1: [P(mX)]^F \vee [P(nX)]^T \qquad c2: [qm]^T \qquad c3: [qn]^F$$

$Res(c2,c3)$: $\qquad\qquad\qquad\qquad\qquad\qquad\qquad\quad c4: [qm = qn]^F$

$Dec(c4)$: $\qquad\qquad\qquad\qquad\qquad\qquad\qquad\qquad\quad c5: [m = n]^F$

$Func(c5)$ (s_ι is a new Skolem constant): $\qquad c6: [ms = ns]^F$

$Leib(c6)$ ($p_{\iota \to o}$ is a new Skolem constant): $\quad c7: [p(ms)]^T \qquad c8: [p(ns)]^F$

Note that resolving $c2$ and $c3$ immediately against $c1$ does not lead to a solvable unification constraint. Instead we made a detour to the pre-unification part of the calculus and modified the clauses $c2$ and $c3$ in an extensionally appropriate way. Now $c2$ and $c3$ have their counterparts in $c7$ and $c8$, but in contrast to $c2$ and $c3$ the new clauses can successfully be resolved against $c1$. $\square$

The proofs of the other examples are discussed in [Ben97].

Remark 6 (Optimization of Extensionality). Note the order in which the extensionality rules were applied in the examples above. For a practical implementation these examples suggest the following **extensionality treatment** of unification constraints: First decompose the unification constraint as much as possible. Then use rule *Func* to add as many arguments as possible to both hand sides of the resulting unification constraints. And last use rule *Leib* and/or *Equiv* to finish the extensionality treatment. In this sense the above rules can be combined to form only one rule *Ext-Treat*.

Remark 7 (Rule Leib). Due to an idea of Frank Pfenning every refutation which uses rule *Leib* can possibly be done without this rule by resolving against the extensional modified unification constraint instead, and hence rule *Leib* may be superfluous. For example the application of rule *Leib* in the proof of example **E5** can be replaced by an immediate resolution step between clause $c1$ and $c6$: $c7: [P(mX)]^F \vee [P(nX) = (ms = ns)]^F$. And by pre-unification ($P \leftarrow \lambda Y_\iota.(ms = Y)$ and $X \leftarrow s$) we immediately get the empty clause. Note that in this case it is essential that unification constraints are encoded as negative equality literals (see Remark 5).

However, there are two reasons why rule *Leib* seems to be very appropriate. First the completeness proof with respect to Henkin models seems to be more complicated without rule *Leib* and isn't done yet. Additionally the experience from the implementation work of the system LEO is, that rule *Func* eases the implementation and the integration of heuristics. See [Ben97] for a more detailed discussion.

4   Soundness and Completeness

Theorem 3 (Soundness of $\mathcal{ER}$). *The calculus $\mathcal{ER}$ is sound with respect to Henkin semantics.*

Proof. The soundness of $\mathcal{HORES}$ is discussed in detail in [Koh94], the only major difference to the first-order case is the treatment of Skolemization, which has been discussed in [Mil83].

   The soundness of the three new extensionality rules are obvious, as they do only apply the two extensionality principles and the Leibniz definition, which are valid in Henkin models.

   For the completeness result, we will need a series of disjunction Lemmata, which are well-known for first-order logic, and which can be proven with the same techniques, only considering the extra inference rules of $\mathcal{ER}$ in the inductions.

Lemma 1. *Let $\Phi, \Delta, \Gamma_1, \Gamma_2 \subseteq wff^{cl}(\Sigma)$ and $\mathbf{A}, \mathbf{B} \in wff^{cl}(\Sigma)$. We have*

1. *If $CNF(\Phi * \mathbf{A}) \vdash_{\mathcal{ER}} \square$ and $CNF(\Phi * \mathbf{B}) \vdash_{\mathcal{ER}} \square$, then $CNF(\Phi * \mathbf{A} \vee \mathbf{B}) \vdash_{\mathcal{ER}} \square$*
2. *If $CNF(\Phi * \neg \mathbf{A} * \mathbf{B}) \vdash_{\mathcal{ER}} \square$ and $CNF(\Phi * \mathbf{A} * \neg \mathbf{B}) \vdash_{\mathcal{ER}} \square$, then $CNF(\Phi * \neg(\mathbf{A} \equiv \mathbf{B})) \vdash_{\mathcal{ER}} \square$*

Proof. For the proof of the first assertion we first verify that $CNF(\Phi * \mathbf{A} \vee \mathbf{B}) = CNF(\Phi) \cup CNF(\mathbf{A}) \sqcup CNF(\mathbf{B})$, where $\Gamma \sqcup \Delta = := \{\mathbf{C} \vee \mathbf{D} | \mathbf{C} \in CNF(\mathbf{A})\}, \mathbf{D} \in CNF(\mathbf{B})\}$. Then we use that $\Phi \cup \Gamma_1 \sqcup \Gamma_2 \vdash_{\mathcal{ER}} \square$, provided that $\Phi \cup \Gamma_1 \vdash_{\mathcal{ER}} \square$ and $\Phi \cup \Gamma_2 \vdash_{\mathcal{ER}} \square$. The second involves a tedious but straightforward calculation.

Lemma 2 (Lifting Lemma). *Let Φ be a set of clauses and σ a substitution, then Φ is refutable by $\mathcal{ER}$, provided that $\theta(\Phi)$ is.*

Proof. The claim is proven by an induction on the structure of the refutation $\mathcal{D}_\theta: \theta(\Phi) \vdash_{\mathcal{ER}} \square$ be a refutation of $\theta(\Phi)$ constructing a refutation $\mathcal{D}$ for Φ that is isomorphic to $\mathcal{D}_\theta$.

   For this task it is crucial to maintain a tight correspondence $\omega: \Phi \longrightarrow \theta(\Phi)$ between the respective clause sets. This is formalized by a **clause set isomorphism**, i.e. a bijection of clause sets, that corresponding clauses are isomorphic, i.e. for a ω respects literal polarities and is compatible with θ, i.e. for any literal $\mathbf{N}^\alpha$ we have $\omega(\mathbf{N}) = \theta(\mathbf{N})$. The main difficulty with lifting properties in higher-order logic is the fact that due to the existence of predicate variables at the head of formulae, the propositional structure of formulae can change during instantiation. For instance if $\theta(F) = \lambda X_\alpha. GX \vee p$, and $\mathbf{A}^\mathsf{T} = Fa^\mathsf{T}$, then the pre-literal $\theta(F)$ is split $\mathcal{D}_\theta$ but not in the $\mathcal{ER}$-derivation already constructed. The solution of this problem is to apply the rule *Prim* with a suitable general binding $\mathcal{G}^\vee_{\alpha \to o} = \lambda X_\alpha.(H^1 X) \vee (H^2 X)$ and obtain a pre-literal $(H^1 a \vee H^2 a)^\mathsf{T}$, to which can be split in order to regain a clause set isomorphism. Since $\mathcal{G}^\vee_{\alpha \to o}$ is more general than $\theta(F)$ there is a substitution ρ, such that $\theta(F) = \rho(\mathcal{G}^\vee_{\alpha \to o})$, therefore $\omega((H^1 a \vee H^2 a)^\mathsf{T}) = \theta'((H^1 a \vee H^2 a)^\mathsf{T})$ where $\theta' = \theta \cup \rho$.

Theorem 4 (Completeness of $\mathcal{ER}$). *The calculus $\mathcal{ER}$ is complete with respect to Henkin semantics.*

Proof. Let Γ_Σ be the set of Σ-sentences which cannot be refuted by calculus $\mathcal{ER}$ ($\Gamma_\Sigma := \{\Phi \subseteq \mathit{wff}_o^{cl}(\Sigma)|\mathrm{CNF}(\Phi) \nvdash_{\mathcal{ER}} \Box\}$), then we show that Γ_Σ is a saturated abstract consistency class for Henkin models. This entails completeness of $\mathcal{ER}$ by theorem 1.

Let $\Phi \in \Gamma_\Sigma$. We show that Φ mets the conditions required in definition 1:

∇_c Suppose that $\mathbf{A}, \neg\mathbf{A} \in \Phi$. Since $\mathbf{A}$ is atomic we have $\mathrm{CNF}(\Phi * \mathbf{A} * \neg\mathbf{A}) = \mathrm{CNF}(\Phi) * [\mathbf{A}]^T * [\mathbf{A}]^F$ and hence we can derive $\Box$ with *Res* and *Triv*. This contradicts our assumption.

In all of the remaining cases, we show the contrapositive, e.g. in the next case we prove, that for all $\Phi \in \Gamma_\Sigma$, if $\Phi * \neg\neg\mathbf{A} * \mathbf{A} \notin \Gamma_\Sigma$, then $\Phi * \neg\neg\mathbf{A} \notin \Gamma_\Sigma$, which entails the assertion.

$\nabla_\neg$ If $\mathrm{CNF}(\Phi * \neg\neg\mathbf{A} * \mathbf{A}) \vdash_{\mathcal{ER}} \Box$, then also $\mathrm{CNF}(\Phi * \neg\neg\mathbf{A}) \vdash_{\mathcal{ER}} \Box$, since $\mathrm{CNF}(\Phi * \neg\neg\mathbf{A} * \mathbf{A}) = \mathrm{CNF}(\Phi * \neg\neg\mathbf{A})$.

$\nabla_{\beta\eta}$ Analog to $\nabla_\neg$, since $\mathrm{CNF}(\Phi * \mathbf{A} * \mathbf{A}_{\downarrow_{\beta\eta}}) = \mathrm{CNF}(\Phi * \mathbf{A})$.

$\nabla_\vee$ If $\mathrm{CNF}(\Phi * \mathbf{A} \vee \mathbf{B} * \mathbf{A}) \vdash_{\mathcal{ER}} \Box$ and $\mathrm{CNF}(\Phi * \mathbf{A} \vee \mathbf{B} * \mathbf{B}) \vdash_{\mathcal{ER}} \Box$, then $\mathrm{CNF}(\Phi * \mathbf{A} \vee \mathbf{B}) \vdash_{\mathcal{ER}} \Box$ by lemma 1(3).

$\nabla_\wedge$ If $\mathrm{CNF}(\Phi * \neg(\mathbf{A} \vee \mathbf{B}) * \neg\mathbf{A} * \neg\mathbf{B}) \vdash_{\mathcal{ER}} \Box$, then $\mathrm{CNF}(\Phi * \neg(\mathbf{A} \vee \mathbf{B})) \vdash_{\mathcal{ER}} \Box$, since $\mathrm{CNF}(\Phi * \neg(\mathbf{A} \vee \mathbf{B}) * \neg\mathbf{A} * \neg\mathbf{B}) = \mathrm{CNF}(\Phi * \neg(\mathbf{A} \vee \mathbf{B}))$.

$\nabla_\forall$ By the lifting lemma 2.

$\nabla_\exists$ Let $\mathrm{CNF}(\Phi * \neg\Pi\mathbf{F} * \neg\mathbf{F}w) \vdash_{\mathcal{ER}} \Box$ and note that $\mathrm{CNF}(\Phi * \neg\Pi\mathbf{F} * \neg\mathbf{F}w) = \mathrm{CNF}(\Phi * \neg\mathbf{F}w' * \neg\mathbf{F}w)$. Now let w'' be any new constant symbol which does not occur in Φ or $\mathbf{F}$. Since also w and w' do not occur in Φ or $\mathbf{F}$ it is easy to verify that their is a derivation $\mathrm{CNF}(\Phi * \neg\mathbf{F}w'') \vdash_{\mathcal{ER}}^{D'} \Box$, where each occurrence of $\neg\mathbf{F}w'$ or $\neg\mathbf{F}w$ is replaced by $\neg\mathbf{F}w''$. Hence $\mathrm{CNF}(\Phi * \neg\Pi\mathbf{F}) \vdash_{\mathcal{ER}} \Box$.

∇_b We show that if $\mathrm{CNF}(\Phi * \neg(\mathbf{A} \doteq^o \mathbf{B}) * \neg\mathbf{A} * \mathbf{B}) \vdash_{\mathcal{ER}} \Box$ and $\mathrm{CNF}(\Phi * \neg(\mathbf{A} \doteq^o \mathbf{B}) * \mathbf{A} * \neg\mathbf{B}) \vdash_{\mathcal{ER}} \Box$, then $\mathrm{CNF}(\Phi * \neg(\mathbf{A} \doteq \mathbf{B}) \vdash_{\mathcal{ER}} \Box$. Note that $\mathrm{CNF}(\Phi * \neg(\mathbf{A} \doteq \mathbf{B})) = \mathrm{CNF}(\Phi * \neg\Pi(\lambda P.\neg PA \vee PB)) = \mathrm{CNF}(\Phi) * [rA]^T * [rB]^F$, with Skolem constant $r_{o \to o}$. Now consider the following derivation

$$\frac{\dfrac{[r\mathbf{A}]^T \quad [r\mathbf{B}]^F}{\dfrac{[r\mathbf{A} \doteq r\mathbf{B}]^F}{\dfrac{[\mathbf{A} \doteq \mathbf{B}]^F}{\mathrm{CNF}(\neg(\mathbf{A} \equiv \mathbf{B}))} \; Equiv} \; Dec} \; Res}$$

Hence $\mathrm{CNF}(\Phi * \neg(\mathbf{A} \doteq \mathbf{B})) \vdash_{\mathcal{ER}} \mathrm{CNF}(\Phi * \neg(\mathbf{A} \doteq \mathbf{B})) \cup \mathrm{CNF}(\neg(\mathbf{A} \equiv \mathbf{B}))$ and we get the conclusion as a simple consequence of lemma 1(4).

∇_q We show that if $\mathrm{CNF}(\Phi * \neg(\mathbf{F} \doteq^{\alpha \to \beta} \mathbf{G}) * \neg(\mathbf{F}w \doteq^\beta \mathbf{G}w)) \vdash_{\mathcal{ER}} \Box$, then $\mathrm{CNF}(\Phi * \neg(\mathbf{F} \doteq \mathbf{G})) \vdash_{\mathcal{ER}} \Box$. Note that $\mathrm{CNF}(\Phi * \neg(\mathbf{F} \doteq \mathbf{G}) * \neg(\mathbf{F}w \doteq \mathbf{G}w)) = \mathrm{CNF}(\Phi * \neg\Pi(\lambda Q.\neg Q\mathbf{F} \vee Q\mathbf{G}) * \neg\Pi(\lambda P.\neg P(\mathbf{F}w) \vee P(\mathbf{G}w))) = \mathrm{CNF}(\Phi) * [q\mathbf{F}]^T * [q\mathbf{G}]^F * [p(\mathbf{F}w)]^T * [p(\mathbf{G}w)]^F$ and that $\mathrm{CNF}(\Phi * \neg(\mathbf{F} \doteq \mathbf{G})) = \mathrm{CNF}(\Phi) * [r\mathbf{F}]^T * [r\mathbf{G}]^F$, where $p_{\beta \to o}, q_{(\alpha \to \beta) \to o}$ and $r_{(\alpha \to \beta) \to o}$ are new Skolem constants. Now consider the following derivation:

$$\frac{[r\mathbf{F}]^T \quad [r\mathbf{G}]^F}{[r\mathbf{F} \doteq r\mathbf{G}]^F} \; Res$$

$$\frac{}{[\mathbf{F} \doteq \mathbf{G}]^F} \; Dec$$

$$\frac{}{[\mathbf{F}s \doteq \mathbf{G}s]^F} \; Func$$

$$\frac{[t(\mathbf{F}s)]^T}{[t(\mathbf{G}s)]^F} \; Leib$$

Here again s_α and $t_{\beta \to o}$ are new Skolem constants. Hence $\mathrm{CNF}(\Phi) * [r\mathbf{F}]^T * [r\mathbf{G}]^F \vdash_{\mathcal{ER}} \mathrm{CNF}(\Phi) * [r\mathbf{F}]^T * [r\mathbf{G}]^F * [t(\mathbf{F}s)]^T * [t(\mathbf{G}s)^F$.

Now the conclusion follows from the assumption since s, t and r are only renamings of the Skolem symbols w, p and q and all do not occur in Φ.

To see that Γ_Σ is saturated let $\mathbf{A} \in \mathit{wff}_o(\Sigma)$ and $\Phi \subseteq \mathit{wff}_o^{cl}(\Sigma)$ with $\Phi \not\vdash_{\mathcal{ER}} \square$. We have to show that $\Phi * \mathbf{A} \not\vdash_{\mathcal{ER}} \square$ or $\Phi * \neg\mathbf{A} \not\vdash_{\mathcal{ER}} \square$. For that suppose $\Phi \not\vdash_{\mathcal{ER}} \square$, but $\Phi * \mathbf{A} \vdash_{\mathcal{ER}} \square$ and $\Phi * \neg\mathbf{A} \vdash_{\mathcal{ER}} \square$. By lemma 1(3) we get that $\Phi * \mathbf{A} \vee \neg\mathbf{A} \vdash_{\mathcal{ER}} \square$, and hence, since $\mathbf{A} \vee \neg\mathbf{A}$ is a tautology, it must be the case that $\Phi \vdash_{\mathcal{ER}} \square$, which contradicts our assumption.

5 Conclusion

We have presented an extensional higher-order resolution calculus that is complete relative to Henkin model semantics. The treatment of the extensionality principles – necessary for the completeness result – by specialized (goal-directed) inference rules practical applicability, as an implentation of the calculus in the LEO-System [BK98] shows.

Acknowledgments The work reported here was funded by the Deutsche Forschungsgemeinschaft under grant HOTEL. The authors are grateful to Peter Andrews and Frank Pfenning for stimulating discussions.

References

[ABI+96] Peter B. Andrews, Matthew Bishop, Sunil Issar, Dan Nesmith, Frank Pfenning, and Hongwei Xi. TPS: A theorem proving system for classical type theory. *Journal of Automated Reasoning*, 16(3):321–353, 1996.

[And71] Peter B. Andrews. Resolution in type theory. *Journal of Symbolic Logic*, 36(3):414–432, 1971.

[And72] Peter B. Andrews. General models descriptions and choice in type theory. *Journal of Symbolic Logic*, 37(2):385–394, 1972.

[And86] Peter B. Andrews. *An Introduction to Mathematical Logic and Type Theory: To Truth Through Proof.* Academic Press, 1986.

[And89] Peter B. Andrews. On Connections and Higher Order Logic. *Journal of Automated Reasoning*, 5:257–291, 1989.

[Bar84] H. P. Barendregt. *The Lambda Calculus.* North Holland, 1984.

[Ben97] Christoph Benzmüller. A calculus and a system architecture for extensional higher-order resolution. Research Report 97-198, Department of Mathematical Sciences, Carnegie Mellon University, Pittsburgh,USA, June 1997.

[BK97] Christoph Benzmüuller and Michael Kohlhase. Model existence for higher-order logic. SEKI-Report SR-97-09, Universität des Saarlandes, 1997.

[BK98]   Christoph Benzmüller and Michael Kohlhase. LEO, a higher-order theorem prover. to appear at CADE-15, 1998.

[dB72]   Nicolaas Govert de Bruijn. Lambda calculus notation with nameless dummies, a tool for automatic formula manipulation, with an application to the Church-Rosser theorem. *Indagationes Mathematicae*, 34(5):381–392, 1972.

[Göd31]   Kurt Gödel. Über formal unentscheidbare Sätze der Principia Mathematica und verwandter Systeme I. *Monatshefte der Mathematischen Physik*, 38:173–198, 1931.

[Hen50]   Leon Henkin. Completeness in the theory of types. *Journal of Symbolic Logic*, 15(2):81–91, 1950.

[Hue73]   Gérard P. Huet. A mechanization of type theory. In Donald E. Walker and Lewis Norton, editors, *Proc. IJCAI'73*, pages 139–146, 1973.

[JP76]   D. C. Jensen and T. Pietrzykowski. Mechanizing ω-order type theory through unification. *Theoretical Computer Science*, 3:123–171, 1976.

[Koh94]   Michael Kohlhase. *A Mechanization of Sorted Higher-Order Logic Based on the Resolution Principle*. PhD thesis, Universität des Saarlandes, 1994.

[Koh95]   Michael Kohlhase. Higher-Order Tableaux. In P. Baumgartner, et al. eds, *TABLEAUX'95*, volume 918 of *LNAI*, pages 294–309, 1995.

[Mil83]   Dale Miller. *Proofs in Higher-Order Logic*. PhD thesis, Carnegie-Mellon University, 1983.

[Smu63]   Raymond M. Smullyan. A unifying principle for quantification theory. *Proc. Nat. Acad Sciences*, 49:828–832, 1963.

X.R.S : Explicit Reduction Systems - A First-Order Calculus for Higher-Order Calculi

Bruno Pagano

LIP6 — Université Pierre et Marie Curie — Paris (France)
Bruno.Pagano@lip6.fr

Abstract. The $\lambda_\Uparrow$-calculus is a confluent first-order term rewriting system which contains the λ-calculus written in de Bruijn's notation. The substitution is defined explicitly in $\lambda_\Uparrow$ by a subsystem, called the $\sigma_\Uparrow$-calculus. In this paper, we use the $\sigma_\Uparrow$-calculus as the substitution mechanism of general higher-order systems which we will name *Explicit Reduction Systems*. We give general conditions to define a confluent XRS. Particularly, we restrict the general condition of orthogonality of the classical higher-order rewriting systems to the orthogonality of the rules initiating substitutions.

1 Introduction

Rewriting systems are widely used to model computation. Usually, the first-order ones represent algebraic abstract types and the higher-order ones describe functionality. The main difference between them is that the higher-order ones contain bound variables. So in the first-order case the substitution is only the grafting operation, and in the higher-order case the substitution has to avoid capture of variables.

Another point of view to model functionality is to embed a binding mechanism into a first-order framework. Abadi and al. have proposed the $\lambda\sigma$-calculus [ACCL90] which encodes the λ-calculus as a first-order term rewriting system. Variables are represented by de Bruijn's indices, so that the binder λ is coded by a unary operator. The process of substitution is made explicit; substitutions are recorded as environments and the application of a given substitution to a term is decomposed into elementary steps described by rewriting rules. The calculus of substitution, denoted by σ is canonical. The β-reduction is simply the initiation of some σ steps. In this system, the metavariables of higher-order rewriting systems are simply the variables of the free algebra. This original $\lambda\sigma$-calculus has several variants collectively called the λ-calculi with explicit substitution. They differ on their confluence and termination properties [ACCL90, CHL96, Les94, Kes96, KR96, Mel95]. These systems are interesting because they can express more precisely some computations on λ-terms as the mechanisms of compilation[Cur91, HMP96]. Here we shall use the $\lambda_\Uparrow$-calculus

C. Kirchner and H. Kirchner (Eds.): Automated Deduction, CADE-15
LNAI 1421, pp. 72–87, 1998. © Springer–Verlag Berlin Heidelberg 1998

which is left linear, confluent and weakly terminating. We will call $\sigma_{\Uparrow}$ the subsystem of $\lambda_{\Uparrow}$ performing the substitution.

Dowek, Hardin and Kirchner have shown in [DHK95] how we can use the calculi with explicit substitution to reduce higher-order unification to first-order equationnal unification in a suitable theory. In [DHKP96], they show that the general algorithm for higher-order unification with explicit substitutions can be specialized to the case of *higher-order patterns*[Mil91].

Our purpose in this paper is to use $\sigma_{\Uparrow}$ to define higher-order rewriting systems in a first-order framework. We call such rewriting systems *explicit reduction systems* (XRS). In such a system, the operators are defined by a signature, giving their arity. They are either *data operators* (i.e. with non binding power) or *binding operators*. We introduce the notion of *binding arity*, which allows us to classify the operators according to their binding power. The rule performing the substitution into the operands of a given operator is simply deduced from its binding arity. The system includes also rules expressing computation. The computation rules for binding operators, called higher-order computation rules (HC-rules), initiate substitution process, according to the binding arity. Computation rules of data operators, called first-order computation rules (FC-rules), involve no substitution.

We focus on confluence properties. When they are defined by an orthogonal set of rewriting rules, higher-order rewriting systems are confluent on terms (that is metaterms without metavariables). Van Oostrom and van Raamsdonk have weakened the condition to weak orthogonality[OR94]. But this refinement is still rather strong. The clear separation between data and binding operators allows us to have weaker conditions than the usual orthogonality to ensure the confluence of an XRS. We will show that a system defined by a confluent set of FC-rules and an orthogonal set of HC-rules, is confluent (if some coherence between the binding arity and the HC-rules of a binding operator is assumed).

The paper is divided in five sections including this introduction. The second section is the presentation of the explicit substitution calculus we will use. We show its main properties, i.e. confluence and strong termination. In the third section, we define formally an XRS. We give a sufficient condition to establish the confluence of an XRS. In the fourth section, we express the sufficient condition by local properties on the rewriting rules of a XRS. We illustrate the different cases with examples. In the last section, we present related works and some hints on future developments.

2   Calculus of Explicit Substitution: The σ_Γ-Calculus

Let Γ be a signature (with one or several sorts) and V be a set of variables. The free algebra built upon Γ and V is denoted by Γ_V. The substitution on Γ_V is defined by the canonical homomorphic extension of a mapping of variables on terms. The computations on Γ_V are usually described by a set of rewriting rules.

Γ_V is a first-order language. In contrast, the λ-calculus is a higher-order one as it has a binding operator, λ, which changes the status of variables. The variable

x, free in a term a, becomes bound in $\lambda x.a$. The computation is performed by the β-rule: $(\lambda x.a)\ b \rightarrow a\{x \rightarrow b\}$. Here, the notation $\{x \rightarrow b\}$ denotes the *higher-order substitution*: it is different from the one on Γ_V, because the capture of variables has to be avoided.

However, the λ-calculus has not a handy syntax to manage general rewriting, data types must be coded with complex λ-terms. So, we may wish to extend λ-calculus with data structures or, going the other way, to extend first-order rewriting systems with a binding mechanism to recover functionality. This leads to higher-order rewriting. Since the *combinatory reduction systems* (CRS) of Klop[Klo80], many formalisms have been introduced to provide syntactical definitions for higher-order rewriting. After the CRS of Klop came the *expression reduction systems* (ERS) of Khasidashvili[Kha90], the *interaction systems* of Asperti and Laneve[AL94], the *higher-order rewriting systems* (HRS) of Nipkow[Nip93], etc. The description of these different formalisms is given by van Raamsdonk in [vR96]. She enlights the links between all these presentations by a translation in her proper higher-order formalism. These higher-order rewriting systems share the following points.

- There is a distinction between variables and metavariables. The metavariables are the *first-order variables*: they cannot be bound, they are the variables of the free algebra underlying the TRS. The variables are the *higher-order variables*: they can be bound, so they are the variables of the λ-calculus.
- Metaterms belong to the term algebra defined by a signature, a set of variables and a set of metavariables. Terms are those metaterms containing no metavariable.
- Each presentation offers at least one symbol of abstraction as the λ of the λ-calculus.
- The rewriting relation on the terms is defined via rewriting rules on metaterms and assignments, which are some kind of substitutions of metavariables.
- They have a substitution calculus close to the λ-calculus one. The substitutions concern variables. As usual, α-conversion cannot be avoided.
- As in the λ-calculus, the application of a rewriting rule involves some substitution steps.

As explained in [DHK95], higher-order substitution cannot be described via the first-order one. But, with de Bruijn's notation, it is possible to replace the binding operator λ, by an unary operator, still denoted λ, and to encode higher-order substitution by a set of first-order rules. This is the purpose of the lambda-calculi with explicit substitution. The $\lambda\sigma$-calculus was the first introduced, by Abadi and al. in [ACCL90]. It is a first-order language with two sorts, *term* and *substitution*. It has a set of rules, σ, which performs higher-order substitution step by step and which is canonical. The system $\lambda\sigma$ is obtained by adding to σ the rule called (Beta), which, roughly speaking, launches the substitution of the argument b in the body of the function λa. The σ-normal ground terms of sort *term* are simply λ-terms in de Bruijn's notation. The variables of sort *term* are the metavariables, they permit to express contexts as open terms. The terms of sort *substitution* are roughly lists of terms, they can be understood as environments. The first-order variables of sort *substitution* can be seen as names for some parts of environments still to be instantiated. The rewriting system $\lambda\sigma$ is not confluent[CHL96] but it is confluent on terms without metavariables of sort substitution[Rio93].

In [HL89, CHL96], a second calculus, called the $\lambda_{\Uparrow}$-calculus, was defined. It differs from $\lambda\sigma$ in the way environments are managed, and it is confluent. When typed, $\lambda\sigma$ and $\lambda_{\Uparrow}$ are only weakly normalizing [Mel95, Gou97]. Later on, several other calculi were derived from $\lambda\sigma$ [Les94, Kes96] or built from $\lambda\sigma$-calculus with named variables [Rio93] or designed directly from the coding of the higher-order substitution in the de Bruijn's notation [KR96]. Apart the calculus introduced by Muñoz in [Muñ97], the set of terms of these calculi are not first-order free algebras. Usually, they are confluent on their set of terms and some of them are strongly normalizing.

We start with the substitution part of the $\lambda_{\Uparrow}$-calculus to describe a calculus on environments. We want to encode different binding mechanisms and also first-order data types. So the signature of the $\sigma_{\Uparrow}$-calculus is extended by a set of operators, Γ, which are unspecified. So Γ plays the role of a set of signature parameters. Our aim is to define sufficient conditions on Γ to obtain a confluent calculus of environments. This calculus is called σ_Γ-calculus, and its term algebra is called $\Gamma_{\Uparrow}$, where Γ is the parameter signature. We have chosen to describe an untyped formalism, but as in the $\lambda_{\Uparrow}$-calculus[Rio93], it is possible to add types.

The Term Algebra

Let *integer*, *term* and *substitution* be three sorts. The terms of $\Gamma_{\Uparrow}$ are defined by the following rules:

integer	n	=	1	$S(n)$		
term	a	=	x_t	n	$a[s]$	$f(a,\ldots,a)$ $(\forall f \in \Gamma)$
environment	s	=	x_s	id	$\uparrow$	$\Uparrow(s)$ $a.s$ $s \circ s$

where Γ is a set of symbols with a given arity.

The expressions x_s and x_t are metavariables respectively of sort *term* and *substitution*, there is no metavariable of sort *integer*. The expressions of sort *integer* represent de Bruijn's indices and they are denoted by naturals $(1, 2, \ldots, n, n+1)$. They encode the variables of higher-order rewriting systems. The expressions of sort *term* $f(\ldots)$ represent binding or data expressions, according to the rules of calculation on f. The term $a[s]$ represents an expression a to be evaluated in an environment s, that is the *closure* of a in s. The environments are lists of terms written with the cons operator (.). The empty environment is denoted by *id*. $\uparrow$ (pronounce *shift*) is a special environment and $\Uparrow()$ (pronounce *lift*) is an operator on environment, both of them help to perform renaming. The symbol $\circ$ denotes the composition of environments.

Example 1. Let Γ be a set containing an unary symbol which is denoted λ and a binary symbol App also denoted by juxtaposition (App(a,b) is denoted by $(a\ b)$). The sort of *terms* of $\Gamma_\Uparrow$ is

$$\text{term}\quad a\quad =\quad x_t\ \mid\ \mathrm{n}\ \mid\ a\,[s]\ \mid\ \lambda(a)\ \mid\ (a\ a)$$

The algebra of terms defined by the signature Γ is exactly the $\lambda_\Uparrow$-calculus's one.

Example 2. Now, we consider the signature Γ containing the two previous symbols of the λ-calculus and three data operators $(0,\mathrm{Succ}(.),+(.,.))$ encoding the naturals's data type and the addition.

$$a\quad =\quad x_t\ \mid\ \mathrm{n}\ \mid\ a\,[s]\ \mid\ \lambda(a)\ \mid\ (a\ a)\ \mid\ 0\ \mid\ \mathrm{Succ}(a)\ \mid\ a+a$$

$\Gamma_\Uparrow$ encodes the algebra of terms of an extension of the λ-calculus.

Let's remark that we have only encoded the syntactic aspects of an higher-order rewriting system, but not the computational aspects. Metavariables are unchanged, and variables become de Bruijn's indices. At this level, there is no difference between a binder (like the λ of the two previous examples) and a data symbol (like the operators 0 and Succ).

The Rewriting Relation

Let Γ be a signature, the main difference between the free algebra Γ_V and the algebra of term $\Gamma_\Uparrow$ is the introduction of the environments and of the operator of closure $(.[.])$. We introduce them to extend Γ_V with a mechanism of explicit substitution defined by first-order rules.

Example 3. We consider the signature of the example 2; if x is a variable, $a = x+0$ is a term of Γ_V. Using a meta-theory, one can define *the term a where x is substituted by the term* $\mathrm{Succ}(0)$ to be the Γ_V-term $\mathrm{Succ}(0)+0$.
In $\Gamma_\Uparrow$, the term a is encoded for instance by the term $1+0$. There exists a different term, which is $(1+0)\,[\mathrm{Succ}(0).id]$, to express the sentence *"the term $1+0$ where the de Bruijn's natural 1 is substituted by the term* $\mathrm{Succ}(0)$*"*. In $\Gamma_\Uparrow$, the term $\mathrm{Succ}(0)+0$ is a third different term.
In this section, we will define a rewriting relation σ_Γ such as:

$$(1+0)\,[\mathrm{Succ}(0).id]\ \xrightarrow{\ \sigma_\Gamma\ }\ \mathrm{Succ}(0)+0$$

The rewriting relation on $\Gamma_\Uparrow$ is defined by two sets of rewriting rules. The first one is the usual $\sigma_\Uparrow$-calculus, as defined in [CHL96], where we have removed the rules for the λ-abstraction and the application. These operators are not basic symbols of $\Gamma_\Uparrow$, but they may be reintroduced as operators of Γ (example 1). The $\sigma_\Uparrow$-rules are listed in the figure 1.
The second set of rules is defined according to the intended binding power of the operators of Γ.

$$(a[s])[t] \xrightarrow{clos} a[s \circ t]$$
$$n[\uparrow] \xrightarrow{vs1} n{+}1$$
$$n[\uparrow \circ s] \xrightarrow{vs2} n{+}1[s]$$
$$1[a.s] \xrightarrow{fvc} a$$
$$1[\Uparrow(s)] \xrightarrow{fvl1} 1$$
$$1[\Uparrow(s) \circ t] \xrightarrow{fvl2} 1[t]$$
$$n{+}1[a.s] \xrightarrow{rvc} n[s]$$
$$n{+}1[\Uparrow(s)] \xrightarrow{rvl1} n[s \circ \uparrow]$$
$$n{+}1[\Uparrow(s) \circ t] \xrightarrow{rvl2} n[s \circ (\uparrow \circ t)]$$
$$a[id] \xrightarrow{id} a$$

$$(s \circ t) \circ u \xrightarrow{ass} s \circ (t \circ u)$$
$$a.s \circ t \xrightarrow{map} a[t].(s \circ t)$$
$$\uparrow \circ (a.s) \xrightarrow{sc} s$$
$$\uparrow \circ \Uparrow(s) \xrightarrow{sl1} s \circ \uparrow$$
$$\uparrow \circ \Uparrow(s) \circ t \xrightarrow{sl2} s \circ (\uparrow \circ t)$$
$$\Uparrow(s) \circ \Uparrow(t) \xrightarrow{l1} \Uparrow(s \circ t)$$
$$\Uparrow(s) \circ (\Uparrow(t) \circ u) \xrightarrow{l2} \Uparrow(s \circ t) \circ u$$
$$\Uparrow(s) \circ (a.t) \xrightarrow{le} a.(s \circ t)$$
$$id \circ s \xrightarrow{il} s$$
$$s \circ id \xrightarrow{ir} s$$
$$\Uparrow(id) \xrightarrow{li} id$$

Fig. 1. $\sigma_{\Uparrow}$-rules

Definition 1 (Binding arity). *Let f be an operator of arity n of Γ.*

- *The binding arity of f is a n-tuple $(p_1, \ldots, p_n)$ of naturals.*
- *If one of the $p_i s$ is different from 0, the operator is said to be a* binder.
- *If all the $p_i s$ are 0, the operator is said to be a* data operator.

The binding arity of an operator expresses how many de Bruijn's naturals are linked in each argument of the operator. For instance, the binding arity of the unary symbol λ is (1), because this operator links the indice 1 in its argument. A data operator binds no indice in any of its arguments. The notion of binding arity is close to the higher-order rewriting systems's one as Khasidashvili[Kha90] or Asperti-Laneve[AL94] define it. Here, the definition is more arithmetical because we use the de Bruijn's naturals.

Definition 2 (Propagation rule). *In accordance with its binding arity, each symbol is associated to a rewriting rule which expresses how an environment is propagated to the arguments of the operator. If f is a symbol of binding arity $(p_1, \ldots, p_n)$, it is associated with the rule σ_f:*

$$f(a_1, \ldots, a_n)[s] \xrightarrow{\sigma_f} f(a_1[\Uparrow^{p_1}(s)], \ldots, a_n[\Uparrow^{p_n}(s)])$$

Where $\Uparrow^0(s)$ stands for s and $\Uparrow^{p+1}(s)$ stands for $\Uparrow(\Uparrow^p(s))$.

In this first-order setting, the operator $\Uparrow()$ acts as a revealer of the binding power of operators. There is another way to express the binding effect of operators which is borrowed from the $\lambda\sigma$-calculus. Instead of introducing the symbol

$\Uparrow()$ in the signature, we can define it as an abbreviation : $\Uparrow(s) = 1.(s \circ \uparrow)$. This leads to a weaker confluent result for the binding reduction but to a better one for extensionality.

Definition 3 (The relation σ_Γ). *Let Γ be a signature. The set of the rewriting rules on $\Gamma_\Uparrow$ containing the rules of $\sigma_\Uparrow$ and the rules σ_f for each $f \in \Gamma$ is denoted by σ_Γ. We identify the set of rules and the relation they induce, so σ_Γ denoted also a rewriting relation on $\Gamma_\Uparrow$-terms.*

The first-order rewriting system defined by $\Gamma_\Uparrow$ and the reduction σ_Γ is called the σ_Γ-calculus.

Example 4. We illustrate the definition of the σ_Γ-calculus with the example of the $\lambda_\Uparrow$-calculus. Let Γ be the signature of the example 1 containing an unary symbol λ and a binary symbol denoted by juxtaposition. The symbol coding the application is not a binder, so it has the binding arity $(0,0)$. The symbol λ codes the lambda-abstraction, so it is a binder. It abstracts the first variable of his argument as the λ of the de Bruijn's formalism. So, its binding arity is (1). With the associated rules, we have exactly defined the $\sigma_\Uparrow$-calculus:

$$(a\ b)[s] \xrightarrow{\sigma_{(..)}} a[s]\ b[s] \qquad\qquad (\lambda a)[s] \xrightarrow{\sigma_\lambda} \lambda(a[\Uparrow(s)])$$

The λ-term $\lambda x.(x\ y)$ can be coded in the de Bruijn's formalism (and in the same way in the $\sigma_\Uparrow$-calculus) by the term $\lambda(1\ 2)$. In the $\sigma_\Uparrow$-calculus, this term where the first free indice is substituted by a term t is represented by the first order term $\lambda(1\ 2)[t.id]$. Let's examine the $\sigma_\Uparrow$-normalization of this term :

$$
\begin{aligned}
\lambda(1\ 2)[t.id] &\xrightarrow{\sigma_\lambda} \lambda((1\ 2)[\Uparrow(t.id)]) \xrightarrow{\sigma_{(..)}} \lambda(1[\Uparrow(t.id)]\ 2[\Uparrow(t.id)]) \\
&\xrightarrow{fvl1} \lambda((1\ 2[\Uparrow(t.id)])) \xrightarrow{rvl1} \lambda((1\ 1[(t.id)\circ\uparrow])) \\
&\xrightarrow{map} \lambda((1\ 1[t[\uparrow].(id\circ\uparrow)])) \xrightarrow{rvl1} \lambda((1\ t[\uparrow]))
\end{aligned}
$$

We remark, that the indice 1 is unchanged because it is protected by its link with the binder λ. The indice 2 has been substituted by the closure $t[\uparrow]$ which is the term t where all the free indices are incremented to take act that the term is now under the binder λ.

Proposition 1 (Strongly normalization). *The relation σ_Γ is terminating.*

Proposition 2 (Local confluence). *The relation σ_Γ is locally confluent.*

Proof. The proofs are easily deducted from the proofs in [CHL96].   □

Corollary 1 (Confluence). *The relation σ_Γ is confluent.*

The σ_Γ-calculus is a substitution calculus for the signature Γ. It has the usual properties of such a calculus: confluence and strong normalization. Moreover, it is a calculus of environments, so it is possible to propagate heterogeneously substitutions into a term.

Notice than even if the σ_Γ-calculus implements substitutions on terms, this is a first-order left linear term rewriting system. These properties will be very useful to obtain the confluence results of the following sections.

Moreover, the confluence of the σ_Γ-calculus is in the sense of first-order order term rewriting systems, i.e. with terms containing variables. In a classical implicit calculus of substitution, we have only the *ground confluence*, i.e. on terms containing variables (here de Bruijn's naturals) but containing no metavariables (here variables).

3   Explicit Reduction Systems : X.R.S

In the previous section, we have associated to each term algebra induced by a signature Γ a first-order term rewriting system $< \Gamma_\Uparrow, \sigma_\Gamma >$ which is confluent and strongly terminating. As we have already suggested, this system can be seen as a general calculus of substitution for a set of binding and data operators. Now, these operators have also a *computing power*, which we describe by a set of rules called informally computation rules and denoted by $\mathcal{R}_\Gamma$. Some conditions are required on $\mathcal{R}_\Gamma$ in order to obtain the confluence of the system $\sigma_\Gamma + \mathcal{R}_\Gamma$. They express some compatibility between substitution and computation rules of a given operator, or they give general and classical conditions on rules, like the left linearity. Such a set of rewriting rules satisfying these conditions is called an explicit reduction system (XRS) and is defined as follows.

Definition 4. Explicit reduction systems (XRS)
Let Γ be a signature, and let $\mathcal{R}_\Gamma$ be a set of rewriting rules on $\Gamma_\Uparrow$. All the rewriting rules $(l \rightarrow r) \in \mathcal{R}_\Gamma$ verify:

1. l is not a variable. All variables of r occur in l.
2. l is linear (a variable occur at most only one time).
3. l is a term of Γ_V (i.e. it contains only operators of Γ or variables of sort term).

The term rewriting system defined by the term algebra $\Gamma_\Uparrow$ and the rewriting relation $(\sigma_\Gamma \cup \mathcal{R}_\Gamma)$ is said to be the explicit reduction system *defined by Γ and $\mathcal{R}_\Gamma$; it is noted* XRS $[\Gamma_\Uparrow, \mathcal{R}_\Gamma]$.

The left linearity is not needed to define a not ambiguous term rewriting system but the example of the surjective pairing[Klo90] prompts us to banish systems which are not linear when we consider higher-order rewriting systems, especially when they are not typed. Moreover, the left linearity is an essential condition for our proofs of confluence. The third condition expresses than the left members cannot contain a substitution. The ERSs of [Kha90], where there is an explicit symbol for substitutions, have the same condition. This is not a restriction because our goal is not to define rewriting rules on substitutions, the reduction σ_Γ is designed to play this role.

Notice that right members which are always of sort *term*, can contain closures. The computation rules can create substitutions. Such rules, introducing substitutions, are said to be *higher-order computation rules* (HC-rules). If a computation rule does not introduce a substitution, then it describes a data simplification and it is called a *first-order computation rule* (FC-rule). Left and right members of such a FC-rule are expressions of the free algebra Γ_V.

Example 5. To illustrate that, we show how to define the λ-calculus with pairs. We keep the symbols λ and $(.\,.)$ of the previous examples, and we add two unary data symbols $\mathtt{fst}$ and $\mathtt{snd}$ and a binary data symbol $< .,. >$. The associate σ_Γ-rules are:

$$\mathtt{fst}(a)[s] \xrightarrow{\sigma_{fst}} \mathtt{fst}(a[s]) \qquad \mathtt{snd}(a)[s] \xrightarrow{\sigma_{snd}} \mathtt{snd}(a[s])$$

$$< a, b > [s] \xrightarrow{\sigma_{<>}} < a[s], b[s] >$$

The relation $\mathcal{R}_\Gamma$ is defined by the two projections and the β-reduction. The two projections are FC-rules:

$$\mathtt{fst}(< a, b >) \xrightarrow{proj1} a \qquad \mathtt{snd}(< a, b >) \xrightarrow{proj2} b$$

And the β-reduction is a HC-rule: $(\lambda(a)\ b) \xrightarrow{Beta} a[b.id]$.

For instance, we define a function swapping the components of a pair by the following term $(\lambda < \mathtt{snd}(1), \mathtt{fst}(1) >)$. The reduction of the application of this function to the pair $< a, b >$ is :

$$\lambda\,(< \mathtt{snd}(1), \mathtt{fst}(1) >)\ \ < a, b >$$

$$\xrightarrow{Beta}\ < \mathtt{snd}(1), \mathtt{fst}(1) > [< a, b > .id]$$
$$\xrightarrow{\sigma_{<>}}\ < \mathtt{snd}(1)[< a, b > .id]\,,\ \mathtt{fst}(1)[< a, b > .id] >$$
$$\xrightarrow{\sigma_{snd}\ \sigma_{fst}}\ < \mathtt{snd}(1[< a, b > .id])\,,\ \mathtt{fst}(1[< a, b > .id]) >$$
$$\xrightarrow{fvc\ fvc}\ < \mathtt{snd}(< a, b >)\,,\ \mathtt{fst}(< a, b >) >$$
$$\xrightarrow{proj2\ proj1}\ < b, a >$$

So, $\mathcal{R}_\Gamma$ is the union of a set of substitution rules and a set of computation rules. There must be some agreement between these two sets of rules: the higher-order computation rules of a given binding operator f must be coherent with its binding arity. So we have to require a coherence condition, which is defined as follows.

Definition 5.

A relation $\mathcal{R}$ is said coherent with σ_Γ (or σ_Γ-coherent) if and only if the following diagram can be closed:

$$
\begin{array}{ccc}
f & \xrightarrow{\ \mathcal{R}\ } & g \\
\sigma_\Gamma \downarrow & & \vdots\, \sigma_\Gamma^* \\
h & \dashrightarrow & i \\
& \sigma_\Gamma^* \mathcal{R} \sigma_\Gamma^* &
\end{array}
$$

The σ_Γ-coherence asserts the adequation between the binding of de Bruijn's integers induced by the rules of σ_f and the rewriting rules of $\mathcal{R}$. For instance, the (Beta) rule, mentioned above, is σ_Γ-coherent if and only if the rules σ_λ and $\sigma_{(..)}$ are:

$$(\lambda a)[s] \xrightarrow{\sigma_\lambda} \lambda(a[\Uparrow (s)]) \quad \text{and} \quad (a\ b)[s] \xrightarrow{\sigma_{(..)}} a[s]\ b[s]$$

The symbol λ is a binder, i.e. this symbol is linked with some de Bruijn's integers. The $\Uparrow$ operator manages the fact that an external substitution does not concern these bound integers.

Definition 6.

A relation $\mathcal{R}$ satisfies the σ_Γ-diamond property if and only if the following diagram can be closed:

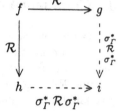

This property expresses the diamond property of the relation $\mathcal{R}$ modulo the relation σ_Γ. This is a very strong requirement. For instance, even in forgetting the σ_Γ^* steps, this property is not verified by the β-rule of the λ-calculus. But, we know how to build a relation B, verifying $\beta \subset B \subset \beta^*$, which has the diamond property — for instance, by the Taït-Martin-Löf method. So, most of the $\mathcal{R}_\Gamma$ systems will not verify directly this property. However, it may be possible to define the analogous of the relation B.

Proposition 3. *If a relation $\mathcal{R}$ is σ_Γ-coherent and has the σ_Γ-diamond property, then the relation $(\sigma_\Gamma^* \mathcal{R} \sigma_\Gamma^*)$ has the diamond property.*

Proof. This proposition is inspired by the Yokouchi's lemma stated in [CHL96]. □

Theorem 1. *Let S be a relation on $\Gamma_\Uparrow$. If S is σ_Γ-coherent, if S has the σ_Γ-diamond property and if $\mathcal{R} \subset S \subset \mathcal{R}^*$ then the XRS $[\Gamma, \mathcal{R}]$ is confluent.*

Proof. It is immediate to establish that $(\mathcal{R} \cup \sigma_\Gamma) \subset (\sigma_\Gamma^* S \sigma_\Gamma^*) \subset (\mathcal{R} \cup \sigma_\Gamma)^*$. We know that $(\sigma_\Gamma^* S \sigma_\Gamma^*)$ is strongly confluent. So $(\mathcal{R} \cup \sigma_\Gamma)$ is confluent. □

Definition 7.

Two relations $\mathcal{R}$ and S σ_Γ-commute if and only if they satisfy the following diagram:

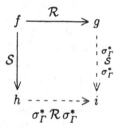

Notice that if a relation $\mathcal{R}$ σ_Γ-commutes with itself, then $\mathcal{R}$ has the σ_Γ-diamond property.

Theorem 2. *Let $\{\mathcal{R}_i\}_{1 \leq i \leq n}$ a finite family of reductions on $\Gamma_{\Uparrow}$. If*

1. for all i, $\mathcal{R}_i$ is σ_Γ-coherent,
2. for all i and j, $\mathcal{R}_i$ and $\mathcal{R}_j$ σ_Γ-commute,

then the relation $(\sigma_\Gamma^* \mathcal{R}_1 \sigma_\Gamma^* \ldots \sigma_\Gamma^* \mathcal{R}_n \sigma_\Gamma^*)$ satisfies the diamond property.

Proof. This a consequence of the proposition 3.   □

4   Confluence of XRSs

In the previous section, in the theorems 1 and 2, we have given conditions on $\mathcal{R}_\Gamma$ which cannot be asserted by a simple inspection of left members. Here, we show how to define a confluent XRS with local conditions on the rewriting rules defining $\mathcal{R}_\Gamma$. Having a different approach for the FC-rules and the HC-rules, we give families of confluent XRS. We illustrate with examples.

4.1   The $\lambda_{\Uparrow}$-Calculus

Applying our formalism to the λ-calculus leads to the $\lambda_{\Uparrow}$-calculus as we have presented it in a previous example. The signature Γ has two elements: the first one is a binary data symbol $((..))$ and the second one is an unary symbol (λ) with the binding arity (1). The β-reduction is coded by the single HC-rule named Beta: $(\lambda a \ b) \xrightarrow{Beta} a[b.id]$.

Proposition 4. *The parallelization of the relation $\xrightarrow{Beta}$ is σ_Γ-coherent and has the σ_Γ-diamond property.*

Proof. This proof is made in [CHL96]. In this case, the parallelization of Beta has the diamond property.

Corollary 2. *The $\lambda_{\Uparrow}$-calculus (i.e. XRS $[\{\lambda, (.\ .)\}, Beta]$) is confluent.*

Proof. The proposition 4 gives the hypothesis of the theorem 1.   □

4.2   The $\lambda_{\Uparrow}$-Calculus with Data Structures

λ-calculus may be extended with data-structures. Here, as we have defined λ-calculus as an XRS, we define extensions of λ-calculus as XRSs (so as extensions of $\lambda_{\Uparrow}$-calculus). Such a XRS must be defined by a signature including the $\lambda_{\Uparrow}$-calculus one (i.e the symbols of application and abstraction with their associated rule σ_f). The rewriting rules of the XRS must be the *Beta* rule or first-order computation rules.

Let Σ be the signature of the first-order operators of the data structures. The computations on these data structures are described by a set of rewriting rules on σ-terms called $\mathcal{R}_\Sigma$.

We consider the signature $\Gamma = \Sigma \cup \{\lambda, (..)\}$. Notice that Σ cannot contain the operator λ because it is not a first-order operator; but the application can be a data operator of Γ. We consider the rewriting systems $\mathcal{R}_\Sigma$ as a rewriting system on $\Gamma_\uparrow$-terms, called $\mathcal{R}$. We assume the following hypothesis:

1. $\mathcal{R}_\Sigma$ is left linear and confluent on Σ_V.
2. (*Beta*) is orthogonal with $\mathcal{R}$ (i.e. there is no critical pair between a $\mathcal{R}$-rule and (*Beta*)).
3. For all f of Σ, the binding arity of f is $(0, 0, \ldots, 0)$.
4. $\sigma_\Gamma = \sigma_\lambda \cup \sigma_{(..)} \cup \sigma_\Sigma$.
5. $\mathcal{R}_\Gamma = (Beta) \cup \mathcal{R}$.

So, we have defined an extension of λ-calculus with only data symbols and first-order rules. We have divided the computation calculus in the β-reduction on one side, and a confluent first-order rewriting system on the other side.

Definition 8. *We define the relation $B\|$ by the rules:*

$$\frac{}{s \xrightarrow{B\|} s} \qquad \frac{s \xrightarrow{B\|} s'}{\Uparrow(s) \xrightarrow{B\|} \Uparrow(s')} \qquad \frac{a \xrightarrow{B\|} a' \quad s \xrightarrow{B\|} s'}{a.s \xrightarrow{B\|} a'.s'} \qquad \frac{s \xrightarrow{B\|} s' \quad t \xrightarrow{B\|} t'}{s \circ t \xrightarrow{B\|} s' \circ t'}$$

$$\frac{a \xrightarrow{B\|} a' \quad s \xrightarrow{B\|} s'}{a[s] \xrightarrow{B\|} a'[s']} \qquad \frac{a_1 \xrightarrow{B\|} a_1' \quad \ldots \quad a_n \xrightarrow{B\|} a_n'}{f(a_1 \ldots a_n) \xrightarrow{B\|} f(a_1' \ldots a_n')} \Gamma_f \qquad \frac{a \xrightarrow{B\|} a' \quad b \xrightarrow{B\|} b'}{(\lambda a)\, b \xrightarrow{B\|} a'[b'.id]}$$

Lemma 1. *The relation $B\|$ is σ_Γ-coherent and has the σ_Γ-diamond property.*

Proof. This is the same proof that for the proposition 4. □

Lemma 2. *The relations $B\|$ and $\mathcal{R}^*$ commute.*

Proof. Beta and $\mathcal{R}_\Sigma$ are orthogonal. It is not difficult to extend the property to the parallelization of *Beta*. □

Lemma 3. *The relation $\mathcal{R}^*$ has the σ_Γ-diamond property.*

Proof. This is a natural consequence of the confluence of $\mathcal{R}_\Sigma$. □

Lemma 4. *The relation $\mathcal{R}^*$ is σ_Γ-coherent.*

Proof. We use the properties of the σ_Γ-normal forms of the terms and the fact that all the rules are FC-rules.

Theorem 3. *The* XRS $[\Gamma, \mathcal{R}_\Gamma]$ *is confluent.*

Proof. The relations $B\|$ and $\mathcal{R}^*$ satisfy the hypothesis of the theorem 2, so the relation $\sigma_\Gamma^* B \| \sigma_\Gamma^* \mathcal{R}^* \sigma_\Gamma^*$ satisfies the diamond property.

Moreover, $\mathcal{R}_\Gamma \subset \sigma_\Gamma^* B \| \sigma_\Gamma^* \mathcal{R}^* \sigma_\Gamma^* \subset \mathcal{R}_\Gamma^*$, so $\mathcal{R}_\Gamma$ is a confluent relation.   □

So, we obtain for XRS the same confluence conditions as Müller had for the left-linear algebraic extensions of the λ-calculus in [Mül92]. He asked the algebraic rewriting rules to be not *variable applying*, i.e. the left members of rules must not contain a variable in the left-hand side of an application. We have the same restriction, but it is required to obtain the orthogonality between *Beta* and the first-order rules.

4.3   Calculi with New Binders

In our previous examples, the only binder was λ and the only rule which creates a substitution was (*Beta*). Our main concern is to describe a calculus with several binders and several ways to create substitutions. For instance we want to consider a binder emulating a fix-point or pattern-matching on data structures.

Example 6. The rule $(Y\ a)\ b \longrightarrow (a\ (Y\ a))\ b$ is described with an operator of binding arity (2) associated to the rule $(\lambda_{rec}\ a)\ b \longrightarrow a[\lambda_{rec}\ a.b.id]$.

Example 7. The ML like matching rules on Peano's integer

$$(\texttt{match } 0 \texttt{ with } 0 \ \to \ a \ | \ S(n) \ \to \ b) \ \longrightarrow \ a$$
$$(\texttt{match } Succ(p) \texttt{ with } 0 \ \to \ a \ | \ S(n) \ \to \ b) \ \longrightarrow \ (b\ p)$$

can be expressed by a binder for the second match with a binding arity $(0, 1)$.

$$\texttt{match}(a, b)\ 0 \ \longrightarrow \ a$$
$$\texttt{match}(a, b)\ Succ(p) \ \longrightarrow \ b\,[p\,.id]$$

Notice that these rewriting rules have a left member which is a term of Γ_V, but their right member contain a closure. In such cases, the σ_Γ-coherence of $\mathcal{R}_\Gamma$ needs to extend the conditions given the first-order rules.

Definition 9. *The relations $\mathcal{R}$ and σ_Γ are said compatible if and only if for each rule $l(x_1 \ldots x_n) \longrightarrow r(x_1 \ldots x_n)$ of $\mathcal{R}$, for each term $a_1, \ldots, a_n$ and for each substitution s; there exists unique integers $p_1, \ldots, p_n$ such as:*

$$l(a_1 \ldots a_n)[s] \xrightarrow{\sigma_\Gamma^*} l(a_1[\Uparrow^{p_1}(s)] \ldots a_n[\Uparrow^{p_n}(s)])$$

$$r(a_1 \ldots a_n)[s] \stackrel{\sigma_\Gamma^*}{=} r(a_1[\Uparrow^{p_1}(s)] \ldots a_n[\Uparrow^{p_n}(s)])$$

Remark that this definition given in a typed context implies that the relation $\mathcal{R}_\Gamma$ has the subject reduction property.

Proposition 5. *If $\mathcal{R}$ and σ_Γ are compatible together, then $\mathcal{R}^*$ is σ_Γ-coherent.*

This proposition generalizes the property established in the previous section to prove the proposition 4 for the first-order rules.

Proof. Notice that the only critical pair within a $\mathcal{R}_\Gamma$-rule and a σ_Γ-rule is with terms like $l(a_1 \ldots a_n)[s]$ because l cannot contain a symbol .[.] .   □

Proposition 6. *If $\mathcal{R}$ is an orthogonal system then $\mathcal{R}^*$ satisfies the σ_Γ-diamond property.*

The two previous propositions are sufficient to prove the confluence of XRS coding orthogonal higher-order rewriting systems. We retrieve the results of the other formalisms for higher-order rewriting.

Now, we merge results for first-order algebraic extensions and results for higher-order orthogonal extensions. We show than the orthogonality is needed only for higher-order rules but not for first-order ones.

Proposition 7. *Let Γ be a signature. Let $\mathcal{R}^1$ and $\mathcal{R}^>$ two sets of rewriting rules on $\Gamma_\Uparrow$ such as:*

1. *$\mathcal{R}^>$ is orthogonal and orthogonal with rules of $\mathcal{R}^1$,*
2. *$\mathcal{R}^1$ contains only left-linear FC-rules,*
3. *$\mathcal{R}^1$ is confluent on Γ_V,*

then there exists a relation S such as $S \subset (\sigma_\Gamma \cup \mathcal{R}^1 \cup \mathcal{R}^>)^* \subset S^*$ and which is confluent.

Proof. Let $\mathcal{R}^>$ be the set $\{r_1, \ldots, r_n\}$.
Let S be the relation $(\sigma_\Gamma^* \mathcal{R}^{1^*} \sigma_\Gamma^* r_1^* \sigma_\Gamma^* \ldots \sigma_\Gamma^* r_n^* \sigma_\Gamma^*)$. Using the properties of first-order reduction and properties of orthogonal reduction previously demonstrated and using the proposition 2, we have the confluence of S.   □

Corollary 3. *With the hypothesis of the preceding proposition, the explicit reduction system XRS $[\Gamma_\Uparrow, \mathcal{R}^1 \cup \mathcal{R}^>]$ is confluent.*

5   Discussion and Conclusion

In [BR96], Bloo and Rose "generalize explicit substitution to CRS". Their aim is to transform a CRS into an *explicit substitution CRS*, this ESCRS is still a CRS which inherits the properties of confluence and of strong normalization of the original CRS. XRSs are slightly different: an XRS defines a higher-order rewriting system as a first-order rewriting system. Another difference between [BR96] and us is the choice of the calculus with explicit substitution. The authors use an explicit substitution calculus with name. We use the $\lambda_\Uparrow$-calculus which is not normalizing even for simply typed λ-terms[Mel95] but which is confluent on terms containing variables when an ESCRS is only *ground confluent*.

We discuss now the main advantages and the major limitations of the XRSs. In our point of view, it is simplier to express an intuitive higher-order rewriting system in the XRS's formalism because a first order rule is coded by itself. The de Bruijn's integers cancel all name clash problems. In such a formalism, we only need grafting as substitution mechanism. Using de Bruijn's naturals, the HC rewriting rules are less intuitive, but they express exactly where a symbol binds a variable and how a reduction rule performs a substitution. We gain benefits of explicit substitutions when we want to implement a XRS, because there is no particular treatment for the substitution. And last but not least, a XRS is a first order term rewriting system: so all technics, algorithms and implementations on first-order rewriting systems are available on XRSs.

But the $\lambda_{\Uparrow}$-calculus, and by casualty XRS, has several defaults. One of them, as it has been shown by Melies[Mel95], is that this calculus is not strongly terminating with simply typed terms. But Goubault[Gou97] has shown that there are terminating strategies to perform this calculus, in most of the cases, this is sufficient. This proof cannot be trivially extended to the XRS cases, so one of our further works will be to express conditions to have weak normalization of XRS.

Another exploitable aspect of the XRS is a singular property of the weak calculi with explicit substitution. With explicit substitution, it is possible to define a confluent weak λ-calculus[Cur91, HMP96]. In XRS, we have a syntactic way to differentiate binders and others data symbols. This can be used to define weak calculi on higher-order rewriting systems, in this case we conjecture that XRS are strongly normalizing, if the data rewriting part is.

References

[ACCL90]   M. Abadi, L. Cardelli, P.-L. Curien, and J.-J. Lévy. Explicit substitutions. In *Principles of Programming Languages*, pages 31–46, 1990.

[AL94]   A. Asperti and C. Laneve. Interaction systems 1: The theory of optimal reductions. *Mathematical Structures in Computer Science*, 4:457–504, 1994.

[BR96]   R. Bloo and K.H. Rose. Combinatory reduction systems with explicit substitution that preserve strong normalisation. In *Rewriting Techniques and Applications*, pages 169–183, 1996.

[CHL96]   P.-L. Curien, T. Hardin, and J.-J. Lévy. Confluence properties of weak and strong calculi of explicit substitutions. *Journal of the ACM*, 43(2):362–397, March 1996.

[Cur91]   P.-L. Curien. An abstract framework for environment machines. *Theoretical Computer Science*, 82, 1991.

[DHK95]   G. Dowek, T. Hardin, and C. Kirchner. Higher-order unification via explicit substitutions. In *Logic in Computer Science*, 1995.

[DHKP96]   G. Dowek, T. Hardin, C. Kirchner, and F. Pfenning. Unification via explicit substitutions: the case of higher-order patterns. In *Logic Programming*, pages 259–273, 1996.

[Gou97]   J. Goubault. Weak normalization of $\lambda\sigma$-calculus. GDR-AMI, 1997.

[HL89]   T. Hardin and J.-J. Lévy. A confluent calculus of substitutions. In *France-Japan Artificial Intelligence and Computer Science Symposium*, 1989.

[HMP96]   T. Hardin, L. Maranget, and B. Pagano. Functional back-ends within the lambda-sigma calculus. In *International Conference on Functional Programming*, pages 25–33, 1996.

[Kes96]   D. Kesner. Confluence properties of extensional and non-extensional lambda-calculi with explicit substitutions. *Lecture Notes in Computer Science*, 1103:184–??, 1996.

[Kha90]   Z.O. Khasidashvili. Expression reduction systems. In *Proceedings of I. Vekua Institute of Applied Mathematics*, volume 36, pages 200–220, 1990.

[Klo80]   J.W. Klop. *Combinatory Reduction Systems*. PhD thesis, University of Amsterdam, 1980.

[Klo90]   J.W. Klop. Term rewriting systems. Technical report, Centrum voor Wiskunde en Informatica, 1990.

[KR96]   F. Kamareddine and A. Rios. Generalized-reduction and explicit substitution. *Lecture Notes in Computer Science*, 1140:378–??, 1996.

[Les94]   P. Lescanne. From $\lambda\sigma$ to λv: A journey through calculi of explicit substitutions. In *Principles of Programming Languages*, pages 60–69, 1994.

[Mel95]   P.-A. Mellies. Typed lambda-calculi with explicit substitutions may not terminate. In *Typed Lambda Calculi and Applications*, 1995.

[Mil91]   D. Miller. A logic programming language with lambda-abstraction, function variables, and simple unification. *Journal of Logic and Computation*, pages 497–536, 1991.

[Mül92]   F. Müller. Confluence of the lambda calculus with left-linear algebraic rewriting. *Information Processing Letters*, 41:293–299, 1992.

[Muñ97]   C. Muñoz. Meta-theoretical properties of λ_ϕ: A left-linear variant of λ_σ. Technical Report RR-3107, Unité de recherche INRIA-Rocquencourt, Février 1997.

[Nip93]   T. Nipkow. Higher-order critical pairs. In *Proceedings of Logic in Computer Science*, pages 342–349, 1993.

[OR94]   V. Oostrom and F. Raamsdonk. Weak orthogonality implies confluence: The higher-order case. *Lecture Notes in Computer Science*, 813:379–??, 1994.

[Rio93]   A. Rios. *Contributions à l'étude des Lambda-calculs avec Substitutions Explicites*. PhD thesis, Université PARIS 7, 1993.

[RM95]   K. H. Rose and R. R. Moore. *Xy-pic Reference Manual*, 1995.

[vR96]   F. van Raamsdonk. *Confluence and Normalization for Higher-Order Rewriting*. PhD thesis, University of Amsterdam, 1996.

About the Confluence of Equational Pattern Rewrite Systems*

Alexandre Boudet and Evelyne Contejean

LRI, CNRS URA 410
Bt. 490, Universit Paris-Sud, Centre d'Orsay
91405 Orsay Cedex, France

Abstract. We study the confluence of higher-order pattern rewrite systems modulo an equational theory E. This problem has been investigated by Mayr and Nipkow [13], for the case of rewriting modulo a congruence à la Huet [8]. The case we address here is rewriting using matching modulo E as done in the first-order case by Jouannaud and Kirchner [10].
The theory is then applied to the case of AC-theories, for which we provided a complete unification algorithm in [1]. It happens that the AC-unifiers may have to be constrained by some flexible-flexible equations of the form $\lambda x_1 \cdots \lambda x_n.F(x_1,\ldots,x_n) = \lambda x_1 \cdots \lambda x_n F(x_{\pi(1)},\ldots,x_{\pi(n)})$, where F is a free variable and π a permutation. This situation requires a slight technical adaptation of the theory.

Introduction

Using equations as a programming language is very tempting because very natural. A theory of term rewriting systems (TRSs) has been developed so as to make this paradigm effective by orienting the equations into rewrite rules (in order to gain efficiency) while restoring the completeness by a *completion* process [11,9]. Completion relies on a *critical pair lemma* which shows that whenever a term t can be rewritten using rules $l_1 \to r_1$ and $l_2 \to r_2$ in two different terms s_1 and s_2, then either s_1 and s_2 rewrite (maybe in several steps) to a common reduct, or there exists a *critical pair* between $l_1 \to r_1$ and $l_2 \to r_2$. The critical pairs are obtained by unifying a left-hand side of a rule with a subterm of a left-hand side of a rule.

Some equations (like commutativity) cannot be oriented into terminating rewrite rules, hence the need of rewriting *modulo* an equational theory. The confluence of a terminating rewrite system R modulo an equational theory E (denoted by R/E) has been studied by Huet [8]. Jouannaud and Kirchner use a different reduction (denoted hereafter by R^E), in which E-equality steps can be performed only *under* the position to be rewritten [10]. *Matching modulo E*

---

* This research was supported in part by the EWG CCL, the HCM Network CONSOLE, and the "GDR de programmation du CNRS".

C. Kirchner and H. Kirchner (Eds.): Automated Deduction, CADE-15
LNAI 1421, pp. 88–102, 1998. © Springer–Verlag Berlin Heidelberg 1998

is used for rewriting instead of standard matching. On the other hand, a weaker notion of confluence suffices and the rewrite rules do not need to be left-linear.

A major drawback of using equations as a programming language is that they lack the expressiveness for providing higher-order features. Hence the idea of *higher-order rewrite systems* (HRSs) which allow to define functions by means of rewrite rules over terms of the simply-typed lambda calculus. Actually HRSs are difficult to handle since the decidability of higher-order matching is still an open problem [4,17] and higher-order unification is known to be undecidable [7,5]. Matching and unification being crucial for reduction and deduction respectively, we need to restrict our attention to *pattern rewrite systems*, which are HRSs where the left-hand sides of the rules are *patterns*. Patterns are the largest subset of the terms of the simply-typed lambda calculus for which higher-order unification is known to be decidable [14]. Nipkow [16] has proved a critical pair lemma for pattern rewrite systems (PRSs) and Mayr and Nipkow [13] have lifted the theory of rewriting modulo an equational theory of Huet [8] to the case of PRSs [13]. On the other hand, Boudet and Contejean have provided an *AC*-unification algorithm for higher-order patterns [1]. The purpose of the present work is to lift the theory of Jouannaud and Kirchner [10] to the higher-order case, and to apply it to pattern rewrite systems modulo *AC*, completing the following table:

	R	R/E	R^E
First-order TRSs	Knuth–Bendix 70 Huet 81	Huet 80	Jouannaud–Kirchner 86
Higher-order PRSs	Nipkow 91	Mayr–Nipkow 97	*This paper*

We give now a simple motivating example. For this, we have to use some terminology that will be defined later, but a little background about term rewriting should suffice to follow the example.

Example 1. We consider the two base types elt and mset, having in mind to define a map function on multisets of elt. We will use the following constant function symbols:

```
empty    : mset
mk-mset : elt→ mset
union    : mset→ mset→ mset
map      : (elt→ elt)→ mset→ mset
```

and we consider the following rewrite rules:

1. $\mathrm{map}(\lambda x.F(x), \mathrm{empty}) \rightarrow \mathrm{empty}$
2. $\mathrm{map}(\lambda x.F(x), \mathrm{union}\,(\mathrm{mk\text{-}mset}(E), M)) \rightarrow \mathrm{union}(\mathrm{map}(F, M),$
$$\mathrm{mk\text{-}mset}(F(E)))$$

3. $\mathrm{map}(\lambda x.x, M) \rightarrow M$

The third rule is just an optimization for avoiding to apply identity to all the elements of a multiset. Consider now the term t (obtained by superposing the left-hand size of rule 3. in the left-hand size of rule 2.):

$$t \equiv \mathtt{map}(\lambda x.x, \mathtt{union}(\mathtt{mk\text{-}mset}(E), M))$$

The term t rewrites by rule 3. to

$$s_1 \equiv \mathtt{union}\ (\mathtt{mk\text{-}mset}(E), M)$$

which is no longer reducible. On the other hand, rule 2. applies to t yielding the term

$$s_2' \equiv \mathtt{union}(\mathtt{map}(\lambda x.x, M), \mathtt{mk\text{-}mset}(\lambda x.x(E)))$$

After a β-reduction and an application of the rule 3., the term s_2' reduces to the irreducible term

$$s_2 \equiv \mathtt{union}(M,\ \mathtt{mk\text{-}mset}(E))$$

Hence, the term t can be reduced to two different irreducible terms s_1 and s_2.

But s_1 and s_2 are in fact equal modulo the associativity and commutativity of union.

1   Preliminaries

We assume the reader is familiar with simply-typed lambda-calculus, and term rewriting. Given a set $\mathcal{B}$ of *base types*, the set $\mathcal{T}$ of all *types* is the closure of $\mathcal{B}$ under the (right-associative) function space constructor $\rightarrow$. The *simply-typed lambda-terms* are generated from a set $\biguplus_{\tau \in \mathcal{T}} V_\tau$ of *typed variables* and a set $\biguplus_{\tau \in \mathcal{T}} C_\tau$ of *typed constants* using the following construction rules:

$$\frac{x \in V_\tau}{x\ :\ \tau} \qquad \frac{c \in C_\tau}{c\ :\ \tau} \qquad \frac{s\ :\ \tau \rightarrow \tau' \quad t\ :\ \tau}{(s\,t)\ :\ \tau'} \qquad \frac{x\ :\ \tau \quad s\ :\ \tau'}{(\lambda x.s)\ :\ \tau \rightarrow \tau'}$$

The order of a base type is 1, and the order of an arrow type $\tau \rightarrow \tau'$ is the maximum of the order of τ plus 1 and the order of τ'. The order of a term is the order if its type.

Some background is available in *e.g.* [6,3] for lambda-calculus and term rewriting systems. We shall use the following notations: $\lambda x_1 \cdots \lambda x_n.s$ will be written $\lambda \overline{x_n}.s$, or even $\lambda \overline{x}.s$ if n is not relevant. If in a same expression $\overline{x}$ appears several times it denotes the same sequence of variables. In addition, we will use the notation $t(u_1, \ldots, u_n)$ or $t(\overline{u_n})$ for $(\cdots (t\ u_1) \cdots u_n)$. If π is a permutation of $(1, \ldots, n)$, $\overline{x_n}^\pi$ stands for the sequence $x_{\pi(1)}, \ldots, x_{\pi(n)}$. The free (resp. bound) variables of a term t are denoted by $fv(t)$ (resp. $bv(t)$). The *positions* of a term t are words over $\{1, 2\}$, Λ is the empty word and $t|_p$ is the subterm of t at position p. More precisely, $t|_\Lambda = t$, $(t_1\ t_2)|_i = t_i$ for $i \in \{1, 2\}$, and $(\lambda x.t)|_1 = t$. The notation $t[u]_p$ stands for a term t with a subterm u at position p. $\mathcal{P}os(t)$ is the set of positions of a term t. We shall write $p \leq q$ if $q = p \cdot p'$ for some p', and $p \| q$ if neither $p \leq q$ nor $q \leq p$ hold. $bv(t, p)$ is the set of variables that are bound in t above position p.

Unless otherwise stated, we assume all terms to be in η-expanded, β-normal form, the η-expanded, β-normal form of a term t being denoted by $t \uparrow_\beta^\eta$.

A *substitution* σ is a mapping from a finite set of variables to terms of the same type. If $\sigma = \{x_1 \mapsto t_1, \ldots, x_n \mapsto t_n\}$, the *domain* of σ is $Dom(\sigma) = \{x_1, \ldots, x_n\}$ and the *set of variables introduced by* σ is $VCod(\sigma) = fv(t_1) \cup \cdots \cup fv(t_n)$. The order of a substitution is the maximum of the orders of the variables in its domain. When applying a substitution σ to a term t, we will always assume that $VCod(\sigma) \cap bv(t) = \emptyset$ in order to avoid variable captures. In this case, $t\sigma$ denotes the term $\lambda \overline{x_n}.t(t_1, \ldots, t_n) \uparrow_\beta^\eta$. We define $\theta_1 + \theta_2$ by $x(\theta_1 + \theta_2) = x\theta_2$ if $x \in Dom(\theta_2)$, $x\theta_1$ otherwise.

2   Equational Pattern Rewrite Systems

Definition 1. *A pattern is a term of the simply-typed λ-calculus in β-normal form in which the arguments of a free variable are η-equivalent to distinct bound variables.*

For instance, $\lambda xyz.f(H(x,y), H(x,z))$ and $\lambda x.F(\lambda z.x(z))$ are patterns while $\lambda xy.G(x, x, y)$, $\lambda xy.H(x, f(y))$ and $\lambda xy.H(F(x), y)$ are not patterns.

Lemma 1. *Let s be a pattern, p a position of s and θ a substitution such that $bv(s,p) \cap Dom(\theta) = \emptyset$. Then $(s|_p)\theta = s\theta|_p$.*

Let $E = \{l_1 \simeq r_1, \ldots, l_n \simeq r_n\}$ a set of *axioms* such that l_i and r_i are terms of a same base type, for $1 \leq i \leq n$. The *equational theory* $=_E$ generated by E is the least congruence[1] containing all the instances of the axioms of E (by abuse of notation, we will confuse E and $=_E$). For instance, the associative-commutative (AC) theory of $+$ is the equational theory generated by

$$AC(+) = \{(x+y) + z \simeq x + (y+z), x + y \simeq y + x\}$$

A substitution σ is an *E-unifier* of s and t if $s\sigma$ and $t\sigma$ are equivalent modulo $\eta\beta$-equivalence and the theory $=_E$, which we write $s\sigma =_{\beta\eta E} t\sigma$. A *complete set of E-unifiers* of s and t is a set Σ of substitutions such that every σ in Σ is an E-unifier of s and t and for every E-unifier θ of s and t, there exist $\sigma \in \Sigma$ and ρ such that $\theta =_{\beta\eta E} \sigma\rho$. The relation $=_E$ coincides with the reflexive, symmetric, transitive closure $\overset{*}{\leftrightarrow}_E$ of the relation $\rightarrow_E$ defined by $s \rightarrow_E t$ if there exist a position p of s, an equation $l \simeq r \in E$ and a substitution θ such that $s|_p = l\theta$ and $t = s[r\theta]_p$.

Since we consider only terms in η-long β-normal form, the following result from Mayr and Nipkow will allow us to restrict our attention to $=_E$ instead of $=_{\beta\eta E}$:

Theorem 1 ([13]). *For any terms u and v, $u =_{\beta\eta E} v$ if and only if $u \uparrow_\beta^\eta =_E v \uparrow_\beta^\eta$.*

The above theorem extends a result by Tannen where the equational theory is assumed to be defined by first-order equations [2].

---

[1] *i.e., compatible also with application and abstraction, in our context.*

Definition 2. *A rewrite rule is a pair $<l, r>$ of terms, denoted by $l \rightarrow r$ such that l is not a free variable, l and r are of the same base type and $fv(r) \subseteq fv(l)$. If l is a pattern, then $l \rightarrow r$ is a pattern rewrite rule. A set of rewrite rules is called a higher-order rewrite system (HRS). A set of pattern rewrite rules is called a pattern rewrite system (PRS). A HRS R induces a rewriting relation $\rightarrow_R$ on terms defined by $s \rightarrow_R t$ iff there exist $l \rightarrow r \in R$, $p \in Pos(s)$ such that $s|_p = l\theta$ and $t = s[r\theta]_p$ for some substitution θ. If necessary, we shall use one or more of the subscripts $s \rightarrow_R t$, $s \rightarrow_{l \rightarrow r} t$, $s \rightarrow_p t$, $s \rightarrow_\theta t$ to specify the rewrite system, the rule, the position and the substitution used in the reduction. The subscript $s \rightarrow_{\geq p} t$ means that the reduction occurred under position p. Where σ and θ are two substitutions, we shall write $\sigma \rightarrow_R \theta$ if for any variable $x \in Dom(\sigma) \cup Dom(\theta)$ $x\sigma \rightarrow_R x\theta$.*

For any binary relation $\rightarrow$, $\stackrel{=}{\rightarrow}$ will denote its reflexive closure, $\stackrel{*}{\rightarrow}$ its reflexive transitive closure.

Definition 3. *Let R be a pattern rewrite system and E an equational theory whose axioms have patterns as left-hand and right-hand sides. $<R, E>$ is called an equational PRS.*
We write $s \rightarrow_{R^E} t$ if $s|_p =_E u$ for some u and $s[u]_p \longrightarrow_{R,p} s[v]_p = t$. In other words, R^E denotes the relation $\stackrel{*}{\longleftrightarrow}_{E, \geq p} \longrightarrow_{R,p}$.

Lemma 2. *Let $<R, E>$ be an equational PRS such that E is collapse-free. Let s, s' be two terms in η-long, β-normal form, and θ, θ' two substitutions such that $s \stackrel{*}{\rightarrow}_{R^E} s'$ and $\theta \stackrel{*}{\rightarrow}_{R^E} \theta'$. Then $s\theta \stackrel{*}{\rightarrow}_{R^E} s'\theta'$.*

The proof is very similar to the proof in [13]:

Proof. By induction on (i) the order of θ and (ii) the number of steps in the proof $s \stackrel{*}{\rightarrow}_{R^E} s'$. Several cases are to be considered:

1. When $n = 0$ ($s = s'$), we proceed by induction on the structure of s. The term s is in β-normal form: $s = \lambda \overline{x_m}.a(\overline{s_k})$ and by induction hypothesis $s_i\theta \stackrel{*}{\rightarrow}_{R^E} s_i\theta'$.

   (a) If $a \notin Dom(\theta)$, then $a \notin Dom(\theta')$. Indeed, $a\theta \stackrel{*}{\rightarrow}_{R^E} a\theta'$ and $a\theta = a$. But the left-hand sides of the rules are not free variables and E is collapse-free, hence the case $a =_E l\sigma$ for some rule $l \rightarrow r$ is impossible and $a\theta = a\theta' = a$. We have $s\theta = \lambda \overline{x_m}.a(\overline{s_k\theta}) \stackrel{*}{\rightarrow}_{R^E} \lambda \overline{x_m}.a(\overline{s_k\theta'}) = s'\theta'$.

   (b) If $a \in Dom(\theta)$, let $a\theta = \lambda \overline{y_k}.t$ (we know that a requires k arguments) and $a\theta = \lambda \overline{y_k}.t \rightarrow_{R^E} a\sigma \stackrel{*}{\rightarrow}_{R^E} a\theta'$. There exist $l \rightarrow r \in R$, $p \in Pos(a\theta)$ and θ'' such that $a\theta|_p =_E l\theta''$ and $a\sigma = a\theta[r\theta'']_p$. But $l\theta''$ is of a base type and the rewriting takes place below $\lambda \overline{y_k}$ in $\lambda \overline{y_k}.t$. Hence $a\sigma = \lambda \overline{y_k}.t''$ and $t'' \stackrel{*}{\rightarrow}_{R^E} t'$. Let $\delta = \{y_k \mapsto s_k\theta\}$ and $\delta' = \{y_k \mapsto s_k\theta'\}$. By induction hypothesis, $s_i\theta \stackrel{*}{\rightarrow}_{R^E} s_i\theta'$, hence $\delta \stackrel{*}{\rightarrow}_{R^E} \delta'$. Now, a has type $\overline{\tau_k} \rightarrow \tau$ whose order is strictly greater than the order of each τ_i, hence, the order of θ is strictly greater than that of δ and δ'. We have $t \stackrel{*}{\rightarrow}_{R^E} t'$ and $\delta \stackrel{*}{\rightarrow}_{R^E} \delta'$ and by the induction hypothesis, $t\delta \stackrel{*}{\rightarrow}_{R^E} t'\delta'$. Finally,

$$s\theta = \lambda \overline{x_m}.(a\theta)(\overline{s_k\theta}) \downarrow_\beta = \lambda \overline{x_m}.t\delta \stackrel{*}{\rightarrow}_{R^E} \lambda \overline{x_m}.t'\delta' = s\theta'$$

2. Assume now that $s \xrightarrow{*}_{R^E} s' \rightarrow_{R^E} s''$. By the induction hypothesis, $s\theta \xrightarrow{*}_{R^E} s'\theta'$. We are left to show that $s'\theta' \xrightarrow{*}_{R^E} s''\theta'$. Since $s' \rightarrow_{R^E} s''$, there exist $l \rightarrow r \in R$, θ'' and $p \in \mathcal{D}om(s')$ such that $s'|_p = l\theta''$ and $s'' = s'[r\theta'']_p$. We proceed by induction on the length of position p.

   (a) If $p = \Lambda$, then $s' = l\theta''$, $s'' = r\theta''$, hence $s'\theta' =_E l\theta''\theta'$ and $s''\theta' = r\theta''\theta'$. We have $s'\theta' \xrightarrow{\Lambda}_{R^E} s''\theta'$.

   (b) If $|p| \geq 1$ and $s' = \lambda x.t'$ and $s'' = \lambda x.t''$ with $t' \rightarrow_{R^E} t''$, by induction hypothesis, $t'\theta' \xrightarrow{*}_{R^E} t''\theta'$ and $s'\theta' = \lambda x.t'\theta' \xrightarrow{*}_{R^E} \lambda x.t''\theta' = s''\theta'$.
   Finally if $|p| \geq 1$ and $s' = a(\overline{s'_k})$ and $s'' = a(\overline{s''_k})$, there exists an s'_i such that $s'_i \rightarrow_{R^E} s''_i$ (for $j \neq i$, $s'_j = s''_j$). By the induction hypothesis, $s'_i\theta' \rightarrow_{R^E} s''_i\theta'$. If $a \notin \mathcal{D}om(\theta')$, $s'\theta' = a(\overline{s'_k\theta'}) \xrightarrow{*}_{R^E} a(\overline{s''_k\theta'}) = s''\theta'$. If $a \in \mathcal{D}om(\theta')$, $a\theta' = \lambda\overline{y_k}.t$, define $\delta = \{y_k \mapsto s'_k\theta'\}$ and $\delta' = \{y_k \mapsto s''_k\theta'\}$. Again, the order of δ' and δ'' is strictly smaller than that of θ and θ'. By induction hypothesis, $t\delta \xrightarrow{*}_{R^E} t\delta'$.
   Hence, $s'\theta' = (a\theta')(\overline{s'_k\theta'}) \downarrow_\beta = t\delta \xrightarrow{*}_{R^E} t\delta' = s''\theta'$.

The following definition is borrowed from Mayr and Nipkow [13]. It is useful for keeping track of the bound variables above a position p when considering a subterm at position p and for avoiding to have non-disjoint variable sets when superposing left-hand sides of rewrite rules.

Definition 4. *An $\overline{x_k}$-lifter of a term t away from a set W of variables is a substitution $\sigma = \{F \mapsto F\rho(\overline{x_k}) \mid F \in fv(t)\}$, where ρ is a renaming such that $Dom(\rho) = fv(t)$, $VCod(\rho) \cap W = \emptyset$ and $F\rho$ has type $\tau_1 \rightarrow \cdots \rightarrow \tau_k \rightarrow \tau$ if x_i has type τ_i for $1 \leq i \leq k$ and F has type τ.*

Lemma 3 (adapted from [13]). *Consider two patterns l_1 and l_2, p a non-variable position of l_1 (i.e. $l_1|_p \notin fv(l_1)$). Let $\{\overline{x_k}\} = bv(l_1, p)$ and σ an $\overline{x_k}$-lifter of l_2 away from $fv(l_1)$. Then $\lambda\overline{x_k}.(l_1|_p)$ and $\lambda\overline{x_k}.l_2\sigma$ are E-unifiable iff there exist two substitutions θ_1 and θ_2 such that $l_1|_p\theta_1 =_E l_2\theta_2$ and $\{\overline{x_k}\} \cap VCod(\theta_1) = \emptyset$.*

We close this section by making precise the assumptions we make in the rest of the paper. They are similar to those of Jouannaud and Kirchner in the first-order case.

Assumptions In the sequel $<R, E>$ denotes an equational pattern rewrite system. Moreover E is assumed to be a *simple equational theory* that is a theory such that there is no proof $s =_E t$ where s and t are in η-long β-normal form and t is a strict subterm of s. This implies in particular that the sets of free variables of the left-hand and right-hand sides of the axioms of E are the same and are not reduced to a variable. We also assume that the relation $R/E := (=_E \rightarrow_R =_E)$ is terminating. This implies that $R/E \cup sst$ is terminating, where sst is the strict subterm relation.

3   Critical Pairs and Coherence Pairs

Similarly as in the work of Jouannaud and Kirchner [10], we need to consider not only critical pairs, but also *coherence pairs* to take into account the interactions of R and E. Standard completion relies upon the fact that the local confluence amounts to the joinability of critical pairs. Then, confluence is obtained via Newman's lemma [15] with the additional termination assumption. In our case, as in Jouannaud and Kirchner's paper, we need to put together the assumptions of joinability of the critical pairs, and of the coherence pairs, plus the termination of R/E to get the confluence. In this section, we give two technical lemmas (lemmas 5 and 6), which correspond to the "interesting" peaks. The next section is devoted to the confluence.

Definition 5 (Critical pairs of R^E). *Let $l_1 \to r_1$ and $l_2 \to r_2$ be two rewrite rules in an equational PRS $<R, E>$, and $p \in \mathcal{P}os(l_1)$ such that*

- $fv(l_1) \cap bv(l_1) = \emptyset$,
- *the symbol at position p in l_1 is not a free variable,*
- $\lambda\overline{x_k}.l_1|_p\theta =_E \lambda\overline{x_k}.l_2\sigma\theta$, *where $\{\overline{x_k}\} = bv(l_1, p)$ and σ is an $\overline{x_k}$-lifter of l_2 away from $fv(l_1)$ and $\theta \in CSU_E(\lambda\overline{x_k}.l_1|_p, \lambda\overline{x_k}.l_2\sigma)$ such that $\mathcal{D}om(\theta) \cup \{\overline{x_k}\} = \emptyset$.*

Then $<r_1\theta, l_1[r_2\sigma]_p\theta>$ is an E-critical pair of $l_2 \to r_2$ on $l_1 \to r_1$ at position p. The set of all E-critical pairs of $<R, E>$ is denoted by $CP(R^E)$.

The following lemma is straightforward in the first-order case, but requires a proof here, due to the presence of λ-binders. It states that when there is a critical pair, then there exists a corresponding critical peak.

Lemma 4. *If $<u_1, u_2> \in CP(R^E)$ then there exists a term s such that $s \to_{R,\Lambda} u_1$ and $s \to_{R^E} u_2$.*

Proof. $<u_1, u_2> \in CP(R^E)$ implies by definition that $u_1 = r_1\theta$ and $u_2 = l_1[r_2\sigma]_p\theta$, where $\overline{x_k} = bv(l_1, p)$ and σ is an $\overline{x_k}$-lifter of l_2 away from $fv(l_1)$ and θ is an E-unifier of $\lambda\overline{x_k}.l_1|_p$ and $\lambda\overline{x_k}.l_2\sigma$. Let $s = l_1\theta$. Then $s \to_{R,\Lambda} r_1\theta \equiv u_1$ with the rule $l_1 \to r_1 \in R$. On the other hand, we have

$$
\begin{aligned}
\lambda\overline{x_k}.(l_1|_p\theta) &\equiv (\lambda\overline{x_k}.l_1|_p)\theta && \text{using } \alpha\text{-conversion if necessary} \\
&=_E (\lambda\overline{x_k}.l_2\sigma)\theta && \text{by definition of critical pairs} \\
&\equiv \lambda\overline{x_k}.(l_2\sigma\theta) && (\mathcal{D}om(\theta) \cup Cod(\theta)) \cap \overline{x_k} = \emptyset
\end{aligned}
$$

hence $l_1|_p\theta =_E l_2\sigma\theta$.
But $l_1|_p$ is a pattern and $bv(l_1, p) = \{\overline{x_k}\} \cap \mathcal{D}om(\theta) = \emptyset$: by lemma 1, $l_1|_p\theta \equiv l_1\theta|_p$.
Hence $l_1\theta|_p \equiv l_1|_p\theta =_E l_2\sigma\theta$. Finally

$$
s \equiv l_1\theta \equiv l_1\theta[l_1\theta|_p]_p \overset{*}{\leftrightarrow}_{E,\geq p} l_1\theta[l_2\sigma\theta]_p \to_{R,p} l_1\theta[r_2\sigma\theta]_p \equiv u_2
$$

Definition 6 (Coherence pairs of R on E). *A* coherence pair *of R on E is a critical pair of R on $E \cup \{r \simeq l \mid l \simeq r \in E\}$. The set of coherence pairs of R on E is denoted by $CHP(R, E)$.*

Definition 7. *Two terms s and t are R^E-joinable if there exist two terms s' and t' such that $s \xrightarrow{*}_{R^E} s'$ and $t \xrightarrow{*}_{R^E} t'$ and $s' \xleftrightarrow{*}_E t'$.*

Definition 8.

- R^E *is* confluent *if whenever there exist s, s_1, s_2 such that $s \xrightarrow{*}_{R^E} s_1$ and $s \xrightarrow{*}_{R^E} s_2$, then s_1 and s_2 are R^E-joinable.*
- R^E *is* coherent *if whenever there exist s, s_1, s_2 such that $s \xleftrightarrow{*}_E s_1$ and $s \xrightarrow{*}_{R^E} s_2$, then s_1 and s_2 are R^E-joinable.*

Lemma 5. *Assume that for all critical pairs $<u_1, u_2> \in CP(R^E)$, u_1 and u_2 are R^E-joinable. Consider a peak of the form:*

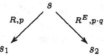

Then s_1 and s_2 are joinable in the following way:

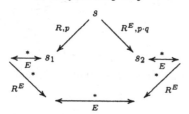

Proof. Two cases are to be considered:
1. The redexes do not overlap.
$s|_p = l_1\theta_1$, $s_1 \equiv s[r_1\theta_1]_p$, $q = q_1 \cdot q_2$ with $l_1|_{q_1} = F(\overline{x_k})$ where F is a free variable. $F\theta_1$ is of the form $\lambda \overline{x_k}.t$. Let $\theta_1' = \theta_1 + \{F \mapsto \lambda \overline{x_k}.t[r_2\theta_2]_{q_2}\}$. Now $t|_{q_2} = (F(\overline{x_k})\theta_1)|_{q_2} = (l_1|_{q_1}\theta_1)|_{q_2} = (l_1\theta_1)|_{q_1}|_{q_2}$ (because l_1 is a pattern and applying θ_1 creates no new redex).
$F\theta_1 = \lambda \overline{x_k}.t \rightarrow_{R^E} \lambda \overline{x_k}.t[r_2\theta_2]_{q_2} = F\theta_1'$. Hence $\theta_1 \xrightarrow{=}_{R^E} \theta_1'$. By lemma 2, $r_1\theta_1 \xrightarrow{*}_{R^E} r_1\theta_1'$.

Let H be a new variable and $l_0 = l_1[H(\overline{x_k})]_{q_1}$. let $\theta_0 = \theta_1 \cup \{H \mapsto F\theta_1'\}$ and $\theta_0' = \theta_1 + \{F \mapsto F\theta_1'\}$. We have $\theta_1 \xrightarrow{=}_{R^E} \theta_1'$, hence $\theta_0 \xrightarrow{=}_{R^E} \theta_0'$. Now,

$$s_2|_p = (l_1\theta_1)[r_2\theta_2]_q$$
$$= (l_1\theta_1)[F(\overline{x_k})\theta_1']_{q_1}$$
$$= l_0\theta_0 \xrightarrow{*}_{R^E} l_0\theta_0'$$
$$= l_1\theta_1' \rightarrow_R r_1\theta_1'$$

We are in the following situation:

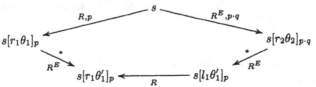

2. The two redexes overlap.
$s|_p = l_1\theta_1$ and $l_1|_q$ is defined and is not a free variable. $s|_{p \cdot q} =_E l_2\theta_2$.

$$l_1\theta_1|_q = l_1|_q\theta_1 \qquad \text{by lemma 1}$$
$$= s|_{p \cdot q} =_E l_2\theta_2$$

Let $\{\overline{x_k}\} = bv(l_1, q)$ and let σ be an $\overline{x_k}$-lifter of l_2 away from $fv(l_1)$, and ρ the renaming associated with σ. Define θ_0 as $\theta_0 = \theta_1 \cup \theta'_2$ with $\theta'_2 = \{F\rho \mapsto \lambda\overline{x_k}.F\theta_2 \mid F \in fv(l_2)\}$. We meet the hypotheses of lemma 3:
  $\lambda\overline{x_k}.l_1|_q$ and $\lambda\overline{x_k}.l_2\sigma$ are E-unifiable by θ_0: $(\lambda\overline{x_k}.l_1|_q)\theta_0 =_E (\lambda\overline{x_k}.l_2\sigma)\theta_0$.
  There exists $\theta \in CSU_E(\lambda\overline{x_k}.l_1|_q, \lambda\overline{x_k}.l_2\sigma)$ such that $\theta_0 =_E \theta\delta$, for some substitution δ. Hence there exist a critical pair $<r_1\theta, (l_1[r_2\sigma]_q)\theta>$ and the corresponding critical peak, which is joinable by hypothesis:

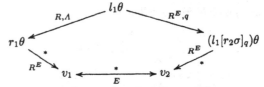

We apply δ to this diagram (remember that $\theta_0 =_E \theta\delta$).

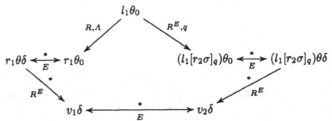

Now, $l_1\theta_0 = l_1(\theta_1 \cup \theta'_2) = l_1\theta_1$ because $fv(l_1) \cap \text{Dom}(\theta'_2) = \emptyset$.
$r_1\theta_0 = r_1(\theta_1 \cup \theta'_2) = r_1\theta_1$ because $fv(r_1) \subseteq fv(l_1)$.
We have $(l_1[r_2\sigma]_q)\theta_0 = (l_1\theta_0)[r_2\sigma\theta_0]_q = l_1\theta_1[r_2\theta_2]_q$. It is now sufficient to plug the whole diagram in the context $s[\cdot]_p$ to get the result.

Note that if in the above proof r_1 is not a variable, then the positions of the E-equality steps in $r_1\theta_0 \longleftrightarrow^*_E r_1\theta\delta$ are not Λ. Under our assumption that E has no variables as left-hand sides or right-hand sides of its axioms, a slightly stronger result holds when an E-equality step is applied above an R^E- step:

Lemma 6. *Assume that for all coherence pairs $<u_1, u_2> \in CP(R^E, E)$, u_1 and u_2 are R^E-joinable. Consider a proof of the form:*

Then s_1 and s_2 are joinable in the following way:

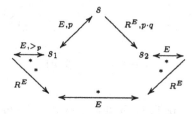

4 Confluence

Contrarily as in [13], and similarly as in [10], we cannot consider separately the properties of local confluence, local coherence and termination. Indeed, to prove the local coherence, we need the coherence, confluence and termination in the induction hypothesis. We can now state our main result:

Theorem 2. *Assume that for all critical pair $<u_1, u_2> \in CP(R^E)$ u_1 and u_2 are R^E-joinable and that for every coherence pair $<u_1, u_2> \in CHP(R, E)$ u_1 and u_2 are R^E-joinable. Assume in addition that the relation $R/E = (=_E \rightarrow_R =_E)$ is terminating. Then R^E is confluent (and coherent).*

The proof is similar to that by Jouannaud and Kirchner in the first-order case. We just give the different cases to be considered, the measure we use for our induction and we develop just one case which illustrates why local confluence cannot be proved separately.

We define a *general peak* as a proof of the following form:

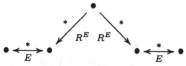

and we show that the extremes of every general peak are R^E-joinable.

There are 4 types of general peaks, and for each type, we define a measure. The first component of our measure is a term. The first components are compared using the union of the strict subterm relation and the relation R/E (two E-equal terms are considered the same). The second component is 1 if the peak really has R^E-steps in both directions, 0 otherwise. The third component is the number of E-equality steps at the top of the peak. The last two components are compared using the usual ordering on naturals.

- type 1: There are R^E-steps in both directions and the first R^E steps of the peak occur at comparable positions p and $p \cdot q$.

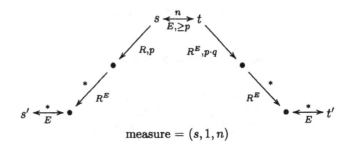

$$\text{measure} = (s, 1, n)$$

- type 2: There are R^E-steps in both directions and the first R^E steps of the peak occur at some parallel positions p and q.

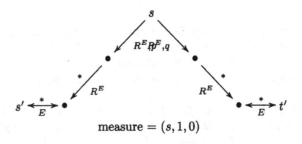

$$\text{measure} = (s, 1, 0)$$

- type 3: There is no R^E-step on one side of the peak.

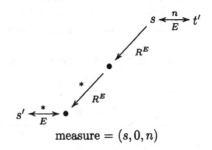

$$\text{measure} = (s, 0, n)$$

- type 4: There is no R^E-step in the peak.

$$s' \xleftrightarrow[E]{*} t'$$
$$\text{measure} = (s', 0, 0)$$

The following picture corresponds to the peaks of type 1 with measure $(s, 1, 0)$.

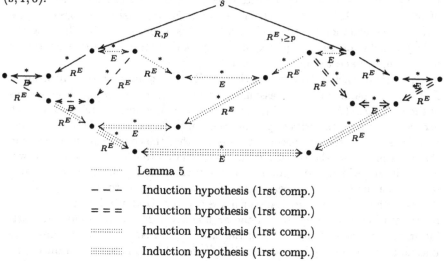

.... Lemma 5

– – –   Induction hypothesis (1rst comp.)

= = =   Induction hypothesis (1rst comp.)

:::::::::: Induction hypothesis (1rst comp.)

:::::::::: Induction hypothesis (1rst comp.)

The original peaks are drawn with plain arrows, and the various dashed arrows show how the peaks are joinable. Note that all our hypotheses are needed in the induction.

5   Application to AC Theories

In [1], we presented an AC-unification algorithm for higher-order patterns. It happens that AC-unification problems do not have minimal complete set of unifiers. Indeed, the equations of the form $\lambda \overline{x}.F(\overline{x}) = \lambda \overline{x}.F(\overline{x}^{\pi})$, while trivially solvable, have an infinite complete set of unifiers $\{\sigma_1, \sigma_2, \cdots\}$ such that σ_{n+1} is strictly more general than σ_n. This was noticed by Qian and Wang [18] who give the following example:

Example 2 ([18]). Consider the equation $e \equiv \lambda xy.F(x, y) = \lambda xy.F(y, x)$ in the AC-theory of $+$. For $m \geq 0$, the substitution

$$\sigma_m = \{F \mapsto \lambda xy.G_m(H_1(x, y) + H_1(y, x), \ldots, H_m(x, y) + H_m(y, x))\}$$

is an AC-unifier of e. Every solution of e is an instance of some σ_i and σ_{n+1} is strictly more general than σ_n.

On the other hand, the algorithm presented in [1] computes a finite complete set of *constrained AC-unifiers* Σ. A constrained AC-unifier is $\sigma|C$ where σ is a substitution and C a conjunction of flexible-flexible equations of the form $\lambda \overline{x}.F(\overline{x}) = \lambda \overline{x}.F(\overline{x}^{\pi})$. Every AC-unifier of an equation e is then an instance of σ satisfying C for some $\sigma|C \in \Sigma$.

AC-critical pairs will hence be represented by $<r_1\theta, l_1[r_2\sigma]_p\theta>|C$, where $l_1 \to r_1$ and $l_2 \to r_2$ are two rewrite rules and $\theta|C$ is a constrained AC-unifier of $\lambda\bar{x}^k.l_1|_p$ and $\lambda\bar{x}^k.l_2\sigma$ as given in definition 5. As usual, $<u_1, u_2>|C$ represents all the equations $u_1\delta = u_2\delta$ such that δ is a solution of C. Checking the R^{AC}-joinability of $<u_1, u_2>|C$ requires to check that for all the above mentioned $u_1\delta = u_2\delta$, $u_1\delta$ and $u_2\delta$ are R^{AC}-joinable.

We briefly sketch how to check the R^{AC}-joinability of the constrained R^{AC}-critical pairs. First, we assume that for each F appearing in equations of the form $\lambda\bar{x}.F(\bar{x}) = \lambda\bar{x}.F(\bar{x}^\pi)$, the sequences of λ-bound variables above each occurrence of F in the critical pair are the same. This can be acheived by using α-conversion if necessary. Second, we assume that the constraint is *saturated* in the following sense: the set of permutations related to each F is saturated wrt composition, yielding a subgroup G_F of the permutation group of the arguments of F. Once the G_Fs have been computed, we can assume that $F(\bar{t})$ and $F(\bar{t}^\pi)$ do not both occur in the critical pair if $\pi \in G_F$. The computation of a canonical representation of the sequence of the arguments of F can be computed starting from the leaves of the terms of the critical pair. Now, it is clear that if an unconstrained critical pair $<u_1, u_2>$ is R^{AC}-joinable, so is the constrained critical pair $<u_1, u_2>|C$. The difficulty is to show that if the unconstrained critical pair is irreducible, then there exists a solution δ of C such that $<u_1\delta, u_2\delta>$ is irreducible. This is the purpose of the following proposition:

Proposition 1. *Let $<R, AC>$ be an AC pattern rewrite system. Let t be a term, and C a conjunction of equations of the form $\lambda\bar{x}.F(\bar{x}) = \lambda\bar{x}.F(\bar{x}^\pi)$. Let G_F be the subgroup of permutations generated by the permutations of the equations involving F in C. We assume that t has not both occurrences of $F(\bar{t})$ and $F(\bar{t}^\pi)$ for $\pi \in G_F$. If t is not R^{AC}-reducible, then there exists an instance of t by a solution of C which is irreducible.*

Proof (Sketched). The result is straightforward if R is left-linear. The only case when applying a solution of C to an irreducible term t turns t into a reducible term is when this makes two non AC-equal subterms $F(\bar{t_n})$ and $F(\bar{t'_n})$ AC-equal. Assume that $\{\bar{t_n}\}$ contains a term t_i which does not appear in $\{\bar{t'_n}\}$ (or the converse). The substitution $\delta = \{F \mapsto \lambda\bar{x} \cdot \Sigma_{\pi \in G_F} H(x_{\pi(i)})\}$ is a solution of C but $F(\bar{t_n})\delta$ contains an occurrence of $H(t_i)$ while $F(\bar{t'_n})\delta$ does not, hence the two terms cannot be AC-equal.

We assume now that the sets of terms occurring in $\{\bar{t_n}\}$ and $\{\bar{t'_n}\}$ are the same. The sequences $\bar{t_n}$ and $\bar{t'_n}$ can be completed in $\bar{t_m}$ and $\bar{t'_m}$ respectively in such a way to obtain the same associated multisets. Now, there exists a permutation π such that $\bar{t'_m} = \bar{t_m}^\pi$. If $\pi \in G_F$, it operates only on the n first elements, hence $\bar{t'_n} = \bar{t_n}^\pi$. But both $F(\bar{t_n})$ and $F(\bar{t'_n}) = F(\bar{t_n}^\pi)$ appear in t, a contradiction.

We are left to consider the case when $\pi \notin G_F$. If for every $\pi' \in G_F$, $\bar{t'_n} = (t_{\pi(1)}, \ldots, t_{\pi(n)}) \neq \bar{t_n}^{\pi'}$, then the substitution $\delta = \{F \mapsto \lambda\bar{x_n}.\Sigma_{\pi' \in G_F} H(\bar{x_n}^{\pi'})\}$ is a solution of C. But $F(\bar{t_n})\delta$ has no occurrence of $H(t_{\pi(1)}, \ldots, t_{\pi(n)})$ while $F(\bar{t'_n})\delta$ has one. The two terms are not AC-equal. Finally, if there exists $\pi' \in G_F$ such that $(t_{\pi(1)}, \ldots, t_{\pi(n)}) = \bar{t_n}^{\pi'}$, then π operates only on the n first elements, hence $n = m$. Now $\overline{t_n}^{\pi} = \overline{t_n}^{\pi'}$ and $\pi \neq \pi'$ because $\pi \notin G_F$. Hence $\pi = \theta\pi'$ for some θ which permutes only identical t_is (this means that $\overline{t_n} = \overline{t_n}^{\theta}$). We have $F(\overline{t_n'}) = F(\overline{t_n}^{\theta^{-1}\pi}) = F(\overline{t_n}^{\pi'})$ with $\pi' \in G_F$. Again, both $F(\overline{t_n})$ and $F(\overline{t_n'}) = F(\overline{t_n}^{\pi'})$ appear in t, a contradiction.

Corollary 1. *Let $<R, AC>$ be an AC pattern rewrite system. Let $<u_1, u_2> \mid C$ be a constrained critical pair of $<R, AC>$. The terms $u_1\delta$, and $u_2\delta$ are R^{AC}-joinable for every solution δ of C if and only if u_1 and u_2 are R^{AC}-joinable.*

6 Conclusion

We have proposed a theory of pattern rewrite systems modulo an equational theory. The assumptions we make on both the rewrite system and the equational theory are very similar to those considered by Jouannaud and Kirchner in the first-order case. In particular, while AC meets the assumptions on E, our work will need to be significantly extended for dealing with non-simple theories (the first that comes to mind being ACU). We will investigate the possibility to extend Marché's theory of S-normalized rewriting [12] to PRSs. For this, it will also be necessary to design unification algorithms for other theories than AC. The AC-unification algorithm proposed in [1] should extend to the usual extensions of AC.

References

1. Alexandre Boudet and Evelyne Contejean. AC-unification of higher-order patterns. In Gert Smolka, editor, *Principles and Practice of Constraint Programming*, volume 1330 of *Lecture Notes in Computer Science*, pages 267–281, Linz, Austria, October 1997. Springer-Verlag.
2. Val Breazu-Tannen. Combining algebra and higher-order types. In *Proc. 3rd IEEE Symp. Logic in Computer Science, Edinburgh*, July 1988.
3. Nachum Dershowitz and Jean-Pierre Jouannaud. Rewrite systems. In J. van Leeuwen, editor, *Handbook of Theoretical Computer Science*, volume B, pages 243–309. North-Holland, 1990.
4. Gilles Dowek. Third order matching is decidable. In *Proc. 7th IEEE Symp. Logic in Computer Science, Santa Cruz*, pages 2–10. IEEE Comp. Society Press, 1992.
5. Warren D. Goldfarb. Note on the undecidability of the second-order unification problem. *Theoretical Computer Science*, 13:225–230, 1981.
6. R. Hindley and J. Seldin. *Introduction to Combinators and λ-calculus*. Cambridge University Press, 1986.
7. Gérard Huet. *Résolution d'équations dans les langages d'ordre* $1, 2, \ldots \omega$. Thèse d'Etat, Univ. Paris 7, 1976.
8. Gérard Huet. Confluent reductions: abstract properties and applications to term rewriting systems. *Journal of the ACM*, 27(4):797–821, October 1980.
9. Gérard Huet. A complete proof of correctness of the Knuth-Bendix completion algorithm. *Journal of Computer and System Sciences*, 23:11–21, 1981.

10. Jean-Pierre Jouannaud and Hélène Kirchner. Completion of a set of rules modulo a set of equations. *SIAM Journal on Computing*, 15(4), November 1986.
11. Donald E. Knuth and Peter B. Bendix. Simple word problems in universal algebras. In J. Leech, editor, *Computational Problems in Abstract Algebra*, pages 263–297. Pergamon Press, 1970.
12. Claude Marché. Normalized rewriting: an alternative to rewriting modulo a set of equations. *Journal of Symbolic Computation*, 21(3):253–288, 1996.
13. Richard Mayr and Tobias Nipkow. Higher-order rewrite systems and their confluence. *Theoretical Computer Science*, 192(1):3–29, February 1998.
14. D. Miller. A logic programming language with lambda-abstraction, function variables, and simple unification. In P. Schroeder-Heister, editor, *Extensions of Logic Programming*. LNCS 475, Springer Verlag, 1991.
15. M. H. A. Newman. On theories with a combinatorial definition of 'equivalence'. *Ann. Math.*, 43(2):223–243, 1942.
16. T. Nipkow. Higher order critical pairs. In *Proc. IEEE Symp. on Logic in Comp. Science*, Amsterdam, 1991.
17. Vincent Padovani. *Filtrage d'ordre supérieur*. PhD thesis, Université de Paris VII, 1996.
18. Zhenyu Qian and Kang Wang. Modular AC-Unification of Higher-Order Patterns. In Jean-Pierre Jouannaud, editor, *First International Conference on Constraints in Computational Logics*, volume 845 of *Lecture Notes in Computer Science*, pages 105–120, München, Germany, September 1994. Springer-Verlag.

Unification in Lambda-Calculi with if-then-else

Michael Beeson

Department of Mathematics and Computer Science
San Jose State University
San Jose, California 95192, USA
beeson@mathcs.sjsu.edu

Abstract. A new unification algorithm is introduced, which (unlike previous algorithms for unification in λ-calculus) shares the pleasant properties of first-order unification. Proofs of these properties are given, in particular uniqueness of the answer and the most-general-unifier property. This unification algorithm can be used to generalize first-order proof-search algorithms to second-order logic, making possible for example a straighforward treatment of McCarthy's circumscription schema.[1]

1 Introduction

The origins of this work lie partly in an attempt to build a theorem-prover capable of implementing John McCarthy's work on circumscription. Circumscription is a second-order axiom schema, and cannot, in its full generality, be reduced to first-order. Indeed, it does not seem any easier to build a theorem-prover to handle all cases of circumscription than to handle second-order logic in general.

Second-order logic uses λ-terms to define predicates, and hence any attempt to mechanize second-order logic necessarily will involve unification of λ-terms. Huet [Huet 1975] introduced an algorithm for unifying terms in λ-calculus, and Miller and Nadathur [Miller and Nadathur 1988] introduced an extension of Prolog to a fragment of second-order logic (in fact higher-order logic) based on a similar unification algorithm. However, it turned out that Huet's algorithm isn't enough to handle circumscription. The difficulty is not hard to understand: Suppose we want $Q(1) = 1$ and $Q(2) = 0$ (Q can be thought of as a predicate by treating 1 as true and 0 as false). Huet's unification, given the problem $Q(1) = 1$, is only going to produce $\lambda x.1$ and $\lambda x.x$ as possible values of Q, neither one of which satisfies $Q(2) = 0$. Moreover, it is unpleasant that Huet's notion of unification does not have "most general unifiers". These difficulties are related; when the right notion of unification is defined, there are "more" unifiers, and there is also a "minimal" or "most general" unifier, of which all the others are "extensions".

This paper contains the definition of this new unification algorithm, and the proof that it always produces a most general unifier.

---

[1] Research partially supported by National Science Foundation grant number CCR-9528913.

C. Kirchner and H. Kirchner (Eds.): Automated Deduction, CADE-15
LNAI 1421, pp. 103–118, 1998. © Springer–Verlag Berlin Heidelberg 1998

2   Related Work

This unification algorithm can be used to extend to second-order logic the "backwards Gentzen" theorem-prover described for first-order logic in [Beeson 1991].

As far as I know, the new unification algorithm presented here makes possible the first direct implementation of circumscription, i.e. using second-order logic directly in proof search. Lifschitz has given a method of reducing some cases of circumscription to first-order logic, where it seems certain that existing theorem-provers could handle the transformed problem, although the experiment hasn't actually been carried out([Lifschitz 1985]). A theorem-prover described in [Baker-Ginsberg 1989] and [Ginsberg 1989] is related to circumscription via Lifschitz's result, but does not involve circumscription in its mechanism. Experiments with this algorithm in automatic deduction by circumscription will be described elsewhere.

3   λ-Calculus and Definition by Cases

We are interested in applications of unification to various logical systems, including second-order logic and various type theories. All of these logics can be expressed as subsystems of λ-calculus, so it is natural to study unification in the general setting of λ-calculus. However, the definition of unification that we introduce requires an if-then-else operator, which does not exist in pure untyped lambda calculus, although the required operator can be defined in various typed calculi. In order to prove our theorems once instead of many times, we extend the usual λ-calculus to include the minimally required rules for definition by cases. We call the extended system λD. It is formed by adding to the ordinary λ-calculus a new constant $\mathbf{d}$ for definition by cases. The expression $d(x, a, a, b)$ means "if $x = y$ then a else b". The system and corresponding reduction relation are specified by the following reduction rules. In these rules, equality means "reduces to".

$$\mathbf{d}(x, x, a, b) = a$$

$$\mathbf{d}(x, y, Zy, Zx) = Zx$$

$$\mathbf{d}(x, y, y, x) = x$$

$$\mathbf{d}(x, y, a, a) = a$$

Taking $Z = \lambda x.x$ and $Z = \lambda x.a$, the last two rules follow as equalities from the second, but as reduction rules instead of just equalities they are not superfluous.

A natural question is whether λD satisfies the Church-Rosser theorem. J. W. Klop showed that it does not (private correspondence). Equality of terms in λD is defined by the transitive closure of the relation "a and b have a common reduct". The following theorem shows that in spite of the failure of Church-Rosser, λD is consistent and indeed is a conservative extension of $\lambda \eta$, for equations between closed terms.

Theorem. *Let P and Q be two closed terms not containing* **d**, *and suppose $P = Q$ in λD-calculus. Then $P = Q$ already in λ-calculus.*

The proof of this theorem is long and technical, and the strict length limit on papers in this volume prohibits its inclusion. To avoid dependency on this result, one can work instead in a typed λ-calculus. To be specific, we consider simply-typed λ-calculus with one ground type, as described in Appendix A of [Barendregt 1981]. To this system we can consistently add a constant **d** of each sensible type such that in $\mathbf{d}(a, b, x, y)$, a and b are of ground type and x and y are of the same type (not necessarily ground), and postulate the laws $\mathbf{d}(a, b, x, y) = x$ if $a = b$ and y otherwise. Then the typed versions of the **d**-laws of λD are valid. The reader with doubts about the theorem just stated can read the rest of the paper as being about this system of typed λ-calculus instead of λD.

We write $t \cong s$ to mean $tx = sx$, where x is a variable not contained in t or s.[2] Note that extensional equality is preserved under reduction: if $a \cong b$ and a reduces to a' and b reduces to b' then $aa' \cong bb'$.

The second **d**-rule above then takes the form

$$\lambda x.\mathbf{d}(x, a, Za, Zx) \cong Z$$

This form of the rule will be used in the most-general-unifier calculation in a subsequent section.

4 λ-Calculus and Logic

It is well-known that second-order logic can be defined in λ-calculus (see [Barendregt 1981], p. 570, for basic references, and [Prawitz 1967] for full details). We specify a few notational matters that will be needed to support the proofs in this paper.

It will be convenient to consider λ-calculus as enlarged with a stock of constants, as well as variables. Technically we can just regard half of the usual variables as "constants"; unification will only instantiate the variables, but not the constants. Note that constants can still be used for λ-abstraction, i.e. from within the λ-calculus they are just like variables.

When logic is translated into lambda-calculus, the "object variables" (variables of the logic) become constants in lambda-calculus, as do the constants and function symbols and predicate symbols of the logic. Also the quantifiers and logical symbols such as $\land$ and $\rightarrow$ become constants or constant terms (containing no variables) of λ-calculus. The variables of λ-calculus are used as "metavariables" to range over terms of logic. When we look for a proof of a theorem $\exists x A(x)$, we first replace x by a metavariable $\mathbf{X}$ and search for a proof of $A(\mathbf{X})$. We hope that eventually unification will "instantiate" $\mathbf{X}$ to some term. In λ-calculus, the

---

[2] The η-reduction rule in λ-calculus says that $\lambda x.tx$ reduces to t. This is not a rule of the usual λ calculus, but it has been extensively studied. We deliberately use the relation $t \cong s$ rather than equivalence in $\lambda\eta$-calculus, to avoid the technical complications of adding η-reduction and the **d**-rules to λ-calculus at the same time.

logical metavariable **X** becomes a variable, and the object variable x of the logic becomes a constant of λ-calculus.

Second-order logic has two kinds of variables, first-order and second-order. It is customary to use capital letters for second-order variables. This conflicts with the Prolog convention, in which capital letters are used for metavariables. We therefore use boldface for logical metavariables; but in λ-calculus, we use lower-case letters for variables, as usual. Second-order logic permits the formation of λ-terms which are thought of as comprehension terms, i.e. $\lambda x.a(x)$ intuitively represents the set of x such that $a(x)$. Such terms translate directly into λ-terms of λ-calculus, where a λ-term is thought of as a predicate, taking values **T** or **F**.

In logic, predicates and functions can have more than one argument, but in λ-calculus, "currying" is used; that is, $f(x, y)$ is an abbreviation for $(fx)y$. Thus the translation of an atomic formula $P(x, y)$ will be in curried form.

5   A New Unification Algorithm

Huet pointed out in [Huet 1975] that equations involving second-order variables in general have many solutions, even if we require the solutions to be definable by λ-terms. For example, $X(1) = 1$ could be solved by $X = \lambda x.x$ or by $X = \lambda x.1$. Hence, he said, we cannot expect unique "most general unifiers" as in first-order logic, and he went on to give a unification algorithm that produces many unifying substitutions. As pointed out in the introduction, in applications the solutions produced by Huet's algorithm do not suffice, partly because the algorithm does not produce terms for functions defined by cases, but only by pure λ-terms.

One approach to the problem, which I first tried, is to allow terms for functions that are only partially defined. This probably works, but it requires many details, as the necessary formal systems are not in the literature. Here we take a different approach: we allow unification to produce answers containing a new variable. Instead of having some values (which aren't needed to solve the equation at hand) be undefined, we just leave them *unspecified*, by using a new free variable.

To lead up to the definition of unification, we will give an important case of the definition first. Consider the problem of unifying $X(t)$ with s, where X is a variable and t and s are constant terms. To solve this unification problem, we let Y be a new variable and take $X = \lambda x.\mathbf{d}(x, t, s, Yx)$. More precisely, we return the substitution θ whose value on X is the term $\lambda x.\mathbf{d}(x, t, s, Yx)$. Think of this as "if $x = t$ then s else unspecified".

To understand this definition, consider an example: when we unify $X(0)$ with 1, we get $X = \lambda x.\mathbf{d}(x, 0, 1, Yx)$, which takes the value 1 at 0, and elsewhere is "unspecified", that is, has the value Yx where Y is a new variable. By contrast, Huet's unification would give only the constant function $X = \lambda x.1$. Consider a second example: unify $X(1)$ with 1. Huet's unification would give two distinct answers: $X = \lambda x.1$ and $X = \lambda x.x$. Our answer is "more general" than each of these, and more general than infinitely many other special answers obtained by specifying other values of X than $X(1)$. The "most general" answer specifies only $X(1)$, leaving the other values unspecified.

However, in that definition of what it means to unify $X(t)$ and s, it is important that t and s were constant terms. Consider the problem of unifying $X(z)$ and $a(z)$, where a is constant. Do we want $X = \lambda x.\mathbf{d}(x, z, a(z), Yx)$? Well, in some cases we might, but in other cases we want $X = \lambda x.(a(x) \vee Yx)$. For example, if we are trying to prove in second-order logic that $\exists X(a(z) \rightarrow X(z))$, we will first replace X by a metavariable $\mathbf{X}$ and then try to unify $\mathbf{X}(z)$ with $a(z)$. We want to get $X = \lambda z.a(z)$ or some answer more general than that, such as $X = \lambda z.(a(z) \vee Y(z))$.

This raises an issue which could/should have been considered already in ordinary unification: scope restrictions.[3] When a theorem-prover replaces a quantifier by a metavariable, there is a restriction on the (object) variables that can occur in the answer substitution when it is eventually found. In the above example, when X is replaced by $\mathbf{X}$, the restriction is that the eventual value of $\mathbf{X}$ is not allowed to contain a free occurrence of z. In [Beeson 1991], a simply-programmed inference program allows "wrong" unifications to be temporarily considered and rejected later. An improvement to the program, suggested by N. Shankar, keeps track of these restrictions and rejects unifications that violate them immediately. Considering unification in second-order logic or lambda-calculus brings this "trick" into focus: it should be part of the *definition* of unification. That is, unification takes place relative to a finite set of restrictions on the possible values of variables; these restrictions are part of the input to the unification algorithm. Whether we take $X = \lambda z(a(z) \vee Y(z))$ or $X = \lambda z\mathbf{d}(x, z, a(z), Yx)$ will depend on whether z is forbidden to X or not, i.e. whether X is restricted from taking values depending on z.

We now make these ideas precise.

Definitions. *A restriction is a pair consisting of a variable (of lambda-calculus) and a (possibly empty) list of constants.[4] An environment is a finite list of restrictions.[5] If $\langle x, r \rangle$ is a member of the environment E we say that the variable x occurs in E or is mentioned in E, and that all the members of the list r are forbidden to x in E. We say a compound term t is forbidden to x in E if it contains a free occurrence of any constant that is forbidden to x in E. A substitution is a function from variables to terms. The substitution σ is legal for environment E provided $\sigma(x)$ is defined for all x that occur in E and that $\sigma(x)$ does not contain free occurrences of any variable or constant forbidden to x in*

---

[3] Although scope restrictions are not considered in the usual definitions of Robinson unification, they have been considered before in the literature: see [Miller 1992] and the connection method of Bibel and Andrews, as explained for example in [Wallen 1990].

[4] Intuitively, the eventual value of the variable is not allowed to depend on the members of the list.

[5] Intuitively, an environment lists all the variables in use so far, whether or not their eventual values are restricted, together with any restrictions so far imposed.

E. The substitution σ unifies terms t and s relative to E if for some substitution χ whose restriction to E is the identity, we have $t\sigma\chi = s\sigma\chi$.[6]

The inputs to the unification algorithm are two terms t and s to be unified and an environment E. We say that t and s are to be unified "relative to" the environment E. One output of the unification algorithm is a substitution σ which is legal for E, such that $t\sigma = s\sigma$. The usual notion of unification is obtained by taking an environment E with no restrictions on any of the variables occurring in E. But note that the use of restrictions, even in first-order unification, corresponds to the actual use of unification in theorem-proving.

The unification algorithm has a second output, which is a new environment enlarging the input environment E. Here "enlarging" means simply that new variables may have been added.

The algorithm produces an answer substitution only if it succeeds. It can also fail, by terminating but producing a special signal for failure instead of an answer substitution and new environment. And, at least *a priori*, it might fail to terminate.

We now give the precise definition of our unification algorithm. We will suppress mention of the environment, both in input and output, writing **unify**(t, s) as usual to denote the output substitution σ. When it is necessary to mention the environment it will be by way of "z is forbidden to x", which means "z is forbidden to x in E, where E is the input environment". When we say, "Y is a new variable", we mean that Y is a variable not occurring in the input environment E, and it is implicit that the output environment will include the new variable Y. It must be remembered that **failure** is a possible result of **unify**(t, s).

If a and b are terms containing no variables, and $a = b$ in λD, then **unify**(a, b) succeeds, producing the empty substitution. If a and b are terms containing no variables and not containing **d**, and a and b reduce to distinct normal forms, then **unify**(a, b) fails.[7]

If a and b are literally identical terms (which may contain variables) then **unify**(a, b) succeeds, producing the identity substitution.

Next, if either input term permits a β-reduction at top level, the following rules are used:

$$\textbf{unify}(t, (\lambda x.a)s) = \textbf{unify}(t, a[s/x])$$

$$\textbf{unify}((\lambda x.a)t, s) = \textbf{unify}(a[t/x], s)$$

Next, there are two clauses in the definition of **unify** for each of the reduction rules involving **d**. These rules take the forms

$$\textbf{unify}(t, s) = \textbf{unify}(t', s)$$

$$\textbf{unify}(s, t) = \textbf{unify}(s, t')$$

---

[6] That is, $t\sigma = s\sigma$ for some values of the the variables not in E.

[7] The restriction to **d**-free terms is necessary because of the failure of Church-Rosser in λD; if one uses typed λ-calculus one can dispense with this.

where t is the left side of the reduction rule and t' is the right side. From now on, we will be dealing with inputs which, while not necessarily normal, permit no reduction at top-level.

To unify $X(t)$ and s, where t and s are not forbidden to X, we take $X = \lambda x \mathbf{d}(x, t, s, Yx)$. To unify $X(t_1, t_2)$ and s, where t_1, t_2 and s are not forbidden to X, we take

$$X = \lambda x_1 x_2(\mathbf{d}(x_1, t_1, \mathbf{d}(x_2, t_2, s, Y_2 x), Y_1 x))$$

where Y_1 and Y_2 are new variables, and similarly for unifying $X(t_1, \ldots, t_n)$ and s.

To unify a variable x with a term t, as in Robinson unification we fail if t contains x (the "occurs check"). We also fail if t contains any variable forbidden to x. Otherwise, we succeed with output substitution $x = t$.

We have to define when two λ-terms unify. We want to require $\text{Sunify}(\lambda x.t, \lambda x.s) = \mathbf{unify}(t, s)$,S where the variable x is regarded on the right as a constant forbidden to all other variables. Technically we can't change a variable to a constant in mid-stream, and besides we also need to unify two λ-terms with different bound variables after suitable renaming of the bound variables. The simplest way to handle this is to define

$$\mathbf{unify}(\lambda x.a, \lambda y.b) = \mathbf{unify}(a[z/x], b[z/y])$$

where z is a new constant, i.e. not contained in a or b (or the input environment), and the input environment on the right lists z as forbidden to all the variables. This prevents, for example, $\lambda x.f(x)$ from unifying with $\lambda x.f(a)$.

In λ-calculus, there are no function and predicate symbols, except the application term formation symbol, Ap. Officially $x(y)$ is the term $Ap(x, y)$. Here our definition corresponds to Robinson unification. To unify ts with pq, we first unify t with p. If this fails, we fail. If it succeeds with substitution σ, we then unify $s\sigma$ and $q\sigma$. Note, however, that the output environment of the first unification becomes the input environment for the second unification. The output is the result of the second unification.

The above clauses define *first-order unification*. This notion of unification will support first-order inference (since it generalizes Robinson unification), but it is not yet sufficient to support second-order inference, in particular the circumscription examples. Consider for example the inference problem in which we have $az \to Xz$. We want to find a value for X more general than $X = \lambda z.az$. If, for example, we also have $bz \to Xz$ we should be able to find by two successive unifications, something more general than $X = \lambda z.(az \lor bz)$. The following additional clause in the definition of unification will permit this:

To unify Xz and az, where z is a constant forbidden to X, we take $X = \lambda z.(az \lor Yz)$, where Y is a new variable. (The convention here is that z can be a single variable or can be $z_1 \ldots z_n$.) More generally, if s is a term containing a constant (or constants) z forbidden to X, to unify Xz and s, we take $X = \lambda z.(s \lor Yz)$. The constant z will be forbidden to Y in the output environment, along with any other constants forbidden to X.

Note that the substitution σ which has been defined in this last clause to unify two terms t and s need not satisfy $t\sigma = s\sigma$, since with $t = Xz$ and $s = az$

we have $t\sigma = az \vee Yz$ and $s\sigma = az$. But if we define χ to be the substitution giving Y (which is not part of the input environment) the value $\lambda z.\mathbf{F}$ then we have $t\sigma\chi = s\sigma\chi$, so σ does unify t and s.

There are also mixed cases, where some of the variables are forbidden to X and some are not. For example, to unify Xxz and axz, where z is forbidden to X and x is not, we take $X = \lambda z.\mathbf{d}(x,t,(axz \vee Yz),Ux)$, where Y and U are fresh variables. The general case is only notationally more complex.

Note that unification can fail to terminate on inputs which have no normal form; for example $\mathbf{unify}(\Omega, x)$ fails to terminate where Ω is any term with an infinite β-reduction sequence. On the other hand $\mathbf{unify}(\Omega, \Omega)$ does succeed. Usually we will be interested in unifying normal terms, and in that case unification always terminates, as the following theorem shows.

Theorem. *Let t and s be normal terms, and let E be an environment containing all variables in t or s. Then $\mathbf{unify}(t,s)$ terminates, and if it terminates successfully, the output substitution unifies t and s relative to E.*

Proof: By induction on the complexity (depth) of t and s. Since they are normal terms, all subterms are normal, and the clauses of **unify** that correspond to reduction rules are never used. The other clauses make recursive calls only to **unify** applied to subterms of t and s, which by induction hypothesis do terminate. We still have to prove that $\mathbf{unify}(t,s)$ unifies t and s. This is obvious for Robinson unification, but now the definition of "unifies" is more general, involving "some values of the new variables", so there is something to be proved, even for the old clauses in the definition. The induction steps corresponding to the new clauses have been given above, in the course of the definition. Consider the proof that $\mathbf{unify}(ts,pq)$ really unifies ts and pq. Let $\sigma = \mathbf{unify}(t,p)$. Then by hypothesis $t\sigma\chi = p\sigma\chi$ for some χ which is the identity on the input environment E. Let $\tau = \mathbf{unify}(s\sigma, q\sigma)$. By induction hypothesis $s\sigma\tau\eta = q\sigma\tau\eta$ for some η which is the identity on E', the environment including E and any new variables introduced by σ. Since E contains all variables in s and q, τ is the identity on any new variables introduced by σ, and since E' is the input environment for the call producing τ, η is the identity on any new variables introduced by τ. Define $\beta = \eta\tau = \tau\eta$, the union of these two disjoint substitutions. Then we will prove $(ts)\sigma\tau\beta = (pq)\sigma\tau\beta$. Note that $\chi\tau = \tau\chi$ since χ is non-identity only on new variables introduced by σ, but τ is the identity on these variables. We calculate as follows:

$$(ts)\sigma\tau\beta =$$
$$(t\sigma\tau\beta)(s\sigma\tau\beta) =$$
$$(t\sigma\tau\chi)(s\sigma\tau\eta) =$$
$$(t\sigma\chi\tau)(s\sigma\tau\eta) =$$
$$(p\sigma\chi\tau)(q\sigma\tau\eta) =$$
$$(p\sigma\tau\chi)(q\sigma\tau\eta) =$$
$$(p\sigma\tau\beta)(s\sigma\tau\beta) = (pq)\sigma\tau\beta$$

Since $\sigma\tau$ is the output substitution $\mathbf{unify}(ts,pq)$, this completes the proof.

6   The Most General Unifier

Since substitutions are functions whose values are terms, equality between substitutions is defined in terms of equaltiy of terms. In systems allowing λ-terms, equality of terms involves the notion of reduction, rather than syntactic identity, so the notion of equality of substitutions is correspondingly more complicated. In the applications we have in mind, variables will denote functions or predicates, not only individuals. Therefore, the substition which gives a variable the value t should be equal to the substitution which gives the same variable the value s, if s and t are extensionally equal. As explained above, we write $t \cong s$ to mean $tx = sx$, where x is a variable not contained in t or s. We now define two substitutions θ and μ to be a *equal on an environment E* provided $\theta X \cong \mu X$ for all variables X in E.

The notion of one substitution being "more general" than another is defined almost as usual. The usual definition is this: θ is more general than μ if there is a substitution γ such that $\theta\gamma = \mu$. The fact that our unification algorithm introduces "new" variables requires relativizing this definition, as follows:

Definition. *Given an environment E, θ is more general than μ, relative to E, if there is a substitution γ such that $\theta\gamma = \mu$ on E. That is, for all variables X in the finite set E, we have $X\theta\gamma \cong X\mu$.*

It will sometimes happen that γ is defined on variables not in the original environment E. For example, if θ is the substitution produced by unifying terms t and s, and E is the set of variables occurring in t or s, then γ may be defined on some of the "new" variables introduced by the unification algorithm.

Because reduction is allowed in determining equality, the concept of one substitution being more general than another is more complex than in first-order logic, as the following example will illustrate.

Example: Consider the problem $X(1) = 1$. The answer substitution is $X = \lambda x.\mathbf{d}(x, 1, 1, Y(x))$. Both the answers produced by Huet's algorithm can be obtained, up to extensional equivalence, from this answer by instantiating Y to one of the values $Y = \lambda x.x$ or $Y = \lambda x.1$. If we substitute these values for Y and reduce to normal form, we obtain

$$\mathbf{d}(x, 1, 1, (\lambda x.x)(1)) = \mathbf{d}(x, 1, 1, x) = x$$

$$\mathbf{d}(x, 1, 1, (\lambda x.1)(1)) = \mathbf{d}(x, 1, 1, 1) = 1$$

Hence the answer substitution produced by our second-order unification algorithm is more general than each of Huet's two answers. It is also more general than any of the infinitely many variable-free solutions, such as

$$X = \lambda x.\mathbf{d}(x, 1, 1, \mathbf{d}(x, 2, 0, 3)).$$

Theorem. *(Most general unifier) Let E be an environment. Suppose that p and q are normal terms in λD. Suppose that for some substitution θ legal for E, $p\theta$ and $q\theta$ are identical. Then p and q unify, and the answer substitution is legal for E, and more general than θ.*

Proof: The proof is by induction on the complexity of the term p. If p is a variable, then **unify**(p, q) succeeds with answer substitution χ given by $p\chi = q$. Take $\beta = \theta$. Then to show $\chi\beta = \theta$ it will suffice to show $p\chi\beta = p\theta$, since χ is the identity on variables other than p. But $p\chi\beta = q\theta$ since $p\chi = q$, and $q\theta = p\theta$ by hypothesis, so $p\chi\beta = p\theta$ as desired. The case when q is a variable is treated similarly. We may henceforth suppose that neither p nor q is a variable.

Suppose p is a constant. Then $p\theta$ is p. Therefore $q\theta$ is also p, so q (since it isn't a variable) is p too. Hence **unify**(p, q) succeeds, returning the identity substitution. Similarly if q is constant.

Now we may assume that p and q are both λ-terms or application terms. Since $p\theta$ and $q\theta$ are identical, either both p and q are application terms, or both of them are λ terms. First consider the case of two λ-terms, $\lambda x.t$ and $\lambda x.s$. Suppose these unify with substitution θ. Then θ is not defined on x, and $t\theta = s\theta$ (for some values of variables outside the environment). Let T and S be the result of replacing z by a new (forbidden) constant in t and s. Let $\chi = $ **unify**(T, S); by induction hypothesis this succeeds and χ is more general than θ. Since the new constant does not occur in the values of χ, χ unifies $\lambda x.t$ and $\lambda x.s$ also, completing this case.

Now consider unifying two application terms, one of which is of the form $X(s)$ with X a variable. Let $\chi = $ **unify**$(X(s), t)$, where t and s are normal terms not forbidden to X in E. Then by definition of unification,

$$X\chi = \lambda z.\mathbf{d}(x, s, t, Y(x)) \tag{1}$$

where Y is a new variable (outside E). Suppose

$$X(s)\theta = t\theta \tag{2}$$

We want to find a substitution β such that $\theta = \chi\beta$ on E. By (2) we have

$$(X\theta)(s\theta) = t\theta \tag{3}$$

Define β so that $Y\beta = X\theta$, and $Z\beta = Z\theta$ for all variables Z in the environment E (including the case $Z = X$). Calculate:

$$
\begin{aligned}
X\chi\beta &= (\lambda x.\mathbf{d}(x, s, t, Y(x)))\beta \\
&= \lambda x.\mathbf{d}(x, s\beta, t\beta, (Y\beta)(x)) \\
&= \lambda x.\mathbf{d}(x, s\theta, t\theta, (Y\beta)(x)) \\
&= \lambda x.\mathbf{d}(x, s\theta, t\theta, (X\theta)(x)) \\
&= \lambda x.\mathbf{d}(x, s\theta, (X\theta)(s\theta), (X\theta)(x))
\end{aligned}
$$

by (3). In view of the identity $Z \cong \lambda x.\mathbf{d}(x, a, Za, Zx)$, (which is just another expression of the second $\mathbf{d}$-rule), applied with $Z = X\theta$, we have

$$X\chi\beta = X\theta$$

Note that this is the step requiring the use of extensional equality. We cannot make this step go through using only β-reduction in the definition of equality of substitutions; and in view of the examples, this seems quite natural. The case in which we have $t_1, \ldots, t_n$ instead of t is handled similarly.

Now consider the case of unifying $X(z)$ and s, where X is a variable and z is a constant forbidden to X in E, and s contains z. By hypothesis, $(X\theta)(z\theta) = (s\theta)$. Since z is constant, $z\theta = z$, so $(X\theta)z = (s\theta)$. Since θ is legal for X in E, by hypothesis, $X\theta$ does not contain z. Let $a = \lambda w.s[w/z]$, so a does not contain z. Therefore $X\theta \cong a\theta$, i.e. $(X\theta)w = (a\theta)w = s[w/z]$ for any variable or constant w.

Let χ be the result of the unification algorithm, so $X\chi z = az \lor Yz$. Define β to agree with θ on variables occurring in E, and $Y\beta = \lambda z\mathbf{F}$. Then

$$
\begin{aligned}
X\chi\beta w &= (\lambda z(az \lor Yz)\beta)w \\
&= (\lambda z((a\beta)z \lor \mathbf{F})\mathbf{w} \\
&= (\lambda z((a\beta)z))w \\
&= (a\beta)w \\
&= (a\theta)w \\
&= (X\theta)w
\end{aligned}
$$

Therefore $X\chi\beta \cong X\theta$ as desired. On any variable U other than X, we have $(U\chi\beta)w = U\beta = (U\theta)w$. Hence $\chi\beta = \theta$ as substitutions. This completes the cases corresponding to the new clauses in the definition of unification.

We still have to check the other cases of application terms, which correspond to ordinary unification. Consider the case when $p = f(t_1, t_2)$ and $q = f(s_1, s_2)$. In λ-calculus, there are no function symbols *per se* except the binary symbol $\mathbf{ap}$ for application. Usually we don't write $\mathbf{ap}$ explicitly but just write $p(q)$ or pq for $\mathbf{ap}(p, q)$. So officially the only possibility here is $f = \mathbf{ap}$; but this one case is as difficult as the general case in first-order unification, of course.

Let $\chi = \mathbf{unify}(p, q)$. We want to show that for some β we have $\chi\beta = \theta$. We have, by definition of the unification algorithm, $\chi = \chi_1\chi_2$ where

$$\chi_1 = \mathbf{unify}(t_1, s_1) \tag{4}$$

$$\chi_2 = \mathbf{unify}(t_2\chi_1, s_2\chi_1) \tag{5}$$

Assume $p\theta = q\theta$. Then

$$t_1\theta = s_1\theta \tag{6}$$

$$t_2\theta = s_2\theta \tag{7}$$

Then by induction hypothesis, (4), and (6), we have for some β_1,

$$\theta = \chi_1\beta_1 \tag{8}$$

By (7) and (8), we have

$$t_2\chi_1\beta_1 = s_2\chi_1\beta_1 \tag{9}$$

By (5) and the induction hypothesis, we have for some β

$$\chi_2\beta = \chi_1\beta_1 \tag{10}$$

By (9), we have

$$\chi\beta = \chi_1\chi_2\beta = \chi_1\beta_1 = \theta$$

This completes the case in which p and q are binary compound terms with the same function symbol. In case p and q are unary compound terms with the same function symbol, apply the induction hypothesis to the arguments. In case p is a variable not occurring in q, the answer substitution $\chi = \mathbf{unify}(p,q)$ is given by $p\chi = q$, and χ is the identity on other variables. Since by hypothesis $p\theta = q\theta$, we have $p\theta = p\chi\theta$. Since χ is the identity on other variables than p, we have $\theta = \chi\theta$, so θ itself is the desired β. This completes the proof.

7   Unification and Second-Order Logic

We now return to the connection between unification and second-order logic. Space does not permit a detailed development; we will just describe the system of second-order logic briefly and give an example deduction using unification.

Each of the four quantifier rules has to be taken twice, once for first-order quantifiers and once for second-order quantifiers. In addition there are the λ-rules:

$$\frac{\Gamma \Rightarrow A[t/x]}{\Gamma \Rightarrow (\lambda x.A)t}$$

$$\frac{\Gamma, A[t/x] \Rightarrow \phi}{\Gamma, (\lambda x.A)t \Rightarrow \phi}$$

These rules permit us to reduce λ-terms when trying to construct a proof bottom-up. These rules were implemented at the same time as first-order logic, in the prover GENTZEN [Beeson 1991], but only simple second-order deductions could be performed by GENTZEN, because a powerful second-order unification algorithm was missing. GENTZEN could find the correct instances of mathematical induction for certain proofs, but could not do circumscription proofs, for example.

We define a system **LD** of second order logic with definition by cases. The intuitive idea is

$$\mathbf{d}(x,y,a,b) = a \text{ if } \mathbf{x} = \mathbf{y} \text{ else } \mathbf{b}$$

In second-order logic, we can take

$$\mathbf{d}(x, y, A, B) = (x = y \rightarrow A) \wedge (x \neq y \rightarrow B)$$

so it is not necessary to add a constant $\mathbf{d}$ to second-order logic. However, since $\mathbf{d}$ figures in our unification algorithm and hence in our theorem-prover, the implemented version of second-order logic does contain a constant $\mathbf{d}$.

The λ-rules allow us to reduce λ-terms, but in $\mathbf{LD}$ we also need to reduce $\mathbf{d}$-terms. Therefore $\mathbf{LD}$ includes the following rules, which we call the $\mathbf{d}$-rules:

$$\frac{\Gamma \Rightarrow A}{\Gamma \Rightarrow \mathbf{d}(x, x, A, B)}$$

$$\frac{x \neq y, \Gamma \Rightarrow B}{\Gamma \Rightarrow \mathbf{d}(x, y, A, B)}$$

$$\frac{y \neq x, \Gamma \Rightarrow B}{\Gamma \Rightarrow \mathbf{d}(x, y, A, B)}$$

$$\frac{B, \Gamma \Rightarrow C}{x \neq y, \mathbf{d}(x, y, A, B), \Gamma => C}$$

$$\frac{B, \Gamma \Rightarrow C}{y \neq x, \mathbf{d}(x, y, A, B), \Gamma => C}$$

$$\frac{A, \Gamma \Rightarrow C}{\mathbf{d}(x, x, A, B), \Gamma => C}$$

Note that if $\mathbf{d}(x, y, A, B)$ is regarded as an abbreviation, these rules are derived rules of inference. It follows that proofs in $\mathbf{LD}$ can be translated into proofs in $\mathbf{L}$; moreover the same is true of cut-free proofs. It is therefore a matter of convenience only whether we take $\mathbf{d}$ as defined or primitive.

Extend second-order logic by allowing "metavariables" to stand in place of terms. Call this system $\mathbf{LDM}$. Second-order logic $\mathbf{LD}$ and its extension $\mathbf{LDM}$ can be translated into λ-calculus by standard techniques. We will be explicit about those "standard techniques." We distinguish some of the variables of λ-calculus and call them *constants*, agreeing not to use them for other purposes. We then specify some constants of λ-calculus to stand for the propositional connectives and for $\forall$ and $\exists$. We denote these constants by the same symbols $\forall$ and $\exists$. Then the translation A' of A is given by

$$(\forall x A)' = \forall(\lambda x. A')$$

$$(\exists x A)' = \exists(\lambda x. A')$$

The translation commutes with the propositional connectives. Identifying formulas of second-order logic with their translations, we can regard unification as defined on formulas of second-order logic. Predicate symbols are simply constants of λ-calculus.

The following lemma is essentially the formalization in second-order logic of the correctness theorem for the unification algorithm.

Lemma. *Let A and B be two formulas of second-order logic* **LDM**. *Let the environment E include all variables in A or B. Suppose* **unify**(A, B) *succeeds with answer substitution* θ. *Then* **LD** *proves* $A\theta\chi \leftrightarrow B\theta\chi$, *for some substitution* χ *which is the identity on E.*

Proof: By induction on the computation of **unify**(A, B). The proof is omitted to meet the length limit.

Robinson's unification algorithm is the key to theorem-proving in first-order logic, whether one combines it with resolution or with "backwards Gentzen" methods, or uses it in an equational theorem-prover. The extensions to the unification algorithm introduced here will have applications in automated deduction, also independent of whether one uses resolution or some other method of proof search.

In [Beeson 1991] one can find the Prolog source code for a theorem-prover for first-order logic, based on bottom-up construction of cut-free proofs in a Gentzen sequent calculus. The prover uses metavariables to stand for as-yet-undetermined terms, and instantiates these metavariables by unification when the proof construction reaches leaf nodes of the proof tree (axioms). We will not assume familiarity with this prover, but only with the general idea of backwards proof-search in a sequent calculus, introducing metavariables when (certain) quantifiers are stripped away, and instantiating the metavariables later by unification. The prover described in [Beeson 1991] can be extended to second-order logic by changing the unification algorithm to the one given in this paper.

We will describe how it proves the theorem

$$a \neq b \Rightarrow \exists X(X(a) \wedge \neg X(b)).$$

First, the quantifier will be "opened up" and the variable X replaced by a metavariable. In [Beeson 1991] we used capital letters for metavariables; this clashes with the convention that capital letters are used in second-order logic for second-order variables, so here we use $\mathbf{X}$ for a metavariable. The goal is now

$$a \neq b \Rightarrow \mathbf{X}(a) \wedge \neg\mathbf{X}(b).$$

This goal is divided into two goals,

$$a \neq b \Rightarrow \mathbf{X}(a) \tag{11}$$

and

$$a \neq b \Rightarrow \neg\mathbf{X}(b) \tag{12}$$

GENTZEN will work on 11 first. It will unify $\mathbf{X}(a)$ with **true**, instantiating the metavariable $\mathbf{X}$ as

$$\mathbf{X} = \lambda x.\mathbf{d}(x, a, \mathbf{true}, \mathbf{Y}x) \tag{13}$$

producing the new goal

$$a \neq b \Rightarrow \lambda x.\mathbf{d}(x, a, \mathbf{true}, \mathbf{Y}x)a.$$

The clause implementing the $\Rightarrow$ λ-rule then applies, reducing the goal to

$$a \neq b \Rightarrow \mathbf{d}(a, a, \mathbf{true}, \mathbf{Y}x).$$

Then a **d**-rule applies, producing the goal

$$a \neq b \Rightarrow \mathbf{true}$$

which is an axiom. Now GENTZEN begins to work on (12), with the metavariable **X** instantiated as in 13. Specifically, the goal is

$$a \neq b \Rightarrow \neg \lambda x.\mathbf{d}(x, a, \mathbf{true}, \mathbf{Y}x)b$$

The rule $\Rightarrow \neg$ is applied, producing the goal

$$\lambda x.\mathbf{d}(x, a, \mathbf{true}, \mathbf{Y}x)b, a \neq b \Rightarrow \mathbf{false}$$

The $\lambda \Rightarrow$ rules is applied, producing the goal

$$\mathbf{d}(b, a, \mathbf{true}, \mathbf{Y}b), a \neq b \Rightarrow \mathbf{false}$$

One of the **d**-rules now applies, producing the new goal

$$\mathbf{Y}b, a \neq b \Rightarrow \mathbf{false}$$

The axiom clause now makes a call to **unify**($\mathbf{Y}b$, **false**), instantiating **Y** as

$$Y = \lambda y.\mathbf{d}(y, b, \mathbf{false}, \mathbf{Z}y)$$

for a new metavariable **Z**. This makes the attempt to prove $\mathbf{X}a \wedge \neg \mathbf{X}b$ succeed, returning the answer substitution

$$X = \lambda x.\mathbf{d}(x, a, \mathbf{true}, \lambda y.\mathbf{d}(y, b, \mathbf{false}, \mathbf{Z}y)x)$$

The proof produced, rewritten in tree form, is as follows, with

$$t = \lambda x.\mathbf{d}(x, a, \mathbf{true}, \lambda y.\mathbf{d}(y, b, \mathbf{false}, \mathbf{Z}y)x) :$$

$$
\cfrac{
  \cfrac{a \neq b \Rightarrow \mathbf{true} \qquad
    \cfrac{
      \cfrac{
        \cfrac{
          \cfrac{\mathbf{false} \Rightarrow \mathbf{false}}
                {\mathbf{d}(b, b, \mathbf{false}, \mathbf{Z}b), a \neq b \Rightarrow \mathbf{false}}
        }{(\lambda y.\mathbf{d}(y, b, \mathbf{false}, \mathbf{Z}y))b, a \neq b \Rightarrow \mathbf{false}}
      }{\mathbf{d}(b, a, \mathbf{true}, (\lambda y.\mathbf{d}(y, b, \mathbf{false}, \mathbf{Z}y))b), a \neq b \Rightarrow \mathbf{false}}
    }{
      \cfrac{a \neq b, \quad tb \Rightarrow \mathbf{false}}
            {a \neq b \Rightarrow \neg tb}
    }
  }{
    \cfrac{a \neq b \Rightarrow \mathbf{d}(a, a, \mathbf{true}, \lambda y.\mathbf{d}(y, b, \mathbf{false}, \mathbf{Z}y)a)}
          {a \neq b \Rightarrow ta}
  }
}{
  \cfrac{a \neq b \Rightarrow ta \wedge \neg tb}
        {a \neq b \Rightarrow \exists X(Xa \wedge \neg Xb)}
}
$$

This proof illustrates the use of the first new clause in the definition of unification. The circumscription examples use the second new clause as well.

References

[Baker-Ginsberg 1989] A. Baker and M. Ginsberg. A theorem prover for prioritized circumscription. *Proceedings of the Eleventh International Joint Conference on Artificial Intelligence*, pp. 463–467, Morgan Kaufmann, Los Altos, Calif. (1989).

[Barendregt 1981] H. P. Barendregt. *The Lambda Calculus: Its Syntax and Semantics.* North-Holland, Amsterdam (1981).

[Beeson 1991] M. Beeson. Some applications of Gentzen's proof theory in automated deduction. In Schroeder-Heister (ed.), *Extensions of Logic Programming*, Lecture Notes in Artificial Intelligence **475**, Springer-Verlag, Berlin/ Heidelberg/ New York (1991).

[Ginsberg 1989] M. Ginsberg. A circumscriptive theorem prover. *Artificial Intelligence* **39**, No. 2 (1989).

[Huet 1975] G. Huet. A unification algorithm for typed λ-calculus. *Theoretical Computer Science* **1** (1975) 27–52.

[Lifschitz 1985] V. Lifschitz. Computing circumscription. *Proceedings of the Ninth International Joint Conference on Artificial Intelligence*, pp. 121–127, Morgan Kaufmann, Los Altos, Calif. (1985).

[McCarthy 1986] J. McCarthy. Applications of circumscription to formalizing common-sense knowledge. *Artificial Intelligence* **28** (1986) 89–116.

[Miller 1992] D. Miller. *Unification under a mixed prefix.* Journal of Symbolic Computation **14** (1992) 321–358.

[Miller and Nadathur 1988] D. Miller and G. Nadathur. An Overview of λ-Prolog In *Proceedings of the Fifth International Symposium on Logic Programming, Seattle, August 1988.*

[Prawitz 1967] D. Prawitz. Completeness and Hauptsatz for second order logic. *Theoria 33*, 246-258.

[Synder 1990] W. Snyder. Higher-order E-unification. In M. E. Stickel (ed.), *CADE-10, Tenth International Conference on Automated Deduction* 573-587 Springer-Verlag (1990).

[Wallen 1990] *Automated Deduction in Nonclassical Logics.* MIT Press, Cambridge, MA (1990)

System Description: An Equational Constraints Solver

Nicolas Peltier

Laboratory LEIBNIZ-IMAG
46, Avenue Félix Viallet 38031 Grenoble Cedex FRANCE
Nicolas.Peltier@imag.fr
Phone: (33) (0)4 76 57 48 05

1 Equational Formulae: Definition and Solvability

Equational formulae are first-order formulae containing only "=" as a predicate symbol. A substitution σ is a *solution* of an equational formula $\mathcal{F}$ iff $\mathcal{F}\sigma$ is valid in the finite tree algebra (i.e. when = is interpreted as the syntactic equality on the Herbrand universe). Equational formulae have many applications in the domains of Automated Deduction, Artificial Intelligence and Computer Science (program verification, negation in logic programming [5,13,3], inductive proofs [6], model building [4,1,19] etc.). They have been studied by many authors for several years. In particular, the validity problem for equational formulae in the empty theory has been proven to be decidable [15,12,14,9].

Example 1. Let $\Sigma = \{0, succ\}$. $\forall z.x \neq succ(z) \land succ(y) = succ(succ(x))$ is an equational formula. This formula has a unique solution : $\{x \rightarrow 0, y \rightarrow succ(0)\}$.

In this paper, we describe a system, called Ecs_{Atinf}, able to solve equational formulae. Ecs_{Atinf} is a part of the Inference Laboratory ATINF developed in the LEIBNIZ laboratory since 1985 (see [2] for more details about ATINF). It is also a key component of our system for simultaneous search for refutations and models $RAMC_{ATINF}$[1]. To the best of our knowledge Ecs_{Atinf} is the only system for solving equational constraints in the public domain[1].

2 Solving Equational Formulae

Given a sorted signature Σ and an equational formula $\mathcal{F}$, Ecs_{Atinf} automatically computes the set of solutions of $\mathcal{F}$. For doing that, it uses the quantifier-elimination algorithm presented in [9] in order to transform first-order formulae into a disjunction of formulae in a so-called definition with constraints solved form, from which the solution of the initial formula can be easily extracted. The

---

[1] of course there exists other implementations [17,10,11]. However, we do not succeed in getting any of them.

C. Kirchner and H. Kirchner (Eds.): Automated Deduction, CADE-15
LNAI 1421, pp. 119–123, 1998. © Springer–Verlag Berlin Heidelberg 1998

notion of definition with constraints can be seen as the analogous of the notion of most general unifiers for unification problems: it gives the general form of the solutions of the initial formula[2]. A formula $\mathcal{F}$ is in *definition with constraints* solved form iff it is $\bot$ of if it is of the form $\exists u_1, \ldots, u_k.(\bigwedge_{i=1}^{n} x_i = t_i \wedge \bigwedge_{i=1}^{m} y_i \neq s_i)$, where the x_i's and y_i's are variables, for all $i \leq n$, x_i occurs only once in $\mathcal{F}$, for all $i \leq m$, y_i does not occurs in s_i.

The algorithm transforming each first-order formula into a definition of constraints is given in [9]. It is specified as a set of rewriting rules, containing in particular the usual unification rules (decomposition, occur check, clash, replacement), specific rules for eliminating quantifiers (universality of parameter and explosion rules) and some boolean transformation rules (for example distributivity rules). We do not recall here the definition of these rules (the interested reader can consult [9]). Ecs$_{\text{Atinf}}$ uses some special strategies increasing the efficiency of the system. In particular, the application of the costly explosion and distributivity rules are *delayed*, and if possible *avoided*. Roughly speaking, the resolution process is divided into two steps. During the first one, Ecs$_{\text{Atinf}}$ tries to eliminate the universal quantifiers occurring in the formula. For doing that it uses a standard unification algorithm for solving unification problems occurring in the formula, then it applies the universality of parameters rules. Finally, the distributivity and explosion rules are applied. The distributivity rule allows one to put the formula in conjunctive normal form (which is necessary for the elimination of universal quantifiers) and the explosion rule is needed for eliminating parameters occurring at non root positions in disequations. During the second step, the system uses the unification and explosion of disjunction rules to transform the formula into a disjunction of definition with constraints. Boolean transformation rules are used to simplify the formula at both steps.

3   Using Ecs$_{\text{Atinf}}$

The syntax used by our system is very close to the one of the theorem prover OTTER [16] (which is very well known and widely used in Automated Deduction). Some further features (such as the use of sort symbols) are allowed for the definition of the formula. Constant or function symbols are defined using the command: `declare(s(f(s1,s2,...,sn)))`, where $s_1, \ldots, s_n, s$ are sort symbols and f is a symbol of profile $s_1, \ldots, s_n \rightarrow s$. Formulae are defined using the command: `formula(name(x1,...,xn))` (where `name` is the name of the formula, and `x1,...,xn` the free variables) followed by the formula itself. Previously defined formula can be reused in defining a new formula : for example the commands `formula(p(x)). (x = a).` and `formula(q). (all y. p(y))` define a

---

[2] In [9], it is shown that any formula in definition with constraints solved form distinct from $\bot$ as a solution. Moreover, an algorithm is given for enumerating the solutions of a formula in definition with constraints solved form.

formula $p = \forall y.(y = a)^3$. The symbols $\vee, \wedge, \Rightarrow, \Leftrightarrow$ are respectively denoted by `|`, `&`, `->`, `<->`. Universal and existential quantified formulae are denoted by `(all x1,...,xn F)` and `(exists x1,...,xn F)`. $\neq$ is denoted by `!=`. The command `solve(name)` transforms the formula **name** into a disjunction of definition with constraints. Some flags and parameters allow the user to control some parts of the resolution process.

Ecs$_{\text{Atinf}}$ has been coded in C. It can be freely downloaded by the WEB, from http://leibniz.imag.fr/ATINF/Nicolas.Peltier/. It is self documented and examples of input files and experimental results are included.

Example We give below an example of problem that can be treated by our system.

```
% functional symbol declaration (optional)
declare(top(a)).
declare(top(f(top))).
declare(top(g(top,top))).

signature = { a,f,g }. % definition of the signature

formula(prob).    % formula to solve
(f(A) =f(B) | (all Z. ((Z = a) | (A != g(Z,Z)))))).

solve(prob).

% Definition with constraint solved form

prob = (exists T,U,S ((-(T = U) & (A = g(U,T)))
| (A = g(U,a)) | (A = a) | (A = f(S)) | (A = B)))

Run Time: 0.01
```

4 Future Work

Numerous extensions have been proposed to the algorithm in [9] (see for example [7]). Algorithms for solving equational formulae in some particular non empty theories have been proposed and some extensions of the constraint language have been considered. In particular, algorithms have been proposed for terms with integer exponents [18], membership constraints [8], some classes of higher order formulae, ordering constraints etc. Some of these extensions could be included in our software in the future. We have proposed in [19] some improvements to the constraints solving algorithm of [9]. These improvements consist mainly in a new more suitable definition of "solved form" (allowing in particular the

---

[3] This feature is particularly useful for model verification applications: it allows in particular to use Ecs$_{\text{Atinf}}$ to evaluate formulae in eq-interpretation, i.e. in Herbrand interpretations defined by equational formulae. See [4,19] for details.

occurrence of some universal quantifiers in the definition with constraints) and a more careful control on the application of the key rules of distributivity and explosion (different from the one of [8], see [19]). These extensions will also be included into our system in the near future.

References

1. C. Bourely, R. Caferra, and N. Peltier. A method for building models automatically. Experiments with an extension of Otter. In *Proceedings of CADE-12*, pages 72–86. Springer, 1994. LNAI 814.
2. R. Caferra and M. Herment. A generic graphic framework for combining inference tools and editing proofs and formulae. *Journal of Symbolic Computation*, 19(2):217–243, 1995.
3. R. Caferra and N. Peltier. Decision procedures using model building techniques. In *Proceeding of Computer Science Logic, CSL'95*, pages 130–144. Springer, LNCS 1092, 1996.
4. R. Caferra and N. Zabel. A method for simultaneous search for refutations and models by equational constraint solving. *Journal of Symbolic Computation*, 13:613–641, 1992.
5. A. Colmerauer. Equations and inequations on finite or infinite trees. In *FGCS'84*, pages 85–99, November 1984.
6. H. Comon. Inductive proofs by specification transformation. In *Proc. of RTA 89*. Springer, 1989.
7. H. Comon. Disunification: a survey. In Jean-Louis Lassez, Gordon Plotkin, editors. Computational logic: Essays in Honor of Alan Robinson. MIT Press, 1991.
8. H. Comon and C. Delor. Equational formulae with membership constraints. *Information and Computation*, 112(2):167–216, August 1994.
9. H. Comon and P. Lescanne. Equational problems and disunification. *Journal of Symbolic Computation*, 7:371–475, 1989.
10. C. Delor. Transformation de problèmes équationels. Internal report, Ecole Normale Supérieure, Paris (in French), 1989.
11. S. Klingenbeck. *Counter Examples in Semantic Tableaux*. PhD thesis, University of Karlsruhe, 1996.
12. K. Kunen. Answer sets and negation as failure. In J. L. Lassez, editor, *Proceeding of the Fourth International Conference on Logic Programming*, pages 219–227. The MIT Press, May 1987.
13. D. Lugiez. A deduction procedure for first order programs. In F. Levi and M. Martelli, editors, *Proceedings of the sixth International Conference on Logic Programming*, pages 585–599. The MIT Press, July 1989.
14. M. Maher. Complete axiomatizations of the algebras of finite, rational and infinite trees. In *Proceedings of the Third Annual Symposium on Logic in Computer Science*, pages 248–357. IEEE Computer Society, 1988.
15. A. Mal'cev. *The Metamathematics of Algebraic Systems: Collected Papers 1936–1967*, chapter Axiomatizable classes of locally free algebra of various type, pages 262–281. Benjamin Franklin Wells editor, North Holland, 1971. chapter 23.
16. W. W. McCune. *OTTER 3.0 Reference Manual and Guide*. Argonne National Laboratory, 1994.
17. M. Mehl. Gleichungsdefinierte probleme. lösungsmethoden und anwendungen bei algebraischen spezifikationen. Projekarbeit, Universität Kaiserlautern (in German), 1988.

18. N. Peltier. Increasing the capabilities of model building by constraint solving with terms with integer exponents. *Journal of Symbolic Computation*, 24:59–101, 1997.
19. N. Peltier. *Nouvelles Techniques pour la Construction de Modèles finis ou infinis en Déduction Automatique*. PhD thesis, Institut National Polytechnique de Grenoble, 1997.

System Description: CRIL Platform for SAT *

Bertrand Mazure, Lakhdar Saïs, and Éric Grégoire

CRIL – Université d'Artois,
rue de l'Université SP 16
F-62307 Lens Cedex, FRANCE.
{mazure,sais,gregoire}@cril.univ-artois.fr

Abstract. The CRIL multi-strategy platform for SAT includes a whole family of local search techniques and some of the best Davis and Putnam strategies for checking propositional satisfiability. Most notably, it features an optimized tabu-based local search method and includes a powerful logically complete approach that combines the respective strengths of local and systematic search techniques. This platform is a comprehensive toolkit provided with most current SAT instances generators and with various user-friendly tools.

1 Introduction

CRIL multi-strategy platform for SAT provides the user with a selection of both local and systematic search techniques. More precisely, it includes many variants of Selman et al. local search [6,7] techniques that prove efficient in showing the consistency of SAT instances. In particular, it features an optimized tabu-based local search method called TSAT [4]. It also includes a powerful logically complete approach that combines the power of local search methods with the completeness of Davis and Putnam procedure (DP), allowing both large satisfiable and unsatisfiable instances to be proved [5]. It thus shows that local search methods can play a key role with respect to proving unsatisfiability.

In this system description paper, the focus is laid on the main two salient features of the CRIL platform: an optimized tabu-based local search method and its use as an heuristic to guide the branching strategy of DP.

The platform is available by anonymous ftp at ftp.lifl.fr in directory: /pub/projects/SAT. It has been developed in standard ANSI C and should run on most UNIX systems. Our implementation and experimentations have been conducted on 133, 166 and 200 Pentium under Linux 2.0.30. All the available search techniques have been implemented by us (when these techniques have been previously proposed by other authors, our implementation is as efficient as the original code).

---

* The development of the CRIL platform for SAT was supported in part by the Ganymède II project of the *Contrat de plan État/Région Nord–Pas-de-Calais*.

C. Kirchner and H. Kirchner (Eds.): Automated Deduction, CADE-15
LNAI 1421, pp. 124–128, 1998. © Springer–Verlag Berlin Heidelberg 1998

The other various software tools are described in an interactive help module. Thanks to its open-ended architecture, the platform can easily be augmented with other techniques, heuristics, options and generators.

2   TSAT: A Brief Description

TSAT departs from basic GSAT by making a systematic use of a tabu list of variables in order to avoid recurrent flips and thus escape from local minima. This allows a better and more uniform coverage of the search space. More precisely, TSAT keeps a fixed length - chronologically-ordered FIFO - list of flipped variables and prevents any of the variables in the list from being flipped again during a given amount of time. The length of the tabu list has been experimentally optimized (for K-SAT instances) with respect to the size of the problems [4]. TSAT proves very competitive w.r.t. most families of SAT instances.

3   DP + Local Search: A Brief Description

Let us now describe a basic algorithm using Selman et al. local search GSAT-like procedures to guide the branching strategy of logically-complete algorithms based on DP [1].

TSAT (or another local search procedure) is run to deliver the next literal to be assigned by DP[1]. This literal is selected as the one with the highest score according to the following counting. A trace of TSAT is recorded: for each literal, taking each flip as a step of time, we count the number of times the literal appears in the falsified clauses. (Intuitively, it seemed to us that the most often falsified clauses should normally belong to an inconsistent kernel of the SAT instance if this instance is actually inconsistent. This hypothesis proves most often correct).

Such an approach can be seen as using the trace of TSAT as an heuristic for selecting the next literal to be assigned by DP, and a way to extend the partial assignment made by DP towards a model of the SAT instance when this instance is satisfiable. Each time DP needs to select the next variable to be considered, such a call to TSAT can be performed w.r.t. the remaining part of the SAT instance. This algorithm is given in Figure 1. Let us stress that this combination schema was simply designed to show its feasibility: in this respect, it is a very primitive one that can be optimized in several ways [5].

4   Experimental Results

In Fig. 2, TSAT [4], GSAT with Random Walk Strategy [6,7] and WSAT [3] are compared on hard random 3-SAT instances using 500 instances for each problem size at the threshold. (#clauses/#variables = 4.25).

In Table 1, a significant sample of our extensive experimentations is given, showing the obtained dramatical performance improvement, in particular for

---

[1] Independly, a close approach has been proposed in [2].

<u>Procedure</u> DP+TSAT ;
Input: a set of clauses S;
<u>Output</u>: a satisfying truth assignment of S if found,
          or a definitive statement that S is inconsistent;
Begin
  Unit_propagate(S);
  <u>if</u> the empty clause is generated
  <u>then</u> <u>return</u> (*false*);
  <u>else</u>
      <u>if</u> all variables are assigned
      <u>then</u> <u>return</u> (*true*);
      <u>else</u>
          begin
              <u>if</u> TSAT(S) succeeds
              <u>then</u> <u>return</u> (*true*);
              <u>else</u>
                  begin
                      p := the most often falsified literal during TSAT search;
                      <u>return</u> (DP+TSAT($S \wedge p$) $\vee$ DP+TSAT($S \wedge \neg p$));
                  <u>end</u>;
          <u>end</u>;
<u>End</u>.

Fig. 1. DP + TSAT: basic version

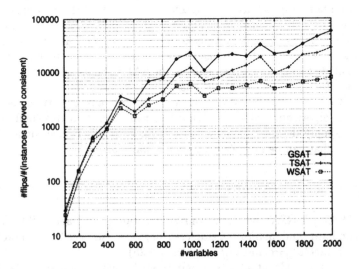

Fig. 2. Results for hard random 3-SAT instances

classes of inconsistent SAT instances. Also, very good results are obtained for consistent instances; indeed, DP+TSAT is as efficient as local search techniques since DP+TSAT begins with a call to them.

Table 1. DIMACS problems[2]

Instances	Sat	Size		Inc. Ker.[3]		DP+FFIS			DP+TSAT		
		Var.	Cla.	Var.	Cla.	assign.	choices	time	assign.	choices	time
AIM series:											
1.6-no-3	No	100	160	51	57	3E+07	2E+06	214 s71	178	16	0s26
1.6-yes1-2	Yes	100	160	***	***	495858	30052	4s3 9	77	6	0s08
2.0-no-1	No	100	200	18	19	4E+07	2E+06	349 s52	46	5	0s10
2.0-yes1-1	Yes	100	200	***	***	706388	31274	7s4 1	81	8	0s15
1.6-no-1	No	200	320	52	55	***	***	> 8h	240	16	0s58
1.6-yes1-3	Yes	200	320	***	***	***	***	> 9h	232	11	0s32
2.0-no-3	No	200	400	35	37	***	***	> 15h	120	10	0s42
2.0-yes1-1	Yes	200	400	***	***	2E+09	7E+07	218 59s45	291	27	1s21
1.6-no-1	No	50	80	20	22	12072	895	0s 09	72	8	0s06
1.6-yes1-1	Yes	50	80	***	***	1540	84	0s 01	37	6	0s05
2.0-no-1	No	50	100	21	22	54014	2759	0s 43	52	5	0s05
2.0-yes1-1	Yes	50	100	***	***	2878	176	0s 03	11	3	0s03
BF series:											
0432-007	No	1040	3668	674	1252	9E+08	6E+06	19553s44	115766	870	85s25
1355-075	No	2180	6778	82	185	317628	2047	18s88	4602	28	26s23
1355-638	No	2177	4768	83	154	***	***	>17h	6192	32	32s57
2670-001	No	1393	3434	79	139	***	***	>25h	490692	4822	519s40
SSA series:											
0432-003	No	435	1027	306	320	133794	1570	1s79	1338	16	0s80
2670-130	No	1359	3321	552	669	***	***	>33h	2E+07	79426	8040s64
2670-141	No	986	2315	579	1247	3E+08	2E+06	6350s77	1E+07	92421	6639s44
7552-038	Yes	1501	3575	***	***	***	***	>13h	29	1	0s34
7552-158	Yes	1363	3034	***	***	1639	78	0s19	12	1	0s29
7552-159	Yes	1363	3032	***	***	1557	84	0s21	12	1	0s25
7552-160	Yes	1391	3126	***	***	1457	76	0s18	1	1	0s30

References

1. Davis, M., Putnam, H.: A Computing Procedure for Quantification Theory. Journal of the Association for Computing Machinery, **7**, pp. 201–215.
2. Crawford, J.: Solving Satisfiability Problems Using a Combination of Systematic and Local Search. Working notes of the DIMACS Workshop on Maximum Clique, Graph Coloring, and Satisfiability (1993).
3. McAllexter, D., Selman, B., Kautz, H.A.: Evidence for Invariants in Local Search. Proceedings of the Fourteenth National Conference on Artificial Intelligence (AAAI'97) (1997) pp. 321–326.
4. Mazure, B., Saïs, L., Grégoire, É.: Tabu Search for SAT, Proceedings of the Fourteenth National Conference on Artificial Intelligence (AAAI'97), (1997) pp. 281–285.

---

[2] In the table, "> n H" means that we gave up after the problem had not been solved within n hours of CPU time.

[3] "Inc. Ker." in the table means "Inconsistent Kernel".

5. Mazure, B., Saïs, L., Grégoire, É.: Detecting Logical Inconsistencies. Proceedings of Mathematics and Artificial Intelligence Symposium (1996) pp. 116-121, extended version in Annals of Mathematics and Artificial Intelligence (1998).
6. Selman, B., Levesque, H., Mitchell, D.: A New Method for Solving Hard Satisfiability Problems. Proceedings of the Tenth National Conference on Artificial Intelligence (AAAI'92) (1992) pp. 440–446.
7. Selman, B., Kautz, H.A., Cohen, B.: Local Search Strategies for Satisfiability Testing. Proceedings of the DIMACS Workshop on Maximum Clique, Graph Coloring, and Satisfiability (1993).

System Description: Proof Planning in Higher-Order Logic with λ*Clam*

Julian Richardson*, Alan Smaill, and Ian Green

Department of Artificial Intelligence, Edinburgh University,
80 South Bridge, EH1 1HN, Scotland.
{julianr,smaill,img}@dai.ed.ac.uk

1 Introduction

Proof planning [4] is an approach to theorem proving which encodes heuristics for constructing mathematical proofs in a meta-theory of *methods*. The *Clam* system, developed at Edinburgh [3], has been used for several years to develop proof planning, in particular proof plans for induction. It has become clear that many of the theorem-proving tasks that we would like to perform are naturally higher-order. For example, an important technique called *middle-out reasoning* [6] uses meta-variables to stand for some unknown objects in a proof, to be instantiated as the proof proceeds. Domains such as the synthesis and verification of software and hardware systems, and techniques such as proof critics [7], benefit greatly from such middle-out reasoning. Since in these domains the meta-variables often become instantiated with terms of function type, reasoning with them is naturally higher-order, and higher-order unification is a vital tool.

One of our motivations for studying induction is that it is an important technique for reasoning about programs. Reasoning about programs (functions, predicates) is naturally higher-order, and although it is possible to reason about such objects in a first-order meta-theory, in order to do so we would have to modify our existing *Clam* methods to deal with proper treatment of λ bindings, β reduction etc. The reasoning is much clearer if we use higher-order logic as the meta-theory.

λ*Clam* is a higher-order prototype of *Clam*, written in λ*Prolog*, a higher-order version of Prolog. The meta-theory is based on higher-order logic, which simplifies reasoning about higher-order objects and allows many of the proof plans developed in *Clam* to be transferred to the higher-order setting without significant modifications. This is important because *Clam* constitutes a significant knowledge base for (inductive) proof. The use of λProlog gives us a powerful meta-theory which allows methods to be written concisely and declaratively, further enhancing one of the advantages of proof planning which is that it produces plans which are understandable to the human user.

* The authors gratefully acknowledge the support of EPSRC grant GR/L/11724 and British Council grant ROM/889/95/70 and for the comments of their colleagues in the Mathematical Reasoning Group and of the referees.

C. Kirchner and H. Kirchner (Eds.): Automated Deduction, CADE-15
LNAI 1421, pp. 129–133, 1998. © Springer–Verlag Berlin Heidelberg 1998

As well as being able to prove higher-order theorems which *Clam* cannot, λ *Clam* is also capable of proving many first-order theorems.

In this system description we introduce λ *Clam* and discuss some of its applications.

2   Higher-Order Theorems

λ *Clam* has already demonstrated its ability to produce proof plans for higher-order theorems. Although *Clam* can sometimes prove higher-order theorems by pretending they are first-order (for example treating λ as a function symbol), this is not very flexible and the standard proof plan for induction is easily broken, partly because there is no proper treatment of binding. By contrast, λ *Clam* is able to reason correctly in such proofs and the standard proof plan for induction then works for many higher-order theorems. We have applied λ *Clam* to a number of higher-order theorems involving for example map functions or limits (including the well-known lim+ example), ordinal arithmetic, and a fixpoint theorem.

3   Program Synthesis

In a constructive logic, a program can be synthesised by proving a statement of the form $\forall \overline{x} \, \exists \overline{z} \, spec(\overline{x}, \overline{z})$. Program synthesis involves finding existential witnesses for $\overline{z}$, which in turn involves manipulating terms of functional type. Program synthesis in *Clam* has been hampered by the lack of higher-order unification needed for rewriting functional terms, and when the specification or rewrite rules contain embedded quantifiers and λ abstraction, first-order rewriting often produces ill-formed terms which had subsequently to be filtered out. The scoping of variables in the target program corresponds in the synthesis task to logical dependencies in the proofs. These are hard to deal with in the presence of meta-variables. A higher-order logic such as that in λ *Clam* gives a transparent treatment of these dependencies, and prunes out ill-formed witnesses as part of the planning process. A number of program synthesis examples have been successfully tackled.

4   Higher-Order Rippling

While many methods in λ *Clam* are just ports of *Clam*'s methods to λ *Clam*'s more expressive meta-language, higher-order logic challenges some heuristics which work in first-order logic. In particular, the *rippling* heuristic [2] requires modification. Rippling guides term rewriting in order to preserve certain subterms (the *skeleton*) of the induction conclusion which correspond to subterms of the induction hypothesis. Subterms of the skeleton which are preserved by first-order rewriting can in the higher-order case be removed from the term by β-reduction. The solution taken in λ *Clam* is to define rippling in terms of *higher-order embeddings* [8] and check that the skeleton of a term is preserved after every application of a rewrite rule. This is less efficient than the rippling used in *Clam*, but is guaranteed to deal with β-reduction in a sound way.

For example, in a program synthesis example from [8], introduction of a higher-order meta-variable for the program to be synthesised and applying structural induction on one of the input lists leads to a blocked step case:

$$l, m, t, n_0 \, list(nat), h \, nat$$
$$\forall x \, x \in t \vee x \in m \to x \in n_0$$
$$\vdash \forall x. \boxed{x = h \vee \underline{x \in t \vee x \in m}}^{\uparrow} \to x \in (N \, h \, t \, m \, n_0)$$

The proof is unblocked by allowing rippling to instantiate the meta-variable N by higher-order unification to the term $\lambda uvwz \, (N_1 \, u \, v \, w \, z) :: (N_2 \, u \, v \, w \, z)$. The proof can then proceed and the instantiations for N_1 and N_2 are determined by higher-order unification. Note that the scope of the universally quantified variable x is inside the scope of the meta-variable N, and the unification algorithm correctly prevents N from becoming instantiated to a term containing x. Incorporating such constraints directly into the meta-theory by using higher-order logic and unification results in a cleaner and more robust treatment than is possible in *Clam*.

5 Problems in Higher-Order Proof Planning

Implementing a proof planning system in higher-order logic gives us great power and expressiveness, but naturally comes with problems of its own. β, η and α conversion, and constraints imposed by variable scoping, disturb the simple syntactic notion of rewriting which we have in first-order logic. This causes problems for rippling, for example (see §4 above).

In the higher-order case, most general unifiers do not generally exist, and λProlog returns multiple unifiers on backtracking. This introduces an additional source of search into proof. The tight search control provided by proof planning helps to keep this problem to a minimum. Often we know the form of the unifier which we want and sometimes we can restrict the unifier to be of this form by appropriate partial instantiation of the terms before applying unification. Sometimes this is not possible, and then it is necessary to filter through the stream of unifiers for the right one. Sometimes λProlog returns unifiers which are at first sight surprising, but on further inspection turn out to be exactly what is required. A feature which is lacking in λProlog which would be very useful is to be able to specify the order in which unifiers are returned by prioritising the order in which projection, imitation etc are applied.

6 Implementation

Whereas the *Clam* system is written in Prolog, λ*Clam* is written in λProlog. While Prolog's foundations lie in Horn clause logic, λProlog is based on hereditary Harrop formulae. As well as the ability to treat higher-order functions and relations as first-class, λProlog is also modular and typed. We use the Prolog/MALI [1] implementation of λProlog, which compiles to C code and is fast, and memory-efficient.

The characteristic features of λProlog are very convenient for our application. The meta-level type system of terms, formulae, sequents, rewrite rules etc. is naturally realised using λProlog types. Higher-order rewriting is easily defined, in the style of [5]; the planning machinery is defined is a similar way. The library system exploits λProlog's modules and *goal implication*, $\Theta \Rightarrow G$ which allows a goal G to be executed in the context of some extra clauses Θ, which in our case are the definitions of rewrite rules, etc. of the relevant background theory.

Input to $\lambda\,Clam$ is currently via a simple command line, and output is either as plain text or as LaTeX.

The system is still under construction and changing rapidly, so is not yet ripe for distribution, but further information and ultimately distribution is available on the WWW at http://dream.dai.ed.ac.uk/systems/lambda-clam.

7 Further Work

On the program synthesis side, we plan to experiment further with the synthesis of functional and logic programs.

More generally, we plan to gradually move our proof planning applications from *Clam* to $\lambda\,Clam$. A first step in this direction is to adapt *Clam*'s induction strategy to higher-order logic, implement proof critics, and develop a graphical user interface. Given such a basis, we will be in a good position to extend existing work on synthesis and verification of software and hardware systems.

8 Conclusion

This system description outlines the $\lambda\,Clam$ system for proof planning in higher-order logic. The usefulness and feasibility of applying higher-order proof planning to a number of types of problem is outlined, in particular the synthesis and verification of software and hardware systems. The use of a higher-order meta-theory overcomes problems encountered in *Clam* because of its inability to reason properly about higher-order objects. $\lambda\,Clam$ is written in λProlog.

References

1. P. Brisset and O. Ridoux. The architecture of an implementation of LambdaProlog: Prolog/Mali. In *Proceedings of the Workshop on Implementation of Logic Programming, ILPS'94, Ithaca, NY*. The MIT Press, November 1994.
2. A. Bundy, A. Stevens, F. van Harmelen, A. Ireland, and A. Smaill. Rippling: A heuristic for guiding inductive proofs. *Artificial Intelligence*, 62:185–253, 1993. Also available from Edinburgh as DAI Research Paper No. 567.
3. A. Bundy, F. van Harmelen, C. Horn, and A. Smaill. The Oyster-Clam system. In M. E. Stickel, editor, *10th International Conference on Automated Deduction*, pages 647–648. Springer-Verlag, 1990. Lecture Notes in Artificial Intelligence No. 449. Also available from Edinburgh as DAI Research Paper 507.
4. Alan Bundy. The use of explicit plans to guide inductive proofs. In R. Lusk and R. Overbeek, editors, *9th Conference on Automated Deduction*, pages 111–120. Springer-Verlag, 1988. Longer version available as DAI Research Paper No. 349.

5. A. Felty. A logic programming approach to implementing higher-order term rewriting. In L-H Eriksson et al., editors, *Second International Workshop on Extensions to Logic Programming*, volume 596 of *Lecture Notes in Artificial Intelligence*, pages 135–61. Springer-Verlag, 1992.
6. J. T. Hesketh. *Using Middle-Out Reasoning to Guide Inductive Theorem Proving.* PhD thesis, University of Edinburgh, 1991.
7. A. Ireland and A. Bundy. Productive use of failure in inductive proof. *Journal of Automated Reasoning*, 16(1–2):79–111, 1996. Also available as DAI Research Paper No 716, Dept. of Artificial Intelligence, Edinburgh.
8. A. Smaill and I. Green. Higher-order annotated terms for proof search. In J. von Wright, J. Grundy, and J Harrison, editors, *Theorem Proving in Higher Order Logics*, volume 1125 of *Lecture Notes in Computer Science*, pages 399–414. Springer, 1996. Also available as DAI Research Paper 799.

System Description: An Interface Between CLAM and HOL*

Konrad Slind[1], Mike Gordon[1], and Richard Boulton[2] and Alan Bundy[2]

[1] University of Cambridge Computer Laboratory
[2] Department of Artificial Intelligence, University of Edinburgh

Abstract. The CLAM proof planner has been interfaced to the HOL interactive theorem prover to provide the power of proof planning to people using HOL for formal verification, *etc.* The interface sends HOL goals to CLAM for planning and translates plans back into HOL tactics that solve the initial goals. The project homepage can be found at http://www.cl.cam.ac.uk/Research/HVG/Clam.HOL/intro.html.

1 Introduction

CLAM [3] is a proof planning system for Oyster, a tactic-based implementation of the constructive type theory of Martin-Löf. CLAM works by using formalized pre- and post-conditions of Oyster tactics as the basis of plan search. These specifications of tactics are called *methods*. The planning-level reasoning may abstract the object-level reasoning, giving proof planning a heuristic element. Soundness is nevertheless guaranteed since proofs are constructed solely by sound tactics. Due to the heuristic aspect, the tactic application may be unsuccessful but in practice this is very rare. Experience also shows that the search space for plans is often tractable: CLAM has been able to automatically plan many proofs. A particular emphasis of research has been inductive proofs.

HOL [5] is a general-purpose proof system for classical, higher-order predicate calculus; it has been used to formalize many areas of interest to computer scientists and mathematicians. The HOL system has been criticized on the basis that it does not provide a high level of proof automation. Such remarks are often based on ignorance, since the HOL system now provides powerful simplifiers, automatic first order provers (both tableaux and model elimination), a semi-decision procedure for a useful fragment of arithmetic, and a co-operating decision procedure mechanism [1]. However, HOL lacks automation for many important areas. A good case in point is *induction*. Induction is certainly a central proof method, but in HOL, as in many other systems, the user must interactively control the application of induction.

---

* Research supported by the Engineering and Physical Sciences Research Council of Great Britain under grants GR/L03071 and GR/L14381.

C. Kirchner and H. Kirchner (Eds.): Automated Deduction, CADE-15
LNAI 1421, pp. 134–138, 1998. © Springer–Verlag Berlin Heidelberg 1998

These two systems have been linked to make the inductive proof methods of CLAM available to users of HOL, and also to give CLAM users access to the large libraries of tactics and theories available in HOL. CLAM is currently implemented in Prolog and HOL in Standard ML.

2   The Interface

In the current design, the HOL process is in control, treating CLAM as an intelligent remote tactic. The CLAM and HOL processes communicate over sockets. The sequence of operations is illustrated in Figure 1.

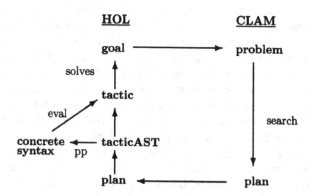

Fig. 1. System Structure

First, the HOL formula (goal) to be proved is translated into the syntax of Oyster's logic. This is then passed to CLAM, which searches for a proof. CLAM returns either a proof plan or an indication of failure. Supporting definitions, induction schemes, and lemmas are passed from HOL to CLAM in a similar way, prior to any proof attempts. CLAM acknowledges them with a handshaking message.

For successful proof attempts HOL receives a proof plan which it attempts to translate into corresponding tactics. If this is successful — which it normally is — the compound tactic is applied to the original HOL goal. Somewhat surprisingly, the plans CLAM produces based on specifications of Oyster tactics also work for a suite of purpose-written HOL tactics, despite the differences between the Oyster and HOL logics. These differences (and the heuristic aspects of planning) cannot lead to a non-theorem being 'proved' in HOL because HOL invokes its own tactics in checking the proof. Simply accepting as a theorem any goal for which CLAM finds a plan would be unsound.

3   Translation of the Object Language

In our work, CLAM has been modified to provide some independence from Oyster and the built-in types and induction schemes of the CLAM library. The library mechanism and Oyster's well-formedness checks have been bypassed. This allows any HOL types and definitions to be used without having to make corresponding definitions in Oyster. Modification of CLAM to suit the classical higher-order logic used by the HOL system has largely been avoided by exploiting correspondences between syntactic features of HOL's logic and the constructive type theory of Oyster/CLAM. The Oyster type theory has not been changed and no new methods have been written, though one for classical propositional reasoning might assist in some examples.

The HOL logic is translated to the syntax used by CLAM as follows. **F** (falsehood) is translated to the empty type and **T** (truth) to the type used to represent truth in CLAM. Conjunction translates to a product type, disjunction to a disjoint union type, implication to a function type, and negation to a function type between the argument of the negation and the empty type. Quantifications become dependent types. Equality between booleans is translated to if-and-only-if and other HOL equalities become equalities in CLAM. Other HOL terms are translated almost directly into the corresponding type-theoretic constructs.

Types in HOL are distinct from formulas/terms and so are translated separately. This is largely straightforward, although type variables required some thought. In HOL, type variables are implicitly universally quantified, but in CLAM they have to be bound. Thus, at the top level, the variables introduced for HOL type variables are quantified by placing them in the first type universe, $u(1)$. As Felty and Howe [4] point out, the domain should really be restricted to the *inhabited* types of $u(1)$ since HOL types have to be non-empty. However, for the kinds of proof under consideration this will be of no consequence and as pointed out earlier can not lead to inconsistency in HOL.

Differences in the lexical conventions of the HOL logic and those of CLAM (which are essentially those of Prolog) require some translation of constant and variable names. The translation table is retained for use in translating the proof plan to a HOL tactic.

4   Tactic Generation

A proof plan is translated into a composition of 'atomic' tactics in HOL, each of which corresponds to a method of CLAM. Currently, there are about twelve atomic tactics that form the basis of the translation.

Tactic generation takes place in two stages, as can be seen in Figure 1. First, an abstract syntax representation (**tacticAST**) of the tactic is derived from the plan. The abstract syntax is then used to generate either a tactic (an ML function) for direct application to the goal or a textual representation (ML concrete syntax) of the tactic for inclusion in a file. Direct translation into a tactic allows the plan to be applied to the goal without parsing and evaluating ML code. On the other hand, the generation of concrete syntax (by **pp**) allows the tactic to be inserted in ML tactic scripts and used in HOL sessions where CLAM may not be present, *i.e.*, it provides persistence.

One of the challenges in translating plans to tactics is tracking (in HOL) the variables introduced into the proof by CLAM. For example, consider an induction step in a plan: the step cases (and sometimes the base cases) introduce new bound variables. Later in the plan, these variables may become free as a result of specialization. Still later, a term with such free variables may be generalized. For HOL to make the same generalization step, the HOL goal must have corresponding occurrences of the same term (and hence corresponding occurrences of the same free variables). Therefore the proof plan must provide sufficient information for the names of bound variables in induction schemes to be ascertained.

5   Examples Performed

Examples that have been planned by CLAM and proved in HOL using the interface include commutativity of multiplication (over the naturals) and a number of theorems about lists including some known to be difficult to automate. The interest in many of these examples is not primarily the theorem, which is usually fairly simple, but rather in how CLAM found the proof, by making multiple and nested inductions and generalizations. Here are a few concrete examples:

$\forall x\ y.$ REVERSE (APPEND $x\ y$) = APPEND (REVERSE y) (REVERSE x)
$\forall x\ m\ n.$ APPEND (REPLICATE $x\ m$) (REPLICATE $x\ n$) = REPLICATE $x\ (m+n)$
$\forall x\ m\ n.$ FLAT (REPLICATE (REPLICATE $x\ n$) m) = REPLICATE $x\ (m*n)$

The functions here are curried. APPEND concatenates two lists, REVERSE reverses a list, FLAT flattens a list of lists into one list (by iterated concatenation), and REPLICATE $x\ n$ generates a list of n copies of x.

6   Conclusions

Two mechanized reasoning systems, one interactive with a large library of theories and many significant examples (HOL), and the other a largely automatic prover (CLAM), have been connected to provide a potentially useful tool for formal verification. The inductive methods of CLAM complement existing proof tools in HOL. Although the system is still very much a prototype, early results are promising. A more detailed, though less up-to-date, description of the system is available as a technical report [2]. Future goals include extending the range of formulas handled, more extended interaction between the two systems (*e.g.*, recursive dialogues), and testing on medium to large examples.

References

1. R. J. Boulton. Combining decision procedures in the HOL system. In *Proceedings of the 8th International Workshop on Higher Order Logic Theorem Proving and Its Applications*, volume 971 of *Lecture Notes in Computer Science*. Springer, 1995.
2. R. Boulton, A. Bundy, K. Slind, and M. Gordon. A Prototype Interface between CLAM and HOL. Research Paper 854, Department of Artificial Intelligence, University of Edinburgh, June 1997.
3. A. Bundy, F. van Harmelen, J. Hesketh, and A. Smaill. Experiments with proof plans for induction. *Journal of Automated Reasoning*, 7(3):303–324, 1991.
4. A. P. Felty and D. J. Howe. Hybrid interactive theorem proving using Nuprl and HOL. In *Proceedings of the 14th International Conference on Automated Deduction (CADE-14)*, volume 1249 of *Lecture Notes in Artificial Intelligence*. Springer, 1997.
5. M. J. C. Gordon and T. F. Melham, editors. *Introduction to HOL: A theorem proving environment for higher order logic*. Cambridge University Press, 1993.

System Description: LEO – A Higher-Order Theorem Prover*

Christoph Benzmüller and Michael Kohlhase

Fachbereich Informatik, Universität des Saarlandes, Germany
chris|kohlhase@cs.uni-sb.de

Many (mathematical) problems, such as Cantor's theorem, can be expressed very elegantly in higher-order logic, but lead to an exhaustive and un-intuitive formulation when coded in first-order logic.

Thus, despite the difficulty of higher-order automated theorem proving, which has to deal with problems like the undecidability of higher-order unification (HOU) and the need for primitive substitution, there are proof problems which lie beyond the capabilities of first-order theorem provers, but instead can be solved easily by an higher-order theorem prover (HOATP) like LEO. This is due to the expressiveness of higher-order Logic and, in the special case of LEO, due to an appropriate handling of the extensionality principles (functional extensionality and extensionality on truth values).

LEO uses a higher-order Logic based upon Church's simply typed λ-calculus, so that the comprehension axioms are implicitly handled by $\alpha\beta\eta$-equality. LEO employs a higher-order resolution calculus $\mathcal{ERES}$ (see [3] in this volume for details), where the search for empty clauses and higher-order pre-unification [6] are interleaved: the unifiability preconditions of the resolution and factoring rules are residuated as special negative equality literals that are treated by special unification rules. In contrast to other HOATP's (such as TPS [1]) extensionality principles are build in into LEO's unification, and hence do not have to be axiomatized in order to achieve Henkin completeness.

Architecture

LEO's architecture is based on a standard set-of-support strategy, extended in order to fulfill the requirements specific to higher-order logic. Furthermore, it uses a higher-order variant [7] of Graf's substitution tree indexing [4] and its implementation is based on the KEIM [5] toolkit which provides most of the necessary data structures and algorithms for a HOATP. The four cornerstones of LEO's architecture (see the figure for details see [2]) are the set of usable clauses (USABLE), the set of support (SOS) – well known from theorem provers such as OTTER – and two new constructions: The set of extensionally interesting clauses (EXT) and the set of HOU continuations (CONT). The motivation for

---

* The work reported in this paper was supported by the Deutsche Forschungsgemeinschaft in grant HOTEL.

C. Kirchner and H. Kirchner (Eds.): Automated Deduction, CADE-15
LNAI 1421, pp. 139–143, 1998. © Springer–Verlag Berlin Heidelberg 1998

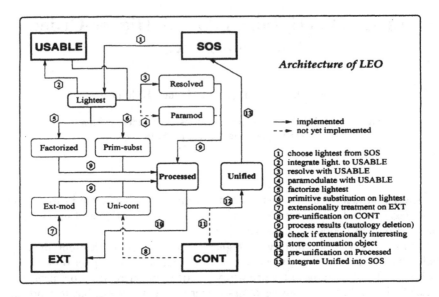

these two additional sets comes from the main idea of using HOU as a filter in order to eliminate in each loop all those newly derived clauses from the search space, which cannot be pre-unified within the given search depth limit (specified by a flag). Unfortunalety this filter is too strong and eliminates clauses which are nevertheless important for the refutation. Such clauses are preserved from elimination and put into CONT or EXT.

In each cycle, Leo selects the lightest clause from SOS and resolves it against all clauses in USABLE, factorizes it and applies primitive substitutions – the higher-order pre-unifiers that license this are not directly computed but residuated as unification literals. In a first-order theorem prover, these processed clauses would simply be integrated into the SOS after unification. A HOATP would thereby loose completeness for two reasons:

- There may be clauses which are non-unifiable within the given unification depth limit, but which have solutions beyond this limit. Upon reaching the depth limit, the unification procedure generates the clauses induced by the open leaves of the unification tree. These are stored in CONT for further processing by pre-unification.
- There are clauses which are not pre-unifiable at all, but which might be necessary for a refutation, if one takes the extensionality principles into account (these are stored in EXT for extensionality treatment).
  As an example consider the unification constraint $[\lambda X_\iota.a_o \vee b_o = \lambda X_\iota.b_o \vee a_o]^F$, which is not pre-unifiable, but leads to a refutation if one applies the extensionality rules to it (first *Func*, then *Equiv*, rest straightforward).

Of course it would be theoretically sufficient to integrate the clauses in CONT and EXT directly into the SOS, but the experiments show that it is better to subject them to specialized heuristics and filters and possibly delay their further processing.

Leo employs a higher-order substitution-tree indexing method [7], for example in the subsumption tests during incorporation into the SOS. Since full HOU is undecidable, it is only possible to use an imperfect filter that rules out all literals where simplification of the induced unification literals fails. However, it is impossible to use these techniques to select possible resolutions and factorizations, since co-simplification does not take extensionality into account – see example 1 below, where the refutation would be impossible, since the set of possible resolutions found by indexing is empty.

Experiments

Leo is able to solve a variety of simple higher-order theorems such as Cantor's theorem and it is specialized in solving theorems with embedded propositions.

Example 1 (Embedded Propositions). $pa \wedge pb \Rightarrow p(a \wedge b)$, where $p_{o \to o}, a_o$ and b_o are constants. Despite it's simplicity, this theorem cannot be solved automatically by any other HOATP such as Tps or Hol.

The clause normal form of the problem consists of three clauses

$$[p(a \wedge b)]^F \qquad [pa]^T \qquad [pb]^T$$

Leo inserts the first one into the SOS and the others into USABLE. In the first cycle $[p(a \wedge b)]^F$ is resolved against $[pa]^T$ and $[pb]^T$ yielding the clauses $[p(a \wedge b) = pa]^F$ and $[p(a \wedge b) = pb]^F$. These are simplified to $[a \wedge b = a]^F$ and $[a \wedge b = b]^F$ and subsequently stored in EXT, since their unification constraints are of boolean type, which makes them extensionally interesting. Since unification fails on these the SOS becomes empty now, leaving extensionality treatment as the only option for further processing. This now interprets the equalities as logical equivalences and yields (after subsumption) the clauses

$$[a]^F \vee [b]^F \qquad [b]^T \qquad [a]^T$$

from which an empty clause can be derived in two resolution steps.

Among the examined examples are also some interesting theorems about sets, where the application of the extensionality principles are essential for finding a proof.

Example 2. $2^{\{X|pX\}} \cap 2^{\{X|qX\}} = 2^{\{X|pX \wedge qX\}}$, where $p_{\iota \to o}$ and $q_{\iota \to o}$ are two arbitrary predicates. In Leo we code this theorem as:

$$\mathcal{P}(\lambda X_\iota.pX) \cap \mathcal{P}(\lambda X_\iota.qX) = \mathcal{P}(\lambda X_\iota.pX \wedge qX)$$

where the power-set $\mathcal{P}$ stands for $\lambda X_{\iota \to o}.\lambda Y_{\iota \to o}.Y \subset X$ and $\cap, \subset$ are similarly defined from $\wedge, \Rightarrow$. The current default heuristic of Leo's clause normalization procedure, does not replace the negated theorem by it's Leibniz formulation, but generates the following clause consisting of exactly one unification constraint

$$[(\lambda X_{\iota \to o}.(\forall Y_\iota.XY \Rightarrow pY) \wedge (\forall Y_\iota.XY \Rightarrow qY)) = (\lambda X_{\iota \to o}.(\forall Y_\iota.XY \Rightarrow (pY \wedge qY)))]^F$$

This unification constraint is not pre-unifiable, but note that the two functions on both hand sides can be identified with the help of the extensionality principles. Thus a higher-order theorem prover without extensionality treatment would either give up or would have to use the extensionality axioms, provided they are available in the search space. LEO instead makes use of its extensionality rules and first derives the following clause with rule *Func* (s_ι is a new Skolem constant):

$$[(\forall Y.sY \Rightarrow pY) \wedge (\forall Y.sY \Rightarrow qY)) = (\forall Y.sY \Rightarrow (pY \wedge qY)))]^F$$

Next LEO applies the rule *Equiv*, which first replaces the primitive equality symbol by an equivalence and second applies clause normalization. By this we get 12 new first-order clauses, and the rest of the proof is straightforward.

Similar examples are those discussed in [10]. When coding these theorems as above, then LEO discovers all proofs (except those for examples 56 and 57, where too many simple first-order clauses were generated), most of them within one second on a Pentium Pro 200. On these examples LEO outperforms well known first-order ATPs like SPASS, OTTER, PROTEIN, GANDALF and SETHEO (see http://www-irm.mathematik.hu-berlin.de/~ilf/miz2atp/mizstat.html). Especially example 111, which cannot be solved by any of the above provers, is trivial for LEO (10msec on a Pentium Pro 200).

Conclusion and Availability

The next logical steps to enhance the deductive power of LEO will be to extend the system to sorted logics [8], to extend the indexing scheme from co-simplification to higher-order pattern unification [9], to fine-tune the heuristics for extensionality treatment and finally to extend the system by a treatment for primitive equality.

The source code and proof examples (including detailed proofs for the example discussed above and those for the problems in [10]) are available via http://www.ags.uni-sb.de/projects/deduktion/projects/hot/leo/.

References

1. P. B. Andrews, M. Bishop, S. Issar, D. Nesmith, F. Pfenning, and H. Xi. TPS: A theorem proving system for classical type theory. *Journal of Automated Reasoning*, 16(3):321–353, 1996.
2. C. Benzmüller. A Calculus and a System Architecture for Extensional Higher-Order Resolution. Research Report 97-198, Department of Mathematical Sciences, Carnegie Mellon University, Pittsburgh,USA, June 1997.
3. C. Benzmüller and M. Kohlhase. Extensional Higher-Order Resolution. *Proc. CADE-15*, this volume, 1998.
4. P. Graf. *Term Indexing*. Number 1053 in LNCS. Springer Verlag, 1996.
5. X. Huang, M. Kerber, M. Kohlhase, E. Melis, D. Nesmith, J. Richts, and J. Siekmann. Keim: A toolkit for automated deduction. In Alan Bundy, editor, *Proc. CADE-13*, number 814 in LNAI, pages 807–810, 1994. Springer Verlag.
6. G. P. Huet. An unification algorithm for typed λ-calculus. *Theoretical Computer Science*, 1:27–57, 1975.
7. L. Klein. Indexing für Terme höherer Stufe. Master's thesis, FB Informatik, Universität des Saarlandes, 1997.
8. M. Kohlhase. *A Mechanization of Sorted Higher-Order Logic Based on the Resolution Principle*. PhD thesis, Universität des Saarlandes, 1994.

9. D. Miller. Unification under a mixed prefix. *Journal of Symbolic Computation*, 14:321–358, 1992.
10. Z. Trybulec and H. Swieczkowska. Boolean properties of sets. *Journal of Formalized Mathematics*, 1, 1989.

Superposition for Divisible Torsion-Free Abelian Groups

Uwe Waldmann

Max-Planck-Institut für Informatik, Im Stadtwald,
66123 Saarbrücken, Germany, uwe@mpi-sb.mpg.de

Abstract. Variable overlaps are one of the main sources for the inefficiency of AC or ACU theorem proving calculi. In the presence of the axioms of abelian groups or at least cancellative abelian monoids, ordering
restrictions allow us to avoid some of these overlaps, but inferences with
unshielded variables remain necessary. In divisible torsion-free abelian
groups, for instance the rational numbers, every clause can be transformed into an equivalent clause without unshielded variables. We show
how such a variable elimination algorithm can be integrated into the
cancellative superposition calculus. The resulting calculus is refutationally complete with respect to the axioms of divisible torsion-free abelian
groups and allows us to dispense with variable overlaps altogether. If
abstractions are performed eagerly, the calculus makes it furthermore
possible to avoid the computation of AC unifiers and AC orderings.

1   Introduction

If we want to tackle real life problems with an automated theorem prover, the
prover must operate in a heterogeneous world. In fields of application like program verification, it has to deal with uninterpreted function and predicate symbols that are specific for a particular domain, as well as with standard algebraic
structures or theories, such as the natural numbers, or abelian groups, or orderings. So both mathematical and meta-mathematical reasoning is required.

Unfortunately, handling algebraical theories naïvely by standard theorem
proving techniques leads to an explosion of the search space: As axioms like commutativity or associativity allow inferences with every clause containing a sum
as a subterm, they are extremely prolific. But the obvious alternative, namely
coupling a decision procedure for some algebraic theory to a theorem prover
in a black-box fashion, does not work well either: The requirement of sufficient
completeness practically excludes uninterpreted function symbols; and even in
situations where sufficient completeness is not a too restrictive requirement, insufficient communication between the general prover and the external decision
procedure makes the latter almost useless. It is therefore crucial to the performance of a prover that specialized techniques to work efficiently within standard
theories are not only coupled to but integrated tightly into the prover.

C. Kirchner and H. Kirchner (Eds.): Automated Deduction, CADE-15
LNAI 1421, pp. 144–159, 1998. © Springer–Verlag Berlin Heidelberg 1998

Typical examples of such techniques can be found in the superposition [2] and the AC-superposition calculus [1,9]. The former may be considered as the result of incorporating the equality axioms into the resolution calculus; the latter extends superposition further by integrating associativity and commutativity, using AC-unification and extended clauses. In both cases, inferences with the theory axioms and certain inferences involving variables can be shown to be superfluous. Together with strengthened ordering restrictions and redundancy criteria, this leads to a significant reduction of the search space. However, reasoning with the associativity and commutativity axioms remains difficult for an automated theorem prover, even if explicit inferences with the AC axioms can be avoided. There are two reasons for this: To begin with, the AC-unifiability problem is NP-complete, and minimal complete set of AC-unifiers may even have doubly exponential size. If the theory contains also the identity law

$$x + 0 \approx x, \tag{U}$$

then AC-unification can be replaced by ACU-unification, but the minimal complete set is still simply exponential. Furthermore, typical AC theorem proving calculi require an inference between literals $u_1 + \cdots + u_k \approx s$ and $v_1 + \cdots + v_l \approx t$ (via extended clauses) whenever *some* u_i is unifiable with *some* v_j [1,5,9]. Obviously, a variable in a sum can be unified with any part of any other sum—in this situation unification is completely unable to limit the search space.

In algebraic structures that are richer than abelian semigroups or monoids, it may be possible to mitigate the second problem by integrating additional axioms into the calculus. For instance, in the presence of the cancellation axiom

$$x + y \approx x + z \Rightarrow y \approx z, \tag{K}$$

or the inverse axiom

$$x + (-x) \approx 0, \tag{Inv}$$

(which implies (K)), the ordering conditions of the inference rules can be refined in such a way that only *maximal summands* u_i and v_j have to be overlapped (Ganzinger and Waldmann [3,7], Marché [4], Stuber [6]). In this way, the number of variable overlaps can be greatly reduced; however, inferences with unshielded, i.e., potentially maximal, variables remain necessary.

In non-trivial divisible torsion-free abelian groups (e. g., the rational numbers and rational vector spaces), the abelian group axioms ACUInv are extended by the torsion-freeness axioms

$$kx \approx ky \Rightarrow x \approx y \tag{T}$$

(for all $k \in \mathbf{N}^{>0}$), the divisibility axioms[1]

$$k \ div\text{-}by_k(x) \approx x \tag{Div}$$

---

[1] In non-skolemized form: $\forall k \in \mathbf{N}^{>0} \ \forall x \ \exists y : ky \approx x$.

(for all $k \in \mathbf{N}^{>0}$), and the non-triviality axiom[2]

$$a \not\approx 0 . \qquad\qquad (\text{Nt})$$

In such structures every clause can be transformed into an equivalent clause without unshielded variables. When we try to integrate this variable elimination algorithm into the superposition calculus, however, a typical discrepancy between computer algebra methods and first-order theorem proving methods becomes visible. In the variable elimination algorithm, the clauses are ordered with respect to the number of their variables: the less variables a clause has, the smaller it is. In superposition and related calculi, variables are objects that may be instantiated with small or with large terms, and the clause ordering has to be stable under instantiation. Consequently, the variable elimination algorithm is not necessarily a simplification in the superposition calculus: some ground instances of the transformed clause may be too large. It turns out, however, that all the critical instances can be handled by case analysis.

The resulting calculus requires neither extended clauses, nor variable overlaps, nor explicit inferences with the axioms ACUKT. Furthermore, even AC unification can be avoided, if clauses are fully abstracted eagerly.

2 Preliminaries

We work in a many-sorted framework and assume that the function symbol $+$ is declared on a sort G. If t is a term of sort G and $n \in \mathbf{N}$, then nt is an abbreviation for the n-fold sum $t + \cdots + t$; in particular, $0t = 0$ and $1t = t$.

A function symbol is called free, if it is different from 0 and $+$. A term is called atomic, if it is not a variable and its top symbol is different from $+$. We say that a term t occurs at the top of s, if there is a position $o \in \mathrm{pos}(s)$ such that $s|_o = t$ and for every proper prefix o' of o, $s(o')$ equals $+$; the term t occurs in s below a free function symbol, if there is an $o \in \mathrm{pos}(s)$ such that $s|_o = t$ and $s(o')$ is a free function symbol for some proper prefix o' of o. A variable x is called shielded in a clause C, if it occurs at least once below a free function symbol in C, or if it does not have sort G. Otherwise, x is called unshielded.

We say that an ACU-compatible ordering $\succ$ has the multiset property, if whenever a ground atomic term u is greater than v_i for every i in a finite non-empty index set I, then $u \succ \sum_{i \in I} v_i$.

From now on we will work *only* with ACU-congruence classes, rather than with terms. So *all* terms, equations, substitutions, inference rules, etc., are to be taken modulo ACU, i.e., as representatives of their congruence classes. The symbol $\succ$ will always denote an ACU-compatible ordering that has the multiset property and is total on ground ACU-congruence classes.[3]

---

[2] In non-skolemized form: $\exists y\colon y \not\approx 0$.

[3] For ground terms, such an ordering can be obtained for instance from the recursive path ordering with precedence $f_n \succ \ldots \succ f_1 \succ + \succ 0$ and multiset status for $+$ by comparing normal forms w.r.t. $x + 0 \to x$ and $0 + x \to x$. As we will see in

Without loss of generality we assume that the equality symbol $\approx$ is the only predicate of our language. Hence a literal is either an equation $t \approx t'$ or a negated equation $t \not\approx t'$, where t and t' have the same sort. The symbol $\dot\approx$ denotes either $\approx$ or $\not\approx$. A clause is a finite multiset of literals, usually written as a disjunction.

Let A be a ground literal $nu + \sum_{i \in I} s_i \dot\approx mu + \sum_{j \in J} t_j$, where u, s_i, and t_j are atomic terms, $n \geq m \geq 0$, $n \geq 1$, and $u \succ s_i$ and $u \succ t_j$ for all $i \in I$, $j \in J$. Then u is called the maximal atomic term of A, denoted by $mt(A)$.

The ordering $\succ_L$ on literals compares lexicographically first the maximal atomic terms of the literals, then the polarities (negative $\succ$ positive), then the multisets of all non-zero terms occurring at the top of the literals, and finally the multisets consisting of the left and right hand sides of the literals. The ordering $\succ_C$ on clauses is the multiset extension of the literal ordering $\succ_L$. Both $\succ_L$ and $\succ_C$ are noetherian and total on ground literals/clauses.

We denote the entailment relation modulo equality and ACUKT by $\models_{\text{ACUKT}}$. In other words, $\{C_1, \ldots, C_n\} \models_{\text{ACUKT}} C_0$ if and only if $\{C_1, \ldots, C_n\} \cup \text{ACUKT} \models C_0$.

3   Cancellative Superposition

The cancellative superposition calculus (Waldmann [7]) is a refutationally complete variant of the standard superposition calculus (Bachmair and Ganzinger [2]) for sets of clauses that contain the axioms ACUK and (optionally) T. It requires neither extended clauses, nor explicit inferences with the axioms ACUKT, nor symmetrizations. Compared with standard superposition or AC superposition calculi, the ordering restrictions of its inference rules are strengthened: Inferences are not only limited to maximal sides of maximal literals, but also to maximal summands thereof. As shielded variables of sort G are non-maximal, this implies in particular that there are no overlaps with such variables.

The inference system $\Re$ of the cancellative superposition calculus[4] consists of the inference rules *cancellation*, *equality resolution*, *standard superposition*, *cancellative superposition*, *abstraction*, *standard equality factoring*, and *cancellative equality factoring*. Ground versions of these rules are given below.

The following conditions are common to all the inference rules: Every literal involved in some inference must be maximal in the respective premise (except for the last but one literal in *equality factoring* inferences). A positive literal involved in a *superposition* or *abstraction* inference must be strictly maximal in the respective clause. In all *superposition* and *abstraction* inferences, the left premise is smaller than the right premise. In *standard superposition* and *abstraction* inferences, if s is a proper sum, then t (or w, respectively) occurs in a maximal atomic subterm of s.

Sect. 7, the compatibility requirement becomes practically void if clauses are fully abstracted eagerly.

[4] In [7], this inference system is denoted by $CS\text{-}Inf_{N>0}$.

Cancellation

$$\frac{C' \vee mu + s \mathrel{\dot{\approx}} m'u + s'}{C' \vee (m - m')u + s \mathrel{\dot{\approx}} s'}$$

if $m \geq m' \geq 1$ and $u \succ s$, $u \succ s'$.

Equality Resolution

$$\frac{C' \vee u \mathrel{\not\approx} u}{C'}$$

if either $u = 0$ or u does not have sort G.

Standard Superposition

$$\frac{D' \vee t \approx t' \qquad C' \vee s[t] \mathrel{\dot{\approx}} s'}{D' \vee C' \vee s[t'] \mathrel{\dot{\approx}} s'}$$

if s does not have sort G or t occurs below a free function symbol in s, and $s[t] \succ s'$, $t \succ t'$.

Canc. Superposition

$$\frac{D' \vee nu + t \approx t' \qquad C' \vee mu + s \mathrel{\dot{\approx}} s'}{D' \vee C' \vee \psi s + \chi t' \mathrel{\dot{\approx}} \chi t + \psi s'}$$

if $m \geq 1$, $n \geq 1$, $\psi = n/\gcd(m,n)$, $\chi = m/\gcd(m,n)$, and $u \succ s$, $u \succ s'$, $u \succ t$, $u \succ t'$.

Abstraction

$$\frac{D' \vee nu + t \approx t' \qquad C' \vee s[w] \mathrel{\dot{\approx}} s'}{C' \vee y \mathrel{\not\approx} w \vee s[y] \mathrel{\dot{\approx}} s'}$$

if $n \geq 1$, $w = mu + q$ occurs in s immediately below some free function symbol, $m \geq 1$, $nu + t$ is not a subterm of w, and $u \succ t$, $u \succ t'$, $s[w] \succ s'$.

Standard Eq. Factoring

$$\frac{C' \vee u \approx v' \vee u \approx u'}{C' \vee u' \mathrel{\not\approx} v' \vee u \approx v'}$$

if u, u', and v' do not have sort G, and $u \succ u'$, $u \succ v'$.

Canc. Eq. Factoring

$$\frac{C' \vee nu + t \approx n'u + t' \vee mu + s \approx s'}{C' \vee \psi t + \chi s' \mathrel{\not\approx} \chi s + \psi t' \vee nu + t \approx n'u + t'}$$

if $m \geq 1$, $n > n' \geq 0$, $\nu = n - n'$, $\psi = m/\gcd(m,\nu)$, $\chi = \nu/\gcd(m,\nu)$, and $u \succ s$, $u \succ s'$, $u \succ t$, $u \succ t'$.

The inference system $\mathfrak{K}$ is sound with respect to ACUKT: For every inference with premises $C_1, \ldots, C_n$ and conclusion C_0, we have $\{C_1, \ldots, C_n\} \models_{\text{ACUKT}} C_0$.

Unification and equality constraints are the two commonly used devices to lift resolution-style inference systems from ground to non-ground formulae. The latter technique is generally preferable in practice: Constraint superposition subsumes the so-called basic strategies and hence leads to a significant reduction of the number of possible inferences. Furthermore, constraints allow to delay the computation of unifiers. This is particularly advantageous in AC or ACU calculi, as the number of AC- or ACU-unifiers may be (doubly) exponential with respect to the size of the inputs. In our context, the use of constraints is not quite unproblematic, since, depending of the structure of the constraint, variable elimination may be prohibited. For simplicity, we restrict ourselves in this paper to lifting via unification.

To lift the inference rules *equality resolution*, *standard superposition*, and *standard equality factoring* to non-ground premises, we proceed as in the standard superposition calculus (Bachmair and Ganzinger [2]), so that for instance the *standard superposition* rule has the following form:

Standard Superposition

$$\frac{D' \vee t \approx t' \quad C' \vee s[w] \approx s'}{(D' \vee C' \vee s[t'] \approx s')\sigma}$$

if the following conditions are satisfied:

- w is not a variable.
- s does not have sort G or w occurs below a free function symbol in s.
- σ is a most general ACU-unifier of t and w.
- $s[w] \not\preceq s', t \not\preceq t'$.

As long as all variables in our clauses are shielded, we can lift the inference rules *cancellation*, *cancellative superposition*, and *cancellative equality factoring* in a similar way as the *standard superposition* rule. We only have to take into account that, in a clause $C = C' \vee A$, the maximal literal A need no longer have the form $mu + s \approx s'$, where u is the unique maximal atomic term. Rather, a literal such as $f(x) + 2f(y) + b \not\approx c$ may contain several (distinct but ACU-unifiable) maximal atomic terms u_k with multiplicities m_k, where k ranges over some finite non-empty index set K. We obtain thus $A = \sum_{k \in K} m_k u_k + s \approx s'$, where $\sum_{k \in K} m_k$ corresponds to m in the ground literal above. As in the *standard superposition* rule, the substitution σ that unifies all u_k (and the corresponding terms v_l from the other premise) is applied to the conclusion. For instance, the *cancellative superposition* rule has now the following form:

Cancellative Superposition

$$\frac{D' \vee A_2 \quad C' \vee A_1}{(D' \vee C' \vee A_0)\sigma}$$

if the following conditions are satisfied:

- $A_1 = \sum_{k \in K} m_k u_k + s \approx s'$.
- $A_2 = \sum_{l \in L} n_l v_l + t \approx t'$.
- $m = \sum_{k \in K} m_k \geq 1, n = \sum_{l \in L} n_l \geq 1$.
- $\psi = n/\gcd(m,n), \chi = m/\gcd(m,n)$.
- u is one of the u_k or v_l ($k \in K, l \in L$).

- σ is a most general ACU-unifier of all u_k and v_l $(k \in K, l \in L)$.
- $u \not\leq s$, $u \not\leq s'$, $u \not\leq t$, $u \not\leq t'$.
- $A_0 = \psi s + \chi t' \approx \chi t + \psi s'$.

The lifted versions of the rules *cancellation* and *cancellative equality factoring* are obtained analogously. The only inference rule for which lifting is not so straightforward is the *abstraction* rule. Here we have to take into account that the term to be abstracted out may be a sum containing variables at the top [7].

In the presence of unshielded variables, it is still possible to devise lifted inference rules that produce only finitely many conclusions for a given tuple of premises. These rules, however, show the familiar weakness of AC-superposition calculi: Variable overlaps become necessary for completeness, leading to an enormous growth of the search space. We do not repeat these rules here, as we will show in the following sections that the additional theory axioms DivInvNt make it possible to eliminate unshielded variables completely.

The elimination of unshielded variables happens in two steps. First we show that every clause is logically equivalent to a clause without unshielded variables. Then this elimination algorithm has to be integrated into the cancellative superposition calculus. Our main tool for the second step is the concept of redundancy.

Let $C_0, C_1, \dots, C_k$ be clauses and let θ be a substitution such that $C_i\theta$ is ground for all $i \in \{0, \dots, k\}$. If there are inferences (other than *abstraction* inferences)

$$\frac{C_k \ \dots \ C_1}{C_0}$$

and

$$\frac{C_k\theta \ \dots \ C_1\theta}{C_0\theta}$$

then the latter is called a ground instance of the former. Ground instances of *abstraction* inferences are defined analogously, except that $C_0\theta$ is no longer required to be ground.

Let N be a set of clauses, let $\overline{N}$ be the set of ground instances of clauses in N. An inference is called ACUKT-redundant with respect to N if for each of its ground instances with conclusion $C_0\theta$ and maximal premise $C\theta$ we have $\{ D \in \overline{N} \mid D \prec_c C\theta \} \models_{\text{ACUKT}} C_0\theta$.[5] A clause C is called ACUKT-redundant with respect to N, if for every ground instance $C\theta$, $\{ D \in \overline{N} \mid D \prec_c C\theta \} \models_{\text{ACUKT}} C\theta$.

A set N of clauses is called saturated with respect to an inference system, if every inference from clauses in N is ACUKT-redundant with respect to N.

Theorem 1. *The inference system $\mathfrak{K}$ is refutationally complete with respect to ACUKT, that is, a $\mathfrak{K}$-saturated set of clauses is unsatisfiable modulo ACUKT if and only if it contains the empty clause (Waldmann [7]).*

---

[5] For *abstraction* inferences one has to consider all ground instances $C_0\theta\rho$ of $C_0\theta = y \not\approx w\theta \lor C_0'\theta[y]$ with $y\rho \prec w\theta$.

In the cancellative superposition calculus, the main application of the redundancy concept is simplification: A prover produces a saturated set of clauses by computing inferences according to some fair strategy and adding the conclusions of non-redundant inferences to the current set of clauses. At any time of the saturation process, the prover is permitted to replace a clause by an equivalent set of new clauses, provided the new clauses make the simplified clause redundant. As we will see later, in the new calculus for divisible torsion-free abelian groups, redundancy is already essential to prove the refutational completeness of the inference rules themselves.

4   Variable Elimination

It is well-known that the theory of divisible torsion-free abelian groups allows quantifier elimination: For every formula over 0, $+$, and $\approx$ there exists an equivalent quantifier-free formula. In particular, every closed formula over this vocabulary is provably true or false. In the presence of free function symbols (and possibly other sorts), there is of course no way to eliminate all variables from a clause, but we can at least give an effective method to eliminate all *unshielded* variables. Using this elimination algorithm, we will then construct a new inference system that is closed under clauses without unshielded variables.

Let x be a variable of sort G. We define a binary relation $\rightarrow_x$ over clauses by

CancelVar $C' \vee mx + s \mathrel{\dot{\approx}} m'x + s' \quad \rightarrow_x \quad C' \vee (m-m')x + s \mathrel{\dot{\approx}} s'$
if $m \geq m' \geq 1$.

ElimNeg $C' \vee mx + s \not\approx s' \quad \rightarrow_x \quad C'$
if $m \geq 1$ and x does not occur in C', s, s'.

ElimPos $C' \vee m_1 x + s_1 \approx s_1' \vee \ldots \vee m_k x + s_k \approx s_k' \quad \rightarrow_x \quad C'$
if $m_i \geq 1$ and x does not occur in C', s_i, s_i', for $1 \leq i \leq k$.

Coalesce $C' \vee mx + s \not\approx s' \vee nx + t \mathrel{\dot{\approx}} t'$
$\rightarrow_x \quad C' \vee mx + s \not\approx s' \vee \psi t + \chi s' \approx \psi t' + \chi s$
if $m \geq 1$, $n \geq 1$, $\psi = m/\gcd(m,n)$, $\chi = n/\gcd(m,n)$, and x does not occur at the top of s, s', t, t'.

Lemma 2. *If $C_0 \rightarrow_x C_1$, then $\{C_1\} \models_{\text{ACUKT}} C_0$ and $\{C_0\} \cup \text{DivInvNt} \models_{\text{ACUKT}} C_1$. If $C_0\theta$ is a ground instance of C_0, then $\{C_1\theta\} \models_{\text{ACUKT}} C_0\theta$.*

Proof. If $C_0 \rightarrow_x C_1$ by *CancelVar*, the equivalence of C_0 and C_1 modulo ACUKT follows from cancellation; for *Coalesce*, from cancellation and torsion-freeness. The soundness of *ElimNeg* follows from the divisibility and and inverse axiom, for *ElimPos* it is implied by torsion-freeness and non-triviality [7].   □

Lemma 3. *The relation $\to_x$ is noetherian.*

If $C_0 \to_x C_1$, then every variable or atomic term occurring (negatively) in C_1 occurs also (negatively) in C_0. Consequently, if x occurs in both C_0 and C_1, and x is unshielded in C_0, then x is unshielded in C_1. Conversely, it is easy to check that every clause in which x occurs unshielded is reducible with respect to $\to_x$. Hence, if C_1 is a normal form of C_0 with respect to $\to_x$, and x occurs unshielded in C_0, then x does not occur in C_1.

The binary relation $\to_{\text{elim}}$ over clauses is defined in such a way that $C_0 \to_{\text{elim}} C_1$ if and only if C_0 contains an unshielded variable x and C_1 is a normal form of C_0 with respect to $\to_x$. As $C_0 \to_{\text{elim}} C_1$ implies $\text{var}(C_1) \subset \text{var}(C_0)$, and as the number of variables in a clause is finite, the relation $\to_{\text{elim}}$ is obviously noetherian. For any clause C, let $\text{elim}(C)$ denote some (arbitrary but fixed) normal form of C with respect to the relation $\to_{\text{elim}}$.

Lemma 4. *For every clause C, $\text{elim}(C)$ contains no unshielded variables.*

Lemma 5. *For every clause C, every variable or atomic term occurring (negatively) in $\text{elim}(C)$ occurs also (negatively) in C. For every ground instance $C\theta$, every atomic term occurring (negatively) in $\text{elim}(C)\theta$ occurs also (negatively) in $C\theta$.*

Lemma 6. *For every clause C, $\{C\} \cup \text{DivInvNt} \models_{\text{ACUKT}} \text{elim}(C)$ and $\{\text{elim}(C)\} \models_{\text{ACUKT}} C$. For every ground instance $C\theta$, $\{\text{elim}(C)\theta\} \models_{\text{ACUKT}} C\theta$.*

Using the technique sketched so far, every clause C_0 can be transformed into a clause $\text{elim}(C_0)$ that does not contain unshielded variables, follows from C_0 and the divisible torsion-free abelian group axioms, and implies C_0 modulo ACUKT. Obviously, we can perform this transformation for all initially given clauses before we start the saturation process. However, the inference system $\mathfrak{K}$ is not closed under clauses without unshielded variables, i.e., inferences from clauses without unshielded variables may produce clauses with unshielded variables. To eliminate these clauses *during* the saturation process, logical equivalence is not sufficient: We have to require either that the transformed clause $\text{elim}(C_0)$ makes the original clause C_0 redundant, or at least that it makes the inference producing C_0 redundant.

The second condition it slightly easier to satisfy: Let ι be an inference with maximal premise C and conclusion C_0. For the redundancy of C_0 it is necessary that each of its ground inferences $C_0\theta$ follows from ground instances of clauses in N that are smaller than $C_0\theta$. For the redundancy of ι, it is sufficient that for each ground instance of ι, $C_0\theta$ follows from ground instances of clauses in N that are smaller than $C\theta$. As demonstrated by the following example, however, even the latter property is not guaranteed for our variable elimination algorithm.

Example 7. Let the ordering on constants be given by $b \succ c$ and consider the clause

$$C \;=\; 3x \not\approx c \lor x + f(z) \approx 0 \lor f(x) + b \approx f(y).$$

A cancellation inference ι from C yields

$$C_0 \;=\; 3x \not\approx c \vee x + f(z) \approx 0 \vee b \approx 0.$$

The conclusion C_0 contains the unshielded variable x. Eliminating x from C_0, we obtain

$$\mathrm{elim}(C_0) \;=\; c + 3f(z) \approx 0 \vee b \approx 0.$$

Now let $\theta = \{x \mapsto b,\, z \mapsto b\}$, then

$$\mathrm{elim}(C_0)\theta \;=\; c + 3f(b) \approx 0 \vee b \approx 0$$

is not only strictly larger than

$$C_0\theta \;=\; 3b \not\approx c \vee b + f(b) \approx 0 \vee b \approx 0,$$

but even strictly larger than

$$C\theta \;=\; 3b \not\approx c \vee b + f(b) \approx 0 \vee f(b) + b \approx f(b).$$

Hence the clause $\mathrm{elim}(C_0)$ makes neither C_0 nor the inference ι, which produces C_0, redundant.

To integrate the variable elimination algorithm into the cancellative superposition calculus, it has to be supplemented by a case analysis technique.

5   Pivotal Terms

Let ι be an inference. We call the unifying substitution that is computed during ι and applied to the conclusion the pivotal substitution of ι. (For *abstraction* inferences and all ground inferences, the pivotal substitution is the identity mapping.) If A is the last literal of the last premise of ι, we call $A\sigma$ the pivotal literal of ι. Finally, if u_0 is the atomic term that is cancelled out in ι, or in which some subterm is replaced or abstracted out,[6] then we call $u_0\sigma$ the pivotal term of ι.

Two properties of pivotal terms are important for us: First, whenever an inference ι from clauses *without* unshielded variables produces a conclusion *with* unshielded variables, then all these unshielded variables occur in the pivotal term of ι. Second, no atomic term in the conclusion of ι can be larger than the pivotal term of ι.

Lemma 8. *In every ground inference, the pivotal term is maximal among the atomic terms occurring in the premises, and the pivotal literal is maximal among the literals of the premises.[7]*

---

[6] More precisely, u_0 is the maximal atomic subterm of s containing t (or w) in *standard superposition* or *abstraction* inferences, and the term u in all other inferences.

[7] This lemma does not hold, if selection functions are taken into account. Neither does it hold for the *merging paramodulation* rule of Bachmair and Ganzinger [2].

Lemma 9. *Let ι be an inference from clauses without unshielded variables, let $\iota\theta$ be a ground instance of ι. Then the pivotal term of $\iota\theta$ is a ground instance of the pivotal term of ι.*

Whenever we talk about a ground instance $\iota\theta$ of an inference ι, we assume without loss of generality that θ is defined on all variables of the pivotal term u_0 of ι, and that the pivotal term of $\iota\theta$ is $u_0\theta$.

Lemma 10. *Let ι be an inference from clauses without unshielded variables; let C_0 be the conclusion and σ be the pivotal substitution of ι. Let C be some premise of ι (if ι is an abstraction inference: the second premise). If t is an atomic term that occurs in $C\sigma$, but not in C_0, then t is a subterm of the pivotal term of ι.*

Corollary 11. *Let ι be an inference from clauses without unshielded variables. Then every variable that is unshielded in the conclusion of ι occurs in the pivotal term of ι.*

Lemma 12. *Let ι be a non-abstraction inference with maximal premise C and conclusion C_0; let $D_0 = \mathrm{elim}(C_0)$. Let $\iota\theta$ be a ground instance of ι, and let $A\theta$ be the pivotal literal of $\iota\theta$. If $C\theta \preceq_c D_0\theta$, then the multiset difference $D_0\theta \setminus C_0\theta$ contains a literal $A_1\theta$, such that $A_1\theta$ has the same polarity as $A\theta$ and the pivotal term of $\iota\theta$ occurs in $A_1\theta$.*

Lemma 13. *Let ι be a non-abstraction inference from clauses without unshielded variables with maximal premise C, conclusion C_0, pivotal literal A, and pivotal term u; let $D_0 = \mathrm{elim}(C_0)$. Let $\iota\theta$ be a ground instance of ι. If $C\theta \preceq_c D_0\theta$, then the multiset difference $D_0 \setminus C_0$ contains a literal A_1, such that:*

- *A_1 has the same polarity as A,*
- *there is an atomic term u_1 occurring at the top of A_1,*
- *for every minimal complete set U of ACU-unifiers of u and u_1, there is a $\tau \in U$ such that $C_0\theta$ is a ground instance of $C_0\tau$.*

Furthermore, for every $\tau \in U$, $C_0\tau$ has no unshielded variables.

A similar lemma can be proved for *abstraction* inferences.

6   Integration of the Elimination Algorithm

Using the results of the previous section, we can now transform the inference system $\mathfrak{K}$ into a new inference system that is closed under clauses without unshielded variables. The new system $\mathfrak{D}$ is given by two meta-inference rules:

Eliminating Inference

$$\frac{C_n \;\; \ldots \;\; C_1}{\operatorname{elim}(C_0)}$$

if the following condition is satisfied:

$-\;\dfrac{C_n \;\; \ldots \;\; C_1}{C_0}$ is a $\mathfrak{K}$-inference.

Instantiating Inference

$$\frac{C_n \;\; \ldots \;\; C_1}{C_0 \tau}$$

if the following conditions are satisfied:

- $-\;\dfrac{C_n \;\; \ldots \;\; C_1}{C_0}$ is a $\mathfrak{K}$-inference with pivotal literal A and pivotal term u.
- The multiset difference $\operatorname{elim}(C_0) \setminus C_0$ contains a literal A_1 with the same polarity as A.
- An atomic term u_1 occurs at the top of A_1.
- τ is contained in a minimal complete set of ACU-unifiers of u and u_1.

Lemma 14. *Let N be a set of clauses without unshielded variables. If every $\mathfrak{D}$-inference from clauses in N is redundant with respect to N, then every $\mathfrak{K}$-inference from clauses in N is redundant with respect to N.*

Proof. This follows from the definition of $\mathfrak{D}$, Lemma 13, and Lemma 6.   □

Example 15. Let us consider once more the cancellation inference ι from Ex. 7:

$$\frac{3x \not\approx c \;\vee\; x + f(z) \approx 0 \;\vee\; f(x) + b \approx f(y)}{3x \not\approx c \;\vee\; x + f(z) \approx 0 \;\vee\; b \approx 0}$$

We denote the premise of ι by C and the conclusion by C_0. The conclusion contains one unshielded variable, namely x, which occurs in the pivotal term $f(x)$. Eliminating x from C_0, we obtain

$$\operatorname{elim}(C_0) \;=\; c + 3f(z) \approx 0 \;\vee\; b \approx 0 .$$

The multiset difference $\operatorname{elim}(C_0) \setminus C_0$ equals $\{c + 3f(z) \approx 0\}$; the pivotal term $f(x)$ and $f(z)$ are ACU-unifiable. The singleton set containing the substitution $\tau = \{x \mapsto z\}$ is a minimal complete set of ACU-unifiers. Applying τ to C_0 we obtain the clause

$$C_0 \tau \;=\; 3z \not\approx c \;\vee\; z + f(z) \approx 0 \;\vee\; b \approx 0 .$$

The clause $\operatorname{elim}(C_0)$ makes all ground instances $\iota\theta$ redundant that satisfy $C\theta \succ_c \operatorname{elim}(C_0)\theta$, that is, in particular, all ground instances with $x\theta \succ z\theta$. The only remaining ground instances are those where $x\theta = z\theta$; these are made redundant by $C_0 \tau$.

Theorem 16. *If a set of clauses is saturated with respect to $\mathfrak{D}$ and none of the clauses contains unshielded variables, then it is also saturated with respect to $\mathfrak{K}$.*

Of course, the calculus $\mathfrak{D}$ is sound only for sets of clauses that contain the axioms of non-trivial divisible torsion-free abelian groups, that is ACUKT $\cup$ DivInvNt. The axioms ACUKT are already integrated into the cancellative superposition calculus; hence, no inferences with these axioms are required. Does the same hold for DivInvNt? If there are no clauses with unshielded variables, then a non-*abstraction* inference with, say, the inverse axiom is only possible if the maximal atomic term $-x$ of the inverse axiom overlaps with a maximal atomic term in another clause, that is, if the negation function occurs in another clause. Similarly, for a non-*abstraction* inference with one of the divisibility axioms $k\ div\text{-}by_k(x) \approx x$ it is necessary that some other clause contains the function symbol $div\text{-}by_k$. The only inferences that are possible if the negation function or the symbol $div\text{-}by_k$ does not occur otherwise are *abstraction* inferences where the theory axiom is the first premise. Note that in this case the conclusion does not depend on the first premise; so, although there are infinitely many divisibility axioms, it suffices to compute *one* such inference. In fact, as we will show in the next section, by performing abstraction eagerly, *abstraction* inferences and inferences with DivInvNt during the saturation process can be avoided completely.

7   Abstraction

A clause C is called fully abstracted, if no non-variable term of sort G occurs below a free function symbol in C. Every clause C can be transformed into an equivalent fully abstracted clause abs(C) by iterated rewriting

$$C[f(\ldots,t,\ldots)] \quad \rightarrow \quad x \not\approx t \vee C[f(\ldots,x,\ldots)],$$

where x is a new variable and t is a non-variable term of sort G occurring immediately below the free function symbol f in C.

Let us define a new inference system $\mathfrak{D}^{abs}$ that contains exactly the inference rules of $\mathfrak{D}$ with the exception of the *abstraction* rule. As *abstraction* inferences from fully abstracted clauses are impossible, the following theorem is an obvious consequence of Thm. 16.

Theorem 17. *If a set of fully abstracted clauses is saturated with respect to $\mathfrak{D}^{abs}$ and none of the clauses contains unshielded variables, then it is also saturated with respect to $\mathfrak{K}$.*

The following two lemmas show that, for effective saturation of a set of clauses with respect to $\mathfrak{D}^{abs}$, it is sufficient to perform full abstraction once in the beginning.

Lemma 18. *Let C be a fully abstracted clause. Then elim(C) is fully abstracted.*

Lemma 19. *Let ι be a $\mathfrak{D}^{abs}$-inference (or more generally, $\mathfrak{D}$-inference) from fully abstracted clauses without unshielded variables. Then the conclusion of ι is a fully abstracted clause without unshielded variables.*

If we replace every clause C in the input of the inference system by the logically equivalent clause $\mathrm{elim}(\mathrm{abs}(C))$ before we start the saturation process, then all the clauses produced by $\mathfrak{D}^{abs}$-inferences are again fully abstracted and do not contain unshielded variables.

Full abstraction is not unproblematic from an efficiency point of view. It increases the number of variables and the number of incomparable terms in a clause, which both add to the number of inferences in which this clause can participate.[8]

On the other hand, the cancellative superposition calculus requires many *abstraction* inferences anyway, Furthermore, full abstraction has several important advantages for an implementation: First, if all clauses are fully abstracted, then the terms that have to be compared or unified during the saturation have the property that they do not contain the operator $+$. For such terms, ACU-unification and syntactic unification are equivalent. Thus we may reformulate $\mathfrak{D}^{abs}$ in terms of syntactic unification. In an implementation of the calculus, this means that efficient indexing techniques for non-AC calculi become available again. Secondly, full abstraction greatly enlarges the assortment of orderings with which the calculus can be parameterized: We are no longer restricted to the small number of known ACU-orderings, but may use an arbitrary reduction ordering over terms not containing $+$ that is total on ground terms and for which 0 is minimal: As every ordering of this kind can be extended to an ordering that is ACU-compatible and has the multiset property (Waldmann [8]), the completeness proof is still justified. In particular, full abstraction allows us to use classes of orderings that are more efficient in practice than LPO or RPO, for instance the Knuth-Bendix ordering. Finally we note that, if all clauses are fully abstracted, then the negation function or the symbols $div\text{-}by_k$ can occur only at the top of a clause. In this case, it is easy to eliminate them initially from all non-theory clauses, so that there is no need for further inferences with the theory clauses DivInvNt during the saturation.

8   Conclusions

To a large extent, the inefficiency of AC theorem proving methods is due to the necessity of variable overlaps. Some of these overlaps can be avoided in algebraic structures that are richer than abelian semigroups: Calculi for cancellative abelian monoids or abelian groups exclude inferences involving shielded variables by means of ordering restrictions; besides, many occurrences of unshielded variables can be eliminated by appropriate simplification techniques. Some overlaps with variables in sums remain necessary, however.

---

[8] Note that *equality resolution* inferences with the new variables that are introduced by abstraction are prohibited by the ordering restrictions, though.

In the case of divisible torsion-free abelian groups, such as the rational numbers or rational vector spaces, unshielded variables can be eliminated completely. We have presented two calculi for first-order equational theorem proving that integrate this variable elimination algorithm into the cancellative superposition calculus. The resulting calculi are refutationally complete without requiring variable overlaps or explicit inferences with the clauses ACUKT.

Our two calculi differ in the way they handle abstraction. The calculus $\mathfrak{D}$ contains an explicit *abstraction* inference rule with the usual ordering restrictions. By contrast, for the calculus $\mathfrak{D}^{abs}$ it is required that all input clauses are fully abstracted in advance. Full abstraction is detrimental to the search space, as it increases the number of inferences in which a clause can participate. On the other hand, it allows us to dispense with ACU-unification and ACU-orderings. Both these operations are costly likewise, and being able to avoid them greatly simplifies the integration of the calculus into existing theorem provers, whose performance depends crucially on efficient indexing data structures. It remains to be investigated whether full abstraction is generally advantageous in practice.

Acknowledgments: I would like to thank Harald Ganzinger for helpful discussions and in particular for pointing out to me that abstraction allows us to avoid ACU-unification completely. I also want to thank Jürgen Stuber for his comments on a previous version of this paper.

References

1. Leo Bachmair and Harald Ganzinger. Associative-commutative superposition. In Nachum Dershowitz and Naomi Lindenstrauss, eds., *Conditional and Typed Rewriting Systems, 4th International Workshop, CTRS-94*, Jerusalem, Israel, July 13–15, 1994, LNCS 968, pp. 1–14. Springer-Verlag.
2. Leo Bachmair and Harald Ganzinger. Rewrite-based equational theorem proving with selection and simplification. *Journal of Logic and Computation*, 4(3):217–247, 1994.
3. Harald Ganzinger and Uwe Waldmann. Theorem proving in cancellative abelian monoids (extended abstract). In Michael A. McRobbie and John K. Slaney, eds., *Automated Deduction – CADE-13, 13th International Conference on Automated Deduction*, New Brunswick, NJ, USA, July 30–August 3, 1996, LNAI 1104, pp. 388–402. Springer-Verlag.
4. Claude Marché. Normalized rewriting: an alternative to rewriting modulo a set of equations. *Journal of Symbolic Computation*, 21(3):253–288, March 1996.
5. Michaël Rusinowitch and Laurent Vigneron. Automated deduction with associative-commutative operators. *Applicable Algebra in Engineering, Communication and Computing*, 6(1):23–56, January 1995.
6. Jürgen Stuber. Superposition theorem proving for abelian groups represented as integer modules. In Harald Ganzinger, ed., *Rewriting Techniques and Applications, 7th International Conference, RTA-96*, New Brunswick, NJ, USA, July 27–30, 1996, LNCS 1103, pp. 33–47. Springer-Verlag.
7. Uwe Waldmann. *Cancellative Abelian Monoids in Refutational Theorem Proving*. PhD thesis, Universität des Saarlandes, Saarbrücken, Germany, 1997. http://www.mpi-sb.mpg.de/~uwe/paper/PhD.ps.gz.

8. Uwe Waldmann. Extending reduction orderings to ACU-compatible reduction orderings. http://www.mpi-sb.mpg.de/~uwe/paper/ACUExt.ps.gz. Submitted, 1997.
9. Ulrich Wertz. First-order theorem proving modulo equations. Technical Report MPI-I-92-216, Max-Planck-Institut für Informatik, Saarbrücken, Germany, April 1992.

Strict Basic Superposition

Leo Bachmair[*][1] and Harald Ganzinger[**][2]

[1] Comp. Sci. Dept., SUNY at Stony Brook, NY 11794, U.S.A.,
leo@cs.sunysb.edu
[2] MPI Informatik, D-66123 Saarbrücken, Germany,
hg@mpi-sb.mpg.de

Abstract. In this paper we solve a long-standing open problem by show-ing that strict superposition—that is, superposition without equality factoring—is refutationally complete. The difficulty of the problem arises from the fact that the strict calculus, in contrast to the standard calcu-lus with equality factoring, is not compatible with arbitrary removal of tautologies, so that the usual techniques for proving the (refutational) completeness of paramodulation calculi are not directly applicable. We deal with the problem by introducing a suitable notion of *direct rewrite proof* and modifying proof techniques based on candidate models and counterexamples in that we define these concepts in terms of, not se-mantic truth, but direct provability. We introduce a corresponding con-cept of redundancy with which strict superposition is compatible and that covers most simplification techniques. We also show that certain superposition inferences *from* variables are redundant—a result that is relevant, surprisingly, in the context of equality elimination methods.

1 Introduction

Superposition, the main deductive inference rule in completion, combines unifi-cation with the replacement of subterms by equal terms. In ordered completion, which is the variant relevant for theorem proving, the key restriction imposed on inferences is that only *maximal* sides of equation be used to replace subterms of *maximal* sides of other equations, where terms are compared in a given ordering. Completion deals only with unit equations, but various extensions of superposi-tion to non-unit clauses have been proposed, see (Bachmair & Ganzinger 1994) for a detailed discussion. The natural additional restrictions on clausal inferences are that the literals involved in an equational replacement be *maximal* in their respective clauses. But proving that such a restricted version of paramodulation (which superposition is in the clause context) is refutationally complete turned out to be an elusive problem.

* Work supported in part by NSF under grants INT-9314412 and CCR-9510072.
** Work supported in part by DFG under grants Ga 261/7-1 and Ga 261/8-1, and by the ESPRIT Basic Research Working Group 22457 (CCL II).

C. Kirchner and H. Kirchner (Eds.): Automated Deduction, CADE-15
LNAI 1421, pp. 160–174, 1998. © Springer–Verlag Berlin Heidelberg 1998

The superposition calculi introduced in Bachmair & Ganzinger (1990) impose all the restrictions, but contain additional inference rules, such as equality factoring, that need to be applied to certain (non-Horn) clauses. The calculus ZK proposed by Zhang & Kapur is closely related to superposition. It is less restrictive in that replacements are allowed in non-maximal terms of maximal negative equations, but on the other hand contains no equality factoring or similar inference rule. In (Zhang & Kapur 1988), ZK was claimed to be refutationally complete, even in the presence of eager simplification of clauses by a variant of contextual rewriting that is sufficiently strong to eliminate all tautologies. However, Bachmair & Ganzinger (1990) have shown that tautology deletion renders ZK incomplete. Since then refutational completeness of ZK when tautologies are not eliminated, has remained an open problem.

In (Bachmair & Ganzinger 1990, Bachmair & Ganzinger 1994) it was shown that superposition can be combined with a variety of simplification techniques including those known from completion. A general notion of redundancy based on logical entailment from smaller clauses justifies the admissibility of these techniques. In this context tautologies are always redundant and can be deleted at any point during the theorem proving process. The proof techniques developed in these papers are therefore not directly applicable to ZK. It was also not clear to what extent other simplification techniques, such as subsumption or (standard or contextual) rewriting, are compatible with ZK. (The question is especially important from a practical point of view, as calculi that do not allow reasonably strong simplification mechanisms are virtually useless for automated theorem proving.)

In this paper we study strict superposition – superposition without equality factoring. We prove that this calculus, which is a substantially more restrictive version of ZK, is not only refutationally complete, but is also compatible with a notion of redundancy that covers most, though not all, of the major simplification techniques. Our results are obtained by introducing a suitable notion of *direct rewrite proof* and modifying proof techniques based on candidate models and counterexamples. We define these concepts, not in terms of semantic truth, but in terms of direct provability. Another contribution of this paper is that it makes the method of candidate models and counterexamples more transparent, separating the two central concepts: (i) the reduction of counterexamples by inferences, and (ii) notions of redundancy that provide approximate characterizations of clauses that cannot be minimal counterexamples. Reasoning about strict superposition requires "weak" counterexamples and, therefore, a weaker notion of redundancy. Lifting is more complicated for strict superposition and requires the techniques of basic superposition (Bachmair, Ganzinger, Lynch & Snyder 1992, Nieuwenhuis & Rubio 1992a). We describe the basic ideas and concepts; proofs can be found in (Bachmair & Ganzinger 1997).

2 Preliminaries

We assume the usual notions and notations about equational clauses, rewrite systems, and reduction orderings. For simplicity, we assume that equality, denoted by the symbol $\approx$, is the only predicate. (Equations are taken to be symmetric, so that we do not distinguish between atoms $s \approx t$ and $t \approx s$.) An *equality (Herbrand) interpretation* is a congruence on ground terms over the given signature.

Let $\succ$ be a reduction ordering (on terms). We say that a set of ground equations I is a *convergent ground rewrite system* (with respect to $\succ$) if (i) all equations $s \approx t$ in I are orientable with respect to $\succ$ (i.e., either $s \succ t$ or $t \succ s$) and (ii) the corresponding set of oriented *rewrite rules* is confluent (in the usual sense). We use such convergent ground rewrite systems to represent equality interpretations. An atom $s \approx t$ is true in the *interpretation represented by I* if, and only if, there exists a *rewrite proof* for $s \approx t$ (written $s \Downarrow_I t$). For simplicity, we will usually speak of the "interpretation I" when in fact we mean the interpretation *represented by I*.

A well-founded ordering $\succ$ on ground literals and ground terms is called *admissible* if (i) the restriction of $\succ$ to literals is a total ordering, (ii) the restriction of $\succ$ to ground terms is a total reduction ordering, and (iii) if L and L' are literals, then $L \succ L'$ whenever (iii.1) $\max(L) \succ \max(L')$ or (iii.2) $\max(L) = \max(L')$, and L is a negative, and L' is a positive literal.[1] If $\succ$ is an admissible ordering, its multi-set extension (which we usually denote by the same symbol) is a well-founded ordering on clauses that is total on ground clauses. We call such clause orderings *admissible* as well. The essence of condition (iii) is that replacing the maximal term in a literal by a smaller term yields a smaller literal in any admissible ordering. By condition (iii.2) clauses in which the maximal term occurs in a negative literal are larger than clause with the same maximal term, but occurring only in positive literals. Condition (iii) circumscribes the relationship between the term and literal orderings, but leaves some flexibility for extending a given term ordering to literals. For instance, comparisons between literals with the same maximal may take into account the respective minimal terms.

The calculi in this paper are parameterized by an admissible clause ordering. From now on, let $\succ$ denote an arbitrary, but fixed admissible ordering.

3 Strict and Non-strict Superposition

We first consider ground clauses only. The extension of our results to general clauses is discussed in Section 7.

The inference rules of *strict (ground) superposition* SS are shown in Figure 1.[2] The ordering constraints imposed on superposition inferences restrict equational replacements so that only maximal terms of maximal equations in the second

---

[1] Here $\max(L)$ denotes the maximal term (with respect to $\succ$) of a literal L. We will also use $\max(D)$ to denote the maximal literal in a clause D.

[2] In order to simplify matters technically, we do not consider selection functions on negative literals. But all the results can be extended appropriately.

Positive (ground) superposition

$$\frac{C \vee s \approx t \quad D \vee w[s] \approx v}{w[t] \approx v \vee C \vee D}$$

where (i) $s \succ t$, (ii) $w \succ v$, (iii) $(s \approx t) \succ C$, (iv) $(w \approx v) \succ D$, and (v) $(w \approx v) \succ (s \approx t)$.

Negative (ground) superposition

$$\frac{C \vee s \approx t \quad D \vee w[s] \not\approx v}{w[t] \not\approx v \vee C \vee D}$$

where (i) $s \succ t$, (ii) $w \succ v$, (iii) $(s \approx t) \succ C$, and (iv) $(w \not\approx v) \succeq \max(D)$.

Reflexivity resolution

$$\frac{s \not\approx s \vee C}{C}$$

where $(s \not\approx s) \succeq \max(C)$.

Ordered Factoring

$$\frac{C \vee s \approx t \vee s \approx t}{C \vee s \approx t}$$

where $(s \approx t) \succeq \max(C)$.

Fig. 1. Strict (ground) superposition calculus SS

---

premise (the *negative premise*) are replaced by the minimal term of the maximal equation of the first (the *positive*) premise.

The calculus ZK (Zhang & Kapur 1988) is a predecessor of SS. The positive superposition rule in ZK imposes constraints (i) and (ii), but not (v), whereas (iii) and (iv) are slightly different due to differences in the literal orderings. For negative superposition the important restriction (ii) is dropped, and (unordered) factoring may be applied to both positive and negative literals.

Strict superposition is not compatible with tautology elimination. For example, the set of clauses

$$a \not\approx b \vee a \approx c$$
$$b \approx c$$
$$a \not\approx b \vee a \not\approx d$$

where a, b, and c are constants, is unsatisfiable. However, if we choose an ordering $a \succ b \succ c$, then only the tautology $b \not\approx b \vee a \not\approx c \vee a \approx c$ can be derived by strict superposition.[3] In other words, strict superposition is not refutationally complete in combination with tautology deletion. In the less restrictive calculus ZK the empty clause can be derived from these clauses, even when one deletes tautologies. But the following example from (Bachmair & Ganzinger 1990) demonstrates that ZK is not compatible with tautology deletion either:

---

[3] This example was communicated to us by Chris Lynch.

$$c \not\approx d$$
$$b \approx d$$
$$a \not\approx d \vee a \approx c$$
$$a \approx b \vee a \approx d$$

If $a \succ b \succ c \succ d$, only the tautology $a \not\approx d \vee b \approx c \vee a \approx d$ can be obtained by ZK.[4]

In (Bachmair & Ganzinger 1990) we had introduced extended superposition calculi that are refutationally complete and compatible with tautology deletion. The *(non-strict) superposition* calculus S consists of SS plus the following *equality factoring* rule:

Equality factoring
$$\frac{C \vee s \approx t \vee s \approx t'}{C \vee t \not\approx t' \vee s \approx t'}$$

where $(s \approx t) \succ (s \approx t')$, $s \succ t$, and $(s \approx t) \succ C$.

Equality factoring combines resolution (of a clause with a certain instance of the transitivity axiom) and factoring as the following derivation shows:

$$\frac{C \vee s \approx t \vee s \approx t' \quad (x \not\approx y \vee y \not\approx z \vee x \approx z)[t'/z]}{\dfrac{C \vee t \not\approx t' \vee s \approx t' \vee s \approx t'}{C \vee t \not\approx t' \vee s \approx t'}}$$

The inference rule obviously applies only to non-Horn clauses.

4   Candidate Models and Counterexamples

A powerful method for proving the refutational completeness of deductive calculi is centered around the concept of candidate models and reduction of counterexamples. The main feature in our current presentation is the clear separation between *local* aspects of reducing counterexamples (by inferences) and *global* methods for characterizing counterexamples. The latter also lead to general notions of redundancy: a clause is inherently redundant if it can never become a minimal counterexample.

4.1   Basic Concepts

If $\mathcal{I}$ is an (clausal) inference system, we denote by $\mathcal{I}(N)$ the set of all clauses that can be derived by applying an inference in $\mathcal{I}$ to premises in N. Suppose we have a mapping I, called a *model functor*, that assigns to each set N of ground clauses not containing the empty clause, an (equality) Herbrand interpretation I_N, called a *candidate model* (for N). If I_N is indeed a model of N, then N is

---

[4] ZK employs a slightly different literal ordering in which the polarity of a literal is ignored, so that $a \approx c \succ a \not\approx d$. These technical differences are not significant, though.

satisfiable. Otherwise, N contains clauses, called *counterexamples* (for I_N), that are false in I_N. If a counterexample exists at all, then N also contains a minimal counterexample with respect to the clause ordering $\succ$. We say that $\mathcal{I}$ has the *reduction property for counterexamples* (with respect to I) if, whenever C is a minimal counterexample for I_N, then there exists an inference in $\mathcal{I}$ from C (and possibly additional premises from N) with a conclusion D that is smaller than C (i.e., $C \succ D$) and is also a counterexample for I_N. Inference systems that have the reduction property for counterexamples are refutationally complete in the following sense.

Proposition 1. *If $\mathcal{I}$ has the reduction property for counterexamples and if N is closed under $\mathcal{I}$, that is, $\mathcal{I}(N) \subseteq N$, then N either contains the empty clause, or else is satisfiable.*

Our approach to proving refutational completeness is based on establishing the reduction property for counterexamples. A key advantage of this approach is that it naturally leads to a very general notion of redundancy.

First observe that only inferences that reduce minimal counterexamples are essential. A clauses that can never become a minimal counterexample is inherently redundant. Of course, the difficulty is to characterize such clauses. The following approximate characterization captures many, but not all, inherently redundant clauses.

We say that a ground clause C (not necessarily in N) is *redundant* with respect to a set N of ground clauses if there exist clauses $C_1, \ldots, C_k$ in N such that $C_1, \ldots, C_k \models C$ and $C \succ C_i$. Let $\mathcal{R}(N)$ denote the set of redundant clauses with respect to N, and let us call N *saturated up to redundancy* with respect to $\mathcal{I}$ if $\mathcal{I}(N \setminus \mathcal{R}(N)) \subseteq N \cup \mathcal{R}(N)$. Let us also denote by N_C the set of clauses D in N with $C \succ D$. If a clause C is redundant in N then it is not only entailed by N_C, but also by $N_C \setminus \mathcal{R}(N)$, the subset of non-redundant clauses in N smaller than C. Note that the admissible ordering $\succ$ provides the link between the redundancy criterion $\mathcal{R}$ and the inference system $\mathcal{I}$.

Proposition 2. *Let $\mathcal{I}$ be a sound inference system with the reduction property. If N is saturated up to redundancy with respect to $\mathcal{I}$, then it is unsatisfiable if, and only if, it contains the empty clause.*

In previous papers, e.g., (Bachmair & Ganzinger 1994), we also formalized the notion of theorem proving processes, as sequences of individual steps of deduction (of new clauses) and deletion (of redundant clauses). Under certain fairness assumptions, theorem proving sequences result in saturated clause sets, and thus represent refutationally complete theorem proving strategies. (A key property is that redundancy of clauses is preserved under deduction and deletion, so that redundant clauses can always be eliminated.) These investigations are essential for effectively and efficiently constructing saturated sets of clauses, but orthogonal to the topic of the present paper. The key question we consider next is how to construct a model functor I so that a given inference system $\mathcal{I}$ has the reduction property for counterexamples with respect to I.

4.2 Constructing Candidate Models

The definition of the model functor I will be monotone for downward closed subsets of N. More precisely, whenever C and D are two clauses with $C \preceq D$, then $I_{N_C} \subseteq I_{N_D} \subseteq I_N$. The sets I_{N_C} will be defined by induction over the given clause ordering, via auxiliary sets of rewrite rules $E_{N,C}$ designed so that in many cases a clause C true in $I_{N_C} \cup E_{N,C}$.

Let C be any given ground clause (not necessarily in N) and suppose that $E_{N,C'}$ and $I_{N_{C'}}$ have already been defined for all clauses C' for which $C \succ C'$. Then

$$I_{N_C} = \bigcup_{C \succ C'} E_{N,C'}.$$

Moreover, $E_{N,C} = \{s \approx t\}$ if C is a clause in N of the form $D \vee s \approx t$ such that (i) D is a counterexample for $I_{N_C} \cup \{s \approx t\}$, (ii) $(s \approx t) \succ D$ and $s \succ t$, and (iii) s is irreducible by I_{N_C}. In that case, we also say that C *produces* the equation (or rule) $s \approx t$. In all other cases, $E_{N,C} = \emptyset$. Finally, we define $I_N = \bigcup_C E_{N,C}$ as the set of all equations produced by the clauses in N.[5] Whenever the set N is known from the context or assumed to be arbitrary then we will omit the index N from I_N, I_{N_C}, and $E_{N,C}$.

Clauses that produce equations are called *productive*. We say that a clause $C \vee s \approx t$ is *reductive for* $s \approx t$ if $(s \approx t) \succ C$ and $s \succ t$. Productive clauses are reductive. Only clauses in N can produce an equation for I_N. A productive clause C is false in I_C, but true in $I_C \cup E_C$, whereas the subclause D remains a counterexample for $I_C \cup E_C$. By condition (ii) the maximal term in a productive clause cannot appear in a negative literal. The sets I_C and I_N are constructed in such a way that they are left-reduced rewrite systems with respect to $\succ$ and, therefore, convergent. It can also be shown that if D is a clause in N, and if C and D' are other clauses such that $D' \succ D \succ C$, then C is true in I_D if, and only if, it is true in $I_{D'}$.

Let us explain this definition by means of an example. Suppose we have constants $a \succ b \succ c \succ d$. The following table lists a set of clauses (in descending order from the top) plus the rewrite rules that are produced.

C	E_C	remarks
$a \approx b \to a \approx d$		true in I_C
$a \approx d \to b \approx c$		false in I_C and I
$c \approx d \to a \approx c, b \approx c$	$a \approx c$	reductive and false in I_C
$\to c \approx d$	$c \approx d$	reductive and false in I_C

All but the second clause are true in the candidate model $I = \{c \approx d, a \approx c\}$. A negative superposition inference

$$c \approx d \to a \approx c, b \approx c \quad a \approx d \to b \approx c$$
$$\overline{c \approx d, c \approx d \to b \approx c, b \approx c}$$

---

[5] Note that I is well-defined; that is, if $N = M$ then $I_N = I_M$. This can be easily verified by induction over the clause ordering.

between the third (productive) clause and the counterexample yields a smaller counterexample $c \approx d$, $c \approx d \rightarrow b \approx c$, $b \approx c$ for I. In general, if a clause C such as $a \approx d \rightarrow b \approx c$ is false in I_C, its maximal term a must be reducible by a rule in I_C (that was produced by some clause C' in N_C). Thus there is a negative superposition inference with a conclusion smaller than C. Moreover, condition (i) ensures that this conclusion is also a counterexample. Other kinds of counterexamples can be reduced in a similar way (but by different inferences).

Theorem 1. *Let N be a set of ground clauses not containing the empty clause and C be the minimal counterexample in N for I_N. Then there exists an inference in S from C such that*

(i) *its conclusion is a counterexample for I_N that is smaller than C; and*

(ii) *if the inference is a superposition inference then C is its negative premise and the positive premise is a productive clause.*

Part (i) of the theorem states that S has the reduction property and, hence, is refutationally complete and compatible with the removal of redundant clauses. Part (ii) provides further restrictions that may be used to define a notion of redundancy for inferences.

Let us now apply the construction to the critical example from Section 3.

clauses C	E_C	remarks
$a \approx b,\ a \approx c \rightarrow$		true
$\rightarrow a \approx b,\ a \approx c$		minimal counterexample
$\rightarrow b \approx c$	$b \approx c$	reductive and false in I_C

The clause $D = a \approx b$, $a \approx c$ is non-productive, for if $a \approx b$ were produced, then $a \approx c$ would become true and condition (i) be violated. Equality factoring can be used to reduce this kind of counterexample. We have seen in Section 3 that a contradiction can also be derived if one computes inferences with tautologies. But this alternative requires that we relax the notion of counterexamples so that certain tautologies can be considered "weak" counterexamples for some interpretations. The modified, proof-theoretic techniques will be developed next.

5   Weak Counterexamples

Let R be a ground rewrite system. An equation $s \approx t$ is said to have a *direct rewrite proof* in R if, and only if, $s \downarrow_{R_{s,t}} t$ where $R_{s,t}$ denotes the set of equations $l \approx r$ in R such that $s \approx t \succeq l \approx r$ in the given literal ordering.

For example, if R contains two equations, $a \approx b$ and $b \approx c$, where $a \succ b \succ c$, then $a \approx c$ has a rewrite proof in R, but not a direct rewrite proof. In a direct rewrite proof no rewrite rules may be used that are larger than the equation to be proved.

We call a ground clause C a *weak counterexample* for R if, and only if, (i) for each negative literal $u \not\approx v$ in C we have $u \downarrow_R v$ and (ii) no positive equation in C has a *direct* rewrite proof in R. Clearly, any counterexample is also a weak counterexample, but the converse is not true in general.

We say an inference system $\mathcal{I}$ has the *reduction property for weak counterexamples* (with respect to a model functor I) if whenever a (nonempty) clause C in N is the minimal weak counterexample for I_N then there exists an inference in $\mathcal{I}$ from C (and possibly additional premises in N) with a conclusion D that is smaller than C and also a weak counterexample for I_N.

Proposition 3. *If $\mathcal{I}$ has the reduction property for weak counterexamples and N is closed under $\mathcal{I}$, that is, $\mathcal{I}(N) \subseteq N$, then N either contains the empty clause or else is satisfiable.*

Weak counterexamples suggest an obvious modification in the notion of redundancy. A ground clause C (not necessarily in N) is said to be *(weakly) redundant* with respect to a set N of ground clauses if for any convergent ground rewrite system R (with respect to $\succ$) for which C is a weak counterexample there exists a weak counterexample D in N for R such that $C \succ D$. Let $\mathcal{R}^w(N)$ denote the set of redundant clauses (based on weak counterexamples) with respect to N, and let us call N *saturated up to weak redundancy* with respect to $\mathcal{I}$ whenever $\mathcal{I}(N \setminus \mathcal{R}^w(N)) \subseteq N \cup \mathcal{R}^w(N)$.

Note that if no clause in $N \setminus \mathcal{R}^w(N)$ is a weak counterexample for an interpretation R then no clause in N can be a weak counterexample for R either, and, hence, R is a model for N. Conversely, if C in $\mathcal{R}^w(N)$ is a weak counterexample for R then $N \setminus \mathcal{R}^w(N)$ also contains a (smaller) weak counterexample for R.

Proposition 4. *Let $\mathcal{I}$ be a sound inference system with the reduction property for weak counterexamples. If a set N is saturated up to weak redundancy with respect to $\mathcal{I}$, then it is unsatisfiable if and only if it contains the empty clause.*

In applying these concepts to strict superposition, we modify the previous definition of a model functor I_N by replacing "counterexample" by "weak counterexample". Let I_N^w denote the modified functor. Note that the modified condition (i) for productive clauses C essentially requires that C be a weak counterexample for I_C^w. (If $C = D \vee s \approx t$ is a weak counterexample for I_C^w, no positive literal in D has a direct rewrite proof in $I_C^w \cup \{s \approx t\}$, even if it is of the form $s \approx u$. As the clause is reductive for $s \approx t$, we have $(s \approx t) \succ (s \approx u)$ so that $s \approx t$ cannot be applied in any direct rewrite proof of $s \approx u$.)

We now obtain a different candidate model $I^w = \{a \approx b, \, b \approx c\}$ for the above example

C	I^w	remarks
$a \approx b, \, a \approx c \rightarrow$		minimal weak counterexample
$\rightarrow a \approx b, \, a \approx c$	$a \approx b$	reductive and false in I_C
$\rightarrow b \approx c$	$b \approx c$	reductive and false in I_C

The clause $a \approx b, \vee \, a \approx c$ is productive now and may be used to reduce the counterexample to a tautology $b \approx b, \, a \approx c \rightarrow a \approx c$ that is a smaller weak counterexample for I^w! In fact, strict superposition does have the reduction property for weak counterexamples and, hence, is refutationally complete for ground clauses.

Theorem 2. *Let N be a set of ground clauses not containing the empty clause. Let C be the minimal weak counterexample in N for I_N^w. Then there exists an inference in SS from C such that*

(i) *its conclusion is a weak counterexample for I_N^w smaller than C; and*

(ii) *if the inference is a superposition inference (left or right) then C is its negative premise and the positive premise is a productive clause.*

6 Simplification Afforded by Weak Redundancy

We next briefly investigate to what extent the main simplification techniques in superposition theorem proving can be used in the context of weak redundancy. We discuss the ground case. For the non-ground case additional consideration have to be taken into account, cf. Section 7.

In general, simplification is a derivation step (on sets of clauses) of the form $N \cup \{C\} \vdash N \cup \{D\}$ where C and D are logically equivalent clauses with $C \succ D$, and C is in $\mathcal{R}^w(N \cup \{D\})$. In other words, simplification allows one to replace a clause C by a simpler clause D, provided C is redundant.

Simplification by standard term rewriting is admissible.

Reduction:

$$N \cup \{s \approx t, \ C \vee w[s] \approx u\} \vdash N \cup \{s \approx t, \ C \vee w[t] \approx u\},$$

if (i) $s \succ t$, (ii) $w[s] \approx u \succeq s \approx t$, and (iii) $w[s] \approx u \succ w[t] \approx u$.

Soundness is trivial. The clause $C \vee w[s] \approx u$ is redundant in $\{s \approx t, \ C \vee w[t] \approx u\}$ as direct rewrite proofs of $s \approx t$ and $w[t] \approx u$ with respect to a convergent rewrite system can be combined into a direct rewrite proof of $w[s] \approx u$. Note that, depending on the literal ordering, the constraint (iii) is not necessarily implied by (i) and (ii). Simplifying a negative literal is essentially similar, except that the constraint (ii) is redundant.

Tautology elimination necessarily has to be weaker than usual. Here is an admissible variant.

Direct tautology elimination:

$$N \cup \{C\} \vdash N$$

if C is of the form $C_n \vee C_p \vee w[s] \approx t$, where (i) C_n the subclause of all negative literals in C, (ii) $w[s] \neq s$ and $w[s] \succeq t$, and (iii) there exists a term u with $s \succ u$, such that both $C_n \vee s \approx u$ and $C_n \vee w[u] \approx t$ are tautologies.

With the specified restrictions, any convergent rewrite system in which the equations in C_n are true admits a rewrite proof of $w[s] \approx w[u]$ (hence of $w[s] \approx t$) using only rules in which the maximal term is smaller than $w[s]$.

Proper subsumption works as usual.

Subsumption:

$$N \cup \{C, \ C \vee D\} \vdash N \cup \{C\}$$

In sum, we have shown that with certain additional restrictions, the usual simplification techniques for standard superposition are also admissible for the strict variant.

7 Lifting

In refutational theorem proving, one usually reasons about non-ground clauses by considering their ground instances. As shown in the full paper (Bachmair & Ganzinger 1997), equational replacements in the "substitution part" of a weak counterexample might result in clauses that are no longer weak counterexamples. Therefore, the lifting argument for standard superposition does not work, and we need to restrict ourselves to "reduced" instances of clauses, like in basic superposition (Bachmair et al. 1992, Nieuwenhuis & Rubio 1992a).

Basic strategies are conveniently formulated with constrained clauses (Nieuwenhuis & Rubio 1992b), but since in this paper we are mainly concerned with a solution to the lifting problem, we shall only employ a simple marking schema to specify those subterm positions in ground clauses on which equational replacements are not allowed. We essentially need to distinguish between (unmarked) positions that were present in the original clauses, and (marked) positions that were introduced by substitutions applied as part of inferences. For that purpose, we use the notation $C \cdot \sigma$, where C is a non-ground clause and σ a ground substitution, to denote a ground instance $C\sigma$. Expressions $C \cdot \sigma$ are also called *closures*. The clause part C of a closure is also called its *skeleton*.[6] Positions in $C\sigma$ that are at or below a variable in C are called *substitution positions* (or *marked* positions). Admissible orderings are defined as before, though an ordering may now depend on the distinction between unmarked and substitution positions (in cases where the maximal terms and the polarity of two literals are the same, cf. Section 8).

A notion central to the lifting of basic inference systems is that of a reduced closure. We say that a literal L is *order-reducible* (at position p) by an equation $s \approx t$, if s is the subterm of L at position p, $s \succ t$, and $L \succ (s \approx t)$. (In any admissible ordering, a negative literal is order-reducible by $s \approx t$ if and only if it is reducible by $s \approx t$. A positive literal $u \approx v$ is order-reducible by $s \approx t$ only if $(u \approx v) \succ (s \approx t)$ in the literal ordering.) A literal is *order-reducible by R* if it is order-reducible by some equation in R. A ground clause is said to be *reduced* with respect to R if it is not order-reducible with respect to R at any substitution position.

The basic variant of positive superposition can be formulated as follows:

Positive basic superposition

$$\frac{(C \vee s \approx t) \cdot \sigma \quad (D \vee w[s'] \approx v) \cdot \sigma}{(w[t] \approx v \vee C \vee D) \cdot \sigma}$$

where $s\sigma = s'\sigma$, and (i) $s\sigma \succ t\sigma$, (ii) $w\sigma \succ v\sigma$, (iii) $(s \approx t) \cdot \sigma \succ C \cdot \sigma$, (iv) $(w \approx v) \cdot \sigma \succ D \cdot \sigma$, and $(w \approx v) \cdot \sigma \succ (s \approx t) \cdot \sigma$, and (v) s' is not a variable

---

[6] We assume that the variables in the *skeleton* C of a closure $C \cdot \sigma$ are α-convertible to achieve variable disjointness wherever needed. In particular, any two closures can always be written as $C \cdot \sigma$ and $D \cdot \sigma$, respectively, with a common substitution σ.

This is essentially the standard superposition rule applied to closures. Other inference rules are obtained in a similar way from the non-basic rules. Note that condition (v) ensures that subterm replacements never take place at substitution positions. Another characteristic property of the basic variant is that skeleton positions in the conclusion correspond to skeleton positions in the premises so that no new skeleton positions are ever generated.

In investigating the reduction property for SBS we assume that candidate models I^w for sets of ground clauses N are defined as before. Produced equations inherit their marked substitution positions from the producing clause.

A set of ground clauses N is said to be *reduced* if any clause C in N is reduced with respect to I_C^w. By the monotonicity of I^w, and properties of the clause orderings, we observe that if C is reduced with respect to I_C^w it is also reduced with respect to I_N^w. No clause greater than or equal to C can produce a rule that is smaller than some literal in C. We say that a reduced subset M of N is *maximal* if it contains all clauses in N that are reduced with respect to I_M^w.

Proposition 5. *Any set of clauses contains a maximal reduced subset.*

A maximal reduced subset M is obtained (inductively) as the set of all clauses C such that C is reduced with respect to $I_{M_C}^w$.

Theorem 3. *Let N be a reduced set of clauses not containing the empty clause and C be the minimal weak counterexample in N for I_N^w. Then there exists an inference in SBS from C such that*

(i) *its conclusion D is a weak counterexample for I_N^w that is smaller than C and reduced with respect to I_N^w; and*

(ii) *if the inference is a superposition inference then C is its negative premise, and the positive premise is a productive clause.*

Part (i) states that SBS has the reduction property for weak counterexamples in reduced sets of closures. It in addition asserts that the smaller counterexample is again a reduced closure, which is important for effective saturation.

A set of closures N is called *schematic* if there exists a set of (general) clauses M such that N is the set of closures $C \cdot \sigma$, where C is a clause in M and σ is an arbitrary ground substitution. The reduction property of SBS implies its refutational completeness for schematic sets of closures. We will, however, right away state a stronger result which shows that SBS is also compatible with a suitable notion of redundancy. The new redundancy criterion is the same as $\mathcal{R}^w$ except that it refers to *reduced* weak counterexamples. Let us call a closure C *redundant* with respect to a set of closures N if for all convergent (with respect to $\succ$) rewrite systems R for which C is a weak counterexample and reduced, N contains a reduced weak counterexample D for R such that $C \succ D$. By $\mathcal{R}^c(N)$ we denote the set of closures redundant with respect to N. A set N is called *saturated up to redundancy* with respect to SBS if $\mathsf{SBS}(N \setminus \mathcal{R}^c(N)) \subseteq N \cup \mathcal{R}^c(N)$.

Theorem 4. *Let N be a set of closures that is saturated up to redundancy with respect to SBS and contains a schematic subset K, such that every closure in $N \setminus K$ is a logical consequence of K. Then N either contains the empty closure, or else is satisfiable.*

Whenever N is the closure under SBS (ignoring inferences involving redundant closures) of some initially given set N_0 of (general) clauses then the set K of ground instances of N_0 is schematic and, hence, this theorem can be applied.

8   Optimized Variable Chaining

The preceding completeness results hold for all admissible orderings. We shall now define a particular subclass of such orderings that prohibit certain superposition inferences *from* variables.

First we define a "complexity measure" c on marked literals as follows: $c(L) = (\max(L), P, V)$, where (i) P is 1 if the literal is negative, and 0, otherwise; and (ii) V is 1 if L is of the form $[\neg](x \approx v) \cdot \sigma$, with x a variable and $\max(L) = x\sigma$, and V is 0, otherwise. Such triples are compared lexicographically, using the given term ordering in the first component and using $1 > 0$ for the bits P and V in the other components. We may then consider the class of admissible orderings on marked literals which are compatible with this complexity measure in that $L \succ L'$ whenever $c(L) \succ c(L')$. Note that the V bit makes literals in which the maximal term lies entirely within the substitution part larger than other literals with the same maximal term and polarity.

The significance of these particular literal orderings is that they allow us to exclude positive top-level superposition inferences *from* variables.

Theorem 5. *If $\succ$ is a literal ordering as specified above, then no positive superposition inferences from a variable into the topmost position of another positive equation are possible in $\mathsf{SBS}^\succ$.*

Proof. For positive superposition inferences of the form

$$\frac{(C \vee s \approx t) \cdot \sigma \quad (D \vee s' \approx v) \cdot \sigma}{(t \approx v \vee C \vee D) \cdot \sigma}$$

(with $s\sigma = s'\sigma$ and s' not a variable) we observe that s cannot be a variable as otherwise the constraint $(w \approx v) \cdot \sigma \succ (s \approx t) \cdot \sigma$ associated with the inference would be violated. (The maximal terms and the polarities of the two literals in question are identical. But if s is a variable, the V bit in $c((s \approx t) \cdot \sigma)$ is 1, whereas in $c((w \approx v) \cdot \sigma)$ it is 0.

Superposition through variables is extremely prolific since unification is no effective filter in such cases. Superpositions into substitution positions, in particular variables, are excluded in SBS, regardless of the ordering. With the specific class of literal orderings (that are based on arbitrary reduction orderings on terms), no positive superposition inferences *from* a skeleton variable into the topmost position of any other positive equation is required either. This observation has been crucial for recent results on equality elimination transformations (Bachmair, Ganzinger & Voronkov 1997).

9 Conclusions

In this paper we solve a long-standing open problem by showing that the superposition calculus ZK by Zhang & Kapur (1988) is refutationally complete provided certain tautologies are not eliminated. More generally, we have shown that slight restrictions of the usual simplification and redundancy elimination techniques are compatible with strict basic superposition, a substantially more restrictive calculus than ZK. We have proved completeness for a large class of admissible orderings on terms and literals. In particular one may choose literal orderings that avoid positive superposition inferences *from* variables into the top position of positive equations.

The results about strict superposition can be also extended to the case of ordered chaining calculi for general transitive relations. One can show (Bachmair & Ganzinger 1997) that transitivity (or composition) resolution inferences, the corresponding generalizations of the equality factoring inference, as they were required in (Bachmair & Ganzinger 1995) can also be dispensed with at the expense of a weaker notion of redundancy.

On the methodological level, we believe that the presentation in the current paper makes the underlying proof techniques more transparent, as it separates the two main components, reduction of counterexamples by inferences and characterizations, via redundancy, of clauses that cannot become counterexamples. Constructions similar to our candidate models for superposition have been sketched, but not formalized with mathematical rigor, by Zhang (1988). Related ideas can already be found in Brand's proof of his equality elimination method (Brand 1975). The present definitions, including redundancy, originated from (Bachmair & Ganzinger 1990), where, however, the exposition is technically considerably more involved, mainly because counterexample reduction and redundancy are dealt with simultaneously. Pais & Peterson (1991) have given a similar proof of the completeness of superposition with merging paramodulation (a variant that was also introduced in (Bachmair & Ganzinger 1990), but without presenting a general concept of redundancy. Strict superposition, as we have explained above, requires that the semantic concept of counterexamples be replaced by a proof-theoretic notion based on direct rewrite proofs.

From a theoretical point of view, strict basic superposition is rather appealing in that two critical issues for equational theorem proving, how to deal with transitivity and disjunction, respectively, are clearly separated. It remains to be seen whether strict basic superposition is the method of choice in practice. Due to the technical complications with the basic setup and with restricted simplification, implementing the calculus efficiently appears to be a non-trivial task.

Acknowledgements. We are grateful to Chris Lynch for his comments on this paper and, in particular, for pointing out a bug in the preliminary version.

References

Bachmair, L. & Ganzinger, H. (1990), On restrictions of ordered paramodulation with simplification, *in* M. Stickel, ed., 'Proc. 10th Int. Conf. on Automated Deduction, Kaiserslautern', Vol. 449 of *Lecture Notes in Computer Science*, Springer-Verlag, Berlin, pp. 427–441.

Bachmair, L. & Ganzinger, H. (1994), 'Rewrite-based equational theorem proving with selection and simplification', *J. Logic and Computation* **4**(3), 217–247. Revised version of Technical Report MPI-I-91-208, 1991.

Bachmair, L. & Ganzinger, H. (1995), Ordered chaining calculi for first-order theories of binary relations, Research Report MPI-I-95-2-009, Max-Planck-Institut für Informatik, Saarbrücken, Saarbrücken. Revised version to appear in JACM.
URL: www.mpi-sb.mpg.de/~hg/pra.html#MPI-I-95-2-009

Bachmair, L. & Ganzinger, H. (1997), Strict basic superposition and chaining, Research Report MPI-I-97-2-011, Max-Planck-Institut für Informatik, Saarbrücken, Saarbrücken.
URL: www.mpi-sb.mpg.de/~hg/pra.html#MPI-I-97-2-011

Bachmair, L., Ganzinger, H., Lynch, C. & Snyder, W. (1992), Basic paramodulation and superposition, *in* D. Kapur, ed., 'Automated Deduction — CADE'11', Vol. 607 of *Lecture Notes in Computer Science*, Springer-Verlag, Berlin, pp. 462–476.

Bachmair, L., Ganzinger, H. & Voronkov, A. (1997), Elimination of equality via transformation with ordering constraints, Research Report MPI-I-97-2-012, Max-Planck-Institut für Informatik, Saarbrücken, Saarbrücken.
URL: www.mpi-sb.mpg.de/~hg/pra.html#MPI-I-97-2-012

Brand, D. (1975), 'Proving theorems with the modification method', *SIAM J. Comput.* **4**, 412–430.

Nieuwenhuis, R. & Rubio, A. (1992*a*), Basic superposition is complete, *in* 'ESOP'92', Vol. 582 of *Lecture Notes in Computer Science*, Springer-Verlag, Berlin, pp. 371–389.

Nieuwenhuis, R. & Rubio, A. (1992*b*), Theorem proving with ordering constrained clauses, *in* 'Automated Deduction — CADE'11', Vol. 607 of *Lecture Notes in Computer Science*, Springer-Verlag, Berlin, pp. 477–491.

Pais, J. & Peterson, G. (1991), 'Using forcing to prove completeness of resolution and paramodulation', *J. Symbolic Computation* **11**, 3–19.

Zhang, H. (1988), Reduction, superposition and induction: Automated reasoning in an equational logic, PhD thesis, Rensselaer Polytechnic Institute, Schenectady, New York.

Zhang, H. & Kapur, D. (1988), First-order theorem proving using conditional rewrite rules, *in* E. Lusk & R. Overbeek, eds, 'Proc. 9th Int. Conf. on Automated Deduction', Vol. 310 of *Lecture Notes in Computer Science*, Springer-Verlag, Berlin, pp. 1–20.

Elimination of Equality via Transformation with Ordering Constraints

Leo Bachmair[*][1], Harald Ganzinger[**][2], and Andrei Voronkov[3]

[1] Comp. Sci. Dept., SUNY at Stony Brook, NY 11794, U.S.A.,
leo@cs.sunysb.edu
[2] MPI Informatik, D-66123 Saarbrücken, Germany,
hg@mpi-sb.mpg.de
[3] Comp. Sci. Dept., Uppsala U., S 751 05 Uppsala, Sweden,
voronkov@csd.uu.se

Abstract. We refine Brand's method for eliminating equality axioms by (i) imposing ordering constraints on auxiliary variables introduced during the transformation process and (ii) avoiding certain transformations of positive equations with a variable on one side. The refinements are both of theoretical and practical interest. For instance, the second refinement is implemented in Setheo and appears to be critical for that prover's performance on equational problems. The correctness of this variant of Brand's method was an open problem that is solved by the more general results in the present paper. The experimental results we obtained from a prototype implementation of our proposed method also show some dramatic improvements of the proof search in model elimination theorem proving. We prove the correctness of our refinements of Brand's method by establishing a suitable connection to basic paramodulation calculi and thereby shed new light on the connection between different approaches to equational theorem proving.

1 Introduction

Efficient techniques for handling equality are a key component of automated reasoning systems. The most successful approaches to date are based on refinements of paramodulation, such as the superposition calculus, but these are unfortunately not fully compatible with tableau-based provers or model elimination methods. Various attempts have been made recently to improve the handling of equality in such provers (Moser, Lynch & Steinbach 1995, Degtyarev & Voronkov 1996b, Degtyarev & Voronkov 1996a), but they usually require subtle interactions between paramodulation-based and model elimination-based subcomponents and therefore are difficult to integrate into existing provers. Most

---

[*] Work supported in part by NSF under grants INT-9314412 and CCR-9510072.
[**] Work supported in part by DFG under grants Ga 261/7-1, 8-1, and by the ESPRIT Basic Research Working Group 22457 (CCL II).

C. Kirchner and H. Kirchner (Eds.): Automated Deduction, CADE-15
LNAI 1421, pp. 175–190, 1998. © Springer–Verlag Berlin Heidelberg 1998

current model elimination provers rely instead on preprocessing steps that transform formulas from logic with equality into logic without equality, see the survey (Schumann 1994).

Brand's modification method (Brand 1975), which consists of three steps. First, terms are flattened by introducing new auxiliary variables, so that only variables occur as arguments of function symbols. The axioms expressing the monotonicity properties of equality are not needed for the resulting flat clauses. Second, all symmetric variants of a clause (which are obtained by switching the arguments of equations) are added to the given set of clauses, so that the symmetry axioms of equality may be dispensed with. Third, the transitivity axioms are internalized by splitting positive equations $s \approx t$ into (clauses that represent) implications $t \approx x \to s \approx x$ with a new auxiliary variable x, called a "link" variable.

In this article, we improve Brand's modification in various ways. We systematically add ordering constraints during the transformation process, so as to be able to better control the theorem proving process on the transformed clauses. For example, a link variable x will be constrained via $s \succ x$ and $t \succeq x$ to terms smaller than s and smaller than or equal to t. Ordering constraints intuitively reflect assumptions about the form of equational proofs of $s \approx t$ and are related to rewrite techniques as used in paramodulation and superposition calculi. The rationale for transitivity elimination is that a sequence of equational replacements

$$s = s_0 \approx s_1 \approx \ldots \approx s_n = t$$

(using equations $s_i \approx s_{i+1}$) can be simulated by a sequence of resolution inferences from the goal clause $s \not\approx z \lor t \not\approx z$ and (clauses representing the) equivalences $s_i \approx x_i \leftrightarrow s_{i+1} \approx x_i$, plus a final resolution step with the reflexivity axiom $x \approx x$ that instantiates the link variables. The ordering constraints ensure that the variables x_i can only be instantiated by *minimal* terms among the s_i and block the search for alternative equational proofs that apply the same equations but differ in the instantiation of the link variables.

Aside from the ordering constraints, we also propose more subtle changes to the transformation process. In particular, we never split a positive equation $t \approx x$ where the right-hand side is already a variable. This may seem to be a minor technical aspect, but the optimization (Moser & Steinbach 1997) has been implemented in the Setheo model elimination theorem prover and is crucial for that prover's successful performance on many equational problems (Ibens & Letz 1997).[1] The completeness of this optimization (without any ordering constraints) had been an open problem[2] that follows from the more general results in the present paper. Our completeness proof is comparatively simple,

---

[1] The optimized transformation avoids the generation of negative equations $x \not\approx y$ between two variables. Model elimination or resolution inferences with such literals correspond to paramodulation inferences into or from variables, most of which are redundant and ought to be avoided.

[2] The proof in (Moser & Steinbach 1997) contains a non-trivial gap which this paper closes.

but draws on rather non-trivial results about basic superposition, some of which have been obtained only very recently (Bachmair & Ganzinger 1997). In essence, we show how refutational proofs by strict basic superposition with flat clauses can be simulated by resolution with the corresponding transformed clauses. In addition to the theoretical results, we also report on experiments with model elimination theorem which appear to indicate the practical usefulness of the proposed method in that context.

This extended abstract does not contain all proofs. For details we refer to the full paper in (Bachmair, Ganzinger & Voronkov 1997).

2   Preliminaries

The transformations described below will be applied to clauses with equality. We use the symbol $\approx$ to denote the equality predicate and assume, for simplicity, that this is the only predicate in the original language. A different symbol $\simeq$ is used to denote the predicate that replaces equality as part of the transformation process. Semantically, the difference between the two symbols is that $\approx$ is interpreted as a congruence relation, whereas no restrictions are imposed on the interpretation of $\simeq$. In other words, the original formulas with $\approx$ are interpreted in a logic with equality, whereas the transformed formulas with $\simeq$ are interpreted in a logic without equality. The aim is to design transformations so that the original clause set is satisfiable in an equality interpretation if, and only if, the transformed clause set is satisfiable in general.

Formally, a *clause* is a disjunction of literals; a literal being either an atomic formula or the negation thereof. Negated equality atoms are written as $s \not\approx t$ or $s \not\simeq t$, respectively. Disjunction is associative and commutative, and hence clauses may be viewed as multisets of literals. The *empty clause* is denoted by $\Box$. By an *equational clause* we mean a clause that contains only $\approx$, but not $\simeq$. Satisfiability and logical consequence (denoted by $\models$) are defined in the usual way, with the proviso that the interpretation of $\approx$ has to be a congruence (while $\simeq$ may be interpreted as an arbitrary binary relation).[3]

Substitutions will be denoted by the letters σ, τ and ρ. Variable renamings are substitutions sending variables to variables. The result of applying a substitution σ to an expression (e.g., a clause or term) E is denoted $E\sigma$. We write $E[s]$ to indicate that s is a subterm of E and write $E[t]$ to denote the expression obtained from E by replacing one specified occurrence of s by t. We also write $E(s)$ to indicate that s occurs in E and denote by $E(t)$ the result of simultaneously replacing *all* occurrences of s in E by t.

A *constraint* is a, possibly empty, conjunction of atomic formulas $s = t$ (called an *atomic equality constraint*) or $s \succ t$ or $s \succeq t$ (called *atomic ordering constraints*). The empty conjunction is denoted by $\top$. The letters γ and δ are used to denote constraints. A *constrained clause* is a pair of a clause C and a

---

[3] On one or two occasions we will explicitly relax the restriction on the interpretation of $\approx$.

constraint γ, written as $C \cdot \gamma$. We call C the *clause part* and γ the *constraint part* of $C \cdot \gamma$.

A substitution σ is said to be a *solution of an atomic equality constraint* $s = t$ if $s\sigma$ and $t\sigma$ are syntactically identical. It is a *solution of an atomic ordering constraint* $s \succ t$ (with respect to a completable reduction ordering $>$) if $s\sigma > t\sigma$; and a solution of $s \succeq t$ if it is a solution of $s = t$ or $s \succ t$. Finally, we say that σ is a *solution of a general constraint* γ if it is a solution of all atomic constraints in γ. A constraint is *satisfiable* if it has a solution.

A *ground instance* of a constrained clause $C \cdot \gamma$ is any ground clause $C\sigma$ such that the constraint $\gamma\sigma$ is satisfiable. A constrained clause C is *more general* than a constrained clause $\mathcal{D}$, denoted $\mathcal{D} \subseteq C$, if every ground instance of $\mathcal{D}$ is also a ground instance of C. We call two constrained clauses C and $\mathcal{D}$ *equivalent* if $C \subseteq \mathcal{D}$ and $\mathcal{D} \subseteq C$, i.e. when C and $\mathcal{D}$ have the same ground instances.

Constraints γ_1 and γ_2 are *equivalent* with respect to a set V of variables if for every solution σ_1 of γ_1 there exists a solution σ_2 of γ_2 such that σ_1 and σ_2 agree on the variables in V, and vice versa. We shall identify constrained clauses $C \cdot \gamma_1$ and $C \cdot \gamma_2$ when the constraints γ_1 and γ_2 are equivalent with respect to the variables in C. In this case $C \cdot \gamma_1$ and $C \cdot \gamma_2$ are equivalent. We identify a constrained clause $C \cdot \top$ with the unconstrained clause C. A *contradiction* is a constrained clause $\square \cdot \gamma$ with an empty clause part such that the constraint γ is satisfiable. A clause is called *void* if its constraint is unsatisfiable. A void clause has no ground instances and therefore is redundant.

A set S of constrained clauses is *satisfiable* if the set of all its ground instances is satisfiable. Evidently, removal of void clauses and replacement of clauses by equivalent ones preserves the (un)satisfiability of S.

If $\mathcal{I}$ is an inference system and N is a set of clauses then $\mathcal{I}(N)$ denotes the set of clauses that can be derived by applying an inference rule in $\mathcal{I}$ to premises in N. Likewise, $\mathcal{I}^*(N)$ denotes the set of clauses that can be derived from N by repeated application of inferences in $\mathcal{I}$. In all calculi of this paper the premises of inference rules are assumed to have disjoint variables, which can be achieved by renaming.

3   Transformations

Given a set of equational clauses N, we apply various transformation rules and replace the equality predicate $\approx$ by the predicate $\simeq$ to obtain a modified clause set N', such that the transformed set N' is satisfiable if, and only if, the original set N is *equationally* satisfiable. Each part of the transformation process is designed to eliminate certain equality axioms and can be described by a set of (schematic) transformation rules to be applied to clauses. If R is a set of such transformation rules, we say that a (constrained) clause is in *R-normal form* if no rule in R can be applied to it. Most of the transformations described below define normal forms that are unique up to renaming of variables. If N is a set of (constrained) clauses, we denote by $R(N)$ the set of all R-normal forms of clauses in N.

3.1 Elimination of Monotonicity

A clause is said to be *flat* if variables are the only proper subterms of terms. Thus, $f(x) \not\approx y \vee h(x) \approx a$ is flat, but $f(f(x)) \approx x$ and $f(a) \approx x$ are not. A constrained clause $C \cdot \gamma$ is called flat if its clause part C is flat (but the constraint part γ may contain non-flat terms).

It is fairly straightforward to flatten clauses by abstracting subterms via introduction of new variables. This can be described by a set M of (schematic) transformation rules

$$C(s) \cdot \gamma \Rightarrow (s \not\approx x \vee C(x)) \cdot \gamma$$

where x is a variable not occurring in C and s is a non-variable term that occurs at least once as an argument of a function symbol in C. The rules in M are called *subterm abstraction rules*.

For example, the unit clause $i(x) * x \approx e$ contains one nested non-variable subterm, namely $i(x)$. Subterm abstraction yields a clause $i(x) \not\approx z \vee z * x \approx e$ that is unique up to renaming of the new variable z. The unit clause $i(y) \approx i(x * y) * x$ contains three nested non-variable terms, $i(y)$, $i(x * y)$, and $x * y$, which are eliminated in three steps to yield a transformed clause

$$i(y) \not\approx x_1 \vee i(x_3) \not\approx x_2 \vee x * y \not\approx x_3 \vee x_1 \approx x_2 * x.$$

A (constrained) clause is flat if, and only if, it is in M-normal form. The M-normal forms of a clause are unique up to renaming of the newly introduced variables (and hence we will speak of *the* M-normal form). Our interest in flat clauses stems from the following result:

Proposition 1 (Brand 1975). *Let N be a set of equational clauses and N' be obtained from N by replacing each clause by its M-normal form. Then N has an equality model if, and only if, N' has a model in which the predicate $\approx$ is interpreted as an equivalence (but not necessarily a congruence) relation.*

In other words, the monotonicity axioms are not needed for testing satisfiability of flat equational clauses. Note that for obtaining flat clauses we need not abstract *all* occurrences of a subterm at once. With the rewrite system M the multiple occurrences of the nested term $g(x)$ in

$$f(g(x)) \not\approx h(x) \vee h(g(x)) \approx x$$

are eliminated all at once to yield the M-normal form

$$g(x) \not\approx z \vee f(z) \not\approx h(x) \vee h(z) \approx x.$$

We may instead abstract the different occurrences separately to obtain a different flat clause,

$$g(x) \not\approx z_1 \vee g(x) \not\approx z_2 \vee f(z_1) \not\approx h(x) \vee h(z_2) \approx x.$$

3.2   Partial Elimination of Reflexivity

We may use equality constraints to get rid of certain undesirable negative equality literals:

$$(x \not\approx y \vee C) \cdot \gamma \Rightarrow C \cdot (\gamma \wedge x = y)$$

where x and y are variables. This transformation is called *reflexivity resolution* as it represents an instance of resolution with the reflexivity axiom. We denote the corresponding set of transformation rules by R.

3.3   Elimination of Symmetry

Next we replace the equality predicate $\approx$ by the predicate $\simeq$ and eliminate the need for the symmetry axioms. Positive equality literals are eliminated by *positive symmetry elimination* rules:

$$(C \vee s \approx t) \cdot \gamma \Rightarrow (C \vee s \simeq t) \cdot \gamma$$
$$(C \vee s \approx t) \cdot \gamma \Rightarrow (C \vee t \simeq s) \cdot \gamma$$

If a clause C contains n positive equality literals, then clearly n transformation steps will eliminate all positive occurrences of equality. There are 2^n different normal forms, *all* of which need to be retained to eliminate symmetry. For example, from the clause

$$g(x) \not\approx z \vee f(z) \not\approx h(x) \vee h(z) \approx x$$

we obtain both

$$g(x) \not\approx z \vee f(z) \not\approx h(x) \vee h(z) \simeq x$$

and

$$g(x) \not\approx z \vee f(z) \not\approx h(x) \vee x \simeq h(z).$$

Negative occurrences of $\approx$ can in principle be simply replaced by $\simeq$, but we prefer a slightly refined transformation that moves variables to the right-hand side.[4] The following *negative symmetry elimination* rules achieve this purpose:

$$(s \not\approx t \vee C) \cdot \gamma \Rightarrow (s \not\simeq t \vee C) \cdot \gamma \qquad \text{if } s \text{ is not a variable}$$
$$(s \not\approx t \vee C) \cdot \gamma \Rightarrow (t \not\simeq s \vee C) \cdot \gamma \qquad \text{if } s \text{ is a variable, but } t \text{ is not}$$

The normal forms produced by these additional transformation rules are unique, as at most one rule can be applied to any negative equality literal.[5]

We denote by S the set of all positive and negative symmetry elimination rules. If a clause contains n positive equality literals, then 2^n different S-normal forms can be derived from it. Two S-normal forms that can be derived from the same clause are said to be *symmetric variants* of each other.

---

[4] The advantage is that fewer splitting rules (described below) will be applicable.

[5] Negative literals $x \not\approx y$, with variables x and y, are not eliminated by symmetry elimination, but by reflexivity resolution.

3.4   Elimination of Transitivity

The transitivity axioms are eliminated by splitting positive and negative equality literals via introduction of so-called "link variables." The idea is the same as in Brand's method, but we also introduce constraints on variables, which necessitates slightly different transformations from Brand's, as will be explained below.

We have both *positive* and *negative splitting* rules of the form:

$$(C \vee s \simeq t) \cdot \gamma \Rightarrow (C \vee t \not\simeq z \vee s \simeq z) \cdot (\gamma \wedge t \succeq z \wedge s \succ z)$$
$$(C \vee s \not\simeq t) \cdot \gamma \Rightarrow (C \vee t \not\simeq z \vee s \not\simeq z) \cdot (\gamma \wedge t \succeq z \wedge s \succeq z)$$

where t is *not* a variable and z is a variable not occurring in C, s or t. The variable z is called a *link variable* (between s and t) and the corresponding constraints are called *link constraints*.

We emphasize that equality literals are *not* split if the right-hand side is already a variable. This is different from Brand's method, where literals are split regardless of whether the right-hand side is a variable or not.

We do not split equality literals with a variable on the right-hand side, but still may add corresponding ordering constraints, as expressed by the following *positive* and *negative link constraint* rules:

$$(C \vee s \simeq x) \cdot \gamma \Rightarrow (C \vee s \simeq x) \cdot (\gamma \wedge s \succ x)$$
$$(C \vee s \not\simeq x) \cdot \gamma \Rightarrow (C \vee s \not\simeq x) \cdot (\gamma \wedge s \succeq x)$$

where the constraints $s \succ x$ and $s \succeq x$, respectively, must not be contained in γ already.[6]

By T we denote the set of all splitting and link constraint rules. The T-normal form of a clause is unique up to renaming of link variables.

The flat clause (with empty constraint)

$$i(x) \not\simeq x_1 \vee x_1 * x \simeq e$$

is transformed by T to the constrained clause

$$(i(x) \not\simeq x_1 \vee e \not\simeq y \vee x_1 * x \simeq y) \cdot (i(x) \succeq x_1 \wedge e \succeq y \wedge x_1 * x \succ y),$$

whereas its symmetric variant

$$i(x) \not\simeq x_1 \vee e \simeq x_1 * x$$

is transformed to

$$(i(x) \not\simeq x_1 \vee x_1 * x \not\simeq y \vee e \simeq y) \cdot (i(x) \succeq x_1 \wedge x_1 * x \succeq y \wedge e \succ y).$$

Observe that the constraint of the last clause is unsatisfiable if e is a minimal ground term with respect to the given ordering $\succ$. In other words, the clause is

---

[6] There is no point in introducing the same constraint repeatedly.

void in that case, and the constraint $e \succeq y$ in the other clause can be simplified to $e = y$.

Note. The example indicates that it is not necessary to apply subterm abstraction to a *minimal* constant c, as the corresponding constraint $c \succeq x$ associated with the abstraction of c can be simplified to $x = c$. Also, Skolem constants that occur only negatively need not be abstracted.

4   Preservation of Satisfiability

The sets M, R, S, and T contain all the transformation rules we need. They eliminate all equality axioms, except reflexivity. Thus, for any set of clauses N, let $CEE(N)$ be the clause set $T(S(R(M(N)))) \cup \{x \simeq x\}$.[7] Our main result can then be stated as follows:

Theorem 1. *A set N of unconstrained equational clauses is equationally unsatisfiable if and only if the transformed set $CEE(N)$ is unsatisfiable.*

It is not difficult to prove that if N is equationally satisfiable, then the transformed set $CEE(N)$ is satisfiable. (In other words, the transformations are all sound.) The difficult part is to show that $CEE(N)$ is unsatisfiable, whenever N is equationally unsatisfiable.

It suffices to establish this property for $M(N)$ or, generally, for sets of flat (unconstrained) clauses. For that purpose we introduce a refutationally complete calculus for flat equational clauses (the "flat basic superposition calculus") and show that all inferences in this calculus are reflected by logical consequences on the transformed clauses. This will imply, in particular, that a transformed set of clauses is unsatisfiable whenever a contradiction can be derived from the original clauses by flat basic superposition.

The inference rules of the *flat basic superposition* calculus are depicted in Figure 1. We should point out that in the presentation of superposition calculi, one usually identifies (as we have done here) a literal $s \approx t$ with $t \approx s$ (and similarly for negative literals $s \not\approx t$). This calculus is a slimmed-down version of a strict basic superposition calculus restricted to flat clauses, and the following theorem is a direct consequence of the results in (Bachmair & Ganzinger 1997).

Theorem 2. *Let N be a set of flat unconstrained equational clauses. The following statements are equivalent:*
1. *N is equationally unsatisfiable;*
2. *$FBS^*(N)$ contains a contradiction;*
3. *$(R \circ FBS)^*(R(N))$ contains a contradiction.*
Moreover, if N is a set of flat clauses, then so are the sets $FBS^*(N)$ and $(R \circ FBS)^*(R(N))$.

By contrast to previous formulations of basic superposition, FBS has no equality factoring inferences, and no positive (top-level) superposition inferences *from*

---

[7] CEE is an acronym for "constrained equality elimination".

Positive flat basic superposition

$$\frac{(C \vee s \approx t) \cdot \gamma \quad (D \vee u \approx v) \cdot \delta}{(C \vee D \vee t \approx v) \cdot (\gamma \wedge \delta \wedge s = u \wedge s \succ v \succ t)} ,$$

where neither s nor u is a variable.

Negative flat basic superposition

$$\frac{(C \vee s \approx t) \cdot \gamma \quad (D \vee u \not\approx v) \cdot \delta}{(C \vee D \vee t \not\approx v) \cdot (\gamma \wedge \delta \wedge s = u \wedge s \succ t \wedge s \succ v)} ,$$

where u is not a variable.

Reflexivity resolution

$$\frac{(C \vee s \not\approx t) \cdot \gamma}{C \cdot (\gamma \wedge s = t)} .$$

Factoring

$$\frac{(C \vee s \approx t \vee u \approx v) \cdot \gamma}{(C \vee s \approx t) \cdot (\gamma \wedge s = u \wedge t = v)} ,$$

where $s\sigma = u\sigma$ and $t\sigma = v\sigma$, for some variable renaming σ.

Fig. 1. Flat Basic Superposition FBS

---

variables, and factoring is restricted to atoms with identical term skeletons. make it possible to state in the Lemma below a connection between flat basic superposition and the transformation system CEE, forming the core of our completeness proof.

Lemma 1. *Let N be a set of flat constrained equational clauses simplified with respect to reflexivity resolution (so that $\mathsf{R}(N) = N$). If $\mathcal{D}$ is a clause in $\mathsf{R} \circ FBS(N)$, then any $\mathsf{T} \circ \mathsf{S}$-normal form of $\mathcal{D}$ is a logical consequence of $\mathsf{T} \circ \mathsf{S}(N) \cup \{x \simeq x\}$.*[8]

Proof. Let $\mathcal{D}$ be the simplified (by R) conclusion of an inference in FBS from premises in N and let $\mathcal{C}$ be in $\mathsf{T} \circ \mathsf{S}(\mathcal{D})$. For demonstrating that $\mathcal{C}$ is logically implied by $\mathsf{T} \circ \mathsf{S}(N) \cup \{x \simeq x\}$ we will usually apply resolution-based reasoning, followed by some strengthening of the constraint.

We prove the assertion by a case analysis over the inferences in FBS. Let

$$\frac{(C \vee s \approx t) \cdot \gamma \quad (D \vee u \approx v) \cdot \delta}{(C \vee D \vee t \approx v) \cdot (\gamma \wedge \delta \wedge s = u \wedge s \succ t \wedge u \succ v \succ t)}$$

be an inference by positive flat basic superposition from premises in N. Then neither s nor u is a variable. Also, the conclusion $\mathcal{D}$ is already simplified by R as any clause in N has this property by assumption. Any $\mathsf{T} \circ \mathsf{S}$-normal form of $\mathcal{D}$ has the form

---

[8] We use the symbol $\circ$ to denote composition of operators. Thus, $\mathsf{T} \circ \mathsf{S}(N) = \mathsf{T}(\mathsf{S}(N))$.

$$C = (C' \vee D' \vee E) \cdot (\gamma \wedge \delta \wedge \lambda_{C'} \wedge \lambda_{D'} \wedge s = u \wedge s \succ t \wedge u \succ v \succ t \wedge \varepsilon).$$

where (i) $C' \cdot (\gamma \wedge \lambda_{C'})$ and $D' \cdot (\delta \wedge \lambda_{D'})$ are $\mathsf{T} \circ \mathsf{S}$-normal forms of $C \cdot \gamma$ and $D \cdot \delta$, respectively; (ii) the subclause E and the link constraints ε for the literals in E depend on (a) whether the new equation $t \approx v$ has been oriented into $t \simeq v$ or $v \simeq t$ during S normalization; and (b) on the result of T normalization, depending on whether or not t or v are variables.[9]

(i) *Variant $t \simeq v$, and v is a variable.* Then C has the form

$$(C' \vee D' \vee t \simeq v) \cdot (\gamma \wedge \delta \wedge \lambda_{C'} \wedge \lambda_{D'} \wedge s = u \wedge s \succ t \wedge u \succ v \succ t \wedge t \succ v)$$

Evidently, the constraint part of C is unsatisfiable, that is, C is void, hence trivially follows from $\mathsf{T} \circ \mathsf{S}(N)$.

From now on, to simplify notation, we shall omit the "side-literals" C' and D' as well as the respective "standard constraints" $\gamma \wedge \delta \wedge \lambda_{C'} \wedge \lambda_{D'}$ which are inherited from the C and D subclauses of the respective premises and their $\mathsf{T} \circ \mathsf{S}$ normal forms.

(ii) *Variant $t \simeq v$, and v is not a variable.* Here, C has the form

$$(v \not\simeq x \vee t \simeq x) \cdot (s = u \wedge s \succ t \wedge u \succ v \succ t \wedge v \succeq x \wedge t \succ x),$$

or, equivalently,

$$(v \not\simeq x \vee t \simeq x) \cdot (s = u \wedge u \succ v \succ t \succ x) \tag{1}$$

with x a fresh link variable. As neither s nor u is a variable, $\mathsf{T} \circ \mathsf{S}(N)$ contains the clauses $(u \not\simeq x \vee v \simeq x) \cdot (u \succeq x \wedge v \succ x)$ and $(s \not\simeq y \vee t \simeq y) \cdot (s \succeq y \wedge t \succ y)$, with link variables x and y. Consider the resolution inference

$$\frac{(u \not\simeq x \vee v \simeq x) \cdot (u \succeq x \wedge v \succ x) \quad (s \not\simeq y \vee t \simeq y) \cdot (s \succeq y \wedge t \succ y)}{(v \not\simeq y \vee t \simeq y) \cdot (s \succeq y \wedge t \succ y \wedge u \succeq x \wedge v \succ x \wedge s = u \wedge y = x)}.$$

Since x and y are variables not occuring in s, t, u, v, the conclusion of this inference is equivalent to

$$(v \not\simeq x \vee t \simeq x) \cdot (t, v \succ x \wedge s, u \succeq x \wedge s = u) \tag{2}$$

The clause (2) is more general than (1) since the constraint $s = u \wedge u \succ v \succ t \succ x$ implies the constraint $t, v \succ x \wedge s, u \succeq x$. We have shown, as was required, that (1) is a logical consequence of $\mathsf{T} \circ \mathsf{S}(N)$.

(iii) *Variant $v \simeq t$, t is a variable.* After simplifying the constraint, C has the form

$$(v \simeq t) \cdot (s = u \wedge s \succ t \wedge u \succ v \succ t). \tag{3}$$

---

[9] When we say that a constraint γ has the form $\gamma' \wedge \gamma''$ we assume matching modulo associativity, commutativity, *and* idempotence of conjunction.

In this case, consider the resolution inference

$$\frac{(s \simeq t) \cdot (s \succ t) \quad (u \not\simeq x \lor v \simeq x) \cdot (u \succeq x \land v \succ x)}{(v \simeq x) \cdot (s \succ t \land u \succeq x \land v \succ x \land s = u \land t = x)}$$

from premises in $\mathsf{T} \circ \mathsf{S}(N)$. Since x does not occur in s, t, u, v, the conclusion of this inference is equivalent to

$$(v \simeq t) \cdot (u \succeq t \land s, v \succ t \land s = u) \tag{4}$$

which is more general than (3).

(iv) *Variant $v \simeq t$, t is not a variable.* In this case, C is equivalent to

$$(t \not\simeq x \lor v \simeq x) \cdot (s = u \land s \succ t \land u \succ v \succ t \succeq x), \tag{5}$$

with a fresh variable x. C can be derived from $\mathsf{T} \circ \mathsf{S}(N)$ via the inference

$$\frac{(t \not\simeq y \lor s \simeq y) \cdot (t \succeq y \land s \succ y) \quad (u \not\simeq x \lor v \simeq x) \cdot (u \succeq x \land v \succ x)}{(t \not\simeq y \lor v \simeq x) \cdot (t \succeq y \land s \succ y \land u \succeq x \land v \succ x \land s = u \land y = x)} .$$

Since x and y are variables not occuring in s, t, u, v, the conclusion of this inference is equivalent to

$$(t \not\simeq x \lor v \simeq x) \cdot (t, u \succeq x \land s, v \succ x \land s = u) \tag{6}$$

which is more general than (5).

The cases of the other inferences in FBS are dealt with in a similar way. The details are included in the appendix.

By inductive application of this lemma we obtain the desired property for flat clauses:

Theorem 3. *Let N be a set of flat equational clauses without constraints. Then N is equationally satisfiable if and only if $\mathsf{T} \circ \mathsf{S} \circ \mathsf{R}(N) \cup \{x \simeq x\}$ is satisfiable.*

Proof. It can easily be shown that $\mathsf{T} \circ \mathsf{S} \circ \mathsf{R}(N) \cup \{x \simeq x\}$ is satisfiable whenever N is equationally satisfiable. Suppose that N is equationally unsatisfiable, and let N' denote $\mathsf{R}(N)$. By the completeness of flat basic superposition, we may infer that $(\mathsf{R} \circ \mathsf{FBS})^*(N')$ contains a contradiction. The set N', and all sets $(\mathsf{R} \circ \mathsf{FBS})^k(N')$ are simplified (with respect to R) flat equational clauses to which we may (inductively) apply the above lemma. Therefore, all clauses in $\mathsf{T} \circ \mathsf{S}((\mathsf{R} \circ \mathsf{FBS})^*(N'))$ are logical consequences of $\mathsf{T} \circ \mathsf{S} \circ \mathsf{R}(N) \cup \{x \simeq x\}$. As the $\mathsf{T} \circ \mathsf{S}$ normal form of a contradiction is also a contradiction, $\mathsf{T} \circ \mathsf{S} \circ \mathsf{R}(N) \cup \{x \simeq x\}$ must be unsatisfiable.

5   Related Transformations

Let us now briefly discuss the connection of our method to other transformation methods. Brand's original method is not directly comparable to our method. The main difference (aside from the fact that we use constraints) is that Brand uses only a positive splitting rule,

$$(C \vee u \simeq v) \Rightarrow (C \vee v \not\simeq z \vee u \simeq z),$$

but no negative splitting rule. However, the positive splitting rule is applied even if the right-hand side v of an equality literal is a variable. With Brand's method the clause

$$f(g(x)) \not\approx h(x) \vee h(g(x)) \approx x$$

is transformed into two clauses

$$g(x) \not\simeq z \vee f(z) \not\simeq h(x) \vee x \not\simeq y \vee h(z) \simeq y$$

and

$$g(x) \not\simeq z \vee f(z) \not\simeq h(x) \vee h(z) \not\simeq y \vee x \simeq y,$$

whereas our transformation results in different (constrained) clauses

$$(g(x) \not\simeq z \vee f(z) \not\simeq z_1 \vee h(x) \not\simeq z_1 \vee h(z) \simeq x) \cdot$$
$$(g(x) \succeq z \wedge f(z), h(x) \succeq z_1 \wedge h(z) \succ x)$$

and

$$(g(x) \not\simeq z \vee f(z) \not\simeq z_1 \vee h(x) \not\simeq z_1 \vee h(z) \not\simeq y \vee x \simeq y) \cdot$$
$$(g(x) \succeq z \wedge f(z), h(x) \succeq z_1 \wedge h(z) \succeq y \wedge x \succ y).$$

It is not possible, though, to simply add link constraints to Brand's original transitivity elimination rule.

For example, Brand's transitivity elimination with link constraints, when applied to the *unsatisfiable* set of unit clauses $a \approx b$, $a \approx c$ and $b \not\approx c$ yields a set of constrained clauses

$$(b \not\simeq x \vee a \simeq x) \cdot (b \succeq x \wedge a \succ x)$$
$$(a \not\simeq x \vee b \simeq x) \cdot (a \succeq x \wedge b \succ x)$$
$$(c \not\simeq x \vee a \simeq x) \cdot (c \succeq x \wedge a \succ x)$$
$$(a \not\simeq x \vee c \simeq x) \cdot (a \succeq x \wedge c \succ x)$$
$$b \not\simeq c$$

that is *satisfiable* (in combination with the reflexivity axiom $x \simeq x$), given an ordering in which $c \succ b \succ a$! (The first and third clause contain the unsatisfiable constraint $a \succ x$ and hence are void. The remaining clauses, along with $x \simeq x$, are satisfiable even without the constraints.) In short, ordering constraints are not compatible with Brand's original transformations.

The method implemented in the Setheo prover (Moser & Steinbach 1997) can be described with our transformation rules, except that no link constraints are introduced. Positive equations with a variable on the right-hand side are not split, and hence negative equations with a non-variable right-hand side must be split also.

For example, the three unit clauses $f(x) \approx x$, $g(x) \approx x$ and $f(x) \not\approx g(x)$ are unsatisfiable. However, if negative equality literals are not split, we obtain a satisfiable set of clauses $f(x) \simeq x$, $f(x) \not\simeq y \lor x \simeq y$, $g(x) \simeq x$, $g(x) \not\simeq y \lor x \simeq y$, $f(x) \not\approx g(x)$, and $x \simeq x$.

Let us conclude this section with an example. The presentation of group theory by three equations, $x * e \approx x$, $x * i(x) \approx e$, and $(x * y) * z \approx x * (y * z)$, is transformed with our method into the following set of constrained clauses:

$$x * e \simeq x$$
$$x * e \not\simeq u \lor x \simeq u \quad \cdot \quad x \succ u$$
$$i(x) \not\simeq u \lor x * u \simeq e \quad \cdot \quad i(x) \succeq u$$
$$x * y \not\simeq u \lor y * z \not\simeq v \lor u * z \not\simeq w \lor x * v \simeq w \quad \cdot$$
$$u * z \succeq w \land x * v \succ w \land x * y \succeq u \land y * z \succeq v$$
$$x * y \not\simeq u \lor y * z \not\simeq v \lor x * v \not\simeq w \lor u * z \simeq w \quad \cdot$$
$$x * v \succeq w \land u * z \succ w \land x * y \succeq u \land y * z \succeq v$$

where $\succ$ refers to a lexicographic path ordering induced by the precedence relation $i > * > e$ and constraints have been simplified accordingly. Note that with Brand's modification or with equality elimination as used in Setheo one gets an additional clause,

$$i(x) \not\simeq z \lor x * z \not\simeq w \lor e \simeq w.$$

This clause can be omitted, as its associated constraint $e \succ w$ is unsatisfiable in the given ordering.

6   Experiments

We present some experimental results with the Protein prover (Baumgartner & Furbach 1994) on certain simple problems in group theory. In the figure 6, "L" means that the goal was attempted in the presence of a previously proved lemma. In the table we list runtimes and number of computed inferences ("K" denotes kilo, and "M" denotes mega inferences) for four kinds of transformation. The "B" column depicts the results for Brand's original modification. "S" refers to the method that is implemented in Setheo with splitting of both positive and negative equations that have no variable right-hand side, without attaching ordering constraints. "Ss" is like "S" except that Skolem constants in the goals have not been abstracted. Compared with Brand's method, the Setheo method avoids more of those inferences which correspond to superposition into or from variables. However, it comes at the expense of also splitting negative equations. The experiments show that the price to pay is indeed very high so that in some of our experiments, "S" performs much worse than Brand's original method. However, if disequations $s \not\simeq t$ in which t is a Skolem constant of the goal are not split we obtain a uniform and more significant improvement. Finally, "C" is CEE transformation, using the presentation of group theory as presented

Problem	ord	number of inferences				time [sec]			
		B	S	Ss	C	B	S	Ss	C
$x * e \approx x$	–	1.3M	21.4K	1.5K	**578**	123	2.1	0.16	**0.1**
$i(i(x)) \approx x$	1	4.7M	∞	83.6M	**15.5K**	508	∞	10191	**4.8**
$i(i(x)) \approx x$	2	∞	∞	∞	**178K**	∞	∞	∞	**84**
$i(i(x)) \approx x$	3	4.7M	∞	83.6M	**15.5K**	502	∞	10191	**4.8**
$x * i(x) \approx e$	1	4.1K	288K	288K	**461**	0.4	30	30.4	**0.1**
$x * i(x) \approx e$	2	2.4M	17.5M	17.6M	**671**	272	2204	2204	**0.2**
$i(x) * (x * y) \approx y$ L	1	19.5K	267K	267M	**3.8K**	1.9	28	28.3	**0.9**
$i(x) * (x * y) \approx y$ L	2	∞	∞	∞	**12.2M**	∞	∞	∞	**3235**
$i(x) * (x * y) \approx y$	1	**9.1M**	∞	∞	24M	**950**	∞	∞	10574
$i(x) * (x * y) \approx y$	2	∞	∞	∞	∞	∞	∞	∞	∞

Fig. 2. Benchmarks on a 167MHz UltraSparc for simple problems in group theory

in Section 5. We have implemented constraint inheritance and checking in a straightforward manner. Ordering constraints are collected through additional arguments of predicate symbols. (As to what extent the additional predicates affect Protein's proof strategy, we do not know.) The first subgoal of any (non-unit) clause first calls upon a satisfiability check (implemented in Prolog) for the accumulated constraint at this point. Constraint solving was implemented incompletely by simply checking independent satisfiability of each inequality in any conjunction of inequalities. A complete constraint solving which is available for large classes of lexicographic path orderings, is very expensive and does not seem to reduce the number of inferences by another order of magnitude.

Protein is extremely sensitive to how the clauses and the literals in a clause, respectively, are ordered. In the examples we have experimented with three different orderings of the subgoals in the goal clause. In ordering 1 the variable definitions for inner subterm positions precede those of the outer positions. This ordering seems to work better with Protein most of the time. Ordering 2 is the inverse of ordering 1. Ordering 3 is some mixture of orderings 1 and 2. Orderings 2 and 3 coincide for the CEE transformation. For ordering 2, the speedups obtained from the optimization are much more dramatic. This seems to indicate that with the constraints the performance of model elimination is somewhat less dependent on subgoal selection strategies. In particular upon backtracking, ordering constraints prevent one from searching redundant alternative proofs of subgoals.

Although these experiments are far from being conclusive, it appears as if the CEE transformation can have a dramatic effect on proof search. Except for one case, proofs using CEE transformation were found much faster, usually by several orders of magnitude. With the rather incomplete method of constraint satisfiability checking, the price paid on each single inference seems affordable.

As said before, Protein proof search is too much dependent on the ordering of clauses and of subgoals within clauses. It would be interesting to see the effect of our improvements on Setheo where dynamic goal selection strategies result in a more predictable behavior and find proofs more often, also for less trivial problems than the ones studied in our experiments (Ibens & Letz 1997).

7   Conclusions

We have described a refined variant of Brand's modification method via ordering constraints that also improves equality elimination as implemented in the prover Setheo. Our theoretical results imply that equality handling in Setheo is indeed refutationally complete (which was an open problem). The completeness proof draws on recent results about basic superposition and thus establishes a connection between the theory underlying local saturation-based methods, such as paramodulation and superposition, and optimizations of equality handling in global theorem proving methods, such as model elimination and semantic tableau-methods.

Our experiments seem to indicate that with the ordering constraints the search space in model elimination theorem proving is indeed drastically reduced. This does not imply, however, that our results are of immediate practical significance as global theorem proving methods appear to be inherently limited in their ability of handling equality efficiently.

Acknowledgements. We are grateful to J. Steinbach for his comments on this paper and for his help in clarifying the relationship to (Moser & Steinbach 1997).

References

Bachmair, L. & Ganzinger, H. (1997), Strict basic superposition and chaining, Research Report MPI-I-97-2-011, Max-Planck-Institut für Informatik, Saarbrücken, Saarbrücken.
URL: www.mpi-sb.mpg.de/~hg/pra.html#MPI-I-97-2-011

Bachmair, L., Ganzinger, H. & Voronkov, A. (1997), Elimination of equality via transformation with ordering constraints, Research Report MPI-I-97-2-012, Max-Planck-Institut für Informatik, Saarbrücken, Saarbrücken.
URL: www.mpi-sb.mpg.de/~hg/pra.html#MPI-I-97-2-012

Baumgartner, P. & Furbach, U. (1994), PROTEIN: A *PROv*er with a *T*heory *E*xtension *IN*terface, in A. Bundy, ed., 'Automated Deduction — CADE-12. 12th International Conference on Automated Deduction.', Vol. 814 of *Lecture Notes in Artificial Intelligence*, Nancy, France, pp. 769–773.

Brand, D. (1975), 'Proving theorems with the modification method', *SIAM Journal of Computing* **4**, 412–430.

Degtyarev, A. & Voronkov, A. (1996a), Equality elimination for the tableau method, in J. Calmet & C. Limongelli, eds, 'Design and Implementation of Symbolic Computation Systems. International Symposium, DISCO'96', Vol. 1128 of *Lecture Notes in Computer Science*, Karlsruhe, Germany, pp. 46–60.

Degtyarev, A. & Voronkov, A. (1996b), What you always wanted to know about rigid *E*-unification, in J. Alferes, L. Pereira & E. Orlowska, eds, 'Logics in Artificial Intelligence. European Workshop, JELIA'96', Vol. 1126 of *Lecture Notes in Artificial Intelligence*, Évora, Portugal, pp. 50–69.

Ibens, O. & Letz, R. (1997), Subgoal alternation in model elimination, *in* D. Galmiche, ed., 'Automated Reasoning with Analytic Tableaux and Related Methods', Vol. 1227 of *Lecture Notes in Artificial Intelligence*, Springer Verlag, pp. 201–215.

Moser, M., Lynch, C. & Steinbach, J. (1995), Model elimination with basic ordered paramodulation, Technical Report AR-95-11, Fakultät für Informatik, Technische Universität München, München.

Moser, M. & Steinbach, J. (1997), STE-modification revisited, Technical Report AR-97-03, Fakultät für Informatik, Technische Universität München, München.

Schumann, J. (1994), 'Tableau-based theorem provers: Systems and implementations', *Journal of Automated Reasoning* 13(3), 409–421.

A Resolution Decision Procedure for the Guarded Fragment

Hans de Nivelle

Centrum voor Wiskunde en Informatica,
PO BOX 94079, 1090 GB Amsterdam,
the Netherlands,
email: nivelle@cwi.nl

Abstract. We give a resolution based decision procedure for the guarded fragment of [ANB96]. The relevance of the guarded fragment lies in the fact that many modal logics can be translated into it. In this way the guarded fragment acts as a framework explaining the nice properties of these modal logics. By constructing an effective decision procedure for the guarded fragment we define an effective procedure for deciding these modal logics.

1   Introduction

The guarded fragment was inspired in [ANB96], (see also [Benthem96]) by the following observations: **(1)** Many propositional modal logics have very good properties, they are decidable, have the finite model property, and interpolation. **(2)** These modal logics can be translated into first order logic, using a standard (relational) translation based on the Kripke frames:

$$\Box A \Rightarrow \forall s' R(s, s') \to \cdots \qquad \Diamond A \Rightarrow \exists s' R(s, s') \wedge \cdots$$

The fragment of first order formulae that can be a translation of a modal formula must also have these properties. This leads to the following question: What makes this set of translations of modal formulae so nice? One explanation could be the fact that modal logic translates into the 2-variable fragment, which is decidable. This is not sufficient. The logic K can be translated into the 2-variable fragment, but most other modal logics cannot. Also the 2-variable fragment lacks interpolation, although it is decidable.

The guarded fragment is based on the observation that in the translations all quantifiers are *conditional* in an accessibility condition, i.e. they all have the form: for all worlds s' for which $R(s, s')$, something holds in s'. This leads to a definition of the *guarded fragment* in which all universal quantifiers occur as $\forall \overline{x}(G(\overline{x}, \overline{y}) \to \Phi(\overline{x}, \overline{y}))$, where G is an atom. It turns out that this fragment, although it still cannot explain all modal logics, has good model theoretic properties. There are

C. Kirchner and H. Kirchner (Eds.): Automated Deduction, CADE-15
LNAI 1421, pp. 191–204, 1998. © Springer–Verlag Berlin Heidelberg 1998

more perspectives for generalization (see [Benthem97]), than from the 2-variable fragment, as the 3-variable fragment is already undecidable.

Among the logics that can be translated into the guarded fragment are the modal logics $K, D, T, S5$, many arrow logics, and weak predicate logics, (see [Benthem96]). Logic $S4$ does not fit, because of the transitivity axioms.

In this paper we develop a resolution decision procedure for the guarded fragment. We define guarded clauses, and show that first order guarded formulae can be translated into sets of guarded clauses. After that we show that sets of guarded clause sets are decidable using techniques that are standard in the field of resolution decision procedures. The restriction of resolution that has to be used is based on an *ordering refinement*. All of the major theorem provers (SPASS, [Wbach96], OTTER [McCune95], and Gandalf, [ATP97]) support orderings, although not exactly the one that we need. We have implemented our strategy as an option in a general purpose, resolution theorem prover.

In [Ohlbach88a] and [Ohlbach88b], the *functional* translation of modal logics is introduced, as opposed to the *relational* translation which is the one that we use. In the functional translation, the accessibility relation is translated into many function symbols, instead of one relation symbol. It is argued there that this has the advantage of resulting in a decision procedure, and that relational translation does not result in a decision procedure. We show that it is possible to obtain a decision procedure, using the relational translation.

Another approach to theorem proving in modal logics can be found in [FarHerz88] and [EnjFar89]. Instead of translating the modal formula, resolution rules are defined, that work directly in the modal logic. The rules are complicated and for each modal logic, a new calculus has to be designed. In [Nivelle93], [Nivelle92], these problems were partially overcome. A generic approach to resolution in propositional modal systems was defined there, but the rules are still complicated, and computationally costly. A resolution based decision procedure based on the guarded fragment is generic, and the effort of implementation is low.

2   The Guarded Fragment

In this section we briefly introduce the guarded fragment:

Definition 1. *A term is* functional *if it is not a constant, nor a variable. The guarded fragment of first order logic ($\mathcal{GF}$) is recursively built up as follows:*

1. $\top$ *and* $\bot$ *are in* $\mathcal{GF}$.
2. *If A is an atom, such that none of its arguments is is functional, then $A \in \mathcal{GF}$.*
3. *If $A \in \mathcal{GF}$, then $\neg A \in \mathcal{GF}$.*
4. *If $A, B \in \mathcal{GF}$, then $A \vee B$, $A \wedge B$, $A \rightarrow B$, $A \leftrightarrow B \in \mathcal{GF}$.*
5. *If $A \in \mathcal{GF}$ and a is an atom, for which (a) all arguments of a are non-functional, (b) every free variable of A is among the arguments of a, then $\forall \bar{x}(a \rightarrow A) \in \mathcal{GF}$, for every sequence of variables $\bar{x}$.*

6. *If $A \in \mathcal{GF}$ and a is an atom, for which* **(a)***every argument of a is a nonfunctional,* **(b)***every free variable of A is among the arguments of a, then* $\exists \overline{x}(a \wedge A) \in \mathcal{GF}$.

The atoms a are called the guards. *The guards may have repeated arguments, and they do not need to occur in some fixed order. So $a(y, x, x, y)$ is allowed as guard. Each occurrence of a quantifier can have a different guard.*

Example 1. The formulae $\forall x(a(x, y) \to b(x, y))$ and $\exists x(a(x, y) \wedge b(x, y))$ are in $\mathcal{GF}$. Also the formulae $\forall xy(a(x, y) \to b(x, y))$ and $\exists xy(a(x, y) \wedge b(x, y))$. The formulae $\forall x(a(x) \to b(x, y))$ and $\exists x(a(x) \wedge b(x, y))$ are not. The formula

$$\forall x(a(x, y) \to \forall z(b(y, z) \to c(y, z) \wedge d(y, z)))$$

is guarded. The formula

$$\exists x(a(x, y) \wedge \forall z(b(y, z) \to c(y, z) \vee d(x, z)))$$

is not guarded. The formula

$$\forall x_1 x_2 x_3 [R(x_1, x_2) \to R(x_2, x_3) \to R(x_1, x_3)],$$

which expresses transitivity, is not guarded. The modal formula $\Diamond(\Box a \wedge b)$ translates into $\exists x[R(c, x) \wedge (\forall y R(x, y) \to a(y)) \wedge b(y)]$, which is guarded, as we promised in the introduction. (c is the present world).

3   Resolution

We briefly review some notions:

Definition 2. *We assume a fixed, infinite set of function/constant symbols F, a fixed, infinite set of predicate/propositional symbols P, and a fixed, infinite set of variables V. The set of* terms *is recursively defined as follows:* **(1)** *A variable is a term.* **(2)** *If $t_1, \ldots, t_n$, with $n \geq 0$, are terms, and $f \in F$, then $f(t_1, \ldots, t_n)$ is a term. If $t_1, \ldots, t_n$, with $n \geq 0$, are terms, and $p \in P$, then $p(t_1, \ldots, t_n)$ is an* atom. *A* literal *is an atom A, or its negation $\neg A$. Atoms of the form A are called* positive. *Atoms of the form $\neg A$ are called* negative. *A* clause *is a finite set of literals. A term that contains no variables is called* ground. *A term of the form c is called* constant. *A term of the form $f(t_1, \ldots, t_n)$, with $n > 0$, is called* functional.

Definition 3. *We define some complexity measures for atoms/clauses/literals: Let A be an atom/term. The* depth *of A is recursively defined as follows:* **(1)** *If A is a variable, then $\mathrm{Depth}(A) = 1$.* **(2)** $\mathrm{Depth}(f(t_1, \ldots, t_n))$ *equals the maximum of $\{1, 1 + \mathrm{Depth}(t_1), \ldots, 1 + \mathrm{Depth}(t_n)\}$. The depth of a literal equals the depth of its atom. The depth of a clause c equals the maximal depth of a literal in c, or -1 for the empty clause. The depth of a set of clauses equals the depth of the deepest clause.*

Let A be an atom/term. The vardepth *of A is recursively defined as follows:*
(1) If A is ground, then $\mathrm{Vardepth}(A) = -1$, *(2) If A is a variable, then*
$\mathrm{Vardepth}(A) = 0$, *(3) Otherwise* $\mathrm{Vardepth}(f(t_1,\ldots,t_n))$ *equals the maximum*
of $\{1 + \mathrm{Vardepth}(t_1), \ldots, 1 + \mathrm{Vardepth}(t_n)\}$. *The vardepth of a literal equals the*
vardepth of its atom. The vardepth of a clause c equals the maximal depth of a
literal in c. The vardepth of the empty clause is defined as -1. The vardepth of
a set of clauses C is defined as the maximal vardepth of a clause in C.
Let A be an atom/literal/clause. $\mathrm{Var}(a)$ *is defined as the set of variables that*
occur in A.
Let A be an atom/literal/clause. $\mathrm{Varnr}(A)$ *equals the size of* $\mathrm{Var}(A)$. *If C is a*
set of clauses, then $\mathrm{Varnr}(C)$ *equals maximal number of variables that occur in*
a clause of C.
Let A be a literal. The complexity *of A, written as $\#A$ equals the total number*
of function/constant/variable occurrences in it.

So $\mathrm{Depth}(p(X)) = 2$, and $\mathrm{Vardepth}(p(X)) = 1$. This is because the Vardepth is
defined by the depth at which variable X occurs, where the Depth is defined by
the depth that X creates. For a literal A holds that $\mathrm{Vardepth}(A) = -1$ implies
that A is ground. $\mathrm{Vardepth}(A) = 0$ is not possible. $\mathrm{Vardepth}(A) = 1$ means that
A is non-ground, but has no non-ground, functional arguments. $\mathrm{Vardepth}(A) > 1$
means that A is non-ground, and has non-ground, functional arguments.

Definition 4. *A* substitution *is a finite set of variable assignments of the form*
$\{V_1 := t_1, \ldots, V_n := t_n\}$, *such that $V_i \neq t_i$, and $V_i = V_j \Rightarrow t_i = t_j$. The first*
conditions ensures non-redundancy, the second condition ensures consistency.
We write $A\Theta$ for the effect of Θ on term A.
If Θ_1 and Θ_2 are substitutions, then the composition of Θ_1 and Θ_2 is defined as
the substitution $\{v := v\Theta_1\Theta_2 \mid v \neq v\Theta_1\Theta_2\}$. We write $\Theta_1 \cdot \Theta_2$ for the composition
of Θ_1 and Θ_2.
For two literals A and B a unifier *is a substitution Θ, such that $A\Theta = B\Theta$. A*
most general unifier Θ is a substitution such that $A\Theta = B\Theta$, and $\forall \Theta'\ A\Theta' =$
$B\Theta' \Rightarrow \exists \Sigma\ \Theta' = \Theta \cdot \Sigma$.

The notion of mgu was introduced by J. A. Robinson in [Robinson65].

Definition 5. *We define the ordered resolution rule, and factorization rule: Let*
$\sqsubset$ *be an order on literals. Let $\{A_1\} \cup R_1$ and $\{\neg A_2\} \cup R_2$ be two clauses, s.t. (1)*
$\{A_1\} \cup R_1$ *and $\{\neg A_2\} \cup R_2$ have no variables in common, (2) for no $A \in R_1$,*
it is the case that $A_1 \sqsubset A$, (3) for no $A \in R_2$, it is the case that $A_2 \sqsubset A$, and
(4) A_1 and A_2 have mgu Θ. Then the clause $R_1\Theta \cup R_2\Theta$ is called a resolvent.
Let $\{A_1, A_2\} \cup R$ be a clause, such that A_1 and A_2 have an mgu Θ. The clause
$\{A_1\Theta\} \cup R\Theta$ *is called a* factor *of $\{A_1, A_2\} \cup R$.*

It is also possible to restrict factorization by the ordering, but we prefer not to
do that, since we are not certain that this improves efficiency.

4   Covering Literals

Most resolution decision procedures rely on the notion of (weakly) covering literals. The guarded fragment is no exception.

Definition 6. *A literal A is* covering *if every functional subterm t of A contains all variables of A. A literal A is* weakly covering *if every functional, non-ground subterm t of A contains all variables of A.*

Covering and weakly covering literals are typically the result of skolemization, when the prefix ends in an existential quantifier. If an atom $a(\overline{x}, y)$ in the scope of $\forall \overline{x} \exists y$ is skolemized the result equals $a(\overline{x}, f(\overline{x}))$, which is covering. If $a(\overline{x}, y)$ contains ground terms, then the result is weakly covering.

The main property of (weakly) covering literals is that they do not grow (too much) when they are unified. Theorem 1 states that when two weakly covering literals are unified, the maximal depth of a variable does not grow. Theorem 2 states that there are no new ground terms in the result, unless the result is completely ground.

Theorem 1. *Let A and B be weakly covering literals that have an mgu Θ. Let $C = A\Theta = B\Theta$. Then: (1) C is weakly covering, (2) Vardepth(C) $\leq$ Vardepth(A), or Vardepth(C) $\leq$ Vardepth(B), and (3) Varnr(C) $\leq$ Varnr(A) or Varnr(C) $\leq$ Varnr(B).*

For a proof, see [FLTZ93] or [Nivelle98].

Theorem 2. *Let $C = A\Theta = B\Theta$ be the most general unifier of two weakly covering literals. If C is not ground by itself, then every ground term of C occurs either in A or in B.*

For a proof see [Nivelle98] or [FLTZ93].

This shows that literals resolved upon do not grow, but it is also necessary to show that side literals can be bounded by the literals resolved upon. First we show that the side literals will be weakly covering. After that we show that they are not too deep:

Theorem 3. *Let A and B be literals and let Θ be a substitution such that (1) Var(A) $\subseteq$ Var(B), (2) A is weakly covering, (3) B is weakly covering, (4) $B\Theta$ is weakly covering. Then $A\Theta$ is weakly covering.*

See [FLTZ93], or [Nivelle98] for a proof.

Lemma 1. *If (1) Var(A) $\subseteq$ Var(B), (2) A is weakly covering, (3) B is weakly covering, (4) Vardepth(A) $\leq$ Vardepth(B), then Vardepth($A\Theta$) $\leq$ Vardepth($B\Theta$).*

5   Transformation to Clausal Normal Form

Since clauses are a restricted subset of first order logic, we need a transformation of first order logic to clausal normal form. The standard clause transformations do not work, since they would not lead to a decision procedure. We first define the notion of 'guarded' for clause sets, after that we show that a first order formula in $\mathcal{GF}$ can be effectively translated into a guarded clause set.

Definition 7. *A clause set C is called* guarded *if its clauses are guarded. A clause c is called* guarded *if it satisfies the following conditions:*

1. *The literals $A \in c$ are weakly covering.*
2. *If c is not ground, then there is a literal $A \in c$ with $\mathrm{Vardepth}(A) = 1$, such that $\mathrm{Var}(A) = \mathrm{Var}(c)$, and A is negative. ($\mathrm{Vardepth}(A) = 1$ means that all arguments of A are a constant or a variable)*
3. *If $\mathrm{Vardepth}(A) > 1$, then $\mathrm{Var}(A) = \mathrm{Var}(c)$. ($\mathrm{Vardepth}(A) > 1$ iff A has a non-ground argument that is functional)*

The negative literal of Condition 2 is the guard.

As a consequence every ground clause is guarded. We give a few examples:

Example 2. Clause $\{p(0, s(0)), q(s(s0))\}$ is guarded because it is ground. The clause $\{\neg\, p(X), \neg\, q(X, Y), r(f(X, Y))\}$ is guarded by $\neg\, q(X, Y)$. The clause $\{\neg p(X), \neg q(Y), r(f(X, Y))\}$ is not guarded. Adding the literal $\neg\, a(X, Y, X, X, Y)$ would make the clause guarded.

The first steps of the translation are completely standard. We define the translation operators for sets of formulae, rather than formulae. This makes it possible that an operators splits a formula into more than one formula.

Definition 8. *Let $C = \{F_1, \ldots, F_n\}$ be a set of formulae. We define $\mathrm{Na}(C)$ as the result of replacing $A \leftrightarrow B$ by $(\neg\, A \vee B) \wedge (\neg\, B \vee A)$, and replacing $A \to B$ by $\neg\, A \vee B$ in all the F_i.*
The negation normal form of $C = \{F_1, \ldots, F_n\}$ is obtained by moving negations inward as far as possible, by deleting double negations, and by deleting $\top$ and $\bot$ as much as possible. We write $\mathrm{NNF}(C)$ for the negation normal form of C.

The advantage of the negation normal form is that it makes the polarities of the subfomulae explicit.
In order to proceed, we need a variation of the structural transformation. Structural transformations replace certain subformulae by fresh names, together with a definition of the name. Structural translations are studied in [BFL94]. They are called structural there, because more is preserved of the structure of the formula than when the formula is factored into clausal normal form. Our structural transformation is different from the one there, as we only replace universally quantified subformulae, and in a specialized manner:

Definition 9. *Let $C = \{F_1, \ldots, F_n\}$ be a set of guarded formulae in negation normal form.* $\text{Struct}_{\mathcal{GF}}(F)$ *is obtained by making the following replacements in the F_i as long as possible: As long as there is an F_i which can be written as $F_i[\forall \overline{x}(\neg a \vee A)]$, where F_i is not empty, (i.e. the quantifier is inside some context), let $\overline{y}$ be the free variables of a, that are not among the $\overline{x}$. So $\overline{y}$ contains exactly the free variables of $\forall \overline{x}(\neg a \vee A)$.*
Let α be a fresh predicate name that does not occur in an F_i. Then add

$$\forall \overline{x}\overline{y}(\neg a \vee \neg \alpha(\overline{y}) \vee A)$$

to C. (Thus increasing n by 1) Replace $F_i[\forall \overline{x}(\neg a \vee A)]$ by $F_i[\alpha(\overline{y})]$.

The next step is Skolemization. Skolemization is the replacement of existential quantifiers by fresh function symbols in the preceding universal quantifiers.

Definition 10. *Let $C = \{F_1, \ldots, F_n\}$ be a set of formulae in NNF. The* Skolemization *is obtained as follows:*
As long as one of the F_i contains an existential quantifier, do the following: Write $F_i = F_i[\exists y A]$, where $\exists y A$ is not in the scope of another existential quantifier. Let $x_1, \ldots, x_n$ be the universally quantified variables, in the scope of which A occurs. Replace $F_i[\exists y A]$ by $F_i[A[y := f(x_1, \ldots, x_n)]]$.

There exist more sophisticated ways for Skolemization leading to smaller, or more general Skolem terms ([OWbach95]), but we cannot use them here. The reason for this is that optimized Skolem translations try to remove irrelevant variables from the Skolem terms $f(v_1, \ldots, v_n)$. This would destroy Condition 3 of Definition 7.

Definition 11. *Let $C = \{F_1, \ldots, F_n\}$ be a set of formulae in NNF containing no existential quantifiers: The* clausification *of C, written as $\text{Cls}(C)$ is the result of the following replacements* **(1)** *Replace $A \vee (B \wedge C)$ by $(A \vee B) \wedge (A \vee C)$.* **(2)** *Replace $(A \wedge B) \vee C$ by $(A \vee C) \wedge (B \vee C)$.* **(3)** *Replace $\forall x A$ by $A[x := X]$, where X is a designated variable symbol not occurring in A.* **(4)** *If one of the F_i has form $A \wedge B$, then replace F_i by A and B separately.*

We now have to show that the transformations translate formulae in $\mathcal{GF}$ into guarded clause sets. Transformation Na and NNF are unproblematic, since the result is still in $\mathcal{GF}$. There is only the small problem that in Condition 5 in Definition 1, the formula $\forall(\overline{x}a \rightarrow A)$ has to be replaced by $\forall \overline{x}(\neg a \vee A)$. It will turn out that Condition 6 can be completely dropped for formulae in NNF.

Theorem 4. *Let $C \in \mathcal{GF}$. Then* **(1)** *$C' = (\text{Na}; \text{NNF})(C) \in \mathcal{GF}$. (using the modification for the negation normal form),* **(2)** *$C'' = \text{Struct}_{\mathcal{GF}}(C') \in \mathcal{GF}$,* **(3)** *$(\text{Sk}; \text{Cls})(C'')$ is a guarded clause set.*

Proof. We study the steps made in the transformation: Na and NNF can be characterized by a set of rewrite-rules, none of which introduces a free variable in a formula. Let $\Phi = \forall \overline{x}(a \rightarrow A)$ or $\Phi = \exists \overline{x}(a \wedge A)$ be a guarded quantification.

Φ will remain guarded under any rewrite step completely inside A. Similarly if A occurs in the X or Y of a rewrite rule $(X \text{ op } Y) \Rightarrow \Phi(X, Y)$ then A is copied without problems. The only possible problem is when $\forall \overline{x}(a \rightarrow A)$ rewrites to $\forall \overline{x}(\neg a \vee A)$, but for this case we extended the definition of the guarded fragment. Next we consider $\text{Struct}_{\mathcal{GF}}$. The formula $\forall \overline{xy}[\neg a \vee \neg \alpha(\overline{y}) \vee A]$ is guarded, since a is a guard, and A is not affected. Any quantification in which $\forall \overline{x}(\neg a \vee A)$ occurs remains guarded when it is replaced by $\alpha(\overline{y})$, because no new free variables are introduced. Quantifications inside A are not affected by this operation.

For Skolemization note that every existential quantifier occurs either outside the scope of any $\forall$-quantifier, in that case it will be replaced by a constant, or in the A of a guarded formula $\forall \overline{x}(\neg a \vee A)$, where A does not contain any universal quantifiers. In this case the existential quantifier will be replaced by a functional term $f(\overline{x})$, where $\overline{x}$ contains exactly the set of variables occurring in the guard. The result is a formula in which all universal quantifiers are guarded, and all functions are Skolem functions. They are either constants or contain all variables of the guarded quantification in which they occur.

After that the formulae $\forall \overline{x}(\neg a \vee A)$ will be factored into guarded clauses

$$\forall \overline{x}(\neg a \vee A_1), \ldots, \forall \overline{x}(\neg a \vee A_n),$$

and the result is a guarded clause set. Every non-ground functional term in an A_i is obtained by Skolemization, and contains exactly the free variables of a. This ensures that the literals in A_i are weakly covering, because every variable occurring in A_i occurs in a.

Example 3. The guarded formula

$$\exists x \ n(x) \wedge \forall y[a(x, y) \rightarrow \neg \exists z < p(x, z) \wedge (\forall x \ a(x, z) \rightarrow (b(z, z) \wedge c(x, x)) \ ) >]$$

is translated as follows: First (Na; NNF) results in

$$\exists x \ n(x) \wedge \forall y[\neg a(x, y) \vee \forall z < \neg p(x, z) \vee (\exists x \ a(x, z) \wedge (\neg b(z, z) \vee \neg c(x, x)) \ ) >].$$

After that $\text{Struct}_{\mathcal{GF}}$ results in the following set of formulae:

$$\exists x[\ n(x) \wedge \alpha(x)], \quad \forall xy[\neg a(x, y) \vee \neg \alpha(x) \vee \beta(x)],$$

$$\forall xz[\neg p(x, z) \vee \neg \beta(x) \vee (\exists x \ a(x, z) \wedge (\neg b(z, z) \vee \neg c(x, x)) \ )].$$

Then Sk results in:

$$n(c) \wedge \alpha(c), \quad \forall xy[\neg a(x, y) \vee \neg \alpha(x) \vee \beta(x)],$$

$$\forall xz[\neg p(x, z) \vee \neg \beta(x) \vee (a(f(x, z), z) \wedge (\neg b(z, z) \vee \neg c(f(x, z), f(x, z)) \ ))].$$

Clausification produces:

$$\{n(c)\} \quad \{\alpha(c)\} \quad \{\neg a(X, Y), \neg \alpha(X), \beta(X)\}$$
$$\{\neg p(X, Z), \neg \beta(X), a(f(X, Z), Z)\}$$
$$\{\neg p(X, Z), \neg \beta(X), \neg b(Z, Z), \neg c(f(X, Z), f(X, Z))\}$$

6   The Resolution Strategy

Now that we have transformed the guarded formulae into a guarded clause set, we can define the resolution strategy. The strategy is defined by the following order. In order to prove that it is a decision procedure we have to show that the set of clauses that can be derived is finite, and that the strategy is complete.

Definition 12. *We define the following order* $\sqsubset$ *on literals:* **(1)** $A \sqsubset B$ *if* $\text{Vardepth}(A) < \text{Vardepth}(B)$, *or* **(2)** $A \sqsubset B$ *if* $\text{Var}(A) \subset \text{Var}(B)$.

Note that the cases are not disjunctive. It is easily checked that $\sqsubset$ is an order on guarded clause sets, so every clause has maximal literals. If a clause c contains non-ground functional terms, then the literals with maximal Vardepth are maximal. Otherwise at least the guard is maximal. It is always the case that every maximal literal of a clause c contains all variables of c.

Lemma 2. *Let C be a finite set of guarded clauses. Let $\overline{C}$ be the set of clauses that can be derived from C by $\sqsubset$-ordered resolution, and by unrestricted factorization. Then:* **(1)** *Every clause in $\overline{C}$ is guarded.* **(2)** $\text{Varnr}(\overline{C}) \leq \text{Varnr}(C)$. **(3)** $\text{Vardepth}(\overline{C}) \leq \text{Vardepth}(C)$.

Proof. We use induction on the derivation. A clause in $\overline{C}$ is either a clause from C, derived by resolution, or derived by factorization.
For initial clauses from C, the situation is trivial.

Let c be obtained from two guarded clauses c_1 and c_2 by resolution. We show that **(1)** c is guarded, **(2)** $\text{Varnr}(c) \leq \text{Varnr}(c_1)$ or $\text{Varnr}(c) \leq \text{Varnr}(c_2)$, and that **(3)** $\text{Vardepth}(c) \leq \text{Vardepth}(c_1)$ or $\text{Vardepth}(c) \leq \text{Vardepth}(c_2)$. Write $c_1 = \{A_1\} \cup R_1$, $c_2 = \{A_2\} \cup R_2$, where A_1 and A_2 are the complementary literals resolved upon. Let Θ be the mgu that was used. If both c_1 and c_2 are ground, then the result is immediate. If one of c_1, c_2 is ground, say c_1, then $A_2\Theta = A_1\Theta = A_1$ is ground, and $R_2\Theta$ is ground, because $\text{Var}(R_2) \subseteq \text{Var}(A_2)$. Because of this c must be ground. Then c is guarded, $\text{Vardepth}(c) = -1$, and $\text{Varnr}(c) = 0$.
If both c_1 and c_2 are non-ground, then let d be the maximum of $\text{Vardepth}(c_1)$ and $\text{Vardepth}(c_2)$. Let n be the maximum of $\text{Varnr}(c_1)$ and $\text{Varnr}(c_2)$. By Theorem 1, $\text{Vardepth}(A_1\Theta) = \text{Vardepth}(A_2\Theta) \leq d$, and $\text{Varnr}(A_1\Theta) = \text{Varnr}(A_2\Theta) \leq n$. Since $\text{Vardepth}(R_i) \leq \text{Vardepth}(A_i)$, and $\text{Var}(R_i) \subseteq \text{Var}(A_i)$, using Lemma 1, $\text{Vardepth}(R_i\Theta) \leq \text{Vardepth}(A_i\Theta)$ and $\text{Var}(R_i\Theta) \subseteq \text{Var}(A_i\Theta)$. This together ensures that $\text{Vardepth}(R_1\Theta \cup R_2\Theta) \leq d$, and $\text{Varnr}(R_1\Theta \cup R_2\Theta) \leq n$.
It remains to show that c is guarded. Using Theorem 1 and Theorem 3 it follows that every literal in $R_i\Theta$ is weakly covering.
We still have to show that for every $B \in c$ with $\text{Vardepth}(B) > 1$, it is the case that $\text{Var}(B) = \text{Var}(c)$, and that c contains a negative literal G, s.t. $\text{Vardepth}(G) = 1$ and G contains all variables of c.

Assume without loss of generality that $\text{Vardepth}(A_1) \leq \text{Vardepth}(A_2)$. If A_2 is a guard of c_2, then A_1 is not a guard, because guards are negative. Because in that case $\text{Vardepth}(A_1) = \text{Vardepth}(A_2) = 1$, we can exchange c_1 and c_2. So we may assume that A_2 is not a a guard, and $\text{Vardepth}(A_1) \leq \text{Vardepth}(A_2)$. Let G be a guard of c_2. We have $G \in R_2$.

The mgu Θ has the property that for every variable X of c_2, the result $X\Theta$ is either ground or a variable, because otherwise Theorem 1 would be violated. It follows easily that $G\Theta$ contains all variables of $R_2\Theta$, and every literal $B\Theta \in R_2\Theta$ with $\text{Vardepth}(B\Theta) > 1$ contains all variables of $G\Theta$.

$G\Theta$ also contains all variables of $R_1\Theta$. Because $\text{Var}(R_1) \subseteq \text{Var}(A_1)$ we have $\text{Var}(R_1\Theta) \subseteq \text{Var}(A_1\Theta)$. From $\text{Var}(A_2) \subseteq \text{Var}(G)$ it follows that that $\text{Var}(A_2\Theta) = \text{Var}(A_1\Theta) \subseteq \text{Var}(G\Theta)$.

It remains to show that every literal $B\Theta$ in $R_1\Theta$, with $\text{Vardepth}(B\Theta) > 1$ contains all variables of $G\Theta$. If $\text{Vardepth}(B\Theta) > 1$, then either $\text{Vardepth}(B) > 1$, or $\text{Vardepth}(B) = 1$, and a variable in B was replaced by a non-ground, functional term. In both cases $\text{Vardepth}(A_1) > 1$ and $\text{Var}(B\Theta) = \text{Var}(A_1\Theta) = \text{Var}(A_2\Theta)$. Because of the property above of Θ it must be the case that $\text{Vardepth}(A_2) > 1$. But then $\text{Var}(A_2) = \text{Var}(G)$ and $\text{Var}(A_2\Theta) = \text{Var}(G\Theta)$.

Let c be obtained from c_1 by factorization. We show that **(1)** c is guarded, **(2)** $\text{Varnr}(c) \leq \text{Varnr}(c_1)$, and **(3)** $\text{Vardepth}(c) \leq \text{Vardepth}(c_1)$. If c is ground then the situation is trivial, otherwise we have $c_1 = \{A_1, A_2\} \cup R$, and $c = \{A_1\Theta\} \cup R\Theta$, where Θ is the mgu of A_1 and A_2.

It is sufficient to show that for every variable X of c_1, the result $X\Theta$ is either a variable or ground.

We may assume that $\text{Vardepth}(A_1) \leq \text{Vardepth}(A_2)$. By Theorem 1, $\text{Vardepth}(A_2\Theta) \leq \text{Vardepth}(A_2)$. This implies that at least for all variables in A_2 the result is a variable or ground. Now if $\text{Vardepth}(A_2) > 1$, then A_2 contains all variables of c_1, and we are ready. Otherwise $\text{Vardepth}(A_1) = \text{Vardepth}(A_2) = 1$. In that case the desired property of Θ is immediate.

It remains to show that the set of clauses is finite. For this we need:

Lemma 3.   *1. Let c be a non-ground factor of clause c_1. Clause c contains no ground terms, which are not in c_1.*

  2. Let c be a non-ground resolvent of clauses c_1 and c_2. Then c contains no ground terms, that are not in c_1 or c_2.

  3. Let c be a resolvent of c_1 and c_2, where c_1 is ground, and c_2 is non-ground. Then $\text{Depth}(c) \leq \text{Depth}(c_1)$ or $\text{Depth}(c) \leq \text{Depth}(c_2)$.

  4. Let c be a resolvent of c_1 and c_2, which are both ground. Then $\text{Depth}(c) \leq \text{Depth}(c_1)$, or $\text{Depth}(c) \leq \text{Depth}(c_2)$.

Part (1) and (2) follow from Theorem 2. Part (3) and (4) are easily checked.

Lemma 4. *Let C be a finite set of guarded clauses. Let $\overline{C}$ be its closure under $\sqsubset$-ordered resolution, and factoring (unrestricted). Then $\overline{C}$ is finite in size.*

Proof.   The difficulty is that, although Vardepth($\overline{C}$) $\leq$ Vardepth(C), and Varnr($\overline{C}$) $\leq$ Varnr(C), we have no upper bound for the ground terms.

Let C_{ng} be the set of non-ground clauses in C. Let $\overline{C}_{ng}$ be the set of non-ground clauses that can be derived from C_{ng}. (So, $\overline{C}_{ng}$ is the total set of non-ground clauses that can be derived)

It follows from Lemma 3 that $\overline{C}_{ng}$ does not contain a ground term that is not in C_{ng}. Hence $\overline{C}_{ng}$ is finite in size.

After that $\overline{C}$ can be obtained from $\overline{C}_{ng}$ by deriving only ground clauses. It follows from Lemma 3, that $\overline{C}$ is finite in size.

It remains to show the completeness. The order is non-liftable, i.e. does not satisfy $A \sqsubset B \Rightarrow A\Theta \sqsubset B\Theta$, for example we have:

1. $p(s(0), X) \sqsubset p(0, s(X))$ and $p(X, s(0)) \sqsubset p(s(X), 0)$. The substitution $\{X := 0\}$ results in a conflict.
2. Also $\neg\, p(X, X) \sqsubset \neg\, q(X, Y)$ and $\neg\, q(X, X) \sqsubset \neg\, p(X, Y)$. The substitution $\{X := Y\}$ results in a conflict.

The completeness proof is based on the resolution game ([Nivelle94], or [Nivelle95]). We need some technical preparation: A literal A is *normal* if variable X_{i+1} occurs only after an occurrence of variable X_i. (When the literal is written in the standard notation. We assume a fixed enumeration of the variables). We write $\overline{A}$ for the normalization of A. Every literal A can be renamed into exactly one normal literal, called the *normalization* of A. If two literals are renamings of each other, they have the same normalization.

Definition 13. *Let $\Theta = \{V_1 := t_1, \ldots, V_n := t_n\}$ be a substitution. The complexity of Θ, written as $\#\Theta$ equals $\#t_1 + \cdots + \#t_n$.*

Theorem 5. *Resolution, using $\sqsubset$ is complete for guarded clause sets.*

Proof. Let C be an unsatisfiable guarded clause set. Let $\overline{C}$ be the set of clauses that can be obtained from C using $\sqsubset$-ordered resolution, and $\sqsubset$-ordered factoring. We show that $\overline{C}$ must contain the empty clause.

Write $C = \{c_1, \ldots, c_n\}$. Let $\Theta_{1,1}, \ldots, \Theta_{1,l_1}, \ldots, \Theta_{n,1}, \ldots, \Theta_{n,l_n}$ be a list of substitutions such that the set of clauses $c_1\Theta_{1,1}, \ldots, c_1\Theta_{1,l_1}, \ldots, c_n\Theta_{n,1}, \ldots, c_n\Theta_{n,l_n}$ is propositionally unsatisfiable. We have each $l_i \geq 0$. We call this clause set the Herbrand set.

First we annotate each clause in the Herbrand set with its representing clauses as follows: For each $c_i = \{A_1, \ldots, A_p\}$ and substitution $\Theta_{i,j}$, the set C_{hb} contains the clause

$$\{A_1\Theta_{i,j} : A_1, \ldots, A_p\Theta_{i,j} : A_p\}.$$

The objects of the form $a : A$ are called *indexed literals*. Extend the order $\sqsubset$ to indexed literals by $(a : A) \sqsubset (b : B)$ iff $A \sqsubset B$. Then define the following resolution and factoring rule for indexed clause sets:

resolution From $\{a\colon A_1\} \cup R_1$ and $\{\neg\, a\colon A_2\} \cup R_2$ derive $R_1\Theta \cup R_2\Theta$.
factoring From $\{a\colon A_1, a\colon A_2\} \cup R$ derive $\{a\colon A_1\Theta\} \cup R\Theta$.

In both cases Θ is the mgu. The result of Θ on an indexed literal $b\colon B$ is defined as $b\colon(B\Theta)$. The literals resolved upon, and one of the literals factored upon must be maximal.

Given this resolution and factoring rule, let $\overline{C}_{hb}$ be the closure of C_{hb}. It is clear that if we can prove that $\overline{C}_{hb}$ contains the empty clause, then $\overline{C}$ contains the empty clause.

In order to do this define the following resolution game $\mathcal{G} = (P, \mathcal{A}, \prec)$, and initial clause set $C_{\mathcal{G}}$:

- The set P of literals equals the set of literals that occur in the Herbrand set.
- The initial indexed clause set $C_{\mathcal{G}}$ consists of the following indexed clauses: For each indexed clause $\{a_1\colon A_1, \ldots, a_p\colon A_p\}$ in C_{hb}, there is the following clause in $C_{\mathcal{G}}$:

$$\{a_1\colon(k, \overline{A}_1), \ldots, a_p\colon(k, \overline{A}_p)\}.$$

  Here $k = \#\Theta$, where Θ is the substitution that makes $a_i = A_i\Theta$. The $\overline{A}_1, \ldots, \overline{A}_p$ are the normalizations of the $A_1, \ldots, A_p$.
- The set $\overline{C}_{\mathcal{G}}$ is defined as $C_{\mathcal{G}}$, but taking $\overline{C}_{hb}$ as a starting point, instead of C_{hb}.
- The set $\mathcal{A}$ of attributes is obtained from $\overline{C}_{\mathcal{G}}$ as the set of $(k, \overline{A})$, for which there is an indexed literal $a\colon(k, \overline{A})$ in $\overline{C}_{\mathcal{G}}$.
- The order $\prec$ is defined from: $a_1\colon(i_1, C_1) \prec a_2\colon(i_2, C_2)$ if **(1)** $i_1 < i_2$, or **(2)** $i_1 = i_2$ and $(\mathrm{Varnr}(C_1) < \mathrm{Varnr}(C_2)$ or $\mathrm{Vardepth}(C_1) < \mathrm{Vardepth}(C_2))$.

This completes the resolution game.

If we can show that $\overline{C}_{\mathcal{G}}$ contains the empty clause then we are done, since this implies that $\overline{C}_{hb}$ contains the empty clause.

We show that $\overline{C}_{\mathcal{G}}$ contains the empty clause by showing that it is a saturation of $C_{\mathcal{G}}$, based on $\mathcal{G}$.

Let $c_1 = \{a\colon(k_1, \overline{A}_1)\} \cup R_1$ and $c_2 = \{\neg\, a\colon(k_2, \overline{A}_2)\} \cup R_2$ be clauses in $\overline{C}_{\mathcal{G}}$, for which $a\colon(k_1, \overline{A}_1)\}$ and $\neg\, a\colon(k_2, \overline{A}_2)$ are maximal. Let $d_1 = \{a\colon A_1\} \cup S_1$ and $d_2 = \{\neg\, a\colon A_2\} \cup S_2$ be the clauses in $\overline{C}_{hb}$ from which d_1 and d_2 originate. Then $a\colon A_1$ and $\neg\, a\colon A_2$ must be maximal in d_1 and d_2. For if some literal in d_1 would be larger, the corresponding literal in c_1 would also be larger, in c_1, since all the k in the (k, B) of the indices are equal. The same is true for d_2. Because of this d_1 and d_2 have a resolvent d. We must show that the clause $c \in \overline{C}_{\mathcal{G}}$, resulting from d is a reduction of the resolvent of c_1 and c_2.

If one of the literals $b\colon B$ from R_1 is replaced by $b\colon B\Sigma$, (where Σ is the mgu), then $b\colon(k, B)$ can be replaced by $b\colon(k', B\Sigma)$, where $k' < k$. The same is true for the literals from R_2. This ensures that the result is a reduction. The situation in the case of factoring is analogous.

The order $\sqsubset$ as we have defined it here is very basic, and it could be refined further to improve the efficiency. Every order $\sqsubset' \supseteq \sqsubset$ can be used to decide the guarded fragment.

7   Conclusions & Further Work

We have shown that it is possible to effectively decide the guarded fragment by resolution. The proof that the resolution refinement is complete and terminating could be used as proof for the decidability of this fragment, but they offer more than that. They also define practical decision procedures, using refinements that are standard to the theorem proving community.

Future work should be the comparison of the complexity of the procedures with the theoretical complexity results obtained in [Graedel97]. Also some solution should be found for transitivity axioms. Transitivity axioms are non-guarded, and it has been shown in [Graedel97] that adding transitivity axioms leads to undecidability. Nevertheless there are modal logics ($S4$, and $K4$) based on transitive frames, that are decidable. So it must be possible to combine some weaker version of the guarded fragment with transitivity. Another point to look at is back translation. As some people prefer to see proofs in modal logic, rather than proofs in first order logic, it is useful to look into possiblities of translating the proofs in the guarded fragment back to proofs in the modal logics.

References

[ANB96]   H. Andréka, J. van Benthem, I. Németi, Modal Languages and Bounded Fragments of Predicate Logic, ILLC Research Report ML-96-03, 1996.

[BFL94]   M. Baaz, C. Fermüller, A. Leitsch, A Non-Elementary Speed Up in Proof Length by Structural Clause Form Transformation, In LICS 94.

[BL94]   M. Baaz, A. Leitsch, On Skolemization and Proof Complexity, Fundamenta Informatica, Vol. 20-4, 1994.

[Benthem96] J. van Benthem, Exploring Logical Dynamics, CSLI Publications, Stanford, California USA, 1996.

[Benthem97] J. van Benthem, Dynamic Bits and Pieces, LP-97-01, Research Report of the Institute for Logic, Language and Information, 1997.

[BGG96]   E. Börger, E. Grädel, Y. Gurevich, The Classical Decision Problem, Springer Verlag, Berlin Heidelberg, 1996.

[Catach91] L. Catach, TABLEAUX, a general theorem prover for modal logics, Journal of automated reasoning 7, pp. 489-510, 1991.

[CL73]   C-L. Chang, R. C-T. Lee, Symbolic Logic and Mechanical Theorem Proving, Academic Press, New York, 1973.

[DG79]   B. Dreben, W.D. Goldfarb, The Decision Problem, Solvable Classes of Quantificational Formulas, Addision-Wesley Publishing Company, Inc. 1979.

[EnjFar89] P. Enjalbert, L. Fariñas del Cerro, Modal resolution in clausal form, Theoretical Computer Science 65, 1989.

[FarHerz88] L. Fariñas del Cerro and A. Herzig, linear modal deductions, CADE '88, pp. 487-499, 1988.

[FLTZ93]   C. Fermüller, A. Leitsch, T. Tammet, N. Zamov, Resolution Methods for the Decision Problem, Lecture Notes in Artificial Intelligence 679, Springer Verlag, 1993.

[Fitting88] M. Fitting, First-order modal tableaux, Journal of automated resoning 4, pp. 191-213, 1991.

[Fitting91]   M. Fitting, Destructive Modal Resolution, Journal of Logic and Computation, volume 1, pp. 83-97, 1990.

[Foret92]   A. Foret, Rewrite rule systems for modal propositional logic, Journal of logic programming 12, pp. 281-298, 1992.

[Graedel97]   E. Grädel, On the Restraining Power of Guards, manuscript, 1997.

[Joyner76]   W. H. Joyner, Resolution Strategies as Decision Procedures, J. ACM 23, 1 (July 1976),l pp. 398-417, 1976.

[Ladner77]   R.E. Ladner, The computational complexity of provability in systems of modal propositional logic, SIAM Journal on Computing 6, pp 467-480, 1977.

[McCune95]   W. W. McCune, Otter 3.0 Reference Manual and Guide, Argonne National Laboratory, Mathematics and Computer Science Division, can be obtained from **ftp.mcs.anl.gov**, directory **pub/Otter**, 1995.

[Nivelle92]   H. de Nivelle, Generic modal resolution, Technical Report 92-90, Delft University of Technology, fac. TWI, 1992.

[Nivelle93]   Generic Resolution in Propositional Modal Systems, in LPAR 93, Springer Verlag Berlin, 1993.

[Nivelle94]   Resolution Games and Non-Liftable Resolution Orderings, in CSL 94, pp. 279-293, Springer Verlag, 1994.

[Nivelle95]   H. de Nivelle, Ordering Refinements of Resolution, Ph. D. Thesis, Delft University of Technology, 1995.

[Nivelle98]   H. de Nivelle, Resolution Decides the Guarded Fragment, ILLC-Report CT-1998-01, 1998.

[Ohlbach88a]   H.J. Ohlbach, A resolution calculus for modal logics, PhD thesis, Universität Kaiserslautern, 1988.

[Ohlbach88b]   H.J. Ohlbach, A resolution calculus for modal logics, CADE '88, pp. 500-516, 1988.

[OWbach95]   H-J. Ohlbach, C. Weidenbach, A note on Assumptions About Skolem Functions, Journal of Automated Reasoning 15, Vol. 2, pp. 267-275, 1995.

[Robinson65]   J. A. Robinson, A Machine Oriented Logic Based on the Resolution Principle, Journal of the ACM, Vol. 12. pp. 23-41, 1965

[ATP97]   The CADE-13 Automated Theorem Proving System Competition, Journal of Automated Reasoning Special Issue, Vol. 18, No. 2, Edited by G. Sutcliffe and C. Suttner, 1996.

[Tammet90]   T. Tammet, The Resolution Program, Able to Decide some Solvable Classes, in COLOG-88, Springer LNCS, pp. 300-312, 1990.

[Wbach96]   C. Weidenbach, (Max-Planck-Institut für Informatik), The Spass & Flotter Users Guide, Version 0.55, can be obtained from **ftp.mpi-sb.mpg.de**, directory **pub/SPASS**, 1997.

[Zamov72]   N.K. Zamov, On a Bound for the Complexity of Terms in the Resolution Method, Trudy Mat. Inst. Steklov 128, pp. 5-13, 1972.

Combining Hilbert Style and Semantic Reasoning in a Resolution Framework

Hans Jürgen Ohlbach

Dept. of Computing, Imperial College
180 Queen's Gate, London SW7 2BZ
h.ohlbach@doc.ic.ac.uk *

Abstract. Many non-classical logics can be axiomatized by means of Hilbert Systems. Reasoning in Hilbert Systems, however, is extremely inefficient. Most inference methods therefore use the semantics of a logic in one kind or another to get more efficiency. In this paper a combination of Hilbert style and semantic reasoning is proposed. It is particularly tailored for cases where either the semantics of some operators is not known, or it is second-order, or it is just too complicated to handle, or flexibility in experimenting with different versions of a logic is required. First-order predicate logic is used as a meta-logic for combining the Hilbert part with the semantics part. Reasoning is done in a (theory) resolution framework. The basic method is applicable to many different (monotonic propositional) non-classical logics. It can, however, be improved by treating particular formulae in a special way, as rewrite rules, as theory unification or theory resolution rules, even as recursive calls to a theorem prover. Examples for all these cases are presented in the paper.

1 Introduction

The simplest and most flexible way of defining a logic is by means of a Hilbert System. Theorem proving with a Hilbert System, however, is very inefficient because one has to generate all theorems until eventually the candidate formula appears, if it appears at all. More efficient methods such as natural deduction, tableaux or translation into predicate logic, use the semantics of the logic in one way or another.

Unfortunately, purely semantic approaches are not always applicable. They are particularly difficult if the semantics is not first-order expressible, or if it is just too complicated, as for example with neighbourhood semantics for classical modal logics [2]. Semantic methods for theorem proving are almost impossible if a user wants to experiment with different Hilbert axiomatizations of a logic without analysing its semantics each time a new variant is tried. This may be the case in applications where combinations of various logics for example time,

---

* This work was supported by the EPSRC Research Grant GR/K57282.

C. Kirchner and H. Kirchner (Eds.): Automated Deduction, CADE-15
LNAI 1421, pp. 205–219, 1998. © Springer–Verlag Berlin Heidelberg 1998

belief, causality, obligations, are to be used, and the interaction axioms are not in some well-known class.

The approach presented in this paper is a compromise between Hilbert style reasoning for getting maximal flexibility and semantics based reasoning for getting efficiency. If a first-order semantics for some connective is known, it is used as a kind of translation rule for eliminating this connective. In addition, Hilbert axioms and rules can be formulated, with quantification over formula variables. The formula variables are left in the systems and treated in a special way. The semantics based translation rules, the specification of the semantic structures, the Hilbert axioms and rules, and the theorem to be proven all become part of a first-order axiomatization. Ordinary resolution theorem proving is possible, but still too inefficient, therefore special algorithms and control mechanisms are needed to guide the proof search. The way, first order logic is used in this approach, is similar to the way Manzano has translated modal and dynamic logic into many-sorted logic [5]. The difference is that Manzano needs infinitely many first-order comprehension axioms. The comprehension axioms essentially introduce names for formulae. The effect of the comprehension axioms can be achieved by encoding formulae as terms. It turns out that the creation of these terms is not necessary in many cases. In certain cases, however, it is needed and must be carefully controlled.

Only the basic techniques are presented in this paper. Optimised algorithms and control structures for more efficient proof search in particular logics are sketched, but not investigated in detail.

2   Hilbert Systems

A Hilbert System is a kind of grammar for generating the theorems of a logic. It consists of *axioms* '$\vdash \varphi$' and *inference rules* 'from $\vdash \varphi_1, \ldots, \vdash \varphi_n$ derive $\vdash \varphi$'. A Hilbert System specifies the properties of each logical connective and axiomatizes their interactions. The Hilbert System for classical propositional logic, for example, can be easily extended with non-classical operators, by just adding more axioms and inference rules. In particular, the interaction between the non-classical and the classical connectives can be specified to any degree. If $\Box$ is one of the non-classical connectives, then for example $\Box(p \wedge q)$ does not automatically imply $\Box(q \wedge p)$, unless this is somehow specified in the Hilbert System, although conjunction $\wedge$ alone is commutative.

Hilbert Systems are also very convenient for combining different logics. The Hilbert Systems of the component logics are just joined together, and some interaction axioms are added. This specifies the combined logic.

Hilbert Systems can be encoded in first-order predicate logic (FOL) using a *theorem* predicate. The formulae of the given logic are encoded as predicate logic terms. The axioms $\vdash \varphi$ become unit clauses *theorem*(φ) where the predicate variables become FOL variables. The inference rules become Horn clauses. Hilbert style reasoning then corresponds to forward UR-resolution. Theorem proving in this style, however, is extremely inefficient [6]. In particular, this kind of reasoning does not provide a decision procedure, although the logic itself may be decidable. Nevertheless, the standard encoding of (finite) Hilbert System in FOL shows that the inference problem is first-order, and that it is at least semi-decidable, even if the semantics of the logic may have second-order features.

3 Semantics as Translation Rules

Most of the popular logics enjoy a semantics which can be expressed in FOL. For example the semantics of the classical connective $\wedge$ (conjunction) is

$$m \models \varphi \wedge \psi \text{ iff } m \models \varphi \text{ and } m \models \psi.$$

Using a binary predicate $T(\varphi, m)$ (φ is true in model m), this can be expressed as a FOL equivalence

$$\forall p, q \ \forall m \ (T(p \wedge q, m) \ \Leftrightarrow \ (T(p, m) \wedge T(q, m))). \tag{1}$$

The semantics of the other classical connectives can be expressed in the same way:

$$\forall p, q \ \forall m \ (T(p \vee q, m) \Leftrightarrow (T(p, m) \vee T(q, m))) \tag{2}$$

$$\forall p, q \ \forall m \ (T(p \Rightarrow q, m) \Leftrightarrow (T(p, m) \Rightarrow T(q, m))) \tag{3}$$

$$\forall p, q \ \forall m \ (T(p \Leftrightarrow q, m) \Leftrightarrow (T(p, m) \Leftrightarrow T(q, m))) \tag{4}$$

$$\forall p \ \forall m \ (T(\neg p, m) \Leftrightarrow \neg T(p, m)) \tag{5}$$

The symbols $\wedge$ (conjunction), $\vee$ (disjunction) $\Rightarrow$ (implication), $\Leftrightarrow$ (equivalence) and $\neg$ (negation) are used at the formula level and (infix) at the term level because they have the same meaning.

Examples for 'T-encoded' semantics of non-classical operators are:

$$\forall p \ \forall m \ (T(\Box p, m) \Leftrightarrow \forall m' \ R(m, m') \Rightarrow T(p, m')) \tag{6}$$

$$\forall p \ \forall m \ (T(\Diamond p, m) \Leftrightarrow \exists m' \ R(m, m') \wedge T(p, m')) \tag{7}$$

$$\forall p \ \forall m \ (T(\Box p, m) \Leftrightarrow \forall \gamma \ T(p, \gamma(m))) \tag{8}$$

$$\forall p \ \forall m \ (T(\Diamond p, m) \Leftrightarrow \exists \gamma \ T(p, \gamma(m))) \tag{9}$$

$$\forall p \ \forall m \ (T(\circ p, m) \Leftrightarrow T(p, m + 1)) \tag{10}$$

$$\forall p, q \ \forall m \ (T(p \rightarrow q, m) \Leftrightarrow \forall m' \ R(m, m') \Rightarrow (T(p, m') \Rightarrow T(q, m'))) \tag{11}$$

(6) and (7) represent Kripke's possible worlds semantics for the modal operators $\Box$ and $\Diamond$ for modal logics above K. R is the accessibility relation [2]. (8) and (9) describe the corresponding 'functional' semantics for modal logics above KD [8]. The γs are 'accessibility functions' mapping worlds m to accessible worlds $\gamma(m)$. The correspondence between the semantics in terms of the accessibility relation and the semantics in terms of the accessibility functions is

$$R(x, y) \Leftrightarrow \exists \gamma \ \gamma(x) = y.$$

(10) represents the semantics of the temporal *next* operator ○ in an integer-like time structure, and (11) is the possible worlds semantics of intuitionistic implication.

Let us call these equivalences the *T-encoded semantics* of the corresponding connectives and operators. The T-encoded semantics can be used to rewrite (translate) a term-encoded formula to the formula level of predicate logic. For example $T(\Box(p \wedge q)), m)$ can be rewritten to $\forall m' \ (R(m, m') \Rightarrow T(p \wedge q, m'))$ using (6) and then further to $\forall m' \ (R(m, m') \Rightarrow (T(p, m') \wedge T(q, m')))$ using (1).

Definition 1 (Semantic Normalising). *Given a set S of T-encoded semantics for some operators, let $\pi_S(T(\varphi, m))$ be the formula obtained by applying the equivalences in S to $T(\varphi, m)$ exhaustively from left to right. $\pi_S(T(\varphi, m))$ is the semantically normalised or S-normalised formula.*   ◁

Semantic normalising is an equivalence preserving transformation. That means $(S \wedge T(\varphi, m)) \Leftrightarrow (S \wedge \pi_S(T(\varphi, m)))$.

If S represents the semantics of *all* the connectives and operators occurring in some (ground) formula φ, then $\forall m \ \pi_S(T(\varphi, m))$ is essentially a FOL-translated non-classical formula. These kind of translations have been investigated for a number of logics, and with different translation functions corresponding to different presentations of the semantics [10,8,9]. The only difference is that in most of the other translation methods, in the final result of the translation, literals $T(p, m)$ are usually replaced with $p(m)$. If φ is ground, and p is a constant, this makes no difference.

In this paper, however, we also consider the cases with *predicate variables*. If p is a predicate variable then there is a big difference between $T(p, m)$ and $p(m)$. The first literal is first-order, whereas the second literal is second-order. For literals of the first kind, the Herbrand Theorem applies. Whenever there is a refutation proof for some theorem, then there is also a ground refutation proof, where the variable p in $T(p, m)$ is instantiated with a term-encoded formula. This cannot be guaranteed for literals $p(m)$ with predicate variables p. Therefore in this case $p(m)$ is stronger than $T(p, m)$. Since in the Hilbert System predicate variables implicitly quantify over formulae, the first-order version $T(p, m)$, but not the second-order version $p(m)$ is appropriate.

Furthermore, we consider the cases where S does not contain T-encoded semantics for *all* the connectives. For example if S only contains the semantics of the classical connectives, then $\pi_S(T(\Box(p \wedge q) \vee r, m)) = T(\Box(p \wedge q), m) \vee T(r, m)$. The '$\wedge$' inside the $\Box$ cannot be rewritten at this step. It might be rewritten after some inference steps which bring the $\wedge$ to the top-level of the term. Using this feature of our approach one can deal with very weak non-classical operators, which do not preserve the properties of other connectives when they occur nested within the weak non-classical operator.

With the binary predicate T, we can encode Hilbert axioms as unit clauses and inference rules as Horn clauses.

Definition 2 (T-Encoding). *A Hilbert axiom* $\vdash \varphi$ *with predicate variables* p_1, ..., p_n *is T-encoded as*

$$\forall p_1, \ldots, p_n \ \forall w \ T(\varphi, w).$$

An inference rule 'from $\vdash \varphi_1, \ldots, \vdash \varphi_k$ *infer* $\vdash \varphi'$ *with predicate variables* $p_1, \ldots, p_n$ *is T-encoded as*

$$\forall p_1, \ldots, p_n (\forall m \ T(\varphi_1, m)) \wedge \ldots \wedge (\forall m \ T(\varphi_k, m)) \Rightarrow (\forall m \ T(\varphi, m)).$$

If φ *is a Hilbert axiom or rule then let* $\tau(\varphi)$ *be its T-encoding.*

A S-normalised T-encoded Hilbert axiom $\vdash \varphi$ *is* $\forall p_1, \ldots, p_n \ \forall w \ \pi_S(T(\varphi, m))$.
A S-normalised T-encoded Hilbert rule has the form

$$\forall p_1, \ldots, p_n (\forall m \ \pi_S(T(\varphi_1, m))) \wedge \ldots \wedge (\forall m \ \pi_S(T(\varphi_k, m))) \Rightarrow (\forall m \ \pi_S(T(\varphi, m)))$$

$\lhd$

For example the K-axiom '$\vdash \Box p \wedge \Box(p \Rightarrow q) \Rightarrow \Box q$' for modal logic is T-encoded as

$$\forall p, q \ \forall m \ T(\Box p \wedge \Box(p \Rightarrow q) \Rightarrow \Box q, m) \tag{12}$$

and S-normalised without using a semantics of the $\Box$-operator to

$$\forall p, q \ \forall m \ T(\Box p, m) \wedge T(\Box(p \Rightarrow q), m) \Rightarrow T(\Box q, m). \tag{13}$$

The necessitation rule 'from $\vdash \varphi$ derive $\vdash \Box\varphi$' is T-encoded as

$$\forall p \ (\forall m \ (T(p, m)) \Rightarrow (\forall m \ T(\Box p, m))). \tag{14}$$

If in addition S contains (6) as T-encoded semantics of the $\Box$-operator then the S-normalised version of the K-axiom and the necessitation rule become tautologies. (This means that the possible worlds semantics of $\Box$ with binary accessibility relation is sound with respect to the Hilbert System consisting of the propositional part plus the K-axiom and the necessitation rule).

Translations of Hilbert axioms into predicate logic are used in correspondence theory for modal logic [10] and other non-classical logics. The translation of Hilbert axioms is correlated with properties of the accessibility relation. For example it is well known that the T-axiom $\vdash \Box p \Rightarrow p$ corresponds to the reflexivity of the accessibility relation in standard Kripke semantics. Technically this correspondence can be shown by proving that the standard translation $\forall p \ \forall m \ ((\forall m' \ R(m, m') \Rightarrow p(m')) \Rightarrow p(m))$ of the T-axiom is equivalent to $\forall m \ R(m, m)$. This in turn can be shown using quantifier elimination algorithms [4,1]. The crucial step, however, is the first one where the implicit quantification over all formulae in the Hilbert axiom is turned into a second-order quantification over a predicate variable. The interpretation of a predicate variable may be a set which cannot be represented as the truth set of a formula. Therefore quantifying over second-order predicate variables in general is stronger than quantifying over first-order term-encoded formula variables. In many cases, however, this is in fact equivalent. Showing this equivalence is the kernel of the corresponding completeness proofs.

The T-encoding of a Hilbert axiom is *not* second-order. Predicate variables in atoms $T(p, m)$ are still ordinary first-order variables. Moreover, in Herbrand models they are interpreted as term-encoded formulae. Therefore the problem that makes completeness proofs difficult for semantics with respect to Hilbert axiomatizations does not exist in our case.

Definition 3 (Mixed Problem Specification). *A mixed problem specification $(S, F, H, \neg Th)$ consists of a set S of T-encoded semantics, a set F of axioms for restricting the semantic structures, a set H of T-encoded Hilbert axioms and rules and a negated T-encoded candidate theorem of the form $\exists p \forall q \exists m \, \neg T(\varphi, m)$.*

It represents the problem of proving $\forall p \exists q \exists m \, T(\varphi, m)$ in the logic specified by S, F and H.

The problem specification is S-normalised if all atoms $T(\varphi, m)$ in $F, H, \neg Th$ are S-normalised.

The connectives with a semantics definition in S are the defined connectives. All other connectives are the undefined or axiomatized connectives.

This schema is not the most general one. In some logics, for example in relevance logic, a theorem is supposed to hold only in some selected world 0. In this case one must refute the formulae $\exists p \forall q \, \neg T(\varphi, 0)$ instead of the formula with the $\exists m$ quantification. For most logics it is obvious how to adapt this schema. ◁

(1) – (11) are examples for S. (12) and (14) are examples for H. F may contain for example the reflexivity axiom for the accessibility relation R used in (6). It may also contain the restrictions on the assignment which is necessary for intuitionistic logic: for all propositional constants p:

$$\forall m, m' \, (T(p, m) \wedge R(m, m') \Rightarrow T(p, m')).$$

The formulae in F may actually be represented by theory unification algorithms, or by theory resolution or constraint rules [7].

4   Theorem Proving

A T-encoded mixed problem specification is first-order and can be given to any FOL theorem prover. Let us illustrate the combination of S-normalising and resolution with a simple example from modal logic.

Example 1. Suppose we want to prove $\Box(p \wedge q) \Rightarrow \Box p$ from the K-axiom and the necessitation rule, and we want to use only the semantics of the classical connectives. That means, the S-part of the mixed problem specification (Def. 3) $(S, F, H, \neg Th)$ consists of (1) – (5) only. F is empty, and H contains the K-axiom. The S-normal form of the T-encoded K-axiom (12) is

$$\neg T(\Box p, w), \neg T(\Box(p \Rightarrow q), w), T(\Box q, w). \tag{15}$$

The clause form of the necessitation rule (14) is

$$\neg T(p, f(p)), T(\Box p, w) \tag{16}$$

where f is a Skolem function. The negation of the T-encoded theorem $\Box(p \land q) \Rightarrow \Box p$ is rewritten to

$$T(\Box(a \land b), w_0) \tag{17}$$

$$\neg T(\Box a, w_0) \tag{18}$$

where a, b and w_0 are Skolem constants. Two resolution steps with (15) (17) and (18) yield

$$\neg T(\Box(a \land b \Rightarrow a), w_0). \tag{19}$$

This is resolved with the T-encoded necessitation rule (16).
The resolvent $\neg T(a \land b \Rightarrow a, f(a \land b \Rightarrow a))$ is rewritten to

$$T(a, f(a \land b \Rightarrow a))$$
$$T(b, f(a \land b \Rightarrow a))$$
$$\neg T(a, f(a \land b \Rightarrow a))$$

which finally yields the empty clause.   ◁

The usual theorems to be proven in non-classical logics either have only universally quantified variables, or they are ground. The negated and Skolemized theorems are ground in both cases. The S-normalised negated theorems may not be ground, but the formula part in general is still ground. Therefore the main part of the reasoning deals with ground terms. Formula variables come from T-encoded Hilbert axioms and rules. For example, resolution with the first or third literal of the T-encoded K-axiom (13) introduces a variable. To keep the formula part ground one can either control the resolution in a special way, or one can turn them into theory resolution rules. In case of the K-axiom, the second alternative is the better option. The other alternative would be to prefer resolution with the second literal $\neg T(p \Rightarrow q, w)$ such that both p and q are instantiated. This, however, would mean that unification with some $T(\varphi, m)$ requires to decompose φ into an implication. This is possible, but the unifier would not be unique. Therefore, it is easier to turn the T-encoded K-axiom into a theory resolution rule:

$$\frac{T(\Box\varphi, m), C \qquad m\lambda = m'\lambda}{(\neg T(\Box(\varphi \Rightarrow \psi), m), C, D)\lambda} \quad \begin{array}{l} m\lambda = m'\lambda \\ \psi \text{ is not of the form } \varphi_1 \Rightarrow \ldots \Rightarrow \varphi \Rightarrow \ldots \varphi_n \end{array} \tag{20}$$

The T-encoded necessitation rule can also be turned into a theory resolution rule which calls the theorem prover recursively:

$$\frac{\neg T(\Box\varphi, m), C \quad \forall m \ T(\varphi\sigma, m) \text{ can be proved.}}{C\sigma.} \tag{21}$$

If φ is ground, then σ is always empty. If φ has free predicate variables $p_1, \ldots, p_k$, then '$\forall m \ T(\varphi\sigma, m)$' indicates that $\exists p_1, \ldots, p_m \ \forall m \ T(\varphi, m)$ has to be proved, and the bindings for $p_1, \ldots, p_k$ have to be returned. A consequence of Herbrand's theorem for FOL is that if the given theorem is provable at all, then there are a finite number of ground substitutions $\sigma_1, \ldots, \sigma_l$ such that $(\forall m T(\varphi\sigma_1, m)) \lor \ldots \lor$

$(\forall m T(\varphi \sigma_l, m))$ can be derived. If in addition, the semantics of all defined operators is sound and complete with respect to a standard Hilbert system (which is a Horn clause theory) then there is only one such σ, and this can easily be extracted from a refutation proof. In most monotonic logics, this is a reasonable assumption. Therefore, (21) has been formulated with only one such σ. However, there may be different proofs for the theorem $\exists p_1, \ldots, p_m \; \forall m \; T(\varphi, m)$ with different substitutions σ. As an example, consider $\exists p \; \forall m \; T(a \wedge b \Rightarrow p, m)$. This has the solutions $p \mapsto a$, $p \mapsto b$ and $p \mapsto (a \wedge b)$. All of them might be necessary.

In the modal logic K, where there is no other Hilbert axiom or rule besides K and necessitation, the system consisting of S-normalising, ordinary resolution and the above theory resolutions between clauses of the negated theorem is a decision procedure for theorems whose negation is ground. This is the case because none of the rules introduces deeper nestings of modal operators, and the recursive call of the procedure in (21) gets a formula with one modal operator less. That means nested recursion eventually has only a propositional formula to check, and this is decidable. Furthermore, the condition in (20), which is the only rule that introduces new terms, ensures that the generated nested implications are bounded.

The same method is a decision procedure for classical modal logics with either the RE-rule 'from $\vdash \varphi \Leftrightarrow \psi$ infer $\vdash \Box\varphi \Leftrightarrow \Box\psi$' or the RM rule 'from $\vdash \varphi \Rightarrow \psi$ infer $\vdash \Box\varphi \Rightarrow \Box\psi$', and no other condition. The RE-rule can be turned into the theory resolution rule

$$\frac{T(\Box\varphi, m), C \quad m\lambda = m'\lambda}{\frac{\neg T(\Box\psi, m'), D \; \forall m \; (T(\varphi\sigma, m) \Leftrightarrow T(\psi\sigma, m)) \text{ can be proved.}}{(C, D)\sigma\lambda.}} \tag{22}$$

The RM-rule can be turned into the theory resolution rule

$$\frac{T(\Box\varphi, m), C \quad m\lambda = m'\lambda}{\frac{\neg T(\Box\psi, m'), D \; \forall m \; (T(\varphi\sigma, m) \Rightarrow T(\psi\sigma, m)) \text{ can be proved.}}{(C, D)\sigma\lambda.}} \tag{23}$$

The usual semantics for these logics is formulated in terms of neighbourhood relations (minimal model semantics) [2], which is not easy to turn into a decision procedure.

Example 2. The cooperation between the theory resolution rule derived from the K-axiom (20), the recursive invocation of the theorem prover in the necessitation rule (21), and a T-encoded further Hilbert axiom, the D-axiom $\vdash \Box\varphi \Rightarrow \Diamond\varphi$ illustrates how to deal with formula variables. The clause form of the T-encoded D-axiom is

$$\neg T(\Box p, m), \neg T(\Box \neg p, m) \tag{24}$$

Suppose we want to refute $\Box a$, $\Box b$ and $\Box c$ in the modal logic KD, where a, b and c are complex formulae such that $a \wedge b \wedge c$ is inconsistent. The T-encoding is

$$T(\Box a, m_0) \tag{25}$$

$$T(\Box b, m_0) \tag{26}$$

$$T(\Box c, m_0) \tag{27}$$

The first step can be an ordinary resolution between (25) and (24), instantiating p with a. The resolvent is $\neg T(\Box\neg a, m_0)$. Applying (20) to (26) this resolvent yields $\neg T(\Box(b \Rightarrow \neg a), m_0)$. (20) is applied to (27) and the second resolvent again. The result is $\neg T(\Box(c \Rightarrow b \Rightarrow \neg a), m_0)$. Now the necessitation rule (21) is applicable because $c \Rightarrow b \Rightarrow \neg a$ is equivalent to $\neg(a \wedge b \wedge c)$, which, by assumption, is valid. The result is the empty clause.

If the second literal in (24), $\neg T(\Box\neg p, m)$ is preferred by some ordering strategy (see below), then there is no ordinary resolution possible. Instead we have to start with an application of (20). The result is $\neg T(\Box(a \Rightarrow \neg p), m_0), \neg T(\Box p, m_0)$ where p is still a variable. In this case, one can apply the necessitation rule (21) directly and find a substitution σ such that $a \Rightarrow \neg p$ becomes valid. The recursive invocation of the theorem prover has to solve the problem $\exists p \, \forall m \, T(a \Rightarrow \neg p, m)$. This is negated and normalised to two unit clauses, $T(a, f(p))$ and $T(p, f(p))$. Using (5) or the corresponding rule for the negation symbol (28) below yields the empty clause with the substitution $p \mapsto \neg a$. The result of the recursive invocation of the theorem prover and the application of the necessitation rule is $\neg T(\Box\neg a, m_0)$. The next steps are the same as above.   ◁

4.1   Ordered Resolution

S-normalising yields clauses with literals $T(\varphi, m)$, where φ is either a predicate constant or a predicate variable or a term with an undefined connective as top-level function. A strategy for controlling the resolution steps is now to use the T-encoded axioms and Hilbert rules for bringing the defined connectives to the top-level of the terms, such that they can be rewritten again. The application of the necessitation rule after (19) above had this effect. The classical term $a \wedge b \Rightarrow a$ inside the $\Box$-operator was brought to the top-level, and S-rewriting did the rest.

Technically, this can be achieved by *ordered resolution*. The ordering must be such that the literals $T(\varphi, m)$ with maximal number of functions in φ are chosen as the maximal terms. In many cases, in particular if the resolution partner is ground, this guarantees that the resolvents have smaller term-encoded formulae than their parent clauses such that resolution eventually terminates. Usually the choice of the maximal literal is obvious. In the clauses corresponding to (1 – 11) it is the (unique) literal with the defined connective. (This in turn guarantees that the equivalences are used from left to right only.) In (15) it is $T(\Box(p \Rightarrow q), w)$, in (16) it is $T(\Box p, w)$. It is also obvious in the T-encoded S-normal form for many of the well-known modal axioms, with $\Box$ as undefined operator:

name	axiom	T-encoded	maximal literal
D	$\Box p \Rightarrow \Diamond p$	$\neg T(\Box p, m), \neg T(\Box\neg p, m)$	second literal
T	$\Box p \Rightarrow p$	$\neg T(\Box p, m), T(p, m)$	first literal
4	$\Box p \Rightarrow \Box\Box p$	$\neg T(\Box p, m), T(\Box\Box p, m)$	second literal
5	$\neg\Box p \Rightarrow \Box\neg\Box p$	$T(\Box p, m), T(\Box\neg\Box p, m)$	second literal
B	$p \Rightarrow \Box\neg\Box p$	$\neg T(p, m), T(\Box\neg\Box\neg p)$	second literal.

Ordered resolution is complete, but it does not necessarily force termination of resolution sequences. The critical cases are clauses where the maximal literal

$T(p, m)$ or $\neg T(p, m)$ has just a variable p as its first argument, i.e. there are no connectives at all in the term-encoded formulae of the other literals in the clause. In this case, applying the T-encoded semantics definitions for rewriting and simplifying terms only is not sufficient. The ordering strategy can, and should not, stop resolution from instantiating p with the term in the left-hand side of a T-encoded semantics definition, thus performing potentially infinitely many further resolutions. In fact, resolution should not be stopped at the variable level, as the following example demonstrates.

Consider the clause $T(p, m), T(p, m')$ where m and m' are different, but do not contain the variable p. Instantiating p with $p_1 \wedge p_2$ and resolving with the clause form of (1) yields the four clauses $T(p_1, m), T(p_1, m')$ and $T(p_1, m), T(p_2, m')$ and $T(p_2, m), T(p_1, m')$ and $T(p_1, m), T(p_2, m')$. The first and the third clause are equivalent to the original one, but the two others are (equivalent) proper generalisations of the original clause. Repeating this operation, however, gives us nothing new. The same happens to negated literals $\neg T(p, m), \neg T(p, m')$ if the T-encoded semantics of $\vee$ is used.

Therefore we define a *linearised S-normalisation* for the classical connectives $\wedge$ and $\vee$: in clauses where a predicate variable p occurs twice or more either positive (i.e. in the form $T(p, m)$) or negative, and p does not occur in the second argument of T, resolve with the semantics definitions (1) and (3) until the condensed and non-subsumed clauses have only one occurrence of each predicate variable in positive or negative form.

Proposition 1. *Resolution between the maximal literals of the clauses corresponding to the semantics definitions (1) and (3) and linearised S-normalised clauses with no nested formula terms, is redundant.* ◁

In the proof one can easily check that all resolvents are subsumed.

Unfortunately the condition that the predicate variables do not occur in the second argument of the T-predicate is necessary. Predicate variables may occur in this argument if the clause contains Skolem functions. Then it may be necessary to instantiate predicate variables, i.e. to use the semantics definitions in the reverse way for building up term-encoded formulae again. Example 4 in the next section demonstrates this effect.

Resolution with the T-encoded semantics of the negation (5) is also not redundant in the above sense. For example, the two clauses $T(p, m)$ and $T(a, m)$ where p is a variable, are contradictory. The empty clause, however, can only be derived by instantiating p with $\neg a$, rewriting $T(\neg a, m)$ to $\neg T(a, m)$ and then resolving it to the empty clause.

The semantics (5) of the negation connective is therefore best turned into theory resolution and factoring rules:

$$\frac{\begin{array}{ll} T(p,m), C & m\sigma = m'\sigma \\ T(\varphi, m'), D & p\sigma = \neg\varphi \end{array}}{(C, D)\sigma} \tag{28}$$

$$\frac{T(p,m), \neg T(\varphi, m'), C \quad m\sigma = m'\sigma, p\sigma = \neg\varphi}{(\neg T(\varphi, m'), C)\sigma}$$

$$\frac{\neg T(p,m), T(\varphi, m'), C \quad m\sigma = m'\sigma, p\sigma = \neg\varphi}{(T(\varphi, m'), C)\sigma.}$$

This is compatible with ordered resolution, where $T(\neg p, m)$ is chosen as the maximal literal in (5). Therefore it is complete.

5   Semantics plus Hilbert Axioms

T-encoded Hilbert axioms are particularly suited for logics with a semantics which is appropriate for translation into predicate logic, but where the class of semantic structures is not first-order axiomatizable. The second-order properties of the semantics usually correspond to particular Hilbert axioms. With some key examples, we show that it is possible to use the basic semantics for translation, whereas the critical Hilbert axioms are just T-encoded, and not turned into conditions on the semantic structures which maybe second-order. This simplifies the proof procedures considerably. Moreover, we do not get the completeness problems related to the transition from implicit quantifiers over formulae in the Hilbert axiom to second-order quantifiers over predicates in the standard translation.

The McKinsey axiom

$$\Diamond\Box\neg p \lor \Diamond\Box p \tag{29}$$

in modal logics defines a frame class which is not first-order axiomatizable [10]. Therefore there is no easy way to get an inference method for a modal logic characterized by the McKinsey axiom. The next example demonstrates that the second-order semantics is not necessary if we keep the McKinsey axiom in the system explicitly.

Example 3. We show that together with the transitivity of the accessibility relation the McKinsey axiom implies $\Diamond(p \Rightarrow \Box p)$ (atomicity). Van Benthem's semantic proof of this theorem uses the axiom of choice ('it is as serious as this' [10]).

Instead of this we use the KD4 possible-worlds semantics (with seriality and transitivity of the accessibility) for the modal operators, and leave the McKinsey axiom essentially as it is. To make the example small enough we use the functional semantics $S = \{(8),(9)\}$.

The T-encoded and S-normalised McKinsey axiom, using (8) and (9) for the modal operators, is

$$\forall p \, \forall w \, ((\exists a \forall x \neg T(p, w : ax)) \lor (\exists b \, \forall y \, T(p, w : by))).$$

The clause form is $\neg T(p, w : a(w, p)x), T(p, w : b(w, p)y).$[1]
The negated theorem $\Box(q \land \Diamond \neg q)$ (with q being a constant symbol) is T-encoded and S-normalised to

$$T(q, w_0 : u) \qquad \text{and} \qquad \neg T(q, w_0 : vc(v)).$$

The empty clause is derivable in two steps using the (transitive[2]) unifier $\{p \mapsto q, w \mapsto w_0, u \mapsto a(w_0, q)x, v \mapsto b(w_0, aq), y \mapsto c(b(w_0, q))\}$.   ◁

Example 4. This example is from temporal logic. To make it more interesting, we choose an integer-like time structure such that an induction axiom holds:

$$\vdash p \land \Box(p \Rightarrow \circ p) \Rightarrow \Box p. \tag{30}$$

This time the $\Box$-operator means 'always in the future' and the $\circ$-operator means 'at the next moment in time'. The induction axiom expresses: 'if p holds now, and at all times t in the future, if p holds at time t then it holds at time $t + 1$, then p will always hold in the future'.
The temporal semantics of the $\Box$- and $\circ$-operators are (functionally[3]) T-encoded as

$$\forall p \, \forall m \, (T(\Box p, m) \Leftrightarrow \forall m' \, T(p, m : m')) \tag{31}$$

$$\forall p \, \forall m \, (T(\circ p, m) \Leftrightarrow T(p, m : 1)) \tag{32}$$

The T-encoded induction axiom[4] is

$$\forall p \, \forall m \, (T(p, m) \land (\forall n \, T(p, m : n) \Rightarrow T(p, m : n1)) \Rightarrow (\forall n \, T(p, m : n))) \tag{33}$$

and the clause form is

$$\neg T(p, m), T(p, m : f(p)), T(p, m : n) \tag{34}$$

$$\neg T(p, m), \neg T(p, m : f(p)1), T(p, m : n) \tag{35}$$

---

[1] The 'world-path notation' $T(p, w : a_1 \ldots a_n)$ is shorthand for
$T(p, a_n(a_{n-1}(\ldots a_1(w))))$. The a_i denote the accessibility functions.

[2] For transitive accessibility relations an 'accessibility function variable' u can be mapped to a string $a_1 \ldots a_k$ of 'accessibility terms'. This reflects that k steps in the transitive accessibility relation can be comprised into one step.

[3] The 'functional' reading of an atom like $T(p, m : m_1 \ldots m_n)$ is that p holds at a time point determined by starting at time point m, applying the function m_1 to m to get to time point $m_1(m)$ and so on. The *next* operator $\circ$ generates a constant 1, which is to be interpreted as the successor function. For example $T(p, m : a1)$ expresses that p holds at time point $a(m) + 1$. Notice that $m : 1a1$ and $m : a11$ as the second argument of the T-predicate denote different time points, because $a(m + 1) + 1$ may be different to $a(m) + 1 + 1$. Terms like $m : a11$ may also be abbreviated as $m : a2$.

[4] This axiom is actually a theorem in the integer time semantics. Unfortunately, it cannot be proved from (31) and (32). Therefore, it must be added explicitly. In general, each Hilbert axiom which is not translated into a theorem of the background theory given by the axiomatization of the semantic structures, has to be added explicitly.

Suppose we want to prove the theorem

$$p \wedge \circ p \wedge \Box(p \Rightarrow \circ \circ p) \Rightarrow \Box p.$$

After negation and translation:

$$T(a, m_0) \tag{36}$$

$$T(a, m_0 : 1) \tag{37}$$

$$\neg T(a, m_0 : x), T(a, m_0 : x2) \tag{38}$$

$$\neg T(a, m_0 : b) \tag{39}$$

Refutation:

$$36, 37, 32, 1^5 \quad T(a \wedge \circ a, m_0) \tag{40}$$

$$40, 34 \quad T(a \wedge \circ a, m_0 : f(a \wedge \circ a)), T(a \wedge \circ a, m_0 : n) \tag{41}$$

$$41 \ S\text{-normalised}, 39^6 \quad T(a, m_0 : f(a \wedge \circ a)) \tag{42}$$

$$T(a, m_0 : f(a \wedge \circ a)1) \tag{43}$$

$$40, 35 \quad \neg T(a \wedge \circ a, m_0 : f(a \wedge \circ a)1), T(a \wedge \circ a, m_0 : n) \tag{44}$$

$$S - \text{normalised}, 39 \quad \neg T(a, m_0 : f(a \wedge \circ a)1), \neg T(a, m_0 : f(a \wedge \circ a)2) \tag{45}$$

$$45, 43 \quad \neg T(a, m_0 : f(a \wedge \circ a)2) \tag{46}$$

$$46, 38(2) \quad \neg T(a, m_0 : f(a \wedge \circ a)) \tag{47}$$

$$47, 42 \quad \text{empty clause.} \tag{48}$$

◁

6 Summary

In this paper a new framework for automated reasoning in non-classical logics is proposed. It combines the translation approach for those operators for which a first-order semantics is known, and reasoning with (translated) Hilbert axioms. The non-classical formulae (including the Hilbert axioms and rules) are encoded as FOL terms. The semantics of some or all connectives and operators is turned into FOL equivalences, which can be used as rewrite rules to lift the term-encoded formulae to the FOL formula level, and for ordinary inference steps.

---

[5] This step actually consists of several different steps. First of all, $T(a, m_0 : 1)$ is turned into $T(\circ a, m_0)$ using (32). Then $T(a, m_0)$ and $T(\circ a, m_0)$ are comprised into $T(a \wedge \circ a, m_0)$ using the T-encoded semantics of $\wedge$ (1). A heuristics for triggering these steps is that in the clauses (34) and (35) a predicate variable occurs in a Skolem function. This causes that a conjunction of instances of the second literal, for example, $T(a, m : f(a)) \wedge T(b, m : f(b))$, is different to $T(a \wedge b, m : f(a \wedge b))$. Therefore one should guide the application of clauses with predicate variables in Skolem functions such that conjunctions appear at the term level.

[6] The second literal, $T(a \wedge \circ a, m_0 : n)$ is S-normalised to $T(a, m_0 : n)$ and $T(\circ a, m_0 : n)$. $T(a, m_0 : n)$ is resolved against $\neg T(a, m_0 : b)$, which leaves the first literal of (41) to be S-normalised.

A problem specification in this framework consists of four different parts:

- The first part is the encoded semantics of the operators. These are equivalences of the form

$$\forall p_1 \ldots p_n \; \forall m \; (T(f(p_1, \ldots, p_n), m) \Leftrightarrow \varphi)$$

where the p_i are formula variables, encoded as ordinary FOL variables, m denotes the model (possible world), and φ is a FOL formula which expresses the semantics of the operator f.
- The second part consists of the specification of the semantic structures. These are usually the axioms characterising the properties of the accessibility relations or accessibility functions. In logics like intuitionistic or relevance logic, restrictions on the assignment of predicate variables have to be added as well.
- The third part consists of T-encoded Hilbert axioms and rules which provide extra information about the operators.
- Finally the fourth part consists of the normalised (negated) theorem to be proved.

All parts are FOL formulae, such that the usual FOL calculi are sound and complete. Nevertheless, more efficiency of the proof search can be gained by treating the formulae in the four parts in a special way. The T-encoded semantics of the operators is mainly used as rewrite rules for lifting the term-encoded formulae to the FOL formula level. Unfortunately, in the presence of universally quantified formula variables in the other parts of the specification they also have to participate in other inference steps. It turns out that they are needed to build up term-encoded formulae again. It seems that this process can be heuristically controlled, for example by the presence of formula variables in Skolem functions. But more case studies with different logics are needed to get more experience on this.

The second part of the problem specification, the restrictions on the semantic structures, can be used as in the usual translation approaches, either for ordinary resolution steps, or they can be turned into theory resolution and theory unification rules. For many cases it is well known how to do this [7,9].

The third part, the T-encoded Hilbert axioms and rules, can also be treated as ordinary clauses, or they can be turned into theory resolution rules. Moreover, it has been shown that the T-encoded Hilbert rules can be turned into recursive calls of the theorem prover. Since particular Hilbert axioms characterized particular logics, it is worthwhile to figure out more efficient treatment for them than just resolution.

The approach proposed in this paper has many knobs and buttons for fine-tuning the proof search. Only a few ideas have been presented in more detail, and a lot more strategies and heuristics have to be developed. Therefore it cannot be recommended to use a standard FOL theorem prover for this kind of problems. Nevertheless, since FOL is used as the general framework, we can make use of all the techniques and results developed for FOL theorem proving.

The approach is very flexible. By representing parts of the specification of a logic as T-encoded Hilbert axioms, critical aspects which make purely semantics-based methods difficult, can be treated in an adequate way. It even works if for some of the connectives there is no known semantics at all. So far, only propositional non-classical logics have been considered. Most of the methods, however, should work for quantified non-classical logics as well. We are investigating the details in the context of Gabbay's self-fibered predicate logic [3], which provides a general semantics for predicates with formulae as arguments.

References

1. Chris Brink, Dov Gabbay, and Hans Jürgen Ohlbach. Towards Automating Duality. *Journal of Computers and Mathematics with Applications*, 29(2):73–90, 1994.
2. B. F. Chellas. *Modal Logic: An Introduction*. Cambridge University Press, Cambridge, 1980.
3. Dov M. Gabbay. Self fibring in predicate logics, fibred semantics and the weaving of logics, part 4, 1996. manuscript.
4. Dov M. Gabbay and Hans Jürgen Ohlbach. Quantifier elimination in second-order predicate logic. In Bernhard Nebel, Charles Rich, and William Swartout, editors, *Principles of Knowledge Representation and Reasoning (KR92)*, pages 425–435. Morgan Kaufmann, 1992.
5. Maria Manzano. *Extensions of First Order Logic*. Cambridge Tracts in Theoretical Computer Science 19, Cambridge University Press, 1996.
6. Williman McCune and Larry Wos. Experiments in automated deduction with condensed detachment. In Deepak Kapur, editor, *Automated Deduction – CADE 11, Lecture Notes in AI, vol. 607*, pages 209–223. Springer Verlag, 1992.
7. Andreas Nonnengart. *A Resolution-Based Calculus for Temporal Logics*. PhD thesis, Universität des Saarlandes, Saarbrücken, Germany, December 1995.
8. Hans Jürgen Ohlbach. Semantics based translation methods for modal logics. *Journal of Logic and Computation*, 1(5):691–746, 1991.
9. Renate A. Schmidt. *Optimised Modal Translation and Resolution*. PhD thesis, Max-Planck-Institut für Informatik, Saarbrücken, 1997.
10. Johan van Benthem. Correspondence theory. In Gabbay Dov M and Franz Guenthner, editors, *Handbook of Philosophical Logic, Vol. II, Extensions of Classical Logic, Synthese Library Vol. 165*, pages 167–248. D. Reidel Publishing Company, Dordrecht, 1984.

— Invited Talk —
ACL2 Support for Verification Projects

Matt Kaufmann

EDS CIO Services
98 San Jacinto Blvd., Suite 500
Austin, TX 78701, USA
kaufmann@cio2000.eds.com

Abstract. This talk discusses the use of a particular theorem prover,
ACL2, on formal verification projects, particularly in industrial settings.
In addition to describing briefly some existing and ongoing applications
of ACL2, I'll discuss features relevant to formal verification projects.

1 Introduction and Scope

The goal of this talk is to explore features for general-purpose reasoning tools
that are potentially useful for formal verification projects. I'll focus on a particular such tool, ACL2. The name is an acronym for "A Computational Logic for
Applicative Common Lisp."

I'll start by introducing ACL2 and summarizing existing applications of it.
Next, I'll describe briefly a relatively simple application of ACL2, which serves
both to introduce the system and to provide an example of the application of
general-purpose theorem proving in an industrial setting. Finally, I'll discuss
weaknesses and strengths of ACL2 for verification projects, in the hope that this
discussion is of use for other systems as well.

Acknowledgments

I am grateful for feedback from Jim Barnes, Bob Boyer, Bishop Brock, Rich Cohen, Ruben Gamboa, Joe Hill, Larry Hines, Warren Hunt, J Moore, Carl Pixley,
David Russinoff, Jun Sawada, Matt Wilding, and Bill Young. I am particularly
grateful to Joe Hill, manager of the Austin Renovation Center of EDS CIO Services, who has been generous in providing the time to write and present this
paper and talk.

2 About ACL2

This section gives background on ACL2 along with a brief description of some
existing applications. ACL2 is available at the following URL, which also provides
links to introductory "tours", related publications, and the manual.

C. Kirchner and H. Kirchner (Eds.): Automated Deduction, CADE-15
LNAI 1421, pp. 220–238, 1998. © Springer–Verlag Berlin Heidelberg 1998

http://www.cs.utexas.edu/users/moore/acl2/

The system runs under the Unix, Linux, and Macintosh operating systems, and has been built on a number of Common Lisps, including Allegro, GCL, Lispworks, Lucid, and MCL (Macintosh Common Lisp). It requires at least 16 megabytes of main memory, though 32 is definitely preferable (possibly more for large applications).

2.1 Introduction to ACL2

ACL2 was conceived as an applicative re-implementation of the Boyer-Moore theorem prover, Nqthm ([8,9,12]). It also incorporates ideas from Nqthm's Pc-Nqthm interactive enhancement. A list of applications using these systems may be found in [32]. A Web page with over 130 Nqthm-related papers, many with links, may be found at [6].

The ACL2 project was originally begun by Bob Boyer and J Moore in 1989. I started contributing to ACL2 somewhat after that, officially joining the project in 1993. The motivations for creating ACL2 and early design decisions are discussed in [35]. ACL2 is currently maintained by J and me, actually almost entirely now by J.

An ACL2 session consists of *events*, especially definitions and theorems. The logic is based on an applicative subset of the Common Lisp programming language [54]. The definitions may be recursive (possibly mutually recursive), in which case proof obligations are generated. However, there is a "program-only" mode in which the theorem prover is turned off and definitions are accepted with syntactic checks but without any proof required. Functions may be executed using the underlying Common Lisp. Collections of such definitions and theorems may be organized into *books*, a number of which are available with the distribution.

As with any general-purpose prover, interaction is important in using ACL2. The most basic way to control the prover is to prove lemmas that are stored as *rewrite rules*, which may be conditional, for automatic use in later proofs. The user can control which rules are *enabled*, and can prove other types of rules such as *forward-chaining* rules in order to help control the prover. Extensive documentation [34] helps the progression of novice users to totally wacked-out ACL2 weenieheads.

The paper [39] gives a tutorial on how to use Nqthm, and hence ACL2 as well, by way of a heavily-annotated example. The lowest level of the ACL2 logic is described in [37].

Large and multi-user interactive proof efforts with ACL2 have benefited significantly from structuring mechanisms provided by ACL2. These are defined rigorously and proved sound in [38].

2.2 Brief Summary of Existing ACL2 Applications

A number of papers describe ACL2 and some of its applications in much more detail than we do here. In particular, [36] provides a concise introduction to

ACL2 and [16] describes two commercial applications related to microprocessor correctness. One is Bishop Brock's behavioral, bit-level accurate specification of the Motorola CAP, a complex digital signal processor, together with correctness proofs for two programs on a pipeline-free version of the model, which in turn was proved suitably equivalent to the original model. See also [15]. The other, [43], describes verification of the microcode-level division algorithm for the AMD-K5^{TM} processor.

More recently, David Russinoff has proved in [47] a related theorem for the square-root microcode running on the AMD-K5^{TM} processor. In later work [48,49] he has proved correctness theorems for several hardware-level implementations of floating-point operations on the AMD-K7^{TM} processor.

Two dissertation projects using ACL2 are underway and show promising results. Verification of a pipelined processor model with variable-length instruction completion times is carried out by Jun Sawada with Warren Hunt in [50,51]. Ruben Gamboa has created a version of ACL2 that can handle irrational numbers, and has used it to verify the Fast Fourier Transform algorithm in [23].

Some of the above work and many applications of Nqthm have reasoned about hardware models and programming languages by formalizing interpreters and proving theorems about them. This technique is illustrated nicely in the tutorial [11]. See also [42].

One fairly intensive application of ACL2 has been to verify parts of its own source code, file `axioms.lisp`. Although such a technique can find bugs, there is clearly a circular aspect to it, which would however be overcome if checkable *proof objects* were created; see Subsection 4.4 for further discussion. Another developer-initiated application of ACL2 has been J Moore's construction of an "nqthm" package, which he has used to prove the major results from the Nqthm file `proveall.events`. Although ACL2 and Nqthm are close cousins, they have different logics. Hence, this exercise provided a good challenge for ACL2, given the goal of minimizing changes required to the Nqthm input.

Let us consider now one more application, in the context of using ACL2 as a simulator.

2.3   Evaluation

Section 2.2 of [16] extols the virtues of ACL2 as a simulator, comparing it to the Signal Processing Workbench simulator for digital signal processing chips.

> The ACL2 model runs several times faster than the compiled SPW model and hence is a potentially valuable debugging tool in its own right.

ACL2 employs the underlying Common Lisp for evaluation, which provides much better performance than one could obtain with, say, a rewrite-rule based evaluation mechanism. One can hope, then, to develop simulator models that have reasonable performance and yet are amenable to formal verification. How does this hope play out in an industrial setting?

Researchers at Rockwell-Collins are investigating the use of ACL2 as a simulator for a Java chip, with the potential for formal verification down the road.

Early results on a "tiny" version of the simulator are promising [25]: ACL2 performed about 2 orders of magnitude slower than a similar simulator written in C, but the Rockwell-Collins team implemented optimizations that removed almost all the deficit. Their model is array-intensive and hence the slower time may be overly pessimistic. Nevertheless, some of the inefficiency appears to be in ACL2's handling of arrays, which we hope to improve.

3 An Application of ACL2 to the Year 2000 Problem

I am fortunate to be working for a group that does Year 2000 COBOL renovations and is interested in the correctness of renovation rules. This section gives a brief introduction to the use of ACL2 to specify and verify correctness of such rules. Although this is a relatively simple application of ACL2, it serves to illustrate its use in an industrial setting. Indeed, a developer of our tool (other than me!) has referred to the verified rules when writing code. More details about this work may be found in [33].

3.1 Introduction

EDS CIO Services uses a suite of in-house tools to fix COBOL code that will fail to work starting in the year 2000. This tool suite uses *transformation rules* to remediate *noncompliant* code (as described below), that is, to translate noncompliant code to compliant code. There is more than one method for doing such remediation, but here we consider the method of *expression replacement*. In particular, we consider the remediation of inequality and equality expressions that are not year-2000 compliant.

The COBOL inequalities and equalities to be considered are quite simple. However, it is easy to make mistakes in their remediations, especially when they involve sums or differences or when there are *non-date* values involved, such as using 000000 to indicate that a date variable is uninitialized. Formal verification is an appropriate vehicle for gaining assurance in such a situation. This is not to denigrate testing, which we also use. However, formal verification provides added assurance as well as a stimulus to write down carefully the properties that are supposed to hold.

Here is a fragment of COBOL that compares two 2-digit years.

```
IF (YY1 < YY2) THEN ...
```

This code is easily seen *not* to be year-2000 compliant: for example, if YY1 has the value 98 and YY2 has the value 03, then this inequality will be false even though 1998 is less than 2003. The EDS tools *remediate* this code as follows.

```
IF ((YY1 < YY2 AND
    (49 < YY1 OR YY2 < 50))
    OR
    (49 < YY1 AND YY2 < 50)) THEN ....
```

We can try to reason out why this is correct, but this task is well-suited to a theorem prover, both to save labor and to gain assurance. An ACL2 theorem given below justifies the remediation shown above.

3.2   Overview of the Correctness Problem

This approach represents COBOL expressions directly in the ACL2 logic. An alternate approach would move up a meta-level, by introducing an expression interpreter (semantic function) for COBOL and reasoning about the values of COBOL expressions under this interpreter. Although I have done some such work, it seemed that enough assurance could be gained by the simpler, direct approach of translating COBOL directly into ACL2.

A *truncated date* is a value intended to represent a year or date that does not include century information. For example, 98 is a truncated date representing the year 1998. The essential idea is to define a *date expansion* function yielding the intended value of a given truncated date, for example, mapping 98 to 1998 but mapping 03 to 2003. For now, we consider only *valid* dates, but in Subsection 3.4 we consider *non-date* values as mentioned above.

This ACL2 work is parameterized by the following integers.

1. *window-bottom*: the base in years of the 100-year window, which is between 0 and 99 (theorems have been proved for selected values)
2. *n*: the number of digits in the date variables under consideration, which could be 2 (year only), 5 (Julian year-day, YYDDD), or 6 (Gregorian year-month-day, YYMMDD)
3. *min-date*: the minimum numeric value of a valid date
4. *max-date*: the maximum numeric value of a valid date

Once the number of digits is fixed, constants *window-top* and *century* are easily defined. The following table shows values for which the base year is 1950.

n	*min-date*	*max-date*	*window-bottom*	*window-top*	*century*
2	00	99	50	49	100
5	00001	99365	50000	49999	100000
6	000101	991231	500000	499999	1000000

A date expansion function is defined in ACL2 as shown below, in terms of these constants. Conventional notation is used below for presentation purposes, rather than the Lisp notation native to ACL2.

DEFINITION:
date(x)
=
if $x <$ *window-bottom* then $x + (20 *$ *century*$)$
 else $x + (19 *$ *century*$)$
fi
Guard: datep(x)

The *guard* above signifies that function 'date' is intended to be applied only to arguments x that satisfy the predicate 'datep'. We return to this point below.

The example remediation shown above in Subsection 3.1 is justified by the 2-digit case of the following theorem. The three cases — 2-digit, 5-digit, or 6-digit dates — are verified separately.

THEOREM: x<y-simple-case
(datep (x) ∧ datep (y))
→ ((date (x) < date (y))
    ↔ ($((x < y)$ ∧ $(($ *window-top* $< x)$ ∨ $(y <$ *window-bottom* $)))$
        ∨ $((*window-top* < x)$ ∧ $(y <$ *window-bottom* $))))$

3.3   Guard Verification

The analog in ACL2 of type-checking is *guard verification*, which catches errors by checking "well-formedness" of definitions and theorems. Recall the guard attached to the definition of 'date':

Guard: datep (x)

The following command checks that all applications of function 'date' are to arguments for which 'datep' holds.

VERIFY GUARDS for 'x<y-simple-case'

ACL2 replies that it must prove the following formula (which it then does, immediately). These proof obligations all come from the guard for '<' asserting that its arguments are rational numbers.

(datep (x) ∧ datep (y)
  →   rationalp (date (x)))
∧ (datep (x) ∧ datep (y)
  →   rationalp (x))
∧ (datep (x) ∧ datep (y)
  →   rationalp (date (y)))
∧ (datep (x) ∧ datep (y)
  →   rationalp (y))

Technical point. Theorems such as 'x<y-simple-case' are stated using a macro 'implies*', defined to be equivalent to the usual 'implies' operator but evaluated lazily: the consequent is evaluated only if the antecedent is true.

MACRO:
implies* (x, y) = list $('$if$, x, y, t)$

If the theorem were stated using 'implies' then guard verification would fail, since 'implies' always evaluates its second argument. A more detailed discussion of guards appears in [36].

3.4   An Example Involving Non-dates

We consider now the possibility that date-holding variables can take on *non-date* values. This situation is common in COBOL programs, where for example a string of spaces may be used as an indicator that a variable is uninitialized. Strings of zeros and nines are sometimes used in this way as well, but generally not in the two-digit case since 00 and 99 represent valid years.

Consider again the statement above,

```
IF (YY1 < YY2) THEN ...
```

but where now the year variables can take on non-date values. The remediation must consider the possibility that the variables have values outside the valid date range of 0 to 99, or more precisely, not lexicographically between the strings '00' and '99'. The resulting remediation appears as follows.

```
IF ((YY1 < YY2 AND
     ('49' < YY1 OR
     YY2 < '50' OR
     YY1 < '00' OR
     '99' < YY2))
   OR
   ('49' < YY1 AND
   YY1 <= '99' AND
   '00' <= YY2 AND
   YY2 < '50')) THEN ....
```

In order to specify this transformation formally, we need to modify the expansion function 'date' defined above to operate appropriately on all possible values of date variables, and we need to introduce an ordering relation on potential COBOL values of date variables.

- pseudo-datep (x) is intended to be true of legitimate, non-date values of COBOL date-holding variables. In many COBOL programs, the number 0 is used this way in the 6-digit case, but not in the 2-digit case, while a string of n spaces is used this way in the n-digit case.
- pseudo-date (x) is intended to return, for a given 'pseudo-datep' x, the appropriate expansion of x. For example, the expansion of the the 6-digit pseudo-date 0, i.e., of 000000, is the 8-digit "general" pseudo-date 00000000; the expansion of the 2-digit pseudo-date consisting of spaces is the 4-digit pseudo-date consisting of spaces; and so on.
- cbl< (x, y) is intended to be true when the COBOL less-than operator holds for x and y, which are each extended dates.

The precise axioms for these functions, for example trichotomy for 'cbl<' on its intended domain, are introduced using the ENCAPSULATE construct of ACL2, and may be found in [33]. ENCAPSULATE encloses a sequence of events (especially, definitions and theorems) and exports only the ones of interest, namely, the ones not marked "LOCAL". See [38] for a careful explanation of the semantics of ENCAPSULATE and justification of the soundness of its implementation. An important feature of ENCAPSULATE is that it is guaranteed to preserve consistency of the theory under development. In fact, it is guaranteed to yield conservative extensions.

Related macros are then defined:

- extended-datep (x) holds for both (century-less) valid dates and pseudo-dates.
- expand-date (x) expands the extended-datep value x: date(x) if x is a datep, else pseudo-date(x).
- cbl$\leq (x, y)$ holds when either cbl$< (x, y)$ holds or x equals y.

ACL2 can be led to prove the following theorem, specifying the correctness of the transformation performed by the EDS tools for 'extended-datep' values.

THEOREM: x<y-general-case
$$(\text{extended-datep}(x) \wedge \text{extended-datep}(y))$$
$$\rightarrow (\quad \text{cbl}< (\text{expand-date}(x), \text{expand-date}(y))$$
$$\leftrightarrow (\quad (\quad \text{cbl}< (x, y)$$
$$\wedge \ (\text{cbl}< (49, x) \vee \text{cbl}< (99, y) \vee \text{cbl}< (x, 0) \vee \text{cbl}< (y, 50)))$$
$$\vee \ (\text{cbl}< (49, x) \wedge \text{cbl}\leq (x, 99) \wedge \text{cbl}\leq (0, y) \wedge \text{cbl}< (y, 50))))$$

3.5   A Simplification Verified

The rules get more complicated when there are arithmetic expressions involved. In fact, we have found bugs by comparing generated code against verified rules. In this subsection we focus on one such rule, and how it was used to simplify a preliminary remediation method.

Our story involves the following fragment of an email message I sent to a tool developer.

> Thanks for sending that code fragment. I think your renovated code is correct, but can be simplified. (I compared with rule RULE-Y_>OP-_X+N/SIMPLE ....)

The relevant rule had been written to an output file generated by ACL2, using annotations in the original input file of definitions and theorems. An excerpt from that output file is shown below. Not shown below is an explanation from the output file that >OP may be interpreted either as > or as >=, and that {X} denotes the century-expanded version of a date X.

```
RULE-Y_>OP_X+N/SIMPLE.
----------
Special case of preceding rule, RULE-Y_>OP_X+N, when we know that X
and Y are valid dates.  Since we always assume that X and Y are
integers when an arithmetic expression is involved, this special case
is completely general in the 2-digit case, where there are no integer
pseudo-dates.
----------
```

```
({Y} >OP ({X} + N))
 ==>
((((Y >OP (X + N))
  AND
  ((X > *WINDOW-TOP*)
   OR (*WINDOW-BOTTOM* > Y)))
 OR
 ((X > *WINDOW-TOP*)
  AND (*WINDOW-BOTTOM* > Y)
  AND (Y >OP ((X + N) - *CENTURY*)))))
```

The EDS tools had been remediating the inequality

```
(WS-MPRDATE-YY - WS-SAVE-YR) > 1
```

as follows.

```
IF ((WS-MPRDATE-YY - WS-SAVE-YR) > 1 AND
    ((49 < WS-SAVE-YR AND 49 < WS-MPRDATE-YY)
     OR
     (WS-SAVE-YR < 50 AND WS-MPRDATE-YY < 50)))
   OR
   (WS-MPRDATE-YY + 99 > WS-SAVE-YR AND
    (49 < WS-SAVE-YR AND WS-MPRDATE-YY < 50)) THEN
```

After looking at the rule above, I suggested the following simplified version.

```
IF ((WS-MPRDATE-YY - WS-SAVE-YR) > 1 AND
    (49 < WS-SAVE-YR OR WS-MPRDATE-YY < 50))
   OR
   (49 < WS-SAVE-YR AND
    WS-MPRDATE-YY < 50 AND
    WS-MPRDATE-YY + 99 > WS-SAVE-YR) THEN
```

It is not difficult to hand-verify correctness of this simplification, but it was comforting that the verification had been done mechanically.

4   Matching Formal Verification Tools with Applications

Numerous tools now exist to automate reasoning in many domains, notably computer systems (hardware and software) and mathematics. It is not surprising that certain tools fit better with certain applications.

Section 5 lists features of ACL2 that support formal verification. However, ACL2 is *not* a particularly good fit for certain formal verification tasks. In fact, some formal verification tasks may not be best suited to any *general-purpose* theorem prover, though certainly a reasonable vision is to create a framework in which general-purpose and special-purpose tools can cooperate (see [52]). The present section considers examples of support for formal verification in tools other than ACL2. They are roughly organized by domain area, though there is considerable overlap.

4.1 Hardware Verification

ACL2 can be used for hardware verification, as demonstrated for example by the work of David Russinoff [48,49] mentioned above. See also [14] for an application of ACL2's relative Nqthm to verification of a gate-level chip design.

However, it is well known that there are virtually automatic hardware-oriented methods and tools that can be used more efficiently than general-purpose approaches, and with less expertise, on certain types of problems. Such tools are gaining acceptance in the semiconductor industry. On a personal note, I recently spent two years at Motorola maintaining its model checker and the front end to its Boolean equivalence checker.

Finite state machine verification may be accomplished efficiently with a model checker (MC). See for example [20,55] for descriptions of the VIS and SMV systems; see [30] for one of many case studies in the literature. Users typically need some training to use a model checker. However, no training in proof is required, which is important in typical hardware design environments where few engineers are likely to have experience with proofs. A major benefit of the tool is the creation of useful counterexample traces. Currently the main drawbacks are capacity (limitations on complexity of the state space) and expressibility of the temporal logic.

Boolean equivalence checking (or *logic checking*, LC) may use methods based on binary decision diagrams [17] and various extensions. However, other methods can also be helpful. For example, the Motorola MET tool [45] also uses simulation to guess *cutpoint* pairs, factoring the problem by suggesting corresponding pairs of nodes that may have the same boolean function of the primary inputs and state elements. It also uses ATPG (automatic test pattern generation) methods to eliminate plausible, but incorrect, guesses.

How do these two methods compare with proof-based methods (TP), used by general-purpose theorem provers and proof checkers? Very broadly speaking, each of the following classes of tools has more automation than the one below it but, in principle at least, somewhat less general applicability.

tool	automation	applicability
LC	essentially automatic	only checks Boolean equivalence
MC	partitioning, abstraction often needed	temporal properties
TP	user builds high-level proof	definitions aid expressiveness

4.2 Abstract Mathematics

General-purpose reasoning systems, including ACL2, can be used to prove theorems of mathematics. Examples using Nqthm may be found for example in [2] and [39], and an ACL2 example in [23] is mentioned above in Subsection 2.2. However, other systems offer certain kinds of support for mathematics reasoning that is not particularly well-supported in ACL2.

- **Domain-specific capabilities.** Geometry theorem proving has benefited from specialized techniques, for example Chou's work described in [18]. Another example is provided by Clarke and Zhao's Analytica prover [19], which leverages off capabilities of Mathematica^{TM}. In general, decision procedures have been developed for numerous domains. Methods for partial and total orders that go beyond decision procedures have been developed by Bledsoe and Hines [5,4,28,27].
- **Higher-order quantification.** ACL2 has only limited support for first-order quantification and even less support in the realm of second-order logic ([7]). In [57] and [58], Young argues that the ACL2 logic is generally quite adequate for verification of computing systems. However, quantification and functional objects are very useful in formalizing mathematics.
- **Theory interpretations** are supported by the IMPS system, [21] providing a useful way to import theory information when a functional substitution is specified, after which they can be used automatically for simplification. ACL2's analogous *functional instantiation* mechanism [7,38] creates proof obligations automatically but does not import rules automatically.
- **Unification and Completion.** Rewrite-based provers such as ACL2 are not a good match for open problems. By comparison, other systems include powerful unification techniques that have been employed successfully on open problems. See for example Argonne's impressive compilation at [1]. A notable success of some such techniques, in particular of associative-commutative unification, has been McCune's use of his EQP prover to solve a problem open for 60 years [41]. These techniques and others, including completion-based techniques have been found to be powerful tools for proof discovery in these two provers and others, for example RRL [31]. ACL2 has no such capabilities.

4.3   Program Verification

ACL2 can be employed for program verification, by using it to reason about interpreters [11]. Indeed, Nqthm has been used extensively for program verification; see for example [32]. Alternatively, ACL2 can be applied to the target of a translator; an example is the work in [49], where ACL2 is the target of a translator from a hardware description language.

However, verification systems targeted to specific languages can generate verification conditions, thus avoiding the need to reason about an interpreter. Such tools have been developed for example at Odyssey Research for reasoning about Ada (see [26]) and VHDL (see [3]). Such tools can hide details of the language semantics and eliminate the need for the user to build explicit proofs by induction.

4.4   A Word About Proof Objects

Some theorem provers generate a formal proof object that can be checked by a much simpler proof-checker. McCune's work mentioned above, for example, employs a proof-checker written in Nqthm to check a proof generated by OT-TER [40] from the original EQP-generated proof. In addition, constructive logic provers such as Coq [29] typically generate proof objects. We would like to add such a capability to ACL2.

5 Some Features of ACL2 Supporting Verification Projects

Below is a "Top 10" countdown of ACL2 features that make it useful for formal verification projects. The following points are worth noting. First, the order below is quite arbitrary; if the order has any meaning at all, then it is very dependent on the particular project and user. Second, this list provides a variety of features that support a variety of users. Novice users will probably employ rather few of these, while even experienced users may be content with only a few favorites. Finally, this list addresses features that directly support *users*. Other features of ACL2 are useful to *developers*: for example, coding ACL2 in itself helps in locating inefficiencies in its execution engine, and coding applicatively enhances maintainability.

10. **The basics**
    - System is *rugged*: users benefit from error checking and useful warnings, usually without surprising breaks or crashes.
    - Careful attention has been paid to *soundness*.
    - *Automated lemma application* supports proof replay in the presence of system modifications. For example, the correctness theorem in [43] was modified or extended several times in response to reviewers' criticisms, with very little modification to existing ACL2 input even when under-lying definitions were modified. See also [56] for a discussion of this "ro-bustness" issue.
    - *Uniformity* of the interface: There is one read-eval-print loop for evalu-ation, definition, and proof.
9. **Guards** [36]; somewhat similar to *predicate subtypes* of PVS [44], guards support:
    - *validating specifications*;
    - *efficient execution* (see item 8);
    - *type-free reasoning* as successfully employed by Nqthm, because guards are *separated from the logic* (an earlier version of ACL2 had serious performance problems because guards were used to restrict definitional equations); and
    - *"partial functions"* with a simple semantics and without needless proof overhead.
8. **Efficient execution**
    - *Compilation* into Common Lisp allows:
      - reasonably efficient evaluation, simulation (see also Subsection 2.3);
      - evaluation of ground terms during proofs;

- use of Common Lisp drivers, so that underlying Lisp structures may be employed (for example, property lists).
- Certain operations have *non-applicative implementations*.
  - the ACL2 state
  - property lists
  - arrays
- Declare forms allow execution speeds that can approach those offered by C.

7. **Flexible input**
   - *Macros* provide the full power of applicative Common Lisp programming to create input interfaces. See [13] for a powerful example.
   - *Corollaries* allow separation of the main theorem proved from the rules to be stored.

6. **Advanced prover control**
   - *Rule classes* support metatheoretic reasoning, congruence-based rewriting, destructor elimination, forward chaining, and other techniques (see also item 3 below)
   - Force and case-split allow the proof to proceed when backchaining would fail.
   - *Macro commands* allow users to program the interactive "proof-checker", in a manner similar to those supplied by older systems such as HOL [24].
   - *Computed hints* allow hints to be generated during a proof.
   - Syntaxp allows conditional rewriting to be driven by the shapes of terms.

5. **Modularity**
   - *Structuring mechanisms* are given a logical basis in [38]. They address a point made by John Rushby [46] that it is important to be able to comprehend the overall structure of a proof development. These mechanisms include:
     - encapsulate;
     - local; and
     - books, which allow multiple theories to be included.
   - *Packages* provide multiple namespaces that avoid theory collisions.

4. **Documentation** includes:
   - *manual* in various formats (HTML, on-line, Texinfo, or printed as about 800 pages);
   - *documentation strings*, which may be provided by the user;
   - *query support*, for example to inspect the current sequence of events, to compute macro expansions, or to find rewrite rules for a given function symbol.

3. **Varied automated reasoning support** includes:
   - *conditional rewriting* with some heuristic controls;
   - *type-set* reasoning (providing equality decision procedures);
   - *"fast" clausification*, also BDDs [17] integrated with lists;
   - *managing large terms* using LET — see for example Section 2.2 of [16];
   - *forward chaining*, providing a fast way to prune undesirable backchaining when using conditional rewriting;

- *linear arithmetic* decision procedure, integrated with rewriting — see [10] for a discussion of issues;
- *congruence-based reasoning* — see [22] for an example;
- *built-in clauses* — see [22] for how these can help in admitting recursive definitions;
- *books* provided with the distribution, including arithmetic, defstructure [13], others;
- *meta-reasoning* support, including conditional meta-lemmas; and
- *induction*.

2. **Generality** avoids the effort of developing special-purpose tools, and has several aspects:
   - *scalability*, supported by database queries mentioned in item 4 and by structuring mechanisms mentioned in item 5;
   - *expressiveness of the logic* via
     - recursive definitions,
     - functional instantiation ([7,38]), which provides some second-order-like capabilities, avoiding the need to keep re-proving analogous theorems (see [22] for examples) and
     - first-order quantification (however, with quite limited automated support);
   - *programming language* providing
     - rapid prototyping without proof obligations and
     - flexibility in development efforts, as suggested for example in Subsection 3.5 where documentation is shown that was created using the proof source files;
   - capabilities for *alternate syntax*, provided by an extension of ACL2 [53], which allows input and output to be given in traditional first-order form, and can be used to translate ACL2's Lisp syntax to that form annotated for Latex or HTML. An earlier version has been used to translate formulas for Section 3.

1. **Support for interaction**
   - *Coarse-level interactivity* is supported through incremental development of definitions and theorems, stored as rules.
   - *Lower-level interactivity* is supported via:
     - "proof-checker" interaction allowing for greater control, including case-splitting, user-controlled backchaining, and simplification of specified subterms;
     - "proof trees" providing a concise, "clickable" summary of the proof transcript;
     - break-rewrite, supporting the monitoring of conditional rewrite rules and detailed inspection of the rewrite stack; and
     - useful output that can be analyzed, including especially unsimplifiable formulas and reports of rules used.
   - *Theory control* allows the user to:
     - define *theories* (sets of rules) by employing theory manipulation routines;

- decide which theory is currently in force; and
- define theory invariants to be checked when theories are defined.

- *Experimentation*
  - "Program-only" mode allows rapid prototyping, as mentioned above in item 2.
  - Temporary assumptions may be made via `defaxiom`, `skip-proofs`, and (on uncertified books) `include-book`.
  - Changing your mind is allowed through undoing, and even undoing the "undo".

- *Useful switches and options*
  - "Macro aliases" allow macro names to be used as functions in hints and theories.
  - "Irrelevant" and "unused" formals cause warnings (when enabled).
  - "Invisible" functions can be specified for purposes of the term-order used in stopping certain rewriting loops.
  - Output can be selectively inhibited according to its type (error, warning, observation, prove, event, summary, proof-tree), with even more selective control available in the case of warnings.
  - `Set-compile-fns` controls compilation of newly-defined functions.
  - `Set-measure-function` and `set-well-founded-relation` provide alternate defaults for admitting recursive definitions.
  - `Set-state-ok` allows advanced users to program with state, which is otherwise disallowed (it's potentially dangerous).
  - `Set-verify-guards-eagerness` provides default for performance of guard verification on definitions.
  - The `term-table` gives a list of terms, employed for catching errors in a proposed metafunction by checking that it maps each of these terms to a syntactically-legal term.

- *Tables* are used not only to implement many of the items above, but also to allow users to record information in the database.

6   Conclusion

General-purpose automated reasoning tools have been improving both in *raw deductive power* and in *general usability*. This talk has discussed some weaknesses and strengths of ACL2 in these areas, though focusing largely on general usability. I believe that the important challenges for improving such tools for use in verification projects lie more in the realm of general usability than in the realm of raw deductive power.

References

1. Argonne National Laboratory, Mathematics and Computer Science Division. A Summary of New Results in Mathematics Obtained with Argonne's Automated Deduction Software. URL http://www-c.mcs.anl.gov/home/mccune/ar/new_results/index.html

2. D. Basin and M. Kaufmann. The Boyer-Moore Prover and Nuprl: An Experimental Comparison. In: *Proceedings of the First Workshop on "Logical Frameworks"*, Antibes, France, May 1990. See also Technical Report 58, Computational Logic, Inc., URL `ftp://ftp.cs.utexas.edu/pub/boyer/cli-reports/058.ps` or `http://www.cli.com/reports/`.

3. M. Bickford and D. Jamsek. Formal specification and verification of VHDL. In *Proceedings of Formal Methods in Computer-Aided Design (FMCAD'96)*, M. Srivas and A. Camilleri (eds.), Springer-Verlag, November, 1996,

4. W. Bledsoe. A maximal method for set variables in automatic theorem-proving. In *Machine Intelligence 9*, ed. J. E. Hayes, D. Michie, and L. I. Mikulich. Ellis Harwood Ltd., Chichester, 1979, pp. 53–100.

5. W. Bledsoe. A resolution-based prover for general inequalities. Technical Report ATP-52, University of Texas, Austin, July 1979.

6. R. Boyer. Nqthm Bibliography. URL `ftp://ftp.cs.utexas.edu/pub/boyer/-nqthm/nqthm-bibliography.html`.

7. R. Boyer, D. Goldschlag, M. Kaufmann, and J Moore. Functional Instantiation in First Order Logic. In *Artificial Intelligence and Mathematical Theory of Computation: Papers in Honor of John McCarthy*, Academic Press, 1991, pp. 7–26.

8. R. Boyer, M. Kaufmann, and J Moore. The Boyer-Moore Theorem Prover and Its Interactive Enhancement. *Computers and Mathematics with Applications*, **5**(2) (1995) pp. 27–62.

9. R. Boyer and J Moore. *A Computational Logic*, Academic Press: New York, 1979.

10. R. Boyer and J Moore. Integrating Decision Procedures into Heuristic Theorem Provers: A Case Study of Linear Arithmetic, In *Machine Intelligence 11*, Oxford University Press, 1988, pp. 83–124.

11. R. Boyer and J Moore. Mechanized Formal Reasoning about Programs and Computing Machines. In R. Veroff (ed.), *Automated Reasoning and Its Applications: Essays in Honor of Larry Wos*, MIT Press, 1996.

12. R. Boyer and J Moore. *A Computational Logic Handbook, Second Edition*. Academic Press: London, 1997.

13. B. Brock. Defstructure for ACL2. URL `http://www.cs.utexas.edu/users/-moore/acl2/reports/b97.ps`.

14. B. Brock and W. Hunt, Jr. The `DUAL-EVAL` Hardware Description Language and Its Use in the Formal Specification and Verification of the FM9001 Microprocessor. *Formal Methods in System Design*, Kluwer Academic Publishers. Volume 11, Issue 1, July, 1997, pp. 71–104.

15. B. Brock and W. Hunt, Jr. Formally Specifying and Mechanically Verifying Programs for the Motorola Complex Arithmetic Processor DSP. 1997 IEEE International Conference on Computer Design, Austin, TX, October 1997, pp. 31–36.

16. B. Brock, M. Kaufmann, and J Moore. ACL2 Theorems about Commercial Microprocessors. In *Proceedings of Formal Methods in Computer-Aided Design (FMCAD'96)*, M. Srivas and A. Camilleri (eds.), Springer-Verlag, November, 1996, pp. 275–293.

17. R. Bryant. Graph Based Algorithms for Boolean Function Manipulation. *IEEE Trans. Comp.*, **C-35**(8), August 1986.

18. S-C. Chou *Mechanical Geometry Theorem Proving* D. Reidel, 1988.

19. E. Clarke and X. Zhao. Analytica: A Theorem Prover for Mathematica. The Journal of Mathematica **3**(1), 56–71, Winter 1993.

20. CMU — School of Computer Science. *Model Checking at CMU*. URL `http://-www.cs.cmu.edu/~modelcheck/`.

21. W. Farmer, J. Guttman, and F. J. Thayer. IMPS: An Interactive Mathematical Proof System. J. Automated Reasoning, 11(2), 213–248, 1993.

22. R. Gamboa. Defthms About Zip and Tie: Reasoning About Powerlists in ACL2. University of Texas Computer Sciences Technical Report No. TR97-02.

23. R. Gamboa. Mechanically Verifying the Correctness of the Fast Fourier Transform in ACL2. To appear in *Third International Workshop on Formal Methods for Parallel Programming: Theory and Applications (FMPPTA)*, Orlando, FL, 1998. URL http://www.lim.com/fuben/research/papers/fft.html.

24. M. Gordon and T. Melham (editors). *Introduction to HOL: A Theorem Proving Environment for Higher-Order Logic.* Cambridge University Press, 1993.

25. D. Greve, M. Wilding, and D. Hardin. Efficient Simulation Using a Simple Formal Processor Model. April, 1998, Rockwell Collins Advanced Technology Center (submitted for publication).

26. D. Guaspari, C. Marceau, and W. Polak. Formal verification of Ada programs. IEEE Trans. Software Engineering, vol. 16, 1990, pp. 1058–1075.

27. L. Hines. Struve: The Strive-based Subset Prover. *Proc. 10th Int'l Conf. Automated Deduction*, July 1990, Kaiserslautern, Germany, Springer-Verlag, pp. 193–206.

28. L. Hines. Strive and integers. In *Proc. 12th Int'l Conf. Automated Deduction*, June 1992, Nancy, France, Springer-Verlag (192), pp. 416–430.

29. G. Huet, G. Kahn, and C. Paulin-Mohring. *The Coq Proof Assistant - A tutorial, Version 6.1.* Technical Report No. 204, INRIA, August 1997 (revised version distributed with Coq). See also URL http://pauillac.inria.fr/coq/.

30. J-Y. Jang, S. Qadeer, M. Kaufmann, and C. Pixley. Formal Verification of FIRE: A Case Study. In: *Proceedings of Design Automation Conference (DAC)*, 1997, pp. 173–177.

31. D. Kapur and H. Zhang. An Overview of Rewrite Rule Laboratory (RRL). *J. Computer and Mathematics with Applications*, 29(2), 1995, pp. 91–114.

32. M. Kaufmann. Response to FM91 Survey of Formal Methods: Nqthm and Pc-Nqthm. Technical Report 75, Computational Logic, Inc., March, 1992. URL ftp://ftp.cs.utexas.edu/pub/boyer/cli-reports/075.ps or http://www.cli.com/reports/.

33. M. Kaufmann. Development and Verification of Year 2000 Conversion Rules using the ACL2 Theorem Prover. *In preparation.*

34. M. Kaufmann and J S. Moore. *ACL2: A Computational Logic for Applicative Common Lisp, The User's Manual.* http://www.cs.utexas.edu/users/moore/acl2/acl2-doc.html#User's-Manual.

35. M. Kaufmann and J Moore. Design Goals for ACL2. In proceedings of: *Third International School and Symposium on Formal Techniques in Real Time and Fault Tolerant Systems*, Kiel, Germany (1994), pp. 92-117. Published by Christian-Albrechts-Universitat. See also Technical Report 101, Computational Logic, Inc. URL http://www.cs.utexas.edu/users/moore/acl2/reports/km94.ps.

36. M. Kaufmann and J Moore. An Industrial Strength Theorem Prover for a Logic Based on Common Lisp. In *IEEE Transactions on Software Engineering* 23(4), April, 1997, pp. 203–213.

37. M. Kaufmann and J Moore. A Precise Description of the ACL2 Logic. URL http://www.cs.utexas.edu/users/moore/acl2/reports/km97a.ps.

38. M. Kaufmann and J Moore. Structured Theory Development for a Mechanized Logic. In preparation. (Earlier version entitled "High-Level Correctness of ACL2: A Story," September, 1995, is distributed with ACL2 release; see http://www.cs.utexas.edu/users/moore/acl2/.

39. M. Kaufmann and P. Pecchiari. Interaction with the Boyer-Moore Theorem Prover: A Tutorial Study Using the Arithmetic-Geometric Mean Theorem. *Journal of Automated Reasoning* 16, no. 1-2 (1996) 181-222.

40. W. McCune. Otter: An Automated Deduction System. URL http://www-c.mcs.anl.gov/home/mccune/ar/otter.

41. W. McCune. Solution of the Robbins Problem. J. Automated Reasoning 19(3), 263–276 (1997).

42. J Moore. An ACL2 Proof of Write Invalidate Cache Coherence. To appear in Proceedings of Computer Aided Verification, CAV'98, Vancouver, June 28–July 2, 1998, Lecture Notes in Computer Science.

43. J Moore, T. Lynch, and M. Kaufmann. A Mechanically Checked Proof of the AMD5$_K$86 Floating-Point Division Program. To appear, *IEEE Trans. Comp.*. See also URL http://devil.ece.utexas.edu/lynch/divide/divide.html.

44. S. Owre, J. Rushby, and N. Shankar. Integration in PVS: Tables, types, and model checking. In Ed Brinksma, editor, *Tools and Algorithms for the Construction and Analysis of Systems (TACAS '97)*, number 1217 in Lecture Notes in Computer Science, Springer-Verlag, Enschede, The Netherlands, April 1997, pp. 366–383.

45. J. Park, C. Pixley, and H. Cho. An Efficient Logic Equivalence Checker for Industrial Circuits. Submitted.

46. J. Rushby. Automated deduction and formal methods. In Rajeev Alur and Thomas A. Henzinger, editors, *Proceedings of the 8th International Conference on Computer Aided Verification*, number 1102 in Lecture Notes in Computer Science, Springer-Verlag, New Brunswick, NJ, July 1996, pp. 169–183.

47. D. Russinoff. A Mechanically Checked Proof of IEEE Compliance of the AMD-K5^{TM} Floating-Point Square Root Microcode. To appear, *Formal Methods in System Design*. URL http://www.onr.com/user/russ/david/fsqrt.html.

48. D. Russinoff. A Mechanically Checked Proof of IEEE Compliance of the Floating Point Multiplication, Division, and Square Root Algorithms of the AMD-K7^{TM} Processor. URL http://www.onr.com/user/russ/david/k7-div-sqrt.html.

49. D. Russinoff. A Case Study in Formal Verification of Register-Transfer Logic: The Floating Point Adder of the AMD-K7^{TM} Processor. In final preparation.

50. J. Sawada and W. Hunt, Jr.. Trace Table Based Approach for Pipelined Microprocessor Verification. In Proceedings of Computer Aided Verification, CAV'97, Lecture Notes in Computer Science 1254, Springer Verlag, 1997, pp. 364–375.

51. J. Sawada and W. Hunt, Jr.. Processor Verification with Precise Exceptions and Speculative Execution. To appear in Proceedings of Computer Aided Verification, CAV'98, Vancouver, June 28–July 2, 1998, Lecture Notes in Computer Science.

52. N. Shankar. Unifying verification paradigms. In Bengt Jonsson and Joachim Parrow, editors, *Formal Techniques in Real-Time and Fault-Tolerant Systems*, volume 1135 of *Lecture Notes in Computer Science*, Springer-Verlag, Uppsala, Sweden, September 1996, pp. 22–39. See also URL http://www.csl.sri.com/ftrtft96.html.

53. M. Smith. Top-level README for IACL2 (Infix ACL2). URL http://www.cs.utexas.edu/users/moore/infix/README.html, April, 1997.

54. G. Steele, Jr. *Common Lisp The Language, Second Edition*. Digital Press, 30 North Avenue, Burlington, MA 01803, 1990.

55. The VIS Group. VIS: A system for Verification and Synthesis. In Rajeev Alur and Thomas A. Henzinger, editors, *Proceedings of the 8th International Conference on Computer Aided Verification*, number 1102 in Lecture Notes in Computer Science, Springer-Verlag, New Brunswick, NJ, July 1996, pp. 428–432. See also URL: http://www-cad.eecs.berkeley.edu/Respep/Research/vis/.

56. M. Wilding. Robust Computer System Proofs in PVS. In C. Michael Holloway and Kelly J. Hayhurst, editors, *LFM97: Fourth NASA Langley Formal Methods Workshop*, NASA Conference Publication, 1997. See also URL http://atb-www.-larc.nasa.gov/Lfm97/.

57. W. Young. Comparing Verification Systems: Interactive Consistency in ACL2. In: *Proceedings of the Eleventh Annual Conference on Computer Assurance*, 1996, pp. 35–45. An expanded version appears in *IEEE Transactions on Software Engineering*, Vol. 23, no. 4, (April, 1997) pp. 214–223. See also URL http://www.cs.-utexas.edu/users/moore/acl2/reports/y96a.ps.

58. W. Young. The Specification of a Simple Autopilot in ACL2. URL http://www.-cs.utexas.edu/users/moore/acl2/reports/y96b.ps.

59. Y. Yu. *Automated Proofs of Object Code for a Widely used Microprocessor*. Technical Report 92, Computational Logic, Inc., May, 1993. URL http://www.cli.-com/reports/files/92.ps.

A Fast Algorithm for Uniform Semi-Unification

Alberto Oliart and Wayne Snyder

Boston University Computer Science Department
111 Cummington St., Boston MA, 02215
{oira,snyder}@cs.bu.edu

Abstract. We present a fast algorithm for uniform semi-unification based on adapting the Huet unification closure method for standard unification. It solves the following decision problem in $O(n^2 \alpha(n)^2)$, where n is the size of the two terms, and α is the functional inverse of Ackermann's function: Given two terms s and t, do there exist two substitutions σ and ρ such that $\rho(\sigma(s)) = \sigma(t)$? In the affirmative case, a solution σ can be constructed within the same time bound. However, if a principal solution (analogous to an mgu) is required, some modifications to the algorithm must be made, and the upper bound increases to $O(n^2 \log^2(n\alpha(n)) \alpha(n)^2)$.

1 Introduction

Semiunification is a combination of matching and unification on first-order terms that has applications in term rewriting, type checking for programming languages, proof theory, and computational linguistics; although it can be defined simply (see following section), it has proved remarkably difficult to analyze precisely. In its general form the problem has been shown to be undecidable [9], with an exceedingly difficult proof. The uniform case is decidable, and various authors have given algorithms (some incorrect), however, a careful analysis of its asymptotic complexity has not as yet been performed.

In this paper we present an algorithm with a time complexity in $O(n^2 \alpha(n)^2)$. Our algorithm is based on the Huet unification algorithm, using a graph representation of the terms. It can generate solutions, although they may not be principal. An algorithm that can find principal solutions in $O(n^2 \log^2(n\alpha(n)) \alpha(n)^2)$ is also presented. Details are found in the thesis of the first author, and in the full paper [12].

After defining the basic notions used in the paper, in Section 3 we give several examples as a motivation for the algorithm, which is presented in Section 4. Section 5 continues Section 3 in showing how to extract the solution from the resulting graph. Section 6 briefly discusses the algorithm which generates principal solutions, and Section 7 gives a sketch of the correctness proof, as well as the complexity results. We conclude with some comparisons with previous work and some final observations.

C. Kirchner and H. Kirchner (Eds.): Automated Deduction, CADE-15
LNAI 1421, pp. 239–253, 1998. © Springer–Verlag Berlin Heidelberg 1998

2   Preliminaries

We assume the standard definition of variables (represented by w, x, y, and z) and first-order terms (represented by the symbols s, t, u, and v) over a fixed signature Σ. A *substitution* is a function from variables to terms almost everywhere equal to the identity (represented by σ and ρ), and the application of a substitution to a term is represented, e.g., in the form $\sigma(s)$. The composition $\sigma\sigma'$ is the function which maps each x to $\sigma'(\sigma(x))$. If σ_1 and σ_2 are substitutions then we say that $\sigma_1 \leq \sigma_2$ iff there is a substitution θ such that $\sigma_2 = \sigma_1\theta$.

We say that a term s *matches onto* t, denoted $s \leq t$, iff there exists a substitution ρ such that $\rho(s) = t$. Two terms s and t *unify* if there exists a σ such that $\sigma(s) = \sigma(t)$.

A *semi-unification* problem is a set of inequalities $\{s_1 \leq^? t_1, \ldots s_n \leq^? t_n\}$ and is solvable if there exist substitutions $\rho_1, \ldots, \rho_n$ and σ such that $\rho_i(\sigma(s_i)) = \sigma(t_i)$ for each i; the σ is called a *semi-unifier* of the set. A semi-unifier σ is *principal* if for any other semi-unifier σ' we have $\sigma \leq \sigma'$. A semi-unification problem is *uniform* when $n = 1$.

The Huet algorithm for standard unification represents terms by directed acyclic graphs (DAGs) with unique (shared) occurrences of variables, see [7, 3, 2]. There are two kinds of arcs in the graph: in addition to normal subterm arcs, we have *equivalence links*; each class in an equivalence relation on the nodes is a tree of links with a *representative* at the root. By following such links to the root, we can check for membership in a class, and by adding a link from one representative to another, we can take the union of two classes. The graph is initialized with a trivial equivalence relation and the algorithm starts by taking the union of the two terms (nodes) to be unified; whenever two classes are unified, if the classes contain distinct function symbols (symbol clash) the algorithm fails; otherwise, if each class contains at least one function symbol then the unification closure axiom

$$f(s_1, \ldots s_n) \cong f(t_1, \ldots t_n) \implies s_1 \cong t_1, \ldots s_n \cong t_n$$

is applied to "push" the equivalence down into the subterms. It is convenient to pick a distinguished function node in the class (if such exists) for the purposes of such propagation. By using fast Union-Find [1] this can be done in almost linear time to calculate the least unification closure. Two tricks ensure fast computation: when two classes are joined, the representative of the larger class is made the representative for the union; and when following links to the root of the tree, paths are collapsed to make the tree as shallow as possible. A final check for acyclicity (in linear time) verifies the existence of a finite solution (otherwise, the solution would be an infinite, rational tree).

3   Examples

We demonstrate our method in this section through examples. The first example shows two terms which are semi-unifiable; this is then modified to demonstrate one failure case (so-called "bad" cycles). A second example that fails to have a solution is also given, but in this case the problem is a "self-loop."

In adapting the unification closure approach to semi-unification, the main difference is that we need to unify terms which, after application of the semi-unifier σ, will have the matching substitution (the ρ) applied to them some number of times. The equivalence links thus have two weights, the source weight and the target weight, which count the number of applications of ρ on each side of the directed link. A link of the form $r \xrightarrow{\;\;n\quad\;m\;\;} s$ says that the term $\rho^n(r)$ is equivalent to the term $\rho^m(s)$, and thus that a σ must be found such that $\rho^n(\sigma(r)) = \rho^m(\sigma(s))$. The creation of such links basically follows the Huet algorithm, except that when a new link is added by "collapsing" two or more links (e.g., in Find), then a corresponding equational inference on these underlying equations must be done; this involves standard rewriting plus some rules which define how ρ behaves on terms. Another difference from the standard algorithm is that cycle checking is more complex. The second phase consists of function **Cycle**, which searches the graphs for a *bad* cycle, which is a loop that corresponds to the derivation of a bad equation of the form $\rho^n(x) = \rho^m(f(\ldots x \ldots))$, with $m \geq n$, which (under suitable completeness conditions for propagating inferences) are necessary and sufficient for non-existence of solutions (see [8]).

3.1   Example 1–A Good Cycle.

The first example is the semi-unification instance $\{f(x, f(y, z)) \leq^? f(f(z, x), x)\}$. In the diagrams, we will denote equivalence links by dashed arrows with source and target weights. After the first call to **Semiunify** we have an equivalence link between the two top nodes; one of the two nodes is choosen as representative arbitrarily:

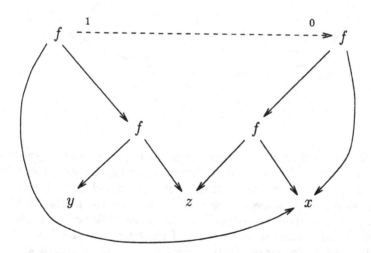

Now the link between the top nodes is pushed down by the recursive calls to **Semiunify** and a link is placed on the left subterms x and $f(z, x)$ and pointed to the latter term as representative. A link $f(y, z) \xrightarrow{\quad 1 \qquad 0 \quad} x$ is then placed on the right subterms.

Since x has a pointer to a class representative, then the link just added will be "repointed" (given a new target) to this representative by adding a new arrow with new weights calculated along the path from $f(y, z)$ to $f(z, x)$. (At this point, function **Semiunify** checks that the names of the functional symbols are the same; and if they were not it would terminate with failure due to symbol clash.) The weights are calculated by simulating the transformation of the equation $\rho(x) = f(z, x)$, represented by the first link added, using the equation $x = \rho(f(y, z))$, by rewriting the left side to obtain $\rho^2(f(y, z)) = f(z, x)$. This gives us the new class link $f(y, z) \xrightarrow{\quad 2 \qquad 0 \quad} f(z, x)$.

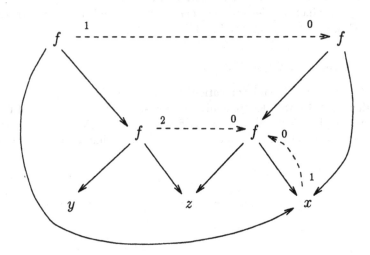

At this point, the new link between $f(y, z)$ and $f(z, x)$ must be pushed down into the subterms. The link is pushed down to y and z, one (say y) is arbitrarily chosen as representative, and then the subterms z and x are linked. Again, the equivalence link between z and x will be repointed so that it joins the representatives of these two terms, and this means building a equivalence link between y and $f(z, x)$; since the class of the latter is larger (with 3 terms) than the class of the former (with 2 terms), the latter is chosen as the new representative. A new link is built, with new weights calculated along the path $y, z, x, f(z, x)$:

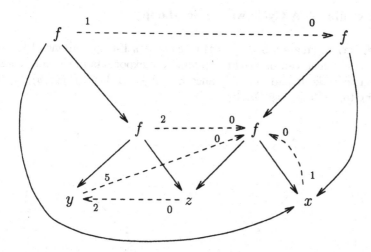

No other links can be added to the DAG after this, and the algorithm would proceed to check for cycles. In fact, the DAG has a cycle, from the link $x \xrightarrow{\;1\quad 0\;} f(z,x)$. Because the cost on x is greater than the cost on $f(z,x)$ this is not a bad cycle, and therefore the instance has a solution. The decision procedure would return **true**.

3.2 Example 2–A Bad Cycle

As an example of an instance with no solution due to a bad cycle consider the instance $f(f(z,x),x) \leq^? f(x,f(y,z))$, which has the same terms, but reversed. In this case, the deduction would proceed as a mirror image to Example 1, but the cycle then ends up having the weights reversed, as the figure shows. This is a bad cycle, corresponding to a bad equation $x = \rho(f(z,x))$ that is not solvable:

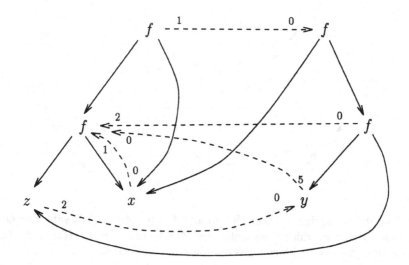

3.3   Example 3–A Cycle with a Self-Loop

Another way to create a bad cycle is to have a "self-loop" on one of the terms in the cycle, which can be used to "pump" the exponents in the corresponding equation to make it bad. The instance is $f(x, f(x, z)) \leq^? f(f(x, y), x)$, corresponding to the following DAG:

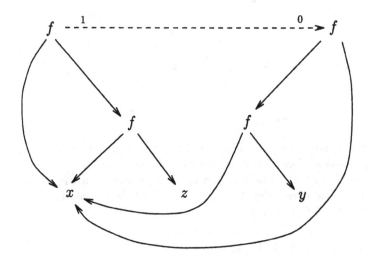

After pushing down the links into the subterms and repointing, we obtain:

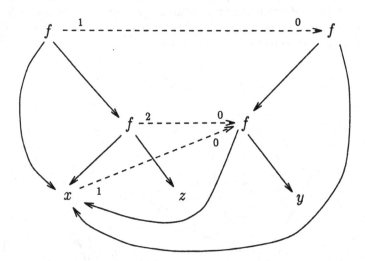

Pushing down the link between $f(x, z)$ and $f(x, y)$ into the left subterms gives us a self-loop on x, which is repointed and thereby moved up to $f(z, y)$. Pushing down onto the right subterms gives us the completed DAG:

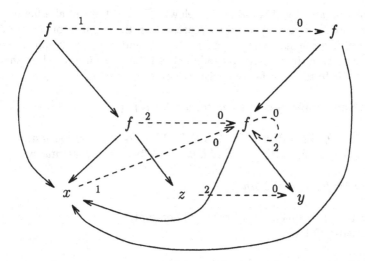

(We do not push self-loops down, as this can lead, as here, to non-termination of the algorithm, and is in fact not necessary.) There is an apparently good loop $x \xrightarrow{\quad 1 \quad\quad 0 \quad} f(x, y)$, however the self-loop participates in this good loop, so that the decision procedure would return **false**, as the instance is not semi-unifiable. The self-loop corresponds to an equation $f(x, y) = \rho^2(f(x, y))$, which can be used to rewrite the one side of the equation $\rho(x) = f(x, y)$ to obtain a bad equation (e.g., $\rho(x) = \rho^2(f(x, y))$). Thus, whenever a self-loop exists on any cycle, it indicates non-unifiability. It is an interesting feature of our decision procedure (compared with, e.g., [8, 15]) that it is only the *presence* of self-loops that needs to be accounted for; no other processing is necessary.

4   The Algorithm

In this section we present the decision procedure used in the above examples.

The graph nodes have the following properties : *class* is a triplet that contains an equivalence link (pointer plus source and target weights) to the representative of the nodes's equivalence class, *children* is the list of subterms of a function node, and *self_loop* is a boolean flag indicating whether this node has an equivalence link to itself with non-trivial weights. Representatives have two additional properties: *size*, the size of the class, used in the union of two classes; and *func*, a pointer to a function node in the class, or **null** if every member of the class is a variable (for function nodes, this pointer is initialized to point to the node itself). This last property is necessary in the unification closure method because representatives might be variables (due to the way that the fast Union-Find algorithm chooses representatives), but when two classes are joined, it is necessary to choose some function node in each class in order to propagate the equivalence down into the subterms.

The decision procedure first calls function **Semiunify** to construct the least unification closure in the graph (the Union function is embedded in the **Semiu-**

nify function and **Find** is discussed below). The most essential difference from the standard case is that weights, representing the number of ρ's applied to each term, are calculated for each link that is added to the graph. If **Semiunify** returns true (indicating no symbol clash) the decision procedure then calls function **Cycle** to check for the existence of "bad" cycles.

boolean **Semiunify**(term s, int n, term t, int m) {

$(n_1, m_1, s') = \textbf{Find}(s);$ // *Find link* $s \xrightarrow{n_1 \quad m_1} s'$ *to representative*   (1)
$(n_2, m_2, t') = \textbf{Find}(t);$ // *Find link* $t \xrightarrow{n_2 \quad m_2} t'$ *to representative*   (2)

// *Check for symbol clash*

if (func(s') != func(t') **and** both are non-null)
    return false;

// *Determine new path between* s' *and* t'

$(w_1, w_2) = \textbf{Getpath}((m_2, n_2), (m, n), (n_1, m_1));$

// *Check for self-loop.*

if ($s' == t'$) {   // *Union not necessary, but have self-loop*
    if ($w_1 \neq w_2$)
        self_loop(s') = **true;**
    return true;   (3)
} **else** {   // *Classes distinct, take union*
    // *Assume, wlog, that size(s') $\geq$ size(t'), so s' is new*
    // *representative. The link to be added here is* $t' \xrightarrow{w_2 \quad w_1} s'$.
    // *The case for size(s') $<$ size(t') is analogous.*

    $class(t') = (w_2, w_1, s');$
    $size(s') = size(s') + size(t');$
    if (func(s') == **null**) **and** (func(t') != **null**)
        func(s') = func(t');   // *func(t') is new function node*
    else if (func(s') != **null**) **and** (func(t') != **null**) {
        // *Calculate link between function nodes and push down*
        $(p_1, q_1, s') = \textbf{Find}(func(s'));$ // *s' and t' are unchanged*   (4)
        $(p_2, q_2, t') = \textbf{Find}(func(t'));$ (5)
        $(k_1, k_2) = \textbf{GetPath}(((p_1, q_1), (w_1, w_2), (q_2, p_2)));$
        return Sulist(subterms(func(s')), k_1, subterms(func(t')), k_2);   (6)
    }
}}

Function **Sulist** traverses the list of subterms of a DAG node and returns true if **Semiunify** returns true for each subterm.

Function **Getpath** returns the weights for a new link to be added to the graph. It receives the weights for three links, which represent the links to be "collapsed". The new link goes from the node that is at the source of the first link to the node that is the target of the last link. Given the pairs of integers $(m_2, n_2), (m, n), (n_1, m_1)$, the pair of weights returned by **Getpath** is (w_1, w_2), where

$$w_1 = max\{m_2, m_2 - n_2 + m, m_2 - n_2 + m - n + n_1\}$$
$$w_2 = w_1 - ((((m_2 - n_2) + m) - n + n_1) - m_1)$$

This corresponds to deriving an equality $\rho^{w_1}(s') = \rho^{w_2}(t')$ from the equalities $\rho^{m_1}(s') = \rho^{n_1}(s)$, $\rho^n(s) = \rho^m(t)$, and $\rho^{m_2}(t') = \rho^{n_2}(t)$. Such an inference is sound according to an appropriate set of rules for equational inference which preserve solvability but not principality of solutions extracted, see [12]. This is because the set includes a rule for cancellation of ρ; e.g., $\rho^2(\sigma(s)) = \rho(\sigma(t))$ is solvable iff $\rho(\sigma'(s)) = (\sigma'(t))$ is, however the solution to the second is "larger" (in fact it is $\sigma\rho$). For a decision procedure this is not an issue, although in order to extract principal solutions, we will need to modify the graph to recover the original links (see below), which accounts for its higher complexity.

Function **Find**(s) is from the fast Union-Find algorithm, but it also calculates the weights of the new "compressed" links constructed in a manner similar to GetPath. It returns the class representative of the class of term s together with the weights that correspond to the "compressed" path from s to the class representative. The function also compresses the path to the representative of any other node that is in the original path from s.

Function **Cycle** checks for "bad cycles" in the terminal graph which indicate the non-existence of solutions. To find cycles this function uses the well-known linear algorithm, while performing a calculation similar to that used in GetPath to derive equational consequences of the equivalence links followed. If a cycle $x \xrightarrow{\ \ n \quad m\ } x$ is found, where $m \leq n$, then this indicates that the system implies a "bad" equation $\rho^m(x) = \rho^n(f(\ldots x \ldots))$, which is sufficient for the non-existence of solutions (cf.[8]). Secondly, if a cycle if any kind involving a node with a self-loop is found, then this is also sufficient for non-existence, since this implies the existence of an equational consequence $\rho^p(s) = \rho^q(s)$, which can be used to "pump" the exponents in the cyclical equation to produce a "bad" equation. If neither of these conditions holds, it can be shown that the graph has a solution.

This algorithm has been implemented in C and tested over a number of months.

5   Extracting a Solution

In this section we present an example of solution extraction, using the instance used in the first example presented in Sec. 3. In order to extract a solution from the final DAG in Example 1, we must use not only the (final) representative arcs, but also the links that were added by the calls to **Semiunify** before "repointing." However, we only need to consider those involving a variable, since those are the only ones that affect the generation of a solution. We must also orient these links according to an ordering on variables, extended to make all non-variable terms smaller than all variables; we thus express the links as dotted arrows according to the ordering:

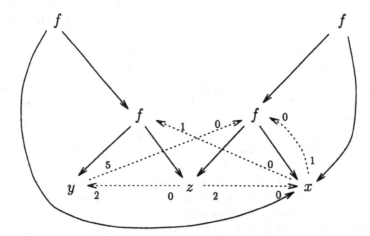

Now we must repoint links, in a manner similar to the decision procedure, and similar to simplification of rewrite rules at the top, so that each variable is the source of at most one arrow. The left side of the simplifier must have a weight which is less than or equal to the left side of the link being simplified. First we simplify $z \xrightarrow{\ 2 \quad 0\ } x$ by $z \xrightarrow{\ 0 \quad 2\ } y$ to obtain $y \xrightarrow{\ 4 \quad 0\ } x$.

Next, we simplify $y \xrightarrow{\ 5 \quad 0\ } f(z,x)$ by the new link $y \xrightarrow{\ 4 \quad 0\ } x$:

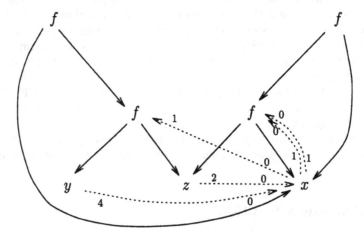

Finally, after simplifying one of the two identical links from x to $f(z,x)$ by the other to obtain a link between $f(z,x)$ and itself (which can be ignored), we obtain the following links; those which have a 0 weight on the left side define the bindings of σ:

$$z \xrightarrow{\ 0 \quad 2\ } y \qquad y \xrightarrow{\ 4 \quad 0\ } x \qquad x \xrightarrow{\ 0 \quad 1\ } f(y,z)$$

This says that $\sigma(x) = \rho(f(y, z))$, $\sigma(y) = y$, $\sigma(z) = \rho(\rho(y))$. By applying renamings as the action of ρ on the variables, we obtain our semiunifier: $\sigma = \{x \mapsto f(y', z'),\ z \mapsto y''\}$.

6 Principal Solution Extraction

We give here a very brief description of the changes needed to extract a principal solution from the graph that results from the call to **Semiunify**. For more details see [12].

The two main issues with the extraction of principal solutions are: keeping all the equivalence links that are encountered during the call to **Semiunify** and also keeping and updating the weights on the self-loops. Also, a total ordering is defined on the variables that appear on the terms.

In order to do this, two more properties of nodes are needed. The first is a pair of numbers to keep the weights of a self-loop, and the second is a list of links for each variable. This list of links contains the set of equivalence links.

In general terms, **Semiunify** must be modified so that all equivalence links are kept for variable nodes, and the weights for the self-loops are kept and updated, by taking greatest common divisors, when a second self-loop is added to a node. GCD is necessary because two self-loops (thought of as rewrite rules) can inter-simplify each other down to a single rule by essentially simulating the process of GCD (cf. [8, 15]).

The self-loops on functional terms are pushed to the variables of the terms, updating the weights accordingly when another self-loop is found. Once this is done, self-loops will be treated as the other links when finding the solution.

The next step is the simplification of the links (thought of as equations), which was described in Sec. 5, until only one link is left for each variable that appears on the graph. This remaining links determine the semiunifier σ, and the matching substitution ρ, as previously illustrated.

Thus the major difference is that more careful processing of the self-loops is necessary, and this necessitates the use of GCD on weights; this turns out to boost the complexity of the method, since GCD is more expensive than addition or subtraction. See the full paper for a more complete description of the algorithm for generating principal solutions.

7 Technical Results

In this section we discuss the technical properties of our algorithm(s): correctness of the decision procedure, soundness of the naive solution extraction algorithm, and soundness and completeness of the modified algorithm which returns principal solutions; in addition we present the complexity of each of these. For reasons of space, the results in this section are merely sketched; the reader is referred to the full paper for a complete treatment.

7.1   Decision Procedure

To prove the correctness of the decision procedure we give an equational semantics to the actions performed by our algorithms (similar to that in [8, 15]). We interpret the class links on the graph as equations on a special terms, called φ-terms, which replace each application of ρ to a term by application of a distinguished new function symbol φ, e.g., a link $s \xrightarrow{\ n \quad m\ } t$ represents the equation $\varphi^n(s) =^? \varphi^m(t)$. Such terms are considered identical up to movement of φ past a function symbol, e.g., $\varphi(f(x))$ is identified with $f(\varphi(x))$.

For any graph G, the set of equations represented by G is

$$E(G) = \{\varphi^n(s) =^? \varphi^m(t) \mid \text{there is an arc } s \xrightarrow{\ n \quad m\ } t \text{ in } G\}$$

For any σ and ρ, the (σ, ρ)-instance of a φ-term t is obtained by replacing, bottom-up, every variable x by $\sigma(x)$, and every $\varphi(t')$ (where t' contains no φ) by $\rho(t')$. A set of φ-equations has a solution iff there exists σ and ρ such that the (σ, ρ)-instance of each equation is an identity.

The set of class links in a graph changes with each call to the functions **Semiunify**, **Find** and **Cycle**, which results in a a sequence of graphs $G_1, G_2, \ldots G_n$, where G_1 has a single link representing the original problem, and G_n is the terminal graph. Correctness of the algorithm is shown in three steps. First, we observe that **Semiunify** calls itself recursively only when two distinct equivalence classes have been joined; since the number of such classes is finite the algorithm must terminate. Second, by considering the cases for changing the graph (marked as lines (1)–(6) in the algorithm), we show that for each i, $E(G_{i+1})$ has a solution iff $E(G_i)$ has a solution. Finally, we prove that $E(G_n)$ has a solution if and only if the call to **Cycle** returns **T**. This is shown in two steps, first proving that $E(G_n)$ has no solution iff it implies an equation of the form

$$\varphi^n(x) = \varphi^m(f(\ldots x \ldots))$$

for some symbol f, and where $n \leq m$ (cf. [8]), and then proving that this condition holds iff there is a cycle of links from x to $f(\ldots x \ldots)$ in the graph, where either there is a self-loop on one of the terms in the cycle, or the accumulation of indices on the links provides for the exponents n and m in a bad equation. **Cycle** returns **T** iff no such cycle can be found.

Lemma 1 Semiunify(s,j,t,k) **and Cycle**(s,t) *returns* **true** *iff there exists* σ *and* ρ *such that* $\rho^j(\sigma(s)) = \rho^i(\sigma(t))$.

To analyze the complexity of our algorithm, we count assignments of a pointer, comparisons of pointers or symbols, and primitive operations on bits. We consider the following points:

- **Semiunify** is called at most n times, where n is the number of symbols in the original equation to be solved;
- A sequence of $O(n)$ calls to Union (implicit in our algorithm) and **Find** can be performed with $O(n\,\alpha(n))$ assignments, comparisons, or additions of two *numbers*, where α is the functional inverse of Ackermann's function [1];

- All other operations add at most a constant number of assignments, comparisons, or additions/subtractions of two *numbers* to each call to **Semiunify**;
- The arithmetic operations of the algorithm may be analyzed as follows: if we start with two numbers of constant size (number of bits), and create a list of $O(m)$ new numbers by addition and subtraction of previous members of the list, we can create numbers of size at most $O(m)$; thus at each step need to do at most $O(m)$ bit operations, which give a total cost of $O(m^2)$ (in our algorithm, $m = n\,\alpha(n)$).

This gives us our complexity result.

Lemma 2 *Under the uniform cost RAM model (counting assignments, comparisons and arithmetic operations), a call to* **Semiunify**(s,j,t,k), *where the combined size of s and t is n symbols, costs* $O(n\,\alpha(n))$. *For a RAM model counting assignments and bit operations, the cost is* $O(n^2\,\alpha(n)^2)$ *assignments, comparisons, or bit operations.*

What is interesting about this result is that the purely symbolic operations cost no more than for standard unification ($O(n\,\alpha(n))$); the dominate cost is for the arithmetic on weights. In Section 8 we compare this result with previous algorithms, which do not closely analyze the cost of the arithmetic.

Finally, we note that a Union-Find problem can be embedded in a Semi-unification problem in a trivial way, which shows that we cannot improve the $O(n\,\alpha(n))$ bound unless we can do the same for Union-Find.

7.2   Naive Solution Extraction

Extracting a solution from the final graph produced by the decision procedure in the affirmative case involves the repointing of arcs in the graph so that each variable is the source of at most one arc, and arcs between variables follow a predetermined ordering on variables; the bindings in the solution can be extracted from these links in a simple way (and reminiscent of the method described in [8]); this can create no more than n new arcs, and hence $O(n)$ arithmetic operations on numbers. The cost for this is $O(n^2)$ assignments and bit operations, which is dominated by the original cost to create the graph. The result is a graph representation of the semi-unifier. Correctness is shown, again, by using the underlying equational semantics.

7.3   Principal Solution Extraction

The second algorithm, briefly described in Section 6, can be proved correct using the equational semantics in a manner similar to the first algorithm. The major difference in terms of complexity is that under certain conditions (viz., two self-loops on the same node in the graph) the implementation of the underlying equational semantics (interreduction of two equations) requires that we find the GCD of two weights in the graph, and this is more expensive than simple addition or subtraction. Using the fastest-known algorithm, we can perform GCD in $O(k\,log^2k)$ bit operations on two k-bit numbers. In the worst case, the arithmetic may involve $O(n\,\alpha(n))$ additions, subtractions, or GCD's, which boosts the overall complexity to $O(n^2\,log^2(n\,\alpha(n))\,\alpha(n)^2)$.

8   Previous Work

The semi-unification problem was introduced in the late 70's in [10] by Lankford and Musser. Purdom presented an algorithm for uniform semi-unification in [14], but his algorithm, as observed in [8], is incorrect. Other decision procedures for the uniform case can be found in [5, 6], in [13], and in [11]. Henglein showed that his algorithm, which finds principal solutions, is in PSPACE.

Perhaps the first rigorous treatment of an efficient algorithm for the problem was given by Kapur et al. in [8]. In this paper, an (exponential) algorithm based on completion, and a method for extracting solutions, was presented, and this leads to a graph-based decision procedure which is shown to terminate in polynomial time; the procedure does not produce solutions. This procedure was the inspiration for our own, but there are significant differences, and our algorithm is not only asymptotically faster, but also much simpler to describe and to implement.

More recently, an efficient algorithm based on the Corbin-Bidoit [4] approach to standard unification was presented by Ruzika [15]; the algorithm does not give principal solutions, and there appears to be a bug (which can perhaps be patched). The claim of quadratic complexity depends on the assumption that arithmetic operations have constant cost; since, as observed above, the cost of the arithmetic dominates the cost of the other operations, we consider this to be unrealistic. Retrofitting fast algorithms for arithmetic (e.g., GCD) into his approach appears to give a complexity of $O(n^3log^2n)$.

9   Conclusions

We have presented the fastest algorithms to date for uniform semi-unification, based on the unification closure method for standard unification. These algorithms have been analyzed thoroughly in the first author's thesis, and the work as a whole is a complete analysis of the algorithmic aspects of deciding the problem and generating solutions. Our decision procedure is asymptotically faster than our method for generating principal solutions. In the context of other algorithms for uniform semi-unification, these results show that approaches to standard unification can be adapted for semi-unification, and the cost in terms of symbolic operations is the same for both problems. However, semi-unification introduces arithmetic for counting the number of ρ's applied to subterms, and this arithmetic dominates the cost of the symbolic operations. Since techniques for unification in linear time depend on acyclicity conditions that can not be obtained in semi-unification, we surmise that our approach is the fastest possible; it may be possible to trim the bound somewhat by a more precise analysis of the arithmetic operations required, however we leave this as a subject for future research.

References

[1] A.V. Aho, J.E. Hopcroft, and J.D. Ullman. *Data Structures and Algorithms.* Addison-Wesley, Reading, MA, 1983.

[2] F. Baader and W. Snyder. Unification theory. In *Handbook on Automated Deduction.* Springer. To be published.

[3] Franz Baader and Tobias Nipkow. *Term Rewriting and All That.* Cambridge University Press, 1998.

[4] J. Corbin and M. Bidoit. A rehabilitation of robinson's unification algorithm. *Information Processing,* 83:909–914, 1993.

[5] F. Henglein. Type inference and semi-unification. In *ACM Conference on Lisp and Functional Programming,* pages 184–197. ACM, 1988.

[6] Fritz Henglein. *Polymorphic Type Inference and Semi-Unification.* PhD thesis, Rutgers University, April 1989. Available as NYU Technical Report 443, May 1989, from New York University, Courant Institute of Mathematical Sciences, Department of Computer Science, 251 Mercer St., New York, N.Y. 10012, USA.

[7] G. Huet. *Résolution d'Equations dans les Langages d'Ordre* $1, 2, \ldots, \omega$. PhD thesis, Université de Paris VII, 1976.

[8] D. Kapur, D. Musser, P. Narendran, and Stillman J. Semi-unification. *Theoretical Computer Science,* 81(2):169–188, April 1991.

[9] A.J. Kfoury, J. Tiuryn, and P. Urzyczyn. The undecidability of the semi-unification problem. *Information and Computation,* 102(1):83–101, January 1993.

[10] D.S. Lankford and D.R. Musser. A finite termination criterion. Unpublished Draft, USC Information Sciences Institute, 1978.

[11] H. Leiss. Semi-unification and type inference for polymorphic recursion. Technical Report INF-2-ASE-5-89, Siemens, Munich, Germany, 1989.

[12] A. Oliart and W. Snyder. Fast algorithms for semi-unification. http://www.cs.bu.edu/faculty/snyder/pubs.html, 1998.

[13] P. Pudlack. On a unification problem related to kreisel's conjecture. *Commentationes Mathematicae Universitatis Carolinae,* 1988. Praguec Czechoslovakia.

[14] P.W. Purdom. Detecting looping simplifications. In *Proc. 2nd Conference on Rewrite Rule Theory and Applications,* volume 250 of *Lecture Notes in Computer Science,* pages 54–62. Springer, Berlin, May 1987.

[15] P. Ruzicka. An efficient decision algorithm for the uniform semi-unification problem. In *16th International Symposium on Mathematical Foundations of Computer Science (MFCS).* Springer, September 1991.

Termination Analysis by Inductive Evaluation

Jürgen Brauburger and Jürgen Giesl

FB Informatik, TU Darmstadt, Alexanderstraße 10, 64283 Darmstadt, Germany
{brauburger, giesl}@informatik.tu-darmstadt.de

Abstract. We present a new approach for automatic termination analysis of functional programs. Several methods have been presented which try to find a well-founded ordering such that the arguments in the recursive calls are smaller than the corresponding inputs. However, previously developed approaches for automated termination analysis often disregard the *conditions* under which the recursive calls are evaluated. Hence, the existing methods fail for an important class of algorithms where the necessary information for proving termination is 'hidden' in the conditions. In this paper we develop the *inductive evaluation* method which analyzes the auxiliary functions occurring in the conditions of the recursive calls. We also discuss an extension of our method to *partial* functions in order to determine their domains automatically. The proposed technique proved successful for termination analysis of numerous algorithms in functional as well as imperative programming languages.

1 Introduction

Proving termination is a central problem in the development of correct software. While most work on the automation of termination proofs has been done for *term rewriting systems* (for surveys see e.g. [Der87,Ste95]) and for *logic programs* (e.g. [UvG88,Plü90,SD94]), in this paper we consider *functional programs*.

A well-known method for termination proofs of LISP functions has been implemented in the NQTHM system of R. S. Boyer and J S. Moore [BM79]. To prove that arguments decrease w.r.t. a well-founded ordering, they use a *measure function* $|.|$ which maps data objects t to natural numbers $|t|$. In their approach, for each recursive call $f(r)$ in an algorithm $f(x)$, an *induction lemma* $\Delta \rightarrow |r| < |x|$ is required. It asserts that under the condition Δ, the argument of the recursive call has a smaller measure than the input. Now it remains to verify $\psi \rightarrow \Delta$ where ψ is the condition under which the recursive call $f(r)$ is performed. While in [BM79] the user has to supply all induction lemmata, the methods in [Wal94b,Gie95c,GWB98] synthesize a certain class of induction lemmata automatically. The technique in [Wal94b] is restricted to one fixed measure function $|.|$, but the approach of [Gie95c,GWB98] also allows an automatic generation of suitable measures by using techniques from the area of *term rewriting systems*.

To synthesize an induction lemma for a recursive call $f(r)$ under the condition ψ, these methods analyze the auxiliary functions occurring in the recursive

C. Kirchner and H. Kirchner (Eds.): Automated Deduction, CADE-15
LNAI 1421, pp. 254–269, 1998. © Springer-Verlag Berlin Heidelberg 1998

argument r. However, auxiliary functions in the *condition* ψ are ignored at this point. Consequently, the previous approaches often fail if the necessary information for the termination proof is given by the functions called in the conditions.

We illustrate this problem in Sect. 2. In Sect. 3 we present the *inductive evaluation* technique which overcomes this drawback by combining termination analysis with methods for *induction theorem proving*. While in Sect. 3 our aim is to show that a procedure terminates for *each* input, in Sect. 4 the method is generalized for termination analysis of functions which terminate for *some* inputs only. In Sect. 5 the techniques are extended for analysis of more complex procedures and Sect. 6 draws some conclusions.

2   Termination of Functional Programs

We regard an eager first-order functional language with free algebraic data types[1] and pattern matching where the patterns have to be exhaustive and exclusive. As an example consider the data types bool and nat (for naturals). The type bool has the nullary *constructors* true and false and the objects of type nat are built with the constructors 0 and s : nat → nat. The following procedures compute the 'less than or equal' relation for naturals and the subtraction function.

function le : nat × nat → bool	function minus : nat × nat → nat
$\mathsf{le}(0, v) = \mathsf{true}$	$\mathsf{minus}(x, y) = \mathsf{if}(\,\mathsf{le}(x, y),$
$\mathsf{le}(\mathsf{s}(u), 0) = \mathsf{false}$	$0,$
$\mathsf{le}(\mathsf{s}(u), \mathsf{s}(v)) = \mathsf{le}(u, v)$	$\mathsf{s}(\mathsf{minus}(x, \mathsf{s}(y)))\,)$

For each data type τ there is a pre-defined conditional function if : $\mathsf{bool} \times \tau \times \tau \to \tau$. These conditionals are the only functions with non-eager semantics, i.e. when evaluating $\mathsf{if}(\psi, t_1, t_2)$, the boolean term[2] ψ is evaluated first and depending on the result of its evaluation either t_1 or t_2 is evaluated afterwards.

An algorithm f is terminating if the inputs are 'greater' than the arguments of the recursive calls. For instance, termination of le can be shown by inventing a measure function $|.|$ satisfying le's *termination hypothesis*

$$|u, v| < |\mathsf{s}(u), \mathsf{s}(v)|. \tag{1}$$

We only regard universally quantified formulas of the form $\forall_{\ldots} \varphi$, where we omit the quantifiers to ease readability. Now 'verification of φ' means proving that φ evaluates to true for all instantiations of its variables with data objects. For termination proofs we extend the specification by a new data type weight, new measure function symbols $|.| : \tau \to \mathsf{weight}$ for each data type $\tau \neq \mathsf{weight}$, and a function symbol $< : \mathsf{weight} \times \mathsf{weight} \to \mathsf{bool}$. To compare *tuples* of terms, we also introduce new n-ary tuple symbols $\mathsf{tuple}_n : \mathsf{weight} \times \ldots \times \mathsf{weight} \to \mathsf{weight}$ for each $n \in \mathbb{N}$, where we often write $|t_1, \ldots, t_n|$ instead of $\mathsf{tuple}_n(|t_1|, \ldots, |t_n|)$. In

---

[1] See [NN96,Sen96,PS97] for extensions of termination analysis to higher-order languages, languages with lazy evaluation strategy, and to non-free algebraic data types.

[2] We use Greek letters φ, ψ, ω to denote boolean terms and often refer to them as 'formulas', where $\neg, \wedge, \vee, \to$ are pre-defined boolean functions with obvious semantics.

the following, we restrict ourselves to interpretations where the universe for objects of type weight is the set of natural numbers $\mathbb{N}$ and where $<$ is interpreted as the usual 'less than' relation on $\mathbb{N}$. For data types $\tau \neq$ weight the corresponding universe must correspond to the set of all constructor ground terms and moreover, all defining equations of the algorithms must be valid (i.e. we only consider *inductive models* of the specification, cf. e.g. [ZKK88,Wal94a,BR95]).

In the area of term rewriting systems, several techniques have been developed to generate suitable interpretations for the measure function symbols $|.|$. For example, termination of le can be proved by using an appropriate *polynomial norm* $|.|_{\text{POL}}$ [Lan79]. A polynomial norm is defined by associating each n-ary constructor c with an n-ary polynomial $\text{POL}(c)$ with integer coefficients. In this way, each data object $c(t_1,..,t_n)$ is mapped to a number, i.e. $|c(t_1,..,t_n)|_{\text{POL}} = \text{POL}(c)(|t_1|_{\text{POL}},..,|t_n|_{\text{POL}})$, where we always demand that the choice of the coefficients ensures that data objects are only mapped to *non-negative* integers. For example, if $|0|_{\text{POL}} = 0$ and $|s(u)|_{\text{POL}} = |u|_{\text{POL}} + 1$, then each data object of type nat is mapped to a natural number, and we have $|u|_{\text{POL}} < |s(u)|_{\text{POL}}$ since $|u|_{\text{POL}}$ is smaller than $|u|_{\text{POL}} + 1$ for each natural number $|u|_{\text{POL}}$.

Similarly, tuple symbols are also associated with polynomials mapping $\mathbb{N}^n$ to $\mathbb{N}$. If $\text{tuple}_2(x, y)$ is associated with $x + y$, then we have $|u, v|_{\text{POL}} < |s(u), s(v)|_{\text{POL}}$, as $|u|_{\text{POL}} + |v|_{\text{POL}} < |u|_{\text{POL}} + 1 + |v|_{\text{POL}} + 1$ holds for all naturals $|u|_{\text{POL}}$ and $|v|_{\text{POL}}$.

If $|.|$ and tuple_2 are interpreted according to the above polynomial norm, then the termination hypothesis (1) is satisfied. Consequently, termination of le is proved. Techniques to generate suitable polynomial norms automatically have been developed in [Ste94,Gie95a], for instance.

Let t^* and r^* denote tuples of terms $t_1,..,t_n$ and $r_1,..,r_n$. To prove termination of f, for every recursive call in a defining equation $f(t^*) = ... f(r^*) ...$ we build a *termination hypothesis* $\psi \rightarrow |r^*| < |t^*|$ where ψ is the condition under which the recursive call $f(r^*)$ is evaluated. (We restrict ourselves to algorithms without recursive calls in conditions.) For instance, the recursive call of minus is evaluated under the condition $\neg\text{le}(x, y)$. So minus' termination hypothesis is

$$\neg\text{le}(x, y) \rightarrow |x, s(y)| < |x, y|. \tag{2}$$

Termination of a functional program f is proved if one finds a polynomial norm such that *all* termination hypotheses of f are satisfied.

As the termination hypothesis (1) of le only contains terms built with constructors, a suitable polynomial norm can easily be generated automatically. However, this is not possible for the termination hypothesis (2) of minus. The reason is that minus calls another algorithm, le. In contrast to (1), the inequality $|t_1, s(t_2)| < |t_1, t_2|$ in minus' termination hypothesis does not have to be satisfied for *all* data objects t_1 and t_2, but only for those where $\neg\text{le}(t_1, t_2)$ is true. To determine these data objects we have to consider the *semantics* of the algorithm le. However, the existing methods for the automated generation of polynomial norms can only be used for termination proofs if the termination hypotheses do not contain *defined symbols*, i.e. function symbols defined by algorithms.

3   Termination Proofs with Inductive Evaluation

To enable automatic termination proofs for algorithms like minus, in this section we develop a calculus which transforms termination hypotheses like (2) into formulas *without* defined symbols. Our calculus operates on pairs $H; C$ where H is a set of formulas possibly containing defined symbols (the hypotheses) and C is a set of formulas without defined symbols (the constraints). The soundness of our calculus guarantees that if $H; C$ can be transformed into $H'; C'$, then every interpretation (of the form as described in Sect. 2) satisfying $H' \cup C'$ also satisfies $H \cup C$. For termination proofs, we initialize H to be the set of termination hypotheses and we let C be empty. Then rules of the calculus are applied repeatedly until we result in a pair $H'; C'$ where the first component H' is empty. By the soundness of the calculus, to prove the termination of the algorithm now it suffices to find a polynomial norm satisfying the constraints C'.

An obvious solution to eliminate the defined symbol le from minus' termination hypothesis is to omit its premise, i.e. we could use the following rule[3].

Premise Elimination	$\dfrac{H \cup \{\psi \to \omega\} \; ; \; C}{H \; ; \; C \cup \{\omega\}}$	if ω does not contain any defined symbols.

This is a sound transformation technique, because every interpretation satisfying ω for *all* instantiations of its variables will also satisfy ω for those instantiations which meet the condition ψ, i.e. $\psi \to |r^*| < |t^*|$ may indeed be transformed into $|r^*| < |t^*|$. Moreover, we also allow the application of this rule if the premise ψ is missing, i.e. for an algorithm like le, the unconditional termination hypothesis (1) can be directly inserted into the set of constraints.

For the termination proof of minus, we would initialize H to be $\{(2)\}$ and C to be empty. Then one application of the premise elimination rule transforms H into the empty set and C into $\{|x, s(y)| < |x, y|\}$. However, in our example this naive solution cannot be used, because this constraint is unsatisfiable. Hence, the termination of minus cannot be proved if the premise of its termination hypothesis is neglected. For that reason, all previous approaches for automatic termination proofs fail with this example.

To enable termination proofs for algorithms like minus we now introduce a new rule which *evaluates* the auxiliary functions in the premises of termination hypotheses. To construct a set of constraints sufficient for the termination hypothesis (2) we use an *induction* w.r.t. the definition of the algorithm le. The base cases of this inductive construction correspond to le's non-recursive defining equations and the step case results from le's recursive (third) equation.

---

[3] In order to obtain constraints without defined symbols, this rule may only be applied if ω contains no calls of auxiliary algorithms. Hence, in this paper we restrict ourselves to termination hypotheses $\psi \to \omega$ where defined symbols may only occur in the *condition* ψ. For algorithms with defined symbols in the arguments of recursive calls, the technique of the present paper is extended by the calculus of [Gie95c,Gie97,GWB98] to eliminate the remaining defined symbols from the *conclusion* ω.

First we perform a case analysis w.r.t. le, i.e. the variables x, y in (2) are instantiated by the patterns of le's defining equations. Instead of (2) we demand

$$\neg le(0, v) \ \rightarrow \ |0, s(v)| < |0, v|, \tag{3}$$

$$\neg le(s(u), 0) \ \rightarrow \ |s(u), s(0)| < |s(u), 0|, \tag{4}$$

$$\neg le(s(u), s(v)) \ \rightarrow \ |s(u), s(s(v))| < |s(u), s(v)|. \tag{5}$$

In order to detect redundant cases, in each resulting formula we now check whether the premise is unsatisfiable. For example, (3) may be omitted as its negated premise $\neg\neg le(0, v)$ can be verified by evaluation of le and $\neg$. As the premises of (3) and (4) are satisfiable, the corresponding proofs must fail.

In the third case (5) we use that each le-call produces a finite sequence of recursive calls. Hence, we assume as an *induction hypothesis* that the termination hypothesis (2) is true for the arguments u and v of le's recursive call, i.e.

$$\neg le(u, v) \ \rightarrow \ |u, s(v)| < |u, v|. \tag{6}$$

To apply the induction hypothesis, we check if the premise of the induction conclusion (5) entails the premise of the induction hypothesis (6), i.e. we prove

$$\neg le(s(u), s(v)) \rightarrow \neg le(u, v). \tag{7}$$

Again, the proof is trivial since $le(s(u), s(v))$ evaluates to $le(u, v)$. For that reason we may now *apply* the induction hypothesis (6), i.e. instead of (5) we demand

$$\neg le(s(u), s(v)) \ \wedge \ |u, s(v)| < |u, v| \ \rightarrow \ |s(u), s(s(v))| < |s(u), s(v)|. \tag{8}$$

The existing techniques for generating polynomial norms expect a set of *inequalities* as constraints, i.e. they cannot treat constraints like $|r_1^*| < |t_1^*| \rightarrow |r_2^*| < |t_2^*|$. To eliminate the inequality in the premise of (8) we use that we restricted ourselves to interpretations where naturals are compared by the usual 'less than' relation. For arbitrary naturals k, l, m, n the conjecture $[m + l \leq n + k] \rightarrow [k < l \rightarrow m < n]$ holds. Hence, instead of (8) we may demand

$$\neg le(s(u), s(v)) \ \rightarrow \ |s(u), s(s(v))| + |u, v| \leq |s(u), s(v)| + |u, s(v)|. \tag{9}$$

Here, $+$ and $\leq$ are new function symbols (on **weight**) and we require that all interpretations map $+$ to the addition and $\leq$ to the 'less than or equal' relation.

In this way, the termination hypothesis (2) can be transformed into the formulas (4) and (9). By eliminating their premises (using the premise elimination rule), we obtain two constraints without defined symbols. Therefore we can now apply the existing techniques to generate a polynomial norm satisfying these constraints. For example, we may use the polynomial norm where $|0|_{\text{POL}} = 0$, $|s(u)|_{\text{POL}} = |u|_{\text{POL}} + 1$, and $\text{tuple}_2(x, y)$ is associated with $(x - y)^2$. (Note that this is a legal polynomial norm, because all tuples of data objects are mapped to non-negative numbers[4].) Hence, termination of minus is proved.

---

[4] In contrast to conventional termination proofs of *term rewriting systems*, for *functional programs* one may use orderings which are not even weakly monotonic, cf.

Recall that during the transformation of minus' termination hypothesis we had to verify the formulas $\neg\neg\mathsf{le}(0, v)$ and (7). To perform the required proofs, we simply applied *symbolic evaluation*, i.e. we used the defining equations as rewrite rules. In general this verification could require an *induction theorem proving system*, e.g. [BM79,ZKK88,Bun$^+$89,Wal94a,BR95,HS96]. However, when testing our method on numerous algorithms, we found that in almost all examples the required conjectures could already be proved by symbolic evaluation.

Let $\psi \to |r^*| < |t^*|$ be a termination hypothesis containing at least the pairwise different variables $y_1, .., y_n$ of the data types $\tau_1, .., \tau_n$. Moreover, let $g : \tau_1 \times .. \times \tau_n \to \tau$ be defined by a terminating algorithm with k defining equations. To ease the presentation, we restrict ourselves to functions g which are defined without using the conditional if (for an extension see Sect. 5).

Then we use the following rule for induction w.r.t. the recursions of g and subsequent evaluation. In this rule, for any terms $p, s_1, \ldots, s_n$ let $p[s^*]$ be an abbreviation for $p[y_1/s_1, \ldots, y_n/s_n]$, i.e. $p[s^*]$ abbreviates $\sigma(p)$ where σ substitutes each y_i by s_i. Moreover, throughout the paper we always assume that the variables occurring in different algorithms are disjoint.

Inductive Evaluation
$$\frac{H \cup \{\psi \to |r^*| < |t^*|\} \ ; \ C}{H \cup \{\varphi_1, .., \varphi_k\} \ ; \ C}$$

If $g(s^*) = q$ is the i-th defining equation of g, then φ_i is defined as follows:

- $\varphi_i := \mathsf{true}$ if $\neg\psi[s^*]$ can be verified,

- $\varphi_i := \psi[s^*] \to$ $\left.\begin{array}{l} \text{otherwise, if } q \text{ contains a term } g(q^*) \\ \text{where } \psi[s^*] \to \psi[q^*] \text{ can be verified,} \end{array}\right\}$
  $|r^*[s^*]| + |t^*[q^*]| \le |t^*[s^*]| + |r^*[q^*]|$

- $\varphi_i := \psi[s^*] \to |r^*[s^*]| < |t^*[s^*]|$ otherwise

---

In our example, for le's first equation we have $s^* = (0, v)$ and φ_1 is true, as $\neg\psi[s^*]$ (i.e. $\neg\neg\mathsf{le}(0, v)$) can be verified. Similarly, φ_2 is (4), i.e. here s^* is $(\mathsf{s}(u), 0)$. For le's recursive equation we have $s^* = (\mathsf{s}(u), \mathsf{s}(v))$ and $q^* = (u, v)$. As the condition (7) could be proved, the resulting formula φ_3 is (9). The following theorem proves that our rule performs a Noetherian induction, since it only allows inductions w.r.t. functions g whose termination has been proved before.

Theorem 1. *If $H; C$ can be transformed into $H'; C'$ by premise elimination and inductive evaluation, then we have $H' \cup C' \models H \cup C$.*

Proof. The soundness of premise elimination is obvious. For inductive evaluation, recall that we restricted ourselves to inductive models I. Now assume that $I \models \varphi_i = \mathsf{true}$ for all i, but there exists a counterexample, i.e. a tuple of constructor ground terms p^* such that $I \models \psi[p^*] = \mathsf{true}$ and $I \not\models |r^*[p^*]| < |t^*[p^*]| = \mathsf{true}$. Let $\prec_g$ be the relation where $p_2^* \prec_g p_1^*$ holds iff evaluation of $g(p_1^*)$ leads to

---

[AG97]. In fact, termination of the algorithm minus from Sect. 2 cannot be proved by any monotonic well-founded ordering. For that reason, in our approach we restricted ourselves to orderings based on polynomial norms, as most other classes of orderings (that are amenable to automation) possess the monotonicity property.

evaluation of $g(p_2^*)$. Then by termination of g we know that $\prec_g$ is well founded. Hence, we may choose p^* to be a *minimal* counterexample w.r.t. $\prec_g$.

There is a defining equation $g(s^*) = q$ (say, the i-th) such that $p^* = \sigma(s^*)$ for some σ. Obviously, $\psi[s^*]$ is satisfiable as its instantiation $\psi[p^*]$ is valid in I. Hence, $\varphi_i \neq$ true. Thus, q must contain a subterm $g(q^*)$ where $\psi[s^*] \to \psi[q^*]$ can be verified. Then $I \models \psi[p^*] =$ true implies $I \models \psi[\sigma(q^*)] =$ true. But as $I(\sigma(q^*)) \prec_g p^*$, due to the minimality of p^*, $I(\sigma(q^*))$ cannot be a counterexample. Hence, we have $I \models |r^*[\sigma(q^*)]| < |t^*[\sigma(q^*)]| =$ true. But then $I \models \varphi_i =$ true implies that p^* is no counterexample either, which leads to a contradiction.   □

To select suitable functions g for inductive evaluation, we use a well-known heuristic from induction theorem proving. For a termination hypothesis $\psi \to |r^*| < |t^*|$, we check whether ψ contains a subterm $g(y_1, .., y_n)$ where y_i are pairwise different variables. Such a term suggests an induction w.r.t. g using $y_1, .., y_n$ as induction variables, cf. e.g. [BM79,ZKK88,Bun⁺89,Wal94a]. Hence, for the termination hypothesis of minus this heuristic suggests inductive evaluation w.r.t. le using the induction variables x and y. Further refined heuristics to choose among several suggested induction relations can be found in [Gie95b].

Inductive evaluation is used for algorithms where the *conditions* of recursive calls have to be analyzed in order to prove termination. In particular, this holds for algorithms like minus where some value is repeatedly increased until it reaches some bound. This class of algorithms is also used extensively in *imperative* programming languages. A straightforward approach to prove termination of imperative programs is to transform them into functional ones and to verify termination of the resulting functions, cf. e.g. [Hen80,GWB98]. For example, the imperative program '$r := 0$; *while* $x > y$ *do* $y := y+1$; $r := r+1$ *od*' is transformed into a function whose termination can be proved analogously to minus. Hence, inductive evaluation is particularly useful when extending termination analysis to imperative programs, cf. [BG98].

4   Termination Analysis for Partial Functions

Up to now we tried to prove that an algorithm terminates *totally*, i.e. for *each* input. In the following, we also regard procedures which terminate for *some* inputs only. For example, consider the data type list with the constructors empty and $\cdot$: nat × list → list where $x \cdot y$ represents the insertion of the number x in front of the list y. Then nextindex(x, y, z) returns the smallest index $i \geq x$ such that z is the i-th element of the list y (where the first element has index 0).

function nth : nat × list → nat
   nth$(u,$ empty$) = 0$
   nth$(0, v \cdot w)) = v$
   nth$(s(u), v \cdot w) =$ nth(u, w)

function eq : nat × nat → bool
   eq$(0, 0)$ = true
   eq$(0, s(v))$ = false
   eq$(s(u), 0)$ = false
   eq$(s(u), s(v)) =$ eq(u, v)

function nextindex : nat × list × nat → nat
   nextindex$(x, y, z) =$ if$($ eq$($nth$(x, y), z), \ x, \ $ nextindex$(s(x), y, z))$

Let '$u.v.w$' abbreviate '$u.(v.w)$'. Hence, nextindex$(2, 5.6.3.5.7.5.$empty$, 5) = 3$. While termination of nth and eq can easily be proved, nextindex(x, y, z) only terminates iff z occurs in y at a position whose index is greater than or equal to x or if $z = 0$ (as nth$(x, y) = 0$ whenever x is not an index of y). Thus, evaluation of nextindex$(2, 5.6.3.5.7.5.$empty$, 6)$ does not halt.

4.1 Termination Predicates

To represent subsets of inputs where procedures like nextindex terminate, in [BG96] we introduced termination predicates. An n-ary boolean function θ_f is a *termination predicate* for an n-ary function f iff θ_f is total and if $\theta_f(t_1, .., t_n) =$ true implies that evaluation of $f(t_1, .., t_n)$ halts. Our aim is to synthesize termination predicates which return true as often as possible, but of course in general this goal cannot be reached as the domains of functions are undecidable.

In [BG96,GWB98], rules for the synthesis of termination predicates are developed. Given an algorithm f and a measure function $|.|$ these rules generate a procedure for θ_f such that $\theta_f(t_1, .., t_n)$ returns true *iff* for $f(t_1, .., t_n)$

(i) the sequence of arguments of (recursive) f-calls decreases under $|.|$ and
(ii) $\theta_g(r_1, .., r_n)$ holds for each resulting auxiliary function call $g(r_1, .., r_n)$.

For example, given $|.|$ the following procedure is synthesized for $\theta_{\text{nextindex}}$.

function $\theta_{\text{nextindex}}$: nat $\times$ list $\times$ nat $\to$ bool
$\theta_{\text{nextindex}}(x, y, z) = $ if$($ eq$($nth$(x, y), z)$, true, if$($ $|s(x), y, z| < |x, y, z|$,
$\qquad\qquad\qquad\qquad\qquad\qquad\qquad\qquad \theta_{\text{nextindex}}(s(x), y, z)$,
$\qquad\qquad\qquad\qquad\qquad\qquad\qquad\qquad$ false $))$

The procedure $\theta_{\text{nextindex}}$ satisfies (i), since under the condition $\neg$eq$($nth(x, y), $z)$ of the only recursive call in nextindex, $\theta_{\text{nextindex}}$ returns true iff the arguments of this recursive call decrease (i.e. $|s(x), y, z| < |x, y, z|$) and if the arguments of the subsequent recursive nextindex-calls decrease under $|.|$, too (i.e. $\theta_{\text{nextindex}}(s(x), y, z)$). Furthermore, (ii) is satisfied since the only auxiliary functions, nth and eq, are total. As the constructors also denote total functions, we may neglect their termination predicates. Note that $\theta_{\text{nextindex}}$ terminates totally by construction since it is called recursively only if the arguments decrease under $|.|$.

4.2 Inductive Evaluation for Partial Functions

The synthesis of termination predicates described in [BG96] requires the user to provide a measure function $|.|$. To get independent from this input, our aim is an automated generation of suitable polynomial norms for termination predicates, such that the corresponding termination hypotheses are satisfied 'as often as possible'[5]. In order to find a suitable choice for the measure $|.|$ in the termination predicate algorithm $\theta_{\text{nextindex}}$, consider the termination hypothesis of nextindex,

$$\neg\text{eq}(\text{nth}(x, y), z) \to |s(x), y, z| < |x, y, z|. \qquad (10)$$

---

[5] For algorithms with auxiliary functions in the recursive *arguments* (instead of the *conditions*), the techniques developed for total termination [Gie95c] can be adapted to partial functions [Bra97], cf. [GWB98].

The formula (10) cannot be transformed into satisfiable constraints, since then total termination of nextindex would be falsely proved. However, we can use inductive evaluation to generate an interpretation that satisfies (10) for a *maximal* number of instances. In this way, we finally obtain a termination predicate for nextindex that is true as often as possible.

In general, the set H of termination hypotheses is transformed into a (possibly empty) set C of inequalities that are satisfied by a polynomial norm. For that purpose we now also use *unsound* transformation rules. However, based on the faulty transformation, for each termination hypothesis $\psi \to |r^*| < |t^*|$ containing the variables x^*, a *soundness predicate* λ is generated such that every interpretation satisfying C also satisfies the restricted termination hypothesis $\lambda(x^*) \wedge \psi \to |r^*| < |t^*|$. So the soundness predicate λ indicates for which data objects the transformation of $\psi \to |r^*| < |t^*|$ into the constraints C is correct[6]. Hence, if we interpret $|.|$ by a polynomial norm satisfying the obtained constraints C, then we can modify the termination predicate algorithm and replace the inequality $|r^*| < |t^*|$ by the corresponding soundness predicate $\lambda(x^*)$.

For instance, to find a suitable measure function for $\theta_{\text{nextindex}}$ we transform the termination hypothesis (10). To exploit the premise $\neg\text{eq}(\text{nth}(x,y),z)$ our heuristic suggests inductive evaluation w.r.t. nth. According to the definition of nth we have to consider two base cases and one step case. For none of these cases the premise is unsatisfiable. In the third case the induction hypothesis may be applied as the formula $\neg\text{eq}(\text{nth}(\text{s}(u), v{\bullet}w), z) \to \neg\text{eq}(\text{nth}(u, w), z)$ can be proved by symbolic evaluation. Thus inductive evaluation and subsequent premise elimination transform (10) into the following inequalities.

$$|\text{s}(u), \text{empty}, z| < |u, \text{empty}, z| \tag{11}$$

$$|\text{s}(0), v{\bullet}w, z| < |0, v{\bullet}w, z| \tag{12}$$

$$|\text{s}(\text{s}(u)), v{\bullet}w, z| + |u, w, z| \leq |\text{s}(u), v{\bullet}w, z| + |\text{s}(u), w, z| \tag{13}$$

Of course, (11)-(13) are unsatisfiable, since nextindex is not totally terminating. Hence, we do no longer demand *all* inequalities but we select a satisfiable *subset* of (11)-(13). For instance, if (11) is rejected, then (12) and (13) are satisfied by the polynomial norm where $|\text{empty}|_{\text{POL}} = |0|_{\text{POL}} = 0$, $|\text{s}(u)|_{\text{POL}} = |u|_{\text{POL}} + 1$, $|v{\bullet}w|_{\text{POL}} = |w|_{\text{POL}} + 1$, and $\text{tuple}_3(x, y, z)$ is associated with $(y - x)^2$.

In general, our aim is to find a maximal satisfiable subset of the inequalities and to reject as few inequalities as possible. As the number of hypotheses is always finite, exhaustive search could be used to determine such a maximal set[7]. Efficiency can be improved if 'probably polynomially satisfiable' inequalities are selected by the heuristics of [Gie95b] which have proved successful in practice.

---

[6] This is similar to the approach of [Pro96] where a *proof predicate* is generated from an unsound induction proof in order to extend faulty conjectures to valid ones.

[7] Rejection of an inequality means that one suspects that the algorithm does not terminate for *any* input corresponding to this inequality. (Otherwise, this rejection will result in a termination predicate which only describes a subset of the domain.)

In our example, we associate the following soundness predicate λ with the faulty transformation of (10) into (12) and (13), where $\lambda(x, y, z)$ is true for all those instantiations of x, y, and z where this transformation is correct.

> **function** λ : nat $\times$ list $\times$ nat $\rightarrow$ bool
> $\lambda(u, \text{empty}, z) = $ false
> $\lambda(0, v \bullet w, z) \quad = $ true
> $\lambda(\text{s}(u), v \bullet w, z) = \lambda(u, w, z)$

The case analysis of λ is given by the case analysis of the algorithm nth which has been used for inductive evaluation of (10). The results of λ are created depending on the transformation steps performed during the inductive evaluation. Since inequality (11) for $y = $ empty has been *rejected*, λ returns false for that case. Analogously, as (12) was kept as a constraint, this results in the value true for $x = 0$ and $y = v \bullet w$. For inputs of the form $\text{s}(u), v \bullet w, z$, the soundness of the transformation depends on the soundness of the transformation for u, w, z, because inequality (13) of the third case has been created by applying the *induction hypothesis*. Hence, in this case the result $\lambda(u, w, z)$ is generated. The procedure λ terminates totally by construction as it is called recursively under the same condition as nth whose total termination has already been verified.

Thus, λ returns true iff the first argument (the natural x) is less than the length of the second argument (the list y). If the inequality $|\text{s}(x), y, z| < |x, y, z|$ in the termination predicate $\theta_{\text{nextindex}}$ is replaced by $\lambda(x, y, z)$, then $\theta_{\text{nextindex}}(x, y, z)$ is true iff z occurs in y at a position $i \geq x$ or if $z = 0$, i.e. we have indeed generated a termination predicate that returns true as often as possible.

To formalize the generation of soundness predicates λ_φ for termination hypotheses φ, we modify the calculus of Sect. 3. The resulting calculus operates on triples $H; C; E$ where the third component E contains the defining equations of the newly synthesized soundness predicates. The correctness of the calculus guarantees that if $H; C; E$ can be transformed into $H'; C'; E'$, then every interpretation satisfying C' and $\lambda_\varphi(x^*) \rightarrow \varphi$ for all $\varphi \in H'$ also satisfies C and $\lambda_\varphi(x^*) \rightarrow \varphi$ for all $\varphi \in H$. Here, the semantics of λ_φ is given by E'.

To use our calculus for termination proofs, we again initialize H with the termination hypotheses and let C and E be empty. Then the rules of the calculus are applied repeatedly until we have obtained a triple of the form $\emptyset; C'; E'$. Now the defining equations E' of the generated soundness predicates are added to our specification. Then by the correctness of the calculus every interpretation satisfying the constraints C' also satisfies the original termination hypotheses $\varphi \in H$ for those inputs where the corresponding soundness predicates λ_φ return true. Hence, if there exists a polynomial norm satisfying C', then in the definitions of termination predicates each inequality $|r^*| < |t^*|$ may be replaced by the soundness predicate for the termination hypothesis $\psi \rightarrow |r^*| < |t^*|$.

In the following rules, let $x_1, .., x_l$ (x^* for short) be the variables in $\psi \rightarrow \omega$ of types $\delta_1, .., \delta_l$ and let $\lambda_{\psi \rightarrow \omega}$ be a new boolean function symbol with the argument types $\delta_1 \times .. \times \delta_l$. As in Sect. 3 we also allow an application of the next two rules if the condition ψ is missing.

Premise Elimination $\quad H \cup \{\psi \to \omega\};\quad C\quad;E$
$\qquad\qquad\qquad\qquad\qquad H\,;\,C \cup \{\omega\}\,; E \cup \{\lambda_{\psi \to \omega}(x^*) = \mathsf{true}\}$
if ω does not contain any defined symbols.

Rejection $\qquad\qquad\qquad\qquad H \cup \{\psi \to \omega\}\,;\, C\,;\, E$
$\qquad\qquad\qquad\qquad\qquad H\,;\, C\,;\, E \cup \{\lambda_{\psi \to \omega}(x^*) = \mathsf{false}\}$

In the third rule, let x^* be the variables of $\psi \to |r^*| < |t^*|$ and to ease readability we write λ instead of $\lambda_{\psi \to |r^*| < |t^*|}$. Let the variables $y_1, .., y_n$ of the types $\tau_1, .., \tau_n$ be contained in x^* and let $g : \tau_1 \times .. \times \tau_n \to \tau$ be defined by a terminating algorithm with k equations. Again $p[s^*]$ abbreviates $p[y^*/s^*]$ and moreover, $\lambda[s^*]$ is used as an abbreviation for $\lambda(x^*[y^*/s^*])$, i.e. $\lambda[s^*]$ abbreviates $\sigma(\lambda(x^*))$ where σ substitutes each y_i with s_i but does not change the remaining variables of x^*.

Inductive Evaluation $\qquad\qquad H \cup \{\psi \to |r^*| < |t^*|\}\,;\,C\,;\,E$
$\qquad\qquad\qquad\qquad H \cup \{\varphi_1, .., \varphi_k\}\,;\,C\,;\,E \cup \{e_1, .., e_k\}$
If $g(s^*) = q$ is the i-th defining equation of g, then φ_i and e_i are defined as

- $\varphi_i := \mathsf{true}$
  $e_i := \lambda[s^*] = \mathsf{true}$ $\qquad\qquad\qquad\left.\right\}$ if $\neg\psi[s^*]$ can be verified,

- $\varphi_i := \psi[s^*] \to |r^*[s^*]| + |t^*[q^*]| \le |t^*[s^*]| + |r^*[q^*]|$ $\left.\right\}$ else, if q contains $g(q^*)$ and
  $e_i := \lambda[s^*] = \lambda[q^*] \wedge \lambda_{\varphi_i}(z^*)$ $\qquad\qquad\qquad$ $\psi[s^*] \to \psi[q^*]$ can be verified,

- $\varphi_i := \psi[s^*] \to |r^*[s^*]| < |t^*[s^*]|,$
  $e_i := \lambda[s^*] = \lambda_{\varphi_i}(z^*)$ $\qquad\qquad\qquad\left.\right\}$ otherwise.

Here, z^* are the variables occurring in φ_i.

Similar to Sect. 3, the heuristic for the application of these rules is that inductive evaluation should be applied first if possible and otherwise, premise elimination is preferable to rejection.

Using this calculus, the termination hypothesis (10) can be inductively evaluated w.r.t. nth. For nth's first equation, φ_1 is $\neg\mathsf{eq}(\mathsf{nth}(u, \mathsf{empty}), z) \to$ (11) and e_1 is the equation $\lambda_{(10)}(u, \mathsf{empty}, z) = \lambda_{(11)}(u, z)$. Similarly, φ_2 is $\neg\mathsf{eq}(\mathsf{nth}(0, v \bullet w), z)$ $\to$ (12) and e_2 is $\lambda_{(10)}(0, v \bullet w, z) = \lambda_{(12)}(v, w, z)$. Finally, for nth's third equation φ_3 is $\neg\mathsf{eq}(\mathsf{nth}(\mathsf{s}(u), v \bullet w), z) \to$ (13) and e_3 is $\lambda_{(10)}(\mathsf{s}(u), v \bullet w, z) = \lambda_{(10)}(u, w, z) \wedge$ $\lambda_{(13)}(u, v, w, z)$. As (11) is rejected and as both (12) and (13) are inserted into the constraints using premise elimination, this results in the defining equations $\lambda_{(11)}(u, z) = \mathsf{false}, \lambda_{(12)}(v, w, z) = \mathsf{true}, \lambda_{(13)}(u, v, w, z) = \mathsf{true}$. Hence, by symbolic evaluation one obtains the algorithm λ given at the beginning of the section. The following theorem shows that our calculus is sound.

Theorem 2. *If $H; C; E$ is transformed into $H'; C'; E'$ by our calculus, then we have $\{\lambda_\varphi(x^*) \to \varphi \mid \varphi \in H'\} \cup C' \cup E' \models \{\lambda_\varphi(x^*) \to \varphi \mid \varphi \in H\} \cup C \cup E$.*

Proof. The soundness of premise elimination and rejection is trivial. For inductive evaluation we proceed as in the proof of Thm. 1. Assume $I \models \lambda_{\varphi_i}(z^*) \to \varphi_i = \text{true}$ and $I \models e_i$ holds for all i, but $I \models \lambda[p^*] = \text{true}$, $I \models \psi[p^*] = \text{true}$, and $I \not\models |r^*[p^*]| < |t^*[p^*]| = \text{true}$ for a minimal counterexample p^*.

Again this implies that for some i-th defining equation $g(s^*) = q$ we have $p^* = \sigma(s^*)$ and q contains a subterm $g(q^*)$ such that $\psi[s^*] \to \psi[q^*]$ can be verified. Thus we have $I \models \psi[\sigma(q^*)] = \text{true}$ and $I \models \lambda[\sigma(q^*)] = \text{true}$ (by $I \models e_i$). As $I(\sigma(q^*))$ is smaller than p^*, it cannot be a counterexample and so we obtain $I \models |r^*[\sigma(q^*)]| < |t^*[\sigma(q^*)]| = \text{true}$. But as $I \models \sigma(\lambda_{\varphi_i}(z^*)) = \text{true}$ (due to $I \models e_i$), p^* cannot be a counterexample either, which is a contradiction. $\square$

This extension of inductive evaluation for termination analysis of partial functions generalizes our first approach, i.e. whenever total termination of f can be verified by the technique of Sect. 3, the technique of the present section can generate a termination predicate θ_f that returns true for each input.

The handling of partial functions is also necessary for termination analysis of *imperative* programs, because when translating imperative programs into functional ones, *while*-loops are often transformed into *partial* functions, as termination of *while*-loops often depends on their contexts, cf. [GWB98].

5   Refinements

In this section we present extensions of our approach which increase its power considerably. As an example regard the following algorithms.

```
function max : list → nat          function add_if_mem : nat × list × list → list
max(empty)    = 0                  add_if_mem(x, empty, z) = z
max(u•empty) = u                   add_if_mem(x, u•y, z)   = if( eq(x, u),
max(u•v•w)   = if( le(u, v),                                   x•z,
                   max(v•w),                                   add_if_mem(x, y, z) )
                   max(u•w) )
```

```
function sort : nat × list → list
 sort(x, y) = if( eq(x, max(y)), x•empty, add_if_mem(x, y, sort(s(x), y)) )
```

Total termination of max and add_if_mem is easily proved (where add_if_mem(x, y, z) returns $x•z$ if x occurs in y and z otherwise[8]). The function sort(x, y) returns a sorted list composed of all elements of y which are greater or equal to x where multiple occurrences of elements are removed. Hence, sort$(0, y)$ sorts the entire list y. This procedure terminates iff x is less than or equal to the maximal element of y (where the maximum of empty is 0). Consider sort's termination hypothesis,

$$\neg\text{eq}(x, \text{max}(y)) \to |\text{s}(x), y| < |x, y|. \tag{14}$$

---

[8] In the algorithm sort, we use add_if_mem$(x, y, \text{sort}(\text{s}(x), y))$ instead of if(member(x, y), $x•$sort$(\text{s}(x), y)$, sort$(\text{s}(x), y)$) to ease the readability of our presentation.

To construct a soundness predicate for (14) according to our heuristic we have to use inductive evaluation w.r.t. the algorithm max. However, for functions like max which are defined using the conditional if, we now have to refine the inductive evaluation rule. For max' recursive (third) equation, the idea is to perform a case analysis w.r.t. its if-condition $\text{le}(u, v)$. We first add the condition $\text{le}(u, v)$ to the condition of (14) and treat max as if it only had the recursive call $\max(v{\cdot}w)$, cf. (17). Then we add the negated condition $\neg\text{le}(u, v)$ instead and now we only regard the recursive call $\max(u{\cdot}w)$, cf. (18). In each resulting case the premise is satisfiable and in both step cases the induction hypothesis can be applied. Hence by inductive evaluation we obtain the following new hypotheses.

$$\neg\text{eq}(x, \max(\text{empty})) \;\rightarrow\; |\text{s}(x), \text{empty}| < |x, \text{empty}| \tag{15}$$

$$\neg\text{eq}(x, \max(u{\cdot}\text{empty})) \;\rightarrow\; |\text{s}(x), u{\cdot}\text{empty}| < |x, u{\cdot}\text{empty}| \tag{16}$$

$$\neg\text{eq}(x, \max(u{\cdot}v{\cdot}w)) \wedge\; \text{le}(u, v) \;\rightarrow\; |\text{s}(x), u{\cdot}v{\cdot}w| + |x, v{\cdot}w| \leq |x, u{\cdot}v{\cdot}w| + |\text{s}(x), v{\cdot}w| \tag{17}$$

$$\neg\text{eq}(x, \max(u{\cdot}v{\cdot}w)) \wedge \neg\text{le}(u, v) \;\rightarrow\; |\text{s}(x), u{\cdot}v{\cdot}w| + |x, u{\cdot}w| \leq |x, u{\cdot}v{\cdot}w| + |\text{s}(x), u{\cdot}w| \tag{18}$$

The generation of soundness predicates proceeds in an analogous way by building $\lambda_{(14)}(x, y)$ according to the algorithm max, where the results of max are replaced by the corresponding soundness predicates for the new hypotheses. For a formal definition of the inductive evaluation rule for conditional algorithms see [BG98].

$$
\begin{aligned}
&\textbf{function } \lambda_{(14)} \,:\, \textsf{nat} \times \textsf{list} \rightarrow \textsf{bool}\\
&\quad \lambda_{(14)}(x, \textsf{empty}) \;\;= \lambda_{(15)}(x)\\
&\quad \lambda_{(14)}(x, u{\cdot}\textsf{empty}) = \lambda_{(16)}(x, u)\\
&\quad \lambda_{(14)}(x, u{\cdot}v{\cdot}w) \;\;= \text{if}(\, \text{le}(u, v), \lambda_{(14)}(x, v{\cdot}w) \wedge \lambda_{(17)}(x, u, v, w),\\
&\qquad\qquad\qquad\qquad\qquad \lambda_{(14)}(x, u{\cdot}w) \wedge \lambda_{(18)}(x, u, v, w)\,)
\end{aligned}
$$

Our heuristic suggests no further inductive evaluation for (15) and (16), since no term $g(y_1, .., y_n)$ with pairwise different y_i occurs in their premises. But then the inequalities in (15) and (16) have to be rejected, since they are unsatisfiable. Thus, both $\lambda_{(15)}$ and $\lambda_{(16)}$ would always be false and hence, the soundness predicate $\lambda_{(14)}$ for sort's termination hypothesis would also return false for each input. Hence, we would obtain an unsatisfiable soundness predicate although evaluation halts for some recursive calls of sort.

To construct a better soundness predicate, we should again perform inductive evaluation on the obtained hypothesis (16). For that purpose the occurring max-term is *symbolically evaluated*. If we replace the term $\max(u{\cdot}\text{empty})$ by its *symbolic value* u then instead of (16) we obtain

$$\neg\text{eq}(x, u) \rightarrow |\text{s}(x), u{\cdot}\text{empty}| < |x, u{\cdot}\text{empty}|. \tag{19}$$

Hence, we extend our calculus by an additional *symbolic evaluation rule* which allows to replace a term $g(t^*)$ in a premise by the term r whenever $g(t^*)$ can be evaluated to r, where C and E do not change.

Now for (19) our heuristic suggests another inductive evaluation w.r.t. eq. We use inductive evaluation as often as possible, but to ensure that it is only applied a finite number of times, we never perform inductive evaluation w.r.t. the same algorithm twice. In our example, if we finally reject the hypothesis (15) and the hypothesis resulting from eq's second equation during the inductive evaluation of (19), then the resulting constraints are satisfied by the polynomial norm $|\mathsf{empty}|_{\mathsf{POL}} = |0|_{\mathsf{POL}} = 0$, $|\mathsf{s}(u)|_{\mathsf{POL}} = |u|_{\mathsf{POL}} + 1$, $|v\bullet w|_{\mathsf{POL}} = |v|_{\mathsf{POL}} + |w|_{\mathsf{POL}}$, where $\mathsf{tuple}_2(x, y)$ is associated with $(y - x)^2$. Hence, we generate soundness predicates $\lambda_{(15)}(x) = \mathsf{false}$, $\lambda_{(17)}(x) = \mathsf{true}$, $\lambda_{(18)}(x) = \mathsf{true}$, and for $\lambda_{(16)}$ we obtain a predicate computing the 'less than or equal' relation on naturals, cf. [BG98]. Thus, the soundness predicate $\lambda_{(14)}(x, y)$ for sort's termination hypothesis is true iff y is non-empty and if x is less than or equal to the maximal element of y. Using this soundness predicate we finally obtain the termination predicate procedure

function θ_{sort} : nat $\times$ list $\to$ bool
$$\theta_{\mathsf{sort}}(x, y) = \mathsf{if}(\,\mathsf{eq}(x, \mathsf{max}(y)),\ \mathsf{true},\ \mathsf{if}(\lambda_{(14)}(x, y),\ \theta_{\mathsf{sort}}(\mathsf{s}(x), y),\ \mathsf{false})\,).$$

The procedure θ_{sort} defines the exact domain of sort, i.e. it returns true iff x is less than or equal to the maximal element of y. Hence, in this way a predicate describing the domain of sort can be generated automatically.

6   Conclusion

We have illustrated that termination of many interesting algorithms cannot be verified if the premises of the termination hypotheses are neglected. Therefore, in this paper we presented the *inductive evaluation* method which analyzes auxiliary functions occurring in the conditions of recursive calls. Our calculus transforms termination hypotheses into inequalities such that existing automated methods can be used to check whether they are satisfied by a polynomial norm. In this way, total termination of algorithms can be proved automatically.

Subsequently, we have generalized our approach for analyzing partially terminating procedures. For that purpose our calculus is extended in order to synthesize *soundness predicates* which are used for the construction of termination predicates describing the domain of the function under consideration.

We combined our method to handle auxiliary functions in the *conditions* with techniques to deal with defined functions in the *arguments* of recursive calls [Gie95b,Gie95c,Gie97,GWB98] and implemented it within the induction theorem prover INKA [HS96]. In this way we obtained an extremely powerful approach for automated termination analysis which performed successfully on a large collection of benchmarks (including all 82 algorithms from [BM79], all 60 examples from [Wal94b], and all 92 examples in [Gie95b] and [BG96]).

See [BG98] for a collection of 36 algorithms whose termination behaviour could not be analyzed with any other automatic method up to now, but where inductive evaluation enables termination analysis without user interaction. For all these examples, termination predicates describing the *exact* domains of the functions could be synthesized. We also applied our approach to *imperative programs* by translating them into equivalent functional programs. In this way, in 33 of 45 examples from [Gri81] the exact domain could be determined automatically.

Acknowledgements. We thank the referees for many helpful suggestions. This work was supported by the DFG (focus program 'Deduktion') under grant no. Wa 652/7-2.

References

[AG97]   T. Arts and J. Giesl. Proving innermost normalisation automatically. In *Proc. RTA-97*, Sitges, Spain, LNCS 1232, 1997.

[BM79]   R. S. Boyer and J S. Moore. *A computational logic.* Academic Press, 1979.

[BR95]   A. Bouhoula and M. Rusinowitch. Implicit induction in conditional theories. *Journal of Automated Reasoning*, 14:189–235, 1995.

[BG96]   J. Brauburger and J. Giesl. Termination analysis for partial functions. In *Proc. 3rd Int. Static Analysis Symp.*, Aachen, Germany, LNCS 1145, 1996. Extended version appeared[9] as Report IBN-96-33, TU Darmstadt, 1996.

[BG98]   J. Brauburger and J. Giesl. Termination analysis with inductive evaluation. Technical Report IBN-98-47, TU Darmstadt, Germany, 1998[9].

[Bra97]   J. Brauburger. Automatic termination analysis for partial functions using polynomial orderings. In *Proc. 4th SAS*, Paris, France, LNCS 1302, 1997.

[Bun+89]   A. Bundy, F. van Harmelen, J. Hesketh, A. Smaill, and A. Stevens. A rational reconstruction and extension of recursion analysis. In *Proc. IJCAI '89*, Detroit, USA, 1989.

[Der87]   N. Dershowitz. Termination of rewriting. *J. Symb. Comp.*, 3:69–115, 1987.

[Gie95a]   J. Giesl. Generating polynomial orderings for termination proofs. In *Proc. RTA-95*, Kaiserslautern, Germany, LNCS 914, 1995.

[Gie95b]   J. Giesl. *Automatisierung von Terminierungsbeweisen für rekursiv definierte Algorithmen.* PhD thesis, Infix-Verlag, St. Augustin, Germany, 1995.

[Gie95c]   J. Giesl. Termination analysis for functional programs using term orderings. In *Proc. 2nd Int. Static Analysis Symp.*, Glasgow, UK, LNCS 983, 1995.

[Gie97]   J. Giesl. Termination of nested and mutually recursive algorithms. *Journal of Automated Reasoning*, 19:1–29, 1997.

[GWB98]   J. Giesl, C. Walther, and J. Brauburger. Termination analysis for functional programs. In W. Bibel and P. Schmitt, editors, *Automated Deduction – A Basis for Applications*, vol. 3. Kluwer Academic Publishers, 1998.

[Gri81]   D. Gries. *The science of programming.* Springer-Verlag, New York, 1981.

[Hen80]   P. Henderson. *Functional programming.* Prentice-Hall, London, 1980.

[HS96]   D. Hutter and C. Sengler. INKA: The next generation. In *Proc. CADE-13*, New Brunswick, USA, LNAI 1104, 1996.

[KZ95]   D. Kapur and H. Zhang. An overview of Rewrite Rule Laboratory (RRL). *J. Computer Math. Appl.*, 29:91–114, 1995.

[Lan79]   D.S. Lankford. On proving term rewriting systems are noetherian. Memo MTP-3, Math. Dept., Louisiana Tech. Univ., Ruston, USA, 1979.

[NN96]   F. Nielson and H. R. Nielson. Operational semantics of termination types. *Nordic Journal of Computing*, 3(2):144–187, 1996.

---

[9] Available   from   http://www.inferenzsysteme.informatik.tu-darmstadt.de/ ~reports/notes/{ibn-96-33.ps,ibn-98-47.ps}.

[PS97]   S. E. Panitz and M. Schmidt-Schauß. TEA: Automatically proving termination of programs in a non-strict higher-order functional language. In *Proc. 4th Int. Static Analysis Symp.*, Paris, France, LNCS 1302, 1997.

[Plü90]   L. Plümer. *Termination proofs for logic programs.* LNAI 446, 1990.

[Pro96]   M. Protzen. Patching faulty conjectures. In *Proc. CADE-13*, LNAI 1104, New Brunswick, USA, 1996.

[SD94]   D. De Schreye and S. Decorte. Termination of logic programs: The neverending story. *Journal of Logic Programming*, 19/20:199–260, 1994.

[Sen96]   C. Sengler. Termination of algorithms over non-freely generated data types. In *Proc. CADE-13*, New Brunswick, USA, LNAI 1104, 1996.

[Ste94]   J. Steinbach. Generating polynomial orderings. *IPL*, 49:85-93, 1994.

[Ste95]   J. Steinbach. Simplification orderings: History of results. *Fundamenta Informaticae*, 24:47-87, 1995.

[UvG88]   J. D. Ullman and A. van Gelder. Efficient tests for top-down termination of logical rules. *Journal of the ACM*, 35(2):345-373, 1988.

[Wal94a] C. Walther. Mathematical induction. In D. M. Gabbay, C. J. Hogger, and J. A. Robinson, editors, *Handbook of Logic in Artificial Intelligence and Logic Programming*, vol. 2. Oxford University Press, 1994.

[Wal94b] C. Walther. On proving the termination of algorithms by machine. *Artificial Intelligence*, 71(1):101–157, 1994.

[ZKK88]   H. Zhang, D. Kapur, and M. S. Krishnamoorthy. A mechanizable induction principle for equational specifications. In *Proc. CADE-9*, Argonne, USA, LNCS 310, 1988.

Admissibility of Fixpoint Induction over Partial Types

Karl Crary

Cornell University

Abstract. Partial types allow the reasoning about partial functions in type theory. The partial functions of main interest are recursively computed functions, which are commonly assigned types using fixpoint induction. However, fixpoint induction is valid only on *admissible* types. Previous work has shown many types to be admissible, but has not shown any dependent products to be admissible. Disallowing recursion on dependent product types substantially reduces the expressiveness of the logic; for example, it prevents much reasoning about modules, objects and algebras.

In this paper I present two new tools, *predicate-admissibility* and *monotonicity*, for showing types to be admissible. These tools show a wide class of types to be admissible; in particular, they show many dependent products to be admissible. This alleviates difficulties in applying partial types to theorem proving in practice. I also present a general least upper bound theorem for fixed points with regard to a computational approximation relation, and show an elegant application of the theorem to compactness.

1 Introduction

One of the earliest logical theorem provers was the LCF system [12, 20], based on the logic of partial computable functions [22, 23]. Although LCF enjoyed many groundbreaking successes, one problem it faced was that, although it supported a natural notion of *partial* function, it had difficulty expressing the notion of a *total* function. Later theorem provers based on constructive type theory, such as Nuprl [5], based on Martin-Löf type theory [19], and Coq [3], based on the Calculus of Constructions [9], faced the opposite problem; they had a natural notion of total functions, but had difficulty dealing with partial functions. The lack of partial functions seriously limited the scope of those theorem provers, because it made them unable to reason about programs in real programming languages where recursion does not always necessarily terminate.

This problem was addressed by Constable and Smith [7], who introduced into their type theory the *partial type* $\overline{T}$, which is like a "lifted" version of T. The type $\overline{T}$ contains all members of T as well as all divergent terms. Using the partial type, partial functions from A to B may be given the type $A \to \overline{B}$. That is, when

C. Kirchner and H. Kirchner (Eds.): Automated Deduction, CADE-15
LNAI 1421, pp. 270–285, 1998. © Springer-Verlag Berlin Heidelberg 1998

applied to an argument in A, such a function either diverges or converges to a result in B.

In a partial type theory, recursively defined objects may be typed using the *fixpoint principle:* if f has type $\overline{T} \to \overline{T}$ then $fix(f)$ has type $\overline{T}$. However, the fixpoint principle is not valid for every type T; it is only valid for types that are *admissible*. This phenomenon was not unknown to LCF; LCF used the related device of fixpoint induction, which was valid only for admissible predicates. When the user attempted to invoke fixpoint induction, the system would automatically check that the goal was admissible using a set of syntactic rules [16].

Despite their obvious uses in program analysis, partial types have seen little use in theorem proving systems [8, 4, 2]. This is due in large part to the fact that too few types have been known to be admissible. Smith, in his doctoral dissertation [24], gave a significant class of admissible types for a Nuprl-like theory, but his class required product types to be non-dependent. The type $\Sigma x{:}A.B$ (where x appears free in B) was explicitly excluded. Partial type extensions to Coq [2] were just as restrictive, assuming function spaces to be the only type constructor. Excluding dependent products is quite a strong restriction; they are used in encodings of modules [18], objects [21], algebras [17], and even such simple devices as variant records. Furthermore, ruling out dependent products disallows reasoning using fixpoint induction as in LCF. (This is explained further in Section 2.3.) Finally, the restriction is particularly unsatisfying since most types used in practice do turn out to be admissible, and may be shown so by metatheoretical reasoning.

In this paper I present a very wide class of admissible types using two devices, a condition called *predicate-admissibility* and a monotonicity condition. In particular, many dependent products may be shown to be admissible. Predicate-admissibility relates to when the limit of a chain of type approximations contains certain terms, whereas admissibility relates to the membership of a single type. The term "predicate-admissibility" stems from its similarity to the notion of admissibility of predicates in domain theory (and LCF), where there has been considerable research (this work was influenced by Igarashi [16], for example), but I will not discuss the connection in this paper. Monotonicity is a simpler condition that will be useful for showing types admissible that do not involve partiality.

The paper is organized as follows: In Section 2 I lay out the theory for which these results are formalized. In Section 3 I prove some computational lemmas needed for the admissibility results. The primary result is a least upper bound theorem for fixed points with regard to a computational approximation relation. This result is quite general, and may be applied more widely than just to the purposes for which I use it. I present my main results in Section 4, beginning with a summary of Smith's admissibility class and then widening the class using predicate-admissibility and monotonicity. Concluding remarks appear in Section 5. Most proofs have been omitted in this paper due to space limitations; those proofs appear in the companion technical report [10].

2   The Type Theory

	Type Formation	Introduction	Elimination
universe i	U_i (for $i \geq 1$)	type formation operators	
disjoint union	$T_1 + T_2$	$inj_1(e)$ $inj_2(e)$	$case(e, x_1.e_1, x_2.e_2)$
function space	$\Pi x{:}T_1.T_2$	$\lambda x.e$	$e_1 e_2$
product space	$\Sigma x{:}T_1.T_2$	$\langle e_1, e_2 \rangle$	$\pi_1(e)$ $\pi_2(e)$
natural numbers	N	$0, 1, 2, \ldots$	assorted operations
equality	$t_1 = t_2 \ in \ T$	$\star$	
partial type	$\overline{T}$		
convergence	$t \ in! \ T$	$\star$	

Fig. 1. Type Theory Syntax

The type theory in which I formalize the results of this paper is a variant of the Nuprl type theory [5] extended with partial types (that is, types containing possibly divergent objects). This theory is a subset of the type theory of Crary [11] and is similar to Smith's theory [24]. The major difference between the theory used here and Smith's is that the latter does not provide a notion of equality; the ramifications of handling equality are discussed in Constable and Crary [6] and at greater length in Crary [11].

2.1   Preliminaries

As data types, the theory contains natural numbers (denoted by N), disjoint unions (denoted by $T_1 + T_2$), dependent products[1] (denoted by $\Sigma x{:}T_1.T_2$), and dependent function spaces (denoted by $\Pi x{:}T_1.T_2$). When x does not appear free in T_2, I write $T_1 \times T_2$ for $\Sigma x{:}T_1.T_2$ and $T_1 \to T_2$ for $\Pi x{:}T_1.T_2$. As usual, alpha-equivalent terms are considered identical. When t_1 and t_2 are alpha-equivalent, I write $t_1 \equiv t_2$.

Types themselves are terms in the theory and belong to a predicative hierarchy of universes, U_1, U_2, U_3, etc. The universe U_1 contains all types built from the base types only (*i.e.*, built without universes), and the universe U_{i+1} contains all types build from the base types and the universes $U_1, \ldots, U_i$. In particular, no universe is a member of itself. Propositions are interpreted as types using the propositions-as-types principle [14], but that is not central to the purposes of this paper.

---

[1] These are sometimes referred to in the literature as dependent sums, but I prefer the terminology to suggest the connection to the non-dependent type $T_1 \times T_2$.

Each type T comes with an intrinsic equality relation denoted by $t_1 = t_2 \in T$. Membership is also derived from this relation; $t \in T$ when $t = t \in T$. The equality relation is introduced into the type theory as the type $t_1 = t_2$ *in* T, which is inhabited by the term $\star$ when $t_1 = t_2 \in T$ and is empty otherwise, provided that $t_1, t_2 \in T$. If either of t_1 or t_2 does not belong to T, then $t_1 = t_2$ *in* T is not well-formed. (Note that $t_1 = t_2 \in T$ is a metatheoretical assertion whereas $t_1 = t_2$ *in* T is a type in the theory.) The empty type *Void* is defined as $0 = 1$ *in* N.

The *partial type* $\overline{T}$ is like a "lifted" version of T; it contains all the members of T as well as all divergent terms. Partial functions from A to B may then be given the type $A \to \overline{B}$. Two terms are equal in $\overline{T}$ if they both diverge, or if they both converge and are equal in T.

Convergence is expressed within the type theory by the type t *in!* T, which is inhabited by the term $\star$ when $t \in \overline{T}$ and t converges, and is empty if $t \in \overline{T}$ but t does not converge. If $t \notin \overline{T}$ then t *in!* T is not well-formed. (Again, note that t *in!* T is a type in the theory, but convergence, which is defined formally below, is a metatheoretical assertion.)

2.2 Computation

Underlying the type theory is the computation system shown in Figure 2. The computation system is defined by a small-step evaluation relation (denoted by $t_1 \mapsto t_2$), and a set of canonical terms. Whether a term is canonical is governed by its outermost operator; the canonical terms are those appearing in the first and second columns of Figure 1. The computation system is call-by-name and contains operators for constructing and destructing functions, pairs and disjoint unions. The computation system also contains various standard operations for computing and analyzing natural numbers, but these are not particularly interesting and are omitted from Figure 2. Of particular interest is the operator *fix*, which allows the recursive definition of objects is evaluated by the rule $fix(f) \mapsto f(fix(f))$.[2] Two important properties of evaluation are that evaluation is deterministic and canonical forms are terminal:

Proposition 1 If $t \mapsto t_1$ and $t \mapsto t_2$ then $t_1 \equiv t_2$. Moreover, if t is canonical then $t \not\mapsto t'$ for any t'.

If $t \mapsto^* t'$ and t' is canonical then I say that t converges (abbreviated $t{\downarrow}$) and t converges to t' (abbreviated $t \Downarrow t'$). Note that if $t \Downarrow t_1$ and $t \Downarrow t_2$ then $t_1 \equiv t_2$ and that if t is canonical then $t \Downarrow t$. If there exists an infinite sequence $t_1, t_2, \ldots$ where $t_i \mapsto t_{i+1}$ then I say that t_1 diverges (abbreviated $t_1{\uparrow}$).

---

[2] The use of a *fix* operator greatly simplifies the presentation of these results (particularly the proof of Theorem 8), but it could be eliminated and replaced with the Y combinator. Similarly, the choice of a call-by-name computation system simplifies the formalism, but is also not critical to the results.

$$\frac{f \mapsto f'}{f e \mapsto f' e} \qquad \frac{t \mapsto t'}{\pi_i(t) \mapsto \pi_i(t')} \qquad \frac{t \mapsto t'}{case(t, x.e_1, x.e_2) \mapsto case(t', x.e_1, x.e_2)}$$

$$\overline{(\lambda x.e)t \mapsto e[t/x]} \qquad \overline{\pi_i(\langle t_1, t_2 \rangle) \mapsto t_i} \qquad \overline{case(inj_i(t), x.e_1, x.e_2) \mapsto e_i[t/x]}$$

$$\overline{fix(f) \mapsto f\, fix(f)}$$

Fig. 2. The Computation System

$t \in T$	iff $t = t \in T$
T $type$	iff $\exists i.\, T = T \in \mathbf{U}_i$
$t_1 = t_2 \in T$	iff $\exists t_1', t_2', T'.\, (t_1 \Downarrow t_1') \wedge (t_2 \Downarrow t_2') \wedge (T \Downarrow T') \wedge$
	$(t_1' = t_2' \in T')$
$inj_1(a) = inj_1(a') \in A + B$	iff $A + B$ $type \wedge a = a' \in A$
$inj_2(b) = inj_2(b') \in A + B$	iff $A + B$ $type \wedge b = b' \in B$
$\lambda x.b = \lambda x.b' \in \Pi x{:}A.B$	iff $\Pi x{:}A.B$ $type \wedge$
	$\forall a, a'.\, a = a' \in A \Rightarrow b[a/x] = b'[a'/x] \in B[a/x]$
$\langle a, b \rangle = \langle a', b' \rangle \in \Sigma x{:}A.B$	iff $\Sigma x{:}A.B$ $type \wedge (a = a' \in A) \wedge (b = b' \in B[a/x])$
$n = n' \in \mathbf{N}$	iff $n \equiv n'$ (n, n' natural numbers)
$\star = \star \in (a = a'\ in\ A)$	iff $(a = a'\ in\ A)$ $type \wedge (a = a' \in A)$
$t = t' \in \overline{T}$	iff $\overline{T}$ $type \wedge (t{\downarrow} \Leftrightarrow t'{\downarrow}) \wedge (t{\downarrow} \Rightarrow t = t' \in T)$
$\star = \star \in (a\ in!\ A)$	iff $(a\ in!\ A)$ $type \wedge a{\downarrow}$

Fig. 3. Type Definitions

The computation system is used to define the relation $t_1 = t_2 \in T$, which specifies the memberships of types and when terms are equal in those types.[3] Part of the definition (for types other than universes) appears in Figure 3; the full definition appears in the companion technical report [10]. This equality relation is constructed to respect evaluation: if $t \in T$ and $t \mapsto t'$ then $t = t' \in T$.

2.3   The Fixpoint Principle

The central issue of this paper is the *fixpoint principle:*

$$f \in \overline{T} \to \overline{T} \Rightarrow fix(f) \in \overline{T}$$

The fixpoint principle allows us to type recursively defined objects, such as recursive functions. Unfortunately, unlike in programming languages, where the

---

[3] Since the definition contains negative occurrences of $t_1 = t_2 \in T$, it is not immediately clear that it is a valid definition. Allen [1] and Harper [13] have shown how such a definition may be converted to a conventional inductive definition.

principle can usually be invoked on arbitrary types, expressive type theories such as the one in this paper contain types for which the fixpoint principle is not valid. I shall informally say that a type is *admissible* if the fixpoint principle is valid for that type and give a formal definition in Section 4. To make maximum use of a partial type theory, one wants as large a class of admissible types as possible.

Smith [24] showed that any type is admissible provided that it is constructed without using *dependent* product spaces (*i.e.*, Σ types) or universes. However, prohibiting dependent products is a strong restriction. Dependent products are used in, for example, encodings of modules [18], objects [21], algebras [17], and even such simple devices as variant records. Furthermore, the restriction also disallows reasoning about programs using the closely related principle of fixpoint induction

$$\frac{P[\bot] \quad P[e] \Rightarrow P[f(e)]}{P[\mathit{fix}(f)]}$$

which may be encoded with the fixpoint principle [24], but only by using dependent products.

In Section 4 I will explore two wide classes of admissible types, one derived from a *predicate-admissibility* condition and another derived from a monotonicity condition. But first, it is worthwhile to note that there are indeed inadmissible types:

Theorem 2 There exist inadmissible types.

Proof. This example is due to Smith [24]. Let T be the type of functions that do not halt for all inputs, and let f be the function that halts on zero, and on any other n immediately recurses with $n - 1$. This is formalized as follows:

$$T \overset{\text{def}}{=} \Sigma h{:}(\mathbb{N} \to \overline{\mathbb{N}}).\,((\Pi x{:}\mathbb{N}.\, h\,x \text{ in! } \mathbb{N}) \to \mathit{Void})$$
$$f \overset{\text{def}}{=} \lambda p.\langle \lambda x.\, \text{if } x \le 0 \text{ then } 0 \text{ else } \pi_1(p)(x - 1), \lambda y.\star\rangle$$

Intuitively, any finite approximation of $\mathit{fix}(f)$ will recurse some limited number of times and then give up, placing it in T, but $\mathit{fix}(f)$ will halt for every input, excluding it from T. Formally, the function f has type $\overline{T} \to \overline{T}$, but $\mathit{fix}(f) \notin \overline{T}$. (The proof of this appears in the companion technical report [10].) Therefore T is not admissible.

3   Computational Lemmas

Before presenting my main results in Section 4, I first require some lemmas about the computational behavior of the fixpoint operator. The central result is that $\mathit{fix}(f)$ is the least upper bound of the finite approximations $\bot, f(\bot), f(f(\bot)), \dots$ with regard to a computational approximation relation defined below. The compactness of fix (if $\mathit{fix}(f)$ halts then one of its finite approximations halts) will be a simple corollary of this result. However, the proof of the least upper bound theorem is considerably more elegant than most proofs of compactness.

3.1   Computational Approximation

For convenience, throughout this section we will frequently consider terms using a unified representation scheme for terms: A term is either a variable or a compound term $\theta(x_{11} \cdots x_{1k_1}.t_1, \ldots, x_{n1} \cdots x_{nk_n}.t_n)$ where the variables $x_{i1}, \ldots, x_{ik_i}$ are bound in the subterm t_i. For example, the term $\Pi x{:}T_1.T_2$ is represented $\Pi(T_1, x.T_2)$ and the term $\langle t_1, t_2 \rangle$ is represented $\langle \rangle (t_1, t_2)$.

Informally speaking, a term t_1 approximates the term t_2 when: if t_1 converges to a canonical form then t_2 converges to a canonical form with the same outermost operator, and the subterms of t_1's canonical form approximate the corresponding subterms of t_2's canonical form. The formal definition appears below and is due to Howe [15]. Following Howe, when R is a binary relation on closed terms, I adopt the following convention extending R to possibly open terms: if t and t' are possibly open then $t \mathrel{R} t'$ if and only if $\sigma(t) \mathrel{R} \sigma(t')$ for every substitution σ such that $\sigma(t)$ and $\sigma(t')$ are closed.

Definition 3 (Computational Approximation)

- Let R be a binary relation on closed terms and suppose e and e' are closed. Then $e \mathrel{C(R)} e'$ exactly when if $e \Downarrow \theta(\vec{x}_1.t_1, \ldots, \vec{x}_n.t_n)$ then there exists some closed $e'' = \theta(\vec{x}_1.t'_1, \ldots, \vec{x}_n.t'_n)$ such that $e' \Downarrow e''$ and $t_i \mathrel{R} t'_i$.
- $e \leq_0 e'$ whenever e and e' are closed.
- $e \leq_{i+1} e'$ if and only if $e \mathrel{C(\leq_i)} e'$
- $e \leq e'$ if and only if $e \leq_i e'$ for every i

The following are facts about computational approximation that will be used without explicit reference. The first two follow immediately from the definition, the third uses determinism and the last is proven using Howe's method [15].

Proposition 4

- $\leq$ and $\leq_i$ are reflexive and transitive.
- If $t \mapsto t'$ then $t' \leq t$ and $t' \leq_i t$.
- If $t \mapsto t'$ then $t \leq t'$ and $t \leq_i t'$.
- (Congruence) If $e \leq e'$ and $t \leq t'$ then $e[t/x] \leq e'[t'/x]$.

3.2   Finite Approximations

With this notion of computational approximation in hand, we may now show that the terms $\bot, f\bot, f(f\bot), \ldots$ form a chain of approximations to the term $\mathit{fix}(f)$. Let $\bot$ be the divergent term $\mathit{fix}(\lambda x.x)$. Since $\bot$ never converges, $\bot \leq t$ for any term t. Let f^i be defined as follows:

$$f^0 \overset{\text{def}}{=} \bot$$
$$f^{i+1} \overset{\text{def}}{=} f(f^i)$$

Certainly $f^0 \leq f^1$, since $f^0 \equiv \bot$. By congruence, $f(f^0) \leq f(f^1)$, and thus $f_1 \leq f_2$. Similarly, $f^i \leq f^{i+1}$ for all i. Thus $f^0, f^1, f^2, \ldots$ forms a chain; I now wish to show that $fix(f)$ is an upper bound of the chain. Certainly $f^0 \leq fix(f)$. Suppose $f^i \leq fix(f)$. By congruence $f(f^i) \leq f(fix(f))$. Thus, since $fix(f) \mapsto f(fix(f))$, it follows that $f^{i+1} \equiv f(f^i) \leq f(fix(f)) \leq fix(f)$. By induction it follows that $fix(f)$ is an upper bound of the chain. The following corollary follows from congruence and the definition of approximation:

Corollary 5 If there exists j such that $e[f^j/x]\downarrow$ then $e[fix(f)/x]\downarrow$. Moreover, the canonical forms of $e[f^j/x]$ and $e[fix(f)/x]$ must have the same outermost operator.

3.3   Least Upper Bound Theorem

In this section I summarize the proof of the least upper bound theorem. To begin, we need a lemma stating a general property of evaluation. Lemma 6 captures the intuition that closed, noncanonical terms that lie within a term being evaluated are not destructed; they either are moved around unchanged (the lemma's first case) or are evaluated in place with the surrounding term left unchanged (the lemma's second case). The variable x indicates positions where the term of interest is found and (in the second case) the variable y indicates which of those positions, if any, is about to be evaluated.

Lemma 6 If $e_1[t/x] \mapsto e_2$, and $e_1[t/x]$ is closed, and t is closed and noncanonical, then either

1. there exists e_2' such that for any closed t', $e_1[t'/x] \mapsto e_2'[t'/x]$, or
2. there exist e_1' and t' such that $e_1 \equiv e_1'[x/y]$, $t \mapsto t'$ and for any closed t'', $e_1'[t'',t/x,y] \mapsto e_1'[t'',t'/x,y]$.

It is worthwhile to note that Propositions 1 and 4 and Lemma 6 are the only general properties of evaluation used in the proof of the least upper bound theorem, and that these properties are true in computational systems with considerable generality. Consequently, the theorem may be used in a variety of applications beyond the computational system of this paper.

Lemma 7 shows that fix terms may be simulated by sufficiently large finite approximations. The lemma is simplified by using computational approximation instead of evaluation for the simulation, which makes it unnecessary to track which of the approximations are unfolded and which are not, an issue that often complicates compactness proofs.

Lemma 7 For all f, e_1 and e_2 (where f is closed and x is the only free variable of e_1), there exist j and e_2' such that if $e_1[fix(f)/x] \mapsto^* e_2$ then $e_2 \equiv e_2'[fix(f)/x]$ and for all $k \geq j$, $e_2'[f^{k-j}/x] \leq e_1[f^k/x]$.

Theorem 8 (Least Upper Bound) For all f, t and e (where f is closed), if $\forall j. e[f^j/x] \leq t$, then $e[fix(f)/x] \leq t$.

There are two easy corollaries to the least upper bound theorem. One is that $fix(f)$ is the least fixed point of f, and the other is compactness.

Corollary 9 (Least Fixed Point) For all closed f and t, if $f(t) \leq t$ then $\mathit{fix}(f) \leq t$.

Proof. Certainly $f^0 \equiv \perp \leq t$. Then $f^1 \equiv f(f^0) \leq f(t) \leq t$. Similarly, by induction, $f^j \leq t$ for any j. Therefore $\mathit{fix}(f) \leq t$ by Theorem 8.   □

Corollary 10 (Compactness) If f is closed and $e[\mathit{fix}(f)/x]\!\downarrow$ then there exists some j such that $e[f^j/x]\!\downarrow$. Moreover, the canonical forms of $e[\mathit{fix}(f)/x]$ and $e[f^j/x]$ must have the same outermost operator.

Proof. Suppose there does not exist j such that $e[f^j/x]\!\downarrow$. Then $e[f^j/x] \leq \perp$ for all j. By Theorem 8, $e[\mathit{fix}(f)/x] \leq \perp$. Therefore $e[\mathit{fix}(f)/x]$ does not converge, but this contradicts the assumption,[4] so there must exist j such that $e[f^j/x]\!\downarrow$. Since $e[f^j/x] \leq e[\mathit{fix}(f)/x]$, the canonical forms of $e[f^j/x]$ and $e[\mathit{fix}(f)/x]$ must have the same outermost operator.   □

4   Admissibility

I am now ready to begin specifying some wide classes of types for which the fixpoint principle is valid. First we define admissibility. The simple property of validating the fixpoint principle is too specific to allow any good closure conditions to be shown easily, so we generalize a bit to define admissibility. A type is *admissible* if the upper bound $t[\mathit{fix}(f)]$ of an approximation chain $t[f^0], t[f^1], t[f^2], \ldots$ belongs to a type whenever a cofinite subset of the chain belongs to the type. This is formalized as Definition 12, but first I define some convenient notation.

Notation 11 For any natural number j, the notation $t^{[j]_f}$ means $t[f^j/w]$, and the notation $t^{[\omega]_f}$ means $t[\mathit{fix}(f)/w]$. Also, the f subscript is dropped when the intended term f is unambiguously clear.

Definition 12 A type T is *admissible* (abbreviated $\mathrm{Adm}(T)$) if:

$$\forall f, t, t'. \, (\exists j. \forall k \geq j. \, t^{[k]} = t'^{[k]} \in T) \Rightarrow t^{[\omega]} = t'^{[\omega]} \in T$$

As expected, admissibility is sufficient to guarantee applicability of the fixpoint principle:

Theorem 13 For any T and f, if T is admissible and $f = f' \in \overline{T} \to \overline{T}$ then $\mathit{fix}(f) = \mathit{fix}(f') \in \overline{T}$.

Proof. $\overline{T}$ *type* since $\overline{T} \to \overline{T}$ *type*. Note that $f^j = f'^j \in \overline{T}$ for every j. Suppose $\mathit{fix}(f)\!\downarrow$. By compactness, $f^j\!\downarrow$ for some j. Since $f^j = f'^j \in \overline{T}$, it follows that $f'^j\!\downarrow$ and thus $\mathit{fix}(f')\!\downarrow$ by Corollary 5. Similarly $\mathit{fix}(f')\!\downarrow$ implies $\mathit{fix}(f)\!\downarrow$. It remains to show that $\mathit{fix}(f) = \mathit{fix}(f') \in T$ when $\mathit{fix}(f)\!\downarrow$. Suppose again that $\mathit{fix}(f)\!\downarrow$. As before, there exists j such that $f^j\!\downarrow$ by compactness. Hence $f^j = f'^j \in T$. Since T is admissible, $\mathit{fix}(f) = \mathit{fix}(f') \in T$.   □

---

[4] Although this proof is non-constructive, a slightly less elegant constructive proof may be derived directly from Lemma 7.

A number of closure conditions exist on admissible types and are given in Lemma 14. Informally, compound types other than dependent products are admissible so long as their component types in positive positions are admissible. Base types—natural numbers, convergence types, and (for this lemma only) equality types—are always admissible. These are essentially Smith's admissible types, except that for a function type to be admissible Smith requires that its domain type also be admissible.

Lemma 14

- $\mathrm{Adm}(A + B)$ if $A + B$ *type* and $\mathrm{Adm}(A)$ and $\mathrm{Adm}(B)$
- $\mathrm{Adm}(\Pi x{:}A.B)$ if $\Pi x{:}A.B$ *type* and $\forall a \in A.\,\mathrm{Adm}(B[a/x])$
- $\mathrm{Adm}(A \times B)$ if $A \times B$ *type* and $\mathrm{Adm}(A)$ and $\mathrm{Adm}(B)$
- $\mathrm{Adm}(\mathbb{N})$
- $\mathrm{Adm}(a = a'\ in\ A)$ if $(a = a'\ in\ A)$ *type*
- $\mathrm{Adm}(\overline{A})$ if $\overline{A}$ *type* and $\mathrm{Adm}(A)$
- $\mathrm{Adm}(a\ in!\ A)$ if $(a\ in!\ A)$ *type*

Proof. The proof follows the same lines as Smith's proof, except that handling equality adds a small amount of complication to the proof. I show the function case by way of example.

Let f, t and t' be arbitrary. Suppose j is such that $\forall k \geq j.\,t^{[k]} = t'^{[k]} \in \Pi x{:}A.B$. I need to show that $t^{[\omega]} = t'^{[\omega]} \in \Pi x{:}A.B$. By assumption $\Pi x{:}A.B\,type$. Both $t^{[j]}$ and $t'^{[j]}$ converge to lambda abstractions, so, by Corollary 5, $t^{[\omega]} \Downarrow \lambda x.b$ and $t'^{[\omega]} \Downarrow \lambda x.b'$ for some terms b and b'. Suppose $a = a' \in A$. To get that $b[a/x] = b'[a'/x] \in B[a/x]$ it suffices to show that $t^{[\omega]}a = t'^{[\omega]}a' \in B[a/x]$. Since $\mathrm{Adm}(B[a/x])$, it suffices to show that $\forall k \geq j.\,t^{[k]}a = t'^{[k]}a' \in B[a/x]$, which follows from the supposition. $\qquad\square$

Unfortunately, Lemma 14 can show the admissibility of a product space only if it is *non-dependent*. Dependent products do not have an admissibility condition similar to that of dependent functions. This reason for this is as follows: Admissibility states that a *single fixed type* contains the limit of an approximation chain if it contains a cofinite subset of that chain. For functions, disjoint union, partial types, and non-dependent products it is possible to decompose prospective members in such a way that admissibility may be applied to a single type (such as the type $B[a/x]$ used in the proof of Lemma 14). In contrast, for a dependent product, the right-hand term's desired type depends upon the left-hand term, which is changing at the same time as the right-hand term. Consequently, there is no single type into which to place the right-hand term.

However, understanding the problem with dependent products suggests a solution, to generalize the definition of admissibility to allow the type to vary. This leads to the notion of *predicate-admissibility* that I discuss in the next section.

4.1 Predicate-Admissibility

Definition 15 A type T is *predicate-admissible* for x in S (abbreviated $\text{Adm}(T \mid x : S)$) if:

$$\forall f, t, t', e.\, e^{[\omega]} \in S \wedge (\exists j.\, \forall k \geq j.\, e^{[k]} \in S \wedge t^{[k]} = t'^{[k]} \in T[e^{[k]}/x]) \Rightarrow$$
$$t^{[\omega]} = t'^{[\omega]} \in T[e^{[\omega]}/x]$$

Predicate-admissibility of the right-hand side (along with admissibility of the left) is sufficient to show the admissibility of a dependent product type:

Lemma 16 The type $\Sigma x{:}A.B$ is admissible if $\Sigma x{:}A.B$ *type* and $\text{Adm}(A)$ and $\text{Adm}(B \mid x : A)$.

Proof. Let f, t and t' be arbitrary. Suppose j is such that $\forall k \geq j.\, t^{[k]} = t'^{[k]} \in \Sigma x{:}A.B$. It is necessary to show that $t^{[\omega]} = t'^{[\omega]} \in \Sigma x{:}A.B$. Both $t^{[j]}$ and $t'^{[j]}$ converge to pairs, so, by Corollary 5, $t^{[\omega]} \Downarrow \langle a, b \rangle$ and $t'^{[\omega]} \Downarrow \langle a', b' \rangle$ for some terms a, b, a' and b'. To get that $a = a' \in A$ it suffices to show that $\pi_1(t^{[\omega]}) = \pi_1(t'^{[\omega]}) \in A$. Since $\text{Adm}(A)$, it suffices to show that $\forall k \geq j.\, \pi_1(t^{[k]}) = \pi_1(t'^{[k]}) \in A$, which follows from the supposition.

To get that $b = b' \in B[a/x]$ (the interesting part), it suffices to show that $\pi_2(t^{[\omega]}) = \pi_2(t'^{[\omega]}) \in B[\pi_1(t^{[\omega]})/x]$. Since $\text{Adm}(B \mid x : A)$, it suffices to show that $\pi_1(t^{[\omega]}) \in A$, which has already been shown, and $\forall k \geq j.\, \pi_1(t^{[k]}) \in A \wedge \pi_2(t^{[k]}) = \pi_2(t'^{[k]}) \in B[\pi_1(t^{[k]})/x]$, which follows from the supposition. □

The conditions for predicate-admissibility are more elaborate, but also more general. I may immediately state conditions for types other than functions. Informally, compound types other than functions are predicate-admissible so long as their component types are predicate-admissible, and base types are always predicate-admissible.

Lemma 17

- $\text{Adm}(A + B \mid y : S)$ if $\forall s \in S.\, (A + B)[s/y]$ *type* and $\text{Adm}(A \mid y : S)$ and $\text{Adm}(B \mid y : S)$.
- $\text{Adm}(\Sigma x{:}A.B \mid y : S)$ if $\forall s \in S.\, (\Sigma x{:}A.B)[s/y]$ *type* and $\text{Adm}(A \mid y : S)$ and $\text{Adm}(B[\pi_1(z), \pi_2(z)/y, x] \mid z : (\Sigma y{:}S.A))$
- $\text{Adm}(\mathbb{N} \mid y : S)$
- $\text{Adm}(a_1 = a_2 \text{ in } A \mid y : S)$ if $\forall s \in S.\, (a_1 = a_2 \text{ in } A)[s/y]$ *type* and $\text{Adm}(A \mid y : S)$
- $\text{Adm}(\overline{A} \mid y : S)$ if $\forall s \in S.\, \overline{A}[s/y]$ *type* and $\text{Adm}(A \mid y : S)$
- $\text{Adm}(a \text{ in! } A \mid y : S)$ if $\forall s \in S.\, (a \text{ in! } A)[s/y]$ *type*

Predicate-admissibility of a function type is more complicated because a function argument with the type $A[e^{[\omega]}/x]$ does not necessarily belong to any of the finite approximations $A[e^{[j]}/x]$. To settle this, it is necessary to require a *coadmissibility* condition on the domain type. Then a function type will be predicate-admissible if the domain is weakly coadmissible and the codomain is predicate-admissible.

Definition 18 A type T is *weakly coadmissible* for x in S (abbreviated WCoAdm($T \mid x : S$)) if:

$$\forall f, t, t', e.\, e^{[\omega]} \in S \wedge (\exists j.\, \forall k \geq j.\, e^{[k]} \in S) \wedge t = t' \in T[e^{[\omega]}/x] \Rightarrow$$
$$(\exists j.\, \forall k \geq j.\, t = t' \in T[e^{[k]}/x])$$

A type T is *coadmissible* for x in S (abbreviated CoAdm($T \mid x : S$)) if:

$$\forall f, t, t', e.\, e^{[\omega]} \in S \wedge (\exists j.\, \forall k \geq j.\, e^{[k]} \in S) \wedge t^{[\omega]} = t'^{[\omega]} \in T[e^{[\omega]}/x] \Rightarrow$$
$$(\exists j.\, \forall k \geq j.\, t^{[k]} = t'^{[k]} \in T[e^{[k]}/x])$$

Lemma 19 Adm($\Pi x{:}A.B \mid y : S$) whenever $\forall s \in S.\, (\Sigma x{:}A.B)[s/y]$ *type* and WCoAdm($A \mid y : S$) and $\forall s \in S, a \in A[s/y].\, $Adm($B[a/x] \mid y : S$)

Clearly coadmissibility implies weak coadmissibility. A general set of conditions listed in Lemma 20 establish weak and full coadmissibility for various types. Weak and full coadmissibility are closed under disjoint union and dependent sum formation, and full coadmissibility is additionally closed under equality-type formation. I use both notions of coadmissibility, rather than just adopting one or the other, because full coadmissibility is needed for equality types but under certain circumstances weak coadmissibility is easier to show (Proposition 21 below).

Lemma 20

- $A + B$ is (weakly) coadmissible for y in S if $\forall s \in S.\, (A + B)[s/y]$ *type* and A and B are (weakly) coadmissible for y in S
- WCoAdm($\Sigma x{:}A.B \mid y : S$) if $\forall s \in S.\, (\Sigma x{:}A.B)[s/y]$ *type* and WCoAdm($A \mid y : S$) and $\forall s \in S, a \in A[s/y].\, $WCoAdm($B[a/x] \mid y : S$)
- CoAdm($\Sigma x{:}A.B \mid y : S$) if $\forall s \in S.\, (\Sigma x{:}A.B)[s/y]$ *type* and CoAdm($A \mid y : S$) and CoAdm($B[\pi_1(z), \pi_2(z)/y, x] \mid z : (\Sigma y{:}S.A)$)
- N is strongly or weakly coadmissible for y in any S
- CoAdm($a_1 = a_2$ in $A \mid y : S$) if $\forall s \in S.\, (a_1 = a_2$ in $A)[s/y]$ *type* and CoAdm($A \mid y : S$)
- $\overline{A}$ is (weakly) coadmissible for y in S if $\forall s \in S.\, \overline{A}[s/y]$ *type* and A is (weakly) coadmissible for y is S
- a *in*! A is strongly or weakly coadmissible for y in S if $\forall s \in S.\, (a$ *in*! $A)[s/y]$ *type*

When T does not depend upon S, predicate-admissibility and weak coadmissibility become easier to show:

Proposition 21 Suppose x does not appear free in T. Then:

- Adm(T) if Adm($T \mid x : S$) and S is inhabited
- Adm($T \mid x : S$) if Adm(T)
- WCoAdm($T \mid x : S$)

There remains one more result related to predicate-admissibility. Suppose one wishes to show $\text{Adm}(T \mid x : S)$ where T depends upon x. There are two ways that x may be used in T. First, T might contain an equality type where x appears in one or both of the equands. In that case, predicate-admissibility can be shown with the tools discussed above. Second, T may be an expression that computes a type from x. In this case, T can be simplified using untyped reasoning [15], but another tool will be needed if T performs any case analysis.

Lemma 22 Consider a type $case(d, x.A, x.B)$ that depends upon y from S. Suppose there exist T_1 and T_2 such that:

- $\forall s \in S.\, d[s/y] \in (T_1 + T_2)[s/y]$
- $\forall s \in S, t \in T_1[s/y].\, A[s, t/y, x]$ *type*
- $\forall s \in S, t \in T_2[s/y].\, B[s, t/y, x]$ *type*

Then the following are the case:

- $\text{Adm}(case(d, x.A, x.B) \mid y : S)$ if $\text{Adm}(A[\pi_1(z), \pi_2(z)/y, x] \mid z : (\Sigma y{:}S.T_1))$ and $\text{Adm}(B[\pi_1(z), \pi_2(z)/y, x] \mid z : (\Sigma y{:}S.T_2))$
- $\text{WCoAdm}(case(d, x.A, x.B) \mid y : S)$ if $\text{WCoAdm}(A[\pi_1(z), \pi_2(z)/y, x] \mid z : (\Sigma y{:}S.T_1))$ and $\text{WCoAdm}(B[\pi_1(z), \pi_2(z)/y, x] \mid z : (\Sigma y{:}S.T_2))$
- $\text{CoAdm}(case(d, x.A, x.B) \mid y : S)$ if $\text{CoAdm}(A[\pi_1(z), \pi_2(z)/y, x] \mid z : (\Sigma y{:}S.T_1))$ and $\text{CoAdm}(B[\pi_1(z), \pi_2(z)/y, x] \mid z : (\Sigma y{:}S.T_2))$

4.2   Monotonicity

In some cases a very simple device may be used to show admissibility. We say that a type is monotone if it respects computational approximation, and it is easy to show that all monotone types are admissible.

Definition 23 A type T is *monotone* (abbreviated $\text{Mono}(t)$) if $t = t' \in T$ whenever $t \in T$ and $t \leq t'$.

Lemma 24 All monotone types are admissible.

Proof. Let f, t and t' be arbitrary and suppose there exists j such that $t^{[j]} = t'^{[j]} \in T$. Since $t^{[j]} \leq t^{[\omega]}$ and $t'^{[j]} \leq t'^{[\omega]}$, it follows that $t^{[j]} = t^{[\omega]} \in T$ and $t'^{[j]} = t'^{[\omega]} \in T$. The result follows directly. □

All type constructors are monotone except universes and partial types, which are never monotone. The proof of this fact is easy [15].

Proposition 25

- $\text{Mono}(A + B)$ if $\text{Mono}(A)$ and $\text{Mono}(B)$
- $\text{Mono}(\Pi x{:}A.B)$ if $\text{Mono}(A)$ and $\forall a \in A.\, \text{Mono}(B[a/x])$
- $\text{Mono}(\Sigma x{:}A.B)$ if $\text{Mono}(A)$ and $\forall a \in A.\, \text{Mono}(B[a/x])$
- $\text{Mono}(\mathbb{N})$, $\text{Mono}(a_1 = a_2 \in A)$, and $\text{Mono}(a \ in! \ A)$

It is worthwhile to note that all these admissibility results are proved constructively, with the exception of the full coadmissibility of partial types, which is necessarily classical (an algorithm that computed the index j could be used to solve the halting problem).

Recall the inadmissible type T from Theorem 2. That type fails the predicate-admissibility condition because of the negative appearance of a function type, which could not be shown weakly coadmissible, and it fails the monotonicity condition because it contains the partial type $\overline{N}$.

5   Conclusions

An interesting avenue for future investigation would be to find some negative results characterizing inadmissible types. Such negative results would be particularly interesting if they could be given a syntactic character, like the results of this paper. Along these lines, it would be interesting to find whether the inability to show coadmissibility of function types represents a weakness of this proof technique or an inherent limitation.

The results presented above provide *metatheoretical* justification for the fixpoint principle over many types. In order for these results to be useful in theorem proving, they must be introduced into the logic. One way to do this, and the way it is presently done in my implementation of partial types in the Nuprl theorem proving system, is to introduce types to represent the assertions $\mathrm{Adm}(T)$, $\mathrm{Adm}(T \mid x : S)$, etc., that are inhabited exactly when the underlying assertion is true (in much that same way as the equality type is inhabited exactly when the equands are equal), and to add rules relating to these types that correspond to the lemmas of Section 4. This brings the tools into the system in a semantically justifiable way, but it is unpleasant in that it leads to a proliferation of new types and inference rules stemming from discoveries outside the logic. It would be preferable to deal with admissibility within the logic. A theory with intensional reasoning principles, such as the one proposed in Constable and Crary [6], would allow reasoning about computation internally. Then these results could be proved within the theory and the only extra rule that would be required would be a single rule relating admissibility to the the fixpoint principle.

However they are placed into the logic, these results allow for recursive computation on a wide variety of types. This make partial types and fixpoint induction a useful tool in type-theoretic theorem provers. It also makes it possible to reason about many recursive programs that used to be barred from the logic because they could not be typed.

References

[1] S. Allen. A non-type-theoretic definition of Martin-Löf's types. In *Second IEEE Symposium on Logic in Computer Science*, pages 215–221, Ithaca, New York, June 1987.

[2] P. Audebaud. Partial objects in the calculus of constructions. In *Sixth IEEE Symposium on Logic in Computer Science*, pages 86–95, Amsterdam, July 1991.

[3] B. Barras, S. Boutin, C. Cornes, J. Courant, J.-C. Filliâtre, E. Giménez, H. Herbelin, G. Huet, C. Muñoz, C. Murthy, C. Parent, C. Paulin-Mohring, A. Saïbi, and B. Werner. *The Coq Proof Assistant Reference Manual.* INRIA-Rocquencourt, CNRS and ENS Lyon, 1996.

[4] D. A. Basin. An environment for automated reasoning about partial functions. In *Ninth International Conference on Automated Deduction*, volume 310 of *Lecture Notes in Computer Science*. Springer-Verlag, 1988.

[5] R. Constable, S. Allen, H. Bromley, W. Cleaveland, J. Cremer, R. Harper, D. Howe, T. Knoblock, N. Mendler, P. Panangaden, J. Sasaki, and S. Smith. *Implementing Mathematics with the Nuprl Proof Development System.* Prentice-Hall, 1986.

[6] R. L. Constable and K. Crary. Computational complexity and induction for partial computable functions in type theory. Technical report, Department of Computer Science, Cornell University, 1997.

[7] R. L. Constable and S. F. Smith. Partial objects in constructive type theory. In *Second IEEE Symposium on Logic in Computer Science*, pages 183–193, Ithaca, New York, June 1987.

[8] R. L. Constable and S. F. Smith. Computational foundations of basic recursive function theory. In *Third IEEE Symposium on Logic in Computer Science*, pages 360–371, Edinburgh, Scotland, July 1988.

[9] T. Coquand and G. Huet. The calculus of constructions. *Information and Computation*, 76:95–120, 1988.

[10] K. Crary. Admissibility of fixpoint induction over partial types. Technical Report TR98-1674, Department of Computer Science, Cornell University, Apr. 1998.

[11] K. Crary. *Type-Theoretic Methodology for Practical Programming Languages.* PhD thesis, Department of Computer Science, Cornell University, Ithaca, New York, 1998. Forthcoming.

[12] M. J. Gordon, A. J. Milner, and C. P. Wadsworth. *Edinburgh LCF: A Mechanised Logic of Computation*, volume 78 of *Lecture Notes in Computer Science*. Springer-Verlag, 1979.

[13] R. Harper. Constructing type systems over an operational semantics. *Journal of Symbolic Computation*, 14:71–84, 1992.

[14] W. Howard. The formulas-as-types notion of construction. In J. P. Seldin and J. R. Hindley, editors, *To H.B. Curry: Essays on Combinatory Logic, Lambda-Calculus and Formalism*, pages 479–490. Academic Press, 1980.

[15] D. J. Howe. Equality in lazy computation systems. In *Fourth IEEE Symposium on Logic in Computer Science*, 1989.

[16] S. Igarashi. Admissibility of fixed-point induction in first-order logic of typed theories. Technical Report AIM-168, Computer Science Department, Stanford University, May 1972.

[17] P. B. Jackson. *Enhancing the Nuprl Proof Development System and Applying it to Computational Abstract Algebra.* PhD thesis, Department of Computer Science, Cornell University, Ithaca, New York, Jan. 1995.

[18] D. MacQueen. Using dependent types to express modular structure. In *Thirteenth ACM SIGACT-SIGPLAN Symposium on Principles of Programming Languages*, pages 277–286, St. Petersburg Beach, Florida, Jan. 1986.

[19] P. Martin-Löf. Constructive mathematics and computer programming. In *Sixth International Congress of Logic, Methodology and Philosophy of Science*, volume

104 of *Studies in Logic and the Foundations of Mathematics*, pages 153–175. North-Holland, 1982.

[20] L. C. Paulson. *Logic and Computation: Interactive Proof with Cambridge LCF.* Cambridge University Press, 1987.

[21] B. C. Pierce and D. N. Turner. Simple type-theoretic foundations for object-oriented programming. *Journal of Functional Programming*, 4(2):207–247, Apr. 1994.

[22] D. Scott. Outline of a mathematical theory of computation. In *Fourth Princeton Conference on Information Sciences and Systems*, pages 169–176, 1970.

[23] D. Scott. Lattice theoretic models for various type-free calculi. In *Fourth International Congress of Logic, Methodology and Philosophy of Science*. North-Holland, 1972.

[24] S. F. Smith. *Partial Objects in Type Theory*. PhD thesis, Department of Computer Science, Cornell University, Ithaca, New York, Jan. 1989.

Automated Theorem Proving in a Simple Meta-Logic for LF

Carsten Schürmann and Frank Pfenning *

Carnegie Mellon University
School of Computer Science
carsten@cs.cmu.edu, fp@cs.cmu.edu

Abstract. Higher-order representation techniques allow elegant encodings of logics and programming languages in the logical framework LF, but unfortunately they are fundamentally incompatible with induction principles needed to reason about them. In this paper we develop a meta-logic $\mathcal{M}_2$ which allows inductive reasoning over LF encodings, and describe its implementation in Twelf, a special-purpose automated theorem prover for properties of logics and programming languages. We have used Twelf to automatically prove a number of non-trivial theorems, including type preservation for Mini-ML and the deduction theorem for intuitionistic propositional logic.

1 Introduction

The logical framework LF [HHP93] has been designed as a meta-language for representing deductive systems which are common in the study of logics and programming languages. It allows concise encodings of many common inference systems, such as natural deduction and sequent calculi, type systems, operational semantics, compilers, abstract machines, etc. (see [Pfe96] for a survey). These representations often lead directly to implementations, either via the constraint logic programming paradigm [Pfe94] or via general search using tactics and tacticals.

The logical framework derives its expressive power from the use of dependent types together with "higher-order" representation techniques which directly support common concepts in deductive systems, such as variable binding and capture-avoiding substitution, parametric and hypothetical judgments, and substitution properties. The fact that these notions are an integral part of the logical framework would seem to make it an ideal candidate not only for reasoning *within* various inference systems, but for reasoning *about* properties of such systems.

Unfortunately, higher-order representation techniques are fundamentally incompatible with the induction principles needed to reason about such encodings (see [DPS97] for a detailed analysis). In the literature three approaches have been

---

* This work was supported by NSF Grant CCR-9619584

C. Kirchner and H. Kirchner (Eds.): Automated Deduction, CADE-15
LNAI 1421, pp. 286–300, 1998. © Springer–Verlag Berlin Heidelberg 1998

studied in order to overcome these problems, while retaining the advantages a logical framework can offer. The first called *schema-checking* [Roh94,RP96] implements meta-theoretic proofs as relations whose operational reading as logic programs realizes the informal proofs. This has been applied successfully in many case studies (see [Pfe96]), but lacks automation. The second is based on reflection via a modal provability operator. At present it is unclear how this idea, developed for simple types in [DPS97], interacts with dependent types, and if it is flexible enough for many of the theorems that can be treated with schema-checking. The third is to devise an explicit (meta-)meta-logic for reasoning about logical framework encodings. For the simpler logical framework of hereditary Harrop formulas this approach has been followed by McDowell and Miller [MM97,McD97] (see Section 5 for a detailed comparison).

In this paper we follow the third approach and develop a simple meta-logic $\mathcal{M}_2$ for LF and sketch its implementation in the Twelf system. $\mathcal{M}_2$ was designed explicitly to support automated inductive theorem proving and has been applied successfully to prove, for example, value soundness and type preservation for Mini-ML, completeness of a continuation stack machine with respect to a natural semantics for Mini-ML, soundness and completeness of uniform derivations with respect to resolution (which is a critical step in the correctness of compilers for logic programming languages), the deduction theorem for intuitionistic propositional logic using Hilbert's axiomatization, and the existence of an embedding of Cartesian closed categories into the simply-typed λ-calculus. In each case we specified only the theorem and the induction variable, the proof was completely automatic in every other respect.

We view Twelf as a special-purpose automated theorem prover for the theory of programming languages and logics. It owes its success to the expressive power of the logical framework combined with the simplicity of the meta-logic which nonetheless allows direct expression of informal mathematical arguments. Its main current limitations are the lack of facilities for incorporating lemmas and for proving properties which require reasoning about *open* LF objects, i.e., objects which may contain free variables. We plan to address the former by adapting standard techniques from inductive and resolution theorem proving and the latter by borrowing successful ideas from schema-checking.

This paper is organized as follows: In Section 2 we briefly describe the logical framework LF and introduce a programming language Mini-ML and a type preservation result as running example. The meta-logic $\mathcal{M}_2$ is introduced in Section 3 which is implemented in the Twelf system which we discuss in Section 4. Section 5 compares the most closely related work before we assess the results and discuss future work.

2 The Logical Framework LF

The type theory underlying the logical framework LF is an extension of the simply-typed λ-calculus by dependent types. It is defined by three syntactic categories of objects, type families, and kinds [HHP93]. We use a for type family constants, c for object constants, and x for variables. Atomic types have the form $a\,M_1\ldots M_n$ and function types $\Pi x : A_1.\,A_2$, which we may write as $A_1 \to A_2$ if x does not occur free in A_2. We assume that constants and variables are declared at most once in a signature and context, respectively. As usual we apply tacit renaming of bound variables to maintain this assumption and to guarantee capture-avoiding substitution.

The LF type theory is defined by a number of mutually dependent judgments which we only summarize here. The main typing judgment is $\Gamma \vdash_\Sigma M : A$ and expresses that object M has type A in context Γ with respect to signature Σ. We generally assume that signature Σ is valid and fixed and therefore omit it from the typing and other related judgments introduced below. We also need to explicitly require the validity of contexts, written as $\vdash \Gamma$ ctx. In a slight departure from [HHP93] we take $\beta\eta$-conversion as our notion of definitional equality, since this guarantees that every well-typed object has an equivalent *canonical form*, that is, a long $\beta\eta$-normal form. The requisite theory may be found in [Coq91].

As a running example we will use Mini-ML in the formulation of [Pfe92] which goes back to [MP91], culminating in an automatic proof of type preservation. While space only permits showing the fragment including abstraction, application, and recursion, our automatic proof also treats the remaining features of Mini-ML including polymorphism and an inductively defined type.

Mini-ML is defined through expressions e, types τ, a typing judgment $\Delta \triangleright e : \tau$, and an evaluation judgment $e \hookrightarrow v$, which are represented as type families

exp : type,
tp : type,
of : exp $\to$ tp $\to$ type, and
ev : exp $\to$ exp $\to$ type,

respectively. Expressions, types, typing rules, and evaluation rules are encoded as object-level constants. The encoding is adequate in the sense that there is a *compositional bijection* between derivations and well-typed objects of appropriate type. For example, using $\ulcorner . \urcorner$ for a generic representation function, we have that derivations of $e \hookrightarrow v$ are in bijective correspondence with closed canonical objects of type ev $\ulcorner e \urcorner \ulcorner v \urcorner$.

Compositionality of the encoding gives us the following substitution lemma "for free", since it can be represented simply by substitution in LF, whose correctness has been proven once and for all [HHP93].

Lemma 1 (Substitution). *If $\Delta \triangleright e' : \tau'$ and $\Delta, x : \tau' \triangleright e : \tau$ then $\Delta \triangleright e[e'/x] : \tau$.*

A substitution lemma of this or a similar form is an important ingredient in many theorems in logic (e.g., cut-elimination, normalization, or the Church-Rosser theorem) or the theory of programming languages (e.g., subject reduction or type preservation).

To demonstrate our theorem prover, we consider the type preservation theorem for Mini-ML. It is proven by structural induction, with repeated applications of *inversion*, which is applicable when the shape of the conclusion determines the inference rule which must have been applied last [Pfe92]. (This proof is also *exactly* the proof found automatically rendered into informal notation.) We write $\mathcal{D} :: J$ if $\mathcal{D}$ is a derivation of a judgment J to avoid two-dimensional notation.

Theorem 1 (Type preservation). *For all expressions e, v, types τ, and derivations $\mathcal{D} :: (e \hookrightarrow v)$ and $\mathcal{P} :: (\cdot \triangleright e : \tau)$, there exists a derivation $\mathcal{Q} :: (\cdot \triangleright v : \tau)$.*

The inductive proof of this theorem is constructive and contains a method for constructing a derivation $\mathcal{Q} :: (\cdot \triangleright v : \tau)$ from $\mathcal{D} :: (e \hookrightarrow v)$ and $\mathcal{P} :: (\cdot \triangleright e : \tau)$. By an extension of the Curry-Howard correspondence one might hope to represent this as an LF function

$$\text{tps} : \Pi E : \exp. \, \Pi V : \exp. \, \Pi T : \text{tp. ev } E \, V \to \text{of } E \, T \to \text{of } V \, T.$$

In fact, if we could exhibit a total function of this type, we would know that type preservation holds. Unfortunately, such a function does not exist in LF, since it would have to be defined by primitive recursion over its fourth argument (the derivation of ev $E \, V$), and primitive recursion is not available in LF. Moreover, straightforward attempts to add primitive recursion render higher-order representations inadequate, as discussed in [DPS97]. Instead we define a meta-logic for LF in which it is possible to express and prove (over the signature encoding Mini-ML):

> For all closed LF objects $E : \exp$, $V : \exp$, $T : \text{tp}$, $D : \text{ev } E \, V$, and $P : \text{of } E \, T$ there exists a closed LF object $Q : \text{of } V \, T$.

By the adequacy of the encodings, the existence of such an LF object Q implies the existence of a typing derivation $\mathcal{Q}$ of $\cdot \triangleright v : \tau$, where $\ulcorner v \urcorner = V$ and $\ulcorner \tau \urcorner = T$, thereby guaranteeing the type preservation property for Mini-ML.

3   The Meta-Logic $\mathcal{M}_2$

The purpose of the meta-logic $\mathcal{M}_2$ is formal reasoning about properties of LF signatures, with the goal of automating the proof of such properties. Since LF signatures implement object languages and their semantics, this provides for automatic proofs of properties of logics and programming languages.

$\mathcal{M}_2$ is a restricted constructive first-order logic where quantifiers range over closed LF objects constructed over a given signature Σ. Its formal definition is a sequent calculus endowed with realizing proof terms.

The formal system of $\mathcal{M}_2$ in its full generality is rather complex. We therefore present here only a restriction of $\mathcal{M}_2$, where pattern matching subjects must be of atomic type. For a complete presentation of the meta-logic we refer the interested reader to the technical report [SP98]. We introduce $\mathcal{M}_2$ in four steps: in Section 3.1 we describe a constructive logic over LF with proof terms which we augment by well-founded recursion in Section 3.2. In Section 3.3 we introduce definition by cases and in Section 3.4 we state the meta-theoretic properties of $\mathcal{M}_2$ which make it an appropriate meta-logic.

$$\frac{\Gamma \vdash \sigma : \Gamma_1 \quad \Gamma; (\Delta_1, \mathbf{x} \in \forall \Gamma_1. F_1, \Delta_2, \mathbf{y} \in F_1[\sigma]) \vdash P \in F_2}{\Gamma; (\Delta_1, \mathbf{x} \in \forall \Gamma_1. F_1, \Delta_2) \vdash \mathbf{let}\ y = \mathbf{x}\ \sigma\ \mathbf{in}\ P \in F_2} \forall L \qquad \frac{(\Gamma, \Gamma_1); \Delta \vdash P \in F}{\Gamma; \Delta \vdash \Lambda \Gamma_1. P \in \forall \Gamma_1. F} \forall R^*$$

$$\frac{(\Gamma, \Gamma_1); (\Delta_1, \mathbf{x} \in \exists \Gamma_1. \top, \Delta_2) \vdash P \in F}{\Gamma; (\Delta_1, \mathbf{x} \in \exists \Gamma_1. \top, \Delta_2) \vdash \mathbf{split}\ \mathbf{x}\ \mathbf{as}\ \langle \Gamma_1 \rangle\ \mathbf{in}\ P \in F} \exists L^* \qquad \frac{\Gamma \vdash \sigma : \Gamma_1}{\Gamma; \Delta \vdash \langle \sigma \rangle \in \exists \Gamma_1. \top} \exists R$$

* Eigenvariable condition: $\vdash \Gamma, \Gamma_1$ ctx

Fig. 1. $\mathcal{M}_2$ without recursion or pattern matching

3.1 A Constructive Sequent Calculus over LF

Formulas in $\mathcal{M}_2$ have the form $\forall x_1 : A_1. \ldots \forall x_n : A_n. \exists y_1 : B_1. \ldots \exists y_m : B_m. \top$ (which we write as $\forall \Gamma_1. \exists \Gamma_2. \top$, where $\Gamma_1 = x_1 : A_1, ..., x_n : A_n$ and $\Gamma_2 = y_1 : B_1, ..., y_m : B_m$). Here all A_i and B_j are LF types, and for a formula to be well-formed the combined context Γ_1, Γ_2 must be a valid LF context.

While this may not seem very expressive, it is sufficient for many theorems in the realm of logic and the theory of programming languages we have examined, since other connectives (such as disjunction) and even more complex quantifier alternations can be incorporated at the level of LF. The main limitation is that the quantifiers range only over closed LF objects of the given types; a generalization is the subject of current research. Assumptions are labelled with proof term variables $\mathbf{x}$ which are used in the proof terms P.

$$\begin{aligned}
\textit{Formulas} \quad & F ::= \forall \Gamma_1. \exists \Gamma_2. \top \\
\textit{Assumptions}\ \Delta ::= & \cdot \mid \Delta, \mathbf{x} \in F
\end{aligned}$$

The main judgment of this sequent calculus is $\Gamma; \Delta \vdash P \in F$, where the LF context Γ makes all Eigenvariables explicit together with their types. The judgment is also indexed by an LF signature Σ which we suppress for the sake of brevity.

The rules for the judgment are in the form of a sequent calculus and defined in Figure 1. Because of the way our search engine actually works and the restriction on quantifier alternations, it is convenient to instantiate all quantified variables of the same kind simultaneously by means of a substitution σ explained below. This applies to the $\forall L$ and $\exists R$ rules, where the latter also incorporates an axiom rule for $\top$. The reader may wish to ignore the proof terms in the first reading, which are not essential until recursion is introduced in Section 3.2.

$$\textit{Substitutions}\ \sigma ::= \cdot \mid \sigma, M/x$$

Valid substitutions map variables in a context Γ' to valid objects in a context Γ. This judgment is written as $\Gamma \vdash \sigma : \Gamma'$ and defined by the following inference rules, which guarantee that dependencies are respected.

$$\frac{}{\Gamma \vdash \cdot : \cdot} \text{subId} \qquad \frac{\Gamma \vdash \sigma : \Gamma' \quad \Gamma \vdash M : A[\sigma]}{\Gamma \vdash (\sigma, M/x) : (\Gamma', x : A)} \text{subDot}$$

When $\Gamma \vdash \sigma : \Gamma'$ and $\Gamma' \vdash M : A$ then we write $M[\sigma]$ for the result of applying the substitution σ to M, and similarly for types, contexts, etc. The result satisfies $\Gamma \vdash M[\sigma] : A[\sigma]$. This is also reflected in our implementation of the system, which employs dependently typed explicit substitutions. We write id_Γ for the identity substitution on Γ satisfying $\Gamma \vdash \mathrm{id}_\Gamma : \Gamma$.

The formulation of the calculus incorporates the structural rules: weakening is implicit in $\exists R$, contraction and exchange are implicit in the left rules $\forall L$ and $\exists L$. The type preservation theorem (Theorem 1) can be expressed in $\mathcal{M}_2$ as

$$\forall E : \exp, V : \exp, T : \mathrm{tp}, D : \mathrm{ev}\ E\ V, P : \mathrm{of}\ E\ T.\ \exists Q : \mathrm{of}\ V\ T.\ \top$$

The variables E, V and T appear as index objects in the types of D, P, and Q and are therefore called *index variables*. Index variables are treated differently from other variables during proof search, as we will see in Section 4. We adopt the convention to omit their quantifier and denote them with bold uppercase names. In this way the theorem can be abbreviated to $\forall D : \mathrm{ev}\ \mathbf{E}\ \mathbf{V}, P : \mathrm{of}\ \mathbf{E}\ \mathbf{T}.\ \exists Q : \mathrm{of}\ \mathbf{V}\ \mathbf{T}.\ \top$.

The system presented in Figure 1 is the core of the meta logic $\mathcal{M}_2$ for LF. In the next two sections we strengthen $\mathcal{M}_2$ by introducing well-founded recursion and definition by cases for closed LF objects. This will allow us to represent many proofs by structural induction, case distinction, and inversion in $\mathcal{M}_2$. A further extension of $\mathcal{M}_2$ is the introduction of conjunction which is required for the representation of mutually inductive proofs, but omitted here for the sake of brevity (see [SP98]).

3.2   Adding Recursion

The recursion operator $\mu \mathbf{x} \in F.\ P$ is the standard fixed point operator at the level of proof terms with the following introduction rule.

$$\frac{\Gamma; \Delta, \mathbf{x} \in F \vdash P \in F}{\Gamma; \Delta \vdash \mu \mathbf{x} \in F.\ P \in F}\ \mathrm{fix}\quad (\text{where } \mu \mathbf{x} \in F.\ P \text{ terminates in } \mathbf{x})$$

It is obvious that a proof term represents a total function only if it terminates independently of the arguments it is applied to. Thus the side condition on the rule. For termination we use arbitrary lexicographic extensions of the subterm ordering on LF objects described in [RP96], all of which are well-founded orderings and easy to check due to the restricted nature of our meta-logic.

3.3   Adding Case Analysis

The context of Eigenvariables Γ in the judgment $\Gamma; \Delta \vdash P \in F$ represents all LF variables which might occur free in the proof term P. Because of the assumption that proof terms are only applied to closed LF objects, all variables in Γ stand for closed LF objects. It is therefore possible to determine all possible cases for the top-level constructor of such objects.

Assume we would like to distinguish all possible cases for a given LF variable x of type A declared in Γ. For simplicity, we assume that A is a base type, even though in the full system [SP98] function types are also permitted which is needed, for example, in the proof of the deduction theorem. The top-level structure of a closed canonical term of base type is always $c\, x_1 \ldots x_n$, where x_i are new variables. If c has type $\Pi x_1 : A_1 . \ldots . \Pi x_n : A_n . B$, then this is a possible candidate for the shape of $x : A$ if B unifies with A.

This idea is very similar to the realization of partial inductive definitions and definitional reflection [SH93], except that dependent types can eliminate more cases statically. Also, because of the higher-order nature of the term language, we need to deal with the undecidability of the full higher-order unification problem. Our solution is to restrict the analysis of possible cases to Miller's higher-order patterns, generalized to the setting of dependent types [Pfe91]. However, we do not restrict our system to patterns statically, since this would preclude, for example, a direct appeal to substitution or substitution lemmas at the level of LF. Instead, we simply rule out definition by cases where determining the possible cases would require unification beyond the pattern fragment.

Formally, we extend the language of proof terms by a case construct.

$$
\begin{array}{lll}
\textit{Patterns} & R ::= \Gamma'; \Gamma'' \rhd M \\
\textit{Cases} & \Omega ::= \cdot \mid \Omega, R \mapsto P \\
\textit{Proof Terms } P ::= \ldots \mid \text{case } x \text{ of } \Omega
\end{array}
$$

The objects M in patterns are strongly restricted by the rules which check valid patterns; usually it will be a constant applied to variable arguments, but because of dependencies, it might be more complex than that. Contexts Γ' and Γ'' are separated for technical reasons, where Γ' contains the variables which will be instantiated when the case subject is matched against the object M, while Γ'' contains those variables which will not be instantiated (although their types could still be instantiated). We always have that $\Gamma', \Gamma'' \vdash M : A'$ for some type A' which is equal to or more specific than the type A of the case subject x.

The judgment for checking the validity of a case construct has the form $\Gamma_1; x : B_x; \Gamma_2; \Delta \vdash_\Sigma \Omega \in F$, where we maintain the invariant that B_x depends on all variables in Γ_1, which therefore collects the variables which will be instantiated by pattern matching. By using the limited permutation properties of LF [HHP93] this can always be established. The following rule then completes the definition of derivability in $\mathcal{M}_2$.

$$
\frac{\Gamma(x) = B_x \qquad \Gamma_1; x : B_x; \Gamma_2; \Delta \vdash_\Sigma \Omega \in F}{\Gamma; \Delta \vdash \text{case } x \text{ of } \Omega \in F} \text{ case}
$$

where $\Gamma_1, x : B_x, \Gamma_2$ must be a valid permutation of Γ, and B_x depends on all variables in Γ_1. The judgment $\Gamma_1; x : B_x; \Gamma_2; \Delta \vdash_\Sigma \Omega \in F$ selects all constants from Σ which are possible constructors for a closed object of type B_x. The rules for the judgment are given in Figure 2. This judgment iterates through the signature Σ, trying each constant c in turn. If the target type B_c unifies with

$$\frac{}{\Gamma_1; x : B_x; \Gamma_2; \Delta \vdash. \ \cdot \in F} \ \text{sigempty}$$

$$\frac{\Gamma_1; x : B_x; \Gamma_2; \Delta \vdash_\Sigma \ \Omega \in F}{\Gamma_1; x : B_x; \Gamma_2; \Delta \vdash_{\Sigma, c: \Pi \Gamma_c. \ B_c} \ \Omega \in F} \ \text{signonuni} \ \ (B_x, B_c \text{ do not unify})$$

$$\frac{\Gamma', \Gamma_2[\sigma]; \Delta[\sigma'] \vdash P \in F[\sigma'] \qquad \Gamma_1; x : B_x; \Gamma_2; \Delta \vdash_\Sigma \ \Omega \in F}{\Gamma_1; x : B_x; \Gamma_2; \Delta \vdash_{\Sigma, c: \Pi \Gamma_c. \ B_c} \ \Omega, (\Gamma'; \Gamma_2[\sigma] \triangleright (c \ \Gamma_c)[\sigma] \mapsto P) \in F} \ \text{siguni}$$

$$\Gamma' \vdash \sigma = \text{mgu} \ (B_x \doteq B_c, x \doteq c \ \Gamma_c) : (\Gamma_1, x : B_x, \Gamma_c)$$
$$\Gamma', \Gamma_2[\sigma] \vdash \sigma' = (\sigma, \text{id}_{\Gamma_2}) : (\Gamma_1, x : B_x, \Gamma_c, \Gamma_2)$$

Fig. 2. Selection rules for $\Gamma_1; x : B_x; \Gamma_2; \Delta \vdash_\Sigma \ \Omega \in F$

the type B_x of the case subject (siguni), a new case is added to Ω. Otherwise, c cannot be a top-level constructor for a closed term M of type B_x and no case is added (signonuni).

In the rules we use $\Pi \Gamma_c. \ B_c$ as a compact notation for the type of the object constant c, where B_c is an atomic type. We write $c \ \Gamma_c$ for the result of applying c to the variables in Γ_c in order, which gives us the most general form of a term in canonical form whose head is c. The side conditions of siguni determine a substitution σ', which instantiates all variables in Γ_1 according to the unification of B_c and B_x, x by $c \ \Gamma_c$, and acts on all variables in Γ_2 as the identity substitution.

3.4 Properties of $\mathcal{M}_2$

The principal property of $\mathcal{M}_2$ which justifies its use for reasoning about closed LF objects is the following.

Theorem 2. *If* $\cdot; \cdot \vdash P \in \forall \Gamma_1. \exists \Gamma_2. \top$ *is derivable for some* P, *then for every closed substitution* $\cdot \vdash \sigma_1 : \Gamma_1$ *there exists a substitution* $\cdot \vdash \sigma_2 : \Gamma_2[\sigma_1]$.

As indicated at the end of Section 2, this, together with the adequacy of the encodings, guarantees the meta-theoretic properties of the object languages we can express in $\mathcal{M}_2$. Note that this is different from and in many ways simpler than a full cut-elimination result for $\mathcal{M}_2$.

The proof of this central property is non-trivial. What we show is that the realizing proof terms P can be used to calculate σ_2 from σ_1. For this purpose, we define a small-step, call-by-value, continuation-passing operational semantics for proof terms P with explicit environments and establish the following three properties.

Type Soundness: Each step in the evaluation of P preserves types and provability in $\mathcal{M}_2$ (the critical idea here is the use of explicit environments rather than substitution, since substitution may render some branches in a case distinction inapplicable, thereby invalidating it).

Progress: At each step we either have a final result, or a rule in the operational semantics applies (the critical step here shows that all possibilities are covered in a definition by cases).

Termination: All reduction sequences terminate (the critical step here uses the well-foundedness restriction on recursion).

Unfortunately, space does not permit us to show the details of this proof or even the definition of the operational semantics. The interested reader is referred to [SP98].

4   Twelf

Twelf is a theorem prover for LF which directly implements the meta-logic $\mathcal{M}_2$ (including mutual induction and distinction by cases over functions). It provides an interactive mode for experimentation and an automatic mode in which only the theorem and the termination ordering are specified. The deduction engine implements only a few elementary operations which are used to formalize the three important basic proof principles: inversion (that is, determining all possible shapes of an LF object from its type), direct proofs (that is, direct construction of an LF object), and appeals to the induction hypothesis. The interactive mode also supports lemma application.

4.1   Elementary Operations

We discuss the elementary operations using the proof of the type preservation theorem as an example. The initial goal

$$\forall D : \text{ev } \mathbf{E}\ \mathbf{V}, P : \text{of } \mathbf{E}\ \mathbf{T}.\ \exists Q : \text{of } \mathbf{V}\ \mathbf{T}.\ \top$$

and the induction principle (induction over D) are specified by the user. Twelf uses only outermost induction, so there is an implicit application of the recursion rule before the real proof process is started. Then Twelf generates subgoals by applying its elementary operations until all subgoals are solved, using the strategy described in Section 4.2.

The most basic step directly constructs a substitution for the existentially quantified variables using the constants from the signature and the universally quantified variables. We call this step *filling*. It is basically a straightforward, iterative-deepening search over an LF signature and is derived from a related implementation of resolution for logic programming [Pfe94].

In our example, such a substitution does not exist for the current state, so the system applies the *splitting* operation which performs a case analysis: it inspects the signature for possible constructors for D and generates a list of three subgoals, automatically updating the context of universal variables.

Case: $D = \text{ev\_lam}$:

$$\forall P : \text{of } (\text{lam } \mathbf{E})\ \mathbf{T}.\ \exists Q : \text{of } (\text{lam } \mathbf{E})\ \mathbf{T}.\ \top$$

Case: $D = \text{ev\_app } D_3\ D_2\ D_1$:

$$\forall D_3 : \text{ev } (\mathbf{E_1'}\ \mathbf{V_2})\ \mathbf{V},\ D_2 : \text{ev } \mathbf{E_2}\ \mathbf{V_2}, D_1 : \text{ev } \mathbf{E_1}\ (\text{lam } \mathbf{E_1'}),$$
$$P : \text{of } (\text{app } \mathbf{E_1}\ \mathbf{E_2})\ \mathbf{T}.\ \exists Q : \text{of } \mathbf{V}\ \mathbf{T}.\ \top$$

Case: $D = \text{ev\_fix } D_1$:

$$\forall D_1 : \text{ev } (\mathbf{E}\ (\text{fix } \mathbf{E}))\ \mathbf{V}, P : \text{of } (\text{fix } \mathbf{E})\ \mathbf{T}.\ \exists Q : \text{of } \mathbf{V}\ \mathbf{T}.\ \top$$

For the sake of brevity, we skip the discussion of the first two subgoals, and continue with the third. Inversion is now applied to P in the informal proof, since there is only one typing rule with a conclusion of the form $\cdot \rhd \textbf{fix } x.\,e : \tau$. In Twelf, inversion is realized by another splitting operation which generates only one subgoal in this example. The other two potential cases (of_lam, of_app) do not need to be considered by Twelf, because their types are incompatible with the type of P. This leaves the subgoal

$$\forall D_1 : \text{ev } (\mathbf{E}\ (\text{fix } \mathbf{E}))\ \mathbf{V},\ P_1 : \Pi x{:}\text{exp. of } x\ \mathbf{T} \to \text{of } (\mathbf{E}\ x)\ \mathbf{T}.\ \exists Q : \text{of } \mathbf{V}\ \mathbf{T}.\ \top.$$

Note, that in this goal the variable P_1 is functional and represents a hypothetical derivation.

It is now possible to appeal to the induction hypothesis in an operation we call *recursion*. The termination condition of the fix-rule requires that it is only applied to a term smaller than $D = \text{ev\_fix } D_1$. According to the termination ordering in [RP96] there is only one possibility, namely D_1.

We cannot appeal to the induction hypothesis without providing a typing derivation as second argument. Formally, the representation of this derivation must be of type 'of $(\mathbf{E}\ (\text{fix } \mathbf{E}))\ \mathbf{T}$'. Twelf searches and finds the term '$P_1\ (\text{fix } \mathbf{E})\ (\text{of\_fix } P_1)$' which represents the result of applying the substitution lemma (Lemma 1) as used in the proof of Theorem 1. If we call the result of the appeal to the induction hypothesis Q_2, we obtain the following subgoal.

$$\forall D_1 : \text{ev } (\mathbf{E}\ (\text{fix } \mathbf{E}))\ \mathbf{V},\ P_1 : \Pi x{:}\text{exp. of } x\ \mathbf{T} \to \text{of } (\mathbf{E}\ x)\ \mathbf{T},\ Q_2 : \text{of } \mathbf{V}\ \mathbf{T}.$$
$$\exists Q_1 : \text{of } \mathbf{V}\ \mathbf{T}.\ \top$$

Twelf is now able to determine in a simple filling step that Q_2 is a possible instantiation for Q_1, thereby completing the ev_fix-branch of the proof. The other two branches can be solved similarly. Twelf then reports the proof term (currently shown in a more readable relational notation as an LF signature, rather than in the functional notation used to define $\mathcal{M}_2$).

4.2 Strategy

The proof strategy of Twelf is a simple combination of the three elementary operations. But each operation must be applied with care because they are inherently expensive in time and space. In particular, we completely avoid backtracking except locally during the filling step. Splitting, filling, and recursion use unification to analyze cases and to select constants. Recursion triggers the calculation of possible recursion arguments according to the termination ordering [RP96].

For a given theorem and induction principle, Twelf attempts to construct a derivation in $\mathcal{M}_2$ using the following strategy:

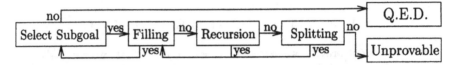

There is a global store of yet to be proven subgoals, initialized with the formula representing the theorem. Once the automated proof process is started, the strategy activates a subgoal and tries to apply a filling operation.

Filling: The filling operation corresponds to an application of the $\exists$R-rule: it is applicable if a substitution instantiating all existentially quantified variables can be constructed. Because index variables occur in the types of non-index variables, it is already enough to determine instantiations for all non-index variables (see Section 2). In general, infinitely many substitutions must be examined, but since our strategy is parameterized by a number to limit the depth of the search space, the employed search algorithm is incomplete but will always terminate (even though failure is sometimes slow).

If Twelf succeeds in constructing the substitution, the current subgoal is successfully completed and the next subgoal is selected if available, otherwise Twelf stops (Q.E.D.). If Twelf fails to construct the desired substitution the strategy tries to apply the recursion operation.

Recursion: The recursion operation corresponds to an application of the $\forall$L-rule, immediately followed by an application of the $\exists$L-rule: Twelf generates all possible recursive calls by constructing substitutions which correspond to the arguments of the recursive call. These substitutions must satisfy the side condition of the fix-rule. Because lower-ranked arguments in a lexicographic termination order actually may increase in size, there are potentially infinitely many different ways to appeal to the induction hypothesis. Moreover results of recursive calls can be used to form new ones. Hence, to avoid an infinite chain of applications of induction hypotheses, our strategy is parameterized by an upper bound on the number of recursive calls. If no new recursive calls can be generated, the strategy tries to apply the splitting operation.

Splitting: The splitting operation corresponds to an application of the case-rule. Twelf selects a universally quantified variable which is not an index variable (see Section 2). Its type is then used to determine all of its possible shapes (sigempty, siguni, and signonuni). For each shape, a new subgoal is created. Twelf then selects among those an active subgoal and tries to apply the filling operation.

Experiment	Ind	Lim	Filling	Splitting	Recursion	Total
Cartesian Closed Categories	1	4	1.000	0.004	0.036	1.099
CPM Completeness	1	20	0.916	0.010	0.117	1.134
CPM Proof equivalence: $\Rightarrow$	1	6	0.226	0.034	0.442	0.951
CPM Proof equivalence: $\Leftarrow$	1	6	0.280	0.033	0.647	1.235
Horn LP Soundness	3	4	4.336	0.004	0.049	4.501
Horn LP Canonical forms	3	4	0.028	0.009	0.107	0.303
Horn LP Completeness	2	4	0.015	0.005	0.039	0.195
Mini-ML Value soundness	1	3	0.016	0.041	0.061	0.172
Mini-ML Type preservation	1	6	0.062	0.521	0.150	0.799
Mini-ML Evaluation/Reduction	1	9	25.397	0.007	0.078	25.546
Hilbert's abstraction theorem	1	4	0.197	0.004	0.010	0.322
Associativity of $+$	1	3	0.009	0.012	0.016	0.063
Commutativity of $+$	2	3	0.092	0.609	4.139	4.877

Fig. 3. Experimental results (in CPU seconds)

Among all universally quantified variables Twelf selects the one which generates the least number of subgoals first (which could be zero if a variable has a dependent type which does not unify with any constructor type—the subgoal succeeds immediately in that case). This heuristic works surprisingly well in all our examples, we leave a refinement to future research. To avoid an infinite loop of splits (applying splits to the children of a previous split), Twelf is parametrized by a splitting limit. Hence, there are two cases when the strategy may stop unsuccessfully: Either there are no further splittable universally quantified variables available, or their types fall outside Miller's pattern fragment. In both cases the strategy stops with the message that a proof could not be found.

4.3 Experimental Results

Twelf has successfully proved several non-trivial theorems automatically. In Figure 3 we give an overview over the experimental results from the areas of programming languages and logics. "Ind" states how many simultaneous induction hypotheses are necessary and "Lim" the maximal size for LF objects (counting variables and constants, excluding index objects). In all examples the splitting limit is 2, and the number of recursive calls in each case is limited to 10. "Total" summarizes time spent for filling, splitting, recursion and miscellaneous tasks such as parsing, and type reconstruction.

All timings are in CPU seconds, include garbage collection, and have been taken on a 300 Mhz Pentium-II machine, running Linux 2.30, New Jersey SML 110, and Twelf 1.2.

In the area of Mini-ML, Twelf was used to prove value soundness, i.e., if $e \hookrightarrow v$ then v is a value, and type preservation (Theorem 1). The third related theorem, namely that if $e \hookrightarrow v$ then e reduces to v was particularly difficult with our strategy, since the search space for reductions is rather unstructured. Most of the time here is spent in failed attempts to fill incomplete subgoals before appeals to the induction hypothesis generate the necessary auxiliary reductions. Twelf also proved completeness of a continuation passing machine (CPM) with respect to a natural semantics for Mini-ML. The proof constitutes a mapping from Mini-ML evaluations to computation traces of the abstract machine. But Twelf cannot verify the soundness direction, because the proof requires complete induction which is currently not supported. Nonetheless, Twelf could prove that the soundness proof (coded by hand) can be mapped onto the completeness proof and vice versa.

In the area of logic, Twelf was used to prove the deduction theorem for intuitionistic propositional logic using Hilbert's axiomatization which is used to translate pure functional programs into combinators. It also proved soundness and completeness of uniform derivations with respect to resolution for Horn-logic. From the area of category theory, it proved that Cartesian closed categories can be embedded into the simply-typed λ-calculus. Finally, we have carried out some more traditional inductions, proving the associativity and commutativity of addition on unary natural numbers. Especially the latter is interesting, since Twelf spends most of its time exploring various ways to apply the rather general induction hypothesis, while in most other examples filling is the most expensive operation.

5   Related Work and Future Work

There have been many mechanized proofs of meta-theoretic properties of logics or programming languages in the literature (see the survey [Pfe96]). Most of these do not use techniques from logical frameworks, but represent the languages via standard inductive types and their semantics by inductively defined predicates. A popular choice for such encodings are de Bruijn indices, since they eliminate the problem of α-conversion from consideration. However, various lemmas regarding substitution must still be shown and used, which severely limits the degree of automation which can be achieved. Most closely related to our own efforts in this area is the work on ALF [Mag95], since ALF also employs dependently typed pattern matching and termination orderings, although without the benefits of higher-order abstract syntax.

Another approach is to represent meta-theoretic proofs as relations in LF, which leaves the progress and termination properties above to an external check on relations [PR92]. In this approach, there is no automation besides type reconstruction. The expressive power of LF makes this feasible, but it remains tedious.

Most closely related to our approach is work by McDowell and Miller [MM97] who also define a higher-order meta-logic $FO\lambda^{\Delta N}$ for a logical framework (hereditary Harrop formulas) and then reason in the meta-logic. Their approach is based entirely on simple types and does not incorporate proof terms, which makes it less suitable for automation. Moreover, in order to establish consistency for their meta-logic, they limit induction to natural numbers, which also complicates automation. In fact, their implementation based on the Pi proof editor [Eri94] is entirely interactive. On the other hand, $FO\lambda^{\Delta\mathbb{N}}$ does not restrict itself to Π_2-formulas. In addition, McDowell has demonstrated the flexibility of his approach in his thesis [McD97] where he also treats a logical framework incorporating linearity. Since the overall architecture is quite similar, this gives us confidence that our approach may be extended to a linear logical framework [CP96], which is planned in future work. We believe that the separation between logical framework and meta-logic, and the separation between definition by cases and well-founded recursion are all critical ingredients in making this idea successful for even richer logical frameworks than LF.

While the set of theorems we can prove at present is already surprisingly rich, they are limited by three factors: (1) we do not attempt to automatically use lemmas, (2) only lexicographic extensions of subterm orderings are permitted to show termination, and (3) $\mathcal{M}_2$ does not support reasoning about *open* LF objects. We believe that (1) and (2) can be addressed by incorporating standard techniques from inductive theorem proving, efficiency improvements such as indexing, and simply allowing more complex termination orderings. Nonetheless, we have currently no plans for developing Twelf into a general-purpose theorem prover, because we feel that its present success owes mostly to its design as a special-purpose prover for properties of programming languages and logics. We are currently investigating how to incorporate ideas from schema-checking [Roh94] and primitive recursion over higher-order abstract syntax [DPS97] into our meta-logical framework in order to make progress on item (3), that is, allow reasoning over terms which may have free variables from certain regular contexts which arise in many practical examples.

References

[Coq91] Thierry Coquand. An algorithm for testing conversion in type theory. In Gérard Huet and Gordon Plotkin, editors, *Logical Frameworks*, pages 255–279. Cambridge University Press, 1991.

[CP96]   Iliano Cervesato and Frank Pfenning. A linear logical framework. In E. Clarke, editor, *Proceedings of the Eleventh Annual Symposium on Logic in Computer Science*, pages 264–275, New Brunswick, New Jersey, July 1996. IEEE Computer Society Press.

[DPS97] Joëlle Despeyroux, Frank Pfenning, and Carsten Schürmann. Primitive recursion for higher-order abstract syntax. In R. Hindley, editor, *Proceedings of the Third International Conference on Typed Lambda Calculus and Applications (TLCA '97)*, pages 147–163, Nancy, France, April 1997. Springer-Verlag LNCS.

[Eri94] Lars-Henrik Eriksson. Pi: An interactive derivation editor for the calculus of partial inductive definitions. In Alan Bundy, editor, *Proceedings of the Twelfth International Conference on Automated Deduction*, pages 821–825. Springer-Verlag LNAI 814, June 1994.

[HHP93] Robert Harper, Furio Honsell, and Gordon Plotkin. A framework for defining logics. *Journal of the Association for Computing Machinery*, 40(1):143–184, January 1993.

[Mag95] Lena Magnusson. *The Implementation of ALF—A Proof Editor Based on Martin-Löf's Monomorphic Type Theory with Explicit Substitution.* PhD thesis, Chalmers University of Technology and Göteborg University, January 1995.

[McD97] Raymond McDowell. *Reasoning in a logic with definitions and induction.* PhD thesis, University of Pennsylvania, 1997.

[MM97] Raymond McDowell and Dale Miller. A logic for reasoning with higher-order abstract syntax: An extended abstract. In Glynn Winskel, editor, *Proceedings of the Twelfth Annual Symposium on Logic in Computer Science*, Warsaw, Poland, June 1997. To appear.

[MP91] Spiro Michaylov and Frank Pfenning. Natural semantics and some of its meta-theory in Elf. In L.-H. Eriksson, L. Hallnäs, and P. Schroeder-Heister, editors, *Proceedings of the Second International Workshop on Extensions of Logic Programming*, pages 299–344, Stockholm, Sweden, January 1991. Springer-Verlag LNAI 596.

[Pfe91] Frank Pfenning. Unification and anti-unification in the Calculus of Constructions. In *Sixth Annual IEEE Symposium on Logic in Computer Science*, pages 74–85, Amsterdam, The Netherlands, July 1991.

[Pfe92] Frank Pfenning. Computation and deduction. Unpublished lecture notes, 277 pp. Revised May 1994, April 1996, May 1992.

[Pfe94] Frank Pfenning. Elf: A meta-language for deductive systems. In A. Bundy, editor, *Proceedings of the 12th International Conference on Automated Deduction*, pages 811–815, Nancy, France, June 1994. Springer-Verlag LNAI 814. System abstract.

[Pfe96] Frank Pfenning. The practice of logical frameworks. In Hélène Kirchner, editor, *Proceedings of the Colloquium on Trees in Algebra and Programming*, pages 119–134, Linköping, Sweden, April 1996. Springer-Verlag LNCS 1059. Invited talk.

[PR92] Frank Pfenning and Ekkehard Rohwedder. Implementing the meta-theory of deductive systems. In D. Kapur, editor, *Proceedings of the 11th International Conference on Automated Deduction*, pages 537–551, Saratoga Springs, New York, June 1992. Springer-Verlag LNAI 607.

[Roh94] Ekkehard Rohwedder. Verifying the meta-theory of deductive systems. Thesis Proposal, February 1994.

[RP96] Ekkehard Rohwedder and Frank Pfenning. Mode and termination checking for higher-order logic programs. In Hanne Riis Nielson, editor, *Proceedings of the European Symposium on Programming*, pages 296–310, Linköping, Sweden, April 1996. Springer-Verlag LNCS 1058.

[SH93] Peter Schroeder-Heister. Rules of definitional reflection. In M. Vardi, editor, *Proceedings of the Eighth Annual IEEE Symposium on Logic in Computer Science*, pages 222–232, Montreal, Canada, June 1993.

[SP98] Carsten Schürmann and Frank Pfenning. Automated theorem proving in a simple meta-logic for LF. Technical Report CMU-CS-98-123, Carnegie Mellon University, 1998.

— Invited Talk —
Deductive vs. Model-Theoretic Approaches to Formal Verification

Amir Pnueli

Weizmann Institute of Science

Abstract. The well-known duality between proof- and model-theoretic approaches in classic logic assumes even greater significance in the application of these approaches for formal verification of software and hardware designs.

In this talk, we will survey the main model-theoretic and deductive approaches to formal verification, as illustrated by enumerative and symbolic model checking techniques and deductive verification systems such as STeP, PVS, HOL, etc. We will motivate the current feeling that only the combination of these dual approaches will enable us to formally verify really complex and large systems. Some proposed ideas about how model-checking and deduction can be effectively combined in a mutually beneficial way will be described, and illustrated on simple case studies.

C. Kirchner and H. Kirchner (Eds.): Automated Deduction, CADE-15
LNAI 1421, pp. 301–301, 1998. © Springer–Verlag Berlin Heidelberg 1998

Automated Deduction of Finite-State Control Programs for Reactive Systems

Robi Malik

Department of Computer Science
University of Kaiserslautern, P.O. Box 3049, 67653 Kaiserslautern, Germany
malik@informatik.uni-kl.de

Abstract. We propose an approach towards the automatic synthesis of finite-state reactive control programs from purely declarative, logic specifications of their requirements. More precisely, if P is a set of propositional temporal logic formulas, representing the environment of a reactive system, and if α is a propositional formula, representing a safety requirement, then we point out how to deduce a most general set C of formulas, representing a control program, such that $P \cup C \models \alpha$.

1 Introduction

In the area of hardware and software development, there is a growing interest in formal methods and tools in order to achieve a more rigorous specification, verification, or automated synthesis of safety-critical circuits. We present an algorithm for the automatic synthesis of finite-state reactive control programs from purely declarative, logic specifications of their requirements.

A specification consists of a set of propositional linear temporal logic formulas, representing the environment of a reactive system, and a safety requirement to be ensured within this environment at all times. Given this input, our synthesis algorithm will compute the description of a *most general* control program which enforces the safety requirement always to hold within the specified environment.

In recent years, a lot of work has been carried out on the formal analysis of finite state systems. The introduction of *symbolic model checking* [2, 19] brought a considerable breakthrough, as far as the *verification* of finite-state systems is concerned. Since then, it became possible to verify ever larger circuits. Our synthesis procedure can be viewed as an extension of symbolic model checking: It does not only check whether a safety condition is satisfied within a given model, it even finds out whether there exists some way of enforcing this safety condition, and if so, it outputs a control program that does so.

The algorithms presented here have also been implemented. By efficient application of *Ordered Binary Decision Diagrams (OBDD's)* [5] for representing state sets, we have successfully synthesized circuits with more than 10^{30} states.

This paper is organized as follows. After this introduction, we begin with a short description of our model for reactive systems. Afterwards we describe our

C. Kirchner and H. Kirchner (Eds.): Automated Deduction, CADE-15
LNAI 1421, pp. 302–316, 1998. © Springer–Verlag Berlin Heidelberg 1998

specification language of *programs stratified in time*, a simple and declarative specification language based on propositional temporal logic, and illustrate its use by means of an example from an actual subway device. Then we show that it is decidable whether a control problem specified by a program stratified in time can be solved, and we present a fixpoint-based algorithm which computes a most general control program satisfying the specification. We conclude with a short discussion of related work and some prospects of future research.

2 Reactive Systems

A *reactive system* is a *control program* (or *controller*) maintaining a continuous interaction with its *environment* [3, 11, 12, 17]. This environment, often also called *plant*, includes all the technical equipment to be supervised by the controller as well as possibly a (human) operator supplying commands. The controller uses a set of *sensors*, through which it receives *inputs* from the plant, describing the plant's present state. From this information, the controller has to compute *outputs*, which are sent back to the plant via so-called *actuators*, causing state changes within the plant and thus influencing the new inputs.

In our model, communication is assumed to be *synchronous* [3], i.e. it is assumed that the controller always has enough time to reply to a message received from the sensors. This assumption, which should be fulfilled by any clocked system, is known to considerably simplify the design of reactive systems.

The goal of *controller synthesis* consists of finding some specific control program, which causes the plant to fulfil certain *requirements*. These requirements have been specified a-priori and describe the *control problem* to be solved. They may describe certain functions to be carried out by the system, but also essential safety constraints that have to be satisfied at all times.

3 The Specification Language

3.1 Propositional Linear Temporal Logic

For the formal specification of reactive systems, we use a simple subset of propositional temporal logic, called LT. We assume that we have a finite alphabet Σ of *propositional variables*, and define the set LT_Σ of *linear time formulas* built from these variables inductively by the following conditions.

- Every symbol $p \in \Sigma$ belongs to LT_Σ.
- LT_Σ contains a special symbol START otherwise not occurring in Σ.
- For all $\alpha, \beta \in \mathrm{LT}_\Sigma$, we have $\neg\alpha \in \mathrm{LT}_\Sigma$, $(\alpha \to \beta) \in \mathrm{LT}_\Sigma$, and $\circ\alpha \in \mathrm{LT}_\Sigma$.

Parentheses will be omitted whenever possible, assuming that $\neg$ and $\circ$ have a higher binding priority than $\to$. Other propositional connectives are defined as abbreviations as usual. The only temporal operators in this language are "START", denoting the initial state, and "$\circ$", representing the so-called *next-state* operator. A sequence of i $\circ$-operators is denoted by $\circ^i$.

This language is supposed to describe a linear temporal logic, therefore its semantics is defined by means of interpretations which are sequences of states, mapping the variables of Σ to 0 or 1 (*true* or *false*) for each instance of time.

Definition 1. A *temporal state* for Σ is a map $I_0 \colon \Sigma \to \{0,1\}$. An *interpretation* I for Σ is a infinite sequence of states, i.e. $I = (I_1, I_2, \ldots)$.

A state I_0 can be uniquely identified with a subset of Σ, namely the set of all $p \in \Sigma$ where $I_0(p) = 1$. Therefore we also regard such sets as states, and sequences of such sets as interpretations. If $\Sigma' \subseteq \Sigma$, it often is convenient to denote the *restriction* of a state or an interpretation I to Σ' by $I|_{\Sigma'}$, and if $I' = I|_{\Sigma'}$, we also write $I \geq I'$.

An interpretation $I = (I_1, I_2, \ldots)$ of the propositional variables in Σ is extended to an interpretation of arbitrary formulas inductively as follows.

- $I_k(\text{START}) = 1$, iff $k = 1$.
- $I_k(\neg\alpha) = 1 - I_k(\alpha)$, for all $\alpha \in \text{LT}_\Sigma$.
- $I_k(\alpha \to \beta) = 1$, iff $I_k(\alpha) = 0$ or $I_k(\beta) = 1$, for all $\alpha, \beta \in \text{LT}_\Sigma$.
- $I_k(\circ\,\alpha) = I_{k+1}(\alpha)$, for all $\alpha \in \text{LT}_\Sigma$.

Definition 2. Let $\alpha \in \text{LT}_\Sigma$, and let $I = (I_1, I_2, \ldots)$ be an interpretation. I is called a *model* for α, $I \models \alpha$, if $I_k(\alpha) = 1$ for every state I_k of I.

It should be noted that, in our definition, a model for α must satisfy the formula α in all its states, i.e. the condition α must hold at all times. This definition enables us to reason conveniently about safety conditions, because we do not have to specify that formulas are supposed to hold "always", and we do not have to reason too much about formulas holding in certain states.

With this definition of a model, the notions of *satisfiability*, *validity*, and *logical consequence* also get slightly non-standard meanings. Yet, they are defined in the usual way, e.g. a formula α is valid if every interpretation is a model for α.

3.2 Programs and Goals

We want to use LT-formulas for specifying reactive control problems. Therefore, we introduce a class of simple temporal logic programs which can be used to describe the plant of a reactive system in an executable and declarative way. There is a wide variety of similar temporal logic languages, many of which offer additional features which we do not need here—see [10] for a survey.

Definition 3. A *(propositional) literal* is a formula of the form p or $\neg p$, for some $p \in \Sigma$. A *propositional formula* is a formula which contains no temporal operator. A *propositional clause* is a formula of the form $L \leftarrow W$, for some propositional formula W and a literal L. L is called the *head* of the clause, and W is called its *body*. A *temporal clause* is a formula which has one of the forms $L \leftarrow \text{START}$ or $\circ L \leftarrow W$, for some propositional formula W and a literal L.

Definition 4. A *program* is a finite set of propositional or temporal clauses.

If P is a program, and $p \in \Sigma$, then we introduce the *definition* of p, $\mathrm{DEF}_P(p)$, as the set of all clauses in P with p occurring in their head. Similarly, for $\Sigma' \subseteq \Sigma$, $\mathrm{DEF}_P(\Sigma')$ denotes the union of the definitions of all the symbols in Σ'.

Definition 5. A *goal* is a formula of the form $\leftarrow W$, where W is a propositional formula.

Our intention is to specify the plant of a reactive system by means of a program as defined above. A goal describes a *safety property* that is supposed to hold within the plant at all times. Often it is useful to consider a program P together with a goal $\leftarrow \alpha$; such a pair $(P, \leftarrow \alpha)$ is called a *control problem*.

The task of *verification* of the conditions α in the environment specified by P, i.e. the task of checking whether $P \models \alpha$, could be approached by techniques of *logic programming*, if we had used *negation as failure* [13] in our negation semantics. But since we use exact negation, *model checking* [6] is more applicable here.

We are interested in the problem of *control program synthesis* which can be stated as follows. "*Given a control problem* $(P, \leftarrow \alpha)$, *find a program* C *such that* $P \cup C \models \alpha$." This problem is more general than the verification problem, to which it becomes equivalent if there are no actuators to be set by the control program. Therefore, the synthesis algorithms presented in section 5 can also be used for the verification of reactive systems, if desired.

3.3 Signatures

In order to obtain a useful specification formalism, we have to distinguish different types of propositional variables. In particular, sensors and actuators have to be treated specially. Therefore, we consider the following subsets of Σ, the set of propositional variables.

- $\mathcal{E}^\circ$, the set of *state variables*,
- $\mathcal{A}$, the set of *actuator variables*,
- $\mathcal{S}$, the set of *sensor variables*, and finally
- $\mathcal{H}$, the set of *auxiliary variables*.

The *state* and *auxiliary* variables are controlled by the plant. We will use state variables to transfer information from the present to the next time interval, while auxiliary variables will be used for intermediate results of computations within a time interval only. State or auxiliary variables may be classified as *sensors* by putting them into the set $\mathcal{S}$, these will be visible to the control program. On the other hand, the set $\mathcal{A}$ of *actuators* consists of those variables that can only be set by the controller.

The sets $\mathcal{E}^\circ$, $\mathcal{A}$, and $\mathcal{H}$ are assumed to be pairwise disjoint, while $\mathcal{S}$ is a subset of $\mathcal{E}^\circ \cup \mathcal{H}$. The interaction between the plant and the controller is defined by the interpretation of the predicate symbols in $\mathcal{S} \cup \mathcal{A}$, the values of the other predicate symbols are hidden from the controller. A program specifying a plant defines which interactions are possible, simply by the set of its models.

3.4   Stratification in Time

Next we impose some syntactical restrictions on programs, but without reducing their expressive power. We want to ensure that programs reflect the meaning of the different sorts of variables introduced by the signature, and to restrict the occurrence of recursion in order to obtain executable specifications.

Definition 6. Let $\Sigma = (\mathcal{E}^{\circ}, \mathcal{H}, \mathcal{A}; \mathcal{S})$ be a signature. A program P is called *Σ-stratified in time*, if it satisfies the following conditions.

- **(ST1)** $\text{DEF}_P(\mathcal{E}^{\circ})$ only consists of temporal clauses.
- **(ST2)** $\text{DEF}_P(\mathcal{H})$ consists of propositional clauses only, and contains no recursion[1].
- **(ST3)** $\text{DEF}_P(\mathcal{A})$ is empty.
- **(ST4)** None of the predicate symbols in $\mathcal{S}$ depends[1] on any of the predicate symbols in $\mathcal{A}$.

Stratification in time enforces that the different types of variables are used as intended. Recursion is prohibited within $\text{DEF}_P(\mathcal{H})$, the propositional part of the program, and therefore can only occur if at least one ∘-operator is involved. Furthermore, the plant cannot impose any restrictions on the interpretations for the actuators in $\mathcal{A}$, which can freely be set by the control program. And finally, the values of the sensors may not depend on the values of the actuators within the same state—this reflects the idea that sensors are supposed to provide information about the plant's current state. Changes of the actuators are assumed to take some time before they can take effect on the sensors again.

Besides, there is another problem to be addressed: since clauses may have negated heads, we can introduce potential contradictions when combining sets of clauses to programs, e.g. by writing $p \leftarrow \alpha$ and $\neg p \leftarrow \beta$ where $\alpha \wedge \beta$ is satisfiable. This undesirable property can be avoided by adding additional constraints.

In spite of all these restrictions, our specification language has been proven to be powerful enough to describe any complete finite automaton without marked states [15]. Actually, stratification in time enforces a *normal form* of programs similar to that presented in [9], and thus general programs can be rewritten equivalently as programs stratified in time. It would even be possible to allow past-time temporal operators in clause bodies, since they can be eliminated by adding some extra variables. Our simple propositional goals are also sufficient to specify any safety property [17].

Besides, programs stratified in time are *executable* [10] in the sense that they can easily be implemented in software or in hardware: because of the restricted use of recursion, there always exists a sequence of order, in which the values for the different variables can be computed successively without backtracking, in order to generate a model.

---

[1] P contains recursion if some predicate $p \in \Sigma$ depends on itself. p depends on q, if there is a propositional clause C in P such that p occurs in the head of C and q occurs in the body of C, or some symbol r depending on q occurs in the body of C.

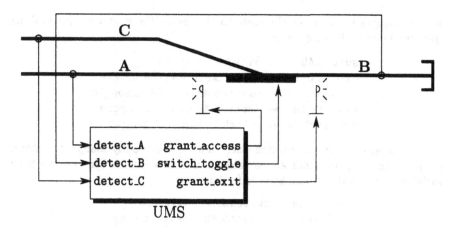

Figure1. A subway U-turn section.

4   An Example

In order to illustrate the benefits of our specification language, we will use it to specify an example adapted from an actual subway device[2]. At a terminus of a subway line, a special "U-turn" section allows trains to switch from one track to another and go back in the opposite direction. A U-turn section consists of three tracks **A**, **B**, **C**, and a switch (figure 1). Trains enter from track **A** and leave via track **C**. In order to transfer safely, they must wait for the switch to connect **A** with **B**, then move to **B** and wait again for the switch to connect **B** with **C** before leaving. Since several trains may move along the tracks, and the switch is not a safe mechanism, accidents may occur if two trains are on the same track, or if a train moves across the switch while it is badly positioned.

An automatic U-turn section management system (UMS) must drive the switch and manage the movement of trains through the section, avoiding accidents. The position of the switch can be controlled by means of an actuator called switch_toggle, and the movement of trains can be controlled by two actuators grant_access and grant_exit, corresponding to traffic lights. If grant_access is activated, a train on track **A** will move towards track **B**, while grant_exit will cause trains to leave track **B** in the opposite direction. Furthermore, the plant contains three sensors detect_A, detect_B, and detect_C, by which the controller can detect the presence of trains on the corresponding tracks.

In order to synthesize a program for the UMS, we specify the behaviour of the plant and the requirements by a program stratified in time and a goal. The plant consists of the switch and some trains. First, we specify the behaviour of the switch. Its state is represented by a state variable switch_AB $\in \mathcal{E}^\circ$, which is true if the switch connects **A** and **B**, and false if it connects **B** and **C**. The actuator

---

[2] A similar problem has been described in [23].

switch_toggle $\in \mathcal{A}$ causes the state to change by the next time interval, as specified by the following clauses:

$$
\begin{aligned}
\text{switch\_AB} \quad &\leftarrow \text{START} \\
\circ\, \text{switch\_AB} \quad &\leftarrow \text{switch\_AB} \land \neg\text{switch\_toggle} \\
\circ\, \neg\text{switch\_AB} \quad &\leftarrow \neg\text{switch\_AB} \land \neg\text{switch\_toggle} \\
\circ\, \text{switch\_AB} \quad &\leftarrow \neg\text{switch\_AB} \land \text{switch\_toggle} \\
\circ\, \neg\text{switch\_AB} \quad &\leftarrow \text{switch\_AB} \land \text{switch\_toggle}
\end{aligned}
$$

Trains can only cross the switch safely, if it is not currently changing its state, i.e. if switch_toggle is not active. This information is stored in two auxiliary variables stable_AB, stable_BC $\in \mathcal{H}$ for later use.

$$
\begin{aligned}
\text{stable\_AB} &\leftrightarrow \text{switch\_AB} \land \neg\text{switch\_toggle} \\
\text{stable\_BC} &\leftrightarrow \neg\text{switch\_AB} \land \neg\text{switch\_toggle}
\end{aligned}
$$

Here we used $L \leftrightarrow W$ as a shorthand for the two clauses $L \leftarrow W$ and $\neg L \leftarrow \neg W$.

Next, we have to model the behaviour of the trains involved. Trains can either be on one of the tracks **A**, **B**, or **C**, or they can be travelling *out*side of the U-turn section, or be *derailed* after crossing the switch unsafely. We will have to encode these five states using three state variables $p_0^i, p_1^i, p_2^i \in \mathcal{E}^\circ$, for each train i. But for the sake of readability, we will use variables pos^i over the five-valued range $\{\text{on\_A}, \text{on\_B}, \text{on\_C}, \text{out}, \text{derailed}\}$ instead. Programs using such multi-valued variables pose no problem, since they can automatically be transformed back into binary programs.

Using multi-valued variables, we thus specify the behaviour of each train i by means of the following clauses:

$$
\begin{aligned}
\text{pos}^i = \text{out} \quad &\leftarrow \text{START} \\
\circ\, \text{pos}^i = \text{out} \quad &\leftarrow \text{pos}^i = \text{out} \land \neg\text{enter}^i \\
\circ\, \text{pos}^i = \text{on\_A} \quad &\leftarrow \text{pos}^i = \text{out} \land \text{enter}^i \\
\circ\, \text{pos}^i = \text{on\_A} \quad &\leftarrow \text{pos}^i = \text{on\_A} \land \neg\text{grant\_access} \\
\circ\, \text{pos}^i = \text{on\_B} \quad &\leftarrow \text{pos}^i = \text{on\_A} \land \text{grant\_access} \land \text{stable\_AB} \land \neg\text{detect\_B} \\
\circ\, \text{pos}^i = \text{on\_B} \quad &\leftarrow \text{pos}^i = \text{on\_B} \land \neg\text{grant\_exit} \\
\circ\, \text{pos}^i = \text{on\_A} \quad &\leftarrow \text{pos}^i = \text{on\_B} \land \text{grant\_exit} \land \text{stable\_AB} \land \neg\text{detect\_A} \\
\circ\, \text{pos}^i = \text{on\_C} \quad &\leftarrow \text{pos}^i = \text{on\_B} \land \text{grant\_exit} \land \text{stable\_BC} \land \neg\text{detect\_C} \\
\circ\, \text{pos}^i = \text{out} \quad &\leftarrow \text{pos}^i = \text{on\_C}
\end{aligned}
$$

It should be noted that this specification is not completely deterministic. For example, we did not specify what happens if a train is on track **A** while access is granted, but without the switch being connected safely. In such a situation, the train's state may change arbitrarily—in particular, it may become **derailed**, and therefore the UMS will have to avoid such situations.

The auxiliary variables enter^i introduce another nondeterministic choice: trains travelling outside the U-turn section may enter at any time, but we assume that two trains never enter simultaneously, and that there always is at least one time interval between the arrival of two trains. Without such assumptions, the UMS will have no chance to avoid collisions. In order to specify the assumptions, we restrict the possible values of enter^i by means of the following clauses.

$$\neg\texttt{enter}^1 \qquad \leftarrow \texttt{just\_entered}$$
$$\neg\texttt{enter}^2 \qquad \leftarrow \texttt{enter}^1 \vee \texttt{just\_entered}$$
$$\circ\,\texttt{just\_entered} \leftarrow \texttt{enter}^1 \vee \texttt{enter}^2$$

For the sake of simplicity, we restrict ourselves to a total of two trains here.

Next, we have to specify the behaviour of the three sensors, which become true if and only if there is a train on the corresponding track. If we still restrict ourselves to two trains, this is easily achieved by the following clauses.

$$\texttt{detect\_}X \leftrightarrow \texttt{pos}^1 = \texttt{on\_}X \vee \texttt{pos}^2 = \texttt{on\_}X \qquad \text{for each } X \in \{\texttt{A},\texttt{B},\texttt{C}\}$$

Finally, we have to specify the requirements to be enforced by the controller. Firstly, trains may never derail, i.e. assume the state **derailed**, and secondly, the UMS must ensure that each track **A**, **B**, and **C** is occupied by at most one train at any time. These properties are expressed by the following simple goals.

$$\leftarrow \neg\texttt{pos}^1 = \texttt{derailed} \wedge \neg\texttt{pos}^2 = \texttt{derailed}$$
$$\leftarrow \neg(\texttt{pos}^1 = \texttt{on\_}X \wedge \texttt{pos}^2 = \texttt{on\_}X) \qquad \text{for each } X \in \{\texttt{A},\texttt{B},\texttt{C}\}$$

We also have to specify that every train entering track **A** eventually reaches track **C**. Such a constraint usually is expressed as a *liveness* condition, which, unfortunately, is not yet possible with our formalism. But in most cases it is not sufficient, that the train arrives "eventually", usually the system will have to obey *real-time constraints*. Therefore, we will specify that a train entering track **A** reaches **C** within at most 7 time intervals.

In order to achieve this, we add to each train i a timer $\texttt{time}^i$, which starts counting when the train enters track **A**, and is reset when it reaches **C**. This counter can attain values from 0 to 7, and has to be mapped to three boolean variables in the same fashion as the $\texttt{pos}^i$ variables above.

$$\texttt{time}^i = 0 \qquad \leftarrow \textsc{Start}$$
$$\circ\,\texttt{time}^i = 0 \qquad \leftarrow \texttt{time}^i = 0 \wedge \neg\texttt{pos}^i = \texttt{on\_A}$$
$$\circ\,\texttt{time}^i = 1 \qquad \leftarrow \texttt{time}^i = 0 \wedge \texttt{pos}^i = \texttt{on\_A}$$
$$\circ\,\texttt{time}^i = k+1 \leftarrow \texttt{time}^i = k \wedge \neg\texttt{pos}^i = \texttt{on\_C} \quad \text{for each } k,\, 0 < k < 7$$
$$\circ\,\texttt{time}^i = 0 \qquad \leftarrow \texttt{pos}^i = \texttt{on\_C}$$

Now we only have to require that no counter ever reaches the critical value 7.

$$\leftarrow \neg\texttt{time}^1 = 7 \wedge \neg\texttt{time}^2 = 7$$

This completes the specification of our control problem. The above clauses can be used as input for our synthesis algorithm in order to generate a correct control program. Our present implementation produced the following output:

$$\texttt{grant\_access} \leftrightarrow \texttt{detect\_A} \wedge \neg\texttt{detect\_B} \wedge \texttt{switch\_AB}$$
$$\texttt{grant\_exit} \leftrightarrow \texttt{detect\_B} \wedge \neg\texttt{switch\_AB}$$
$$\texttt{switch\_toggle} \leftrightarrow \neg\texttt{detect\_B} \wedge \texttt{detect\_A} \wedge \neg\texttt{switch\_AB} \vee$$
$$\texttt{detect\_B} \wedge \texttt{switch\_AB}$$

These automatically generated equations show exactly, how a correct control program has to set its actuators. Given this information, a correct UMS can easily be implemented. As a side note, it is revealed that the sensor **detect_C** is not required to solve this control problem.

5   Control Program Synthesis

In this section, we will show how actually to solve *control problems* without liveness requirements. We consider control problems $(P, \leftarrow \alpha)$, consisting of a Σ-stratified program P specifying a plant and a goal $\leftarrow \alpha$ describing the safety requirements to be enforced.

In this paper, we restrict our attention to signatures $\Sigma = (\mathcal{E}^\circ, \mathcal{H}, \mathcal{A}; \mathcal{E}^\circ)$, i.e. we only consider the case $\mathcal{S} = \mathcal{E}^\circ$. This means that the input to the control program consists of the entire state of the plant—the control program is *"omniscient"* in the sense that it always knows exactly what is going on in the plant. The more general case of *partial observations*, i.e. $\mathcal{S} \subseteq \mathcal{E}^\circ$, has been studied in [15]. Yet, the genuine and simple solution for the controller synthesis problem presented below provides the base for all further results.

5.1   Finite State Representation

So far, we have considered specifications as logic formulas. On the other hand, reactive systems are often described by means of their *state transition relations*—this representation also will turn out useful for our synthesis algorithm. Given the semantics of formulas, such state transition relations can be easily extracted from any program.

All we have to do is to use the set $2^{\mathcal{E}^\circ}$, i.e. the set of all truth assignments for the program's state symbols, as the state set, and the set $2^{\mathcal{A}}$, i.e. the set of all actuator valuations, as a set of actions. This yields the following definition for the state transition relations of a program:

Definition 7. Let $\Sigma = (\mathcal{E}^\circ, \mathcal{H}, \mathcal{A}; \mathcal{S})$ be a signature, and let P be a Σ-stratified program. Then we define the set of *potential initial states* of P by

$$\text{INIT}_P = \{\, I^\circ \subseteq \mathcal{E}^\circ \mid I^\circ(L) = 1 \text{ for all clauses } L \leftarrow \text{START in } P \,\}.$$

For a state $I^\mathcal{E} \subseteq \mathcal{E}^\circ \cup \mathcal{A}$, we define the set of *potential successor states* of $I^\mathcal{E}$,

$$\text{SUCC}_P(I^\mathcal{E}) = \{\, I^\circ \subseteq \mathcal{E}^\circ \mid$$

There exists a state $I \subseteq \Sigma$, such that $I \geq I^\mathcal{E}$, $I \models \text{DEF}_P(\mathcal{H})$, and for every clause $\circ L \leftarrow W$ in P with $I(W) = 1$ we have $I^\circ(L) = 1.\,\}$.

Given these definitions, it is straightforward to see that any program directly corresponds to a finite automaton with state set $2^{\mathcal{E}^\circ}$ and input alphabet $2^{\mathcal{A}}$. Then the function SUCC_P represents the automaton's state transition relation, and INIT_P its initial states.

Conversely, it is possible to prove that every finite automaton can be represented by means of a program stratified in time [15]. Thus, our specification language, although quite simple, is sufficient to specify any finite state control problem, as long as no liveness properties are involved.

5.2 Input/Output Assignments

Let us consider a Σ-stratified control problem[3] for a signature $\Sigma = (\mathcal{E}^\circ, \mathcal{H}, \mathcal{A}; \mathcal{E}^\circ)$. The task of the control program consists of finding an assignment $I^{\mathcal{A}} \subseteq \mathcal{A}$ of the actuators for every state $I^\circ \subseteq \mathcal{E}^\circ$ of the plant, such that these outputs force the plant to fulfil the requirements α in the current state and in every potential successor state.

In general, this will not be possible in every state $I^\circ \subseteq \mathcal{E}^\circ$. Therefore, we are interested in finding sets X of pairs $(I^\circ, I^{\mathcal{A}}) \in 2^{\mathcal{E}^\circ} \times 2^{\mathcal{A}}$, for which the requirements can be enforced. Arbitrary relations $X \subseteq 2^{\mathcal{E}^\circ} \times 2^{\mathcal{A}}$ are called *input/output assignments*. If we write $\mathcal{E} = \mathcal{E}^\circ \cup \mathcal{A}$, we can equivalently represent an input/output assignment by a subset $X \subseteq 2^{\mathcal{E}}$, or an element $X \in 2^{2^{\mathcal{E}}}$.

We are interested in particular input/output assignments, where all combinations of inputs and outputs contained ensure the fulfilment of the requirements. Such input/output assignments are called *secure* and are defined as follows.

Definition 8. Let $\Sigma = (\mathcal{E}^\circ, \mathcal{H}, \mathcal{A}; \mathcal{E}^\circ)$ be a signature, let $\mathcal{E} = \mathcal{E}^\circ \cup \mathcal{A}$, and let $(P, \leftarrow \alpha)$ be a Σ-stratified control problem. A set $X \subseteq 2^{\mathcal{E}}$ is called *secure input/output assignment* for $(P, \leftarrow \alpha)$, if every state $I^{\mathcal{E}} \in X$ satisfies the following properties.

> **(SI1)** for every state $I \geq I^{\mathcal{E}}$ such that $I \models \mathrm{DEF}_P(\mathcal{H})$ we also have $I \models \alpha$.
> **(SI2)** $\mathrm{SUCC}_P(I^{\mathcal{E}}) \in X|_{\mathcal{E}^\circ}$.

Condition (SI1) ensures that all states contained in a secure input/output assignment X meet the safety property stated by the goal $\leftarrow \alpha$. Condition (SI2) requires that no state in X has potential successor states not belonging to X, which might violate the requirements. Every solution to the controller synthesis problem corresponds to a secure input/output assignment.

5.3 The Fixpoint Iteration

Not every secure input/output assignment yields an interesting control program. For example, the empty set always is secure according to the definition. Therefore we need some concept of *maximal* secure input/output assignments.

At this point, we introduce our fixpoint iteration. Its basic idea consists of successively deleting from the set of all states satisfying the safety requirements all those states which may lead to an unsafe successor state, until eventually a secure input/output assignment is found. The iteration begins with the set of valid states, defined as follows.

Definition 9. Let $\Sigma = (\mathcal{E}^\circ, \mathcal{H}, \mathcal{A}; \mathcal{E}^\circ)$ be a signature, let $\mathcal{E} = \mathcal{E}^\circ \cup \mathcal{A}$, and let $(P, \leftarrow \alpha)$ be a Σ-stratified control problem. Then we define the set of *valid states* for $(P, \leftarrow \alpha)$ as

$$\mathrm{SAFE}_{(P, \leftarrow \alpha)} = \{\, I^{\mathcal{E}} \subseteq \mathcal{E} \mid \text{for all } I \geq I^{\mathcal{E}} \text{ with } I \models \mathrm{DEF}_P(\mathcal{H}) \text{ we have } I \models \alpha. \,\}.$$

---

[3] A control problem $(P, \leftarrow \alpha)$ is called Σ-stratified, if P has this property.

Thus, $\text{SAFE}_{(P,\leftarrow\alpha)}$ represents the set of states satisfying condition (SI1) in definition 8. It may happen that some of these states have successor states not belonging to $\text{SAFE}_{(P,\leftarrow\alpha)}$, i.e. violating condition (SI2). These are successively eliminated by the iteration procedure, which is defined by the following operator.

Definition 10. Let $\Sigma = (\mathcal{E}^\circ, \mathcal{H}, \mathcal{A}; \mathcal{E}^\circ)$ be a signature, let $\mathcal{E} = \mathcal{E}^\circ \cup \mathcal{A}$, and let P be a Σ-stratified program. Then we define the operator $\Theta_P \colon 2^{2^{\mathcal{E}}} \to 2^{2^{\mathcal{E}}}$ associated to P as

$$\Theta_P(X) = \{\, I^{\mathcal{E}} \in X \mid \text{SUCC}_P(I^{\mathcal{E}}) \subseteq X|_{\mathcal{E}^\circ} \,\}. \tag{1}$$

For each input/output assignment X, $\Theta_P(X)$ describes the set of those states in X of which all potential successor states can be extended to states in X. Therefore $\Theta_P(X)$ is called the set of *secure states with respect to X*. In some sense, the application of this operator corresponds to condition (SI2) in definition 8, which requires that all successors of states belonging to a secure input/output assignment X can be extended to states in X.

In order to combine the conditions (SI1) and (SI2) represented by the formal concepts of $\text{SAFE}_{(P,\leftarrow\alpha)}$ and Θ_P, we will consider the iteration of the operator

$$\Theta_{(P,\leftarrow\alpha)} \colon 2^{2^{\mathcal{E}}} \to 2^{2^{\mathcal{E}}}; \quad X \mapsto \Theta_P(X) \cap \text{SAFE}_{(P,\leftarrow\alpha)}. \tag{2}$$

This definition ensures that all states in $\Theta_{(P,\leftarrow\alpha)}(X)$ satisfy condition (SI1), for any input/output assignment X. Thus, a subset $X \subseteq 2^{\mathcal{E}}$ is a secure input/output assignment for $(P, \leftarrow\alpha)$, if and only if X is a fixpoint of $\Theta_{(P,\leftarrow\alpha)}$, i.e. if $\Theta_{(P,\leftarrow\alpha)}(X) = X$.

It is easy to prove that Θ_P and $\Theta_{(P,\leftarrow\alpha)}$ are monotonic[4] functions over the complete lattice $2^{2^{\mathcal{E}}}$. But then, by the classical results of Tarski [24], $\Theta_{(P,\leftarrow\alpha)}$ has a greatest fixpoint, which also is the greatest secure input/output assignment for $(P, \leftarrow\alpha)$.

Theorem 1. Let $\Sigma = (\mathcal{E}^\circ, \mathcal{H}, \mathcal{A}; \mathcal{E}^\circ)$ be a signature, let $\mathcal{E} = \mathcal{E}^\circ \cup \mathcal{A}$, and let $(P, \leftarrow\alpha)$ be a Σ-stratified control problem. Then the function $\Theta_{(P,\leftarrow\alpha)}$ has a greatest fixpoint $\hat{H}_{(P,\leftarrow\alpha)}$ which can be characterized as follows.

$$\hat{H}_{(P,\leftarrow\alpha)} = \text{gfp}\,\Theta_{(P,\leftarrow\alpha)} \tag{3}$$
$$= \text{lub}\,\{\, X \subseteq 2^{\mathcal{E}} \mid X \text{ is a secure input/output assignment for } (P, \leftarrow\alpha). \}$$

Thus $\hat{H}_{(P,\leftarrow\alpha)}$, the greatest fixpoint of $\Theta_{(P,\leftarrow\alpha)}$, is the union of all secure input/output assignments for $(P, \leftarrow\alpha)$ and therefore represents the *most general* secure input/output assignment. Hence, $\hat{H}_{(P,\leftarrow\alpha)}$ describes the most general solution for the control problem in the sense that it includes any combination of inputs and outputs, which may be produced by some correct control program.

Furthermore, we observe that the set $\mathcal{E}$ is finite, and thus this fixpoint of $\Theta_{(P,\leftarrow\alpha)}$ can be computed by a finite iteration.

---

[4] $F \colon 2^A \to 2^B$ is called monotonic, if $x \subseteq y$ always implies $F(x) \subseteq F(y)$.

Theorem 2. *Let $\Sigma = (\mathcal{E}^\circ, \mathcal{H}, \mathcal{A}; \mathcal{E}^\circ)$ be a signature, let $\mathcal{E} = \mathcal{E}^\circ \cup \mathcal{A}$, and let $(P, \leftarrow \alpha)$ be a Σ-stratified control problem. Then the greatest fixpoint $\hat{H}_{(P, \leftarrow \alpha)}$ of $\Theta_{(P, \leftarrow \alpha)}$ can be expressed as*

$$\hat{H}_{(P, \leftarrow \alpha)} = \Theta^n_{(P, \leftarrow \alpha)}(2^\mathcal{E}), \text{ for some } n \in \mathbb{N}. \tag{4}$$

This result provides the basis for all algorithms computing solutions of control problems. It shows that the most general solution for a control problem can be computed within a finite number of iteration steps, and therefore can be used to derive correct implementations of the control program.

5.4 Solvability

In this section we will examine the relation between the most general input/output assignment introduced above and the existence of solutions to control problems more closely. First, we have to clarify our notion of a solution.

Definition 11. *Let $\Sigma = (\mathcal{E}^\circ, \mathcal{H}, \mathcal{A}; \mathcal{S})$ be a signature, and let $(P, \leftarrow \alpha)$ be a Σ-stratified control problem. $(P, \leftarrow \alpha)$ is called* solvable *if there exists a signature $\Sigma^C = (\mathcal{E}^C, \mathcal{H}^C \cup \mathcal{A}, \mathcal{S}; \emptyset)$, where $\Sigma \cap \Sigma^C = \mathcal{S} \cup \mathcal{A}$, and a Σ^C-stratified program C, such that $P \cup C \models \alpha$.*

Under these circumstances, C is called a *correct controller* for $(P, \leftarrow \alpha)$, or a *solution* of the control problem. We did not use a signature $\Sigma^C = (\mathcal{E}^C, \mathcal{H}^C, \mathcal{S}; \mathcal{A})$ for the control program, because the outputs $\mathcal{A}$ of this program must depend directly on its inputs $\mathcal{S}$, and thus the control program would violate condition (ST4) for a Σ^C-stratified program.

We are interested in decidable criteria for the solvability of control problems and in some means of computing their solutions. For the case $\mathcal{S} = \mathcal{E}^\circ$ considered here, we obtain a surprisingly simple result: a control problem $(P, \leftarrow \alpha)$ is solvable if and only if every potential initial state of P is covered by the most general secure input/output assignment for $(P, \leftarrow \alpha)$.

Theorem 3. *Let $\Sigma = (\mathcal{E}^\circ, \mathcal{H}, \mathcal{A}; \mathcal{E}^\circ)$ be a signature, and let $(P, \leftarrow \alpha)$ be a Σ-stratified control problem. Then $(P, \leftarrow \alpha)$ is solvable, iff $\text{INIT}_P \subseteq \hat{H}_{(P, \leftarrow \alpha)}|_{\mathcal{E}^\circ}$.*

Thus, in order to check whether a control problem $(P, \leftarrow \alpha)$ is solvable, it suffices to compute the greatest fixpoint $\hat{H}_{(P, \leftarrow \alpha)}$ of $\Theta_{(P, \leftarrow \alpha)}$ and check whether it covers every potential initial state of P. Since this fixpoint can be computed within a finite number of iterations, solvability turns out to be a decidable condition. Moreover, if $(P, \leftarrow \alpha)$ is solvable, the greatest fixpoint $\hat{H}_{(P, \leftarrow \alpha)}$ characterizes the *most general* solution of the control problem.

Example 1. In the U-turn example of section 4, the final fixpoint $\hat{H}$ contains states as follows.

$\hat{H} = \{ \, \{\text{grant\_access}, \text{detect\_A}, \neg\text{detect\_B}, \text{switch\_AB}\},$
$\qquad \{\neg\text{grant\_access}, \neg\text{detect\_A}\}, \{\neg\text{grant\_access}, \text{detect\_B}\},$
$\qquad \{\neg\text{grant\_access}, \neg\text{switch\_AB}\}, \{\text{grant\_exit}, \text{detect\_B}, \neg\text{switch\_AB}\},$
$\qquad \{\neg\text{grant\_exit}, \neg\text{detect\_B}\}, \{\neg\text{grant\_exit}, \text{switch\_AB}\}, \dots \, \}.$

In this list, we have omitted "don't care" variables in states, thus any listed truth assigment represents all the more special truth assignments which assign some value to the variables not mentioned.

Now, such an input/output assignment $\hat{H}$ can easily be transformed into an equivalent set P of propositional clauses such that every state in $\hat{H}$ corresponds to a model for P—it suffices to restate the conditions implied by membership in $\hat{H}$ in an appropriate clausal form.

More precisely, we consider for each actuator a and each truth assignment $I \subseteq \Sigma \setminus \{a\}$ of the other variables, the valuations $I_a = I \cup \{a\}$ and $I_{\neg a} = I \cup \{\neg a\}$, which extend I to interpret a. Apparently, there are four possible cases: (1) $I_a \in \hat{H}$ but $I_{\neg a} \notin \hat{H}$, (2) $I_{\neg a} \in \hat{H}$ but $I_a \notin \hat{H}$, (3) both $I_a, I_{\neg a} \in \hat{H}$, or (4) both $I_a, I_{\neg a} \notin \hat{H}$. In the last two cases we have nothing to do; in the first two cases we must ensure that the value of a always has a certain value in presence of I. Therefore we construct a clause $a \leftarrow W_I$ or $\neg a \leftarrow W_I$, respectively, where W_I is the conjunction of the literals interpreted as *true* by I. Boolean simplification of these clauses yields a program as shown at the end of section 4.

In general, it will turn out that actuators depend on each other in the final solution. In this case, we choose any sequence of order for generating definitions of the actuators, and allow clause bodies to contain actuators occurring in the heads of clauses generated earlier.

The most general solution $\hat{H}_{(P,\leftarrow\alpha)}$ obtained from the iteration procedure may be highly non-deterministic, since it may allow several different combinations of actuator values for the same input. But a deterministic solution can easily be obtained by choosing one of the possible outputs in such cases. It is possible to apply different strategies of choice in order to obtain smaller or better control programs. Actually, the program shown as a solution of our example has been obtained from the most general solution by careful application of such choice criteria.

When implementing the computation of $\hat{H}_{(P,\leftarrow\alpha)}$ and when deriving the final control program, it is not wise to represent input/output assignments as sets, as the above discussion may suggest. In our implementation, we represented state sets *symbolically*, using *Ordered Binary Decision Diagrams (OBDD)* [5]. Using such techniques, our fixpoint iteration can be implemented efficiently. Although the general synthesis problem is known to be in *NP*, OBDD-based representations often remain small, and the iteration procedure behaves well in many practical applications. The solution for the U-turn section example is computed within one second (on a Pentium processor with 133 MHz), and we have successfully solved control problems with more than 10^{30} states.

6   Related Work

Several researchers have addressed the synthesis problem using techniques of *temporal logic theorem proving* [8, 18, 21]. These approaches aim at explicitly constructing a model, i.e. an automaton or a tableau, from a temporal logic specification of the problem to be solved. This model then is interpreted as the desired control program. Our approach appears to be more efficient, since we can use symbolic state space representations and thus avoid explicit model construction.

Ramadge and Wonham suggest a different approach, constructing the control program directly from the specification by means of a fixpoint iteration [4, 22]. Their theory of *supervisory control* provides some basic results on the existence of synthesis algorithms. Our present paper shows how these language-theoretic results can be applied to specifications written in temporal logic. The *supremal controllable language* [25] can be proven to be equivalent to our maximal secure input/output relation, provided that one recasts their asynchronous discrete event systems into our synchronous framework.

The results of supervisory control theory have also been applied to specifications written in the synchronous data-flow language SIGNAL [7], yielding similar results as those presented in this paper. Yet, our approach appears to be simpler, since it is independent from the three-valued logics in SIGNAL and only relies on plain propositional logics.

7 Conclusion

We have proposed an approach to the formal specification and automated synthesis of control programs for finite-state reactive systems: reactive systems can be specified in a purely declarative way, firstly by specifying the behaviour of their environment as a program stratified in time, i.e. a set of PROLOG-like program clauses, and secondly by specifying a safety property to be enforced within this environment as a propositional formula. For a control problem specified by a program stratified in time and a desired safety property, it is decidable whether there exists a solution. We have presented an algorithm based on a fixpoint iteration over the set of all possible control programs, computing a correct solution provided that one exists.

Presently, we are investigating techniques of making our synthesis algorithms more efficient, in order to solve even more complex control problems. We also are exploring possible extensions of control program behaviour to be synthesized, in particular the synthesis of control programs satisfying *liveness* requirements, also under the assumption of *fairness* properties of the plant; some further results on the treatment of *partial observations* are already available [15].

References

1. Burch, J. R., Clarke, E. M., McMillan, K. L.: *Symbolic model checking:* 10^{20} *states and beyond.* Information and Computing **98** (2), 142–170, 1992.
2. Burch, J. R., Clarke, E. M., Long, D. E., McMillan, K. E., Dill, D. L.: *Symbolic model checking for sequential circuit verification.* IEEE Transactions on Computer-Aided Design of Integrated Circuits and systems **13** (4), 1994.

3. Benveniste, A., Berry, G.: *The synchronous approach to reactive and real-time systems.* Proc. IEEE **79** (9), 1270–1282, 1991.
4. Balemi, S., Hoffmann, G. J., Gyugyi, P., Wong-Toi, H., Franklin, G. F.: *Supervisory control of a rapid thermal multiprocessor.* IEEE Transactions on Automatic Control **38** (7), 1040–1059, 1993.
5. Bryant, R. E.: *Graph-based algorithms for boolean function manipulation.* IEEE Trans. Comp. **35** (8), 677–691, 1986.
6. Clarke, E. M., Emerson, E. A., Sistla, A. P.: *Automatic verification of finite-state concurrent systems using temporal logic specifications.* ACM Transactions on Programming Languages and Systems **8** (2), 244–263, 1986.
7. Dutertre, B., Le Borgne, M.: *Control of polynomial dynamical systems: an example.* Tech. Report 2193, INRIA, 1994.
8. Emerson, E. A., Clarke, E. M.: *Using branching time temporal logic to synthesize synchronization skeletons.* Science of Computer Programming **2**, 241–266, 1982.
9. Fisher, M.: *A normal form for first-order temporal formulae.* Proc. 9th International Conference in Automated Deduction, CADE-9, 371–384, Springer, 1992.
10. Fisher, M., Owens, R.: *An introduction to executable modal and temporal logics.* Proc. IJCAI Workshop on Executable Modal and Temporal Logics, 1–20, Springer, 1993.
11. Halbwachs, N.: *Synchronous Programming of Reactive Systems.* Kluwer, 1993.
12. Harel, D., Pnueli, A.: *On the development of reactive systems.* In: *Logics and Models of Concurrent Systems,* ed. K. R. Apt, NATO ASI Series, vol. 13, 477–498, Springer, 1985.
13. Lloyd, J. W.: *Foundations of Logic Programming.* Springer, 1984.
14. Malik, R., Mayer, O.: *Eine Fixpunkt-Semantik für temporal stratifizierte Programme.* Interner Bericht, FB Informatik, Universität Kaiserslautern, 1994.
15. Malik, R.: *Automatische Synthese diskreter Steuerungen aus logischen Spezifikationen.* Shaker Verlag, Aachen, 1998; also available as: Dissertation, FB Informatik, Universität Kaiserslautern, 1997.
16. Manna, Z., Pnueli, A.: *The Temporal Logic of Reactive and Concurrent Systems — Specification.* Springer 1992.
17. Manna, Z., Pnueli, A.: *Temporal Verification of Reactive Systems — Safety.* Springer, 1995.
18. Manna, Z., Wolper, P.: *Synthesis of communicating processes from temporal logic specifications.* Proc. Logics of Programs, 253–281, 1981.
19. McMillan, K. L.: *Symbolic Model Checking.* Kluwer, 1993.
20. Ostroff, J.: *Temporal logic for real-time systems.* Research Studies Press Ltd., Advanced Software Development Series, Taunton, Somerset, 1989.
21. Pnueli, A., Rosner, R.: *On the synthesis of a reactive module.* Proc. 16th ACM Symp. on Principles of Programming Languages POPL '89, 1989.
22. Ramadge, P. J. G., Wonham, W. M.: *The control of discrete event systems.* Proc. IEEE **77** (1), 81–98, 1989.
23. Ratel, C., Halbwachs, N., Raymond, P.: *Programming and verifying critical systems by means of the synchronous data-flow language Lustre.* Software Engineering Notes **16** (5), 112–119, 1991.
24. Tarski, A.: *A lattice-theoretical fixpoint theorem and its applications.* Pacific J. Math. **5**, 285–309, 1955.
25. Wonham, W. M., Ramadge, P. J.: *On the supremal controllable sublanguage of a given language.* SIAM J. Control and Optimization **25** (3), 637–650, 1987.

A Proof Environment for the Development of Group Communication Systems

Christoph Kreitz, Mark Hayden, and Jason Hickey

Department of Computer Science, Cornell University
Ithaca, NY 14853-7501, U.S.A.
{kreitz,hayden,jyh}@cs.cornell.edu

Abstract. We present a theorem proving environment for the development of reliable and efficient group communication systems. Our approach makes methods of automated deduction applicable to the implementation of real-world systems by linking the ENSEMBLE group communication toolkit to the NuPRL proof development system.
We present tools for importing ENSEMBLE's code into NuPRL and exporting it back into the programming environment. We discuss techniques for reasoning about critical properties of ENSEMBLE as well as verified strategies for reconfiguring the ENSEMBLE system in order to improve its performance in concrete applications.

1   Introduction

Group communication via computer networks is used in a wide range of applications [3]. Over the past years the development of a secure and reliable communications infrastructure has become increasingly important. But the current networks are inadequate to support safety-critical applications because considerable technical challenges have not been overcome yet.

First, there is the *performance cost* of modularity. To maximize clarity and code re-use, systems are divided into clean modules, which are designed to operate in a broad number of environments. But when modules are combined in a restricted context, much of the code becomes useless or redundant, leading to unnecessary large execution times. Secondly, there is the *secure implementation problem*: designing and correctly implementing distributed systems is notoriously difficult [3,5]. While in principle it is possible to prove the correctness of theoretical algorithms [19,18,1,20] it is very difficult to transform these idealizations into implementations that can actually be used in real systems. Finally, the *formalization barrier* prevents formal tools for checking software correctness from being used to maximum benefit. These tools are computationally costly and difficult to understand; even well understood type checking algorithms are often viewed as expensive. Few of these tools are integrated into software development environments, nor can they be flexibly and interactively invoked.

C. Kirchner and H. Kirchner (Eds.): Automated Deduction, CADE-15
LNAI 1421, pp. 317–332, 1998. © Springer–Verlag Berlin Heidelberg 1998

In this paper we address these problems by showing how to make methods of automated deduction applicable to the implementation of a real-world system. Our approach links ENSEMBLE [11], a flexible group communication toolkit, to NuPRL [6], a proof system for mathematical reasoning about programs and for rewriting them into equivalent, but more efficient ones.

Because of the similarity between the core of OCAML [16], the implementation language of ENSEMBLE, and *Type Theory*, the logical language of NuPRL, we were able to translate the complete implementation of ENSEMBLE into NuPRL-terms and to apply proof tactics and verified program transformations to the *actual ENSEMBLE code*. This makes it possible to verify critical system properties and to improve its performance in particular applications. NuPRL thus becomes a *logical* programming environment for ENSEMBLE whose capabilities go beyond the usual type-checking and syntactical debugging capabilities of OCAML. It will eventually provide the software development infrastructure and a design methodology for constructing reliable and efficient group communication systems.

In Section 2 we will present the architecture of the logical programming environment, including a brief overview of ENSEMBLE and NuPRL. In Section 3 we describe the representation of the relevant subset of OCAML in Type Theory as well as the tools for importing ENSEMBLE's code into NuPRL and exporting it back into the OCAML environment. In Section 4 we discuss techniques for verifying system properties and in Section 5 we describe proof and rewrite tactics for a verified reconfiguration of ENSEMBLE in a given application-specific context.

2   Architecture of the Logical Programming Environment

The ENSEMBLE toolkit is the third generation of a series of group communication systems that aim at securing critical networked applications. The first system, ISIS [4], became one of the first widely adopted technologies in this area and found its way into Stock Exchanges, Air Traffic Control Systems, and other safety-critical applications. The architecture of HORUS [21], a modular redesign of ISIS, is based on stacking *protocol layers*, which can be combined almost arbitrarily to match the needs of a particular application. Despite its flexibility, HORUS is even faster than ISIS, as the efficiency of its protocol stacks can be improved by analyzing common sequences of operation and reconfiguring the system code accordingly.

However, reconfiguring HORUS protocol stacks is difficult and error prone because its layers are written in C and they are too complex to reason about. Concerns about the reliability of such a technology base for truly secure networked applications led to the implementation of ENSEMBLE [11,12], which is based on HORUS but coded almost entirely in the high-level programming language OCAML [16], a member of the ML [9] language family with a clean semantics. Due to the use of ML, ENSEMBLE turned out to be one of the most scalable and portable, but also one of the fastest existing reliable multicast systems. One of the main reasons for choosing OCAML, however, was to enable formal reasoning about ENSEMBLE's code within a theorem proving environment and to use deduction techniques for reconfiguring the system and verifying its properties.

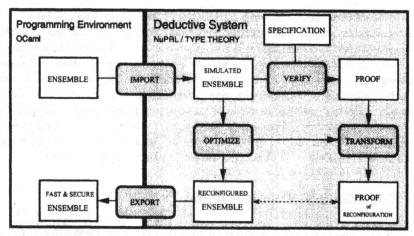

Fig. 1. Verifying and reconfiguring communication systems in NuPRL

Conceptually, each protocol stack is a finite IO-automaton, which could be handled by propositional methods. But reasoning about the *actual* ENSEMBLE *code* requires a theorem proving environment that is capable of expressing the semantics of a real programming language and establishing a correspondence between the implementation of a protocol stack and its formal model.

The NuPRL proof development system [6] is a framework for mathematical reasoning about programs and secure program transformations. Proof strategies, or *tactics*, can be tailored to follow the particular style of reasoning in distributed systems. Tactics also produce (possibly partial) proof objects, which can be used as documentation or reveal valuable debugging information if a verification did *not* succeed. Performance improvements can be achieved by applying *rewrite tactics*, which reconfigure the protocol stack for a particular application.

Because of its expressive formal calculus, NuPRL is well suited for building a reasoning environment for ENSEMBLE. NuPRL's *Type Theory* includes formalizations of the fundamental concepts of mathematics, programming, and data types. It also contains a functional programming language that corresponds to the core of ML. The NuPRL system supports interactive and semi-automatic formal reasoning, conservative language extensions by user-defined concepts, the evaluation of programs, and an extendable library of verified knowledge from various domains. These features make it possible to represent the code of ENSEMBLE and its specifications as terms of NuPRL's formal language and to use NuPRL as a *logical programming environment* (LPE) for ENSEMBLE.

Figure 1 illustrates our methodology for developing efficient and secure communication systems with the logical programming environment. In the first step a well-structured ENSEMBLE protocol stack is be imported into the system, i.e. converted into NuPRL-terms. We can then apply verification tactics to prove critical protocol properties and system invariants. We can also apply optimization tactics to create a fast-track reconfiguration of the protocol stack that is guaranteed to have the same behavior as the original one. We can also prove this fact formally and transform a verification of the original system into one of the reconfigured stack. The latter is then exported back into the programming environment and used as improved and secured part of the application system.

Using this methodology we are able to address the three above-mentioned challenges. By building an environment that treats the actual ENSEMBLE code, we substantially lower the formalization barrier. By providing tactics for reasoning about system properties we address the secure implementation problem. The performance costs of a protocol stack is drastically reduced by applying reconfiguration strategies and exporting their results into the OCAML environment. In the rest of this paper we shall discuss each of these aspects separately.

3 Embedding System Code into NuPRL

In order to enable formal reasoning about the code of an ENSEMBLE protocol stack, we have to convert OCAML programs into terms of the logical language of NuPRL that capture the semantics of these programs and vice versa. For this purpose we have provided a *type-theoretical semantics* for the programming language OCAML that is faithful with respect to the OCAML compiler and manual [16]. We have limited our formalization to the subset of OCAML that is used in the implementation of finite state-event systems like ENSEMBLE, i.e. the functional subset with simple imperative features. By doing this we avoided having to deal with aspects of the language that do not occur when reasoning about protocol stacks but cause unnecessary complications in a rigorous formalization.

We have "implemented" this formalization using NuPRL's definition mechanism: each OCAML language construct is represented by a new NuPRL term that is defined to have the formal semantics of this construct. This *abstraction* is coupled with a *display form*, which makes sure that the formal representation has the same outer appearance as the original code. Thus a NuPRL term represents both the program text of an OCAML program and its formal semantics. Furthermore, the well-formedness and soundness of the new terms with respect to the rest of type theory is proved in separate theorem to make sure that such issues can be handled automatically during verifications and reconfigurations.

We have also developed a formal programming logic for OCAML by describing rules for reasoning about OCAML constructs and rules for symbolically evaluating them. The rules were implemented as NuPRL tactics and are therefore correct with respect to the type-theoretical semantics of OCAML.

Finally, we have created tools that convert OCAML programs into their formal NuPRL representations and store them as objects of NuPRL's library. These tools are necessary to make the actual OCAML-code of an ENSEMBLE protocol stack available for formal reasoning within NuPRL and to keep track of modifications in ENSEMBLE's implementation.

As a result, formal reasoning within NuPRL can now be performed at the level of OCAML programs instead of type theory. All terms representing OCAML programs are displayed in OCAML syntax and individual reasoning and program transformation steps will always preserve the "OCAML-ness" of the terms they are dealing with. This enables system experts who are not necessarily logicians to formally reason about OCAML-programs without having to understand the peculiarities of the underlying theorem proving environment.

In the rest of this section we briefly describe the formalization of OCAML and the tools that translate between OCAML programs and their formal representations. For a full account we refer the reader to our technical report [14].

3.1 Formalizing OBJECTIVE CAML in Type Theory

OCAML [16] is a strongly typed, (almost) functional language, which has been extended with a module system and an object calculus. Its functional core is similar to the language of type theory, but it has a different syntax and contains many additional features.

Standard data types such as arrays, records, queues, etc. and their operations are predefined in OCAML but have to be represented by more fundamental constructs in type theory. In most cases, the formalization is straightforward. Arrays over some type T, for instance, are represented by pairs (lg, a) where $lg \in \mathbb{N}$ is the array's length and $a{:}\mathbb{N}{\rightarrow}T$ the component selector function. Records are represented by dependent functions and variant records by dependent products. But there are also language constructs whose representations are more complex.

Variable-Sized Expressions. In contrast to type-theory, which requires terms to have a fixed number of subterms, OCAML allows expressions with arbitrarily many components. $\{l_1{=}v_1; \ldots; l_n{=}v_n\}$, for instance, denotes a record that has the value v_i at field l_i. This expression can be represented by a function r that on input l_i yields the value v_i, but r can be *described* only through an iterated application of several NuPRL-abstractions: a representation of the empty record $\{\}$ by the constant function $\lambda l.()$ and a representation for record extension by a new field $l_{n+1}{=}v_{n+1}$. Appropriate display forms make sure that a term built from these abstractions is always displayed like the corresponding OCAML-record.

Thus formally OCAML language constructs are not associated with individual NuPRL-abstractions but with *term-generators*, i.e. meta-level programs that construct a NuPRL-term out of one or more abstractions.

Pattern Matching. A convenient feature of OCAML is the support of pattern matching in local abstractions, function definitions, and case-expressions. match *expr* with p_1->$t_1 \ldots p_n$->t_n, for instance, subsequently matches the expression *expr* against the patterns $p_1 \ldots p_n$. If matching succeeds with pattern p_i then the free variables of p_i will be instantiated in t_i and t_i will be evaluated.

Although a pattern looks like a conventional expression, it has an entirely different semantics. Computationally, a pattern p can be viewed as a matching function (or *matcher*) that takes an expression *expr* and a target t, analyzes the structure of *expr*, and returns an instance of t with the free variables of p instantiated. A pattern x, for instance, contains the free variable x and matches against any expression. Applying the matcher to *expr* and t results in $t[expr/x]$.

Since most patterns are constructed from other patterns we also need mechanisms for composing matchers. The paired pattern (p_1, p_2), for instance, expects to be matched against a pair (e_1, e_2). The term e_1 is handed together with t to the matcher p_1 while e_2 and the result of this matching is given to p_2.

Finally, we have to deal with the fact that matching may fail. Therefore, a matcher returns both a modified target expression and a boolean value.

Taking these aspects into account we have implemented a collection of abstractions and display forms for each pattern construct. The abstractions define the term structure and the semantics of a matcher. The display form describes its outer appearance and makes matcher terms look like the original pattern.

Example 1. The abstraction for paired patterns introduces a (higher-order) term with the name Product__Match_Pair and two formal subterms, the submatchers p_1 and p_2, which are separated by a semicolon. The right hand side of the abstraction formalizes the intuition of paired matchers. A display form causes the matcher to appear as simple pair.

$$\frac{\text{Product\_\_Match\_Pair}\{\}(.p_1; .p_2)}{\equiv \;\lambda\text{expr,t. let } e_1, e_2 = \text{expr in}}$$
$$\text{let b,t'} = (p_1 \; e_1 \; \text{targ) in}$$
$$\text{if b then } (p_2 \; e_2 \; \text{t') else (false, t')}$$
$$\underline{p_1, p_2} \equiv \text{Product\_\_Match\_Pair}\{\}(.p_1; .p_2)$$

Imperative Features. For the sake of efficiency OCAML supports imperative features such as assignments, compound statements, and loops, while the primitives of type theory are completely functional. But for formal *reasoning* about OCAML-programs, a representation of imperative features based on a copy semantics is sufficient. Nevertheless, a complete formalization of imperative behavior would require a general model for managing reference variables.

Fortunately, ENSEMBLE's architecture is essentially a finite state-event system. Imperative features only affect the state of a protocol layer and the queue of events that links two layers. Thus we can use a simpler model and represent imperative assignments by functions that modify these two variables. Compound statements and loops are represented by function composition and recursion.

Modules and Object Declarations. OCAML-declarations of user-defined types and functions introduce a name for a new object and bind it to a given expression. Technically, declarations are instructions for the programming environment. In NUPRL they correspond to meta-level programs that add new abstractions and display forms to the library. These *object-generators* also deal with name space management, references to other user-defined objectd, overloading, and similar issues related to the environment of a program.

Similarly, OCAML modules can be considered to be a means for structuring the code. This allows, for instance, using the same name for different functions in different modules and supports a clear and uniform presentation of the protocol layers of ENSEMBLE. In NUPRL modules have to be mapped onto the flat name space of the library. Module declarations thus affect how object-generators determine the names of generated objects or of objects referred to by an identifier.

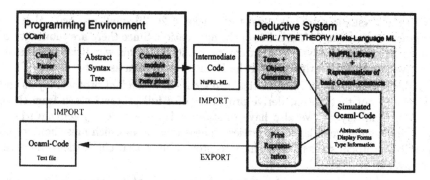

Fig. 2. Translating between OCAML and NUPRL: general methodology

3.2 Conversion Algorithms

Given the formal embedding of OCAML the methodology for importing and exporting system code into NUPRL is straightforward. We have to analyze the syntax of OCAML-programs and create the corresponding term- and object generators. These generators will create appropriate terms and store all declared functions and types as new abstractions in NUPRL's library. In order to ensure faithfulness wrt. the OCAML programming environment we chose the CAMLP4 parser-preprocessor [7], an isolated version of the original OCAML-parser, as a tool for analyzing program text. CAMLP4 generates an abstract syntax tree and then calls an output module for further processing (e.g. pretty-printing or dumping the binary). We have developed an output module that converts the abstract syntax tree it into "intermediate code" consisting of term and object generators. The module generates pieces of text for each node of the syntax tree, distinguishing the various kinds of identifiers, expressions, patterns, types, signature items, and module expressions according to the OCAML specification [7, Appendix A].

Since a parser is restricted to a syntactical analysis of a single text file it cannot solve problems that arise when linking the code of several modules. *Name resolution* (dealing with modules), determining the *role of identifiers* (variable or reference to user-defined object), and overloading (detecting the intended operator via type inference) therefore had to be addressed with meta-level object generators (see Section 4 of our technical report [14] for details).

Translating formal representations of protocol layers back into OCAML source code is easy, because their display is already genuine OCAML code. Since NUPRL already provides a mechanism for printing libraries and proofs we only had to write a function that selects the objects to be printed. The resulting program text can be executed in the OCAML environment without further modifications.

4   Verification of System Properties

The security of distributed systems is usually described by a few critical system properties such as agreement, total message ordering, safe encryption etc., which are achieved by using specific protocols. Group communication systems built with the ENSEMBLE toolkit consist of stacks of 20–30 small protocols that are composed according to the needs of the application. Since there are thousands of different application systems that can be constructed this way it is not possible to give an *a priori* verification of the ENSEMBLE system as such.

Instead, we have to verify critical properties of *individual* protocol layers and develop proof tactics that derive properties of a full protocol stack from those of individual layers. We also have to state and prove *global* system invariants (e.g. independence of layer properties). These Invariants which must hold for all possible protocol stacks and we have to provide tools that check them whenever the system is modified.

One of the advantages of ENSEMBLE's implementation, as far as formal reasoning is concerned, is the simple code structure of protocol layers. Since the protocols are essentially finite state-event machines, the OCAML code contains only nested function applications, sequencing of statements, and simple loops. Correspondingly, many properties of a protocol layer can be proved by straightforward applications of a few fundamental deductive techniques.

- *Function evaluation* is used whenever a newly defined layer function needs to be analyzed. Similarly, the definitions of newly introduced concepts for expressing program properties have to be unfolded.
- *Lemma application* occurs when reasoning about the properties of operations used in the definition of new functions or concepts. This may involve backward (and forward) chaining over implications and *equality substitutions*, depending on which part of the lemma can be used.

  The only difficulty is finding appropriate lemmata in a short amount of time. Efficient lemma application requires a well-organized *formal database* containing verified lemmata about the properties of predefined functions. A strong modularization of this database is necessary to restrict the search space. We are currently developing techniques for constructing this database step by step as new functions and modules are imported into NUPRL.
- *Proof methods* known from first-order theorem proving are used to solve proof subgoals that are conceptually simple but tedious. Similarly simple induction techniques are needed for reasoning about loops.

Usually the syntactical structure of the property to be proved determines how these techniques are to be applied. This makes it possible to write tactics that automate the verification process. To illustrate this process we give an example verification of the central property of Ensemble's Elect protocol layer.

Example 2. The purpose of the Elect layer is to elect a coordinator for groups of processes that do not suspect each other to have failed. For this, each process maintains a list of suspected processes and its own rank in the group. The former will be updated in each cycle, but processes that have been suspected once will remain suspected. A process elects itself as coordinator if all other processes of lower rank are suspected. This guarantees that *each nonempty subgroup of correct processes will always have exactly one coordinator.* The election algorithm can be implemented by the following piece of OCAML-code.[1]

```
type state = { suspects : bool list ;  rank : int }
let handler (state,suspects) =
  let suspects = map2 (or) suspects state.suspects in
   let elect   = (min_rank suspects) >= state.rank in
    let state  = { rank = state.rank; suspects = suspects } in
       (state,elect)
```

To formalize the property we want to verify, we describe a group G of processes by a list of states. Each member m is uniquely identified by its position, or *rank*, in this list, which is assumed to be identical with the value of the rank component of G[m]. The suspects component and each list of new suspects are list of boolean values of exactly the same size as the group. They indicate which group member is suspected to have failed. We introduce two formal abbreviations.

```
G is_well_formed  ≡ ∀m:{1..|G|}. |G[m].suspects|=|G|  ∧  G[m].rank=m
suspects fits G   ≡ ∀m:{1..|G|}. |suspects[m]|=|G|
```

The subgroup SUB of correct processes can be characterized as the set of processes that do not suspect each other but suspect every outsider process.

```
SUB agrees  ≡ ∀m,m':{1..|G|}. m∈SUB ⇒ m'∈SUB ⇔ m' unsuspected_by m
m' unsuspected_by m  ≡ suspects[m][m']=false ∧ G[m].suspects[m']=false
```

A member m elects itself as new coordinator, if the elect-component computed by its handler is true. We define m elects_itself as shorthand for

```
let (state,elect) = handler(G[m],suspects[m]) in  elect=true
```

The property that each nonempty subgroup of correct processes will always have exactly one coordinator can thus be formally sspecified as follows.

```
∀G: state list. G is_well_formed  ⇒
  ∀suspects: B list list. suspects fits G ⇒
    ∀SUB: {1..|G|} list. SUB agrees   ⇒
      ∃₁m:{1..|G|}. m∈SUB ∧ m elects_itself
```

A proof of this property decomposes this specification and then continues as shown in Figure 3 (we used descriptions of proof tactics instead of their NuPRL names). Except for the selection of min(G) in the first step, it can be constructed automatically by the above-mentioned standard techniques, provided that the following lemmata are present in the formal database.

(1) ∀L: B list.   L[min_rank L]=false
(2) ∀L: B list.   ∀j:{0..|L|⁻}. L[j]=false ⇒ min_rank L ≤ j
(3) ∀L1,L2:B list. |L1|=|L2| ⇒
    ∀i:{0..|L1|⁻}. (map2 or L1 L2)[i]=false ⇔ L1[i]=false ∧ L2[i]=false
(4) ∀L:Z list.∀i:Z. i=min(L) ⇔ i∈L ∧ (∀j:Z. j∈L ⇒ i≤j)

The above example is only an illustration of the tasks involved in the verification of a protocol stack. The actual ENSEMBLE implementation of the Elect

---

[1] map2 applies a function with two arguments to two lists. min_rank computes the smallest rank of an entry false in a boolean list.

```
1.-3. G: state list,        suspects: B list list,   SUB: {1..|G|} list
4.-6.. G is_well_formed,     suspects fits G,         SUB agrees
⊢ ∃₁m:{1..|G|}. m ∈ SUB ∧ m elects_itself
BY unfold the definition of ∃₁ and choose m = min(SUB)

   \
    ⊢ min(SUB) ∈ SUB
    BY Lemma (4)
   \
    ⊢ min(SUB) elects_itself
    BY unfold elects_itself, evaluate handler, and convert >=
    ⊢ min_rank (map2 or suspects[min(SUB)]) (G[min(SUB)].suspects)) ≥ G[min(SUB)].rank
    BY unfold is_well_formed and substitute G[min(SUB)].rank=min(SUB)
    ⊢ min_rank (map2 or ... ) ≥ min(SUB)
    BY Lemma (4)
    ⊢ min_rank (map2 or ... ) ∈ SUB
    BY unfold agrees and backward reasoning over hypothesis 6
      \
       ⊢ min(SUB) ∈ SUB
     | BY Lemma (4)
      \
       ⊢ min_rank (map2 or ... ) unsuspected_by min(SUB)
       BY unfold unsuspected_by and apply Lemma (3)
       ⊢ (map2 or ... )[min_rank (map2 or ... )] = false
     | BY Lemma (1)
   \
    7.-9. m:{1..|G|}, m ∈ SUB, m elects_itself
    ⊢ m=min(SUB)
    BY Lemma (4)
       \
        ⊢ m ∈ SUB
      | BY hypothesis 8
        \
         10.-11. j:Z, j ∈ SUB
         ⊢ m≤j
         BY unfold elects_itself, evaluate handler, and convert >=
         9. min_rank (map2 or (suspects[m]) (G[m].suspects)) ≥ m
         ⊢ m≤j
         BY transitivity over hypothesis 9
         ⊢ min_rank(map or (suspects[m]) (G[m].suspects)) ≤ j
         BY Lemma (2)
         ⊢ (map2 or (suspects[m]) (G[m].suspects))[j] = false
         BY apply Lemma (3) and fold unsuspected_by
         ⊢ j unsuspected_by m
         BY unfold agrees and backward reasoning over hypothesis 6
```

Fig. 3. Top-down verification of the Elect protocol layer

protocol layer also contains code for handling various error situations and is about 100 lines long. Because of this, a complete formal specification of protocol layers is rather complex and more difficult to verify. We are currently elaborating formal specifications of ENSEMBLE's protocol layers and the code for layer composition using I/O-automata as in [17]. We intend to use timed automata as a means for specifying synchronization and liveness properties.

The development of verification tactics for protocol stacks is also still in its beginning phase. So far we have developed and implemented a formal programming logic for the embedded subset of OCAML (see Section 4 of our technical report [14] for details) and experimented with small examples like the above. We have also implemented a type-inference algorithm for the embedded subset of OCAML and are currently extending it to provide a more detailed analysis of programs like checking array bounds, division errors, boolean annotations, etc.

Since the formal specifications of individual layers are not very likely to change, it is sufficient to verify them interactively with tactic support. Formal

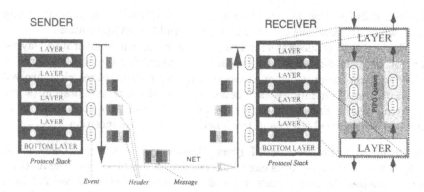

Fig. 4. ENSEMBLE architecture: *Protocol layers are linked by FIFO event queues*

reasoning about application systems can then be done solely on the basis of these formal specifications instead of the real code, which drastically simplifies the reasoning process. We believe that a formalization of the style of reasoning used in Lynch's book [17] may lead to successful verification tactics.

5   Fast-Track Reconfiguration of Protocol Stacks

For the sake of flexibility, ENSEMBLE's protocol layers can be combined almost arbitrarily. Few assumptions are made about adjacent layers and all types of messages (including errors) must be handled within the layer. This approach is safe but it leads to a great amount of redundancy. In most cases a message is simply sent or broadcast and it passes straight through the protocol stack, modifying only a few layer states. Each layer adds a header to the message to indicate how the corresponding receiver layer has to be activated (see Figure 4).

By reconfiguring a layer stack one can achieve a more efficient treatment of these normal cases. For this purpose one has to analyze common sequences of operations, identifying the structure of standard messages and the normal status of a layer's state. Under these conditions the code of the protocol stack can be improved drastically. The result describes a *fast-track* through the protocol stack that can be executed whenever an incoming message and the current state satisfy the conditions. Experiments have shown that a speedup of factor 30–50 can be achieved by function inlining, symbolic code evaluation, dead code elimination, removing the communication overhead between layers, and compressing the headers of standard messages before sending them over the net. Fast-track reconfigurations by hand, however, are time consuming and have a high risk of error because of the code size of typical applications. Without formal support, a reconfiguration of an application system would be infeasible.

We have developed a small set of general tactics that automatically detect pieces of code that can be optimized and rewrite them accordingly. These tactics include function inlining, symbolic evaluation, and knowledge-based simplification. They are based on the derived program evaluation rules mentioned in Section 3 (see also Section 4 of our technical report [14]) and on conditional rewrite rules, which are implemented via substitution and lemma application.

These tactics are successful for a reconfiguration of individual protocol layers. But for the reconfiguration of protocol stacks containing thousands of lines of code they turnead out to be not efficient enough since too much search is involved in the process. Therefore we have developed specialized reconfiguration tactics that avoid search almost completely because by following the code structure of ENSEMBLE's protocol layers and the function for layer composition.

Reconfiguration of Protocol Layers. Besides type and module declarations all ENSEMBLE protocol layers essentially consists of two functions. The function init initializes the layer's state according to a global view state vs and local information ls. The function hdlrs describes how the layer's state is affected when an event is received and which events will be sent out to adjacent layers. Instead of mentioning event queues explicitly, hdlrs transforms the event *handlers* of the stacks above and below the layer. This technique makes it possible to convert a layer l into a functional or an imperative version without modifying its code.

The purpose of a reconfiguration is to optimize the event handler of a protocol stack. A reconfiguration of an individual protocol layer l therefore begins with

$$\text{let (init,hdlr)} = \text{convert l (ls, vs) in } \text{hdlr}(s_l, event)$$

where init describes the initial state, hdlr event handler, and *event* is either an up or downgoing event of the form UpM(ev,msg) or DnM(ev,msg). Assumptions about the "normal case" characterize the type of ev (send, broadcast, etc.), the structure of a header in msg, and the contents of the layer's state s_l.

A reconfiguration first evaluates convert, which has a fixed implementation, and unfolds init and hdlrs. It then evaluates all let-abstractions occurring in hdlr and finally analyzes the outer structure of the event. All these steps could be performed by our general evaluation strategy (a tactic called Red) but a specialized tactic RedLayerStructure can perform them much more efficiently, because the exact order of reductions is fixed.

Afterwards, we have to make use of the assumptions in order to optimize the code further. Since these are usually expressed as equalities, we can use substitution and then reduce the piece of code that was affected. Again, there is a specialized tactic UseHyps for this purpose.

By combining these tactics a reconfiguration of a protocol layer can be performed almost automatically. We have successfully used them in the reconfiguration of several ENSEMBLE layers for various standard situations. In many cases a layer consisting of 300–500 lines of code is reduced to a simple update of the state and a single event that is passed to the next layer.

Verifying a Reconfiguration. A fast-track reconfiguration in NuPRL is more than just a syntactical transformation of program code. Since it is based on substitution and evaluation mechanisms we *know* that under the given assumptions a reconfigured program must be equivalent to the original one. But we can also prove this fact formally after a reconfiguration has been finished. In fact, we get the proof of equivalence almost for free, since all NuPRL substitutions and evaluations also correspond to proof rules in NuPRL.

We have written a tactic that generates the statement of the equivalence theorem from the assumptions, the starting point, and the final result of the reconfiguration and then proves it correct. For the latter, it considers the trace of the reconfiguration as a proof plan and transforms each reconfiguration step into the corresponding proof rule and its parameters. This tactic is completely automated – even in cases where the reconfiguration required some user interaction – and is guaranteed to succeed.

An interesting side effect of this technique is that it also allows us to bypass NuPRL's basic inference system *during a reconfiguration*. Since the correctness of the reconfiguration will be verified anyway, we can simply transform OCAML-programs by meta-level operations, which avoids the overhead of checking each transformation step correct. Experiments have shown that this speeds up the reconfiguration process by a factor of 5 and more since the verification can be executed later in a separate background process.

Reconfiguring Layer Composition. While the reconfiguration of individual layers is mostly straightforward it becomes more complex when layers are composed. In this case the new state is simply a tuple of individual layer states. The composed event handler not only has to deal with outgoing events but also with the events that pass between the composed layers. Since (generated) events may also bounce between the composed layers the function for layer composition (compose) must use unrestricted recursion.

Correspondingly, a reconfiguration of composed layers has to proceed recursively as well while it traces the path of standard events through the composed layers. For instance, upgoing events are first be passed to the lower layer. After the code has been reconfigured accordingly, all emitted downgoing events are stored in the event queue while upgoing events will be passed to the upper layer. Emitted up-events are added to the queue and down-events are passed back into the lower layer. This process continues until all events have left the composed layers. It has been automated by a specialized tactic for reconfiguring composed layers, which performs these steps in an efficient order. Obviously, it only 'succeeds' if the assumptions about incoming event do in fact allow a simplification of the code, since otherwise the generated code may become much bigger.

Reconfiguration of Protocol Stacks. Despite the use of specialized reconfiguration tactics that take into account the specific code structure of ENSEMBLE the performance of the reconfiguration tools does not scale up very well. Due to the size of the code we have to deal with extremely large terms, which is particularly problematic if user interaction is necessary. Tracing events through the code of a full application protocol stack is extremely time consuming as we have to rely on *symbolic* evaluation because we only know the structure of the event.

Reconfiguration in a higher-order proof environment, however, is not restricted to elementary program transformations. In most cases, the result of reconfiguring a protocol stack under a given set of assumptions can easily be

∀Top,Bot, ls,vs, msg,msg₁,msg₂, s_b,s'_b, s_t,s'_t
    let (init,hdlr) = Bot (ls,vs) in hdlr (s_b, UpM(ev,msg)) = (s'_b, [:UpM(ev,msg₁):])
  ∧ let (init,hdlr) = Top (ls,vs) in hdlr (s_t, UpM(ev,msg₁)) = (s'_t, [:UpM(ev,msg₂):])
  ⇒   let (init,hdlr) = (compose Top Bot) (ls,vs) in hdlr ((s_b,s_t), UpM(ev,msg))
        = ((s'_b,s'_t), [:UpM(ev,msg₂):])

Fig. 5. Reconfiguration theorem for linear up-traces

derived from the reconfiguration results for its individual layers. We only have to compose these results according to our knowledge about layer composition.

Formally, we can do this by establishing theorems about the reconfiguration of individual protocol layers and the result of composing reconfigured layers. These formal theorems then serve as *derived inference rules* on a much higher level of abstraction. They compose arbitrary protocol layers in a *single* inference step where a tactic-based reconfiguration would have to execute thousands of elementary steps. This not only leads to a better performance of the reconfiguration process but also a much clearer style of reasoning. Furthermore, system updates can be handled much easier: the modification of a layer's code usually only requires reproving the reconfiguration theorems for this particular layer while the reconfiguration of the stack will remain completely unaffected.

Figure 5 presents a reconfiguration theorem for composing fast-tracks for upgoing events. It deals with the very common case of *linear traces* where an event passes through the stack without generating additional events. In this case each layer Top and Bot yields a queue consisting of a single up-event and the composition of both does the obvious. While the statement of this theorem is simple, its proof is rather complex as we have to reason about the actual code of ENSEMBLE's compose function and reason about the result of all the steps that would usually be executed *during* a reconfiguration. Thus by proving this theorem we remove the deductive burden from the reconfiguration process itself.[2]

Reconfiguration theorems for composing fast-tracks, coupled with reconfiguration theorems for individual protocol layers, lead to a reconfiguration technique that scales up extremely well. We only have to apply the appropriate theorems step-by-step and receive the reconfigured code for the complete stack in linear time with respect to the number of layers that have to be passed by events.

We are currently developing a database of standard reconfigurations for all protocol layers, a series of composition theorems for linear and simple non-linear traces, and a reconfiguration tactic that automatically selects and applies these theorems. We have used this tactic in an example reconfiguration of a simple protocol stack consisting of the four layers Bottom, Mnak, Pt2pt, and Frag with total code size of about 1200 lines. Tracing broadcast events under standard conditions yields only *two lines of code*, which update the state of Mnak and pass the event to the next layer after removing the corresponding four headers.

---

[2] This methodology has already been used successfully for program synthesis [13,2].

6 Conclusion

We have presented a logical programming environment for the development of reliable and efficient group communication systems. Our approach includes algorithms for importing system code into the NuPRL proof development system, semi-automatic reasoning tools for verifying and optimizing this code within the proof environment, and tools for exporting the results back into the programming environment. It is based on a formalization of a subset of the programming language OCAML for which we have developed a type-theoretical semantics.

Recent work on the specification and verification of timed automata [17,1], fault-tolerant systems [20], and protocol stacks for group communication systems [8] has demonstrated that formal reasoning about complex distributed algorithms is feasible. Our approach, however, is the first to make the code of a real-world communication system available for formal reasoning and to combine both verification and code reconfiguration within a single formal framework.

While the import/export mechanisms have already been completed, the degree of automation of our tools for verifying and reconfiguring protocol stacks still has to be improved. For this purpose we will integrate additional tools from the field of automated deduction, such as an extended typechecking algorithm [10], a proof procedure for first-order logic [15], and a proof planner for inductive proofs [2] into the logical programming environment. Furthermore, we are extending our formal database by verified theorems about major reconfiguration and verification steps, which we can then use as derived inference rules. We aim at a modularization of the formal database in order to speed up the search for applicable lemmas. We are also developing a mechanism that automatically adds header compression to a reconfigured stack to further improve the efficiency of the generated code. We intend to apply our reconfiguration and verification tools to a running application system in order to improve its efficiency while hardening its security at the same time.

Although it may take a few years until our tools are mature, we are confident that they will lead to a new design paradigm for distributed systems that yield the high degree of assurance required in many important applications.

References

1. M. Archer & C. Heitmeyer. Mechanical verification of timed automata: A case study. Technical report, Naval Research Laboratory, Washington, DC, 1997.
2. W. Bibel, D. Korn, C. Kreitz, F. Kurucz, J. Otten, S. Schmitt, G. Stolpmann. A multi-level approach to program synthesis. In *Seventh International Workshop on Logic Program Synthesis and Transformation*, LNAI, Springer Verlag, 1998.
3. K. Birman. *Building Secure and Reliable Network Applications*. Manning Publishing Company and Prentice Hall, 1997.
4. K. Birman & R. van Renesse. *Reliable Distributed Computing with the Isis Toolkit*. IEEE Computer Society Press, 1994.
5. T. Chandra, V. Hadzilacos, S. Toueg, B. Charron-Bost. On the impossibility of group membership. *15th ACM Symposium on Principles of Distributed Computing*, pp. 322–330, 1996.

6. R. Constable, et. al., *Implementing Mathematics with the NuPRL proof development system*. Prentice Hall, 1986.
7. D. de Rauglaudre. *Camlp4 version 1.06*. Institut National de Recherche en Informatique et en Automatique, 1997.
8. A. Fekete, N. Lynch, A. Shvartsman. Specifying and using a partitionable group communication service. In *16th ACM Symposium on Principles of Distributed Computing*, 1997.
9. M. Gordon, R. Milner, C. Wadsworth. *Edinburgh LCF: A mechanized Logic of Computation*. LNCS 78, Springer Verlag, 1979.
10. O. Hafızoğulları & C. Kreitz. Dead Code Elimination Through Type Inference. Technical Report TR 98-1698, Cornell University, 1998.
11. M. Hayden. *Ensemble Reference Manual*. Cornell University, 1996.
12. The ENSEMBLE distributed communication system. System distribution and related information. http://www.cs.cornell.edu/Info/Projects/Ensemble
13. C. Kreitz. Formal mathematics for verifiably correct program synthesis. *Journal of the IGPL*, 4(1):75–94, 1996.
14. C. Kreitz. Formal reasoning about communication systems I: Embedding ML into type theory. Technical Report TR97-1637, Cornell University, 1997.
15. C. Kreitz, J. Otten, S. Schmitt. Guiding Program Development Systems by a Connection Based Proof Strategy. In *5th International Workshop on Logic Program Synthesis and Transformation*, LNCS 1048, pp. 137–151. Springer Verlag, 1996.
16. X. Leroy. *The Objective Caml system release 1.06*. Institut National de Recherche en Informatique et en Automatique, 1997.
17. N. Lynch. *Distributed Algorithms*. Morgan Kaufmann Publishers, 1996.
18. P. Lincoln & J. Rushby. A formally verified algorithm for interactive consistency under a hybrid fault model. In *23rd Fault-Tolerant Computing Symposium*, pp. 402–411, 1993.
19. J. Rushby. Formal methods for dependable real-time systems. In *International Symposium on Real-Time Embedded Processing for Space Applications*, pp. 355–366, 1992.
20. J. Rushby. Systematic formal verification for fault-tolerant time-triggered algorithms. In *Dependable Computing for Critical Applications: 6*, pp. 191–210. IEEE Computer Society, 1997.
21. R. van Renesse, K. Birman, & S. Maffeis. Horus: A flexible group communication system. *Communications of the ACM*, 39(4):76–83, 1996.

On the Relationship Between Non-Horn Magic Sets and Relevancy Testing

Yoshihiko Ohta[1], Katsumi Inoue[2], and Ryuzo Hasegawa[3]

[1] Department of Information Engineering, University of Industrial Technology,
Hashimotodai 4-1-1, Sagamihara-shi, Kanagawa 229-1196, Japan
ohta@uitec.ac.jp
[2] Department of Electrical and Electronics Engineering, Kobe University,
Rokkodai, Nada-ku, Kobe 657-8501, Japan
inoue@eedept.kobe-u.ac.jp
[3] Department of Intelligent Systems, Kyushu University,
Kasuga Kouen 6-1, Kasuga-shi, Fukuoka 816-8580, Japan
hasegawa@ar.is.kyushu-u.ac.jp

Abstract. Model-generation based theorem provers such as SATCHMO and MGTP suffer from a combinatorial explosion of the search space caused by clauses irrelevant to the goal (negative clause) to be solved. To avoid this, two typical methods have been proposed. One is *relevancy testing* implemented in SATCHMORE by Loveland *et al.*, and the other is *non-Horn magic sets* that are the extension of Horn magic sets and used for MGTP. In this paper, we define the concept of *weak relevancy testing*, which somewhat relaxes the relevancy testing constraint. Then, we analyze the relationship between non-Horn magic sets and weak relevancy testing in detail, and prove that the total number of interpretations generated by MGTP employing non-Horn magic sets is always the same as that by SATCHMORE using weak relevancy testing. Thus, we find that non-Horn magic sets and weak relevancy testing, although they are completely different approaches, have the same power in pruning redundant branches of a proof tree.

1 Introduction

There have been proposed several theorem provers based on the *model generation* method [7,3]. Basically, the model generation method sets up an interpretation, called a *model candidate*, for a given clause set, and repeats the following: It detects a *violated clause* that is not satisfied under the current interpretation, then extends the interpretation so as to satisfy that clause. Manthey and Bry presented an efficient model-generation based theorem prover SATCHMO [7] written in Prolog. In the model generation method, several different interpretations are generated by extending a current interpretation with a non-Horn clause. We can exploit OR parallelism from non-Horn clauses by independently

C. Kirchner and H. Kirchner (Eds.): Automated Deduction, CADE-15
LNAI 1421, pp. 333–348, 1998. © Springer–Verlag Berlin Heidelberg 1998

exploring each branch (interpretation) of a proof tree caused by case splitting. In particular, a parallel model generation-based theorem prover MGTP [3] has also been developed and achieves high performance on parallel and distributed computer systems.

However, when there are several violated clauses that are not satisfied by a certain interpretation, the computational cost may greatly differ according to the order in which those clauses are evaluated. Especially when a non-Horn clause irrelevant to the given goal is selected, many interpretations generated with the clause would become useless. Thus, in the model generation method, it is necessary to develop a method to suppress the generation of useless interpretations.

To this end, Loveland *et al.* [6] proposed a method to impose a strong restriction on selecting a violated clause to say that no clause need be selected unless all the consequent literals are relevant (be "totally relevant"). In the sequel, we simply call it *relevancy testing* to check if a clause is totally relevant. The relevancy testing is implemented in a simple prover called SATCHMORE (SATCHMO with RElevancy). This implementation takes a dynamic approach, since it computes relevant literals dynamically by utilizing Prolog over Horn clauses, in advance before a violated clause is used for forward chaining.

For the same purpose as above, another method called *non-Horn magic sets* (NHM), which combines bottom-up proving and top-down proving, has also been proposed [4]. The NHM method is based on a static clause transformation, in which a given clause set is transformed to clauses simulating backward reasoning and those for controlling forward reasoning. Although the magic sets method [1] proposed in the field of deductive databases is applicable only to Horn clauses, it has the effect of avoiding the generation of useless facts irrelevant to the given query. Thus, by using the NHM method that extends the magic sets method to make it applicable to non-Horn clauses, it is possible to avoid evaluating useless clauses irrelevant to negative clauses in model-generation based theorem provers for first-order logic.

As mentioned above, the relevancy testing and the NHM methods have been presented to prevent redundant interpretations from being generated by SATCHMO and MGTP. However, the relationship between both methods has not yet been clarified. According to several experimental results having been obtained so far [6,4], it is estimated that relevancy testing and NHM have the same pruning ability. In this paper, we define the concept of *weak relevancy testing* that mitigates the condition of relevancy testing [6], and analyze the relationship between the weak relevancy testing and the NHM methods. Then, we prove that the total number of interpretations generated by the weak relevancy testing method is always the same as that by the NHM method. That is, we clarify that the NHM method is equivalent to the weak relevancy testing in terms of the ability to prune redundant branches of a proof tree generated with the model generation method.

Section 2 of this paper defines the clauses used in model generation theorem provers. Section 3 defines weak relevant literals and gives the SATCHMORE procedure incorporating the weak relevancy testing. Section 4 describes the NHM transformation method and defines the MGTP procedure employing the NHM method. Section 5 proves that both procedures have the same power in pruning redundant branches. Section 6 refers to a case where the relevancy testing [6] is more powerful than the weak relevancy testing, and also compares both methods from other aspects.

2 Notation of Clauses

A *clause* $\neg A_1 \vee \ldots \vee \neg A_n \vee B_1 \vee \ldots \vee B_m$ is represented in either of the following implicational forms:

$$A_1, \cdots, A_n \rightarrow B_1; \cdots; B_m. \tag{1}$$

$$B_1; \cdots; B_m \leftarrow A_1, \cdots, A_n. \tag{2}$$

where A_i $(i = 1, \ldots, n)$ and B_j $(j = 1, \ldots, m)$ are atoms; "," denotes a conjunction, ";" a disjunction, and "$\rightarrow$" an implication. The conjunction $A_1, \cdots, A_n$ is said to be the *antecedent*. The disjunction $B_1; \cdots; B_m$ is said to be the *consequent*. A clause is called a *positive clause* if its antecedent is empty $(n = 0)$, and a *negative clause* if its consequent is empty $(m = 0)$. A special atom "$\bot$" is used to denote the consequent literal of any negative clause. A clause with $m \leq 1$ is called a *Horn clause*; otherwise a clause with $m > 1$ is called a *non-Horn clause*.

Here, we assume that every variable in the consequent of a clause must have its occurrence in the antecedent. A clause that satisfies this condition is said to be a *range-restricted clause*.

Although SATCHMO [7] and SATCHMORE [6] are based on forward reasoning (bottom-up proving) basically, they also provide another variation which employs Prolog over the Horn clause subsets to perform bidirectional reasoning. For this, the given clause set is split into two sets: a Horn clause set BC that is processed directly by Prolog based on backward reasoning (top-down proving) and a clause set FC that is used for forward reasoning. Note that FC contains all non-Horn clauses and may include some Horn clauses. In this paper, the clause form (2) is used to represent Horn clauses in BC, since they are applied backward. On the other hand, the clause form (1) is used for clauses in FC. In MGTP [3], however, as it is based only on forward reasoning, only the clause form (1) is used.

3 Relevancy Testing

This section reviews the relevancy detection algorithm introduced by Loveland *et al.* [6]. They defined an extension of SATCHMO, called *SATCHMORE*, which avoids the uncontrolled use of forward chaining by *relevancy testing* (RT). In RT, the notions of *relevant literals* and *relevant clauses* are introduced to recognize whether each clause used for forward chaining is relevant to proving the unsatisfiability of the axiom set.

Since SATCHMO(RE) utilizes Prolog in its implementation, in order to analyze its properties, we need knowledge about SLD resolution such as *SLD trees*, *SLD derivations*, *SLD refutations*, and *computed answers* (see [5]). In this paper, we assume that the computation rule for SLD resolution always selects the leftmost atom of a goal. We write $BC \vdash (A_1, \ldots, A_n)$ if there is an SLD refutation for $BC \cup \{ \leftarrow (A_1, \ldots, A_n) \}$. It is assumed below that Prolog terminates on any goal for BC. A sufficient way to assure this assumption is that we exclude Horn clauses that cause an infinite loop [6].

Here, we redefine relevant literals and a version of SATCHMORE procedure using such literals. Intuitively, a literal is *relevant* if it can contribute to a derivation of $\perp$ from backward-chaining clauses BC or a derivation of some antecedent of a forward-chaining clause from BC.

Definition 1. Let BC be a set of Horn clauses, and G a conjunction of atoms. Each leftmost atom of any node in the SLD tree for $BC \cup \{ \leftarrow G \}$ is called a *relevant literal* to the derivation of G from BC. The set of all relevant literals to the derivation of G from BC is denoted as $rl(BC, G)$.

Next, we define the relevancy for forward-chaining clauses FC. RT checks whether each clause C in FC is *totally relevant*, that is, whether all the consequent literals are relevant or not, before C is used for forward chaining.

Definition 2. Let R be a set of atoms, and FC a set of clauses. An instance $C\theta$ of a clause C: $(A_1, \ldots, A_n \rightarrow B_1; \ldots; B_m)$ in FC is a *relevant clause in FC relative to* R if θ is a computed answer for $R \cup \{ \leftarrow (B_1, \ldots, B_m) \}$. The set of relevant clauses in FC relative to R is denoted as $rc(R, FC)$.

In the above definition, the set R of atoms usually takes the relevant literals to the derivation of $\perp$ from BC or the *weak relevant literals* defined next. Weak relevant literals are similar to *extended relevant literals* in [6], but they are not equivalent.[1] Considering the correspondence between RT and NHM, we need a minor change to the definition of their extended relevant literals. The detailed comparison between these two will be given in Section 6.

Definition 3. Let BC be a set of Horn clauses, FC a set of clauses, G a conjunction of atoms, and R a set of atoms. The set of *weak relevant literals* to the derivation of G from (BC, FC) relative to R (denoted as $wrl(BC, FC, G, R)$) is defined as:

$$wrl(BC, FC, G, R) = \begin{cases} R, & \text{if } rl(BC, G) \subseteq R; \\ \bigcup_{C \in rc(R \cup rl(BC,G), FC)} wrl(BC, FC, ant(C), R \cup rl(BC, G)), \\ & \text{otherwise,} \end{cases}$$

where $ant(C)$ is the antecedent of C. In particular, an atom in $wrl(BC, FC, \perp, \emptyset)$ is called a *weak relevant literal for* (BC, FC).

---

[1] In Section 6, we will show that the set of extended relevant literals is a subset of the weak relevant literals, which explains the naming of "weak relevant" in this paper.

Note that $wrl(BC, FC, G, R)$ is a monotone function of R. Its computation stops in a finite number of steps whenever the domain is finite.

Example 1. Let BC and FC be as follows.

$$BC: \quad \bot \leftarrow p(X), r(b), \quad \bot \leftarrow p(X), s(b), \quad \bot \leftarrow t(X),$$
$$p(X) \leftarrow q(X), \quad q(a) \leftarrow, \quad q(b) \leftarrow,$$
$$FC: \quad u(X) \rightarrow r(X); s(X), \quad p(X) \rightarrow t(X); u(X).$$

The set of weak relevant literals for (BC, FC) is computed as follows.

1. Let $R_0 = \emptyset$. $rl(BC, \bot) = \{\bot, p(X), q(X), r(b), s(b), t(X)\}$.
2. Let $R_1 = R_0 \cup \{\bot, p(X), q(X), r(b), s(b), t(X)\}$.
   $rc(R_1, FC) = \{(u(b) \rightarrow r(b); s(b))\}$ because $\{X/b\}$ is a computed answer for $R_1 \cup \{\leftarrow (r(X), s(X))\}$. Then, $wrl(BC, FC, \bot, \emptyset) = wrl(BC, FC, u(b), R_1)$.

3. $rl(BC, u(b)) = \{u(b)\}$. Let $R_2 = R_1 \cup \{u(b)\}$.
   $rc(R_2, FC) = \{ (u(b) \rightarrow r(b); s(b)), (p(b) \rightarrow t(b); u(b)) \}$. Then,

   $$wrl(BC, FC, u(b), R_1) = wrl(BC, FC, u(b), R_2) \cup wrl(BC, FC, p(b), R_2).$$

   (a) $rl(BC, u(b)) = \{u(b)\} \subseteq R_2$. Then, $wrl(BC, FC, u(b), R_2) = R_2$.
   (b) $rl(BC, p(b)) = \{p(b), q(b)\}$. Let $R_3 = R_2 \cup \{p(b), q(b)\}$.
   $rc(R_3, FC) = \{ (u(b) \rightarrow r(b); s(b)), (p(b) \rightarrow t(b); u(b)) \}$. Then,

   $$wrl(BC, FC, p(b), R_2) = wrl(BC, FC, u(b), R_3) \cup wrl(BC, FC, p(b), R_3).$$

   i. $rl(BC, u(b)) = \{u(b)\} \subseteq R_3$. Then, $wrl(BC, FC, u(b), R_3) = R_3$.
   ii. $rl(BC, p(b)) = \{p(b), q(b)\} \subseteq R_3$. Then, $wrl(BC, FC, p(b), R_3) = R_3$.

Hence, $wrl(BC, FC, \bot, \emptyset) = \{\bot, p(X), q(X), r(b), s(b), t(X), u(b), p(b), q(b)\}$.

Definition 4. Let BC be a set of Horn clauses. A ground instance $C\theta$ of a range-restricted clause C: $(A_1, \ldots, A_n \rightarrow B_1; \ldots; B_m)$ is *violated in BC* if θ is a computed answer for $BC \cup \{\leftarrow (A_1, \ldots, A_n)\}$ and $BC \not\vdash (B_1; \ldots; B_m)\theta$. In this case, $C\theta$ is also said to be a *violated clause* for BC.

It is easy to see that $C\theta$ is a violated clause for BC iff $C\theta$ is not satisfied by the least Herbrand model of BC.

Now, we define the *SATCHMORE procedure using weak relevant literals*, which we call *SATCHMORE/w*, by the next procedure rt.

Definition 5 (Procedure rt(BC, FC, I)).

Input: BC: a set of range-restricted Horn clauses, FC: a set of range-restricted clauses, I: a set of ground atoms.

Output: *sat/unsat*: the (un)satisfiability of $BC \cup FC$.

1. If $BC \cup I \vdash \bot$, then return *unsat*;
2. Else if any ground clause from $rc(wrl(BC \cup I, FC, \bot, \emptyset), FC)$ is not violated in $BC \cup I$, then return *sat*;

3. Otherwise, let $C\theta$ be a violated clause for $BC \cup I$ such that it is a ground clause from $rc(wrl(BC \cup I, FC, \perp, \emptyset), FC)$. If $\mathbf{rt}(BC, FC, I \cup \{B_j\theta\}) = unsat$ for every consequent atom $B_j\theta$ of $C\theta$, then return $unsat$; else return sat.

Here, each set $I \cup \{B_j\theta\}$ of ground atoms generated in $\mathbf{rt}(BC, FC, I)$ is called a *partial interpretation*. Initially, SATCHMORE/w is called by $\mathbf{rt}(BC, FC, \emptyset)$.

Loveland *et al.* [6] proved the soundness and completeness of their SATCH-MORE procedure using extended relevant literals. With the relationship between the extended relevant literals and the weak relevant literals to be shown in Section 6, SATCHMORE/w can also be shown to be sound and complete. Namely, $BC \cup FC$ is unsatisfiable if and only if $\mathbf{rt}(BC, FC, \emptyset) = unsat$.

Example 2 (cont. from Example 1). Let us consider $\mathbf{rt}(BC, FC, \emptyset)$.

1. Let $R = wrl(BC, FC, \perp, \emptyset) = \{\perp, p(X), q(X), r(b), s(b), t(X), u(b), p(b), q(b)\}$. Then, $rc(wrl(BC, FC, \perp, \emptyset), FC) = \{ (u(b) \rightarrow r(b); s(b)), (p(b) \rightarrow t(b); u(b)) \}$, in which $(p(b) \rightarrow t(b); u(b))$ is violated in BC.
2. (a) $\mathbf{rt}(BC, FC, \{t(b)\})$ returns $unsat$ since $BC \cup \{t(b)\} \vdash \perp$.
   (b) $\mathbf{rt}(BC, FC, \{u(b)\})$: $wrl(BC \cup \{u(b)\}, FC, \perp, \emptyset) = R$. Then, $rc(wrl(BC \cup \{u(b)\}, FC, \perp, \emptyset), FC) = \{ (u(b) \rightarrow r(b); s(b)), (p(b) \rightarrow t(b); u(b)) \}$, in which $(u(b) \rightarrow r(b); s(b))$ is violated in $BC \cup \{u(b)\}$.
      i. $\mathbf{rt}(BC, FC, \{u(b), r(b)\})$ returns $unsat$ since $BC \cup \{u(b), r(b)\} \vdash \perp$.
      ii. $\mathbf{rt}(BC, FC, \{u(b), s(b)\})$ returns $unsat$ since $BC \cup \{u(b), s(b)\} \vdash \perp$.
      Hence, $unsat$ is returned by $rt(BC, FC, \{u(b)\})$.

Therefore, $unsat$ is returned by $rt(BC, FC, \emptyset)$.

Definition 6. Let BC and FC be the same as in Definition 5. A *proof tree by SATCHMORE/w* with respect to (BC, FC) is a tree satisfying the conditions:

1. Each node of the tree is a set of ground atoms;
2. The root node is $\emptyset$;
3. For each node I, if $BC \cup I \vdash \perp$, then I is a leaf node;
4. For each node I, if any ground clause from $rc(wrl(BC \cup I, FC, \perp, \emptyset), FC)$ is not violated in $BC \cup I$, then I is a leaf node;
5. For each non-leaf node I, if $(A_1, \ldots, A_n \rightarrow B_1; \ldots; B_m)\theta$ is both a violated clause for $BC \cup I$ and a ground clause from $rc(wrl(BC \cup I, FC, \perp, \emptyset), FC)$, then I has the children $I \cup \{B_1\theta\}, \ldots, I \cup \{B_m\theta\}$.

Example 3 (cont. from Examples 1 and 2). From Example 2, it is easy to see that the proof tree by SATCHMORE/w with respect to (BC, FC) has the 3 leaves: $\{t(b)\}$, $\{u(b), r(b)\}$ and $\{u(b), s(b)\}$. Here, no partial interpretation including either $t(a)$ or $u(a)$ is generated although the ground clause $(p(a) \rightarrow t(a); u(a))$ from FC is violated in BC. In contrast, the uncontrolled SATCHMO prover [7] generates such interpretations.

4   Non-Horn Magic Sets

This section presents a version of *non-Horn magic sets* (NHM) introduced in [4]. NHM is a natural extension of magic sets [1] to make them applicable to non-Horn clauses. The NHM method in the next definition is called the *depth-first NHM transformation* in [4], which we simply call *NHM* in this paper.

Definition 7. Given a set of clauses S, NHM translates S into $\Theta(S)$, which is defined as follows. For each clause C : $(A_1, \ldots, A_n \to B_1; \ldots; B_m)$ in S, if C is a positive clause ($n = 0$), then the clause C' : $(g(B_1), \ldots, g(B_m) \to B_1; \ldots; B_m)$ is in $\Theta(S)$; otherwise the clauses

$$C_0 : \ g(B_1), \ldots, g(B_m) \to g(A_1), ct_{C,1}(\mathbf{V}_C),$$
$$C_i : \ ct_{C,i}(\mathbf{V}_C), A_i \to g(A_{i+1}), ct_{C,i+1}(\mathbf{V}_C) \quad \text{for } i = 1, \ldots, n-1,$$
$$C_n : \ ct_{C,n}(\mathbf{V}_C), A_n \to B_1; \ldots; B_m,$$

are in $\Theta(S)$, where $\mathbf{V}_C$ is the tuple of all variables appearing in C. Each clause C_k ($0 \le k \le n$) is called the *k-th translation clause* from C.

In the above definition, the new predicate g is a meta-predicate which is an abbreviation of *goal* in [9,4]. Each atom of the form $g(A)$ is called a *goal atom*, while an atom constructed in the original language is called an *object atom*. The new predicate $ct_{C,i}$ ($1 \le i \le n$) is also an abbreviation of $cont_{C,i}$ in [9,4], in which the suffix C is used to identify the original clause, and works as a *supplementary magic predicate* in [2]. Although each C_i ($0 \le i \le n-1$) has a conjunction of two atoms $g(A_{i+1})$ and $ct_{C,i+1}(\mathbf{V}_C)$ in the consequent, we identify C_i with two Horn clauses, $A \to g(A_{i+1})$ and $A \to ct_{C,i+1}(\mathbf{V}_C)$ where A is the antecedent of C_i.

For a set of clauses FC, $hc(\Theta(FC))$ ($\subseteq \Theta(FC)$) is the set of all k-th translation clauses C_k's ($k = 0, \ldots, n-1$) from clauses in FC, and $nhc(\Theta(FC))$ is the set of all n-th translation clauses C_n from clauses in FC ($n > 1$) together with all translation clauses C' from positive clauses in FC. Note that both $\Theta(BC)$ and $hc(\Theta(FC))$ consist of Horn clauses only, while $nhc(\Theta(FC))$ contains both non-Horn clauses and Horn clauses; a Horn clause is in $nhc(\Theta(FC))$ iff FC includes a Horn clause. We also write $\Theta'(BC, FC) = \Theta(BC) \cup hc(\Theta(FC))$.

Example 4. Let BC and FC be the same as in Example 1. $\Theta'(BC, FC)$ consists of:

$$g(\bot) \to g(p(X)), ct_{1,1}(X), \qquad ct_{1,1}(X), p(X) \to g(r(b)), ct_{1,2}(X),$$
$$ct_{1,2}(X), r(b) \to \bot, \qquad g(\bot) \to g(p(X)), ct_{2,1}(X),$$
$$ct_{2,1}(X), p(X) \to g(s(b)), ct_{2,2}(X), \qquad ct_{2,2}(X), s(b) \to \bot,$$
$$g(\bot) \to g(t(X)), ct_{3,1}(X), \qquad ct_{3,1}(X), t(X) \to \bot,$$
$$g(p(X)) \to g(q(X)), ct_{4,1}(X), \qquad ct_{4,1}(X), q(X) \to p(X),$$
$$g(q(a)) \to q(a), \qquad g(q(b)) \to q(b),$$
$$g(r(X)), g(s(X)) \to g(u(X)), ct_{5,1}(X), \qquad g(t(X)), g(u(X)) \to g(p(X)), ct_{6,1}(X),$$

and $nhc(\Theta(FC))$ contains the clauses:

$$ct_{5,1}(X), u(X) \rightarrow r(X); s(X), \tag{3}$$
$$ct_{6,1}(X), p(X) \rightarrow t(X); u(X). \tag{4}$$

As shown in Example 4, clauses in $hc(\Theta(S))$ are not always range-restricted even if all clauses in S are range-restricted [4]. To recover the range-restrictedness, the NHM method in [4] uses the dom predicate [7] and adornments [2]. Here, we use the technique of generalized subsumption [8,9] to handle non-range-restricted Horn clauses, which is shown by the following function Δ.

Definition 8. Let BC be a set of Horn clauses, and E a set of atoms. Then,

$$\Delta(BC, E) = \{ \ B\theta \mid (A_1, \ldots, A_n \rightarrow B) \in BC, \ E \vdash (A_1, \ldots, A_n)\theta,$$
$$\text{where } \theta \text{ is a computed answer for } E \cup \{ \leftarrow (A_1, \ldots, A_n) \},$$
$$\text{and } B\theta \text{ is not any instance of } B' \in E \ \}.$$

The *naive evaluation* $nv(BC, E)$ is defined as:

$$nv(BC, E) = \begin{cases} E, & \text{if } \Delta(BC, E) \subseteq E; \\ nv(BC, E \cup \Delta(BC, E)), & \text{otherwise.} \end{cases}$$

$nv(BC, E)$ is also a monotone function of E.

Now, we redefine a bottom-up proof-procedure for NHM using nv.

Definition 9 (Procedure bp(BC, FC, E)).

Input: BC: a set of Horn clauses, FC: a set of range-restricted clauses, E: a set of atoms.
Output: *sat/unsat*: the (un)satisfiability of $BC \cup FC$.
1. Set $M = nv(BC, E)$. If $M \vdash \bot$, then return *unsat*.
2. Else if any ground clause from FC is not violated in M, then return *sat*;
3. Otherwise, let $C\theta$ be a violated clause for M such that it is a ground clause from FC. If $\mathbf{bp}(BC, FC, M \cup \{B_j\theta\}) = unsat$ for every consequent atom $B_j\theta$ of $C\theta$, then return *unsat*; else return *sat*.

Initially, NHM is called by $\mathbf{bp}(\Theta'(BC, FC), nhc(\Theta(FC)), \{g(\bot)\})$. Here, each set $M \cup \{B_j\theta\}$ of atoms generated in $\mathbf{bp}(BC, FC, E)$ is called a *model candidate*.

Example 5 (cont. from Example 4).
Let us consider $\mathbf{bp}(\Theta'(BC, FC), nhc(\Theta(FC)), \{g(\bot)\})$.

1. Let $M_0 = nv(\Theta'(BC, FC), \{g(\bot)\})$. Then, we have

$$M_0 = \{ \ g(\bot), g(p(X)), ct_{1,1}(X), ct_{2,1}(X), g(t(X)), ct_{3,1}(X), g(q(X)),$$
$$ct_{4,1}(X), q(a), q(b), p(a), p(b), g(r(b)), ct_{1,2}(a), ct_{1,2}(b), g(s(b)),$$
$$ct_{2,2}(a), ct_{2,2}(b), g(u(b)), ct_{5,1}(b), ct_{6,1}(b) \ \}.$$

The ground instance of (4) with the substitution $\{X/b\}$ is violated in M_0.

2. (a) Let $M_1 = nv(\Theta'(BC, FC), M_0 \cup \{t(b)\})$. Then, $M_1 = M_0 \cup \{t(b), \perp\}$. Since $M_1 \vdash \perp$, *unsat* is returned.
   (b) Let $M_2 = nv(\Theta'(BC, FC), M_0 \cup \{u(b)\})$. Then, $M_2 = M_0 \cup \{u(b)\}$. The ground instance of (3) with the substitution $\{X/b\}$ is violated in M_2.
      i. Let $M_3 = nv(\Theta'(BC, FC), M_2 \cup \{r(b)\})$. Then, $M_3 = M_2 \cup \{r(b), \perp\}$. Since $M_3 \vdash \perp$, *unsat* is returned.
      ii. Let $M_4 = nv(\Theta'(BC, FC), M_2 \cup \{s(b)\})$. Then, $M_4 = M_2 \cup \{s(b), \perp\}$. Since $M_4 \vdash \perp$, *unsat* is returned.
   Hence, *unsat* is returned by $\mathbf{bp}(\Theta'(BC, FC), nhc(\Theta(FC)), M_0 \cup \{u(b)\})$. Therefore, *unsat* is returned by $\mathbf{bp}(\Theta'(BC, FC), nhc(\Theta(FC)), \{g(\perp)\})$.

Definition 10. Let BC and FC be the same as in Definition 9. A *proof tree by NHM* with respect to (BC, FC) is a tree satisfying the conditions:

1. Each node of a tree is a set of atoms;
2. The root node is $\{g(\perp)\}$;
3. For each node E, if $nv(\Theta'(BC, FC), E) \vdash \perp$, then E is a leaf node;
4. For each node E, if any ground clause from $nhc(\Theta(FC))$ is not violated in $nv(\Theta'(BC, FC), E)$, then E is a leaf node;
5. For each non-leaf node E, if a ground clause, $(ct_{C,n}(\mathbf{V}_C), A_n \rightarrow B_1; \ldots; B_m)\theta$ or $(g(B_1), \ldots, g(B_m) \rightarrow B_1; \ldots; B_m)\theta$, from $nhc(\Theta(FC))$ is violated in $M = nv(\Theta'(BC, FC), E)$, then E has the children $M \cup \{B_1\theta\}, \ldots, M \cup \{B_m\theta\}$.

Example 6 (cont. from Examples 4 and 5). From Example 5, it is easy to see that the proof tree by NHM with respect to (BC, FC) has the 3 leaves: $M_0 \cup \{t(b)\}$, $M_0 \cup \{u(b), r(b)\}$ and $M_0 \cup \{u(b), s(b)\}$.

5 Equivalence Between NHM and RT

In this section, we show that given a set of clauses, which is either satisfiable or unsatisfiable, the proof tree by SATCHMORE/w is the same as that by NHM except for syntactic differences of their nodes.

Firstly, the next two lemmas state relations between the top-down proof and the bottom-up proof for a set of Horn clauses. These lemmas are proved in [8] in the context of logic programming and deductive databases.

Lemma 1. Let BC be a set of Horn clauses, and G an object atom. Then, for any object atom L, $rl(BC, G) \vdash L$ if and only if $nv(\Theta(BC), \{g(G)\}) \vdash g(L)$.

Lemma 2. Let BC and G be the same as in Lemma 1. Then, for any substitution θ, $BC \vdash G\theta$ if and only if $nv(\Theta(BC), \{g(G)\}) \vdash G\theta$.

The next two corollaries easily follow from Lemmas 1 and 2, respectively.

Corollary 1. *Let BC be a set of Horn clauses, and $G = (A_1, \ldots, A_n)$ ($n \geq$ 1) a conjunction of object atoms. Also, let $\mathcal{G} = \{G_1, \ldots, G_{n-1}\}$ be a set of clauses, where $G_i = (ct_{G,i}(\mathbf{V}_G), A_i \rightarrow g(A_{i+1}), ct_{G,i+1}(\mathbf{V}_G))$ for $i = 1, \ldots, n - 1$. Then, for any object atom L, $rl(BC, G) \vdash L$ if and only if $nv(\Theta(BC) \cup \mathcal{G}, \{g(A_1), ct_{G,1}(\mathbf{V}_G)\}) \vdash g(L)$.*

Corollary 2. *Let BC be a set of Horn clauses, FC a set of clauses, and G any object atom. Then, $BC \vdash G$ and $nv(\Theta'(BC, FC), \{g(\bot)\}) \vdash g(G)$ if and only if $nv(\Theta'(BC, FC), \{g(\bot)\}) \vdash G$.*

Now, we show the relationship between weak relevant literals in RT and goal atoms in NHM.

Theorem 1. *Let FC be a set of range-restricted clauses, and BC a set of range-restricted Horn clauses. Then, for any object atom L, $wrl(BC, FC, \bot, \emptyset) \vdash L$ if and only if $nv(\Theta'(BC, FC), \{g(\bot)\}) \vdash g(L)$.*

Proof. Put $R = wrl(BC, FC, \bot, \emptyset)$, and $M = nv(\Theta'(BC, FC), \{g(\bot)\})$.

(Only-if part) *Assume that $R \vdash L$. We prove that $M \vdash g(L)$ by induction on the number $l \geq 1$ of recursive calls to wrl. We denote the k-th recursive call to wrl as $wrl(BC, FC, G_k, R_k)$ for $k = 1, \ldots, l$.*

In case of $l = 1$, $R_1 = rl(BC, \bot)$, and the result holds by Lemma 1.

In case of $l > 1$, we will prove that $M \vdash g(L)$ when $R_l \vdash L$ and $R_{l-1} \nvdash L$; otherwise the proof is obvious by the induction hypothesis. In this case, L is an instance of a relevant literal to the derivation of $(A_1, \ldots, A_n)\theta$ from BC, where $(A_1, \ldots, A_n)$ is the antecedent of some clause C in $rc(R_{l-1}, FC)$. Then, for the consequent $(B_1; \ldots; B_m)$ of C, $R_{l-1} \vdash (B_1, \ldots, B_m)\theta$. By the induction hypotheses, $M \vdash (g(B_1), \ldots, g(B_m))\theta$. Since C_0 translated from C is contained in $\Theta'(BC, FC)$, $M \vdash (g(A_1), ct_{C,1}(\mathbf{V}_C))\theta$ holds. Moreover, since C_i's ($i = 1, \ldots, n - 1$) translated from C are also contained in $\Theta'(BC, FC)$ and $rl(BC, (A_1, \ldots, A_n)\theta) \vdash L$ holds, $M \vdash g(L)$ holds by Corollary 1.

(If part) *Assume that $M \vdash g(L)$. We prove that $R \vdash L$ by induction on the number $l \geq 0$ of recursive calls to nv. We denote the k-th call to nv as $nv(\Theta'(BC, FC), E_k)$ for $k = 0, \ldots, l$.*

In case of $l = 0$, $E_0 = \{g(\bot)\}$, and the result follows from Definition 3.

In case of $l > 0$, we will prove that $R \vdash L$ when $E_l \vdash g(L)$ and $E_{l-1} \nvdash g(L)$; otherwise the proof is obvious by the induction hypothesis. There are two cases:
Case I. *Consider the case that $g(L)$ is an instance of $g(A_1)\theta$, where*

$$C_0 : (g(B_1), \ldots, g(B_m) \rightarrow g(A_1), ct_{C,1}(\mathbf{V}_C))$$

in $\Theta'(BC, FC)$ is translated from $C : (A_1, \ldots, A_n \rightarrow B_1; \ldots; B_m)$ such that (i) $E_{l-1} \vdash (g(B_1), \ldots, g(B_m))\theta$, and (ii) θ is a computed answer for $E_{l-1} \cup \{ \leftarrow (g(B_1), \ldots, g(B_m)) \}$.

Then, $R \vdash (B_1, \ldots, B_m)\theta$ holds by the induction hypotheses. Here, either $C \in FC$ or $C \in BC$, and each case is analyzed separately:

$C \in FC$: $C\theta$ is an instance of a relevant clause in FC relative to R. Then, the leftmost atom in each node in the SLD tree for $BC \cup \{ \leftarrow (A_1, \ldots, A_n)\theta \}$ is an instance of an element of R. Since L is an instance of $A_1\theta$, $R \vdash L$ holds.

$C \in BC$: $(B_1, \Gamma)\theta$ is an instance of a node in some SLD tree to compute R, where Γ is a conjunction of some atoms. Then, $(A_1, \ldots, A_n, \Gamma)\theta$ appears as a child node of $(B_1, \Gamma)\theta$. Hence, $A_1\theta$ is an instance of the leftmost atom in a node in the SLD tree. Since L is an instance of $A_1\theta$, $R \vdash L$ holds.

Case II. Consider the case that $g(L)$ is an instance of $g(A_{i+1})\theta$, where

$$C_i : (ct_{C,i}(\mathbf{V}_C), A_i \to g(A_{i+1}), ct_{C,i+1}(\mathbf{V}_C))$$

in $\Theta'(BC, FC)$ is translated from $C : (A_1, \ldots, A_n \to B_1; \ldots; B_m)$ such that (i)

$$E_{l-1} \vdash (ct_{C,i}(\mathbf{V}_C), A_i)\theta, \tag{5}$$

and (ii) θ is a computed answer for $E_{l-1} \cup \{ \leftarrow (ct_{C,i}(\mathbf{V}_C), A_i) \}$.

Since $C_j \in \Theta'(BC, FC)$ for every $j = 1, \ldots, i-1$, (5) implies that $E_{l-1} \vdash (g(A_{j+1}), ct_{C,j}(\mathbf{V}_C), A_j)\theta$. In particular, $E_{l-1} \vdash ct_{C,1}(\mathbf{V}_C)\theta$. We have $E_{l-1} \vdash (g(B_1), \ldots, g(B_m), g(A_1))\theta$ by $C_0 \in \Theta'(BC, FC)$. Therefore, $R \vdash (B_1, \ldots, B_m)\theta$ holds by the induction hypothesis. For both $C \in FC$ and $C \in BC$, we can prove that $R \vdash L$ by the similar argument as in Case I. □

Nextly, we show that the number of nodes in depth 1 in the proof tree by SATCHMORE/w is the same as that in the proof tree by NHM. In the following, we assume that the strategy to select a violated clause in SATCHMORE/w and that in MGTP employing NHM are exactly the same.

Theorem 2. Let BC and FC be the same as in Theorem 1. Then, a ground clause $C\theta : (A_1, \ldots, A_n \to B_1; \ldots; B_m)\theta$ from $rc(wrl(BC, FC, \perp, \emptyset), FC)$ is violated in BC if and only if a ground clause $C_n\theta : (ct_{C,n}(\mathbf{V}_C), A_n \to B_1; \ldots; B_m)\theta$ from $nhc(\Theta(FC))$ is violated in $nv(\Theta'(BC, FC), \{g(\perp)\})$.

Proof. Put $M = nv(\Theta'(BC, FC), \{g(\perp)\})$.

(**Only-if part**) Assume that $C\theta$ is a violated clause for BC. Because $C\theta$ is a ground clause from $rc(wrl(BC, FC, \perp, \emptyset), FC)$, for the consequent atoms $B_1, \ldots, B_m$ of C, it holds that $M \vdash (g(B_1), \ldots, g(B_m))\theta$ by Theorem 1. Then, by $C_0 \in \Theta'(BC, FC)$,

$$M \vdash (g(A_1), ct_{C,1}(\mathbf{V}_C))\theta. \tag{6}$$

Since $C\theta$ is a violated clause for BC,

$$BC \vdash (A_1, \ldots, A_n)\theta, \tag{7}$$

$$BC \not\vdash (B_1; \ldots; B_m)\theta. \tag{8}$$

Since $C_i \in \Theta'(BC, FC)$ for $i = 1, \ldots, n-1$, (6), (7) and Corollary 2 imply that

$$M \vdash (g(A_{i+1}), ct_{C,i+1}(\mathbf{V}_C))\theta. \tag{9}$$

Further, by (8) and Corollary 2,

$$M \not\vdash (B_1; \ldots; B_m)\theta. \tag{10}$$

By (7), (9) and Corollary 2, $M \vdash A_n\theta$ holds. Then, by (9) and (10), $C_n\theta$ is violated in M.

(If part) *Suppose that $C_n\theta$ is a violated clause for M. Then,*

$$M \vdash (ct_{C,n}(\mathbf{V}_C), A_n)\theta, \tag{11}$$
$$M \not\vdash (B_1; \ldots; B_m)\theta. \tag{12}$$

Since $C_i \in \Theta'(BC, FC)$ for $i = 1, \ldots, n-1$, (11) implies that

$$M \vdash (g(A_{i+1}), ct_{C,i}(\mathbf{V}_C), A_i)\theta. \tag{13}$$

Next, $C_0 \in \Theta'(BC, FC)$ and (13) imply that

$$M \vdash (g(B_1), \ldots, g(B_m), g(A_1))\theta. \tag{14}$$

Therefore, $wrl(BC, FC, \bot, \emptyset) \vdash (B_1, \ldots, B_m)\theta$ by Theorem 1. Hence, $C\theta$ is a ground clause from $rc(wrl(BC, FC, \bot, \emptyset), FC)$.

Now, by (11), (13) and Corollary 2, $BC \vdash (A_1, \ldots, A_n)\theta$. Further, by (14), (12) and Corollary 2, $BC \not\vdash (B_1, \ldots, B_m)\theta$. Hence, $C\theta$ is violated in BC. □

The next theorem shows that the number of nodes in any depth in the proof tree by SATCHMORE/w is the same as that in the proof tree by NHM. In the following, the *top call to* **rt** *is* $\mathbf{rt}(BC, FC, \emptyset)$, *and the top call to* **bp** *is* $\mathbf{bp}(\Theta'(BC, FC), nhc(\Theta(FC)), \{g(\bot)\})$.

Theorem 3 (Main). *Let FC and BC be the same as in Theorem 1, and I a set of ground atoms. Then, for any ground atom B, a partial interpretation $I \cup \{B\}$ is generated by the top call to* **rt** *if and only if a model candidate $M \cup \{B\}$ is generated by the top call to* **bp**, *where $M = nv(\Theta'(BC, FC), \{g(\bot)\} \cup I)$.*

Proof. **(Only-if part)** *Suppose that a partial interpretation $I \cup \{B\}$ is generated. Let $I_0 = \emptyset$ and $I_1, \ldots, I_l$ ($l \geq 1$) be the sequence of partial interpretations generated by the top call to* **rt** *such that (i) $I_k = I_{k-1} \cup \{B^k\}$ for $k = 1, \ldots, l$ (B^k is a ground atom), and (ii) $I_{l-1} = I$ and $B^l = B$. We prove by induction on the number $l \geq 1$ that the partial interpretation $I_{l-1} \cup \{B^l\}$ is generated only if the model candidate $M_{l-1} \cup \{B^l\}$ is generated by* **bp**, *where*

$$M_{l-1} = nv(\Theta'(BC, FC), \{g(\bot)\} \cup I_{l-1}).$$

In case of $l = 1$, the result follows from Theorem 2.

In case of $l > 1$, assume that the model candidate $M_{k-1} \cup \{B^k\}$ is generated for every $k = 1, \ldots, l-1$, where $M_{k-1} = nv(\Theta'(BC, FC), \{g(\bot)\} \cup I_{k-1})$. Then, $I_0 \subset I_1 \subset \ldots \subset I_{l-2} \subset I_{l-1}$. Similarly, by the monotonicity of nv, $M_0 \subset M_1 \subset \ldots \subset M_{l-2} \subset M_{l-1}$. On the other hand, $M_{k-1} \vdash g(B^k)$ holds for every $k = 1, \ldots, l-1$ by the induction hypothesis and Definitions 8 and 9.

Therefore, $M_{l-1} \vdash (g(B^1), \ldots, g(B^{l-1}))$ holds. Hence, $M_{l-1} = nv(\Theta'(BC \cup I_{l-1}, FC), \{g(\bot)\})$. Now, let $C : (A_1, \ldots, A_n \to B_1; \ldots; B^l; \ldots; B_m)$ be a ground clause from $rc(wrl(BC \cup I_{l-1}, FC, \bot, \emptyset), FC)$ such that C is violated in $BC \cup I_{l-1}$. Then, by Theorem 2, there is a ground instance C_n of the n-th translation clause from C such that C_n is violated in M_{l-1}. This implies that the model candidate $M_{l-1} \cup \{B^l\}$ is generated.

   (If part) *Suppose that a model candidate $M \cup \{B\}$ is generated. Let $M_0, \ldots, M_l$ $(l \geq 1)$ be the sequence of model candidates generated by the top call to **bf** such that (i) $M_0 = nv(\Theta'(BC, FC), \{g(\bot)\})$, (ii) for every $k = 1, \ldots, l$,*

$$M_k = nv(\Theta'(BC, FC), M_{k-1} \cup \{B^k\}) \tag{15}$$

where B^k is a ground atom, and (iii) $M_{l-1} = M$ and $B^l = B$. We prove by the induction on the number $l \geq 1$ that the model candidate $M_{l-1} \cup \{B^l\}$ is generated only if the partial interpretation $I_{l-1} \cup \{B^l\}$ is generated, where I_{l-1} is the minimal set of ground atoms satisfying $M_{l-1} = nv(\Theta'(BC, FC), \{g(\bot)\} \cup I_{l-1})$.

   In case of $l = 1$, the proof is done by Theorem 2.

   In case of $l > 1$, assume that the partial interpretation $I_k = I_{k-1} \cup \{B^k\}$ is generated for every $k = 1, \ldots, l-1$, where $I_0 = \emptyset$.

   By the induction hypothesis and (15), for each $k = 1, \ldots, l-1$, it holds that

$$M_k = nv(\Theta'(BC, FC), \{g(\bot)\} \cup I_k). \tag{16}$$

By (15) and Definitions 8 and 9, $M_{k-1} \vdash g(B^k)$ holds for every $k = 1, \ldots, l$. Further, by Definitions 8 and 9, $M_0 \subset M_1 \subset \ldots \subset M_{l-1}$. Therefore, $M_{l-1} \vdash (g(B^1), \ldots, g(B^{l-1}), g(B^l))$. By this and (16),

$$M_{l-1} = nv(\Theta'(BC \cup I_{l-1}, FC), \{g(\bot)\}).$$

Now, let $C_n : (ct_{C,n}(\mathbf{V}'_C), A_n \to B_1; \ldots; B^l; \ldots; B_m)$ be a ground instance of the n-th translation clause from $C \in FC$ such that C_n is violated in M_{l-1}. Then, by Theorem 2, there is the corresponding clause C that is a ground clause from $rc(wrl(BC \cup I_{l-1}, FC, \bot, \emptyset), FC)$ and violated in $BC \cup I_{l-1}$. Hence, the partial interpretation $I_{l-1} \cup \{B^l\}$ is generated. □

Theorem 3 states that, if SATCHMORE/w generates a partial interpretation then NHM also generates the corresponding model candidate, and vice versa. Namely, there is a one-to-one correspondence between the partial interpretations generated by SATCHMORE/w and the model candidates generated by NHM. In other words, the number of leaves in the proof tree by SATCHMORE/w is exactly the same as that in the proof tree by NHM. Thus, we have shown that non-Horn magic sets and weak relevancy testing, although in which completely different approaches are taken, have the same power in pruning redundant branches of proof trees.

6   Discussion

According to Definition 3, the set of weak relevant literals for $(BC \cup I, FC)$ increases monotonically as a partial interpretation I grows. However, this monotonicity does not hold in the original SATCHMORE [6]. This is because our definition of weak relevant literals wrl (Definition 3) is different from the definition of *extended relevant literals* in [6] in the following sense. The extended relevant literals $xrl(BC, FC, G, R)$ is defined as:

$$xrl(BC, FC, G, R) = \begin{cases} R, & \text{if } rl(BC, G) \subseteq R; \\ R \cup rl(BC, G), & \\ & \text{else if there is a ground clause from} \\ & rc(R \cup rl(BC, G), FC) \text{ which is violated in } BC; \\ \bigcup_{C \in rc(R \cup rl(BC,G), FC)} xrl(BC, FC, ant(C), R \cup rl(BC, G)), & \\ & \text{otherwise,} \end{cases}$$

where $ant(C)$ is the antecedent of C. We here denote SATCHMORE using extended relevant literals [6] as *SATCHMORE/x*, which is defined in the same way as SATCHMORE/w in Definition 5 except that the function xrl is used instead of wrl.

The only difference between SATCHMORE/w and SATCHMORE/x lies in the case that there are several violated and relevant clauses relative to BC. With the additional second condition, the set of extended relevant literals for $(BC \cup I, FC)$ may decrease according to the increase of I. Moreover, the set of extended relevant literals becomes always smaller than the set of weak relevant literals, and thus partial interpretations generated by SATCHMORE/w may not be generated by SATCHMORE/x. In particular, when there are cyclic clauses or equivalences like $(a \equiv e \vee f)$ in the example below, SATCHMORE/x has more power than SATCHMORE/w in pruning redundant branches in proof trees.

Example 7. Suppose that Horn clauses BC and clauses FC are given by

$$BC: \quad \bot \leftarrow p, \quad \bot \leftarrow q, \quad a \leftarrow e, \quad a \leftarrow f, \quad a \leftarrow b, \quad b \leftarrow,$$
$$FC: \quad a \rightarrow e; f, \tag{17}$$
$$a \rightarrow p; q. \tag{18}$$

Then, SATCHMORE/w checks the satisfiability of $BC \cup FC$ by **rt** as follows.

1. $rl(BC, \bot) = \{\bot, p, q\}$. The only relevant clause in FC relative to this set is the clause (18).
2. $rl(BC, a) = \{e, f, b\}$. Then, $rc(rl(BC, \bot) \cup rl(BC, a), FC) = FC$. Computing wrl for each clause in FC, we have $wrl(BC, FC, \bot, \emptyset) = \{\bot, p, q, e, f, b\}$.

3. In the procedure **rt**, a violated clause for BC is nondeterministically selected from the relevant clauses FC. Here, both (17) and (18) are violated in BC. If (17) is selected first, an extra case-splitting is performed.

On the other hand, SATCHMORE/x works differently as follows. At Step 1 above, the additional condition in xrl is checked to see whether the relevant clause (18) is violated in BC. Since this is the case, xrl immediately returns $\{\perp, p, q\}$ as the extended relevant literals for (BC, FC). Hence, the case-splitting with the clause (17) is avoided.

Although SATCHMORE/w is weaker than SATCHMORE/x in the above sense, the notion of weak relevant literals has an advantage too. Since SATCH-MORE/x realizes non-monotone computation of extended relevant literals, it discards all the extended relevant literals computed so far and computes a new one from the scratch. In most cases, this involves recomputation of extended relevant literals that have been computed already. In NHM, on the other hand, due to bottom-up computation, recomputation of goal atoms which correspond to weak relevant literals are completely avoided. This merit is reflected in monotone computation of weak relevant literals in SATCHMORE/w. This is illustrated in the next example.[2]

Example 8. Consider Example 2 again. In Step 2 (b), $\mathbf{rt}(BC, FC, \{u(b)\})$ is computed. Here, SATCHMORE/x would firstly compute the extended relevant literals for $(BC \cup \{u(b)\}, FC)$. In this case, $xrl(BC \cup \{u(b)\}, FC, \perp, \emptyset)$ repeats the same computation as $rl(BC, \perp)$ in computing $rl(BC \cup \{u(b)\}, \perp)$. On the other hand, NHM never recomputes any goal atom by using goal atoms that have been computed in M_0 as shown in Example 5.

7   Conclusion

This paper has shown that the number of leaves of a proof tree generated by the SATCHMORE procedure using weak relevant literals coincides with the number of those by the NHM method. This set of weak relevant literals includes the corresponding set of extended relevant literals. Therefore, there is a case where SATCHMORE which uses extended relevant literals generates a proof tree with fewer leaves than the NHM method. However, unlike SATCHMORE using extended relevant literals, the NHM method has an advantage that it can avoid duplicated computations of *goal* atoms corresponding to elements in the set of weak relevant literals. A major subject of the future is to clarify for what class of input clause sets, the NHM method becomes equivalent to SATCHMORE using extended relevant literals.

References

1. Bancilhon, F., Maier, D., Sagiv, Y., and Ullman, J. D., Magic sets and other strange ways to implement logic programs, in: *Proc. 5th ACM SIGMOD-SIGACT Symp. on Principles of Database Systems*, pp. 1–15, 1986.

---

[2] The cost of recomputation of extended relevant literals by SATCHMORE/x can be exponentially more expensive than that of computing weak relevant literals by SATCHMORE/w for some examples (see [4]).

2. Beeri, C. and Ramakrishnan, R., On the power of magic, *J. Logic Programming*, 10:255–299, 1991.
3. Fujita, H. and Hasegawa, R., A model generation theorem prover in KL1 using a ramified-stack algorithm, *Proc. 8th Int. Conf. on Logic Programming*, pp. 535–548, MIT Press, 1991.
4. Hasegawa, R., Inoue, K., Ohta, Y. and Koshimura, M., Non-Horn magic sets to incorporate top-down inference into bottom-up theorem proving, in: W. McCune (ed.), *Proc. 14th Int. Conf. on Automated Deduction (CADE-14), Lecture Notes in Artificial Intelligence*, 1249, pp. 176-190, Springer, 1997.
5. Lloyd, J. W., *Foundations of Logic Programming*, 2nd Edition, Springer, 1987.
6. Loveland, D. W., Reed, D. and Wilson, D. S., SATCHMORE: SATCHMO with RElevancy, *J. Automated Reasoning*, 14(2):325–351, 1995.
7. Manthey, R. and Bry, F., SATCHMO: a theorem prover implemented in Prolog, in: E. Lusk and R. Overbeek (eds.), *Proc. 9th Int. Conf. on Automated Deduction (CADE-9), Lecture Notes in Computer Science*, 310, pp. 415–434, Springer, 1988.
8. Seki, H., On the power of Alexander templates, *Proc. 8th ACM SIGACT-SIGMOD-SIGART Symp. on Principles of Database Systems*, pp. 150–158, 1989.
9. Stickel, M. E., Upside-down meta-interpretation of the model elimination theorem-proving procedure for deduction and abduction, *J. Automated Reasoning*, 13(2):189–210, 1994.

A Certified Version of Buchberger's Algorithm

Laurent Théry

INRIA, 2004 route des Lucioles, 06902 Sophia Antipolis France
`thery@sophia.inria.fr`

Abstract. We present a proof of Buchberger's algorithm that has been developed in the Coq proof assistant. The formulation of the algorithm in Coq can then be efficiently compiled and used to do computation.

1   Introduction

If we look at the way one can use computers to do mathematics, there is a clear separation between computing, where one uses computer algebra systems, and proving, where one uses theorem provers. The fact that these two aspects are covered separately has obvious drawbacks. On the one hand it is a well-known fact that, because of misuse or implementation errors, one should always double-check the results given by a computer algebra system. This problem is even more crucial for general-purpose computer algebra systems where the library of algorithms is mostly developed by the user community. Extensions of the system are then performed without giving evidence of their applicability or correctness. On the other hand theorem provers usually come with very little computing power. This makes it difficult to complete proofs for which some computing steps are needed.

It would be a real progress if one could unify these two aspects in a single system. It would then be possible to define mathematical objects and both compute and prove properties about them. Building such a system from scratch requires an important effort. A more pragmatic approach consists in complementing existing systems. If we look at computer algebra systems, the situation is somewhat difficult. The languages of general-purpose computer algebra systems have not been designed with the idea that people would like to reason about them. For example, the scope of local variables in Maple [2] is not limited to the procedure where they have been defined. Thus, stating properties of algorithms turns out to be very difficult.

If we look at theorem provers, the main problem is efficiency. While most theorem provers allow us to define algorithms, executing them is inefficient because it is performed inside the prover in an interpretative way. An alternative solution is for the prover to be able to translate its algorithms into another programming language that has a compiler.

Our approach follows the second line. We have chosen the theorem prover Coq [12] to do our experiments. Coq is a prover based on type theory. It manipulates

C. Kirchner and H. Kirchner (Eds.): Automated Deduction, CADE-15
LNAI 1421, pp. 349–364, 1998. © Springer–Verlag Berlin Heidelberg 1998

objects with a rich notion of types which is clearly adequate for mathematical objects. Coq also proposes an extraction mechanism that, given an algorithm defined in the system, generates an implementation in the language Ocaml [14] that can be efficiently compiled.

Is this solution practical? What is the effort involved in trying to certify standard algorithms for computer algebra systems? It is to answer these questions that we decided to work on the proof of correctness of Buchberger's algorithm. We started from a five page description of the algorithm in a standard introduction book [7]. The goal was simple: to develop enough mathematical knowledge in Coq for stating the algorithm and proving its correctness and termination.

The paper is organized as follows. In Section 2 we introduce the Buchberger's algorithm. In Sections 3 and 4 we sketch its proofs of correctness and termination. In Section 5 we explain the main steps of our development and give a running example of the algorithm. Finally we relate our approach to others and draw some conclusions and future work.

2   Buchberger's Algorithm

Buchberger's algorithm is a *completion* algorithm working on polynomials. Given a list of polynomials it returns a completed list that has a particular property. Before presenting the algorithm, we first need to define some basic notions [7].

2.1   Ordered Polynomials

We first consider the usual n variables polynomials over an arbitrary field (A, $+_a, -_a, *_a, /_a, 0_a, 1_a$) with two of their usual operations: addition ($+$) and multiplication by a term ($.$). A polynomial is composed of a list of *terms*. Each term is composed of a *coefficient* and a *monomial*. The set of coefficients is A. The set of monomials is denoted by M_n where n is the number of variables. The set of terms and polynomials are denoted by T_{A,M_n} and P_{A,M_n} respectively.

An *order* $\leq_{M_n}$ over monomials is a binary relation that is transitive, reflexive and antisymmetric. It is *total* if two distinct elements are always comparable. It is *well-founded* if there exists no infinite strictly decreasing sequence of monomials. Finally it is *admissible* if $x_1^0 \ldots x_n^0$ is minimal for the order and if the order is compatible with the multiplication.

Given an admissible well-founded total order $\leq_{M_n}$ over monomials, it is possible to represent a polynomial as a list of terms, such that the list of the corresponding monomials is ordered, i.e. each monomial in the list is strictly greater than the ones at its right. We use 0 and $\dotplus$ to denote the null polynomial and the ordered list constructor respectively. From this representation we get the structural induction theorem for an arbitrary predicate P over polynomials:

$$(P\,0) \wedge (\forall a \in A, \forall p \in P_{A,M_n}, (P\,p) \Rightarrow (P\,(a \dotplus p))) \Rightarrow \forall p \in P_{A,M_n}, (P\,p)$$

We define the transitive relation $<_p$ over polynomials as the smallest relation such that:

- $\forall t \in T_{A,M_n}, \forall p \in P_{A,M_n}, 0 <_p t \dotplus p$
- $\forall a_1, a_2 \in A, \forall m \in M_n, \forall p, q \in P_{A,M_n}, p <_p q \Rightarrow a_1 m \dotplus p <_p a_2 m \dotplus q$
- $\forall a_1, a_2 \in A, \forall m_1, m_2 \in M_n, \forall p, q \in P_{A,M_n},$
  $$m_1 <_{M_n} m_2 \Rightarrow a_1 m_1 \dotplus p <_p a_2 m_2 \dotplus q$$

This relation is well-founded. So we get another important induction principle:

$$(\forall p \in P_{A,M_n}, (\forall q \in P_{A,M_n}, q <_p p \Rightarrow (P\,q)) \Rightarrow (P\,p)) \Rightarrow \forall p \in P_{A,M_n}, (P\,p)$$

2.2   Normal Form

Given the definition of polynomials, it is possible that polynomials carry terms with null coefficient. Equality for polynomials is then understood as the equality without paying attention to terms with null coefficient. To give a more algorithmic account of this notion, we define the function nf that computes the normal form of a polynomial by removing terms with null coefficient:

- $nf(0) = 0;$
- $\forall m \in M_n, \forall p \in P_{A,M_n}, nf(0_a m \dotplus p) = nf(p);$
- $\forall a \in A, \forall m \in M_n, \forall p \in P_{A,M_n}, a \neq 0_a \Rightarrow nf(am \dotplus p) = am \dotplus nf(p).$

2.3   One Step Division, Reduction, and Irreducibility

Since the division over monomials is not total, we first define a relation $divP_{M_n}$:

$$\forall m_1, m_2 \in M_n, divP_{M_n}(m_1, m_2) \iff \exists m_3 \in M_n, m_1 = m_3.m_2$$

Then the division over monomials $/_{M_n}$ is defined as:

$$\forall m_1, m_2 \in M_n, divP_{M_n}(m_1, m_2) \Rightarrow m_1 = (m_1/_{M_n} m_2).m_2$$

We define the one step division $/_p$ over polynomials as follows :

$$\forall m_1, m_2 \in M_n, divP_{M_n}(m_1, m_2) \Rightarrow$$
$$\forall a_1, a_2 \in A, \forall p_1, p_2 \in P_{A,M_n}, a_2 \neq 0_a \Rightarrow$$
$$(a_1 m_1 \dotplus p_1)/_p(a_2 m_2 \dotplus p_2) = p_1 - (a_1/_a a_2)(m_1/_{M_n} m_2).p_2$$

Given a set of polynomials S, it is now possible to define the reduction relation $\rightarrow_S$ as the smallest relation such that:

- $\forall p_1, p_2 \in P_{A,M_n}, \forall t \in T_{A,M_n}, p_1 \rightarrow_S p_2 \Rightarrow t \dotplus p_1 \rightarrow_S t \dotplus p_2$
- $\forall m_1, m_2 \in M_n, divP_{M_n}(m_1, m_2) \Rightarrow$
  $\forall a_1, a_2 \in A, \forall p_1, p_2 \in P_{A,M_n}, a_2 \neq 0_a \Rightarrow$
  $(a_2 m_2 \dotplus p_2) \in S \Rightarrow a_1 m_1 \dotplus p_1 \rightarrow_S (a_1 m_1 \dotplus p_1)/_p(a_2 m_2 \dotplus p_2)$

We say that p is irreducible by $\rightarrow_S$ if $\forall q \in P_{A,M_n}, \neg(p \rightarrow_S q)$. We define the relation $\rightarrow_S^+$ as the reflexive-transitive closure of the relation $\rightarrow_S$ and the reduction till irreducibility $\rightarrow_S^*$ ($p \rightarrow_S^* q$ iff $p \rightarrow_S^+ q$ and q is irreducible by $\rightarrow_S$).

2.4 Spolynomials

We use the infix symbol $\hat{\ }$ to denote the function that computes the least common multiple of two monomials. If we have two polynomials $p = a_1 m_1 \stackrel{\cdot}{+} p_1$ and $q = a_2 m_2 \stackrel{\cdot}{+} p_2$ with $a_1, a_2 \neq 0$, the polynomial $m_1\hat{\ }m_2$ represents the 'smallest' polynomial that can be divided by both polynomials p and q:

$$m_1\hat{\ }m_2 \rightarrow_{\{p\}} q_1 = -(1_a/_a a_1)((m_1\hat{\ }m_2)/_{M_n} m_1).p_1$$

$$m_1\hat{\ }m_2 \rightarrow_{\{q\}} q_2 = -(1_a/_a a_2)((m_1\hat{\ }m_2)/_{M_n} m_2).p_2$$

We define the function $Spoly$ as $Spoly(p, q) = q_2 - q_1$ if the previous conditions on p and q hold and $Spoly(p, q) = 0$ otherwise ($p = 0$ or $q = 0$ or $a_1 = 0$ or $a_2 = 0$).

2.5 Polynomial Ideals

A polynomial *ideal* is a set of polynomials I that is stable under

- addition: $\forall p, q \in I$, $p + q \in I$
- multiplication by a term: $\forall p \in I$, $\forall t \in T_{A,M_n}$, $t.p \in I$.

Given a set of polynomials S, the ideal $<S>$ *generated by* S is the set of polynomials p such that

$$\exists k \in \mathbb{N}, p = \sum_{i<k} t_i.p_i \text{ such that } \forall i < k, t_i \in T_{A,M_n} \text{ and } p_i \in S.$$

It is easy to check that this set is an ideal. Finally a set of polynomials S is said to be a *basis* of an ideal I iff $<S> = I$.

2.6 Gröbner Basis and Buchberger's Algorithm

To be able to decide whether or not a given polynomial belongs to an ideal is an important property that can be used to solve a large number of interesting problems concerning polynomials. We say that a set of polynomials S is a *Gröbner basis* iff

$$\forall p \in P_{A,M_n}, p \in <S> \iff p \rightarrow^*_S 0$$

In other words, a Gröbner basis is characterized by a generated ideal whose only irreducible polynomial is 0. Thus, to check if a given polynomial belongs to an ideal generated by a Gröbner basis, one simply needs to reduce it to an irreducible polynomial and then check if this polynomial is 0 or not. A general result by Hironaka states that, given any ideal generated by a set of polynomials, there exists a Gröbner basis that generates the same ideal. Buchberger's contribution was to give an explicit algorithm for computing a Gröbner basis corresponding to the initial set of polynomials.

    In the presentation of the algorithm below, we manipulate sets of polynomials as lists. The set of set of polynomials is represented by P_{A,M_n} *list*. We also use []

to denote the empty list and the notation $[p|L]$ to represent the list whose head is the polynomial p and whose tail is L.

We first define the function $SpolyL$ that takes a polynomial and two lists of polynomials and returns a list of polynomials:

- $SpolyL(p, L_1, []) = L_1$
- $SpolyL(p, L_1, [q|L_2]) = [Spoly(p, q)|SpolyL(p, L_1, L_2)]$.

This function simply adds to the first list the spolynomials formed by the polynomial and each polynomial of the second list.

The second function $SpolyProd$ computes a reduced set of all possible spolynomials formed from a list of polynomials:

- $SpolyProd([]) = []$
- $SpolyProd([p|L]) = SpolyL(p, SpolyProd(L), L)$.

The third function nfL normalizes each element of a list, removing zero polynomials:

- $nfL([]) = []$
- $nf(p) \neq 0 \Rightarrow nfL([p|L]) = [nf(p)|nfL(L)]$
- $nf(p) = 0 \Rightarrow nfL([p|L]) = nfL(L)$.

We have now enough material to present the algorithm. Among its parameters there is an arbitrary function $reducef$ that takes a polynomial and computes an irreducible polynomial such that:

$$\forall p \in P_{A,M_n} p \rightarrow^*_S reducef(S, p)$$

For the moment, we assume that such a function exists. The algorithm is a completion that takes a pair of lists of polynomials as argument. The first element of the pair represents the basis and the second one the possible candidates to complete the basis:

- $buchf(L_1, []) = L_1$
- $nf(reducef(L_1, p)) \neq 0 \Rightarrow$
      $buchf(L_1, [p|L_2]) = buchf([nf(reducef(L_1, p))|L_1],$
                   $SpolyL(nf(reducef(L_1, p)), L_2, L_1))$
- $nf(reducef(L_1, p)) = 0 \Rightarrow buchf(L_1, [p|L_2]) = buchf(L_1, L_2)$.

If the list of candidates is empty, the basis is returned (first case). If the head of the list of candidates does not reduce to zero, it is added to the basis and the spolynomials computed by $SpolyL$ are added to the list of candidates (second case). If the head of the list of the candidates reduces to zero, a recursive call is made with the tail of the list (third case).

We finally define the function $buch$ that takes a list of polynomials as argument and returns a corresponding Gröbner basis as:

$buch(L) = buchf(nfL(L), SpolyProd(nfL(L)))$.

3 The Proof of Correctness

The correctness of the algorithm can be expressed by two theorems. The first one ensures that the result of the algorithm does not change the generated ideal:
Theorem *BuchStable:*

$$\forall S \in P_{A,M_n} \, list, \ <S> = <buch(S)>$$

The second one states that every member of the ideal reduces to 0:
Theorem *BuchReduce:*

$$\forall S \in P_{A,M_n} \, list, \ \forall p \in <S>, \ p \rightarrow^*_{buch(S)} 0$$

The theorem *BuchStable* is a direct consequence of the three following lemmas:
Lemma *RedStable:*

$$\forall S \in P_{A,M_n} \, list, \ \forall p, q \in P_{A,M_n}, \ p \rightarrow^+_S q \Rightarrow (p \in <S> \iff q \in <S>)$$

Lemma *NfStable:*

$$\forall S \in P_{A,M_n} \, list, \ \forall p \in P_{A,M_n}, \ (p \in <S> \iff nf(p) \in <S>)$$

Lemma *SpolyStable:*

$$\forall S \in P_{A,M_n} \, list, \ \forall p, q \in P_{A,M_n}, \ p \in <S> \wedge q \in <S> \Rightarrow Spoly(p,q) \in <S>$$

The theorem *BuchReduce* needs much more work to be proved. The first step is to prove the three following lemmas:
Lemma *RedCompMinus:*

$$\forall S \in P_{A,M_n} \, list, \ \forall p, q, r \in P_{A,M_n},$$
$$p - q \rightarrow_S r \Rightarrow \exists p_1, q_1 \in P_{A,M_n}, \ p \rightarrow^+_S p_1 \wedge q \rightarrow^+_S q_1 \wedge r = p_1 - q_1$$

Lemma *Red+Minus0:*

$$\forall S \in P_{A,M_n} \, list, \ \forall p, q \in P_{A,M_n},$$
$$p - q \rightarrow^+_S 0 \Rightarrow \exists r \in P_{A,M_n}, \ p \rightarrow^+_S r \wedge q \rightarrow^+_S r$$

Lemma *RedDistMinus:*

$$\forall S \in P_{A,M_n} \, list, \ \forall p, q, r \in P_{A,M_n},$$
$$p \rightarrow_S q \Rightarrow \exists s \in P_{A,M_n}, \ p - r \rightarrow^+_S s \wedge q - r \rightarrow^+_S s$$

To prove the first lemma we just look at the term that has been reduced in $p - q$ and use associative and distributive properties of addition and multiplication by a term. The second lemma is proved by induction on the length of the reduction using the first lemma in the induction case. The third lemma is proved with techniques similar to the first one.

The next step is to show that in order to get the theorem *BuchReduce* it is sufficient to prove that the reduction is confluent:

$$\forall p, q, r \in P_{A,M_n}, \ (p \rightarrow^*_S q \wedge p \rightarrow^*_S r) \Rightarrow q = r$$

Here is the proof:

- We take an arbitrary element p of $<S>$. We want to prove that $p \to_S^* 0$ with the hypothesis that the reduction is confluent.
- By definition $p = \sum_{i<k} t_i.p_i$ with $\forall i < k, t_i \in T_{A,M_n}$ and $p_i \in S$ for some k.
- We proceed by induction on k.
- For $k = 0$, we have $p = 0$ so the property holds.
- Suppose that the property holds for $l < k$.
- By defining $q = \sum_{i<k-1} t_i.p_i$, we get $q \to_S^* 0$ by induction hypothesis.
- We have $p - q = t_k p_k$, with $p_k \in S$. It implies that $p - q \to_S^+ 0$.
- By applying the lemma $Red^+Minus0$, we deduce that there exists an r such that $p \to_S^+ r$ and $q \to_S^+ r$.
- We know that the reduction is confluent and that q reduces to 0. It implies that r reduces to 0. So we get $p \to_S^* 0$. $\square$

We are now ready for the main step of the proof. In order to prove that the reduction is confluent, we show that it is sufficient that every spolynomial formed with polynomials of the basis reduces to 0:

$$(\forall p, q \in S,\ Spoly(p,q) \to_S^* 0) \Rightarrow \to_S^* confluent$$

We first prove two useful lemmas about the order defined in Section 2.1:
Lemma *StructLess:*

$$\forall t \in T_{A,M_n},\ \forall p \in P_{A,M_n},\ p <_p t \ddagger p$$

Lemma *RedLess:*

$$\forall S \in P_{A,M_n} list,\ \forall p, q \in P_{A,M_n},\ p \to_S q \Rightarrow q <_p p$$

Note that the lemma *RedLess* and the fact that $<_p$ is well-founded ensure that the reduction always terminates. Now we can start the proof that the reduction is confluent:

- As the relation $<_p$ is well-founded, we prove that the reduction is confluent by induction on $<_p$ by taking as the main hypothesis that:

$$\forall p, q \in S,\ Spoly(p,q) \to_S^* 0$$

- Consider an arbitrary p, and suppose that

$$\forall q \in P_{A,M_n},\ q <_p p \Rightarrow (\forall r, s \in P_{A,M_n}(q \to_S^* r \wedge q \to_S^* s) \Rightarrow r = s)$$

- We take two arbitrary reductions of p: $p \to_S^* r$ and $p \to_S^* s$ and prove that $r = s$.
- If p is irreducible, the property clearly holds $r = p = s$.
- Otherwise, consider p_1 and p_2 such that $p \to_S p_1 \to_S^* r$ and $p \to_S p_2 \to_S^* s$.
- Because $p_1 <_p p$ and $p_2 <_p p$, it is now sufficient to prove that there exists a p_3 such that $p_1 \to_S^* p_3$ and $p_2 \to_S^* p_3$ to get $r = p_3 = s$ by induction hypothesis.

- We do a case analysis on the nature of the reductions $p \rightarrow_S p_1$ and $p \rightarrow_S p_2$. There are four possible cases:
  1. Suppose $p = t \dotplus q \rightarrow_S t \dotplus q_1 = p_1$ and $p = t \dotplus q \rightarrow_S t \dotplus q_2 = p_2$.
     - Since $q <_p p$, $q \rightarrow_S q_1$, and $q \rightarrow_S q_2$, we get $reducef(S, q_1) = reducef(S, q) = reducef(S, q_2)$ by induction hypothesis.
     - It follows that $p_1 \rightarrow_S^+ t \dotplus reducef(S, q)$ and $p_2 \rightarrow_S^+ t \dotplus reducef(S, q)$.
     - It is then sufficient to take $p_3 = reducef(S, t \dotplus reducef(S, q))$.
  2. Suppose $p \rightarrow_S p/_p q_1 = p_1$ and $p = t \dotplus q \rightarrow_S t \dotplus q_2 = p_2$.
     - By definition of the one step division, there exists a polynomial q_3 such that $p/_p q_1 = q - q_3$.
     - Since $q \rightarrow_S q_2$, by applying the lemma $RedDistMinus$, there exists a polynomial q_4 such that $p_1 = q - q_3 \rightarrow_S^+ q_4$ and $q_2 - q_3 \rightarrow_S^+ q_4$.
     - It is easy to check that $q_2 - q_3 = p_2/_p q_1$, so $p_2 \rightarrow_S^+ q_4$.
     - It is then sufficient to take $p_3 = reducef(S, q_4)$.
  3. Suppose $p = t \dotplus q \rightarrow_S t \dotplus q_1 = p_1$ and $p \rightarrow_S q/_p q_2 = p_2$.
     - This case is just the symmetric of case 2, so the property holds.
  4. Suppose $p \rightarrow_S p/_p q_1 = p_1$ and $p \rightarrow_S p/_p q_2 = p_2$.
     - p, q_1, and q_2 are non-zero polynomials, so $p = am \dotplus p'$, $q_1 = a_1 m_1 \dotplus q_1'$, and $q_2 = a_2 m_2 \dotplus q_2'$ for some $a, a_1, a_2 \in A$, some $m, m_1, m_2 \in M_n$, and some $p', q_1', q_2' \in P_{A,M_n}$.
     - q_1 and q_2 divide p, so m_1 and m_2 divide m. We deduce that there exists m_3 such that $m = m_3.(m_2 \hat{} m_1)$.
     - Using the definition of the one step division, we get that
       $$p_1 - p_2 = (p' - (a/_a a_1)(m/_{M_n} m_1).q_1') - (p' - (a/_a a_2)(m/_{M_n} m_2).q_2')$$
     - By simplifying the previous expression with the spolynomials definition we get $p_1 - p_2 = (am_3).Spoly(q_2, q_1)$.
     - Using the main hypothesis, we have $Spoly(q_2, q_1) \rightarrow_S^* 0$, so we get $p_1 - p_2 \rightarrow_S^* 0$.
     - By applying the lemma $Red^+Minus0$, there exists a polynomial p_4 such that $p_1 \rightarrow_S^+ p_4$ and $p_2 \rightarrow_S^+ p_4$.
     - It is then sufficient to take $p_3 = reducef(S, p_4)$.
- In all four cases, we are able to find such a polynomial p_3, so the property holds. □

Now in order to prove the theorem $BuchReduce$, it is sufficient to show

$$\forall p, q \in buch(S), Spoly(p, q) \rightarrow_{buch(S)}^* 0$$

This property is not immediate because the function $SpolyProd$ does not generate all the possible spolynomials but only a reduced set. The following two lemmas:
Lemma *SpolyId:*

$$\forall p \in P_{A,M_n}, Spoly(p, p) = 0$$

Lemma *SpolySym:*

$$\forall p, q \in P_{A,M_n}, Spoly(p, q) = -Spoly(q, p)$$

ensure that the reduction to 0 of the reduced set implies the reduction of the complete set. This ends the proof of correctness.

4   The Proof of Termination

Except for the function *buchf*, all the proofs of termination of the functions we have been using are trivial: the arguments in recursive calls are always structurally smaller than the initial arguments.

For the termination of the function *buchf* we need a weak version of Dixon's lemma. This lemma states that in every infinite sequence of monomials M_n there exists at least one monomial M_i that divides another monomial M_j such that $i < j$. It follows that if we define the relation $\Re$ over list of polynomials as the smallest relation such that:

$$\forall S \in P_{A,M_n} \textit{ list}, \forall p \in P_{A,M_n},$$
$$p \text{ is irreducible by } \rightarrow_S \wedge p \neq 0 \Rightarrow [p|S] \Re S$$

the relation $\Re$ is well-founded. If now we define the relation $\Re'$ as the smallest relation such that:

- $\forall S, S', T, T' \in P_{A,M_n} \textit{ list}, S \Re S' \Rightarrow (S, T) \Re' (S', T')$
- $\forall S, T \in P_{A,M_n} \textit{ list}, \forall p \in P_{A,M_n}, (S, T) \Re' (S, [p|T])$

$\Re'$ is the lexicographic product of two well-founded relations, so it is well-founded. Then for every recursive call within *buchf* it is easy to show that the argument y of the recursive call and the initial argument x are such that $y \Re' x$. So the function terminates.

5   Formalizing the Proofs Inside a Prover

One of the most satisfying aspect of our work has been to realize how naturally definitions and properties can be expressed in a higher order logic setting. What has been presented in Sections 2, 3 and 4 follows closely the proof development we have done in Coq. However we have avoided to present elements that were too specific to Coq. So we believe that the same definitions and the same proof steps could be used to get the proofs of correctness and termination in any theorem prover like Nuprl [4], HOL [8], Isabelle [18] or PVS [21], that allows the definition of recursive functions. In that respect we hope that what has been presented in the previous sections is a good compromise between the need for the proof to be human readable and the necessary detailed formalization due to mechanical theorem proving. In any case, it is a useful and important exercise to go from a textbook proof like the one in [7] to a proof that is suitable to mechanical theorem proving.

5.1   The Proof Development

The development in Coq is structured in three main parts:

1. The development of generic polynomials is composed of five modules. The module **porder** defines the notions of polynomials as lists of terms where terms are axiomatized and of ordered polynomials using an arbitrary order. Then the modules **seq**, **splus**, **smultm_lm**, and **sminus** define respectively equality, addition, term multiplication, and subtraction over polynomials.
2. The development of the algorithm itself contains five modules. The first two modules **spminus** and **sreduce** define respectively the one step division and the different notions of reduction. The module **def_spoly** defines the notion of spolynomials and proves that the reduction is confluent if all the spolynomials reduce to zero. The module **NBuch** defines an abstract version of the algorithm proving all the results with the help of some hypotheses. Finally, the module **Buch** instantiates the result of **NBuch** proving the different hypotheses.
3. The final part of the development is the instantiation. It is composed by three modules. The module **Monomials** defines monomials. The module **pair** defines terms as pairs of coefficients and monomials. The module **instan** glues all the different modules with the instantiation.

Figure 1 gives some quantitative information on the development. The columns correspond respectively to the number of lines of the module, the number of definitions, the number of theorems, the number of lemmas, and finally the ratio between the number of lines and the different objects defined or proved. Note that these figures do not include two important contributions that we have been using in the proof. A theory of lexicographic exponentiation derived from [17] is provided within the Coq system. It contains the main result needed for proving that reductions always terminate. A contribution by Loïc Pottier [19] gave us a non-constructive proof of the Dixon's lemma[1]. As explained before, this gives us indirectly the termination of the algorithm.

The proof development is around 9000 lines, so it represents an important effort. The proof has been carried out over a period of one year as a part-time activity. When we started, we thought the proof could be carried out in three months. Our first mistake was to underestimate the amount of work needed to formalize polynomials and the usual operations. The second lesson we have learned is that a special care has to be given to the organization of the development. Having a good set of definitions and basic properties is crucial when doing proofs. It is very often necessary to reorganize and reformulate definitions and theorems to increase reusability and productivity.

The other problems we have encountered are more specific to Coq. The entire proof development has been done using an arbitrary ring of coefficients and an arbitrary order. So each theorem of the development is fully quantified in order to allow later instantiation. But when we need to get theorems from a module

---

[1] It is the only non-constructive part of our proof.

Module	Lines	Definitions	Theorems	Lemmas	Ratio
porder	359	8	18	15	8
seq	359	8	17	8	10
splus	726	5	37	1	16
smultm_lm	201	1	19	2	9
sminus	500	4	25	2	16
$Total_1$	2145	26	116	28	12
spminus	380	2	19	0	18
sreduce	1439	16	34	9	24
def_spoly	1135	10	45	3	19
NBuch	455	13	26	0	11
Buch	1334	15	68	0	16
$Total_2$	4743	56	192	12	18
Monomials	408	12	18	4	12
pair	701	11	72	0	8
instan	943	18	11	0	32
$Total_3$	2052	41	101	4	14
Total	8940	123	409	44	15

Fig. 1. Quantitative information on the development

for a given instantiation, we need to operate individually on each of them which is very tedious. This is a well-known problem of modularity for which solutions have been proposed and implemented in other provers (see for example [6]). Clearly modularity is a must if we aim at large proof developments.

The equality we use for polynomials is not the simple structural equality. The polynomials we have defined may contain zero terms but we want to consider as equals those polynomials that only differ for zero terms. Also we want to take into account a possible equality $=_a$ over the elements of A. Using an explicit equality makes proofs harder in Coq because we miss the possibility to replace equals by equals. In order to regain substitutivity, we need to prove a theorem of compatibility for each function and predicate. For example, if $=_p$ denotes our equality over polynomials, it is necessary to prove the theorem:

$$p_1 =_p q_1 \wedge p_2 =_p q_2 \Rightarrow p_1 + p_2 =_p q_1 + q_2$$

to be allowed to replace polynomials in additions. Then proofs often get polluted with tedious steps of manipulation of the equality. In mathematics, the usual trick for avoiding this problem is to implicitly work with quotients. A real benefit could be gained in adding such a capability to Coq.

Finally if we look at Figure 1, the average of 15 lines per definition or theorem shows that proofs are often reasonably short. As a matter of fact, we have made very little use of automation. We mostly use the tactic Auto that simply takes a database of theorems and checks if the goal is a simple consequence of the database and the assumptions using the modus ponens only. It is difficult to evaluate what would be gained if we were doing the proof in a prover that provides more automation. Nevertheless, a specific class of goals we have encountered could largely benefit from automation. In the proof development, we construct the type of polynomials as being {p:term list | (olist p)}, i.e. the lists of terms such that the lists are ordered. In a proof that manipulates polynomials, it is often the case that we get several subgoals which require to prove that a list is ordered so it can be considered as a polynomial. Proving such subgoals is trivial most of the time but having to repeatedly prove them becomes quickly annoying.

5.2   Extracting the Algorithm

Once the development is finished, not only we have the proof of correctness of the algorithm but it is also possible to automatically extract an implementation. The self-contained version of the algorithm gives a 600 line long Ocaml program. The example below uses an instantiation of the algorithm with n variables polynomials for $n = 6$ over $\mathbb{Q}$ and the usual lexicographic order (a > b > c > d > e > f). Instantiating the implementation gives us 5 functions:

1. gen: int -> poly creates the generators;
2. scal: int -> poly -> poly multiplies the polynomial by an integer;
3. plus: poly -> poly -> poly adds two polynomials;
4. mult: poly -> poly -> poly multiplies two polynomials;
5. buch: poly list -> poly list computes the Gröbner basis.

We also write a prettyprinter in Ocaml to make the outputs of computation more readable. In the following, we present an interactive session with the toplevel Ocaml. Command lines are prefixed with # and end with two semicolons. We first define local variables to represent generators:

```
# let a = gen 0;;
val a : poly = a
# let b = gen 1;;
val b : poly = b
# let c = gen 2;;
val c : poly = c
# let d = gen 3;;
val d : poly = d
# let p1 =   gen 6;;
val p1 : poly = 1
```

We then construct the four n-cyclic polynomials for n=4:

```
# let r0 = (plus a (plus b (plus c d)));;
val r0 : poly = a +b +c +d
# let r1 = (plus (mult a b)
              (plus (mult b c) (plus (mult c d) (mult d a))));;
val r1 : poly = ab +ad +bc +cd
```

```
#let r2 = (plus (mult a (mult b c)) (plus (mult b (mult c d))
          (plus (mult c (mult d a)) (mult d (mult a b)))))));;
val r2 : poly = abc +abd +acd +bcd
#let r3 = (plus (mult a (mult b (mult c d))) (scal (-1) p1));;
val r3 : poly = abcd -1
```

and the computation of the Gröbner basis gives:

```
# buch [r3;r2;r1;r0];;
- : poly list = [abcd -1; abc +abd +acd +bcd; ab +ad +bc +cd;
                 a +b +c +d; -b^2d -2bd^2 -d^3; b^2 +2bd +d^2;
                 bcd^2 -bd^3 +c^2d^2 +cd^3 -d^4 -1;
                 bc -bd +c^2d^4 +cd -2d^2;
                 -bd^4 +b -d^5 +d; c^3d^3 +c^2d^4 -cd -d^2;
                 c^3d^2 +c^2d^3 -c -d; c^2d^6 -c^2d^2 -d^4 +1]
```

While the answer of the system for $n = 4$ was immediate, the computation for $n = 5$ had to be aborted after one hour of computation and a process size of more than 100Mb! This is not too surprising: the version of the algorithm is clearly too naive to perform well on large examples.

6   Related Work

Analytica [3] and more recently Theorema [22] propose an extension of the computer algebra system Mathematica [23] with a proving component. The examples they present are promising but their proof engines seem to need further developments in order to handle proofs of the same complexity as the one we have presented here. Also, there have been attempts to develop large fragments of mathematics within theorem provers. One of the first attempt was the Automath project [15]. The current largest attempt is the Mizar project [20]. Some recent efforts include Jackson's work on computational algebra [13] and Harrison's work on real analysis [9]. The focus of these works is mostly on formalizing mathematics inside a prover, so they give very few account of algorithmic aspects. Finally there have been several proposals to exploit a physical link between a prover and a computer algebra system to perform computation (see for example [1]). In [10], there is a discussion of some of the limitations of this approach.

As for the technique of program extraction, it has been demonstrated mostly on toy programs [11], [16]. We believe that our algorithm is one of the first non-trivial examples using this technique.

7   Conclusion and Future Work

While working on this development we had clearly the feeling to be at the frontier between proving and computing. Even if we were mostly in the proving world trying to state properties about polynomials, we were also able to test and compute with these very same polynomials. The situation is not yet ideal and we have described some of the problems we have encountered. Still we hope that this experiment shows that we are not so far from being able to mix proving and computing.

It is interesting to contrast the 9000 lines of the proof development with the 600 lines of the extracted Ocaml implementation of the algorithm. Proving requires much more effort than programming. This is not a surprise. It also indicates that the perspective of developing a completely certified computer algebra system is unrealistic for the moment. The first step in that direction is definitely to increase the knowledge of provers with basic algebraic notions. One third of our proof lines has been used to construct a library of multivariate polynomials. More automation and a better support to structure the development are also mandatory.

The work we have done on Buchberger's algorithm is far from being finished. Our algorithm is a textbook version of a real algorithm. We are aware that we still need to give evidence that with our approach we can obtain an algorithm that can be compared with what is proposed in general-purpose computer algebra systems. In that respect, it is worth noticing that correctness becomes an important issue for optimized versions of the algorithm. The main optimization consists in avoiding to check the reducibility to zero of some spolynomials. A common implementation error is to be too aggressive in the optimization and discard spolynomials that are in fact not reducing to zero. Even in that case, the algorithm can still behave well because the generation of spolynomials is heavily redundant. Testing may not be sufficient to spot this kind of implementation error.

Moreover, we would like to investigate the possibility of obtaining automatically or semi-automatically a textbook version of the proof of correctness of the algorithm directly from our development. In [5], a method is proposed to automatically produce a document in a pseudo-natural language out of proofs in Coq. Applying this method to our complete development seems very promising.

There are several ways in which this initial experiment can be extended. First of all it would be very interesting to see how the same proof looks like in other theorem proving systems. It would give a more accurate view of what current theorem proving technology can achieve on this particular problem. Also, we plan to complement this initial contribution with the certification of other standard algorithms for polynomials such as factorization. Our long term goal is to provide a completely certified kernel for non-trivial polynomial manipulations.

References

1. Jacques Calmet and Karsten Homann. Classification of communication and co-operation mechanisms for logical and symbolic computation systems. In *First International Workshop 'Frontiers of Combining Systems' (FroCoS'96)*, Kluwer Series on Applied Logic, pages 133–146. Springer-Verlag, 1996.
2. Bruce W. Char, Keith O. Geddes, and Gaston H. Gonnet. *First leaves: a tutorial introduction to Maple V.* Springer-Verlag, 1992.

3. Edmund Clarke and Xudong Zhao. Analytica — a theorem prover for Mathematica. Research report, Carnegie Mellon University, 1991.

4. Robert L. Constable, Stuart F. Allen, H.M. Bromley, Walter R. Cleaveland, James F. Cremer, Robert W. Harper, Douglas J. Howe, Todd B. Knoblock, Nax P. Mendler, Prakash Panangaden, James T. Sasaki, and Scott F. Smith. *Implementing mathematics with the Nuprl proof development system*. Prentice Hall, 1986.

5. Yann Coscoy, Gilles Kahn, and Laurent Théry. Extracting text from proofs. In *Typed Lambda Calculus and its Applications*, volume 902 of *LNCS*, pages 109–123. Springer-Verlag, 1995.

6. William M. Farmer, Joshua D. Guttman, and F. Javier Thayer. Little theories. In D. Kapur, editor, *Automated Deduction—CADE-11*, volume 607 of *LNCS*, pages 567–581. Springer-Verlag, 1992.

7. Keith O. Geddes, Stephen R. Czapor, and George Labahn. *Algorithms for computer algebra*. Kluwer, 1992.

8. Michael Gordon and Thomas Melham. *Introduction to HOL: a theorem proving environment for higher order logic*. Cambridge University Press, 1993.

9. John R. Harrison. Theorem proving with the real numbers. Technical Report 408, University of Cambridge Computer Laboratory, 1996. PhD thesis.

10. John R. Harrison and Laurent Théry. Extending the HOL theorem prover with a computer algebra system to reason about the reals. In *Higher Order Logic Theorem Proving and Its Applications*, volume 780 of *LNCS*. Springer-Verlag, August 1995.

11. Doug Howe. Reasoning About Functional Programs in Nuprl. In *Functional Programming, Concurrency, Simulation and Automated Reasoning*, volume 693 of *LNCS*, pages 144–164. Springer-Verlag, 1993.

12. Gérard Huet, Gilles Kahn, and Christine Paulin-Mohring. The Coq proof assistant: A tutorial: Version 6.1. Technical Report 204, INRIA, 1997.

13. Paul B. Jackson. Enhancing the Nuprl proof development system and applying it to computational abstract algebra. Technical Report TR95-1509, Cornell University, 1995.

14. Xavier Leroy. Objective Caml. Available at http://pauillac.inria.fr/ocaml/, 1997.

15. Rob P. Nederpelt, J. Herman Geuvers, and Roel C. De Vrijer, editors. *Selected papers on Automath*. North-Holland, 1994.

16. Christine Paulin-Mohring and Benjamin Werner. Synthesis of ML programs in the system Coq. *Journal of Symbolic Computation*, 15(5-6):607–640, May–June 1993.

17. Lawrence C. Paulson. Constructing Recursion Operators in Intuitionistic Type Theory. *Journal of Symbolic Computation*, 2(4):325–355, December 1986.

18. Lawrence C. Paulson. *Isabelle: a generic theorem prover*, volume 828 of *LNCS*. Springer-Verlag, 1994.

19. Loïc Pottier. Dixon's lemma. Available at ftp://www.inria.fr/safir/pottier/MON/, 1996.

20. Piotr Rudnicki. An overview of the MIZAR projet. In *Workshop on Types and Proofs for Programs*. Available by ftp at pub/csreports/Bastad92/proc.ps.Z on ftp.cs.chalmers.se, June 1992.

21. John M. Rushby, Natajaran Shankar, and Mandayam Srivas. PVS: Combining specification, proof checking, and model checking. In *CAV '96*, volume 1102 of *LNCS*. Springer-Verlag, July 1996.

22. Daniela Vasaru, Tudor Jebelean, and Bruno Buchberger. Theorema: A system for formal scientific training in natural language presentation. Technical Report 97-34, Risc-Linz, 1997.
23. Stephen Wolfram. *Mathematica: a system for doing mathematics by computer.* Addison-Wesley, 1988.

Selectively Instantiating Definitions

Matthew Bishop and Peter B. Andrews

Department of Mathematical Sciences, Carnegie Mellon University,
Pittsburgh, PA 15213, U.S.A.*
mbishop+@cs.cmu.edu, andrews+@cs.cmu.edu
http://www.cs.cmu.edu/~andrews/tps.html

Abstract. When searching for proofs of theorems which contain definitions, it is a significant problem to decide which instances of the definitions to instantiate. We describe a method called *dual instantiation*, which is a partial solution to the problem in the context of the connection method; the same solution may also be adaptable to other search procedures. Dual instantiation has been implemented in TPS, a theorem prover for classical type theory, and we provide some examples of theorems that have been proven using this method. Dual instantiation has the desirable properties that the search for a proof cannot possibly fail due to insufficient instantiation of definitions, and that the natural deduction proof which results from a successful search will contain no unnecessary instantiations of definitions. Furthermore, the time taken by a proof search using dual instantiation is in general comparable to the time taken by a search in which exactly the required instances of each definition have been instantiated. We also describe how this technique can be applied to the problem of instantiating set variables.

1 Introduction

When searching for proofs of theorems which contain definitions, it is a significant problem to decide which instances of the definitions to instantiate. Often, one needs to instantiate some, but not all, of them, and if one does instantiate all of them, one can cause the search space to expand in a very undesirable way. This problem has been noted in [4] and [23], and treatments of it may be found in [6], [8] and [12].

We have found a partial solution to this problem; it involves making each instance of a definition accessible to the search procedure in both its instantiated and its uninstantiated form, and letting the search procedure decide which to use, with a bias in favor of the uninstantiated form. This is very effective in some cases.

* This material is based upon work supported by the National Science Foundation under grant CCR-9624683. This work was supported in part by Intel Corporation through an equipment grant.

C. Kirchner and H. Kirchner (Eds.): Automated Deduction, CADE-15
LNAI 1421, pp. 365–380, 1998. © Springer–Verlag Berlin Heidelberg 1998

This solution to the problem seems particularly well suited to use with the connection method (also known as the matings procedure). We will discuss it as it is implemented in TPS, an automated theorem prover for classical type theory developed at Carnegie Mellon University, based on the ideas in [3] and most recently described in [4].

2   Dual Instantiation

Well-formed formulae (wffs) in TPS are the formulae of Church's type theory[10]. A sentence in TPS is a wff of type o, where o is the type of truth values. Proofs in TPS are presented in the style of [2], and in wffs a dot stands for a left bracket whose mate is as far to the right as is consistent with the pairing of brackets already present. Quantifiers and negations have the smallest possible scope. Omitted brackets associated with the connectives $\wedge$, $\vee$, $\supset$, and $\equiv$ should be restored in that order, giving the connective the smallest possible scope in each case. Type symbols are omitted wherever it is possible to do so without ambiguity.

Any sentence in TPS may contain *abbreviations*, which are typed symbols such as $\subseteq_{o(o\alpha\alpha)(o\alpha\alpha)}$ or TRANSITIVE$_{o(o\alpha\alpha)}$. Each abbreviation is associated with a *definition*[1] — in the case of $\subseteq$ (inclusion between binary relations), the definition is the wff $\lambda P_{o\alpha\alpha}\lambda R_{o\alpha\alpha}\forall x_\alpha\forall y_\alpha.Pxy \supset Rxy$. The process of replacing an abbreviation by its definition, and λ-normalizing the resulting expression if necessary, is referred to as *instantiating* the abbreviation.

Given such a sentence to be proven, we negate it, skolemize, and recursively construct an *expansion tree* [16]. So, for example, if the topmost symbol of the parse tree of the sentence is a conjunction, the expansion tree will consist of a conjunction node whose children are the expansion trees of the conjuncts.

In previous versions of TPS, the user had two options for instantiating abbreviations: either instantiate them all (*full instantiation*), or instantiate none of them. Uninstantiated abbreviations are regarded as constant symbols by the mating-search procedures. A similar choice was available for equalities, which could be instantiated by the Leibniz definition of equality ($x_\alpha = y_\alpha$ becomes $\forall q_{o\alpha}.qx_\alpha \supset qy_\alpha$), or left uninstantiated and treated as constant symbols. (Equalities between sets could also be instantiated using the extensional definition of equality, and those between truth values as equivalences, but for our purposes the essential distinction is between instantiated — by whichever definition — and uninstantiated equalities.)

In the current version of TPS, there is another choice, called dual instantiation. In this case, an atom A which contains an abbreviation is replaced by $A \wedge A'$ if A occurs positively, and by $A \vee A'$ if it occurs negatively, where A' is the result of instantiating the outermost abbreviation in A. A is left as a leaf of the expansion tree, and TPS continues to construct the expansion tree of A' exactly as it would for an ordinary instantiation.

---

[1] The classical terms for *abbreviation* and *definition* are *definiendum* and *definiens*, respectively.

When a vertical path diagram is constructed, as described in [1] and [3], the effect of this is to produce a conjunct, the uppermost literal of which is simply A, and the rest of which is an instantiated version of A. Clearly, since $X \Leftrightarrow (X \wedge X) \Leftrightarrow (X \vee X)$, the truth or falsity of the sentence is unaffected by this.

As an example of the use of dual instantiation, consider the simple theorem, which we call THM136, asserting that the transitive closure of any relation is transitive:

$$\forall r_{o\alpha\alpha} \text{TRANSITIVE .TRANSITIVE-CLOSURE } r$$

where TRANSITIVE is defined as

$$\lambda r_{o\alpha\alpha} \forall a_\alpha \forall b_\alpha \forall c_\alpha . rab \wedge rbc \supset rac$$

and the transitive closure of r is defined to be the relation which relates x to y whenever x is related to y by every transitive relation p which includes r. Thus, the definition of TRANSITIVE-CLOSURE is:

$$\lambda r_{o\alpha\alpha} \lambda x_\alpha \lambda y_\alpha \forall p_{o\alpha\alpha} . r \subseteq p \wedge \text{TRANSITIVE } p \supset pxy$$

After instantiating TRANSITIVE in THM136, it becomes

$$\forall r_{o\alpha\alpha} \forall a_\alpha \forall b_\alpha \forall c_\alpha. \quad \text{TRANSITIVE-CLOSURE } rab$$
$$\wedge \text{ TRANSITIVE-CLOSURE } rbc$$
$$\supset \text{TRANSITIVE-CLOSURE } rac$$

Instantiating TRANSITIVE-CLOSURE produces

$$\forall r_{o\alpha\alpha} \forall a_\alpha \forall b_\alpha \forall c_\alpha. \quad \forall p^1_{o\alpha\alpha} [r \subseteq p^1 \wedge \text{TRANSITIVE } p^1 \supset p^1 ab]$$
$$\wedge \forall p^2_{o\alpha\alpha} [r \subseteq p^2 \wedge \text{TRANSITIVE } p^2 \supset p^2 bc]$$
$$\supset \forall p_{o\alpha\alpha} . r \subseteq p \wedge \text{TRANSITIVE } p \supset pac$$

Negating and skolemizing the above, and putting the result into negation normal form, produces

$$\forall p^1_{o\alpha\alpha} [\sim [R_{o\alpha\alpha} \subseteq p^1] \vee \sim \text{TRANSITIVE } p^1 \vee p^1 A_\alpha B_\alpha]$$
$$\wedge \forall p^2_{o\alpha\alpha} [\sim [R_{o\alpha\alpha} \subseteq p^2] \vee \sim \text{TRANSITIVE } p^2 \vee p^2 B_\alpha C_\alpha]$$
$$\wedge R_{o\alpha\alpha} \subseteq P_{o\alpha\alpha}$$
$$\wedge \text{TRANSITIVE } P_{o\alpha\alpha}$$
$$\wedge \sim P_{o\alpha\alpha} A_\alpha C_\alpha$$

Instantiating the original theorem using full instantiation produces the vertical path diagram in Fig. 1, which clearly corresponds to the wff above. (Terms of the form $X^i p^j$ and $Y^i p^j$ are skolem terms, as are A, B and C, and the labels $\boxed{N}$ have been added for convenience in describing the mating below.)

To find a complete mating for this diagram, it is necessary to duplicate the x^2_α quantifier once and the x^1_α quantifier twice, producing the diagram in Fig. 2. The new copies of a literal $\boxed{N}$ created by duplication will be referred to as $\boxed{N'}$, $\boxed{N''}$ and so on; we will write connected pairs of literals as $\boxed{M - N}$. The complete

$$\forall p^1_{o\alpha\alpha}$$
$$\left[\begin{bmatrix} \boxed{16}\ R_{o\alpha\alpha}[X^0p^1].Y^0p^1 \\ \boxed{17}\ \sim p^1_{o\alpha\alpha}[X^0p^1].Y^0p^1 \end{bmatrix} \vee \begin{bmatrix} \boxed{13}\ p^1_{o\alpha\alpha}[X^1p^1].Y^1p^1 \\ \boxed{14}\ p^1_{o\alpha\alpha}[Y^1p^1].Z^0p^1 \\ \boxed{15}\ \sim p^1_{o\alpha\alpha}[X^1p^1].Z^0p^1 \end{bmatrix} \vee \boxed{12}\ p^1_{o\alpha\alpha}A_\alpha B_\alpha \right]$$

$$\forall p^2_{o\alpha\alpha}$$
$$\left[\begin{bmatrix} \boxed{10}\ R_{o\alpha\alpha}[X^2p^2].Y^2p^2 \\ \boxed{11}\ \sim p^2_{o\alpha\alpha}[X^2p^2].Y^2p^2 \end{bmatrix} \vee \begin{bmatrix} \boxed{7}\ p^2_{o\alpha\alpha}[X^3p^2].Y^3p^2 \\ \boxed{8}\ p^2_{o\alpha\alpha}[Y^3p^2].Z^1p^2 \\ \boxed{9}\ \sim p^2_{o\alpha\alpha}[X^3p^2].Z^1p^2 \end{bmatrix} \vee \boxed{6}\ p^2_{o\alpha\alpha}B_\alpha C_\alpha \right]$$

$$\forall x^2_\alpha \forall y^2_\alpha$$
$$\left[\boxed{5}\ \sim R_{o\alpha\alpha}x^2_\alpha y^2_\alpha \vee \boxed{4}\ P_{o\alpha\alpha}x^2_\alpha y^2_\alpha\right]$$

$$\forall x^1_\alpha \forall y^1_\alpha \forall z^1_\alpha$$
$$\left[\boxed{3}\ \sim P_{o\alpha\alpha}x^1_\alpha y^1_\alpha \vee \boxed{2}\ \sim P_{o\alpha\alpha}y^1_\alpha z^1_\alpha \vee \boxed{1}\ P_{o\alpha\alpha}x^1_\alpha z^1_\alpha\right]$$

$$\boxed{18}\ \sim P_{o\alpha\alpha}A_\alpha C_\alpha$$

Fig. 1. THM136 after full instantiation

$$\forall p^1_{o\alpha\alpha}$$
$$\left[\begin{bmatrix} \boxed{16}\ R_{o\alpha\alpha}[X^0p^1].Y^0p^1 \\ \boxed{17}\ \sim p^1_{o\alpha\alpha}[X^0p^1].Y^0p^1 \end{bmatrix} \vee \begin{bmatrix} \boxed{13}\ p^1_{o\alpha\alpha}[X^1p^1].Y^1p^1 \\ \boxed{14}\ p^1_{o\alpha\alpha}[Y^1p^1].Z^0p^1 \\ \boxed{15}\ \sim p^1_{o\alpha\alpha}[X^1p^1].Z^0p^1 \end{bmatrix} \vee \boxed{12}\ p^1_{o\alpha\alpha}A_\alpha B_\alpha \right]$$

$$\forall p^2_{o\alpha\alpha}$$
$$\left[\begin{bmatrix} \boxed{10}\ R_{o\alpha\alpha}[X^2p^2].Y^2p^2 \\ \boxed{11}\ \sim p^2_{o\alpha\alpha}[X^2p^2].Y^2p^2 \end{bmatrix} \vee \begin{bmatrix} \boxed{7}\ p^2_{o\alpha\alpha}[X^3p^2].Y^3p^2 \\ \boxed{8}\ p^2_{o\alpha\alpha}[Y^3p^2].Z^1p^2 \\ \boxed{9}\ \sim p^2_{o\alpha\alpha}[X^3p^2].Z^1p^2 \end{bmatrix} \vee \boxed{6}\ p^2_{o\alpha\alpha}B_\alpha C_\alpha \right]$$

$$\forall x^2_\alpha \forall y^2_\alpha$$
$$\left[\boxed{5}\ \sim R_{o\alpha\alpha}x^2_\alpha y^2_\alpha \vee \boxed{4}\ P_{o\alpha\alpha}x^2_\alpha y^2_\alpha\right]$$

$$\forall x^{2\,\prime}_\alpha \forall y^{2\,\prime}_\alpha$$
$$\left[\boxed{5'}\ \sim R_{o\alpha\alpha}x^{2\,\prime}_\alpha y^{2\,\prime}_\alpha \vee \boxed{4'}\ P_{o\alpha\alpha}x^{2\,\prime}_\alpha y^{2\,\prime}_\alpha\right]$$

$$\forall x^1_\alpha \forall y^1_\alpha \forall z^1_\alpha$$
$$\left[\boxed{3}\ \sim P_{o\alpha\alpha}x^1_\alpha y^1_\alpha \vee \boxed{2}\ \sim P_{o\alpha\alpha}y^1_\alpha z^1_\alpha \vee \boxed{1}\ P_{o\alpha\alpha}x^1_\alpha z^1_\alpha\right]$$

$$\forall x^{1\,\prime}_\alpha \forall y^{1\,\prime}_\alpha \forall z^{1\,\prime}_\alpha$$
$$\left[\boxed{3'}\ \sim P_{o\alpha\alpha}x^{1\,\prime}_\alpha y^{1\,\prime}_\alpha \vee \boxed{2'}\ \sim P_{o\alpha\alpha}y^{1\,\prime}_\alpha z^{1\,\prime}_\alpha \vee \boxed{1'}\ P_{o\alpha\alpha}x^{1\,\prime}_\alpha z^{1\,\prime}_\alpha\right]$$

$$\forall x^{1\,\prime\prime}_\alpha \forall y^{1\,\prime\prime}_\alpha \forall z^{1\,\prime\prime}_\alpha$$
$$\left[\boxed{3''}\ \sim P_{o\alpha\alpha}x^{1\,\prime\prime}_\alpha y^{1\,\prime\prime}_\alpha \vee \boxed{2''}\ \sim P_{o\alpha\alpha}y^{1\,\prime\prime}_\alpha z^{1\,\prime\prime}_\alpha \vee \boxed{1''}\ P_{o\alpha\alpha}x^{1\,\prime\prime}_\alpha z^{1\,\prime\prime}_\alpha\right]$$

$$\boxed{18}\ \sim P_{o\alpha\alpha}A_\alpha C_\alpha$$

Fig. 2. THM136 after full instantiation and duplication

mating is as follows: $\boxed{16-5}$, $\boxed{17-4}$, $\boxed{13-3}$, $\boxed{14-2}$, $\boxed{15-1}$, $\boxed{10-5'}$, $\boxed{11-4'}$, $\boxed{7-3'}$, $\boxed{8-2'}$, $\boxed{9-1'}$, $\boxed{12-3''}$, $\boxed{6-2''}$, $\boxed{18-1''}$.

Although the required unification depth is not large, there are many literals with flexible heads, and this makes it difficult to rule out connections by unification failure. This, coupled with the increase in the size of the search space caused by duplicating the quantifiers, prevents TPS from finding a proof.

Notice that, in the mating, we have often mated all of the literals in some disjunction with all of the literals in some conjunction (e.g. $\boxed{16-5}$, $\boxed{17-4}$). This happens because we have instantiated some abbreviation that need not have been instantiated: for example, the disjunction containing $\boxed{5}$ and $\boxed{4}$ is an instantiation of $R_{o\alpha\alpha} \subseteq P_{o\alpha\alpha}$, and the conjunctions to which the copies of this are mated ($\boxed{16}$ and $\boxed{17}$, $\boxed{10}$ and $\boxed{11}$) are instantiations of $\sim R_{o\alpha\alpha} \subseteq p^1_{o\alpha\alpha}$ and $\sim R_{o\alpha\alpha} \subseteq p^2_{o\alpha\alpha}$.

Dual instantiation, at first sight, appears to make the problem even worse, since it produces even more literals. The same theorem, instantiated with dual instantiation, gives the vertical path diagram of Fig. 3.

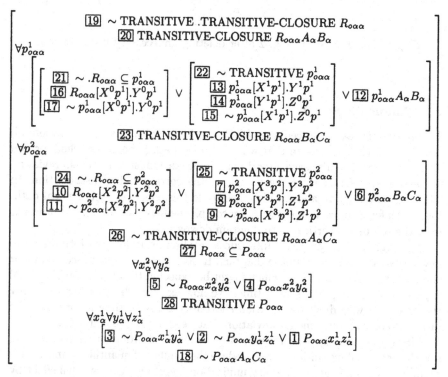

Fig. 3. THM136 after dual instantiation

However, this diagram has a much simpler mating than the previous one:
$\boxed{21-27}$, $\boxed{24-27}$, $\boxed{22-28}$, $\boxed{25-28}$, $\boxed{12-3}$, $\boxed{6-2}$, $\boxed{1-18}$. Note that it is no longer necessary to duplicate any quantifiers.

It is also obvious from this mating that two of the instances of TRANSITIVE, and all of the instances of $\subseteq$, need never have been instantiated at all, since we have not made any connections involving the literals in their instantiations. We can use this information to construct a proof in which no unnecessary instantiations have been performed. To do this, we begin by deleting the unused parts of the vertical path diagram, reducing it to the diagram in Fig. 4. More details about the translation process are given in Section 2.2.

$$
\left[
\begin{array}{l}
\forall p^1_{o\alpha\alpha} \\
\quad \left[\boxed{21} \sim .R_{o\alpha\alpha} \subseteq p^1_{o\alpha\alpha} \vee \boxed{22} \sim \text{TRANSITIVE } p^1_{o\alpha\alpha} \vee \boxed{12}\, p^1_{o\alpha\alpha} A_\alpha B_\alpha \right] \\
\forall p^2_{o\alpha\alpha} \\
\quad \left[\boxed{24} \sim .R_{o\alpha\alpha} \subseteq p^2_{o\alpha\alpha} \vee \boxed{25} \sim \text{TRANSITIVE } p^2_{o\alpha\alpha} \vee \boxed{6}\, p^2_{o\alpha\alpha} B_\alpha C_\alpha \right] \\
\qquad\qquad\qquad \boxed{27}\, R_{o\alpha\alpha} \subseteq P_{o\alpha\alpha} \\
\qquad\qquad \boxed{28}\, \text{TRANSITIVE } P_{o\alpha\alpha} \\
\quad \forall x^1_\alpha \forall y^1_\alpha \forall z^1_\alpha \\
\quad \left[\boxed{3} \sim P_{o\alpha\alpha} x^1_\alpha y^1_\alpha \vee \boxed{2} \sim P_{o\alpha\alpha} y^1_\alpha z^1_\alpha \vee \boxed{1}\, P_{o\alpha\alpha} x^1_\alpha z^1_\alpha \right] \\
\qquad\qquad \boxed{18} \sim P_{o\alpha\alpha} A_\alpha C_\alpha
\end{array}
\right]
$$

Fig. 4. The diagram in Fig. 2 after deleting unnecessary instantiations

2.1 Automatic Search

The automatic search procedures of TPS work well with dual instantiation; all that is required is to ensure that when an open path is being searched for two complementary literals, each literal containing an uninstantiated abbreviation is considered before any of the literals in the corresponding instantiation. In TPS, the construction above will suffice to do this, since on each vertical path, the search for a connection (potentially complementary pair of literals) proceeds from the top of the vertical path diagram downwards.

Although dual instantiation introduces new literals, it does not introduce any new paths into the vertical path diagram. It does, however, introduce a number of new potential connections, which might be expected to cause a combinatorial explosion of the required search time. We now explain why this is not usually the case, and why dual instantiation shortens the search time for most of the proofs which contain some abbreviation that need not be instantiated.

Firstly, we consider the reasons why dual instantiation often reduces the search time. Dual instantiation may reduce the number of quantifier duplications required, by removing unnecessary unification steps. One can see this effect by comparing Fig. 2 with Fig. 3. In the former, TPS would first attempt to unify

x_α^2 with both $X^0 p_{o\alpha\alpha}^1$ and $X^2 p_{o\alpha\alpha}^2$; since this is impossible, it would then have to duplicate the quantifier containing x^2 in order to complete the mating. In the latter, this is unnecessary. Removing unnecessary unification steps also reduces the depth of the unification tree, and hence improves the search time by allowing for stronger constraints on unification. (Since higher-order unification is undecidable, unification in TPS is always given a bound, roughly corresponding to the depth of the tree generated by the algorithm in [14].)

More importantly, an instantiated definition usually consists of more than one literal, and these literals may occur on paths that are not considered consecutively by the search procedure. Consider Fig. 2: the first correct connection that TPS will find is $\boxed{16-5}$. The leftmost open path will then be $\boxed{16}\text{-}\boxed{17}\text{-}\boxed{10}\text{-}\boxed{11}\text{-}\boxed{4}\text{-}\ldots$, and before it can find and add the connection $\boxed{17-4}$, it must consider all the other potential connections that can be made from $\boxed{16}$, $\boxed{17}$, $\boxed{10}$ and $\boxed{11}$. Not only does this waste time, but if any of these connections is acceptable it will be added to the mating and the rest of the search space will be searched until unification failure forces us to backtrack and remove it. Compare Fig. 3: the first correct connection that TPS will find is $\boxed{21-27}$, and this blocks all paths through $\boxed{21}$, $\boxed{16}$ and $\boxed{17}$ at one stroke.

Secondly, we consider the reasons why dual instantiation does not cause a combinatorial explosion in the search space. In the presence of dual instantiation, TPS never considers connections between an uninstantiated literal A and any of the literals of its instantiation A', since such connections cannot possibly be required in the mating. Also, the new uninstantiated literals are simply unable to unify with many of the other literals in the diagram (and when they do unify, the unification constraints that this generates are usually so strong that TPS is seldom sent off down a blind alley; if the connection is wrong, it will become obvious very quickly). This allows us to rule out most possible connections involving the uninstantiated literals almost immediately.

2.2 Proof Translation

Once a complete mating is found, TPS uses it to construct a natural deduction proof of the original theorem. The translation from expansion trees to natural deduction proofs was described in [18]; however, a little more work is required when dual instantiation is used, since the modified expansion tree does not correspond to the original sentence in the usual manner. These changes occur in two steps of the procedure: during merging and after translation.

Merging is the procedure which deletes any unnecessary parts of the tree (in particular, it deletes any subtrees which do not occur in the mating), merges together any redundant branches, applies unification substitutions, and generally cleans up the results prior to translation into a natural deduction proof. During merging, TPS finds each of the points at which dual instantiation was used. These parts of the expansion tree will each be a subtree of the same form as the "dual instantiation" tree in Fig. 5, where A is a literal containing an uninstantiated abbreviation, and A' is a subtree containing the instantiation of A.

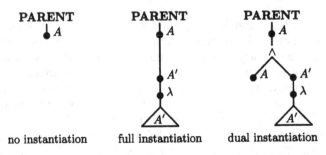

Fig. 5. Internal representations of instantiations

The diagrams in Fig. 5 show the relevant parts of the expansion trees for the three possibilities for instantiation. Note that in the construction of the expansion tree, dual instantiation occurs in several steps: first A is replaced by $A \wedge A$ (by $A \vee A$ if this is a negative occurrence of A), then the conjunction (resp. disjunction) is deepened, and then the rightmost A is instantiated to A' and deepened into an expansion tree. The λ-nodes, which are obtained by λ-normalization of their parent nodes, will not occur if A' is already in λ-normal form.

We now proceed by a case analysis of the leaves of the expansion tree which occur in the complete mating. We assume that unnecessary connections in the mating have already been removed, so that the mating is minimal.

1. If no leaves of the instantiated expansion subtree A' occur in the mating, then regardless of whether the uninstantiated literal A occurs or not, replace the dual expansion subtree with the "no instantiation" expansion subtree.
2. If the uninstantiated literal A does not occur in the mating, but literals from the instantiated expansion subtree A' do occur, replace the dual expansion subtree with the "full instantiation" expansion subtree.
3. Otherwise, if both A and leaves of A' occur in the mating, leave the dual expansion subtree as it is.

The translation from an expansion tree to a natural deduction proof is then performed using the methods of [18], with additional special cases which allow $A \wedge A'$ and $A \vee A'$ to be seen by TPS as equivalent to A under the "Elimination of Definitions" rule. The remaining dual instantiations will occur as either support or planned lines in the proof; for example, the following is a proof fragment corresponding to an introduction of $A \wedge A'$ as a support line:

(l_1)	(hyps)	$\vdash A$	(justification)
(l_2)	(hyps)	$\vdash A \wedge A'$	Edef: l_1
(l_3)	(hyps)	$\vdash A$	Econj: l_2
(l_4)	(hyps)	$\vdash A'$	Econj: l_2

where "Edef" means "by elimination of definitions" and "Econj" means "by elimination of a conjunction". The step from line l_1 to line l_2 corresponds to a dual instantiation of the topmost abbreviation in A, and from this we deduce line l_3 (corresponding to the uninstantiated literal) and line l_4 (corresponding to the instantiated expansion tree). The hypotheses are the same for each line.

After the translation is complete, we produce a more natural proof by replacing these four lines with the following:

| (l_1) | (hyps) | $\vdash A$ | (justification) |
| (l_4) | (hyps) | $\vdash A'$ | Edef: l_1 |

We also change any line in the proof using l_3 as a justification, by justifying it from l_1 instead. No lines in the proof, other than l_3 and l_4, will have been justified from l_2. It is trivial to see that these changes do not affect the validity of the proof.

We omit discussion of the case in which $A \vee A'$ occurs as a planned line; it occurs only rarely and is more technical, since there are several proof fragments which TPS might generate to justify such a planned line.

The other two cases are clearly redundant and cannot happen due to the minimality of the mating. If A is a planned line, it is clearly redundant to instantiate A to $A \wedge A'$ and then justify this new plan by proving both A and A' and introducing a conjunction. Similarly, if A is a support line for some goal G, it is redundant to instantiate A to $A \vee A'$ and then prove G twice, once from A and once from A'.

After these transformations of the natural deduction proof are complete, the resulting natural deduction proof will show no signs of dual instantiation.

2.3   Examples of Theorems Proven Using Dual Instantiation

All the timings quoted below represent the time taken for a complete proof, including translation to natural deduction style, on a Dell System Workstation 400MT, with dual 300 MHz Intel Pentium II processors, running TPS under Allegro Common Lisp.

THM48: $\forall F_{\alpha\beta} \forall G_{\beta\xi}.\text{INJECTIVE}F \wedge \text{INJECTIVE } G \supset \text{INJECTIVE } .F \circ G$ where INJECTIVE is defined by $\lambda f_{\alpha\beta} \forall x_\beta \forall y_\beta . fx = fy \supset x = y$, and $\circ$ is defined by $\lambda f_{\alpha\beta} \lambda g_{\beta\gamma} \lambda x_\gamma f.gx$. In this theorem, both INJECTIVE and $\circ$ must be instantiated; however, the proof time differs depending on the treatment of equality. If equality is instantiated using the Leibniz definition ($x = y$ becomes $\forall q.qx \supset qy$) then the proof takes 3.2 seconds; if equality is not instantiated at all, then it takes 0.1 seconds. Using dual instantiation, we get a proof in 0.2 seconds; note that this is almost as fast as the "cheating" proof in which TPS is told not to instantiate equalities at all.

THM70: $\forall S_{o(o\alpha\alpha)}\text{TRANSITIVE } . \cap . \lambda R_{o\alpha\alpha}.\text{TRANSITIVE } R \wedge SR$
This theorem states that the intersection of a set of transitive relations is transitive. Using dual instantiation, TPS can prove it in 1.2 seconds; without dual instantiation TPS has not found a proof.

THM136: $\forall r_{o\alpha\alpha}\text{TRANSITIVE } .\text{TRANSITIVE-CLOSURE } r$
This is the theorem which was discussed earlier in this paper. Using dual instantiation, TPS can prove this theorem in 0.6 seconds. Without dual instantiation, TPS has not been able to find a proof, even after searching for several weeks.

THM250: $\forall R_{o\alpha\alpha}\forall S_{o\alpha\alpha}.\text{TRCL }[R \cup S] = \text{TRCL }.\text{TRCL } R \cup \text{TRCL } S$

This theorem was suggested by Xiaorong Huang. TRCL is the transitive closure, as before, and $\cup$ is the union of a set of pairs, which is defined by $\lambda A_{o\alpha\alpha}\lambda B_{o\alpha\alpha}\lambda x_\alpha$ $\lambda y_\alpha.Axy \vee Bxy$. Instantiating all of the many abbreviations in this theorem results in a very large vertical path diagram, since TRCL is itself defined in terms of $\subseteq$ and TRANSITIVE, so it is not surprising that TPS cannot prove this using full instantiation. Using dual instantiation, a proof is found in 11.3 seconds.

THM252: $\forall P_{o(o\alpha\alpha)}\forall R_{o\alpha\alpha}\forall S_{o\alpha\alpha}.\text{CL }P[R \cup S] = \text{CL }P.\text{CL }PR \cup \text{CL }PS$

Inspection of the proof of THM250 revealed that the definition of TRANSITIVE was never used, and hence that the theorem is also true of the closure of relations R and S under any property P. We define this closure CL as $\lambda P_{o(o\alpha\alpha)}\lambda r_{o\alpha\alpha}\lambda x_\alpha\lambda y_\alpha\forall q_{o\alpha\alpha}.r \subseteq q \wedge Pq \supset qxy$. This theorem is easier to prove than THM250, although again it requires dual instantiation. The proof is found in 6.5 seconds (of which the actual mating search takes only 0.6 seconds).

THM260: $\forall R_{o\alpha\alpha}.\text{EQUIV-REL }R \supset \text{PARTITION }.\text{EQUIV-CLASSES }R$

This theorem states that the equivalence classes of an equivalence relation form a partition. The proof requires that the definitions of EQUIV-REL, PARTITION and EQUIV-CLASSES, as well as the definitions of REFLEXIVE, TRANSITIVE and SYMMETRIC that they contain, all be fully instantiated. Because of this, we would expect dual instantiation to take longer, since it increases the search space without providing any benefit. The proof with full instantiation takes 1.6 seconds; that with dual instantiation takes 3 seconds.

GAZING-THM43: $\forall S_{o\alpha}\forall T_{o\alpha}\forall U_{o\alpha}.[S \bigtriangleup T] \bigtriangleup U = S \bigtriangleup [T \bigtriangleup U]$

This is example 43 from [6]. $\bigtriangleup$ is the symmetric difference, defined as usual in terms of the abbreviations $\cup$ and $-$. In the proof which TPS finds, all abbreviations must be instantiated, and so dual instantiation will not help. The proof with full instantiation takes 15 seconds; that with dual instantiation takes 18 seconds.

3   Related Work on Instantiating Definitions

In the UT theorem prover described in [8], a technique called *peeking* was implemented. In this technique, each abbreviation was associated with a list of all the predicate symbols in its definition, and an abbreviation would be instantiated if one of these symbols occurred in the goal to be proven. This only allowed for looking ahead a single step at a time (the possibility of further rewriting the predicate symbols in the definition was not considered), and ignored function symbols completely. A different and more specialized approach was used in the theorem prover for set theory which is described in [17]. In both cases, it was possible for an attempted proof to fail due to insufficient instantiation, or to succeed but contain unnecessary instantiations. Dual instantiation is similar in spirit, but allows for multiple-step look-ahead by allowing the uninstantiated and instantiated forms of every abbreviation to occur in the diagram. Furthermore, an attempted proof cannot fail from insufficient instantiation, and if the theorem is eventually proven then the resulting natural deduction proof will contain no unnecessary instantiations.

Gazing, as defined in [21] and [6], is based on the idea of searching for a collection of concepts used in both the hypotheses and the conclusions. This is sometimes described as "building the *common currency*", and is done by constructing a *predicate abstraction space* around the database of rewrite rules which comprise the theory. Proofs in the abstraction space can be constructed in a decidable propositional theory and then generalized (sometimes) to proofs in the original undecidable first-order theory; unfortunately, this generalization is not always possible. The requirement to construct a different abstraction space for each domain, and then to discover by experimentation whether or not the abstraction space is useful in that domain, is a problem with gazing that does not occur with dual instantiation. Gazing also has difficulty with theories containing many function symbols and few predicate symbols, so that although it works well for naïve set theory, it is of little or no use for equational theories. Furthermore, there is still the possibility of either unnecessary or insufficient instantiation. However, gazing also provides a partial solution to the problem of using lemmas and rewrite rules within a theory, whereas dual instantiation does not.

The idea of using abstraction to simplify a search has a long history in artificial intelligence, and further references on this subject can be found in [13]. A theory of abstraction for resolution-based theorem-proving was developed in [19] and [20], and a more generalized theory of abstraction was developed in [13].

Gazing was further developed in [12] (in particular, the handling of function symbols was improved), and is the basis of the ABSFOL theorem prover described in [11]. The idea has also been implemented [22] for a theorem prover using the connection method.

All of the papers mentioned above are concerned mostly with first-order logic.

4   Instantiating Set Variables

In both first-order and higher-order logic, a key step in discovering a proof of a theorem is finding correct instantiations for the variables. In higher-order logic, however, variables with types of the form $(o\alpha)$ will correspond to sets; these variables may require instantiations which cannot be generated by unification alone. For example, it may be necessary to instantiate $p_{o\alpha}$ with the term $\lambda w_\alpha.A_{o\alpha}w \wedge B_{o\alpha}w$, meaning that p is the intersection of the two sets A and B. The problem of instantiating set variables in higher-order proof search has been addressed by papers such as [3], [4], [5], [7] and [9]; we have found that the techniques used for dual instantiation can also help with this problem.

TPS can generate instantiations for set variables incrementally, by first replacing a variable $p_{o\alpha}$ with one of the following:

conjunction $\lambda w_\alpha.p_{o\alpha}^1 w \wedge p_{o\alpha}^2 w$ **universal quantifier** $\lambda w_\alpha \forall x_\gamma p_{o\gamma\alpha}^1 wx$

disjunction $\lambda w_\alpha.p_{o\alpha}^1 w \vee p_{o\alpha}^2 w$ **existential quantifier** $\lambda w_\alpha \exists x_\gamma p_{o\gamma\alpha}^1 wx$

The new set variables p^i in these formulae may then be replaced with similar conjunctions, disjunctions and quantifiers, to generate instantiations of arbitrary depth.

We have added to TPS the ability to generate set variable instantiations which contain some of the abbreviations that occur in the sentence being proven – so that, for example, a sentence containing equality and the definitions TRANSITIVE and SUBSET can generate set variable substitutions for $p_{o\alpha}$ of the following forms:

equality $\lambda w_\alpha . p^1_{\gamma\alpha} w = p^2_{\gamma\alpha} w$ **transitivity** $\lambda w_\alpha . \text{TRANSITIVE} \cdot p^1_{o\gamma\gamma\alpha} w$
subset $\lambda w_\alpha . p^1_{o\gamma\alpha} w \subseteq p^2_{o\gamma\alpha} w$

We refer to these new set variable instantiations as *abbreviational set instantiations*, or ABR instantiations. To construct ABR instantiations, we first search the expansion tree, extracting the formulae stored at each leaf and rewrite node. In these formulae, which will all be of type o, we search for maximal subformulae which contain only variables and constants (but not, for example, quantifiers or abbreviations), and replace these formulae by *blanks* of appropriate types, denoted $\bullet_\tau$. We also generate the negations of any blanked-out formulae with rigid heads, and we add the single formula $\bullet_o$ (in the unlikely event that it isn't generated anyway).

For example, THM136 contained the subformula

$$[r_{o\alpha\alpha} \subseteq p^1_{o\alpha\alpha} \wedge \text{TRANSITIVE } p^1 \supset p^1 a_\alpha b_\alpha]$$

which, when deepened into a subtree of the expansion tree, will generate blanked formulae

$$\bullet_{o\alpha\alpha} \subseteq \bullet_{o\alpha\alpha} \qquad\qquad \text{TRANSITIVE } \bullet_{o\alpha\alpha} \qquad\qquad \bullet_o$$
$$\sim [\bullet_{o\alpha\alpha} \subseteq \bullet_{o\alpha\alpha}] \qquad\qquad \sim [\text{TRANSITIVE } \bullet_{o\alpha\alpha}]$$

These formulae are then combined into larger formulae, using conjunctions, disjunctions and quantifiers exactly as before. Quantified variables are also left blank at this stage. Because of the number of possible combinations, we usually only generate these larger formulae in prenex normal form. Using the formulae above, we can generate

$$\forall \bullet_\alpha . [\sim [\bullet_{o\alpha\alpha} \subseteq \bullet_{o\alpha\alpha}]] \wedge \bullet_o$$

To transform this into a substitution for a variable such as $p_{o\alpha\alpha}$, we add a prefix of lambda-bound variables (in this case, $\lambda w^1_\alpha \lambda w^2_\alpha$), replace the quantified blanks with variables of the appropriate type (in this case, w^3_α), and then replace each of the remaining blanks with a new set variable of appropriate type which takes all of the w-variables as arguments. The blanked-out formula above would thus generate a substitution of the form:

$$\lambda w^1_\alpha \lambda w^2_\alpha \forall w^3_\alpha . [\sim [p^1_{o\alpha\alpha\alpha\alpha\alpha} w^1 w^2 w^3 \subseteq p^2_{o\alpha\alpha\alpha\alpha\alpha} w^1 w^2 w^3]] \wedge p^3_{o\alpha\alpha\alpha} w^1 w^2 w^3$$

Because the formula $\bullet_o$ was definitely generated, all of the substitutions which were generated by the old procedure will also be generated here (since they amount to combining $\bullet_o$ with itself using conjunctions, disjunctions and quantifiers).

ABR instantiations are useful for much the same reasons as dual instantiation: they help to minimize the depth of unification required, and provide stronger unification constraints than the more general set instantiations. In addition, they are more compact than the equivalent substitutions in which the abbreviations have been instantiated, and hence can reduce the size of the vertical path diagram. They also interact well with dual instantiations; several of the examples listed below can only be proven by TPS using both dual instantiation and ABR instantiation.

4.1 Examples of Theorems Proven Using ABR Instantiation

THM15B: $\forall f_{\iota\iota}.\exists g_{\iota\iota}[\text{ITERATE}+\ fg \wedge \exists x_\iota.gx = x \wedge \forall z_\iota.gz = z \supset z = x] \supset \exists y_\iota.fy = y$

This theorem was stated in [15], and was discussed in some detail in [4]. It states that if some iterate g of a function f has a unique fixed point, then f has a fixed point. ITERATE+ is defined by $\lambda f_{\alpha\alpha}\lambda g_{\alpha\alpha}\forall p_{o(\alpha\alpha)}.pf \wedge \forall j_{\alpha\alpha}[pj \supset p.f \circ j] \supset pg$, and the principal problem for TPS is to find the appropriate instantiation for p. This instantiation will be the set of all the functions that commute with f; TPS then proves that g is one such function, and hence that the unique fixed point of g is a fixed point of f. Because TPS now finds the ABR instantiation $\lambda F_{\iota\iota}.f_{\iota\iota}[Fx_\iota] = F.fx$ (instead of the old set instantiation $\lambda g_{\iota\iota}\forall q_{o\iota}.q[g.f_{\iota\iota}x_\iota] \supset q.f.gx$), the proof can now be completed in 4 seconds instead of 1 minute, and the resulting natural deduction proof is more readable and 20% shorter.

THM120I: $\exists R_{o(o\iota)(o\iota)}.\text{REFLEXIVE } R \wedge \text{TRANSITIVE } R \wedge \forall X_{o\iota}\forall Y_{o\iota}.RXY \wedge RYX \supset X \equiv^s Y$

$\equiv^s$ is set equivalence, defined by $\lambda P_{o\alpha}\lambda R_{o\alpha}\forall x_\alpha.Px = Rx$. This theorem says that there is a reflexive, transitive and antisymmetric relation between sets. Using dual instantiation and ABR instantiation, TPS discovers the relation $\equiv^s$ and completes the proof in 10 seconds.

X5211: $y_{o\alpha} = \bigcup .\lambda z_{o\alpha}\exists x_\alpha.yx \wedge z = [= x]$

This says that a set is the union of the unit-sets of each of its elements. (Note that $[= x]$ is the unit set which is normally written as $\{x\}$, since both are equal to $\lambda y.y = x$.) This theorem requires both dual instantiation (of equality) and ABR instantiation in order for TPS to find a proof. It can be proven in 1.3 seconds.

X6104: $\exists i_{o(\alpha\alpha)(\alpha\alpha)}.\forall g_{\alpha\alpha}[ig[\lambda x_\alpha x] \wedge ig.\lambda x.g.gx] \wedge \forall f_{\alpha\alpha}\forall y_\alpha.i[\lambda xy]f \supset fy = y$

This says that there is a relation i between functions such that every function g is related both to the identity function and to $g \circ g$, and that $fy = y$ if the constant function λxy is related to f. The theorem was formulated with the expectation that TPS would discover a proof in which i is the "ITERATE" relation: f is related to g iff g is an iterate of f. However, TPS discovers a short proof in which i is the "commutes with" relation, taking 2.5 seconds in total. Again, this requires both dual instantiation and ABR instantiation.

5 Conclusions and Further Work

We have demonstrated that dual instantiation can provide an effective way to decide which abbreviations to instantiate when searching for a proof using the connection method. Moreover, by using dual instantiation one is guaranteed that the search for a proof cannot possibly fail due to insufficient instantiation, and that if the search succeeds then the resulting natural deduction proof will contain no unnecessary instantiations. This method of instantiation has allowed TPS to prove many previously intractable theorems, and has improved the search time and the readability of the natural deduction proofs produced by TPS for a number of other theorems. Several other lines of enquiry that have been suggested by our work on dual instantiation are outlined below.

5.1 Multiple Instantiation

The method of dual instantiation could easily be generalized to *multiple instantiation*, in which a single abbreviation is allowed to have several different instantiations — so that, for example,

$$A_{o\alpha} = B_{o\alpha} \text{ becomes } [A_{o\alpha} = B_{o\alpha}] \wedge [\forall x_\alpha . Ax \equiv Bx] \wedge [\forall q_{o(o\alpha)} . qA \supset qB]$$

$$P_{o\alpha} \subseteq Q_{o\alpha} \text{ becomes } [P_{o\alpha} \subseteq Q_{o\alpha}] \wedge [P \cap Q = P] \wedge [P \cup Q = Q] \wedge [\forall x_\alpha . Px \supset Qx]$$

By preventing the search procedure from making connections between various instantiations of the same occurrence of an abbreviation, just as we currently forbid connections between the uninstantiated and instantiated abbreviations, it might then be possible to avoid a combinatorial explosion in the size of the search space and yet allow the search procedure to use whichever definition is most natural for a given proof.

We have not yet implemented multiple instantiation in TPS.

5.2 Discovering Abbreviations

It would be very useful to have a theorem prover capable of inventing abbreviations; this would correspond in some way to discovering a mathematical concept and putting it to use. As we remarked earlier in the context of THM136, when an entire conjunction generated from a formula involving an abbreviation is mated to a similar entire disjunction, it is a sign that the abbreviation need not have been instantiated. The converse is also true: whenever a complete mating contains a subset of connections which mate one entire subtree to a negated version of itself, this suggests that the subtree in question might usefully have been replaced by an abbreviation.

TPS is currently capable of discovering such subsets, and of suggesting abbreviations that might shorten the proof. At the moment, this routine is called after the tree is merged (and hence after a proof has already been discovered), and nothing is done with the suggested abbreviations.

References

1. Peter B. Andrews. Theorem Proving via General Matings. *Journal of the ACM*, 28:193–214, 1981.

2. Peter B. Andrews. *An Introduction to Mathematical Logic and Type Theory: To Truth Through Proof.* Academic Press, 1986.

3. Peter B. Andrews. On Connections and Higher-Order Logic. *Journal of Automated Reasoning*, 5:257–291, 1989.

4. Peter B. Andrews, Matthew Bishop, Sunil Issar, Dan Nesmith, Frank Pfenning, and Hongwei Xi. TPS: A Theorem Proving System for Classical Type Theory. *Journal of Automated Reasoning*, 16:321–353, 1996.

5. Sidney C. Bailin and Dave Barker-Plummer. Z-match: An Inference Rule for Incrementally Elaborating Set Instantiations. *Journal of Automated Reasoning*, 11:391–428, 1993. Errata: JAR 12:411–412, 1994.

6. Dave Barker-Plummer. Gazing: An Approach to the Problem of Definition and Lemma Use. *Journal of Automated Reasoning*, 8:311–344, 1992.

7. W. W. Bledsoe. Using Examples to Generate Instantiations of Set Variables. In *Proceedings of IJCAI-83, Karlsruhe, Germany*, pages 892–901, Aug 8-12, 1983.

8. W. W. Bledsoe and Peter Bruell. A Man-Machine Theorem-Proving System. *Artificial Intelligence*, 5(1):51–72, 1974.

9. W. W. Bledsoe and Gohui Feng. Set-Var. *Journal of Automated Reasoning*, 11:293–314, 1993.

10. Alonzo Church. A Formulation of the Simple Theory of Types. *Journal of Symbolic Logic*, 5:56–68, 1940.

11. Fausto Giunchiglia and Adolfo Villafiorita. ABSFOL: a Proof Checker with Abstraction. In M.A. McRobbie and J.K. Slaney, editors, *CADE-13: Proceedings of the 13th International Conference on Automated Deduction*, Lecture Notes in Artificial Intelligence 1104, pages 136–140. Springer-Verlag, 1996.

12. Fausto Giunchiglia and Toby Walsh. Theorem Proving with Definitions. In *Proceedings of AISB 89*, Society for the Study of Artificial Intelligence and Simulation of Behaviour, 1989.

13. Fausto Giunchiglia and Toby Walsh. A Theory of Abstraction. *Artificial Intelligence*, 57(2-3):323–389, 1992.

14. Gerard P. Huet. A Unification Algorithm for Typed λ-Calculus. *Theoretical Computer Science*, 1:27–57, 1975.

15. Ignace I. Kolodner. Fixed Points. *American Mathematical Monthly*, 71:906, 1964.

16. Dale A. Miller. A compact representation of proofs. *Studia Logica*, 46(4):347–370, 1987.

17. D. Pastre. Automatic Theorem Proving in Set Theory. *Artificial Intelligence*, 10:1–27, 1978.

18. Frank Pfenning. *Proof Transformations in Higher-Order Logic.* PhD thesis, Carnegie Mellon University, 1987. 156 pp.

19. D.A. Plaisted. Abstraction Mappings in Mechanical Theorem Proving. In *5th Conference on Automated Deduction*, Lecture Notes in Computer Science 87, pages 264–280. Springer-Verlag, 1980.

20. D.A. Plaisted. Theorem Proving with Abstraction. *Artificial Intelligence*, 16:47–108, 1981.

21. Dave Plummer. *Gazing: Controlling the Use of Rewrite Rules.* PhD thesis, Dept. of Artificial Intelligence, University of Edinburgh, 1987.

22. K. Warren. Implementation of a Definition Expansion Mechanism in a Connection Method Theorem Prover. Master's thesis, Dept. of Artificial Intelligence, Univ. of Edinburgh, 1987.

23. Larry Wos. The Problem of Definition Expansion and Contraction. *Journal of Automated Reasoning*, 3:433–435, 1987.

Using Matings for Pruning Connection Tableaux

Reinhold Letz

Institut für Informatik, Technische Universität München
80290 München, Germany
letz@in.tum.de

Abstract Tableau calculi and the connection method are generally considered as related paradigms in automated deduction. However, in their
essence, the frameworks are based on different concepts, and there is a
large potential for cross-fertilization which is by far not exploited. In
this paper, we demonstrate how the matings concept, which is central
to the connection method framework, can be used to identify significant
redundancies in the search for connection tableau proofs. The redundancies we discuss arise from the fact that different tableaux may encode
the same mating. We concentrate on certain permutations of connection
tableaux that occur when so-called reduction steps are performed in the
tableau construction. Those permutations can be avoided without having
to store the corresponding matings, which would be expensive. Instead
the input formula is augmented with a literal ordering which is used in
the connection tableau calculus to prune certain reduction steps. With
this technique a significant reduction of the search space for almost every non-Horn formula can be achieved. Furthermore, the method can be
implemented very easily and has almost no run-time overhead.

1   Introduction

Currently there is a methodological discussion between members of the tableau
and the connection method community about the essential differences and relations between both frameworks. In this paper, we attempt to contribute to this
discussion by arguing that the central notions are essentially different and that,
from the perspective of automated deduction, there is a large potential of cross-
fertilization between the methods which is by far not recognized and exploited.
We begin with a brief clarification of the inherent principles of both paradigms,
their relations and differences.

Systematically, the tableau method [19] is a *tree-oriented* deductive paradigm
based on the *subformula principle*, which permits a well-founded decomposition
of a formula into certain subformulae. Further typical proof-theoretic virtues of
the framework are the *confluence* of the calculus and the possibility of *saturation*
of a branch (possibly up to a Hintikka set). Traditionally, tableau calculi have no
reference to connections, which is a central concept in automated deduction for

C. Kirchner and H. Kirchner (Eds.): Automated Deduction, CADE-15
LNAI 1421, pp. 381–396, 1998. © Springer–Verlag Berlin Heidelberg 1998

classical logic. In fact, until recently both communities were almost separated.[1]
When integrating connections as a control structure into tableaux [9], the gain is
goal-orientedness, which renders tableaux successful [16] and hence respectable
also in the classical automated deduction community, but at the price of losing
the possibility of branch saturation and confluence.

In the connection or matings method [1,3,4], on the other hand, the notion of
a connection is of central importance. The proof-theoretic kernel of this framework is to call a set of connections M—called *mating*—*spanning* for a formula
if every appropriately defined *path through* the formula contains a connection
from M. First and foremost, the concept of a spanning mating has no deductive
content, it provides just a declarative (graph-theoretic) characterization of logical validity or inconsistency. So both paradigms are essentially different. The
wide-spread misinterpretation that both frameworks be very related has the following simple reason. The most natural method for finding and identifying a
spanning mating as such is to use a tree-oriented path checking procedure which
decomposes the formula, like in the tableau framework, but guided by connections. The majority of those connection *calculi* in [4] can therefore be viewed as
connection *tableau* calculi (although this may be historically unfair). It is important to note, however, that using connection tableau calculi is just one approach
of identifying a spanning mating, and there are procedures imaginable that are
based on completely different paradigms, for example, on resolution.

In this paper, we will stick to the tableau-oriented proof methodology, but
we will demonstrate that the matings concept can be used to identify enormous
redundancies in tableau search procedures. Our considerations are based on the
fact that one can associate a mating with every connection tableau, but this
mapping is highly non-injective, i.e., there may be a large number of tableaux
which encode the same mating. The technique we develop in detail is not aimed
at removing all redundancies based on this "permutation" phenomenon, but the
ones that can be identified in an efficient manner. In particular, it is not necessary
to store the already processed matings during the proof search procedure, which
would be very expensive. Instead, it suffices to define an ordering on the literals
of the input formula, which is then used to prune certain reduction steps in
the connection tableau procedure. The method is integrated into two types of
connection tableau calculi, one *multiplicity*-based, in which a number of variants
of each input clause is generated in a preprocessing phase and no renaming
of input clauses is permitted during the tableau construction, and one with a
dynamic renaming of the input clauses. We prove that the ordering refinement
preserves completeness. The method has a high potential for search pruning,
since it definitely reduces the search space of *every* unsatisfiable input formula

---

[1] As an illustration, note that unification was not used in tableaux before [18], and
the notion of a connection does not even appear in [5]. On the other hand, it was
not widely noticed in the area of automated deduction that calculi like *model elimination* [14,15] or *SLD-resolution* [8] are proof-theoretically better viewed as tableau
calculi, which permits to define the calculi as *cut-free* proof systems. The relation of
connection tableaux with model elimination is discussed, for example, in [11,12].

which permits the application of so-called reduction steps in connection tableaux. Note that this holds for almost every non-Horn formula, which are typically hard to handle in automated deduction.

The paper is organized as follows. In the next section, we shortly review the main concepts and properties of clausal connection tableau calculi. In Section 3, the connection method framework is presented including some new notions and results. In Section 4, we relate properties of matings with properties of tableaux and identify the type of redundancy we wish to remove from the tableau procedures; it is shown that this can be achieved by simply equipping the tableau calculi with literal orderings. Section 5 is devoted to the ground completeness proof of the new literal-ordered connection tableau calculus. In Section 6, the first-order calculi are considered, both the multiplicity and the non-multiplicity oriented ones, and the ground completeness result is lifted to the first-order case. In Section 7, an improvement of the technique is developed using syntactic disequation constraints. In the final section, we compare our work with related approaches and point to some further search pruning methods based on the use of the matings concept.

2   Clausal Tableaux with Connection Conditions

Before starting with the presentation of connection tableaux, the meaning of some basic concepts and notations will be determined. We use standard conventions for denoting terms and literals, variables will be denoted with the letters u, v, x, y (with subscripts). The proof systems we will consider are all working on *clausal formulae*, which are conjunctions $F = c_1 \wedge \cdots \wedge c_n$ of *clauses*. A *clause* is a string of the form $L_1 \vee \cdots \vee L_n$ where the L_i are literals. Occurrences of literals in a clausal formula are denoted with triples $\langle L, i, j \rangle$ where L is the literal at position i of the j-the clause in F. The *complement* $\sim L$ of a literal L is A if L is of the form $\neg A$, and $\neg L$ otherwise. For formulae in clausal form, the calculus of free-variable tableaux [5,13] can be reformulated in a particularly simple and condensed form.

Definition 1. (Clausal tableau) *A clausal tableau is a downward-oriented tree in which all nodes except the root node are labelled with literals (and other control information). For every non-leaf node N in a clausal tableau, the sequence $N_1, \ldots, N_m$ of its immediate successor nodes is called the node family below N; if the nodes $N_1, \ldots, N_m$ are labelled with literals $L_1, \ldots, L_m$, respectively, then the clause $L_1 \vee \cdots \vee L_m$ is termed the tableau clause below N; the tableau clause below the root node is called the start or top clause of the tableau. Let F be a conjunction of clauses; a clausal tableau is said to be a clausal tableau for F if every tableau clause in T is an instance of a clause in F.*

The most successful structural refinement of clausal tableaux concerning automated deduction is to use links or *connections* to guide the proof search. The condition comes in two variants, a weaker one, which we term *path connectedness*, and a stricter one, simply called *connectedness*, which we prefer. The resulting tableau calculi can be formulated as consisting of three inference rules.

Definition 2. (Connection tableau calculus) *Let F be a conjunction of clauses* $c_1 \wedge \cdots \wedge c_n$.

(Start rule) *At the beginning, select a clause from F and take it as top clause of the tableau. All new branches are considered as open.*

Then select an open branch B in the current tableau with leaf node N (called subgoal) and literal label K. Two types of inference rules may be applied.

(Extension rule) *Select a clause c_j from F and rename it, i.e., obtain a variant $c'_j = L_1 \vee \cdots \vee L_m$ in which all variables are different from the variables in T. If there is a most general unifier σ for $\sim K$ and a literal L_i in c'_j, attach a new node family $N_1, \ldots, N_m$ to the subgoal N and label the nodes with the literals $L_1, \ldots, L_m$, respectively. Then consider all new branches as open, except N_i which is considered as closed. Finally, apply the substitution σ to the formulae in the tableau. We will say that the new node family (the clause c_j) was entered at the node N_i (the literal occurrence $\langle L_i, i, j \rangle$).*

(Closure or reduction rule) *If N has an ancestor node N' with literal L on the branch B such that there is a most general unifier σ for $\sim K$ and L, then consider B as closed and apply σ to the tableau.*

The *path connection tableau calculus* is identical except that the extension rule is generalized to the *path extension rule* which permits that *any* node from the branch B may be used as a unification partner for L_i. We mention this variant because it corresponds to the connection calculi in [4]. The connection tableau calculus, on the other hand, is a generalization of (weak) model elimination [14,15]. Completeness proofs can be found in [12] or below.

Although with the integration of connections into the tableau framework the fundamental proof-theoretic property of *confluence*[2] is lost, the new calculus becomes competitive in automated deduction, because it permits a *goal-oriented* search. But, when searching for closed connection tableaux, a systematic branch saturation procedure like in [19] cannot be used. Instead one uses the well-known two-step methodology of iterative deepening search [20]. On each iteration level, only tableaux up to a certain complexity are permitted. The favoured complexity measures are the number of (closed) branches or the maximal depth of a tableau, called *inference* and *depth* bound, respectively. The bounds differ strongly in their worst-case complexities. While it is straightforward to recognize that the verification of the existence of a tableau with k inferences is an NP-complete problem, the corresponding problem for the depth bound seems much harder (it is not even clear whether it is in PSPACE). A combination of both bounds, the *weighted-depth bound*, which is integrated in the theorem prover SETHEO [16,7] turned out to be very successful in practice (although the weighted-depth bound and the depth bound have the same worst-case complexity).

The pure connection tableau calculus contains lots of redundancies. A basic pruning mechanism is *regularity*. It requires that on no branch in a clausal

---

[2] A calculus is confluent if it cannot run into dead ends (see, e.g., [12]).

tableau a literal may appear more than once. A further reduction of the search space can be achieved with methods of *failure caching* [2], which avoid repetitions of subgoal solutions with the same or more special substitutions. Only the *local* variant [11,12] is successful in practice, which was termed *anti-lemma* mechanism in [11]. Failure caching methods, however, are very expensive and difficult to implement. Finally, one should mention additional inference rules like *factorization* or *folding up* [11]. Those may have a proof shortening effect and can be viewed as controlled integrations of the (atomic) cut rule. Although these additional inference rules increase the search space, they may be beneficial if a proof can be found on an earlier iterative-deepening level. It is important to mention the most successful pruning methods of connection tableaux, because we want to investigate whether the new search pruning technique developed in this paper is compatible with those methods.

3 The Connection Method

Based on work by Prawitz [17], the *connection method* was introduced by Andrews [1] and Bibel [3,4]—we shall use Bibel's terminology as reference point. As already mentioned in the Introduction, the kernel of the connection method is not a deductive system, but a declarative syntactic characterization of logical validity or inconsistency. While, in the original papers, the connection method represents logical validity directly, we work with the dual variant representing inconsistency, which makes no difference concerning the employed notions and mechanisms. Furthermore, we work on the clausal case only.

Definition 3. (Path, connection, mating, spanning property) *Given a clausal formula $F = c_1 \wedge \cdots \wedge c_n$, a path through F is a set of n literal occurrences in F, exactly one from each clause in F. A connection in F is a two-element subset $\{\langle K, i, k \rangle, \langle L, j, l \rangle\}$ of a path through F such that K and L are literals with the same predicate symbol, one negated and one not. Any set of connections in F is called a* mating *in F. A mating M is said to be* spanning *for F if every path through F is a superset of a connection in M.*

A conjunction of ground clauses F is unsatisfiable if and only if there is a spanning mating for F. In the first-order case, the notions of multiplicities and unification come into play.

Definition 4. (Multiplicity, unifiable connection, mating) *First, a multiplicity is just a mapping $\mu : \mathbb{N} \longrightarrow \mathbb{N}_0$ which is then applied to clausal formulae, as follows. Given a multiplicity μ and two clausal formulae $F = c_1 \wedge \cdots \wedge c_n$ and $F' = c_1^1 \wedge \cdots \wedge c_1^{\mu(1)} \wedge \cdots \wedge c_n^1 \wedge \cdots \wedge c_n^{\mu(n)}$ where every c_i^k is a variable-renamed variant of c_i, we call F' a (μ-)multiplicity of F. A connection $\{\langle K, i, k \rangle, \langle L, j, l \rangle\}$ is termed* unifiable *if the atoms of K and L are. A mating is* unifiable *if there is a simultaneous unifier for all its connections.*

Theorem 1. *A clausal formula F is unsatisfiable if and only if there is a unifiable spanning mating for a multiplicity of F.* [4]

Since it is decidable whether a clausal formula has a unifiable and spanning mating (more precisely, the problem is complete for the complexity class Σ_2^p in the polynomial hierarchy), the theorem suggests a two-step methodology of *iterative-deepening* proof search, as performed with the connection tableau procedures. The outer loop is concerned with increasing the multiplicity whereas the inner procedure explores the finite search space determined by the given multiplicity. Although there are different methods for identifying a unifiable and spanning mating for some multiplicity of a formula, one of the most natural ways is exemplified with a procedure which is similar to the connection tableau calculi, but without a renaming of the clauses in the given multiplicity.

Definition 5. ((Path) Connection tableau calculus without renaming) *The two calculi are the same as the ones given in the previous section except that*

1. *they work on a multiplicity F' of the input formula,*
2. *no renaming is permitted in a (path) extension step, and*
3. *the computed substitution σ is also applied to the clauses in F'.*

The connection procedure C_1^1 on pages 108f. in [4], for example, is based on the path connection tableau calculus without renaming. There is the following fundamental difference between the two types of calculi. If the regularity (or some similar) condition is added, then, for the calculi without renaming, it is guaranteed that there are only finitely many (path) connection tableaux for each multiplicity of the input formula.

It is interesting to compare both iterative-deepening methodologies. The main difference of this type of tableau calculi from the ones of the previous section is that with multiplicity-based bounds static complexity limits are put on the input multiplicity whereas the tableau complexity is not directly bounded. There are also two important differences concerning the effectiveness of the search pruning mechanisms mentioned above. The first is that the beneficial effect of factorization and folding up (permitting that a proof is found on an earlier iterative-deepening level) cannot occur in the multiplicity-based case, since those rules can only reduce the tableau size, but have no influence on the unifiability and spanning properties of matings. Failure caching is even more problematic in the multiplicity-based case, for the following reason. In order to preserve completeness, not only the solution substitution of a subgoal N has to be considered, but also the substitutions applied to all clauses used in the subrefutation of N. This renders failure caching practically useless in the multiplicity-based case.

Moreover, in the multiplicity-based case, there is an additional source of redundancy which has directly to do with the use of multiplicities. Consider the clausal formula

$$F = \neg P(a) \wedge (P(x) \vee \neg Q(y)) \wedge (Q(a) \vee Q(b)).$$

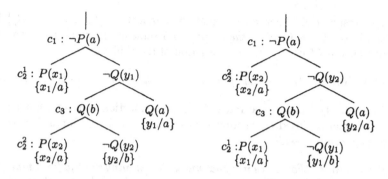

Figure1. Multiplicity-based duplication of connection tableaux.

In Figure 1, two closed connection tableaux for the multiplicity $F' = c_1 \wedge c_2^1 \wedge c_2^2 \wedge c_3$ of F are displayed; also, the attached clause variants and the substitutions to be applied in the inference steps are given.

It is evident that the two tableaux are variants of each other obtainable by exchanging the positions of the clauses c_2^1 and c_2^2. This obvious redundancy can be avoided by using the proviso that any variant c_i^{k+1}, $k > 0$, of an initial clause c_i can be selected for extension only if the clause variant c_i^k in the multiplicity was already used in the tableau. This way the tableau on the right cannot be constructed any more. We assume in the sequel that the tableau construction always complies with this condition.

4 Using Matings for Pruning Connection Tableaux

It is interesting to relate properties of matings with one another and with properties of clausal tableaux. There are the following fundamental refinements of matings.

Definition 6. (Fully connected, minimal mating) *A mating M in a clausal formula F is called* fully connected *if, whenever a literal occurrence in a clause c in F is the member of some connection of M, then every literal occurrence in c is contained in some connection of M. A mating M is called* minimal *if, for every connection $C \in M$, there is a path through F containing only the connection C.*

Proposition 1. *Every unsatisfiable ground clausal formula has a minimal spanning mating, and every minimal spanning mating is fully connected.*

In order to clarify the relation to tableaux with connection conditions, it is more natural to work with the multiplicity-based calculi, since there the literal occurrences and connections in a multiplicity F' of a formula can directly be identified in any tableau for F'. Whenever an extension or reduction step is performed in the construction of a tableau for a multiplicity F' which involves two tableau nodes N and N' with corresponding literal occurrences $\langle K, i, k \rangle$ and

$\langle L, j, l \rangle$, respectively, then we say that the connection $\{\langle K, i, k \rangle, \langle L, j, l \rangle\}$ in F' is *used* in the tableau. With *the mating* of a tableau for F' we mean the set of connections in F' used in the construction of the tableau.

Proposition 2. *The mating of any closed connection tableau is fully connected.*

Note that this is not guaranteed for path connection tableaux. Furthermore, the mating of a closed connection tableau need not be minimal. However, we have the converse result.

Proposition 3. *For every minimal unifiable spanning mating for a multiplicity F' of a clausal formula, there exists a closed connection tableau without renaming for F' with this mating.*

An analysis of the standard connection tableau procedures, including the procedures developed in the connection method community, reveals that in those approaches the generation of a spanning mating is mainly a waste-product, with almost no influence on the pruning of the search space. The matings concept, however, provides a more abstract view on the search space, since it groups tableaux together in equivalence classes. Under certain circumstances, it is not necessary to construct *all* tableaux in such a class but only *one representative*. In order to illustrate this, let us consider the propositional formula

$$(\neg P_1 \vee \neg P_2) \wedge (\neg P_1 \vee P_2) \wedge (P_1 \vee \neg P_2) \wedge (P_1 \vee P_2).$$

As shown in Figure 2, the formula has four closed regular connection tableaux with all-negative start clause $\neg P_1 \vee \neg P_2$. If, however, the involved sets of connections are inspected, it turns out that the tableaux all have the same mating consisting of six connections. In fact, there exists exactly one minimal spanning mating for this formula. The redundancy contained in the tableau framework is that certain tableaux are *permutations* of each other corresponding to different possible ways of *traversing* a set of connections. Under certain circumstances, only one of the tableaux in such an equivalence class has to be considered.

Before we are going to discuss different remedies, we will shortly demonstrate that it is worthwhile to remove this type of redundancy. For this purpose, note that the above formula is a member of a well-known formula class. For every n, let F_n denote the conjunction of all clauses $L_1 \vee \cdots \vee L_n$ where every L_i is either the atom P_i or its negation $\neg P_i$. It is straightforward to check that the number of closed regular connection tableaux with all-negative start clause for an F_n is the value of the rapidly growing function $\nu(n)$ which is recursively defined as: $\nu(1) = 1$ and $\nu(n + 1) = (2^n \times c(n))^{n+1}$. For example, for $n = 3$, we have 4096 proofs and, for $n = 4$, already more than 10^{18}. Each formula in this class, however, has exactly one minimal spanning mating. This illustrates that an enormous reduction of the search space may be obtained when we succeed in avoiding the generation of different tableaux with the same mating.

The question is, how exactly this redundancy can be avoided. A general line of development would be to store all matings that have been considered during

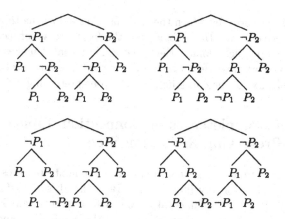

Figure2. Four closed connection tableaux for the same spanning mating.

the tableau search procedure and to ignore all tableaux which encode a mating which was already generated before. This method of *matings caching* is similar in many respects to failure caching [2] and would require an enormous amount of space. Also, it contradicts the general paradigm of proof procedures of the connection tableau type, which can do with very little space. Nevertheless (the amount of space is less than in failure caching and the method is applicable to non-Horn formulae) such a method seems worthwhile to be investigated.

In this paper, however, we will not further pursue this approach. Instead, we will develop a method for avoiding permutations of the type shown in Figure 2 which works with very little additional data structure. On the other hand, this method will not detect every repetition of a mating. To comprehend the method, note that in the example above, the source of the redundancy is that a certain connection can be used both in an extension step and a reduction step. This causes the combinatorial explosion. The idea is now to block certain reduction steps by using an ordering on the literals in the multiplicity F' of the input formula which has to be respected during the tableau construction.

Definition 7. *Let $\prec$ be a partial or total ordering on the literal occurrences of a multiplicity F' of a clausal formula. A reduction step from a subgoal N using an ancestor node N' is said to* preserve the order $\prec$ *if the literal occurrence corresponding to N is not greater than the literal occurrence corresponding to the node at which the node family below N' was entered.*

Applied to the example above, let the literal order $\prec$ be just decreasing with the position in the string F, i.e., $\langle L, k, l \rangle \prec \langle K, i, j \rangle$ if $l > j$ or if $l = j$ and $k > i$. Now consider the top left tableau in Figure 2. The tableau contains two reduction steps, both at tableau nodes with maximal depth, one for the P_1-subgoal on the left and one for the P_2-subgoal on the right. Both reduction steps are order-preserving, since the corresponding literal occurrences $\langle P_1, 1, 4 \rangle$ and $\langle P_2, 2, 4 \rangle$ are not greater than $\langle P_1, 1, 3 \rangle$ and $\langle P_2, 2, 2 \rangle$, respectively. The latter correspond to the nodes by which the node families below the top clause where entered, respectively. All other tableaux in the figure, however, contain at least one reduction step which violates the order $\prec$. Note that it makes absolutely no difference for the pruning effect which order is used. For any total order, exactly one of the tableaux can be constructed with order-preserving reduction steps.

5   Ground Completeness of Connection Tableaux with Order-Preserving Reduction Steps

We will demonstrate now that the developed refinement preserves completeness for ground formulae, for any literal order. Beforehand, some additional terminology is needed and a fundamental lemma will be stated that is employed in the proof. Let S be the set of clauses in a clausal formula F. S and F are called *minimally unsatisfiable* if S is unsatisfiable and every proper subset of S is satisfiable. A clause c is called *relevant* in S and F if there is an unsatisfiable subset of S containing c. Let S be a set of clauses and P a set of literals. With S_{-P} we denote the subset of clauses in S which do not contain literals from P.

Lemma 1. (Mate Lemma) *Let S be an unsatisfiable set of ground clauses. For any literal L contained in any relevant clause c in S, there exists a clause c' in S such that c' contains $\sim L$ and c' is relevant in $\{L\} \cup S_{-\{L\}}$.*

A proof of this lemma can be found, for example, in [10,11]. Note further that, obviously, for any P and S, $P \cup S_{-P}$ implies S. As usual for connection tableaux, we want completeness for regularity, any relevant clause as top clause, and any *subgoal selection function*. A *subgoal selection function* ϕ is a mapping assigning to any open tableau T a subgoal of T. A tableau is said to be *constructed according to* a subgoal selection function ϕ if every inference was performed at the subgoal assigned by ϕ.

Proposition 4. *For any unsatisfiable ground clausal formula F, every relevant clause c in F, every subgoal selection function ϕ, and every literal order $\prec$, there exists a closed regular connection tableau for F with top clause c constructed according to ϕ in which every reduction steps preserves the order $\prec$.*

Proof. We adapt the completeness proof contained in [12] to the ordered case. Accordingly, we first specify a deduction procedure for connection tableaux, and show then by induction that during execution of this procedure an invariant is preserved which eventually leads to a closed tableaux with the required properties.

Tableau procedure. First, attach c as top clause of the tableau T. As long as the tableau is not yet closed, let N with corresponding literal occurrence $\langle L, i, k \rangle$ and corresponding clause c_k in F be the subgoal selected by ϕ, and let P be the set of literals on the branch with subgoal N.

1. if N has an ancestor N' on the branch labelled with $\sim L$, perform a reduction step using N',

2. otherwise, let c_l be a clause in S_{-P} that is relevant in $P \cup S_{-P}$ and contains a *maximal occurrence* $\langle \sim L, j, l \rangle$ of $\sim L$ in S_{-P}, i.e., no literal occurrence of the form $\langle \sim L, r, s \rangle$ in S_{-P} is greater than $\langle \sim L, j, l \rangle$. Enter the clause c_l at $\langle \sim L, j, l \rangle$.

First, we verify that the above procedure solely admits the construction of connection tableaux which are regular and in which the reduction steps preserve the order $\prec$. For the preservation of the literal order, note that, according to the clause selection in the procedure, in previous extension steps, the node at which the node family below N' was entered corresponds to a literal occurrence of L which was maximal in a set containing the clause c_k and hence cannot be smaller than the literal occurrence corresponding to the subgoal N. Regularity is trivially preserved, since, in each extension step, the attached clause must be from the set S_{-P}.

Furthermore, because of the regularity restriction, there can be only branches of finite length. Consequently, the procedure must terminate either because every branch is closed or because no clause exists for an extension step which meets the conditions stated in the procedure. We prove that the second alternative can never occur, since, for any subgoal N, there exists such a clause for extension. This will be shown by induction on the node *depth* (as the depth of a node we take the number of its predecessor nodes). The induction base, $n = 1$, i.e., the possibility of extending the start clause respectively, is evident from the Mate Lemma. For the induction step from depth n to $n + 1$, $n \geq 1$, let N be a subgoal with depth $n+1$ and literal L in the clause c_k, and with P being the set of path literals up to the immediate predecessor of N. By the induction assumption, c_k is relevant in $P \cup S_{-P}$. Let $P' = P \cup \{L\}$. By the Mate Lemma, some clause in $P \cup S_{-P}$ contains $\sim L$ and is relevant in $\{L\} \cup (P \cup S_{-P})_{-\{L\}} = P' \cup S_{-P'}$. Now, one such clause with a maximal occurrence of $\sim L$ can be selected, say c_l. Finally, $c_l \notin P'$, since then N would have been closed by a reduction step, hence $c_l \in S_{-P'}$.   □

6   Matings Pruning in the First-Order Case

Before considering the completeness of the new calculi for the first-order case, we wish to discuss an additional example. While, in the ground case, multiple occurrences of literals in a clause can be removed in a preprocessing phase, for first-order clauses, multiple occurrences may be produced dynamically when certain substitutions are applied. Under certain circumstances, this may lead to redundancies. As an illustration, consider Figure 3, which displays a connection tableau constructed with *depth-first leftmost* subgoal selection function, as indicated with the sequence of inference steps by which the final substitution σ_5 was computed. The arrows point to the nodes (marked with σ_1 and σ_2) at which the respective clauses were entered, the nodes marked with $\sigma_3, \sigma_4, \sigma_5$ were closed with reduction steps. Now, it is essential for the completeness of connection tableaux that *all contrapositives* of a clause be tried during the proof search, that is, the clause c_2 has to be entered at the rightmost literal, too, the difference being that in this case the leftmost subgoal is closed by a reduction step. The resulting tableau, however, is identical to the one displayed in the figure. The same duplication occurs for clause c_3. So we have in total 4 different ways of constructing the same tableau. It can easily be verified that, for *any* total literal order, there is only one way to generate this tableau if the order is preserved by the reduction steps. In applications, for example, the clauses of associativity (in their relational representation) give rise to this type of redundancy during proof search when the underlying formula is non-Horn. This illustrates that, in the first-order case, already for very small examples, the pruning effect can be achieved.

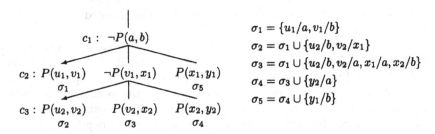

Figure3. Multiple literal occurrences in tableau clauses.

The lifting of the ground completeness to the first-order case is straight-forward, for the connection tableau calculus without renaming, since to every non-root node in a connection tableau one can assign a literal occurrence in the underlying multiplicity, just like in the ground case. However, one precaution has to be taken in order to preserve completeness. It has to do with the proviso that a clause variant c_i^{k+1} of an initial clause c_i can be selected for extension only if the clause variant c_i^k in the multiplicity was already used in the tableau. This condition also imposes a certain restriction on the applicability of inference steps, which may conflict with some literal order. To recognize this, reconsider Figure 1. If we select $P(x_2)$ in c_2^2 greater than $P(x_1)$ in c_2^1, then no closed regular connection tableau exists with the given start clause, and completeness is lost. In general, the literal order has to be *compatible* with the order of clause variants in the multiplicity. i.e., any literal occurrence in a clause c_i^{k+l} must not be greater than any literal occurrence (with the same predicate symbol) in a clause c_i^k.

Proposition 5. *The connection tableau calculus without renaming is complete for any partial or total literal order on the underlying multiplicity that is compatible with the order of the clause variants, plus the other standard conditions stated in Proposition 4.*

The proof is straightforward by using a standard lifting technique [10,12]. The case of connection tableau calculi with renaming is a bit problematic, since there is, at first sight, no notion of a multiplicity. The natural association coming with the definition of the calculus is to associate all nodes in a tableau with literal occurrences in the *input* formula. For example, the literal occurrences $P(x_1)$ and $P(x_2)$ in Figure 1 would be associated with the same literal occurrence $P(x)$ in the input formula F. Obviously, this view is too simple to permit a general identification of connections and matings in such connection tableaux. However, for our restricted application of avoiding permutations by imposing orderings, this simple interpretation will suffice. All literal occurrences in a tableau that are associated with the same literal occurrence in the input formula F will then automatically be treated as equal in any ordering.

Proposition 6. *The connection tableau calculus with renaming is complete for any (partial or total) literal order on the input formula, with the same additional conditions as stated in Proposition 4.*

Proof. The proof is an immediate corollary from Proposition 5, as follows. Let F be an unsatisfiable clausal formula and $\prec$ any literal order on F. Extend $\prec$ to the (partial) order on the multiplicities F' of F by treating every two literal occurrences $\{L, i, c_i^k\}$ and $\{L, i, c_i^l\}$ in F' as equal in $\prec$. Now, by Proposition 5, there is a closed connection tableau T without renaming for some multiplicity F' of F satisfying the ordering and the other requirements. Then T is a closed connection tableau with renaming for F and satisfies the ordering and the other requirements. $\square$

Furthermore, it is straightforward to recognize that this matings technique is compatible with local failure caching. We should mention, however, that there is a strengthening of the connection condition, the so-called *strong* connectedness [10,12], which is not compatible with the matings technique (see pages 184–185 in [10]).

7 From Literal Orderings to Disequation Constraints

In this section, we describe an improvement of the developed method using *disequation constraints*, which are conditions of the form $s \neq t$ on the terms occurring in tableaux and multiplicities. When violated, those constraints immediately initiate a backtracking of the search procedure. A number of pruning methods can be reformulated as such disequation constraints [9,10]. And really, the fact that a node N must not be solved by a reduction step using a predecessor N' (because of an ordering restriction) can be reexpressed as a disequation constraint $\sim K \neq L$, where K and L are the literals at N and N', respectively, with the following precaution.

Definition 8. *Let $\prec$ be any literal order. Whenever a clause is entered at a literal occurrence $\langle L, j, l \rangle$ from a subgoal N with literal occurrence $\langle K, i, k \rangle$ where σ is the respective unifier for $\sim K$ and L, then, for any literal occurrence $\langle L', r, s \rangle \succ \langle L, j, l \rangle$ in the underlying multiplicity F' with unifiable L' and $L\sigma$, a disequation constraint $L' \neq L\sigma$ is generated. The respective set of disequation constraints is associated with the node N and the clause c_s.*

Proposition 7. *The regular connection tableau calculus without renaming and with the conditions stated in Proposition 5 preserves completeness under the additional condition that, for any tableau clause c_s dominated by any node N, the disequation constraints associated with N and c_s have to be satisfied.*

Proof. Assume a clause c_s is dominated by a node N and a constraint associated with N and c_s is violated. This can only be because a literal occurrence $\langle L', r, s \rangle$ in c_s is greater than the literal occurrence at which the clause immediately below N was entered. Either c_s was entered at $\langle L', r, s \rangle$, then c_s cannot be immediately below N and the predecessor of the $\langle L', r, s \rangle$-node would be labelled with the same literal as N, which would violate the regularity. Or c_s was entered at another literal occurrence. Since the $\langle L', r, s \rangle$-node must not be closed by a reduction step using N because of the ordering, another node on the branch must have the same literal as N, which would also violate the regularity.   □

In the renaming variant of connection tableaux, such disequation constraints cannot be imposed on the input clauses, because of the lacking correspondence with clauses in the tableau. But the constraints may be generated at the moment a renaming of an input clause is attached below a node N, in a similar way regularity constraints are generated in the theorem prover SETHEO [16]. This method is currently being implemented in SETHEO. Interestingly, such constraints can prune the search *long before* the failing reduction steps (due to a violation of the order) would cause a backtracking in the search procedure. In the ground case, for example, all constraints have the form $L \neq L$, which permits that all clauses containing constraints associated with a node N may be completely ignored below N.

8   Related Work and Further Research

As already mentioned, so far there has been no real exploitation of properties of matings for proof search in connection tableaux. However, our work is related, at least in methodology, with the approach in [6], which uses the notion of *clause trees* as a static representation tool for describing permutations of resolution derivations. There are the following main differences. First, obviously, matings are general graphs and hence permit a more abstract view than just trees. Furthermore, the use of clause trees for pruning resolution procedures is relatively limited, since the technique is mainly employed as a method for avoiding the derivation of clauses that would be deleted by subsumption anyway.

It is also important to compare the technique developed here with other pruning methods, particularly, with failure caching. As a matter of fact, when a subgoal N is solved by subrefutations with the same mating, this will eventually be detected by failure caching, because the solution substitutions for N must be identical. But, in general, with failure caching this type of redundancy is identified much later than with the matings technique developed here. This may make an enormous difference in search effort, as can be verified with the formula considered in Figure 3. On the other hand, failure caching can avoid redundancies that cannot be captured by any form of matings pruning, not even by full matings caching. This has profound proof-theoretic reasons that are discussed in [10,12]. A further important difference between both methods is that failure caching is more expensive during run-time and by magnitudes more expensive to implement than the matings technique developed here.

We conclude with pointing to some future promising research perspectives using matings information. First, the techniques developed here should be extended to connection tableau calculi with additional inference rules. Furthermore, the potential of full matings caching should be investigated, with the emphasis on minimal matings. For this purpose, practically efficient algorithms for deciding the minimality of matings have to be developed.

Acknowledgements. I would like to thank the referees for their comments.

References

1. P. Andrews. Theorem Proving via General Matings. *Journal of the Association for Computing Machinery*, 28(2):193–214, 1981.
2. O. W. Astrachan and M. E. Stickel. Caching and Lemmaizing in Model Elimination Theorem Provers. *Proceedings of the 11th Conference on Automated Deduction (CADE-11)*, LNAI 607, pages 224–238, Springer, 1992.
3. W. Bibel. On Matrices with Connections. *Journal of the ACM*, 28:633–645, 1981.
4. W. Bibel. *Automated Theorem Proving*. Vieweg, 2nd edition, 1987.
5. M. Fitting. *First-Order Logic and Automated Theorem Proving*, Springer, 2nd edition, 1996.
6. J. D. Horton and B. Spencer. Clause trees: a tool for understanding and implementing resolution in automated deduction. *Artificial Intelligence*, 92:25–89, 1997.
7. O. Ibens and R. Letz. Subgoal Alternation in Model Elimination. In *Proceedings of TABLEAUX'97*, LNAI 1227, pages 201–215, Springer, 1997.
8. R. A. Kowalski and D. Kuehner. Linear Resolution with Selection Function. *Artificial Intelligence*, 2:227–260, 1970.
9. R. Letz, J. Schumann, S. Bayerl, and W. Bibel. SETHEO: A High-Performance Theorem Prover. *Journal of Automated Reasoning*, 8(2):183–212, 1992.
10. R. Letz. *First-Order Calculi and Proof Procedures for Automated Deduction*. PhD thesis, Technische Hochschule Darmstadt, 1993
(http://wwwjessen.informatik.tu-muenchen.de/personen/letz.html).
11. R. Letz, K. Mayr, and C. Goller. Controlled Integration of the Cut Rule into Connection Tableaux Calculi. *Journal of Automated Reasoning*, 13:297–337, 1994.
12. R. Letz. Clausal Tableaux. In W. Bibel, P. H. Schmitt, editors, *Automated Deduction. A basis for applications*, Vol. 1, pages 39–68, Kluwer, 1998.
13. R. Letz. First-order Tableau Methods. In M. D'Agostino, D. Gabbay, R. Hähnle, J. Posegga, editors, *Handbook of Tableau Methods*, Kluwer, 1998.
14. D. W. Loveland. Mechanical Theorem Proving by Model Elimination. *Journal of the ACM*, 15(2):236–251, 1968.
15. D. W. Loveland. *Automated Theorem Proving: a Logical Basis*. North-Holland, 1978.
16. M. Moser, O. Ibens, R. Letz, J. Steinbach, C. Goller, J. Schumann, K. Mayr. SETHEO and E-SETHEO. *Journal of Automated Reasoning*, 18:237–246, 1997.

17. D. Prawitz. An Improved Proof Procedure. *Theoria*, 26:102–139, 1960.
18. S. Reeves. Semantic tableaux as a framework for automated theorem-proving. In C. S. Mellish and J. Hallam, editors, *Advances in Artificial Intelligence (Proceedings of AISB-87)*, pages 125–139, Wiley, 1987.
19. R. M. Smullyan. *First-Order Logic*. Springer, 1968.
20. M. A. Stickel. A Prolog Technology Theorem Prover: Implementation by an Extended Prolog Compiler. *Journal of Automated Reasoning*, 4:353–380, 1988.

On Generating Small Clause Normal Forms

Andreas Nonnengart[1], Georg Rock[2], and Christoph Weidenbach[1]*

[1] Max-Planck-Institut für Informatik, Im Stadtwald, 66123 Saarbrücken, Germany,
{nonnenga, weidenb}@mpi-sb.mpg.de
[2] German Research Center for Artificial Intelligence GmbH, Stuhlsatzenhausweg 3,
66123 Saarbrücken, Germany,
rock@dfki.de

Abstract. In this paper we focus on two powerful techniques to obtain compact clause normal forms: Renaming of formulae and refined Skolemization methods. We illustrate their effect on various examples. By an exhaustive experiment of all first-order TPTP problems, it shows that our clause normal form transformation yields fewer clauses and fewer literals than the methods known and used so far. This often allows for exponentially shorter proofs and, in some cases, it makes it even possible for a theorem prover to find a proof where it was unable to do so with more standard clause normal form transformations.

1 Introduction

Theorem provers for first-order predicate logic usually operate on sets of clauses. However, many problem formulations, in particular problems from application domains such as formal program analysis (verification, model checking) are given in full first-order logic and thus require a transformation into clause normal form (CNF). It is well-known that the quality of such a translation has a great impact on the success of an afterwards applied theorem prover. A CNF of some formula is better than another one if it enables a theorem prover to find a proof/counter-model in a shorter period of time. Since this is an undecidable criterion, there cannot be an optimal algorithm in this sense. Therefore, we employ the following heuristics in our paper: The smaller a set of clauses is the easier a proof or a counter-model can be found. Even the design of an algorithm producing "smallest" CNFs is non-trivial. Nevertheless, we shall show that heading towards small CNFs pays off.

The approach we propose in this paper emphasizes on two major aspects in the CNF transformation of first-order predicate logic formulae. These are *Renaming* and *Skolemization*.

By *Renaming* we mean the replacement of subformulae with some new predicates and adding a suitable definition for these new predicates. This is done

---

* This work was supported by the German science foundation program Deduktion.

C. Kirchner and H. Kirchner (Eds.): Automated Deduction, CADE-15
LNAI 1421, pp. 397–411, 1998. © Springer–Verlag Berlin Heidelberg 1998

whenever there is some evidence that such a step will ultimately lead to fewer and smaller clauses [1]. It shows that the clause set obtained by this method in accordance with the other techniques described below is usually smaller than the corresponding result of any other method used so far, e.g., see the papers by Egly and Rath [7] or Sutcliffe and Pelletier [15].

Moreover, we propose the two *Skolemization* techniques described by Ohlbach and Weidenbach [13] and Nonnengart [12], which turned out to be superior to the standard Skolemization approaches, i.e., they usually result in smaller and/or more general clauses. These methods can be turned into algorithms showing a reasonable behaviour for all examples we tested.

A further aspect of our CNF generator lies in the elimination of redundant clauses. All generated clauses are checked for subsumption and condensation. In addition, tautologies are removed.

We thus finally obtain clause sets which, in many cases (e.g., the halting problem [7], Pelletier's Problem 38 [14]), are smaller than any other CNF known so far.

Our CNF translation procedure consists of the following steps:

1. Obvious simplifications.
2. Renaming: see Section 2.
3. Building negation normal form.
4. Anti-Prenexing: see Section 3.
5. Skolemization: see Section 3.
6. Transformation into conjunctive normal form.
7. Redundancy tests: see Section 4

The first step eliminates redundant operators, quantifiers, the logical constants for truth and falsity and simple, syntactic tautologies. The steps 3 and 6 include the standard procedures for building the respective normal forms [10], except that we use polarity dependent linearization, see Section 2. We call a CNF translation *standard* if step 2 is missing and step 5 is replaced by standard Skolemization [10].

The paper mainly contributes to two aspects of CNF translation: (i) it shows how techniques already established theoretically can be turned into well-behaved algorithms in practice (ii) by an exhaustive experiment over all TPTP-v2.1.0 [19] first-order problems we show that these methods outperform standard CNF translations and simple definitional translations.

The paper is now organized as follows: Section 2 turns the renaming technique due to Thierry Boy de la Tour [1] into an effective algorithm. In Section 3 we discuss our Skolemization techniques and present methods to make them tractable in practice. Concerning redundancy tests, we explain in Section 4 improvements for subsumption/condensation tests. The procedure FLOTTER incorporating all these techniques is put to the test in Section 5. We conclude the paper with a small summary and an outlook in Section 6.

Preliminaries

We assume the reader to be familiar with the syntax, semantics and common notions of first-order logic and resolution-based theorem proving.

Clauses are often denoted by their respective multisets of literals. A clause C is said to *subsume* a clause D, if there exists a substitution σ with $C\sigma \subseteq D$. A clause C is a *condensation* of a clause D if there exists a substitution σ such that C is obtained from $D\sigma$ by the deletion of duplicate literal occurrences, $C \neq D$ and C subsumes D, or, equivalently, if C is a proper factor of D that subsumes D.

A *position* is a word over the natural numbers. The set $pos(\phi)$ of positions of a given formula ϕ is defined as follows: (i) the empty word $\epsilon \in pos(\phi)$ (ii) for $1 \leq i \leq n$, $i.p \in pos(\phi)$ if $\phi = \phi_1 \circ \ldots \circ \phi_n$ and $p \in pos(\phi_i)$ where $\circ$ is a first-order operator. Now, if $p \in pos(\phi)$ we define $\phi|_\epsilon = \phi$ and $\phi|_{i.p} = \phi_i|_p$ where $\phi = \phi_1 \circ \ldots \circ \phi_n$. We write $\psi[\phi]_p$ for $\psi|_p = \phi$. With $\psi[p/\phi]$ where $p \in pos(\psi)$ we denote the formula obtained by replacing $\psi|_p$ with ϕ at position p in ψ.

The polarity of a formula occurring at position π in a formula ψ is denoted by $Pol(\psi, \pi)$ and defined in the usual way: $Pol(\psi, \epsilon) = 1$; $Pol(\psi, \pi.i) = Pol(\psi, \pi)$ if $\psi|_\pi$ is a conjunction, disjunction, formula starting with a quantifier or an implication with $i = 2$; $Pol(\psi, \pi.i) = -Pol(\psi, \pi)$ if $\psi|_\pi$ is a formula starting with a negation symbol or an implication with $i = 1$ and, finally, $Pol(\psi, \pi.i) = 0$ if $\psi|_\pi$ is an equivalence.

2   Renaming

First, let us illustrate the problem with the help of a simple example. Consider the formula

$$\phi_1 \vee \forall x\, \phi_2$$

where we assume that x is the only free variable in ϕ_2. If n is the number of clauses generated by ϕ_1 and m is the number of clauses generated by $\forall x\, \phi_2$ then the overall above formula generates nm clauses. Thus, a nesting of such disjunctions easily leads to an exponential number of clauses. The same holds for nested implications and equivalences. The reason for this exponential explosion is the (exponential) duplication of subformulae obtained by the exhaustive application of the distributivity law. The solution to this problem is *Renaming*, the replacement of subformulae using new predicates. For the above formula, a renaming of ϕ_2 is

$$[\phi_1 \vee \forall x\, P(x)] \wedge \forall x\, (P(x) \supset \phi_2)$$

where P is a new one-place predicate. The renamed formula is not logically equivalent to the first formula, but preserves both satisfiability and unsatisfiability and this suffices for resolution-based theorem proving. Furthermore, the renamed formula generates only $n + m$ clauses. Thus, using a renaming technique, the worst case exponential explosion of the number of clauses generated by a formula can be avoided.

The renaming idea goes back to Tseitin [20] who showed that the introduction of new propositional symbols can result in exponentially shorter proofs. In the context of CNF translation important contributions have been made by Eder [5], Plaisted and Greenbaum [16] and Boy de la Tour [1]. These approaches differ in their respective criteria to decide which subformulae are to be replaced by new predicates. Whereas Plaisted and Greenbaum basically suggested to rename all subformulae up to literals, Boy de la Tour only replaces a subformula if this would decrease the number of eventually generated clauses. Since our goal is to produce short CNFs, we follow the approach of Boy de la Tour. In the following we present the key ideas of Boy de la Tour's technique and show how these ideas can be turned into effective algorithms. Furthermore, we use the notion of formula positions for our definitions which avoids some ambiguities contained in Boy de la Tour's work [1] if the same formula occurs more than once [17].

Let us start with a precise definition of a renaming. Let ψ be a formula and $\phi = \psi|_\pi$ be a subformula of ψ that we want to rename. Let $x_1, \ldots, x_n$ be the free variables in ϕ and let R be an n-place predicate new to ψ. Then the formula

$$\psi[\pi/R(x_1, \ldots, x_n)] \wedge Def_\pi^\psi$$

is a *renaming* of ψ at position π. The formula Def_π^ψ is a polarity dependent definition of the new predicate R:

$$Def_\pi^\psi = \begin{cases} \forall x_1, \ldots, x_n \left[R(x_1, \ldots, x_n) \supset \phi \right] & \text{if } Pol(\psi, \pi) = 1 \\ \forall x_1, \ldots, x_n \left[\phi \supset R(x_1, \ldots, x_n) \right] & \text{if } Pol(\psi, \pi) = -1 \\ \forall x_1, \ldots, x_n \left[R(x_1, \ldots, x_n) \equiv \phi \right] & \text{if } Pol(\psi, \pi) = 0 \end{cases}$$

Now recall that we only want to rename a formula, if the number of clauses generated from the renamed formula is smaller than the number of clauses generated from the original formula. The first crucial point towards this end is to calculate the number of clauses generated by a standard CNF without any reduction. This can be done by the function p defined in Table 1, where $\bar{p}(\psi)$ stands for $p(\neg\psi)$ for any formula ψ. The first column shows the form of ψ and the next two columns the corresponding recursive, top-down calculations for $p(\psi)$ and $\bar{p}(\psi)$, respectively.

ψ	$p(\psi)$	$\bar{p}(\psi)$
$\phi_1 \wedge \ldots \wedge \phi_n$	$\sum_{i=1}^n p(\phi_i)$	$\prod_{i=1}^n \bar{p}(\phi_i)$
$\phi_1 \vee \ldots \vee \phi_2$	$\prod_{i=1}^n p(\phi_i)$	$\sum_{i=1}^n \bar{p}(\phi_i)$
$\phi_1 \supset \phi_2$	$\bar{p}(\phi_1)p(\phi_2)$	$p(\phi_1) + \bar{p}(\phi_2)$
$\phi_1 \equiv \phi_2$	$p(\phi_1)\bar{p}(\phi_2) + \bar{p}(\phi_1)p(\phi_2)$	$p(\phi_1)p(\phi_2) + \bar{p}(\phi_1)\bar{p}(\phi_2)$
$\forall x_1, \ldots x_n\, \phi_1$	$p(\phi_1)$	$\bar{p}(\phi_1)$
$\exists x_1, \ldots x_n\, \phi_1$	$p(\phi_1)$	$\bar{p}(\phi_1)$
$\neg\phi_1$	$\bar{p}(\phi_1)$	$p(\phi_1)$
atomic	1	1

Table 1. Calculating the number of clauses

The calculation for equivalences assumes a polarity dependent linearization: A formula $\psi \equiv \phi$ is transformed into $(\psi \wedge \phi) \vee (\neg\psi \wedge \neg\phi)$ if its polarity is -1. It is transformed into $(\psi \supset \phi) \wedge (\phi \supset \psi)$ if its polarity is $+1$. This linearization avoids generating redundant clauses that are hardly recognizable once the CNF is built.

Second, in order to check whether a renaming yields fewer clauses, we need to calculate the difference between the number of clauses generated with and without a renaming. So let us assume that we want to rename a subformula at position π within a formula ψ. The condition to be checked is

$$p(\psi) \geq p(\psi[\pi/R(x_1,\ldots,x_n)]) + p(Def_\pi^\psi).$$

The obvious problem with this condition is that the function p cannot be effectively computed in general, since it grows exponentially in the size of the input formula. The rest of this section is concerned with solving this problem. Obviously, the formulae ψ and $\psi[\pi/R(x_1,\ldots,x_n)]$ only differ at position π, the other parts of the formulae remain identical. We can make use of this fact by an abstraction of those parts of ψ that do not influence the changed position. This is done by the notion of a coefficient as shown in Table 2. The coefficients

π	$\psi\vert_\tau$	a_π^ψ	b_π^ψ
$\tau.i$	$\phi_1 \wedge \ldots \wedge \phi_n$	a_τ^ψ	$b_\tau^\psi \prod_{j\neq i} \bar{p}(\psi\vert_{\tau.j})$
$\tau.i$	$\phi_1 \vee \ldots \vee \phi_n$	$a_\tau^\psi \prod_{j\neq i} p(\psi\vert_{\tau.j})$	b_τ^ψ
$\tau.1$	$\phi_1 \supset \phi_2$	b_τ^ψ	$a_\tau^\psi p(\psi\vert_{\tau.2})$
$\tau.2$	$\phi_1 \supset \phi_2$	$a_\tau^\psi \bar{p}(\psi\vert_{\tau.1})$	b_τ^ψ
$\tau.i$	$\phi_1 \equiv \phi_2$	$a_\tau^\psi \bar{p}(\psi\vert_{\tau.(3-i)}) + b_\tau^\psi p(\psi\vert_{\tau.(3-i)})$	$a_\tau^\psi p(\psi\vert_{\tau.(3-i)}) + b_\tau^\psi \bar{p}(\psi\vert_{\tau.(3-i)})$
$\tau.1$	$\neg\phi_1$	b_τ^ψ	a_τ^ψ
$\tau.1$	$\forall x_1,\ldots,x_n \phi_1$	a_τ^ψ	b_τ^ψ
$\tau.1$	$\exists x_1,\ldots,x_n \phi_1$	a_τ^ψ	b_τ^ψ
ϵ	ψ	1	0

Table 2. Calculating the coefficients

determine how often a particular subformula and its negation is duplicated in the course of a standard CNF translation. The coefficient a_π^ψ is the factor for the eventual multiplication of $p(\psi\vert_\pi)$ in the CNF and the factor b_π^ψ for the multiplication of $\bar{p}(\psi\vert_\pi)$. The first column of Table 2 shows the form of π, the second column the form of ψ directly above position π (ψ itself if $\pi = \epsilon$) and the next two columns the corresponding recursive, bottom-up calculations that have to be done to compute a_π^ψ and b_π^ψ, respectively. For our starting example formula $\psi = \phi_1 \vee \forall x\, \phi_2$ where we renamed position 2.1, i.e., the subformula ϕ_2, the coefficients are $a_{2.1}^\psi = p(\phi_1)$ (Table 2, seventh, second and last row, first column) and $b_{2.1}^\psi = 0$ (seventh, second and last row, second column). Note that a_π^ψ (b_π^ψ) is always 0 if $Pol(\psi, \pi) = -1$ ($Pol(\psi, \pi) = 1$).

Using the notion of a coefficient, the previously stated condition can be reformulated as

$$a_\pi^\psi p(\phi) + b_\pi^\psi \bar{p}(\phi) \geq a_\pi^\psi + b_\pi^\psi + p(Def_\pi^\psi)$$

where we still assume that $\phi = \psi|_\pi$. Note that since ϕ is replaced by an atom, the coefficients a_π^ψ, b_π^ψ are multiplied by 1 in the renamed version. Depending on the polarity of $\psi|_\pi$ the disequation is equivalent to one of the three disequations:

$$a_\pi^\psi p(\phi) \geq a_\pi^\psi + p(\phi) \qquad\qquad \text{if } Pol(\psi, \pi) = 1$$
$$b_\pi^\psi \bar{p}(\phi) \geq b_\pi^\psi + \bar{p}(\phi) \qquad\qquad \text{if } Pol(\psi, \pi) = -1$$
$$a_\pi^\psi p(\phi) + b_\pi^\psi \bar{p}(\phi) \geq a_\pi^\psi + b_\pi^\psi + p(\phi) + \bar{p}(\phi) \text{ if } Pol(\psi, \pi) = 0$$

Let us examine the most complicated third case in more detail. The other cases can be treated accordingly. The third case can be equivalently transformed into the disequation

$$(a_\pi^\psi - 1)(p(\phi) - 1) + (b_\pi^\psi - 1)(\bar{p}(\phi) - 1) \geq 2$$

Let us abbreviate the product $(a_\pi^\psi - 1)(p(\phi) - 1)$ with p_a and $(b_\pi^\psi - 1)(\bar{p}(\phi) - 1)$ with p_b. Since neither p_a nor p_b can become negative, the disequation holds if (i) $p_a \geq 2$ or (ii) $p_b \geq 2$ or (iii) $p_a \geq 1$ and $p_b \geq 1$. In order to check these conditions, it is sufficient to check whether the coefficients a_π^ψ, b_π^ψ and the number of clauses $p(\phi)$, $\bar{p}(\phi)$ are strictly greater than 1, 2, respectively. This can always be checked in linear (!) time with respect to the size of ψ. For example, $p(\phi) > 1$ holds iff ϕ contains an equivalence or a conjunct with positive polarity or a disjunct with negative polarity or an implication with negative polarity. To sum up, we turned the renaming condition due to Boy de la Tour [1] that requires the computation of exponentially growing functions into a condition that can be checked in linear time and does not require any arithmetic calculation at all.

In fact, all the above is relevant in practice. An older version of FLOTTER [21] computed the values for the number of clauses and coefficients. It turned out that the computation of coefficients and number of clauses significantly shows up in the profiling of FLOTTER. There were even some examples for which the exponential explosion prevented FLOTTER from working properly. After the above explained reformulation all these problems disappeared.

3   Skolemization

A further important step in the clause normal form transformation which is commonly neglected is the so-called *Skolemization* [18] of formulae. It is used to get rid of existentially quantified variables and that by replacing each such occurrence with a Skolem function application. There are usually two kinds of Skolemization techniques described in the literature (see, e.g., [2,10]) which we call *Inner* and *Outer Skolemization* respectively. The two differ mainly in the choice of variables the Skolem functions get as arguments. Outer Skolemization gets those universally quantified variables as arguments in whose scopes the (existentially quantified) subformula under consideration occurs, whereas Inner Skolemization receives all free variables of this very subformula as arguments.

For both kinds of Skolemization it has been shown to be valuable to initially transform the given problem into anti-prenex normal form [6], i.e., quantifiers are moved inwards as far as possible.[1]

Not much effort had been spent until recently to improve these standard Skolemization techniques. Nevertheless, even Skolemization leaves possibilities for improvements. In this paper we want to introduce two such proposals, the Optimized Skolemization [13] and the Strong Skolemization [12].

Definition 1 (Optimized Skolemization). *Let Δ be a sentence in negation normal form, i.e., it contains no implications or equivalences and negations do only occur directly in front of atoms. Moreover, let $\exists x_1, \ldots, x_k\, (\phi \wedge \psi)$ be a subformula of Δ at position π and assume that $\Delta \models \forall y_1, \ldots, y_n \exists x_1, \ldots, x_k\, \phi$ where $\{y_1, \ldots, y_n\}$ denotes the set of free variables of $\exists x_1, \ldots, x_k\, (\phi \wedge \psi)$. Finally, let $f_1, \ldots, f_k$ be new (Skolem) function symbols. We then say that*

$$\forall y_1, \ldots, y_n\, \phi\{x_i \mapsto f_i(y_1, \ldots, y_n)\} \wedge \Delta[\pi/\psi\{x_i \mapsto f_i(y_1, \ldots, y_n)\}$$

can be obtained by a single optimized Skolemization step *from Δ.*

Ohlbach and Weidenbach [13] showed that Optimized Skolemization behaves as desired, i.e., Δ is satisfiable if and only if $\forall y_1, \ldots, y_n\, \phi\{x_i \mapsto f_i(y_1, \ldots, y_n)\} \wedge \Delta[\pi/\psi\{x_i \mapsto f_i(y_1, \ldots, y_n)\}]$ is satisfiable.

Note that Optimized Skolemization requires a theorem prover on its own in order to prove the preliminary condition $\Delta \models \forall y_1, \ldots, y_n \exists x_1, \ldots, x_k\, \phi$. As an example consider the (sub-)problem

$$\forall x, y, z\, (R(x, y) \wedge R(x, z) \supset \exists u\, (R(y, u) \wedge R(z, u)))$$

and assume that $\forall x \exists y\, R(x, y)$ is provable from the whole problem under consideration. With standard Inner Skolemization we would obtain the clauses

$$\neg R(x, y) \vee \neg R(x, z) \vee R(y, f(y, z))$$
$$\neg R(x, y) \vee \neg R(x, z) \vee R(z, f(y, z))$$

With Optimized Skolemization, however, we would end up with the clause set

$$R(y, f(y, z))$$
$$\neg R(x, y) \vee \neg R(x, z) \vee R(z, f(y, z))$$

which is definitely superior to the standard result. In short, the effect of Optimized Skolemization compared to standard (Inner) Skolemization is that some of the literals in the standard result are deleted.

Strong Skolemization differs from Optimized Skolemization in many respects. First of all, like standard (Inner) Skolemization, it is a local method, i.e., it applies only to the subformula under consideration and does not take the whole problem into account. Moreover, it does not require a theorem prover on its own to perform its task. Now, in order to define what Strong Skolemization is about let us first introduce the notion of a *free variable splitting*. Consider the (sub-)formula $\Delta = \exists x_1, \ldots x_k\, (\phi_1 \wedge \ldots \wedge \phi_n)$. The free variable splitting $\langle \overline{z_1}, \ldots, \overline{z_n} \rangle$ consists of n sequences of free variables of Δ such that the sequence $\overline{z_1}$ consists of exactly the free variables occurring in ϕ_1 (without the $x_1, \ldots x_k$) and for each i with $1 < i \leq n$, $\overline{z_i}$ contains all free variables of ϕ_i (again without the $x_1, \ldots x_k$)

---

[1] There is one exception however: Existential quantifiers are not distributed over disjunctions in order to avoid generating unnecessarily many Skolem functions.

which did not yet occur in any of the subformulae $\phi_1, \ldots, \phi_{i-1}$. Evidently, the union of all these sequences contains all the free variables of the given subformula.

Notice that standard Inner Skolemization could then be defined as follows: Replace the subformula $\exists x_1, \ldots x_k \, (\phi_1 \wedge \ldots \wedge \phi_n)$ with $\phi_1^\star \wedge \ldots \wedge \phi_n^\star$ where $\phi_i^\star = \phi_i \{ x_j \mapsto f_j(\overline{z_1}, \ldots, \overline{z_n}) \mid 1 \le j \le k \}$ and $\langle \overline{z_1}, \ldots, \overline{z_n} \rangle$ is the corresponding free variable splitting.[2]

The effect of Strong Skolemization now lies in the replacement of some of these variable sequences with sequences of fresh universally quantified variables. The following definition specifies this.

Definition 2 (Strong Skolemization). *Let Δ be a first-order sentence in negation normal form. Strong Skolemization replaces existentially quantified subformulae of the form $\exists x_1, \ldots x_k \, (\phi_1 \wedge \ldots \wedge \phi_n)$ with*

$$\forall \overline{w_2}, \overline{w_3}, \overline{w_4}, \ldots, \overline{w_n} \; \phi_1 \{ x_i \mapsto f_i(\overline{z_1}, \overline{w_2}, \overline{w_3}, \overline{w_4}, \ldots, \overline{w_n}) \} \; \wedge$$
$$\forall \overline{w_3}, \overline{w_4}, \ldots, \overline{w_n} \; \phi_2 \{ x_i \mapsto f_i(\overline{z_1}, \overline{z_2}, \overline{w_3}, \overline{w_4}, \ldots, \overline{w_n}) \} \; \wedge$$
$$\vdots$$
$$\forall \overline{w_n} \; \phi_{n-1} \{ x_i \mapsto f_i(\overline{z_1}, \overline{z_2}, \ldots, \overline{z_{n-1}}, \overline{w_n}) \} \; \wedge$$
$$\phi_n \{ x_i \mapsto f_i(\overline{z_1}, \overline{z_2}, \ldots, \overline{z_{n-1}}, \overline{z_n}) \}$$

where $\langle \overline{z_1}, \ldots, \overline{z_n} \rangle$ is the free variable splitting of $\exists x_1, \ldots x_k \, (\phi_1 \wedge \ldots \wedge \phi_n)$, each variable sequence $\overline{w_i}$ has length equal to the length of the variable sequence $\overline{z_i}$, and the $f_i, 1 \le i \le k$, are new (Skolem) function symbols.

In a technical report [12] it is shown that Strong Skolemization preserves both satisfiability and unsatisfiability. Evidently, the Strong Skolemization result subsumes what we could possibly get from standard Inner Skolemization (simply instantiate the $\overline{w_i}$ with the corresponding $\overline{z_i}$). Briefly, the effect of Strong Skolemization compared to standard Inner Skolemization is that some of the arguments of the new Skolem functions are replaced with new, universally quantified variables.

Let us again have a look at the example

$$\forall x, y, z \, (R(x, y) \wedge R(x, z) \supset \exists u \, (R(y, u) \wedge R(z, u))).$$

Strong Skolemization would lead us to the clause set

$$\neg R(x, y) \vee \neg R(x, z) \vee R(y, f(y, w))$$
$$\neg R(x, y) \vee \neg R(x, z) \vee R(z, f(y, z))$$

which is almost identical to the standard Skolemization outcome, with one exception, however, the new variable w in the first clause. In fact, this tiny change allows us to perform a condensation step on the first two literals, so that we finally end up with

$$\neg R(x, y) \vee R(y, f(y, w))$$
$$\neg R(x, y) \vee \neg R(x, z) \vee R(z, f(y, z))$$

This result is not quite as strong as the one we obtained from Optimized Skolemization. But notice that it did not require to prove the goal $\forall x \, \exists y \, R(x, y)$ which might actually be hard to prove, provided it is at all provable. In fact, proving such preliminary lemmata can be arbitrarily complicated and so, in case of

---

[2] For simplicity, we assume uniqueness of existentially quantified subformulae.

Optimized Skolemization, suitable restrictions are necessary to ensure that such intermediate steps ultimately terminate. Also, given for instance a subformula of the form $\exists x\ (\phi_1 \wedge \ldots \wedge \phi_n)$, it would be necessary for Optimized Skolemization to consider up to $n!$ (n factorial) intermediate proofs for best performance. This is intractable in practice. Therefore, in FLOTTER only up to n proof attempts are made in such cases, one for each conjunct ϕ_i. Furthermore, all proof attempts performed in the context of Optimized Skolemization are restricted to resolution inferences where the resolvent is strictly shorter than its longest parent clause and the term depth of the resolvent is at most equal to the maximal term depth of a parent clause. Together with subsumption and condensation this restriction guarantees termination of the inference process. Moreover, it serves to detect situations where the formula to be proven is already "contained" in the input formula. Strong Skolemization, on the other hand, is almost as cheap as standard (Inner) Skolemization and requires no intermediate theorems to be proved.

Now recall the example from above. It shows the superiority of both Strong and Optimized Skolemization over standard Skolemization. Also, it suggests to prefer Optimized Skolemization provided the intermediate goal $\forall y, z\,\exists u\ R(y, u)$ is (more or less easily) provable. For this reason, the current FLOTTER implementation first attempts to perform an Optimized Skolemization step and only if this one was not successful a Strong Skolemization step is performed. Such a heuristics has proved to be sensible in practice, although there are examples where an opposite direction would be more effective. For instance consider the formula $\forall x, y\ (R(x, y) \supset \exists z\ (P(z) \wedge Q(x, z) \wedge S(x, y, z)))$ and suppose that the relation R is provably non-empty. Standard Skolemization would then lead us to the clause set

$$\neg R(x, y) \vee P(f(x, y))$$
$$\neg R(x, y) \vee Q(x, f(x, y))$$
$$\neg R(x, y) \vee S(x, y, f(x, y))$$

whereas Strong Skolemization would come up with

$$\neg R(x, y) \vee P(f(v, w))$$
$$\neg R(x, y) \vee Q(x, f(x, w))$$
$$\neg R(x, y) \vee S(x, y, f(x, y))$$

Because of the assumption that R is provably non-empty, sooner or later it may become possible to simplify the first clause of the Strong Skolemization outcome to the unit clause $P(f(v, w))$.

In case of Optimized Skolemization the attempt to prove that $\exists z\ P(z)$ would obviously be successful and so we would finally end up with the clause set

$$P(f(x, y))$$
$$\neg R(x, y) \vee Q(x, f(x, y))$$
$$\neg R(x, y) \vee S(x, y, f(x, y))$$

which is a little less general than what we obtained from Strong Skolemization.

Thus there are examples which suggest to first try an Optimized Skolemization step and then a Strong Skolemization step (if the former was not successful in proving any of the intermediate goals), but also there are examples which propose the other way round. It certainly would be desirable to combine the two techniques more tightly. This however, is a matter of future work.

4   Subsumption and Condensation

Our CNF translation removes tautologies and also checks for subsumption and condensation. Since it is well known that testing subsumption between two clauses is an NP-complete problem, we have to be very careful concerning the construction of our subsumption algorithm, to obtain acceptable behaviour. It was found that the addition of two filters and efficient data structures makes the standard Stillman algorithm [9] a tractable subsumption test. The first filter considers the number of symbols in the clauses. A necessary condition for a clause C to subsume a clause D is that the number of symbols in C is smaller or equal to the number of symbols in D. Recall that we consider clauses to be multisets. In practice, this test allows us to reject about 95% of all subsumption queries that are generated by a matching query to a perfect term index. The second filter independently checks for every literal in clause C whether it can be matched to a literal in D. This reduces the remaining queries by another 70%. Our condensation test is based on matching and subsumption according to algorithms presented by Gottlob and Leitsch [9].

5   Experiments

We apply the techniques introduced in the previous sections to all TPTP-v2.1.0 [19] first-order problems and including two problems that have been extensively discussed in the literature, namely the halting problem [3,7] and problem 38 from the Pelletier problem collection [14,15]. Our CNF translator FLOTTER, its restriction to standard CNF generation, the CNF translator of ILF (see below) and the theorem provers SPASS-v.0.80[3] and OTTER-v3.0.4 [11] are run on Sun Sparc Ultra 170 workstations with 128MB of main memory. All timings are given in seconds and refer to this machine setup. We apply the two different theorem provers solely to validate our heuristics that smaller clause sets very often result in shorter proof times.

The halting problem [3] was first automatically solved by Egly and Rath [7]. They also used a renaming technique for their disjunctive normal form translation and obtained a normal form with 75 conjuncts. Pelletier's problem 38 was discussed in detail by Pelletier and Sutcliffe [15] where they present a CNF with 31 clauses. Applying FLOTTER to these problems yielded the results below, where the Halting Problem is problem COM003+1 and Pelletier's problem 38 is problem SYN67+1 of the TPTP. For the Halting Problem FLOTTER generates 28 clauses and for Pelletier's problem 38 it generates 27 clauses, the smallest CNFs we know so far for these problems. This is due to the fact that FLOTTER made three renamings and applied six times Optimized Skolemization to the Halting Problem and applied no renamings but five times Optimized Skolemization to Pelletier's problem 38.

---

[3] Version 0.80 is not an official distribution, however, the official distribution Version 1.00 includes all FLOTTER features of version 0.80.

The table below shows the results of applying FLOTTER, standard CNF translation (FLOTTER without renaming and improved Skolemization techniques), and the normal form translation contained in ILF [4] to all first-order problems of the TPTP. The table is pretty ugly, but it presents the complete raw material for our analysis and is intended to allow the reader an easy comparison with her/his prover or CNF translator. For the CNF translation of ILF we used the settings definitions-on, recognize_equal_subformulas-on, polarity-on, optimized_skolemization-on, tautology_detection-on. These settings cause a CNF translation close to the one proposed by Plaisted and Greenbaum [16] that is also somewhere between the normal forms generated by the settings p-def. and p-def. red suggested by Egly and Rath [8]. Therefore, we call this normal form *definitional* in the sequel.

We checked all 347 first-order examples from the TPTP. Below only those 95 problems are listed where the number of symbols/clauses generated by FLOTTER and the standard CNF differs. The table shows the problem name the number of clauses/symbols generated by the CNF translators FLOTTER, the standard translation and the definitional translation, the time spent by the CNF translators and the time spent by the provers SPASS and OTTER to solve the respective normal forms. Here, SFL, SST, SDE abbreviates SPASS applied to the FLOTTER, standard and definitional CNF, respectively and OFL, OST, ODE abbreviates the same relations for OTTER. We set a time limit of 120 seconds for the CNF translation and a time limit of 300 seconds for the provers. A "-" indicates that a CNF could not be generated in the time limit and therefore, in the respective row the proof attempts to this CNF are not available, marked "n.a.".

It holds on all 347 examples that the number of clauses/symbols generated by the definitional translation is greater than the number of clauses/symbols generated by FLOTTER. Furthermore, except for the examples SYN007+1.014, SYN522+1 and SYN532+1 even the standard CNF transformation needs less time and produces fewer clauses than the definitional transformation. The increased time consumption of the definitional transformation may be mainly a result of our careful implementation in C compared to a straightforward implementation of the definitional transformation in PROLOG.

Another interesting point to note is that there are cases in which FLOTTER produces a longer clause normal form than the standard one. This occurs for the examples SYN069+1, SYN327+1, SYN351+1 and SYN393+1. This is due to the fact that without renaming these problems produce a highly redundant set of clauses such that the effects of renaming are compensated by the subsumption test. The introduction of new predicate symbols prevents the redundancy tests from being successful for the renamed version. The redundancy is later on detected by both provers such that there are no significant difference in their time spent to solve these four problems. However, these examples show that even an optimal CNF result with respect to the number of clauses is hard to obtain, since it requires a deep global analysis of the problem.

For 65 out of the presented 95 problems, FLOTTER produced fewer clauses than the standard transformation. For our comparison, we do not consider problems where the timing differences of the proof attempts are less than 0.5 seconds or less than 20%. With respect to this restriction, comparing the FLOTTER output with the standard CNF output, SPASS performed worse on four problems and performed better on 26 problems. In particular, there are examples SPASS could only solve using the CNF generated by FLOTTER, but no examples where it was possible for SPASS to solve the standard translation but not the FLOTTER translation. The 4 problems SYN514+1, SYN518+1, SYN520+1 and SYN546+1 where SPASS performed worse are satisfiable problems. SPASS is sufficiently strong to decide these problems, but the timing of SPASS on these problems depends crucially on the ordering in which SPASS applies its Splitting rule [21].

Similar observations can be made by comparing the results produced by OTTER or by comparing the behaviour of the provers on the definitional CNF with the FLOTTER generated clause sets. With respect to some few exceptions, the heuristics that smaller clause sets simplify finding proofs or counter-models holds over the TPTP problem domain. This corresponds to our experience on other problem domains like formal software-reuse problems or problems generated in the course of program verification.

Problem	FLOTTER #cl	#sy	time	STANDARD #cl	#sy	time	DEFINITIONAL #cl	#sy	time	SFL time	SST time	SDE time	OFL time	OST time	ODE time
COM003+1	28	311	0.05	50	1030	0.22	114	788	3.32	0.16	5.31	1.80	1.30	>300	77.14
COM003+2	43	409	0.07	43	445	0.06	192	1609	6.65	0.06	0.07	0.38	0.12	0.11	0.44
COM003+3	19	230	0.03	27	531	0.11	71	536	2.43	0.12	1.08	0.30	0.66	>300	5.57
GRP194+1	12	139	0.13	12	143	0.12	52	430	1.28	0.14	0.13	4.60	5.33	0.88	>300
MGT019+2	12	114	0.04	12	118	0.02	41	292	1.16	0.04	0.05	0.12	>300	>300	>300
MGT023+1	9	119	0.20	9	137	0.03	31	237	0.90	0.05	0.13	0.09	0.54	2.51	3.01
MGT023+2	14	186	0.07	17	352	0.07	49	388	1.49	0.08	1.35	0.14	131.01	111.34	256.80
MGT027+1	16	196	0.10	16	209	0.07	69	520	1.97	3.30	3.74	0.49	0.06	0.10	0.42
MGT028+1	13	203	0.16	14	259	0.04	45	343	1.34	0.09	0.11	0.12	0.06	0.08	0.27
MGT029+1	22	369	0.24	22	379	0.12	70	525	1.94	8.56	5.70	>300	>300	>300	>300
MGT030+1	13	163	0.04	16	322	0.06	45	359	1.38	0.08	0.56	0.13	0.09	0.18	0.33
MGT032+2	8	73	0.02	8	87	0.02	29	223	1.02	0.01	0.02	0.07	0.03	0.02	0.10
MGT035+1	25	424	0.28	25	434	0.14	84	691	2.62	7.97	9.17	>300	1.08	1.54	86.32
MGT035+2	45	667	0.22	45	677	0.16	167	1335	9.72	184.43	144.49	>300	0.48	0.73	>300
MGT038+1	12	103	0.05	12	116	0.03	45	291	1.12	0.15	0.19	0.27	0.08	0.07	0.24
MGT038+2	30	459	0.76	30	465	0.16	121	864	4.93	>300	>300	>300	0.28	0.31	6.45
MGT039+1	19	190	0.06	19	203	0.04	75	504	1.78	0.60	0.76	>300	2.55	2.70	>300
MGT039+2	28	350	0.14	28	363	0.12	116	857	5.14	>300	>300	>300	>300	>300	>300
MSC009+1	26	197	0.04	26	200	0.02	144	967	1.91	0.07	0.06	0.26	0.05	0.05	0.19
PUZ031+1	25	177	0.14	26	186	0.13	104	567	2.60	0.16	0.19	0.65	0.11	0.13	0.36
SET046+1	3	23	0.00	3	26	0.00	17	131	0.63	0.00	0.01	0.03	0.01	0.03	0.06
SYN007+1.014	104	468	0.12	-	-	>120	393	2064	1.05	54.57	n.a.	76.45	48.00	n.a.	39.83
SYN036+1	22	128	0.03	72	1032	0.42	125	752	1.04	0.06	1.32	0.18	0.19	>300	146.43
SYN036+2	24	152	0.04	86	1282	0.47	125	752	1.05	0.09	1.31	0.27	0.54	>300	>300
SYN055+1	8	38	0.01	8	43	0.01	26	116	0.69	0.00	0.01	0.03	0.03	0.02	0.07
SYN056+1	8	52	0.01	9	62	0.01	46	240	0.70	0.02	0.03	0.07	0.03	0.05	0.14
SYN058+1	8	30	0.00	9	40	0.00	26	111	0.66	0.02	0.01	0.03	0.01	0.02	0.06
SYN059+1	9	40	0.02	16	120	0.02	57	319	0.76	0.02	0.02	0.07	0.03	0.09	0.27
SYN066+1	6	42	0.00	6	50	0.00	26	161	0.79	0.02	0.01	0.02	0.02	0.03	0.07
SYN067+1	27	457	03.55	55	1076	0.69	115	851	1.68	20.33	>300	0.56	>300	>300	0.47
SYN068+1	7	34	0.01	7	40	0.01	22	117	0.66	0.01	0.02	0.06	0.02	0.03	0.06
SYN069+1	12	67	0.00	11	81	0.01	36	208	0.84	0.01	0.03	0.07	0.03	0.05	0.13
SYN070+1	9	60	0.01	9	65	0.02	31	176	0.79	0.01	0.00	0.07	0.03	0.04	0.12
SYN074+1	7	80	0.01	7	85	0.01	42	427	1.00	0.13	0.08	0.12	0.37	0.76	>300
SYN075+1	7	80	0.01	7	85	0.01	42	427	1.01	0.14	0.09	0.11	0.42	0.54	>300
SYN076+1	17	182	0.05	34	906	0.11	102	966	1.86	>300	>300	>300	>300	>300	>300
SYN077+1	7	68	0.03	7	79	0.01	46	370	0.87	0.12	0.17	0.98	22.94	251.63	70.34
SYN078+1	5	31	0.01	7	52	0.01	33	201	0.82	0.01	0.02	0.07	0.04	0.15	0.15
SYN082+1	4	39	0.01	4	47	0.00	24	202	0.62	0.01	0.02	0.04	0.03	0.04	0.10
SYN084+1	7	49	0.03	11	130	0.03	51	357	0.70	0.02	0.03	0.07	0.07	0.56	0.30
SYN327+1	6	47	0.01	4	28	0.00	14	112	0.64	0.00	0.00	0.03	0.03	0.02	0.15

Problem	FLOTTER			STANDARD			DEFINITIONAL			SFL	SST	SDE	OFL	OST	ODE
	#cl	#sy	time	#cl	#sy	time	#cl	#sy	time	time	time	time	time	time	time
SYN348+1	24	684	0.19	64	2944	0.43	70	905	1.60	0.36	0.40	0.29	>300	>300	>300
SYN349+1	10	144	0.05	10	208	0.02	43	532	1.05	0.04	0.04	0.09	168.64	0.46	>300
SYN351+1	6	74	0.02	4	52	0.01	21	256	1.05	0.01	0.03	0.50	0.03	0.02	0.43
SYN365+1	6	33	0.02	6	36	0.03	19	102	0.57	0.01	0.01	0.03	0.10	0.12	0.33
SYN374+1	5	34	0.00	6	44	0.01	49	302	0.68	0.01	0.01	0.05	0.03	0.06	4.49
SYN375+1	3	15	0.01	3	17	0.00	45	246	0.59	0.01	0.01	0.04	0.02	0.02	0.08
SYN377+1	3	16	0.01	3	18	0.00	45	246	0.61	0.01	0.01	0.02	0.01	0.02	0.07
SYN393+1	16	84	0.01	8	36	0.01	63	326	0.59	0.03	0.01	0.03	0.05	0.03	0.10
SYN414+1	7	48	0.03	11	93	0.02	55	392	0.84	0.02	0.01	0.07	0.02	0.06	0.35
SYN415+1	7	44	0.02	10	96	0.02	49	294	0.72	0.04	0.10	0.14	0.11	86.69	0.80
SYN418+1	504	5480	3.60	1158	22515	30.63	-	-	>120	3.87	32.63	n.a.	>300	>300	n.a.
SYN419+1	436	4636	2.61	1040	19949	21.94	-	-	>120	3.43	31.03	n.a.	>300	>300	n.a.
SYN420+1	605	6871	5.32	1617	30557	71.45	-	-	>120	22.59	114.18	n.a.	>300	>300	n.a.
SYN421+1	547	5508	3.83	-	-	>120	-	-	>120	5.20	n.a.	n.a.	>300	n.a.	n.a.
SYN422+1	529	6221	4.26	902	17375	18.21	-	-	>120	7.29	75.47	n.a.	>300	>300	n.a.
SYN423+1	629	6379	5.44	1190	21004	28.06	-	-	>120	20.06	66.92	n.a.	132.68	>300	n.a.
SYN424+1	765	8402	8.67	-	-	>120	-	-	>120	13.12	n.a.	n.a.	>300	n.a.	n.a.
SYN425+1	531	5645	4.72	1103	20830	33.29	-	-	>120	4.69	29.82	n.a.	>300	n.a.	n.a.
SYN426+1	724	8247	8.87	1673	37067	82.60	-	-	>120	44.38	164.36	n.a.	>300	>300	n.a.
SYN427+1	765	8385	9.21	-	-	>120	-	-	>120	87.14	n.a.	n.a.	>300	n.a.	n.a.
SYN428+1	700	7470	6.88	1641	31373	60.20	-	-	>120	9.51	98.31	n.a.	>300	>300	n.a.
SYN429+1	735	8436	7.72	1210	23473	33.43	-	-	>120	24.11	32.07	n.a.	>300	>300	n.a.
SYN513+1	392	4124	2.27	894	17379	19.30	-	-	>120	2.46	11.98	n.a.	>300	>300	n.a.
SYN514+1	279	3606	2.16	438	7898	6.57	-	-	>300	15.73	n.a.	n.a.	>300	>300	n.a.
SYN515+1	89	920	0.22	216	5007	2.54	239	1307	5.67	0.16	0.92	1.66	0.18	7.75	0.43
SYN516+1	71	561	0.13	97	1078	0.22	157	817	2.49	0.14	0.21	0.27	0.15	5.71	0.42
SYN517+1	68	654	0.13	76	815	0.16	181	912	2.92	0.18	0.13	0.45	0.34	0.35	0.44
SYN518+1	471	5136	3.20	1184	30854	119.90	-	-	>120	>300	58.35	n.a.	>300	>300	n.a.
SYN519+1	526	5638	3.81	1107	17815	16.40	-	-	>120	>300	>300	n.a.	>300	>300	n.a.
SYN520+1	528	5674	4.71	1008	15536	15.26	-	-	>120	214.52	42.92	n.a.	>300	>300	n.a.
SYN521+1	102	797	0.17	224	4532	2.21	239	1243	4.53	0.15	1.05	0.80	0.17	2.50	0.50
SYN522+1	111	1065	0.24	376	8070	4.86	302	1617	8.10	0.26	2.35	2.80	0.79	6.37	1.47
SYN523+1	53	439	0.08	54	587	0.13	146	716	1.97	0.07	0.10	0.35	0.12	0.16	0.30
SYN524+1	101	1166	0.34	132	2309	0.60	297	1578	8.35	0.32	0.59	2.72	0.27	0.47	2.20
SYN525+1	104	867	0.21	154	1652	0.34	263	1356	5.65	0.22	0.27	1.74	0.55	0.66	0.58
SYN526+1	113	1218	0.28	256	5201	2.01	308	1698	9.98	0.31	1.35	5.27	0.28	1.53	0.67
SYN527+1	84	686	0.15	92	1038	0.21	220	1077	3.56	0.13	0.15	0.70	0.17	0.25	0.48
SYN528+1	121	1180	0.32	202	3020	1.07	300	1566	7.70	0.30	0.48	3.72	0.29	0.64	0.64
SYN529+1	133	1074	0.31	251	3807	1.37	319	1623	7.61	0.24	0.93	1.90	1.06	3.59	1.30
SYN530+1	95	916	0.21	110	1494	0.39	261	1375	6.21	0.28	0.41	3.08	0.40	0.74	0.62
SYN531+1	82	886	0.19	117	1763	0.45	235	1251	5.81	0.22	0.43	2.04	0.29	2.30	1.37
SYN532+1	101	737	0.17	389	6501	9.16	263	1275	4.60	0.15	1.17	1.43	0.37	1.72	0.55
SYN533+1	92	618	0.13	152	1413	0.31	207	1040	3.49	0.14	0.24	0.65	0.17	0.37	0.46
SYN534+1	77	908	0.19	99	1421	0.28	247	1334	6.67	0.19	0.31	5.02	0.22	0.30	0.85
SYN535+1	100	840	0.18	143	2028	0.51	266	1356	5.89	0.16	0.43	1.73	0.18	0.57	0.56
SYN536+1	87	907	0.21	130	1873	0.51	275	1542	9.12	0.19	0.41	5.44	0.36	4.35	1.16
SYN537+1	114	1134	0.29	118	1606	0.40	396	2078	13.69	0.32	0.36	5.71	0.35	0.34	10.79
SYN538+1	138	1769	0.66	208	4562	2.38	456	2536	24.31	0.61	1.31	>300	1.44	1.61	2.67
SYN539+1	152	1756	0.51	203	4053	1.59	499	2749	26.24	0.48	0.92	>300	>300	>300	16.56
SYN540+1	142	1417	0.42	221	2764	0.79	436	2331	18.54	0.40	0.55	13.13	0.41	1.83	2.05
SYN541+1	145	1680	0.54	242	5027	2.82	497	2717	26.22	0.54	1.49	>300	0.36	1.67	2.73
SYN544+1	363	4429	2.64	1139	18275	13.55	-	-	>120	3.82	12.61	n.a.	1.74	233.17	n.a.
SYN545+1	510	5878	4.00	835	16120	16.73	-	-	>120	4.09	11.54	n.a.	>300	>300	n.a.
SYN546+1	521	5983	4.20	1028	21117	28.21	-	-	>120	>300	78.04	n.a.	>300	>300	n.a.
SYN547+1	482	6069	5.80	919	20212	29.25	-	-	>120	7.43	28.82	n.a.	>300	>300	n.a.

6   Conclusion

This paper consists of two major parts: It describes two important ingredients of FLOTTER, which is the realization of a sophisticated clause normal form generator. It also reports on the experimental results obtained from the application of FLOTTER to comparatively huge problem sets.

FLOTTER's most important features for the experiments this paper is concerned with are (i) fast Renaming, (ii) Optimized and Strong Skolemization, and (iii) efficient redundancy tests.

Renaming is based on the method introduced by Boy de la Tour [1]. It is further refined such that the number of clauses, which grows exponentially in the worst case, does not need to be computed. Optimized and Strong Skolemization are variants of standard Skolemization that, in general, lead to fewer, smaller, and more general clauses. The redundancy tests described here are subsumption and condensation. These are based on Stillman's and on Gottlob and Leitsch's algorithms, respectively, with the addition of some effective filters.

Experiments (e.g., on the TPTP library) show the great impact of this kind of CNF generation. FLOTTER outperforms all other considered CNF generators in any sense: It produces fewer, smaller, and more general clauses with fewer symbols in less time. This has a remarkable positive effect on the theorem provers applied to the respective CNF results. Only in a few cases of satisfiable formulae does the clause normal form produced by FLOTTER behave worse than that obtained from a standard or a straightforward definitional translation. The performance of FLOTTER is one of the reasons why SPASS won the first-order division of CASC-14, the CADE theorem proving contest, by solving all selected competition problems.

In the near future the algorithm will be applied to further problem sets. Also there is some further work to be done in the combination of Optimized and Strong Skolemization. In the current implementation Strong Skolemization is only invoked when Optimized Skolemization would end up in a result identical to the standard one. There is some evidence that a more tight combination of the two approaches is possible and valuable. Moreover, there are several techniques not touched in this paper that seem to be valuable for further improvements. This includes, for example, potential reuse of Skolem functions and/or predicate symbols introduced by renaming as described by Egly and Rath [7]. The renaming techniques can also be further refined. If a subformula occurs several times inside a formula (e.g., with respect to α-conversion) it may be the case that the replacement of a single occurrence is worthless but the simultaneous replacement of all occurrences may pay off [16].

Acknowledgements. We are indebted to the ILF group in Berlin for providing the definitional CNF translation. Moreover, we want to thank Uwe Egly and our anonymous reviewers for their valuable comments.

References

1. Thierry Boy de la Tour. An Optimality Result for Clause Form Translation. *Journal of Symbolic Computation*, 14:283–301, 1992.
2. Chin-Liang Chang and Richard Char-Tung Lee. *Symbolic Logic and Mechanical Theorem Proving*. Computer Science and Applied Mathematics. Academic Press, 1973.
3. Li Dafa. The Formulation of the Halting Problem is Not Suitable for Describing the Halting Problem. *Association for Automated Reasoning Newsletter*, 27:1–7, 1994.
4. Ingo Dahn, J. Gehne, Thomas Honigmann, and Andreas Wolf. Integration of Automated and Interactive Theorem Proving in ILF. In *Proceedings of the 14th International Conference on Automated Deduction, CADE-14*, volume 1249 of *LNAI*, pages 57–60, Townsville, Australia, 1997. Springer.
5. Elmar Eder. *Relative Complexities of First Order Calculi*. Artificial Intelligence. Vieweg, 1992.

6. Uwe Egly. On the Value of Antiprenexing. In *Logic Programming and Automated Reasoning, 5th International Conference, LPAR'94*, volume 822 of *LNAI*, pages 69–83. Springer, July 1994.
7. Uwe Egly and Thomas Rath. The Halting Problem: An Automatically Generated Proof. *AAR Newsletter*, 30:10–16, 1995.
8. Uwe Egly and Thomas Rath. On the Practical Value of Different Definitional Translations to Normal Form. In M.A. McRobbie and J.K. Slaney, editors, *13th International Conference on Automated Deduction, CADE-13*, volume 1104 of *LNAI*, pages 403–417. Springer, 1996.
9. Georg Gottlob and Alexander Leitsch. On the Efficiency of Subsumption Algorithms. *Journal of the ACM*, 32(2):280–295, 1985.
10. Donald W. Loveland. *Automated Theorem Proving: A Logical Basis*, volume 6 of *Fundamental Studies in Computer Science*. North-Holland, 1978.
11. William McCune and Larry Wos. Otter. *Journal of Automated Reasoning*, 18(2):211–220, 1997.
12. Andreas Nonnengart. Strong Skolemization. Technical Report MPI-I-96-2-010, Max-Planck-Institut für Informatik, Saarbrücken, Germany, 1996. http://www.mpi-sb.mpg.de/~nonnenga/publications/, submitted.
13. Hans Jürgen Ohlbach and Christoph Weidenbach. A Note on Assumptions about Skolem Functions. *Journal of Automated Reasoning*, 15(2):267–275, 1995.
14. Francis Jeffry Pelletier. Seventy-Five Problems for Testing Automatic Theorem Provers. *Journal of Automated Reasoning*, 2(2):191–216, 1986. Errata: *Journal of Automated Reasoning*, 4(2):235–236,1988.
15. Francis Jeffry Pelletier and Geoff Sutcliffe. An Erratum for Some Errata to Automated Theorem Proving Problems. *Association for Automated Reasoning Newsletter*, 31:8–14, December 1995.
16. David A. Plaisted and Steven Greenbaum. A Structure-Preserving Clause Form Translation. *Journal of Symbolic Computation*, 2:293–304, 1986.
17. Georg Rock. Transformations of First-Order Formulae for Automated Reasoning. Diplomarbeit, Max-Planck-Institut für Informatik, Saarbrücken, Germany, April 1995. Supervisors: H.J. Ohlbach, C. Weidenbach.
18. Thoralf Skolem. Logisch-kombinatorische Untersuchungen über die Erfüllbarkeit oder Beweisbarkeit mathematischer Sätze nebst einem Theoreme über dichte Mengen. *Skrifter utgit av Videnskappsellkapet i Kristiania*, 4:4–36, 1920. Reprinted in: *From Frege to Gödel, A Source Book in Mathematical Logic, 1879-1931*, van Heijenoort, Jean, editor, pages 252–263, Harvard University Press, 1976.
19. Geoff Sutcliffe, Christian B. Suttner, and Theodor Yemenis. The TPTP Problem Library. In Alan Bundy, editor, *Twelfth International Conference on Automated Deduction, CADE-12*, volume 814 of *Lecture Notes in Artificial Intelligence, LNAI*, pages 252–266, Nancy, France, June 1994. Springer.
20. G.S. Tseitin. On the complexity of derivations in propositional calculus. In A.O. Slisenko, editor, *Studies in Constructive Mathematics and Mathematical Logic*. 1968. Reprinted in: *Automation of Reasoning: Classical Papers on Computational Logic*, J. Siekmann and G. Wrightson, editors, pages 466–483, Springer, 1983.
21. Christoph Weidenbach, Bernd Gaede, and Georg Rock. SPASS & FLOTTER, Version 0.42. In M.A. McRobbie and J.K. Slaney, editors, *13th International Conference on Automated Deduction, CADE-13*, volume 1104 of *LNAI*, pages 141–145. Springer, 1996.

Rank/Activity: A Canonical Form for Binary Resolution

J. D. Horton and Bruce Spencer

Faculty of Computer Science, University of New Brunswick
P.O. Box 4400, Fredericton, New Brunswick, Canada E3B 5A3
jdh@unb.ca, bspencer@unb.ca, http://www.cs.unb.ca

Abstract. The rank/activity restriction on binary resolution is introduced. It accepts only a single derivation tree from a large equivalence class of such trees. The equivalence classes capture all trees that are the same size and differ only by reordering the resolution steps. A proof procedure that combines this restriction with the authors' minimal restriction of binary resolution computes each minimal binary resolution tree exactly once.

1 Introduction

A new restriction of binary resolution is proposed in this paper. The restriction is complete in a strong sense, in that every binary resolution proof, up to reordering the resolution steps, is allowed. On the other hand, the restriction prevents multiple versions of the same proof from being constructed. If a given proof is allowed, then no other proof that can be obtained from it by reordering the steps is allowed.

Consider an automated reasoning procedure that takes a set of clauses as input, and resolves pairs of clauses containing complementary literals to generate new clauses. The possible resolutions must be restricted somehow. To do this, let each literal in a clause be either active or inactive, and only let pairs of active complementary literals resolve. Since at the beginning we have no idea which resolution it is best to perform first, all literals in all input clauses are active.

As resolutions occur, some of the literals in newly generated clauses must become inactive. Since we want to have only one acceptable order in which the literals are resolved, the literals in each clause are ordered by a rank function which assigns an integer value to each literal. This rank function must be consistent between a parent clause and a child clause, in that if $rank(a) < rank(b)$ in a parent clause, then $rank(a) < rank(b)$ in the child clause as well. When a clause is resolved on a literal of a given rank, in the newly created child clause all literals of a lesser rank (rank as defined in the parent clause) become inactive, and hence are not allowed to be resolved again. This activity condition also must be inherited from parent literal to child literal, with the following exception. When

C. Kirchner and H. Kirchner (Eds.): Automated Deduction, CADE-15
LNAI 1421, pp. 412–426, 1998. © Springer–Verlag Berlin Heidelberg 1998

two literals that come from different parents merge (or factor) in a child clause, the literal becomes active, regardless of whether the literals in the parent clauses are active or inactive. This exception is very important as completeness is lost if this is not done.

Instead of just keeping the clauses produced, it is important to remember also how a clause is derived. This can be done using clause trees [5], which is where this material was first derived. In this paper we develop the ideas in binary resolution trees [7], which are much more closely related to the proof trees seen in many papers on resolution.

One simple rank function is to assign ranks from 1 to n arbitrarily in an n-literal input clause. When two clauses are resolved, the ranks of the literals in the clause containing the negative resolved literal are the same in the child clause as in the parent clause. The rank of a literal from the parent containing the positive resolved literal receives in the new clause a rank equal to its old rank plus the number of leaf literals in the binary resolution tree containing the negative resolved literal. This method guarantees that the rank function on every clause is one-to-one, and remains between one and the number of leaf literals in every binary resolution tree. In fact if the rank function is applied to the "history path" of every leaf literal, then the rank function remains one-to-one on the set of history paths. We must also specify the rank of merged literals. When two literals are merged, the new literal gets the smaller of the ranks of the literals being merged.

In this example, superscripts denote rank values and a superscript asterisk denotes an inactive literal. When the clause $a^1 \vee b^2 \vee d^3 \vee e^4$ resolves against $a^1 \vee c^2 \vee \neg d^3 \vee f^4$ the result is $a^1 \vee b^{6*} \vee c^{2*} \vee e^8 \vee f^4$. Resolving this against $\neg e^1$ results in a clause that is completely inactive and can never resolve. Note that the rank and activity of the literals in the original clauses are unaffected.

The only requirement on the procedure is that the choice of which resolution to do next has to be fair. If a resolution can be done, then it must be done eventually, at some time in the future, unless one of the resolving clauses is rejected. No resolution can be put off forever. Likewise, no resolution needs to be done more than once. Then the above restriction guarantees that every proof will be found by the procedure, and only once.

2 Background

We use standard definitions [2] for atom, literal, substitution, unifier and most general unifier. Most of the rest of this section originated from [7,8]. In the following a *clause* is an unordered disjunction of literals. We do not use set notation because we do not want multiple occurrences of a literal to collapse to a single literal automatically. Thus our clauses can be viewed as multisets. An atom a *occurs in* a clause C if either a or $\neg a$ is one of the disjuncts of the clause. The clause C *subsumes* the clause D if there exists a substitution θ such that $C\theta \subseteq D$ as sets. A *variable renaming substitution* is one in which every variable maps to a new variable (not in the expression in question), and no two variables map to the same variable. Two clauses C and D are *equal up to variable renaming* if there exists a variable renaming substitution θ such that $C\theta = D$. Two clauses are *standardized apart* if no variable occurs in both. Given two *parent* clauses $C_1 \vee a_1 \vee \ldots \vee a_m$ and $C_2 \vee \neg b_1 \vee \ldots \vee \neg b_n$ that are standardized apart (a variable renaming substitution may be required), their *resolvent* is the clause $(C_1 \vee C_2)\theta$ where θ is the most general unifier of $\{a_1, \ldots, a_m, b_1, \ldots, b_n\}$. The *atom resolved upon* is $a_1\theta$, and the set of *resolved literals* is $\{a_1, \ldots, a_m, \neg b_1, \ldots, \neg b_n\}$.

For each resolution operation we define the resolution mapping ρ from each occurrence of a literal c in each parent clause to either the atom resolved upon if c is a resolved literal, or otherwise to the occurrence of $c\theta$ in the resolvent. We use ρ later to define history paths.

The reader may be missing the usual factoring operation on a clause, which consists of applying a substitution that unifies two of its literals with the same sign and then removing one of these literals. The original definition of resolution [6] does not have this operation. By allowing several literals to be resolved on, instead of merging them before the resolution, we have just one type of internal node in our binary resolution tree, instead of two. De Nivelle uses resolution nodes and factorization nodes [3]. Moreover, an implementation is free to merge or factor literals if desired. Factoring may be seen as an optimization if the factored clause can be used in several resolution steps, since the factoring is done only once.

A binary resolution derivation is commonly represented by a binary tree, drawn with its root at the bottom. Each edge joins a *parent* node, drawn above the edge, to a *child* node, drawn below it. The *ancestors* (*descendants*) of a node are defined by the reflexive, transitive closure of the parent (child) relation. The *proper ancestors* (*proper descendants*) of a node are those ancestors (descendants) not equal to the node itself. Thus the root is a descendant of every node in the tree.

Definition 1. *A binary resolution tree on a set S of input clauses is a labeled binary tree. Each node N in the tree is labeled by a clause label, denoted $cl(N)$. Each node either has two parents and then its clause label is the result of a resolution operation on the clause labels of the parents, or has no parents and is labeled by an instance of an input clause from S. In the case of a resolution, the atom resolved upon is used as another label of the node: the atom label, denoted $al(N)$. Any substitution generated by resolution is applied to all labels of the tree. The clause label of the root of the binary resolution tree is called the* result *of the tree, $result(T)$. A binary resolution tree is* closed *if its result is the empty clause, $\square$.*

For the binary resolution tree in Figure 1 $S = \{a \vee d, \neg a \vee b \vee \neg e, c \vee \neg d, e \vee f \vee g, a \vee b \vee \neg c, \neg a \vee h, \neg h, \neg b, \neg g\}$. The labels of a node N are displayed beside the name of the node and separated by a colon if both labels exist. For example the node N_4 has atom label c, and clause label $a \vee b \vee b \vee f \vee g$. The order between the parents of a node is not defined.

Using the resolution mapping ρ for each resolution operation in the tree, we can trace what happens to a literal from its occurrence in the clause label of some

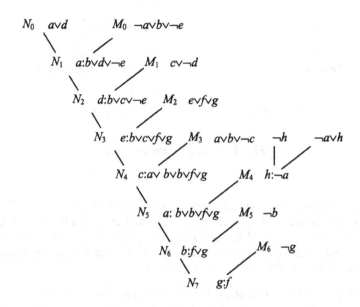

Fig. 1. A binary resolution tree.

leaf, down through the tree until it is resolved away. If all literals are eventually mapped to the atom label of some internal node, the clause label of the root is empty. In this case by soundness of resolution, the clause labels of the leaves is an unsatisfiable set of clauses. Thus we are primarily concerned about tracing the "history" of a literal starting from its appearance in a leaf.

Definition 2 (History Path). *Let a be an occurrence of a literal in the clause label of a leaf node N_0 of a binary resolution tree T. Let $P = (N_0, N_1, \ldots, N_n)$ be a path in T where for each $i = 1, \ldots, n$, N_i is the child of N_{i-1}, ρ_i is the resolution mapping into N_i, and $\rho_i \ldots \rho_2 \rho_1 a$ occurs in $cl(N_i)$, so that a is not resolved upon in P. Further suppose N_n either is the root of T, or has a child N such that $\rho_n \ldots \rho_1 a$ is the atom resolved upon at N. Then P is a history path for a in T. The history path is said to close at N if N exists. The node N_n is the head, the leaf N_0 is the tail and a is the literal of P, written $head(P), tail(P)$ and $literal(P)$, respectively.*

For example in Figure 1, (M_1, N_2, N_3) is a history path for c which closes at N_4. The two history paths for b in Figure 1, corresponding to the two occurrences of b, are (M_3, N_4, N_5) and $(M_0, N_1, N_2, N_3, N_4, N_5)$. Both of these close at N_6. The only history path that does not close is the one for f, which is $(M_2, N_3, N_4, N_5, N_6, N_7)$.

A *rotation* of an edge in a binary tree is a common operation, for example with AVL trees [1]. Before we apply it to binary resolution trees, we review the operation on binary trees. Given the binary tree fragment on the left of Figure 2,

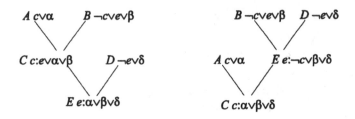

Fig. 2. A binary tree rotation

a rotation is the reassignment of edges so that the tree on the right of Figure 2 is produced. The parent C of E becomes the child of E and the parent B of C becomes the parent of E. If E has a child in T, then C takes that child in T'. In other words, the edges (B, C), (C, E) and (E, F) if it exists, are replaced by the edges (B, E), (E, C) and (C, F) if necessary.

Operation 1 (Edge Rotation) *Let T be a binary resolution tree with an edge (C, E) between internal nodes such that C is the parent of E and C has two parents A and B. Further, suppose that no history path through A closes at E. Then the result of a rotation on this edge is the binary resolution tree T' defined by resolving $cl(B)$ and $cl(D)$ on $al(E)$ giving $cl(E)$ in T' and then resolving $cl(E)$ with $cl(A)$ on $al(C)$ giving $cl(C)$ in T'. Any history path closed at C in T is closed at C in T'; similarly any history path closed at E in T is closed at E in T'. Also, the child of E in T, if it exists, is the child of C in T'.*

A rotation may introduce tautologies to clause labels of internal nodes. For instance, if $al(C)$ occurs in $cl(D)$ then $cl(E)$ in T' may be tautological.

Note that before the rotation, no history path through A closes at E. We do not allow the rotation if history paths through both parents of C close at E. If we did then after the rotation, one of them would not have the opportunity to close, and thus the clause label of the root would change. Before showing that the clause label of the root is not changed (Corollary 1), we prove a slightly more general result, which is also used later.

Definition 3. *Let T_1 and T_2 be two binary resolution trees defined on the same set of input clauses. Then T_1 and T_2 close history paths similarly if there is a one-to-one and onto mapping ν from nodes in T_1 to those in T_2, such that:*

1. *If N is a leaf then $\nu(N)$ is a leaf and both are labeled with instances of the same input clause. Thus there is a natural one to one correspondence, from literals in $cl(N)$ to those in $cl(\nu(N))$. Moreover this mapping of literals provides a mapping from history paths in T_1 to those in T_2, defined so that they start from the same literal in the input clause, up to variable renaming. We represent these other two mappings also with ν. We require for all history paths P in T_1 that $tail(\nu(P)) = \nu(tail(P))$ and $literal(\nu(P)) = literal(P)$ up to variable renaming.*

2. *For every history path P of T_1, P closes at a node N if and only if $\nu(P)$ closes at $\nu(N)$.*

Thus two binary resolution trees close history paths similarly if they resolve the same literals against each other, albeit in a possibly different order.

Lemma 1. *If two binary resolution trees T_1 and T_2 close history paths similarly, the result of T_1 and the result of T_2 are the same, up to variable renaming.*

Proof. Note that $result(T_1)$ and $result(T_2)$ are composed entirely of literals from history paths that do not close, and since the same history paths are closed in each, the same literals are not resolved away. Also the composition of mgu's in T_1 and the composition of mgu's in T_2 are unique up to variable renaming since, given a node N, the same literals are unified at N and $\nu(N)$, up to variable renaming. $\square$

Corollary 1. *Given a binary resolution tree T with an internal node C and its child E, Operation 1 generates a new binary resolution tree and $cl(C)$ in $T' = cl(E)$ in T, up to variable renaming.*

Proof. Observe that Operation 1 produces a tree which closes history paths similarly.$\square$

A rotation changes the order of two resolutions in the tree. Rotations are invertible; after a rotation, no history path through D closes at C, so another rotation at (E, C) can be done, which generates the original tree again. We say that two binary resolution trees are *rotation equivalent* if one can be generated from the other by a sequence of rotations. For instance, the first binary resolution tree in Figure 3 is produced by rotating the edge (N_4, N_5) in Figure 1. The second tree in Figure 3 is then produced by rotating the edge (M_4, N_5). Thus both trees are rotation equivalent to Figure 1. Rotation equivalent is an equivalence relation. It is not surprising that rotation equivalent binary resolution trees must close history paths similarly, but the converse is true as well.

Theorem 2. *Two binary resolution trees T_1 and T_2 are rotation equivalent if and only if they close history paths similarly.*

Proof. Since one rotation of T_1 creates a binary resolution tree that closes history paths similarly to it, so too does the sequence of rotations creating T_2.

The converse is proved by induction on the number of internal nodes. Suppose T_1 and T_2 close history paths similarly. Then they must have the same number n of internal nodes since they have the same number of leaves. If $n = 0$ or $n = 1$ then no rotation is possible and the theorem holds. Let N be a node in T_1 with parents L_1 and L_2 that are leaves. Then in T_2, $\nu(N)$ has proper ancestors $\nu(L_1)$ and $\nu(L_2)$, which also are leaves, and $\nu(N)$ closes only history paths with tails $\nu(L_1)$ and $\nu(L_2)$. We create T_2' by rotating edges so that $\nu(L_1)$ and $\nu(L_2)$ are parents of $\nu(N)$, if this is not already the case. Let C be either parent of $\nu(N)$

and let A and B be the parents of C. If $\nu(L_1)$ and $\nu(L_2)$ are both ancestors of C then neither is an ancestor of the other parent of $\nu(N)$. But $\nu(N)$ must close a history path from that other parent, contradiction. Thus the edge $(C, \nu(N))$ can be rotated, since it is not possible that both A and B contain a history path

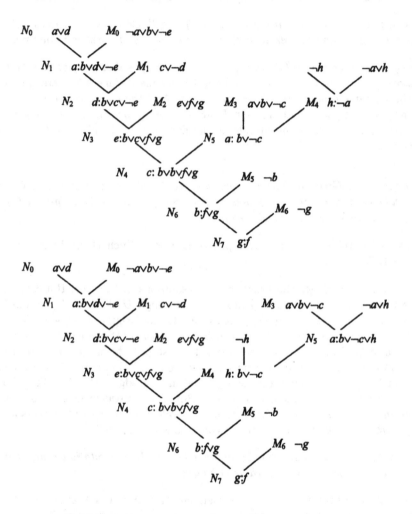

Fig. 3. From Figure 1 rotate (N_4, N_5), then (M_4, N_5)

closing at $\nu(N)$. This rotation reduces the total number of non-leaf ancestors of $\nu(N)$. After a finite number of such rotations, both parents of $\nu(N)$ are leaves. Call this tree T_2'.

Let T_1^* be T_1 with leaves L_1 and L_2 deleted, and let T_2^* be T_2' with leaves $\nu(L_1)$ and $\nu(L_2)$ deleted. Then T_1^* and T_2^* close history paths similarly since

T_1 and T_2' close history paths similarly. By induction T_1^* and T_2^* are rotation equivalent. The sequence of rotations to convert T_1^* to T_2^* will also convert T_1 to T_2', which is rotation equivalent to T_2. $\square$

3   The Rank/Activity Calculus

A rank function must assign a value to every literal in the clause at each node in a given binary resolution tree, in such a way that it orders history paths consistently. Moreover it must assign values to sets of literals if they are unified by a resolution closer to the root of the binary resolution tree. In the following definition a rank function is required to assign values to every set of unifiable literals, even if they are not unified later in the tree. In the informal discussion in the introduction, the rank of a set of literals was given as the minimum of the ranks of the literals unified, but this is not a requirement. The maximum or any other number could be used instead. In the following, if H is a set of history paths in a binary resolution tree T such that (1) some node occurs on all these paths and (2) the literals of these paths are unifiable, then let $literal(H)$ be the multiset of these literals.

Definition 4 (Rank function). *Let $\mathcal{F}$ be a set of binary resolution trees, closed under taking subtrees. Let r assign an integer value to every set of unifiable literals at every node of every tree. Then r is a rank function for $\mathcal{F}$ if r satisfies the following condition in every binary resolution tree T:*

For every pair of disjoint sets H_1 and H_2 of history paths that have two nodes N_1 and N_2 in common:

$$r(literal(H_1), N_1) < r(literal(H_2), N_1) \iff$$

$$r(literal(H_1), N_2) < r(literal(H_2), N_2).$$

Thus r is a rank function if it orders the sets of history paths consistently. In fact the reflexive transitive closure of this relation between sets of history paths, is a partial order.

For example, let T_0 be a binary resolution tree containing a node N_1 and its child N_2. $cl(N) = s \lor p(x) \lor p(y) \lor q(u) \lor q(v)$ where x, y, u and v are variables. At N_1, let r map s to 2, $\{p(x), p(y)\}$ to 4 and $\{q(u), q(v)\}$ to 6. The resolution at N_2 resolves away the s so that $cl(N_2) = p(x) \lor p(y) \lor q(u) \lor q(v)$. If r at N_2 maps $\{p(x), p(y)\}$ to 12, then it must map $\{q(u), q(v)\}$ to a value greater than 12 if r is to be a rank function. In this example H_1 is the history paths for $p(x)$ and $p(y)$ so $literal(H_1)$ is $\{p(x), p(y)\}$, while $literal(H_2)$ is $\{q(u), q(v)\}$.

Next we want to define those binary resolution trees that can be built using the rank/activity restriction. Let N be a node other than the root of a binary resolution tree T. Let $H(N)$ be the set of history paths with N as their head. Then these paths close at the child of N.

Definition 5 (r-compliant). *Let r be a rank function for a binary resolution tree and all its subtrees. Then T is r-compliant if the following condition is true.*

Let N and M be any two nodes such that $H(N)$ also have M in common. Thus M is an ancestor of N. Then $r(literal(H(M)), M) \leq r(literal(H(N)), M)$.

Returning to the example T_0, let $N_2 = M$ and suppose that a new node N is made the child of M. Both $p(x)$ and $p(y)$ are resolved away at N so $cl(N) = q(u) \vee q(v)$. Thus $H(M) = H_1$, the history paths for $p(x)$ and $p(y)$, so $r(literal(H(M)), M) = 12$. Then suppose the child of N resolves away the remaining literals so that $literal(H(N)) = \{q(u), q(v)\}$. Call the resulting tree T_1. We have already assumed that $r(literal(H(M)), M) < r(literal(H(N)), M)$ to make r a rank function. This condition also makes T_1 r-compliant. Note that if one rotates the edge between N and the root, one gets a tree which is rotation equivalent to T_1 but resolves away the q's before the p's. Since r still ranks the p's in M lower than the q's, this tree is not r-compliant. The resolution on the q's has deactivated the p's.

In the general case, the resolution at M's child does not deactivate the set of history paths with head at N. Moreover, this set of history paths is not affected by what happens before they are drawn together at some node by a resolution. Therefore it is created as an active set of literals, which justifies the re-activation of literals when they are merged together. Hence the set is active in N and can be resolved by a rank/activity procedure at N's child. Thus the r-compliant binary resolution trees are precisely those trees that can be constructed using the rank/activity restriction of binary resolution, using the function r as the rank function.

Theorem 3 (Completeness and uniqueness). *Let T be a binary resolution tree. Let r be a rank function for the set of all binary resolution trees that are rotation equivalent to T. Then there is a binary resolution tree T' that is rotation equivalent to T and is r-compliant. Moreover, if the rank function r maps disjoint sets of literals at any given node to different values, then T' is unique.*

Proof. First we prove the existence of T', which implies that the rank/activity restriction is complete. The proof is an induction on the number of nodes in T. If T consists of a single node, then T itself is r-compliant for any rank function defined on T.

We now consider the case in which T has more than one node. Consider any leaf L. The literals of L correspond to history paths that either close at some internal node of T, or pass through to the root of T. Let $N_1, N_2, ..., N_k$ be the nodes that are the heads of history paths with L as the tail, excluding those paths whose heads are the root. Let P_i be the set of history paths with L as the tail and N_i as the head, for $i = 1, 2, ..., k$. We define a pointer $P(L)$, which points from L at some internal node of T. $P(L)$ is the child of the N_j where:

1. $P_j = H(N_j)$;
2. $r(literal(P_j), L) \leq r(literal(P_i), L)$ for all i such that $P_i = H(N_i)$.

The first condition asserts that the literals of P_j are not merged or factored with literals from any other leaf, before being resolved. The second condition asserts that this set of literals has the minimum rank of all sets of literals that satisfy condition (1). If there is more than one choice for $P(L)$ because r is not one-to-one, then any choice of the nodes that satisfy the conditions can be made. Note that if the rank function satisfies the condition of the second part of the theorem, then $P(L)$ must necessarily be unique, even if r itself is not one-to-one. There is some P_i that satisfies condition $P_i = H(N_i)$, since L itself is one of the N_i, as at least one literal of $cl(L)$ must close at L's child, and thus cannot be merged with literals from other clauses first.

Now $P(L)$ is a function that points from the leaves of T into the interior nodes of T. Since the number of leaves is one more than the number of interior nodes, by the pigeon hole principle there must be some node N pointed at by two different leaves, L_1 and L_2. Then $P(L_1) = P(L_2) = N$.

If either parent of N is not L_1 or L_2, then N can be rotated with that parent, since the literals closing at N through that parent cannot come from distinct grandparents of N. Since the set of literals closing at N are not changed by rotation, N can be rotated upward in the tree until its parents are L_1 and L_2 themselves. Now remove L_1 and L_2 from the tree, making N a leaf of a new smaller tree T_1. The function r, restricted to the nodes of T_1 and all its rotation equivalent binary resolution trees, is still a rank function for T_1. By induction T_1 is rotation equivalent to a binary resolution tree T_1' that is r-compliant. Replace the leaf N in T_1' by the subtree with leaves L_1 and L_2, and root N, to get another binary resolution tree T'. T' is rotation equivalent to T, since the rotations of T_1 to T_1' can be mirrored by rotations in binary resolution trees with N replaced by the $L_1 - N - L_2$ subtree.

It remains to show that T' is r-compliant. The only nodes that must be checked are the new nodes L_1 and L_2, as a possible M in the definition of r-compliant. Consider any non-root node N' such that the history paths $H(N')$ have L_1 in common. Then by the choice of $P(L_1)$, $r(literal(H(L_1)), L_1) \leq r(literal(H(N')), L_1)$ by the definition of $P(L_1)$, so that the r-compliant condition is always satisfied at L_1. The same situation applies at L_2. Thus T' is r-compliant. Hence the rank/activity restriction is complete.

If the condition is added that the rank function r does not map two disjoint sets of literals at any node to the same value, then the pointer function chooses a unique node $P(L)$ for any leaf L. Let L, N_i, P_i, be as defined above. Let T^* be any binary resolution tree that is r-compliant and rotation equivalent to T. The history paths of $H(L)$ close at the child of L. Then $r(literal(H(L)), L) \leq r(literal(P_i), L)$ for $i = 1, 2, ..., k$, because T^* is r-compliant. But by the uniqueness condition on r, these ranks must all be distinct. Thus there is a unique j such that $H(L) = P_j$, and $P(L) = $ the child of N_j, by the definition of $P(L)$. Hence $N_j = L$, and $P(L)$ must be the child of L in T^*.

This argument shows that each leaf of T^* has a unique child. The argument can be extended to all the nodes of T^*, by inducting on the height of the subtree above the node. Thus every node, other than the root node, has a uniquely defined child node. It follows that the binary resolution tree T* is unique. $\square$

Consider any bottom up binary resolution proof procedure that keeps all clauses that it generates, and uses the rank/activity restriction. It only constructs proofs that correspond to r-compliant binary resolution trees, where r is the rank function used. One consequence of this theorem is that as long as the proof procedure is fair, in that if a resolution is allowed then it will eventually be performed once, the procedure must construct every possible proof, up to reordering the resolutions. That is, the procedure is refutationally complete. Moreover it will produce a binary resolution tree of minimal size (number of nodes), if it is not halted after the first is found. However only one binary resolution tree is produced for each possible proof, if the rank function is distinct on disjoint sets of literals. As the number of reorderings is typically exponential in the size of the binary resolution tree, this amounts to a considerable saving of work compared to a proof procedure that does not use this restriction.

4   Combining with Minimality

The rank/activity restriction combines well with minimality, another restriction of binary resolution. Minimality [5,7,8] is an extension of the better known regularity restriction [9]. A binary resolution tree is regular if, for every internal node N, the atom label of N is not in the clause label of any descendant of N.

The tree in Figure 1 is irregular because $al(N_1)$ is a and a occurs in $cl(N_4)$. Irregular trees are never necessary. Why resolve away the a twice? One could choose to leave out the resolution at N_1, leaving the a in the clause, do the other resolutions as necessary (not all will be necessary) and later resolve a away, as was done at N_5. We call this operation *surgery* [7,8].

A binary resolution tree is minimal if it is not rotation equivalent to a irregular binary resolution tree. There is a linear time (in the size of the tree) algorithm to detect whether the resolution of two binary resolution trees creates binary resolution tree that is minimal or is non-minimal [7].

Theorem 4. *Let C be an unsatisfiable set of clauses. Let r be a rank function defined on the binary resolution trees that can be constructed with C as the clauses of the leaves. Then there is a minimal r-compliant binary resolution tree with an empty clause at its root. Moreover, one of the smallest binary resolution trees on C with the empty clause at the root is minimal and r-compliant.*

Proof. An irregular binary resolution tree can be manipulated by surgery so that the second identical literal on a branch is resolved away at the same time as the first identical literal. The resulting binary resolution tree is smaller, and the resulting clause at the root subsumes the clause of the original binary resolution tree. (See [8] for a proof.) Thus the smallest binary resolution tree that results in the empty clause must be regular. Since every binary resolution tree is rotation equivalent to one that is r-compliant, so is the smallest one. Rotating nodes cannot turn a minimal binary resolution tree into one that is non-minimal, for if the resulting tree can be rotated into an irregular proof, so too can the original tree. Moreover rotating nodes does not change the size of the binary resolution tree. The theorem follows. □

Corollary 2. *A fair binary resolution procedure that uses both the rank/activity and the minimality restrictions and that keeps all other clauses produced, is refutationally complete.*

Proof. Any subtree of a minimal binary resolution tree is also minimal, since if a subtree can be rotated to be irregular, so can the supertree. Thus to produce a given minimal tree, only minimal trees have to be resolved. By the same proof as Theorem 3, every minimal tree must be rotation equivalent to some tree produced by this procedure. □

5   A Simple Example

The rank/activity restriction, like resolution itself, does not require any specific procedure or approach, so any example is rather arbitrary. However an example may clarify some points. The procedure used below is not recommended as a efficient theorem prover, but has been chosen because it is simple and straightforward.

The procedure grows a list of clauses, starting from a list of the input clauses. The clauses are processed from top to bottom. Each clause in the list, when its turn comes, is resolved in all possible ways with the clauses above it. The generated clauses, if they contain an active literal, are added to the bottom of the list. Those clauses with no active literals are discarded. This procedure is fair so it is complete with the rank/activity restriction. Subsumption is not used.

The rank of a literal is denoted by a superscript following it. If a literal is inactive, an asterisk is placed after the rank. Ranks are kept as discussed in the introduction, so a "size" must be kept for each clause, representing the number of literals in the corresponding binary resolution tree. When a clause that consists only of inactive literals would be generated by a given resolution, the word "inactive" is placed in the diagram where the clause would otherwise appear, but the clause itself is not inserted into the list, and in fact does not even need to be generated. The clause will be inactive if the two resolving literals are the highest ranked active literals in the parent clauses, there are other literals and no merging of literals is possible.

The clauses and literals resolved upon for each new clause are indicated by the notation clause1#:literal-position - clause2#:literal-position.

# Clause	Size	Source
1. p^1	1	input
2. $\neg s^1$	1	input
3. $s^1 \vee \neg r^2$	2	input
4. $\neg q^1 \vee \neg p^2$	2	input
5. $q^1 \vee \neg p^2 \vee r^3$	3	input

Processing clauses 1 and 2 generates no clauses.
Processing clause 3 generates one clause.

6. $\neg r^3$	3	3:1-2:1

Processing clause 4 generates a clause with no active literals, $\neg q^{1*}$. Such inactive clauses are discarded.

inactive   4:1-1:1

Processing clause 5 generates three clauses, one of which is inactive, and another has a merge.

7. $q^{1*} \vee r^3$	4	5:2-1:1
inactive		5:3-3:2
8. $\neg p^2 \vee \neg p^4 \vee r^5$	5	5:1-4:1
merged to $\neg p^2 \vee r^5$		

Processing clause 6 generates one inactive clause.

inactive   6:1-5:3

In processing clause 7, only the active literal needs to be resolved.

inactive	7:2-3:2
inactive	7:2-6:1

Processing clause 8:

9. r^6	6	8:1-1:1
inactive		8:2-3:2
inactive		8:2-6:1

Processing clause 9 ends the procedure.

inactive		9:1-3:2
10.$\square$	8	9:1-6:1

The resulting binary resolution tree is in Figure 4.

In all the procedure has done five resolutions, only one of which, #7, is not used in the proof. A total of eight resolutions were not done because the resulting clause would be inactive. There are nine rotation equivalent binary resolution trees; there is only one r-compliant one, unless the merge is clause 8 is optional.

6   Discussion

This paper presents a canonical form for a large equivalence class of binary resolution trees. For a rank function r that gives different values to disjoint sets of literals, there is a unique r-compliant binary resolution tree that is rotation

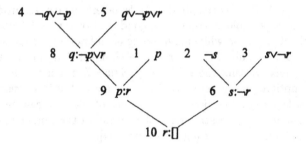

Fig. 4. The example's unique r-compliant binary resolution tree

equivalent to a given binary resolution tree. Rotation equivalent trees do the same resolutions in a different order so this is a natural class to study. The restriction leads to an exponential reduction in the number of proofs in the search space. Implementations need only store an integer rank and a one-bit activity status with each literal, and the check is inference local so it adds little to the overall execution time. Meanwhile it does not eliminate the proof tree of minimum size. Most restrictions of resolution, such as linear, selection function, A-ordered, and lock, do not have all of these properties. Moreover, the minimal restriction [5], an extension of the regular restriction, can be combined with rank/activity.

A-ordered resolution appears to be a somewhat closely related restriction; it makes the smallest atom in the A-ordering the only active atom. However, A-ordering cannot consistently order the literals in first-order logic and all their instances. The rank/activity restriction applies directly to first order logic, since the rank of an occurrence of a literal is not affected by taking instances. In effect, rank/activity resembles an A-ordering restriction that sometimes allows literals to be skipped over, and brought back into the order after they are factored.

In one sense the rank/activity restriction is just a subrestriction of subsumption, because every unclosed binary resolution tree that is prevented from being formed by rank/activity, would eventually rejected by subsumption too. But it is much easier to check activity than it is to check subsumption since subsumption depends on the, often large, size of the set of retained clauses. This work addresses a problem posed by Wos [10]:

> If a strategy could be found whose use prevented a reasoning program
> from deducing redundant clauses, we would have a solution far preferable
> to our current one of using subsumption.

Full scale subsumption cannot be combined with the rank/activity restriction, since totally separate proofs of the same clause need not have the same rank orderings of the literals or activity conditions on the literals. However it is possible to combine a considerable portion of subsumption with the rank/activity restriction. To use rank activity completely, one can delete a subsumed clause D

if the subsuming clause C corresponds to a "smaller" binary resolution tree than D does. It is also possible to combine a good deal of the rank/activity restriction with full subsumption while maintaining completeness. To use subsumption fully, one can activate all of the literals of a clause if that clause subsumes another clause, thus treating the subsuming clause like a new input clause. Of course subsumption guarantees uniqueness of clauses, but in a sense uniqueness is lost in this latter combination, in that proof of a clause can be constructed and then subsumed by a rotation equivalent proof of the same clause. This has been investigated more fully using clause trees [4].

References

1. G. M. Adelson-Velskii and E. M. Landis. An algorithm for the organizaton of information. *Soviet Math. Doklady*, 3:1259–1263, 1962.
2. Chin-Liang Chang and Richard Char-Tung Lee. *Symbolic Logic and Mechanical Theorem Proving*. Academic Press, New York and London, 1973.
3. Hans de Nivelle. Resolution games and non-liftable resolution orderings. *Collegium Logicum, Annals of the Kurt Gödel Society*, 2:1–20, 1996.
4. J. D. Horton and Bruce Spencer. Bottom up procedures to construct each minimal clause tree once. Technical Report TR97-115, Faculty of Computer Science, University of New Brunswick, PO Box 4400, Fredericton, New Brunswick, Canada, 1997.
5. J. D. Horton and Bruce Spencer. Clause trees: a tool for understanding and implementing resolution in automated reasoning. *Artificial Intelligence*, 92:25–89, 1997.
6. J. A. Robinson. A machine-oriented logic based on the resolution principle. *J. ACM*, 12:23–41, 1965.
7. Bruce Spencer and J.D. Horton. Extending the regular restriction of resolution to non-linear subdeductions. In *Proceedings of the Fourteenth National Conference on Artificial Intelligence*, pages 478–483. AAAI Press/MIT Press, 1997.
8. Bruce Spencer and J.D. Horton. Efficient procedures to detect and restore minimality, an extension of the regular restriction of resolution. *Journal of Automated Reasoning*, 1998. accepted for publication.
9. G. S. Tseitin. On the complexity of derivation in propositional calculus. In *Studies in Constructive Mathematics*, Seminars in Mathematics: Mathematicheskii Institute, pages 115–125. Consultants Bureau, 1969.
10. L. Wos. *Automated Reasoning : 33 Basic Research Problems*. Prentice-Hall, Englewood Cliffs, New Jersey, 1988.

Towards Efficient Subsumption

Tanel Tammet

Department of Computing Science, University of Göteborg,
Göteborg, Sweden
tammet@cs.chalmers.se

Abstract. We propose several methods for writing efficient subsumption procedures for non-unit clauses, tested in practice as parts incorporated into the Gandalf family of theorem provers. Versions of Gandalf exist for classical logic, first order intuitionistic logic and type theory.

Subsumption is one of the most important techniques for cutting down search space in resolution theorem proving. However, for many problem categories most of the proof search time is spent on subsumption. While acceptable efficiency has been achieved for subsuming unit clauses (see [7], [2]), the nonunit subsumption tends to slow provers down prohibitively.

We propose several methods for writing efficient subsumption procedures for non-unit clauses, succesfully tested in practice as parts built into the Gandalf family of theorem provers:

- ordering literals according to a certain subsumption measure
- indexing first two literals of each nonunit clause
- pre-computed properties of terms, literals and clauses
- a hierarchy of fast filters for clause-to-clause subsumption
- combining subsumption with clause simplification
- linear search among the strongly reduced number of candidates for back subsumption

The presented methods for substitution were among the key techniques enabling the classical version of Gandalf to win the MIX division of the CASC-14 prover contest in 1997. The approach of the paper is purely empirical, presenting the methods and bringing some statistical evidence.

1 Gandalf Family of Provers

Before continuing with the details of the subsumption methods we will present an overview of the Gandalf family of provers. We use the name Gandalf for the interdependent, code-sharing, resolution-based automated theorem provers we are developing: a resolution prover for first-order intuitionistic logic Tammet [9], for a fragment of Martin-Löf's type theory Tammet [10] and for first-order classical logic (earlier version in Tammet [11]).

C. Kirchner and H. Kirchner (Eds.): Automated Deduction, CADE-15
LNAI 1421, pp. 427–441, 1998. © Springer–Verlag Berlin Heidelberg 1998

1.1   Gandalf for Intuitionistic Logic and Type Theory

The motivation for the intuitionistic version of Gandalf was to build the very first resolution prover for the logic. The type theory version is developed as an assistant for human users of the type theory system ALF, see Magnusson and Nordström [4]. One of our goals was to experiment with the optimised translation methods from type theory to classical logic, presented in Tammet [10]

1.2   Code Sharing and Comparisons

The intuitionistic version presented in Tammet [9] uses the general scheme of building resolution calculi (also called the inverse method) originating from Maslov and Mints [5], augmented with a number of novel search strategies.

Most of the code of the intuitionistic prover is shared with the classical prover. This makes it easy to implement universal low-level resolution strategies, heuristics and engineering solutions, so that they will work both for classical and intuitionistic logic.

Since the resolution proof search in intuitionistic logic typically generates large amounts of non-unit clauses, the efficiency of the subsumption procedure for the non-unit clauses is highly important for the intuitionistic version of Gandalf. Since the same procedure is shared by the intuitionistic and and classical components, the subsumption component is currently one of the most sophisticated parts of the classical version of Gandalf.

However, we note that the top-level search strategies for these logics are still substantially different.

In [9] we observe that for the most of the first-order intuitionistic formulas we have found in the literature, our resolution-based prover compares favourably with the earlier tableaux-based provers.

The similarity of the search paradigm — resolution — and the code for intuitionistic and classical provers also simplifies comparison between the time it takes to prove a formula intuitionistically and classically. Roughly said, in almost all of our experiments the intuitionistic proof search is much harder than the classical proof search.

The current version of Gandalf for the (restricted) type theory uses a modification of the classical prover, with the latter limited to Horn clauses, where classical and intuitionistic provability coincide. The modified classical prover is used as an inference engine in a larger system doing conversions between type theory and classical logic as well as creating proof subtasks by automating structural induction on types. The system always performs the conversion from classical proofs to type theory proofs, which is a relatively complicated part of the system. In particular, we use a separate limited proof search for the conversion only.

1.3   Gandalf for Classical Logic

Although some of our motivations stem from nonclassical logics, we are strongly interested in the classical version in its own right. In particular, Gandalf contains special strategies for program synthesis using classical logic, see Tammet [8] as well as decision strategies based on orderings, see Fermüller et al [1]. The classical version of Gandalf won the prover competition CASC-14 during the CADE-14 in 1997.

Gandalf implements a number of different basic strategies: binary ordered resolution for several orderings, versions of set-of-support resolution, binary unit resolution, hyperresolution. Enhancements are used for cutting off literals and combining different strategies, in particular forward and backward reasoning, into one run. Equality is handled by ordered paramodulation and demodulation.

1.4 Time Slicing

It is universally recognised that there cannot exist any simple search strategies which are feasible for most or all problems. Typically, different strategies have dramatic differences of behaviour on different problems. It is rather common that a proof which would take years to find with one particular search strategy can be found in a few seconds with another.

Selecting possibly suitable strategies and running them either in parallel or one after another is a regular pattern of practical use of provers by humans. We think that it is worthwhile to automatise at least parts of this Las Vegas type strategy selection algorithm in order to obtain better cooperation between runs with different strategies and to assist a human user — in particular, an unexperienced human user — with a powerful expert system also for the meta-level of theorem proving.

The basic idea of the automatic mode in Gandalf — also used during the CASC-14 competition — is time-slicing: Gandalf selects a set of different search strategies, allocates time to these and finally runs the strategies one after another. The motivation is the following: since it is very hard to determine a *single* suitable strategy by some heuristic procedure, it pays off to try a number of possibly suitable strategies.

The selection of strategies and the percentage of time they receive is in a somewhat ad hoc way based on the characteristics of the problem: percentage of horn and almost-horn clauses, the number of clauses, percentage of clauses where literals can be ordered using term and variable depths. For example, in case of small horn problems hyperresolution and binary unit resolution would get most of the time, whereas in case of large non-horn problems several versions of set-of-support would get most of the time.

The set of candidate strategies contains both pure, complete strategies, incomplete combinations (for example, hyperresolution with set-of-support) and strategies with limitations on term depth and clause length. For pure unit equality problems a fixed set of five different strategies was used.

Once the strategies are selected, they are run one after another. There is some cooperation between different strategies - in case enough memory is available, unit clauses derived during running the previous strategies are kept, in order to cut off literals from newly derived clauses. However, for the CASC-14 competition examples this cooperation was very rarely of any use.

1.5 Implementation and Availability

Gandalf is implemented in Scheme. We are using the *scm* interpreter developed by A. Jaffer and the Scheme-to-C compiler *Hobbit* developed by T. Tammet for the scm system.

The source, binaries, manual and other materials are available at http://www.cs.chalmers.se/~tammet/gandalf/.

2 Subsumption: Preliminaries

We use the standard notions of term, literal, unifier, clause and subsumption, see for example Fermüller et al: [1].

A *unit clause* is a clause consisting of a single literal. A term, literal or a clause is *ground* iff it does not contain variables. The *length* of a clause is the number of literals in the clause. The *size* of a term, literal and clause is the number of subterms and literals in it. The *depth* of a literal and a clause is the depth of the deepest term occurring in it.

A literal A *subsumes* a literal B iff there exists a substitution σ such that $A\sigma = B$. A clause C *subsumes* a clause D iff there exists a substitution σ such that $C\sigma \subseteq D$.

The main kinds of subsumption application in a typical resolution prover are *forward* and *backward* subsumption, ordinarily called while processing a newly derived clause.

By *forward subsumption* we mean the process of checking whether any of the input or already derived clauses subsumes the newly derived clause. If yes, then the newly derived clause is eliminated.

By *backward subsumption* we mean the process of eliminating these input and already derived clauses which are subsumed by the newly derived clause.

By *unit* subsumption we mean a special case of subsumption where the subsuming clause is unit.

The Gandalf *given-clause main loop* for inferring and processing clauses keeps two main lists of clauses — *sos* and *usable* — and is similar to most of the other resolution provers (cite from McCune [6]):

```
While (sos is not empty and no refutation has been found)
    1. Let given_clause be the 'lightest' clause in sos;
    2. Move given_clause from sos to usable;
    3. Infer and process new clauses using the inference rules in
            effect; each new clause must have the given_clause as
            one of its parents and members of usable as its other
            parents;  new clauses that pass the retention tests
            are appended to sos;
End of while loop.
```

During the 'process' phase above Gandalf will attempt to forward subsume the clause and if that does not succeed, back subsumption is called. Several clause simplification methods are combined into the forward subsumption process.

Gandalf always generates all the factors of each derived clause. Therefore we prohibit subsumption checks between clauses A and B such that A is longer than B. Should subsumption hold, there will be a shorter factor of A subsuming B.

3   Challenges of Subsumption

The two main reasons why subsumption often takes a large percentage of search time are:

1. Subsumption check has to be called for each newly derived clause C. Each such check must test C against all the existing clauses. Thus the number of clause-to-clause subsumption tests is quadratic to the number of derived clauses. When the latter is large - tens and hundreds of thousands — the square of this number becomes prohibitively large.
2. Checking whether a non-unit clause C of length n subsumes another clause D of length m is a backtracking algorithm which requires m^n literal-to-literal subsumption tests in the worst case. Thus, for long clauses even the time of a single clause subsumption may become prohibitively long.

It is important to consider separately the forward and backward subsumption, as well as unit and nonunit subsumption: the methods for handling these tasks efficiently differ a lot.

The standard way to alleviate problems stemming from the first reason above is the use of special indexing techniques, like discrimination tree indexing and path indexing, see McCune [7].

These indexing methods work very well with forward subsumption, particularly the unit forward subsumption. They are not as good for backward subsumption and they do not give much improvement over the naive linear algorithm in case the average clause length is high.

The standard way to alleviate the problems stemming from the second reason above is to analyse the variable-sharing properties of literals and order the literals accordingly: a literal A which contains a superset of variables in a literal B should be tested before B. This method was proposed and analysed by Leitsch and Gottlob in [3].

4   Importance of Subsumption for Large Non-Horn Problems

When compared to other provers — for example, Otter — Gandalf performs best on large non-Horn clause sets. Most of the industrial verification problems create such sets when converted to the clause form. In mathematics, set theory problems have a similar effect.

For proving non-Horn clause sets it is typically necessary to generate non-unit clauses. The longer they are, the harder the task of subsumption.

Some search strategies, like forward-reasoning hyperresolution, tend to produce relatively short clauses, while others, like backward-reasoning set of support resolution, tend to produce long clauses.

Because most of the existing provers slow down considerably — due to subsumption — when large amounts of long clauses are produced, these provers are preferably used with strategies like hyperresolution, and not with strategies like set of support.

However, for problems which translate into large clause sets — on the order of hundreds of clauses — the forward-reasoning hyperresolution-like strategies are ordinarily a bad choice, since they do not concentrate search on the goal clause(s), as set of support does. However, without fast subsumption, set of support becomes prohibitively slow for large non-Horn clause sets.

Because backward-reasoning tableaux provers do not rely on subsumption to such an extent as the resolution provers do, tableaux systems like SETHEO have been a good choice for finding proofs for large non-Horn clause sets. However, our experience with Gandalf shows that versions of set of support combined with an efficient subsumption procedure are a feasible alternative to the tableaux systems when it comes to proving beforementioned types of problems.

5   Forward Subsumption

5.1   Unit Forward Subsumption

According to McCune [7] the most efficient forward subsumption procedure for unit forward subsumption is obtained by using the full variable-containing discrimination tree. Hence Gandalf keeps all the unit clauses indexed in such a tree and uses the corresponding method for forward subsumption: a newly derived clause $\{L_1, \ldots, L_n\}$ is processed by attempting to forward subsume the literals $L_1, \ldots, L_n$ one after another, with the discrimination tree. No direct clause-to-clause subsumption checks are performed.

Unit Deletion Gandalf combines the following clause simplification method into unit forward subsumption. The discrimination tree leaves contain unit clauses for both negative and positive literals, and in case a literal negative to the checked literal L_i is found at a leaf, the literal L_i is removed from the clause C.

5.2   Nonunit Forward Subsumption

Observe that if the clause D subsumes C, then each literal in D subsumes at least one literal in C.

Several provers combine the discrimination tree with the linear test with a subset of derived clauses. One literal in each nonunit clause is put into the indexed tree. When a new clause C is checked for nonunit subsumption, at first the set S of clauses is retrieved from the tree so that at least one literal in each clause in S subsumes at least one literal in C. The clauses in S are then checked linearly.

Gandalf takes this idea one step further, indexing on **two** literals from each clause. In principle it is possible to extend the indexing to any n literals, in which case the time spent on linear search will diminish, but the time required for searching the tree will grow very fast as n increases. Our choice of indexing on two literals stems mainly from the following empirical considerations:

- It is usually advantageous to concentrate search on shorter clauses. Hence the number of shorter clauses is likely to be bigger than the number of long clauses. Although this varies a lot, two-literal clauses appear to be fairly common during proof searches.
- The balance between the tree search time and the linear test time appears to be acceptable for most problems when two-literal indexing is used.

Each clause D is ordered according to a certain measure $\succ_s$ described later (the idea is that the $\succ_s$-bigger elements of the clause are less likely to subsume a randomly chosen literal) and the $\succ_s$-first two literals L_1 and L_2 are combined into one *pseudo-literal* $P(L_1, L_2)$ which is then added to the discrimination tree in a standard way.

Hence all the two-literal clauses $\{R_1, R_2\}$ are non-unit forward-subsumed by checking first $P(R_1, R_2)$ and then $P(R_2, R_1)$ against the discrimination tree. No direct clause-to-clause subsumption checks are performed.

For longer clauses $\{R_1, R_2, \ldots, R_n\}$ we *do not* carry on subsumption checking by first checking all clauses of length two, then of length three, etc. Instead we use the previously described indexing on two literals for forming a set of *candidate subsuming clauses* which are later used for clause-to-clause subsumption.

In order to create the list of candidate subsuming clauses we first form pseudo-literals

$$P(R_1, R_2), P(R_1, R_3), \ldots, P(R_1, R_n), \ldots, P(R_n, R_{n-1})$$

representing all ordered pairs of literals in the clause. These pseudo-literals are then checked incrementally for finding clauses which contain a pair of literals subsuming both components of the pseudo-literal. A clause $G : \{G_1, G_2, \ldots, G_m\}$ is a subsumption candidate iff for some substitution σ, some literals G_i and G_j and some pseudo-literal $P(R_u, R_v)$ holds $G_i\sigma = R_u$ and $G_j\sigma = R_v$.

The search for subsumption candidates is organised incrementally, by re-using a path in the discrimination tree for the first component literal. For example, once the path for $P(R_1)$ has been found in the discrimination tree, the found path is used for all of

$$P(R_1, R_2), P(R_1, R_3), \ldots, P(R_1, R_n)$$

instead of re-finding the path for $P(R_1)$ for each pseudo-literal.

Unit Deletion Gandalf combines the following clause simplification method into two-literal forward subsumption. The discrimination tree leaves contain two-literal clauses for both negative and positive literals. In case such a two-literal clause $\{\neg L, R\}$ is found at the leaf that the newly derived clause contains literals L' and R' such that $\{L, R\}$ subsumes $\{L', R'\}$, the literal L' is deleted from the newly derived clause.

Linear Test The set of candidate subsuming clauses contains clauses of length three or more. Once the set of candidate subsuming clauses has been built, they are all tested for subsuming the newly derived clause, using the clause-to-clause subsumption check. The optimised algorithm for this test is presented in the next section.

6   Clause-to-Clause Subsumption

We will first consider the importance of ordering the literals in a suitable way.

Consider the task of checking whether the clause $\{L_1, \ldots, L_n\}$ subsumes the clause $\{R_1, \ldots, R_m\}$. In the general case we need to test all the permutations of literals $L_1, \ldots, L_n$ against the clause $\{R_1, \ldots, R_m\}$. A natural way to do this is to use a backtracking algorithm. First a literal L_1 is matched with $R_1, R_2, \ldots$ until such an R_i is found which is subsumed by L_1, giving a certain substitution σ_1. After that we repeat the same search for $L_2\sigma_1$, etc, until each literal L subsumes a literal R. In case some $L_j\sigma_j$ does not subsume any R_k, the search backtraces to L_{j-1}, attempting to find another R_l subsumed by L_{j-1}, giving a different substitution σ'_j.

The crucial issue here is minimising backtracking. Gottlob and Leitsch [3] suggests the following:

1. In case the literal $L_{j-1}\sigma$ does not contain variables, there is no need to attempt subsuming a different R_l, since the new substitution is empty in any case.
2. Strengthening the previous idea: in case the literal $L_{j-1}\sigma$ does not contain variables *which occur in literals to the right:* $L_j, \ldots, L_n$, there is also no need to attempt subsuming a different R_l.
3. Splitting the clause $\{L_1, \ldots, L_n\}$ into subsets which do not share variables enables analysing these components separately.
4. Ordering the literals in $\{L_1, \ldots, L_n\}$ in such a way that the previous considerations would have maximal effect: literals containing more variables should be tested before literals containing fewer variables. For example, if a literal L_i contains all the variables in $\{L_1, \ldots, L_n\}$, and we test it first, then we only need to retry L_i, never any other literal in the clause.
5. Before full test with backtracking, test each literal in $\{L_1, \ldots, L_n\}$ separately: for each L_i there should be at least one literal R_j which is subsumed by L_i.

The suggestions from Gottlob and Leitsch [3] are implemented in Gandalf with certain pragmatical modifications. The most important of these is an ordering of literals which reflects the probability of a literal subsuming another, randomly picked literal.

6.1 Ordering Methods in Gandalf

Observe that almost all the clause-to-clause subsumption tests during the proof search fail. Hence it is useful to look for the failure first. Hence we first try these literals in $\{L_1, \ldots, L_n\}$ which are less likely to subsume randomly picked literals.

The function $ground(A)$ returns 1 if A is ground, 0 otherwise. Functions $size(A)$ and $depth(A)$ return the size and the depth of the literal, respectively. Function $cnum(A)$ returns the number of occurrences of constants in A.

The ordering $A \succ_s B$ is defined in the following way: A and B are compared according to $ground$, $depth$, $size$, $cnum$, in that order. In case any comparison gives a bigger value for A than B, then $A \succ_s B$. In case any comparison gives a bigger value for B than A, then $B \succ_s A$. If the values are equal, the next comparison function is taken.

The proof of the following lemma is easy:

Lemma 1. *If $A \succ_s B$, then A cannot subsume B.*

The main issue is having an ordering which contains many independent comparison functions and satisfies the lemma. We do not claim that this particular order $\succ_s$ is statistically much better than other, similar orders.

The order $\succ_s$ is used in Gandalf in several ways. First, it is used to determine which two literals in the clause should be indexed. Second, it is used for ordering literals in a clause before the clause-to-clause subsumption checks.

We have not implemented splitting the clause into components, as suggested by Gottlob and Leitsch [3], for the reason that most clauses derived during the search typically cannot be split into several non-ground components. The ordering realises the splitting effects for the ground and ground/non-ground components. We have not implemented ordering by variable occurrences either. Instead we prefer larger and deeper literals, which statistically tend to contain more variables than smaller and shallower. We can say that the variable-occurrence ordering suggested in Gottlob and Leitsch [3] is *approximated* by our choice of $\succ_s$, with the latter taking additional considerations into account too.

6.2 Pre-computing the Values

We avoid all costly computations during subsumption. The values of functions $ground$, $depth$, $size$ are $cnum$ are pre-computed when a clause is stored and saved as consecutive bit fields into a special 4-byte integer in the representation of a literal, containing also the name of the leading predicate. Clauses are pre-sorted according to the ordering.

In order to keep track of whether a literal contains variables occurring also in the following literals, each variable occurrence in a literal is decorated with a special data bit, indicating whether there are any later occurrences.

6.3 Hierarchical Filters

Before a full clause-to-clause subsumption test of B with A is performed, a number of fast checks are performed. In most cases these fast checks establish immediately that A cannot subsume B.

As said before, each literal is decorated with the values of *ground*, *depth*, *size* and *cnum*. Similarly, the whole clause and each term is also decorated with these values for the corresponding object.

The set of predicate names occurring in a literal is encoded as a bit string in an integer. This enables very fast checking (using bitwise machine operations) of whether the set of predicate names in A is a subset of predicate names in B.

The hiearchy of tests performed while checking subsumption of B by A is the following (failure of any test causes failure of the whole test):

1. Is A shorter or of equal length to B?
2. Is it the case that $A \succ_s B$ does not hold?
3. Is it the case that $depth(A) \leq depth(B)$, $size(A) \leq size(B)$ and $const(A) \leq const(B)$?
4. Bitwise check: is the set of predicate names in A a subset of predicate names in B?
5. Is it the case that each literal in A subsumes at least one literal in B?
6. Full test: does A subsume B?

The analogues of steps 2 and 3 are used not only before the full subsumption check of clauses, but also before the full subsumption check of literals and all terms. For example, it is always very quickly determined that a ground term cannot subsume a non-ground term, a deep term cannot subsume a shallow term, etc.

7 Back Subsumption

Simple discrimination trees cannot be used for performing the back-subsumption operation efficiently. Thus several alternative indexing methods have been proposed in the literature, see Graf [2]. However, these methods are significantly less efficient than full variable-containing decision trees for forward subsumption. Back subsumption has degraded the performance of many otherwise highly efficient provers.

Gandalf does not use any indexing methods for back subsumption: it uses simple linear search, but tests only a very small percent of existing clauses for back subsumption. Our experiments show that the Gandalf back-subsumption has excellent efficiency. It it is unclear whether indexing methods are at all superior to the Gandalf-style simple linear back subsumption.

Gandalf keeps the list of existing clauses for back subsumption sorted under clause length and the ordering $\succ_s$. Only these clauses are considered for back subsumption for which none of the parameters *length*, *ground*, *depth* and *size* is less than the corresponding parameters of the newly kept clause A.

When back subsumption with A reaches a clause C such that C is shorter than A, none of the following clauses can be back subsumed and the whole back subsumption process is stopped. Similarly, when checking clauses with a certain length l and a clause C such that $A \succ_s C$ is reached, none of the following clauses with length l can be back subsumed, thus all the following clauses with length l are skipped.

Another important restriction is that **only the clauses in the usable list** are back subsumed. Indeed, since clauses in the sos list do not participate in ordinary resolution steps (they may participate in simplification, demodulation and subsumption steps) not much is gained by eliminating some of them with back subsumption. Clauses in the usable list, on the contrary, participate in ordinary resolution and paramodulation steps, hence eliminating some of them may give a noticeable gain in efficiency.

Because of this restriction we separately check each selected clause in sos for forward subsumption before it is moved to usable: it may be subsumed by a clause derived after this selected clause was derived. Since the operation of selecting a new clause is rare, the extra overhead of a forward subsumption check is neglible.

The motivation for the used scheme of back subsumption is the following. Since the problem of deriving an empty clause is undecidable, statistically the average size of the derived clause is growing during the derivation process. However, a newly kept clause can only subsume these of the existing clauses which are not bigger than the newly kept clause. Since it is likely that most of the older clauses are smaller than the newly kept clause, only a small fraction of the old clauses has to be checked. This motivation is further strengthened by the fact that the sos list is normally much larger than the usable list and we only need to back subsume the usable list.

8   Statistics

In order to give some evidence of the efficiency of the proposed methods, we have chosen to present statistics for the problems posed in the no-equality, non-Horn category of the prover competition CASC-14.

The no-equality, non-Horn category is selected since except for back subsumption, the methods presented in the paper are suitable for non-unit subsumption. The problems in the selected category produce large amounts of non-unit clauses and the efficiency of proving them does not rely on factors like efficient paramodulation and demodulation.

First we bring the table with the competition results for the mentioned category. While the speed of nonunit subsumption is certainly not the only important factor for the overall result — notably, SPASS was successful since it derived very few clauses to start with — together with time slicing it was certainly one of the main factors for the success of Gandalf.

Non-Horn with No Equality Category

Problem	Allpaths	Gandalf	I-THOP	Otter	SCOTT	SETHEO	SPASS	TGTP
SET014-2	76.2	15.5	4.2	TO	TO	1.1	0.2	1.0
SET015-2	TO	60.5	TO	TO	TO	TO	148.2	TO
SET013-1	3.0	TO	15.3	TO	TO	TO	81.0	64.1
SET015-1	1.1	30.5	4.7	TO	TO	1.1	64.1	85.1
SET007-1	TO	TO	25.5	TO	TO	57.9	0.7	3.6
SET012-2	9.6	46.0	TO	TO	TO	TO	20.2	11.8
SET011-1	5.6	6.6	4.5	129.1	250.2	1.3	0.0	1.4
SET055-6	3.0	0.1	13.8	0.4	8.7	5.2	0.5	1.8
SET013-2	TO	50.9	TO	TO	TO	TO	TO	TO
ANA002-2	TO	121.4	TO	TO	TO	36.4	TO	TO
SET005-1	78.1	30.3	3.9	281.9	6.7	1.8	0.1	1.3
SET012-1	0.5	30.4	14.0	TO	TO	4.3	2.1	3.8
Attempted	12	12	12	12	12	12	12	12
Solved	8	10	8	3	3	8	10	9
Time	177.1	392.2	85.9	411.4	265.6	109.1	317.1	173.9
Average	22.1	39.2	10.7	137.1	88.5	13.6	31.7	19.3

The abbreviation TO used in the table stands for "timeout".

In the following tables we bring subsumption statistics for the problems in the selected category. The timings and statistics are obtained in a later run than the competition table above. In particular, Gandalf proved successfully (in 18 seconds) the problem SET013-1.

While searching for proofs, Gandalf uses several different search strategies, for example hyperresolution and set of support resolution. Thus the statistics do not depend on one specific strategy, but rather a combination of strategies.

We'd like to turn attention to the ratio of F. full (the number of full, backtracking clause-to-clause subsumption checks performed during forward subsumption) and F. fail (the number of full checks which fail). This indicates that the combination of subsumption candidate selection using the discrimination tree and the fast filtration steps performed during clause-to-clause subsumption is quite precise: approximately five percent of full clause-to-clause subsumption checks succeed.

Also, the number B. full (full backtracking clause-to-clause subsumption checks during back subsumption) is significantly smaller than the corresponding number F. full for forward subsumption.

Explanation of the fields:

- Given: number of given clauses
- Derived: number of derived clauses
- Kept: number of kept clauses
- F. unit: number of forward subsumed unit clauses
- F. double: number of forward subsumed two-literal clauses
- F. long: number of forward subsumed clauses of length three and more
- F. tried: number of clause-to-clause subsumption checks during forward subsumption.
- F. full: number of remaining clause-to-clause forward subsumption checks after fast filters have been passed
- F. fail: number of these remaining clause-to-clause forward subsumption checks (after fast filters have been passed) which failed
- B. full: number of remaining clause-to-clause back subsumption checks after fast filters have been passed

SET014-2

Given	143	Derived	24734	Kept	10154
F. unit	2863	F. double	8309	F. long	2175
F. tried	24828	F. full	12471	F. fail	10208
B. full	2761				

SET015-2

Given	2958	Derived	75368	Kept	20510
F. unit	28790	F. double	14866	F. long	2723
F. tried	65742	F. full	30876	F. fail	28126
B. full	7934				

SET013-1

Given	1366	Derived	14466	Kept	2646
F. unit	1111	F. double	1396	F. long	7377
F. tried	826818	F. full	168118	F. fail	160530
B. full	10011				

SET015-1

Given	5268	Derived	170938	Kept	38451
F. unit	51876	F. double	23190	F. long	24783
F. tried	558302	F. full	412754	F. fail	386724
B. full	27006				

SET007-1

Given	9360	Derived	169975	Kept	30028
F. unit	17578	F. double	49904	F. long	41520
F. tried	3312621	F. full	847768	F. fail	807156
B. full	11027				

SET012-2

Given	2311	Derived	63072	Kept	14775
F. unit	28542	F. double	8984	F. long	1258
F. tried	26489	F. full	12773	F. fail	11471
B. full	7105				

SET011-1

Given	91	Derived	5393	Kept	2695
F. unit	19	F. double	759	F. long	986
F. tried	25610	F. full	9726	F. fail	8541
B. full	2433				

SET055-6

Given	3	Derived	7	Kept	5
F. unit	1	F. double	0	F. long	0
F. tried	0	F. full	0	F. fail	0
B. full	0				

SET013-2

Given	2970	Derived	76086	Kept	20835
F. unit	30332	F. double	15601	F. long	1492
F. tried	43519	F. full	18268	F. fail	16719
B. full	8180				

ANA002-2

Given	4737	Derived	79270	Kept	32779
F. unit	15915	F. double	18260	F. long	10355
F. tried	876717	F. full	246665	F. fail	237277
B. full	7417				

SET005-1

Given	1374	Derived	8152	Kept	3280
F. unit	274	F. double	2654	F. long	1726
F. tried	275975	F. full	117433	F. fail	115824
B. full	10670				

SET012-1

Given	1716	Derived	18885	Kept	4958
F. unit	3169	F. double	4325	F. long	5382
F. tried	293373	F. full	81529	F. fail	75858
B. full	35926				

9　Acknowledgement

This work is supported by the Swedish TFR grant Dnr 96-536.

References

1. C. Fermüller, A. Leitsch, T. Tammet, N. Zamov. Resolution methods for decision problems. *Lecture Notes in Artificial Intelligence vol. 679, Springer Verlag*, 1993.
2. P. Graf. Term Indexing. *Lecture Notes in Computer Science. 1053, Springer Verlag*, 1996.
3. G. Gottlob, A. Leitsch. On the efficiency of subsumption algorithms, *Journa of ACM* **32**(2):280-295, April 1985.
4. L. Magnusson, B. Nordström. The ALF proof editor and its proof engine. In *Types for Proofs and Programs*, pages 213-237, *Lecture Notes in Computer Science vol. 806, Springer Verlag*, 1994.
5. G.Mints. Resolution Calculus for The First Order Linear Logic. *Journal of Logic, Language and Information*, **2**, 58-93 (1993).
6. W.McCune. OTTER 3.0 Reference Manual and Users Guide. Tech. Report ANL-94/6, Argonne National Laboratory, Argonne, IL, January 1994.
7. W. McCune. Experiments with discrimination tree indexing and path indexing for term retrieval. *Journal of Automated Reasoning*, **9**(2):147–167, 1992.
8. T. Tammet. Completeness of Resolution for Definite Answers. *Journal of Logic and Computation*, (1995), vol 4 nr 5, 449-471.
9. T. Tammet. A Resolution Theorem Prover for Intuitionistic Logic. In *CADE-13*, pages 2-16, *Lecture Notes in Computer Science vol. 1104, Springer Verlag*, 1996.
10. T. Tammet, J. Smith. Optimised Encodings of Fragments of Type Theory in First Order Logic. In *Types for Proofs and Programs*, pages 265-287, *Lecture Notes in Computer Science vol. 1158, Springer Verlag*,1996.
11. T. Tammet. Gandalf. *Journal of Automated Reasoning*, **18**(2): 199-204, 1997.

Author Index

Springer
and the
environment

At Springer we firmly believe that an international science publisher has a special obligation to the environment, and our corporate policies consistently reflect this conviction.
We also expect our business partners – paper mills, printers, packaging manufacturers, etc. – to commit themselves to using materials and production processes that do not harm the environment. The paper in this book is made from low- or no-chlorine pulp and is acid free, in conformance with international standards for paper permanency.

 Springer

Lecture Notes in Artificial Intelligence (LNAI)

Lecture Notes in Computer Science